# Formative Experiences

## The Interaction of Caregiving, Culture, and Developmental Psychobiology

This interdisciplinary book offers a unique exploration of the formative effects of children's early life experiences, with an emphasis on interactions among neurodevelopmental, behavioral, and cultural dynamics. The authors draw on insights from psychobiological, clinical, and cross-cultural comparative research that maps the robustness of these developmental dynamics across species and societies. Multidisciplinary case studies focus on specific periods of development, or windows of susceptibility, during which caregiving and other cultural practices potentially have a long-lasting impact on brain and behavior. Chapters describe in detail: how social experience interacts with neurodevelopmental disorders; how epigenetic mechanisms mediate the effects of early environment; the interaction of temperament and environmental influences; the implications of early life stress or trauma for mental health and well-being; and the cultural shaping of sexual development and gender identity. The authors also explore key aspects of and common experiences associated with modern childhood, including teasing, bullying, the function of social play, emotional regulation, and management of attention disorders. The final section translates insights from this work into a fresh appraisal of childrearing practices, clinical interventions, and global public health policy that affect the mental health and well-being of children around the world.

Carol M. Worthman, Ph.D., is Samuel Candler Dobbs Professor of Anthropology and Director of the Laboratory for Comparative Human Biology at Emory University. She combines laboratory, field, and population research for the study of biocultural dynamics in human development, reproduction, and mental and physical health. Her research has spanned twelve countries, including Kenya, South Africa, Nepal, Egypt, Japan, and Papua New Guinea, as well as rural, urban, and semi-urban areas of the United States.

Paul M. Plotsky, Ph.D., is the GlaxoSmithKline Professor of Psychiatry and Behavioral Sciences at Emory University. Plotsky has adjunct appointments in the departments of cell biology and psychology and the Yerkes National Primate Research Center. He is on the faculty of the Graduate Program in Neuroscience, the Endocrine Training Program, the Center for Behavioral Neuroscience, and the undergraduate Neurobiology and Behavior Program. His research is focused on the interaction between genes and the perinatal environment in shaping the developing nervous system. Using rodent and nonhuman primate models in collaboration with clinical researchers, he has developed animal models of vulnerability to a variety of psychiatric and medical diseases.

Daniel S. Schechter, M.D., is the Director of the Consult-Liaison and Parent-Infant Research Units of the Child and Adolescent Psychiatry Service at the Children's Hospital, University Hospitals of Geneva, and the University of Geneva, Faculty of Medicine, Switzerland. He is also Adjunct Assistant Professor of Psychiatry in the Division of Developmental Neuroscience and Behavior and Director of Child Research at the Center for Psychoanalytic Training and Research of the Columbia University College of Physicians and Surgeons. The focus of his research is the understanding of the psychological and neurobiological processes that underlie the intergenerational transmission of violence, trauma, and associated psychopathology during formative early development and in the context of the parent-child relationship. He is currently prospectively exploring pre- and postnatal predictors of individual differences in general child outcome and in response to psychosocial intervention.

Constance A. Cummings, Ph.D., is Project Director of the non-profit The Foundation for Psychocultural Research, which supports interdisciplinary research and scholarship in anthropology, psychiatry, and the behavioral neurosciences, with an emphasis on the interactions between biology and culture. She received her doctorate in theoretical linguistics from New York University.

# Formative Experiences

## The Interaction of Caregiving, Culture, and Developmental Psychobiology

Edited by

**Carol M. Worthman**
Emory University

**Paul M. Plotsky**
Emory University

**Daniel S. Schechter**
Hôpitaux Universitaires de Genève, Switzerland

**Constance A. Cummings**
The Foundation for Psychocultural Research

CAMBRIDGE
UNIVERSITY PRESS

CAMBRIDGE UNIVERSITY PRESS
Cambridge, New York, Melbourne, Madrid, Cape Town, Singapore,
São Paulo, Delhi, Dubai, Tokyo

Cambridge University Press
32 Avenue of the Americas, New York, NY 10013-2473, USA

www.cambridge.org
Information on this title: www.cambridge.org/9780521895033

© Cambridge University Press 2010

First published 2010

Printed in the United States of America

A catalog record for this publication is available from the British Library.

Library of Congress Cataloging in Publication data

Formative experiences : the interaction of caregiving, culture, and developmental
psychobiology / edited by Carol M. Worthman ... [et al.].
    p.  cm.
Includes bibliographical references and index.
ISBN 978-0-521-89503-3 (hardback)
1. Parenting – Cross-cultural studies.   2. Developmental psychobiology.
I. Worthman, C. M. (Carol M.), 1948–   II. Title.
HQ755.8.F67   2010
649'.1–dc22        2009033929

ISBN 978-0-521-89503-3 Hardback

*For children and their families, everywhere: their lives, our future. (CMW)*

*... May we as clinicians, researchers, policy makers, teachers, and parents come together to be inspired by and with them [those children and their families, everywhere] to encourage the most wonderful of formative experiences for generations to come! (DSS)*

# Contents

# List of Figures

# List of Tables

# List of Contributors

**Susan L. Andersen, Ph.D.**
Developmental
Psychopharmacology Laboratory,
McLean Hospital; Harvard Medical
School.

**Carl M. Anderson, Ph.D.**
Harvard Medical School; McLean
Hospital.

**Eileen Anderson-Fye, Ed.D.**
Schubert Center for Child Studies,
Case Western Reserve University;
Center for Culture and Health,
NPI-Semel Institute for
Neuroscience, University of
California, Los Angeles.

**Ronald G. Barr, M.A., M.D.C.M.,
F.R.C.P.C.**
University of British Columbia;
Developmental Neurosciences and
Child Health, Child and Family
Research Institute; Fellow,
Experience-based Brain and
Biological Development Program,
Canadian Institute for Advanced
Research.

**Emily S. Barrett, Ph.D.**
Center for Reproductive
Epidemiology, University of
Rochester Medical Center.

**Anne E. Becker, M.D., Ph.D., Sc.M.**
Harvard Medical School.

**Ursula Bellugi, Ed.D.**
Laboratory for Cognitive
Neuroscience, Salk Institute for
Biological Sciences, La Jolla,
California.

**Marc H. Bornstein, Ph.D.**
Head of Child and Family
Research, National Institute of
Child Health and Human
Development.

**Jean L. Briggs, Ph.D.**
Memorial University
(Newfoundland).

**Stefan Brunnhuber, M.D., M.A.,
Ph.D.**
Universitätskliniken für Psychiatrie
und Psychotherapie, Christian-
Doppler-Klinik, PMU (Austria).

**Amy L. Busch, Ph.D.**
Child Trauma Research Project,
San Francisco General
Hospital.

**Flavia Bustreo, M.D., M.P.H.**
Partnership for Maternal, Newborn
and Child Health, World Health
Organization.

**Jeewook Choi, M.D., Ph.D.**
Harvard Medical School; McLean
Hospital; Catholic University of
Korea, Daejeon St. Mary's Hospital
(Korea).

**Dante Cicchetti, Ph.D.**
University of Minnesota.

**Constance A. Cummings**
The Foundation for Psychocultural
Research

**Michael D. De Bellis, M.D.**
Division of Child and Adolescent
Psychiatry; Healthy Childhood
Brain Development and
Developmental Traumatology
Research Program, Duke
University Medical Center.

**Hillary N. Fouts, Ph.D.**
University of Tennessee.

**Vivette Glover, Ph.D.**
Institute of Reproductive and
Developmental Biology, Imperial
College, London.

**Neal Halfon, M.D., Ph.D.**
UCLA Center for Healthier
Children, Families, and
Communities, School of Public

Health, University of California,
Los Angeles.

**Geoffrey Hall, Ph.D.**
McMaster University.

**Christine M. Heim, Ph.D.**
Emory University School of
Medicine.

**Gilbert Herdt, Ph.D.**
Human Sexuality Studies; National
Sexuality Resource Center, San
Francisco State University.

**Jonathan Hill, M.R.C. Psych.**
Child and Adolescent Psychiatry,
Neuroscience Research
Institute, University of Manchester
(UK).

**Myron A. Hofer, M.D.**
Sackler Institute Professor of
Developmental Psychobiology,
Columbia University; New York
State Psychiatric Institute,
Columbia University.

**Kim L. Huhman, Ph.D.**
Neuroscience Institute and
Department of Psychology; Center
for Behavioral Neuroscience (CBN),
Georgia State University.

**Aaron M. Jasnow, Ph.D.**
Center for Behavioral
Neuroscience, Yerkes National
Primate Research Center, Emory
University.

**Karla Jessen Williamson, Ph.D.**
Educational Foundations, College
of Education, University of
Saskatchewan.

**Laurence J. Kirmayer, M.D.**
Division of Social and Transcultural Psychiatry, McGill University; Culture and Mental Health Research Unit, Institute of Community and Family Psychiatry, Jewish General Hospital, Montréal, Québec.

**Jaap M. Koolhaas, Ph.D.**
University of Groningen.

**Jill E. Korbin, Ph.D.**
Schubert Center for Child Studies, Case Western Reserve University.

**Julie R. Korenberg, M.D., Ph.D.**
The Brain Institute, University of Utah.

**Alice Kuo, M.D., Ph.D., M.Ed.**
University of California, Los Angeles; UCLA Center for Healthier Children, Families and Communities; Community Health and Advocacy Training (CHAT) Program and the Combined Internal Medicine and Pediatrics Residency Program at UCLA.

**Robert Lemelson, Ph.D.**
The Foundation for Psychocultural Research; Center for Culture and Health, NPI-Semel Institute for Neuroscience; University of California, Los Angeles.

**Robert A. LeVine, Ph.D.**
Harvard University.

**Alicia F. Lieberman, Ph.D.**
University of California San Francisco; Child Trauma

Research Program, San Francisco General Hospital.

**Dario Maestripieri, Ph.D.**
University of Chicago.

**Emeran A. Mayer, M.D.**
Center for Neurovisceral Sciences and Women's Health; Center for Neurobiology of Stress; CURE DDRC Division of Digestive Diseases, University of California, Los Angeles.

**Kai M. McCormack, Ph.D.**
Spelman College; Yerkes National Primate Research Center, Emory University.

**Patrick O. McGowan, Ph.D.**
McGill University, Montréal, Québec.

**Michael J. Meaney, Ph.D., PhD, C.Q., F.R.S.C.**
Douglas Institute; Program for the Study of Behaviour, Genes and Environment, McGill University, Montréal, Québec.

**Klaus K. Minde, M.D., F.R.C.P.C.**
McGill University; Anxiety Clinic and Infant Mental Health Clinic, Montréal Children's Hospital.

**Urs M. Nater, Ph.D.**
Emory University School of Medicine, Emory Mind-Body Program, and Centers for Disease Control.

**Emily Ng, B.A.**
University of California, Berkeley.

**Matilda Nowakowski, Ph.D.**
(Candidate)
McMaster University.

**Jaak Panksepp, Ph.D.**
College of Veterinary Medicine,
Washington State University.

**Sergio M. Pellis, Ph.D.**
University of Lethbridge.

**Vivien C. Pellis, Ph.D.**
Canadian Centre for Behavioural
Neuroscience, University of
Lethbridge.

**Paul M. Plotsky, Ph.D.**
Emory University School of
Medicine; Yerkes National Primate
Center.

**Frank W. Putnam, M.D.**
Mayerson Center for Safe and
Healthy Children, Trauma
Treatment Replication Center,
Cincinnati Children's Hospital
Medical Center.

**Keren Rabi, M.A.**
Developmental Biopsychiatry
Research Program, McLean
Hospital; Massachusetts School of
Professional Psychology.

**Judy Reilly, Ph.D.**
San Diego State University;
University of Poitiers (France).

**Christine J. Reinhart, M.Sc.**
University of Lethbridge.

**Jennifer Harris Requejo, Ph.D.,
M.A., M.H.S.**
The Partnership for Maternal,
Newborn and Child Health
(PMNCH), The World Health
Organization (WHO); Johns

Hopkins Bloomberg School of
Public Health.

**Kerry J. Ressler, M.D., Ph.D.**
Howard Hughes Medical Institute,
Center for Behavioral
Neuroscience, Yerkes National
Primate Research Center, Emory
University.

**Linda M. Richter, Ph.D.**
Child Youth Family and Social
Development (CYFSD), Human
Sciences Research Council, Durban,
South Africa.

**M. Mar Sánchez, Ph.D.**
Yerkes National Primate Research
Center, Emory University School of
Medicine.

**Robert Sapolsky, Ph.D.**
Stanford University.

**Daniel S. Schechter, M.D.**
University Hospitals of Geneva
and the University of Geneva,
Faculty of Medicine,
Switzerland; Columbia University
College of Physicians and
Surgeons.

**Louis A. Schmidt, Ph.D.**
McMaster University.

**Sally B. Seraphin, Ph.D.**
McLean Hospital; Harvard Medical
School.

**Yi-Shin Sheu, B.Sc.**
Harvard Medical School; McLean
Hospital.

**Ninik Supartini, Dra.**
International Organization for
Migration (Indonesia).

**Moshe Szyf, Ph.D.**
McGill University, Montréal,
Québec.

**Martin H. Teicher, M.D., Ph.D.**
McLean Hospital; Harvard Medical
School.

**Akemi Tomoda, M.D., Ph.D.**
McLean Hospital; Harvard Medical
School; Kumamoto University
(Japan).

**Gustavo Turecki, M.D., Ph.D.**
Douglas Institute; McGill
University, Montréal, Québec.

**Thomas S. Weisner, Ph.D.**
Semel Institute, University of
California, Los Angeles.

**Christoph Wiedenmayer, Ph.D.**
Columbia University;
Developmental Neuroscience, New
York State Psychiatric Institute.

**James Wilce, Ph.D.**
Blackwell Studies in Discourse and
Culture, Northern Arizona
University.

**Carol M. Worthman, Ph.D.**
Laboratory for Comparative
Human Biology, Emory University.

**Carol Zitzer-Comfort, Ph.D.**
California State University, Long
Beach.

# Foreword

Robert Sapolsky

The field of psychobiology recently lost one of its giants, Seymour "Gig" Levine, who spent a remarkably productive career showing the ways in which early experience shapes the brain and behavior. Although passionately interested in the topic of development, he was realistic enough to admit that it wasn't a subject for everyone – "At some point or other, everyone in our business gets around to doing a development study. After that, either they're hooked forever, or they run away as fast as possible because development's so damn complicated," he once said to me (which I think was meant to taunt me for being in the second category).

Stated in the most low-key manner, the purpose of a volume such as this is not only for the developmental psychobiology obsessives to catch up on the latest work, but also to make such an update readily accessible to the ones who ran away from the subject as fast as possible. Stated more hopefully, this volume can be meant to entice those who did the one-night-stand with the subject into a longer commitment. And stated hegemoni-ously, it can be meant to convince those who fled that they must start studying development.

But when the current state of developmental psychobiology is considered closely, a conclusion must emerge that speaks to all the other psychobi-ologists – tough luck, you've got no choice in the matter, you're already studying the development of brain and behavior. And this is because of two facts, namely the plasticity of the brain and the persistence of developmental effects.

The plasticity cannot be overemphasized. This point was captured by the gerontologist Walter Bortz, when asked if his goal was to eliminate aging – "No, I'm not interested in abnormal development." Now a sound bite like this can be heart-warming, but can easily degenerate into bumper stickers about how today is the first day of the rest of your synapses' lives. What has made the fact of brain development as a life-long process so compelling is that the story is driven by our increasing knowledge of how this actually works. An example of this, relevant to how one must gradually attain maturity, is the extraordinary fact that the frontal cortex does not come fully online until about 25 years of age. This is wildly important. For one thing, this fact informed the decision of the Supreme Court that someone can't be executed for a crime they committed before age 18, because of the immaturity of the brain (although the Court somehow bypassed the fact that something doesn't magically happen to the frontal cortex on the day of your 18th birthday). It gives insight into why schizophrenia so often has a late adolescent onset. It helps explain some of the things your freshman roommate did. And it teaches us that the part of the brain that makes us most uniquely human is the most shaped by environment and least constrained by genetics.

The dictum of development as a life-long process is shown at a more reductive level by the revolution of adult neurogenesis. For the last thousand years, students in Neuro 101 were dutifully taught that the adult brain does not make new neurons. But starting in the 1960s, pioneers like Joseph Altman cried out in the wilderness about how this may not be true, yet it wasn't until the 1990s that the fact of adult neurogenesis was fully demonstrated and widely accepted. The adult brain, particularly the hippocampus, most definitely makes new neurons, and it does so in response to the most interesting circumstances – learning, environmental enrichment, and exercise. Strikingly, such neurogenesis can occur in aged organisms – just another phase of brain development.

So all psychobiologists are ultimately doing development research because of the plasticity of the brain and the fact that it develops throughout the lifetime. The second reason is the persistence of some of the consequences of early experience. A definitive example of this is neonatal handling, a phenomenon first described by Levine, whereby optimal environmental stimulation during the first few weeks of a rat pup's life causes beneficial neurobiological, endocrine, and cognitive changes that persist into adulthood. The changes even last into a rat's old age. And, as a measure of the ethological relevance of this phenomenon, such brain plasticity did not evolve for the benefit of graduate students who like to hold rats. Instead, it turns out to be a surrogate for the effects caused by an optimal style of rodent mothering.

The consequences of early experience can be so persistent as to be multi-generational. Writ small, this concerns the fact that the endocrine changes induced in a female rat by being neonatally stressed will alter the hormonal makeup of her milk when she is a lactating adult, and thereby effect the development of her offspring. Writ larger, this is the truism for both rat and primate that the sort of childhood that individuals experience greatly influences the sort of parents they become. Writ large and pathological, this is the world in which being abused as a child increases the risks of being an abusive parent.

An appreciation of the persistence of the effects of early environmental experience underlines another point, one initially flabbergasting, but ultimately perfectly logical: Environment does not begin at birth. Most obvious is the fact that, say, crack cocaine does not do good things to the fetal brain. Less obvious is the fact that the experiences of a pregnant female will change the hormonal exposure of her fetus, that the endocrine environment of a rodent fetus can even reflect whether the siblings next to her are sisters or brothers. Arguably, the most remarkable example of the persistence of the effects of prenatal environment is the Dutch Hunger Winter phenomenon – people who were fetuses during the catastrophic famine of the winter of 1945 in Nazi-occupied Holland developed "thrifty metabolisms," where the sparseness of fetal nutrition programmed their bodies for a life-long efficiency at storing nutrients. And more than half a century later, the consequences of having been a fetus at that time include a greatly increased risk of obesity, metabolic syndrome, and diabetes.

As noted, an appreciation of the life-long development and plasticity of the brain has been strengthened by uncovering some of the mechanisms underlying such plasticity (e.g., cell cycle regulation in neural progenitor cells). Similarly, mechanisms are being discovered to explain the persistence of some of the effects of early experience. One domain is genetic, e.g., where the likelihood of childhood trauma resulting in adult depression is modulated greatly by polymorphisms in the serotonin transporter gene. Another is epigenetic, e.g., an understanding of how changes in access of transcription factors to promoter elements in DNA can cause persistent silencing of a gene.

So the brain is always developing, and at any given point in life, the brain has been sculpted by all that came before it, even by things long, long before. But this seems to raise a problem. If considered superficially, the elements of persistence and plasticity appear contradictory – on one hand, the consequences of early experience can be huge and so persistent as to be set in stone for a lifetime. Yet, those stones can turn out to be made of plastic, reshaped by adult experience. Permanent effects that are easily changed. Hmm.

The reconciliation, of course, is that effects aren't necessarily permanent, nor are changes necessarily easy. Such contingencies apply when a salutary developmental effect early in life is derailed by adversity in adulthood. But far more important is the opposite situation, when the pathological consequences of early developmental adversity are lessened by salutary interventions later in life. Except when dealing with the most severe developmental adversity, "persistent" doesn't equal "permanent." But the longer you wait to intervene, the harder it will be to help. And if you never try for recovery and assume that it is already too late to make a change, things that you guess to be permanent will always prove to be.

This insight is quite important when considering a nuts-and-bolts biology issue, such as whether gene methylation induced by a certain mothering style in a rat can be reversed. But it is vastly more important when considering whether long-term consequences can be reversed in humans exposed early in life to abuse or deprivation, to a shortage of calories or of love, or to the corrosive effects of being bathed in alcohol as a fetus or bathed in fear and lessons of helplessness once born. It's swell that all us psychobiologists turn out to be closet developmental psychobiologists. But it's essential that the non-psychobiologists become trained to be as well. The extended plasticity of the brain is the moral imperative to try to make things better, while the persistence is the lesson of what happens if society doesn't make the effort.

# Preface

The genesis of this book about development itself has been a developmental process. The structure as well as the source of some of the material derive from a conference held in 2005, entitled "Four Dimensions of Childhood: Brain, Mind, Culture, and Time." Organized and funded by the nonprofit The Foundation for Psychocultural Research (FPR), the meeting was co-sponsored by the University of California, Los Angeles, and The Eunice Kennedy Shriver National Institute of Child Health and Human Development (NICHD, R13HD048149). The conference itself was the product of the vision of FPR founder Robert Lemelson, of discussions by members of the foundation board, and of creative and energetic foundation staff.

The intellectual highlights of the conference drove decisions about formation of the volume. First, we found that the initial focus on advances in developmental neuroscience required expansion to include the equally compelling breakthroughs in epigenetics, genomics, neuroendocrine regulation, and behavioral and social biology. Second, we observed that the interaction among scientists and practitioners around specific cases or findings were particularly revealing. Several sessions at the meeting were organized as case studies, which were then discussed in depth by a panel of researchers from different fields. We found that the diversity of contexts, observations, and perspectives – even within academic disciplines – contributed to a richer understanding of early life experience and its defining moments. Consequently, we set out to identify a complementary set of case studies or research vignettes and then elicited commentary from key thinkers in other fields. Each set includes a developmental biologist, an anthropologist, and a clinician or development psychobiologist. Thus, the book is organized to combine the strengths of integrative essays with those of analytic case studies.

The manifest value represented in the contents of this volume is due to the efforts of the truly stellar contributors. These important thinkers, practitioners, policy makers, and researchers have generously shared their years of scholarship and experience in the pages of this book. Equally necessary to making the book actually happen are the efforts of several different actors. First, there are the aforementioned visionaries – Robert Lemelson and the Board of the FPR – who fashioned the unique mission and programs of the FPR, conceived of this bold integrative project, and supported its completion. The present book represents yet another FPR accomplishment: it is the second title to appear from the conferences they have hosted, the first being *Understanding Trauma: Integrating Biological, Clinical, and Cultural Perspectives*, edited by Laurence Kirmayer, Robert Lemelson, and Mark Barad.

Second are the movers and shakers, and other organizers. These include Irene Sukwadi, Director of the FPR, who provides the organizational genius that keeps everything going. Then there is Dr. Mamie Wong, who made the graphics in this book happen, among other contributions. Emily Ng, prose stylist with flair, helped with initial editing, followed by two further editors, Enid Pearsons and Linda Thompson, who together helped finalize all contributions to the book. Anyone who has been stymied by a bad or sketchy index will appreciate Erin Hartshorn, our indexer. Isabel Roldos, at Emory, assisted in a crucial stage of organization. Eric Schwartz, formerly of Cambridge University Press and now at Princeton University Press, supported and encouraged us in the early stages of this work. We are deeply indebted to our current editor at Cambridge, Simina Calin, for her astute editorial guidance as well as Christie Polchowski and Jeanie Lee for their editorial assistance on this project.

Three of us editors want to offer special recognition to the fourth among us: A brilliant integrative thinker who at the start of the project preferred to remain modestly behind the scenes, yet without whose creativity and attention to every substantive and practical detail, this book would, in fact, not exist. We honor therefore our colleague and co-editor,

Dr. Constance Cummings of the FPR as an essential driving force, organizing spirit, and intellectual catalyst for the volume before you.

Carol M. Worthman
Emory University, United States

Paul M. Plotsky
Emory University, United States

Daniel S. Schechter
Hôpitaux Universitaires de Genève, Switzerland

Constance A. Cummings
The Foundation for Psychocultural Research, United States

# List of Abbreviations

| | |
|---|---|
| 5-HIAA | 5-hydroxyindoleacetic acid (5-HT metabolite) |
| 5-HT | serotonin neurotransmitter |
| 5-HT$_{1A}$ | serotonin receptor |
| 5-HTT | serotonin transporter (gene) |
| 5-HTTLPR | serotonin transporter polymorphism |
| ABN | arched-back nursing (of rat pups) |
| ACE | Adverse Childhood Experience Study |
| ACTH | adrenocorticotropin |
| ADHD | attention deficit hyperactivity disorder |
| ADR Ctx | adrenal cortex |
| ANOVA | analysis of variance |
| AP | anterior pituitary |
| APA | American Psychiatric Association |
| ASB | antisocial behaviors |
| AVP | vasopressin |
| BDNF | brain-derived neurotrophic factor |
| BLA | basolateral complex of the amygdala |
| BNST | bed nucleus of the stria terminalis |
| BPD | bipolar disorder |
| BSQ | Behavioral Style Questionnaire |
| cAMP | cyclic adenosine monophosphate |
| CBP | CREB binding protein |
| CC | corpus callosum |
| Ce | central nucleus of the amygdala |
| CG | cytosine-guanine (dinucleotide sequence) |
| CIFAR | Canadian Institute for Advanced Research |

| COHORTS | Consortium of Health Outcome Research in Transitioning Societies |
|---|---|
| CPA | childhood physical abuse |
| Cr | creatine |
| CREB | cyclic AMP response element binding protein |
| CRF | corticotropin-releasing factor |
| CRH | corticotropin-releasing hormone |
| (C)SA | contact sexual abuse |
| CSF | cerebral spinal fluid |
| CSHCN | children with special health care needs |
| CSI | Commonwealth of Independent States |
| CTS | childhood traumatic stress |
| CV | cerebellar vermis |
| DHEA | dehydroepiandrosterone |
| DID | dissociative identity disorder |
| DNMT | DNA methyltransferase |
| DS | Down syndrome |
| DSM | *Diagnostic and Statistical Manual of Mental Disorders* |
| DTI | diffusion tensor imaging |
| EBBD | Experience-based Brain and Biological Development (program) |
| ECCS | Early Childhood Comprehensive Systems Initiative |
| ECD | early childhood development |
| ECI | early care and education |
| ECIC | Early Childhood Investment Corporation |
| EDI | Early Development Instrument |
| EEA | environment of evolutionary adaptation |
| ELN | elastin (gene) |
| FA | fractional anisotropyy |
| *FKBP5* | gene involved in regulating the HPA axis |
| FL | early focal lesions |
| FRC | family resource center |
| GABA | gamma aminobutyric acid |
| GC | glucocorticoid |
| GMV | grey matter volume |
| GR | glucocorticoid receptor |
| GxE | gene–environment interaction |
| H | histone (protein) |
| HAT | histone acetyltransferase |
| HDAC | histone deacetylase |

| | |
|---|---|
| HDI | Human Development Index |
| HDM | histone demethylase |
| HFA | high functioning autism |
| HMT | histone methyltransferase |
| HP | hippocampus |
| HPA | hypothalamic-pituatary-adrenal (axis) |
| IDEA | Individuals with Disabilities Act |
| ILF | inferior longitudinal fasciculus |
| LCHD | Life Course Health Development (approach) |
| LCN | Salk Institute's Laboratory for Cognitive Neuroscience |
| LG | licking and grooming (of rat pups) |
| LI | language impairment |
| LSCL-33 | Limbic System Checklist-33 |
| MAOA | monoamine oxidase (gene) |
| MAPK | p38 mitogen-activated protein kinase |
| MDGs | Millenium Development Goals (United Nations) |
| Me | medial nucleus of the amygdala |
| mPFC | medial prefrontal cortex |
| MPQ | Multidimensional Personality Questionnaire |
| mPSS | PTSD Symptom Scale |
| NAA | N-acetylaspartate |
| NAcc | nucleus accumbens |
| NE | norepinephrine |
| NMDA | N-methyl-D-aspartate |
| OFC | orbital frontal cortex |
| PFC | prefrontal cortex |
| PFS | perceived financial distress |
| PK | protein kinase |
| PP | protein phosphatase |
| PTSD | posttraumatic stress disorder |
| PVA | parental verbal abuse |
| PVN | paraventricular nucleus |
| RCT | randomized clinical trial |
| ROR | Reach Out and Read |
| SAM | S-adenosyl methionine |
| SERT | serotonin transporter |
| SES | socioeconomic status |
| SISQ | Salk Institute Sociability Questionnaire |
| SNPs | single nucleotide polymorphisms |
| SNS | sympathetic nervous system |

| | |
|---|---|
| SSBS | social support behaviors scale |
| T2-RT | brain transverse magnetization relaxation time |
| TANF | Temporary Assistance to Needy Families |
| TBSS | Tract-based Spatial Statistics |
| TD | typically developing (children) |
| TEI | traumatic events inventory |
| TNF | tumor necrosis factor |
| TRP | tryptophan |
| TSA | HDAC inhibitor |
| UNICEF | United Nations Children's Fund |
| VBM | voxel-based morphometry |
| VBR | voxel-based relaxometry |
| (W)DV | witnessing domestic violence |
| WHO | World Health Organization |
| WM | white matter |
| WS | Williams syndrome |

# Introduction

## Carol M. Worthman and Constance A. Cummings

Anyone who cares for the interests of the young faces a vexing paradox: Dramatically escalating challenges threaten their future even as our knowledge about human development exponentially expands. Global trends including rapid societal changes in family formation, schooling and paid labor participation, escalating refugeeism and migration, and rising rates of AIDS- or conflict-related orphanhood have transformed early rearing environments. Concurrently, advances in the developmental sciences have identified critical elements and mechanisms involved in social and emotional development in humans. Recent molecular research on epigenetics, for instance, not only documents gene-environment interactions that play crucial roles in this process, but also illuminates the significance of the particular context in which a person's early experience unfolds. Both clinical and animal research play leading roles in these advances, by respectively providing in-depth clinical pictures of how development goes awry or is mended, and comparative or experimental material about how the process works. Reciprocally, anthropological studies probe the range of cultural practices, meanings, and ecologies that shape both contexts and experiences.

These key intellectual insights have transformed how we think about development, about culture, and about biology in ways also relevant to policy, prevention, and treatment. Essentially, we have learned that human nature is innately nurtured: Without the social world and its animating culture, we cannot become human. Although how we depend on nurturance is peculiar to humans, such reliance turns out to be widespread among animals. Developmental biology is being revealed as pervasively context-expectant, designed to use typical experience – such as maternal licking in

1

rats or exposure to language in humans – as stimuli that drive the process. Who would have suspected that maternal licking behavior in rats would organize stress reactivity in their offspring, or that there would be analogs to this effect in humans?

Similar findings from across the academic spectrum are altering concepts about parents and parenting practices, and can inform action at the community and clinical levels. Learning that child perception of financial distress predicts psychopathological insult more strongly than does objective poverty casts new light on globalizing material culture and the sources of youth distress. Detailed evidence on the cascading neurodevelopmental, psychobehavioral, and multi-systemic (immune, endocrine, and metabolic) effects of early trauma literally flesh out the sources of health disparity when we learn of the extraordinary rates of trauma reported by clients at a public hospital in Atlanta. Finally, evidence that play is important for learning reciprocity and other social skills gives pause when we notice the relative inattention to play, by both science and society. The rather rudimentary state of knowledge about the developmental effects of play, contrasted with that of trauma, for example, further highlights social conditions and priorities that are mirrored in science.


## FORMATIVE EXPERIENCES: WHY, WHAT, HOW

The view of human nature as nurtured has sharpened attention to changing contexts for child development and highlighted that such contexts comprise evolutionary, historical, cultural, familial, proximal, and genetic dimensions. A consistent motif across these domains is that successful development means becoming competent in the world as it is. From this perspective, there is no single ideal developmental outcome; rather, the process must balance plasticity with resilience to suit the person for the contexts in which s/he needs to function across the life course. With that insight in view, this volume brings to bear a multidisciplinary approach to understanding how early experiences shape human development. Its purpose is to engage development of whole mind/brain/body systems while avoiding "black holism," which includes everything and explains nothing. The contents and organization aim to communicate a working picture of the key insights, conceptual and empirical models, thorny problems, and future prospects of a multidimensional developmental science and practice that is committed to supporting and learning from real-world settings – in clinics, homes, communities, or organizations.

In line with such orientations, some of the particular cross-cutting questions about early experiences that the editors – a biological anthropologist, a developmental psychobiologist, a clinical neuroscientist/child psychiatrist, and a linguist – wanted the book to address include:

- What are the key mechanisms for plasticity and individual differences in early life as experiences start to accrue over time and across cultures?
- What are the key parent-offspring dynamics that shape behavior with long-term – including cross-generational – consequences?
- How do different social and cultural conceptions of childhood – as well as the particular behavioral patterns and roles that children are enjoined to perform in any given society – shape psychobiological development?
- What kinds of social behaviors push the envelope of what is considered normative in a given context?
- What sort of feedback effects do challenging but common experiences such as fear, aggressive behavior, or play fighting have on development?
- How do particular cultural and social ecologies, such as endemically violent societies, psychotropic medication of children, or media exposure guide developmental trajectories?
- How do insights into plasticity and variation inform practices and policy decisions within and across populations?

## TOWARD INTEGRATED MODELS OF DEVELOPMENT

The book reflects an expanding movement, with deep roots in developmental research and practice, to resolve antinomies in western thought commonly captured by mind-body, nature-nurture, and individual-collective distinctions. Through a focus on early experience, the book examines evidence regarding key developmental processes, such as epigenesis, organization of biological stress response systems, or emotion regulation, and traces their formation through multiple levels of analysis, including molecular, systemic, psychobehavioral, familial, and societal. That all these levels occur in concert must somehow be represented in conceptual frameworks that are comprehensive yet realistic. Certainly, treatment of the individual as the unit of analysis has given way to a growing appreciation that a complete understanding of human development is not possible without a consideration of its contexts, including evolutionary history and design, social dynamics and relationships, and cultural settings and ecologies. Chapters provide extended discussion of the evidence and current ideas around these key issues at different levels of analysis, from neuroarchitecture and sensitive periods to cultural differences and social upheavals. As outlined in Table 1, the chapters systematically span a comprehensive range in scale, from molecular to global. We also have encouraged contributors to rifle their drawers of unpublished observations to add

**Table 1** *Formative Experiences Contributor Map: Chapters*

| Chapters | Developmental Psychobiology | | | Clinical Neuroscience | Clinical & Cultural Devel. Psychology | Anthropology | History | Policy | Global Health |
|---|---|---|---|---|---|---|---|---|---|
| | Genetics & epigenesis | Molecular, cellular | Animal studies | Imaging, evaluation, therapies | Theory, treatment | Evolution, ecology, culture, society | History of anthropology, psychiatry, policy | US, non-US | WHO/agencies, epidemiology |
| | *perinatal programming, intergen. transmission, genes: 5-HTT & FKB5* | *language, intergen. trans, sexual dev., sensitive periods, learning, plasticity* | *sensitive periods, early life stress, early abuse, emotion, play* | *trauma, substance abuse, intergenerational transmission* | *cog. dev., aggression, violence, neighborhood, community dynamics, cross-cult. comparison* | *parental care, gender, adolescence* | *human development, political conflict, globalization, equality, restitution* | *child health care systems* | *poverty, health disparities, maternal care, syndemics* |
| Szyf (3) | | | | | | | | | |
| Nowakowski (5) | | | | | | | | | |
| Wiedenmayer (4) | | | | | | | | | |
| Zitzer-Comfort (6) | | | | | | | | | |
| Pellis (16) | | | | | | | | | |
| Panksepp (18) | | | | | | | | | |
| Seraphin (12) | | | | | | | | | |
| Bornstein (2) | | | | | | | | | |
| Herdt (14) | | | | | | | | | |
| LeVine (1) | | | | | | | | | |
| Richter (20) | | | | | | | | | |
| Halfon (19) | | | | | | | | | |
| Requejo (21) | | | | | | | | | |

valuable material not available elsewhere. Panksepp and Jaak, for example, moved beyond reviewing his years of work on the developmental psychobiology of emotion regulation to consider the causes and consequences of widespread psychotropic medication of children diagnosed with attention disorders.

## CASE STUDIES AND COMMENTARIES

Given our central objectives of interdisciplinary communication and practical applicability, we seek to make the contributions accessible and useful to researchers across disciplines. That goal may be best achieved by the case study and response format, which solicits and integrates different interpretations of the same phenomena by experts from developmental neurobiology, clinical sciences, psychology, and cultural, psychological, and biological anthropology. Specific cases and observations can stimulate focused discussion to yield a richly layered analysis when commentators interpret and attempt to explain the same phenomena through very different conceptual and empirical lenses.

Case studies (see Table 2) were selected to span a range of settings and levels of analysis that refract aspects of common issues. These include infant maltreatment in macaques as well as preventive and palliative care for maltreatment and early trauma in humans; conditioned defeat in hamsters as well as the impact of bullying and stigma in Indonesia; contrasting forms of traditional childrearing practices as well as the developmental impact of globalization. Comments about case studies were solicited from scientists, clinicians, or agents who engage development with quite different disciplinary paradigms to build a composite multidimensional picture of the cases. The process reveals synergies as well as gaps in the explanatory frames juxtaposed from diverse lines of research. Similarly, it discovers where and how knowledge can be applied to address suffering, prevent harm, and promote welfare.

## GLOBAL REALITIES, LOCAL APPLICATIONS

At the beginning of this introduction, we noted the irony of escalating risk to children even as understanding development swiftly advances. A logical prescription for that tension is to become more creative and effective in applying what we know about development toward realizing human potential. Of course, it is not that simple. Aforementioned advances in the understanding of gene-environment interactions, for example, do not

**Table 2** *Formative Experiences Contributor Map: Case Studies*

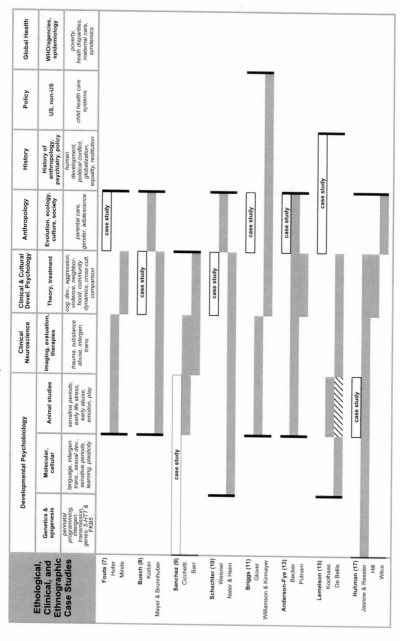

6

readily translate into international policy. Translational work is required, not only from scientists to practitioners, but also from cells to societies, from the experimental to the everyday. The study of development contributes fresh insight into what matters and how things work. New information can help establish priorities and identify whether and how change is possible. With the aim to bridge the gap between scientific progress and real-world challenges, we incorporate case study and policy perspectives that orient academic developments toward pragmatic concerns for addressing the welfare of children, particularly in adverse environments.

There are important reasons for studying development and attempting to apply its lessons under as many conditions as possible. First, there is the matter of equity: The bulk of research on development occurs in western and/or post-industrial societies that represent only a small, privileged fraction of humanity. Second, there is the problem of provincialism. The recognized importance of context and early formative experiences impugns models of human development that are founded on so narrow a sample of human societies and conditions. Expanding the range of inquiry and inclusion necessarily will both test existing assumptions and views, and expose trajectories or mechanisms that were opaque in other settings. Third, differences within populations commonly are found to exceed those among them; comparison of pathways to and consequences of diversity within populations may illuminate sources of difficulty and distress as well as forces for resilience and well-being. Attempts to apply insights from such comparisons can contribute to the urgent necessity to recognize and accommodate diversity, both within and among populations.

The final section deals directly with building contexts that promote child flourishing and health, in domestic, community, state, and global contexts. International leaders in child health, welfare, and policy consider how state-of-the-art knowledge and concepts can be marshaled to address the needs of children around the globe. But such applications will need to be made organically and self-critically in light of local conditions and awareness of likely limitations in the state of the art itself.

The book in its entirety is organized as follows. Section I leads with historical and contemporary overviews of cross-cultural, developmental research on plasticity and variation. This segues into the four core sections (II-V) that anchor the book. The chapters in Section 2 describe in detail how experience interacts with biological development at the molecular, behavioral, social – emotional, and cultural levels. Section 3, "Formative Relationships Within and Across Generations," is entirely comprised of case studies with commentaries from experts in different fields, which capture the complexities of the topic more succinctly and evocatively than do abstract scholarly treatments. Sections IV ("Social and Cultural Contexts of Childhood Development: Normative Settings, Practices, and Consequences") and V ("Fear, Fun, and the Boundaries of Social Experience") interleave case studies and full-length chapters that cover such topics as teasing and emotional regulation, trauma and psychopathology, gender identity, bullying, social defeat, spiritual growth, and play. The concluding Section VI ("Public Health, Education, and Policy Implications") translates current multidisciplinary perspectives reflected in the four core sections into potential pragmatic applications, particularly domestic and global public health and policy. International leaders in child welfare and policy comment briefly on these prospects.

## PROSPECTS

This is a time when the hopeful vision to globalize conditions for human flourishing faces powerful challenges on ecological, political, sociostructural, and existential fronts. The concurrent great advances in understanding development also rest on shaky ground, being limited to a narrow range of human variation that constrains their generalizability. These challenges call on capacities for creativity and collaboration to imagine and enact a more nurturant and responsible world, writ large and small, where formative experiences foster positive human development and diversity. Emerging dialogues and pluralisms – disciplinary, cultural, methodological, and geographical – appear to nurture these capacities. Through such engagements, unexpected changes in perspective are catalyzed, new possibilities and sympathies open, and minds are literally changed. We close with a metaphor of shifts in perspective, regarding how differently societies may view the "past" and the "future." We tend to treat time as a journey advancing into a future that spreads out ahead while the past recedes behind. But imagine thinking of time through a metaphor of the visible, where the past accumulates before us while the invisible future moves up behind us. This possibility conjures a different relationship to experience and urges speculation about what other concepts of time might exist. Metaphors matter: Objectively we know that the future is neither ahead nor behind us, but how we think about it defines our experience and action. By analogy, the perspectives we hold on development exert similar effects, with profound implications for tomorrow's children. We hope that the ideas, models and data presented and debated in this book promote fresh views of development that benefit us all.

# HISTORICAL, CROSS-CULTURAL, AND DEVELOPMENTAL SCIENCE PERSPECTIVES

# ONE

# Plasticity and Variation

## Cultural Influences on Parenting and Early Child Development Within and Across Populations

Robert A. LeVine

This chapter examines two moments in the twentieth century when anthropology made a major contribution to developmental research or was in a position to do so. I seek to clarify what progress has been made up to now and discern what can be done to find a way forward.

The question of whether anthropology can make a central contribution to our understanding of human development has been asked – and answered affirmatively – at least since Margaret Mead (1928, 1930, 1931) raised it in the first third of the 20th century, and numerous times since then by the Whitings (e.g., J. Whiting, 1954; Whiting & Whiting, 1960) and others, including several contributors to this volume. Forceful arguments, vivid illustrations, and empirical evidence have been assembled – repeatedly, recently as well as in the past, and in interdisciplinary forums – to argue the necessity of cross-cultural research on childhood environments and development for a science of human child development and, more specifically, for developmental psychology and psychiatry. Is there any need to make this case again?

Apparently so. All the evidence I am aware of suggests that even in this first decade of the 21st century, with the exception of nutritional science, anthropological, and other cross-cultural studies remain marginal to and of minor significance in the mainstreams of the research disciplines investigating child development (developmental psychology, child psychiatry, pediatrics, and education). This is not to say that there has been no progress in the awareness of cultural factors and the acceptance of comparative evidence in these fields, but such progress is often without implications for the setting of research agendas. Take, for example, *From Neurons to Neighborhoods: The Science of Early Childhood Development* (Shonkoff & Phillips,

2000), the final report of the National Academy of Sciences (NAS) committee on "integrating the science of early childhood development." In Chapter 3, "The Challenge of Studying Culture," although the authors say,

Cultural practices related to early childrearing are highly variable and lead to different developmental outcomes.... Sound scientific thinking asks how and why cultural practices differ and assesses their differential developmental consequences, in both the short and long term. It is therefore essential that the full range of possible effects of contrasting childrearing practices be evaluated objectively. (p. 62)

they also reveal,

[T]he committee began its work with a strong conviction about the importance of culture as a highly salient influence on early childhood development. As our examination of the knowledge base progressed, we became increasingly appreciative of its complexity. In part, this complexity is related to the interdisciplinary nature of the field and its reliance on a wide array of qualitative and quantitative methods. Beyond methodological diversity, however, the committee was struck by the extent to which much of the research on the role of culture in child development is tied to values and personal beliefs.

Thus, the task of assessing the science of culture was exceedingly more complicated than assessing the neurobiology of brain development.... Consequently, this report presents a more bounded analysis of culture than it does of neuroscience. It is important that this discrepancy not be interpreted as an indication of the relative importance of these two domains of study. Quite the contrary, it should be viewed as a strong message both about the significant challenges that face those who investigate the role of culture in early childhood development and the critical need for ongoing methodologically rigorous research in this area. (p. 58)

In effect, their endorsement of cultural research is vitiated by indirect criticisms of it as biased, methodologically deficient, and exceptionally "challenging" and "complicated," in comparison with other lines of research. As complex as cultures may be, however, it is hard to accept that they are more so than the human brain, or that it would have seemed so had there been a cultural anthropologist on the committee. And the abovementioned "critical need" for research "in this area" is mentioned neither in the next chapter's discussion of research strategies for investigating causal influences of child rearing on development under the ethical restraints on experiments with humans – although this has always been one of the prime reasons for cross-cultural research on child rearing – nor in the recommendations of the last chapter. Research in diverse cultures does not find a place on the committee's agenda for future work.

My intention in this paper is not to complain about or explain the child development field's attitude toward anthropological research. The National Academy of Sciences committee's ambivalence will have to stand as emblematic of attitudes prevalent in that field as a whole. My point here is simply that the moment for making a case for anthropological research on child development, and particularly for comparative research that can help identify the boundaries between normal and pathological development, has not yet passed.

Rather than repeating familiar arguments and evidence, I shall examine two episodes in the history of anthropology that opened doors to developmental research and pointed to potential advances, only some of which have been realized: Franz Boas's research on physical growth beginning in 1908 and William Caudill's comparison of Japanese and Americans beginning in 1960.

## FRANZ BOAS AND CHILD DEVELOPMENT

We do not usually think of Franz Boas (1859–1942), a founder of academic anthropology in the United States, as involved with child development except through his students of the 1920s, Margaret Mead and Ruth Benedict. But Boas actually had interests and experience of his own in this field, dating back at least to 1888, when he was hired by G. Stanley Hall, founder of American child psychology, to teach in the Psychology Department at Clark University and conduct a study of physical growth of the immigrant children in Worcester, Massachusetts. This was Boas's first academic position in America. He taught at Clark for three years, from 1889 to 1892, and left as the result of an administrative dispute with Hall in which a majority of faculty members resigned. Years later, however, Boas remembered Hall and the atmosphere of interest in child development at Clark as having stimulated his work on "the influences of environment upon growth" (quoted in Stocking, 1968, p. 165). He published a short paper on the value of anthropometric measures of physical growth in the second issue (1891) of Hall's journal of child study, *The Pedagogical Seminary*, and initiated a longitudinal study of the immigrant children in Worcester, which was discontinued when he left Clark. The following year he published an article, "The Growth of Children," in *Science* (Boas, 1892).

Boas initiated later anthropometric research in Toronto and in Oakland, California. Then in 1908, he undertook an anthropometric study of more than 17,000 European immigrants in New York City, seeking to detect the effects of childhood environments on physical growth. This study stirred controversy when it was published in 1911–1912 and has recently received attention from biological anthropologists, who have reanalyzed the dataset Boas made available in 1928 (Sparks & Jantz, 2002; Gravlee, Bernard, & Leonard, 2003), and even from the *New Yorker* magazine (Pierpont, 2004).

Boas was trained in anthropometric methods by Rudolf Virchow in Berlin in 1883. Virchow, known in medicine as the founder of cellular pathology, was also a leader of German physical anthropology. Boas greatly admired his scientific attitude, radical empiricism, and his liberal political orientation; he was also influenced by Virchow's concept of plasticity or mutability as a basic biological principle that was directly applicable to the physical growth of humans. Boas's exposition of Virchow's ideas in his obituary in *Science* is virtually a charter for his own research on immigrants:

Cells, in the course of their lives, may change their forms according to age and according to the influences to which they are subjected. Such changes take place both in the healthy and the sick organism, and often it is impossible to draw a sharp line between normal physiological, and abnormal or pathological, changes. . . . [I]n reality there is no distinct line of demarcation between physiological and pathological processes, that the latter are only physiological processes which take place under difficult conditions.

[H]is position rests on the general scientific principles that it is dangerous to classify data that are imperfectly known under the point of view of general theories, and that the sound progress of science requires us to be clear at every moment, what elements in the system of science are hypothetical and what are the limits of that knowledge which is obtained by exact observation. (Boas, 1902, reprinted in Stocking, 1974, pp. 38–40)

In other words, human bodies change in response to differing environmental conditions; apparent pathological variations may be normal responses to differing conditions; and the scientist should distinguish what he knows from what he guesses.

In the immigrant studies, Boas was particularly interested in proving that the concept of fixed racial subdivisions among European peoples – based on skeletal, particularly cranial, measurements and held by most physical anthropologists at the time – was inconsistent with the evidence that skeletal dimensions changed with migration. By the time of the New York study in 1908 he was aware that such changes had been shown to occur with rural-urban migration in Europe; thus it seemed predictable that there would be further changes in head form when Europeans came to the United States, as they had been doing in large numbers. Despite his high level of statistical sophistication for 1910 (Tanner, 1959), Boas's New York data required methods of statistical inference that were not yet available. Without computers or even calculators, and with improvised statistical methods, he did as well as he could and came up with restrained descriptions of the evidence and with the conclusion that children of the several ethnic groups changed in cephalic index in migrating to New York, although not in the same direction. He did not attempt to explain which aspects of the environment caused the changes. Boas nevertheless claimed that the data showed that the cephalic indices of children change in a new environment, thereby challenging the doctrine that they were fixed by racial inheritance and setting off a controversy that went on for years.

The recent controversy over Boas's data, however, is not over whether there are fixed racial types based on cranial form that are impervious to environmental influence – no one believes that any more – but rather whether Boas "got it right" in his interpretations of the ambiguous evidence from his study. Using contemporary statistical methods to analyze the corpus of data Boas made publicly available in 1928, one group (Gravlee et al., 2003) concluded that Boas did get it right, whereas another (Sparks & Jantz, 2002) concluded that he did not. They used different analytic methods, but their findings are actually not far apart.

Both groups found that the differences in cephalic index between children born in Europe and those born in New York are small. Gravlee et al. emphasize that these differences are statistically significant (unlikely to occur by chance), whereas Sparks and Jantz emphasize that the differences by birthplace account for a minuscule amount of the variance in cranial measurements (roughly 1 per cent, according to Gravlee et al.). Thus when Sparks and Jantz assess heritability in the data (a measure based on variance), they are able to show that almost all of the variance in cranial form is from genetic rather than environmental factors. But Gravlee et al. find that the parent-child correlations in cephalic index of the foreign-born children average .64, whereas those for the American-born children average only .43, indicating a drop in parent-child similarity because of immigration to the United States and the associated environmental changes in the conditions of early childhood.

I agree with Gravlee et al. that there are unmistakable, perhaps indisputable, signs of environmental influence in these data, but I also agree with Sparks and Jantz that it is remarkable how weak the environmental influence is, particularly given the historic status of this study as definitively falsifying racial types in physical anthropology.

Boas was interested in more than cranial measurements. But because the cephalic index was the criterion for classifying individuals into what he regarded as entirely fictitious racial types that, according to the dominant theory of the time, included cultural and psychological attributes, he publicized the cephalic index data from the New York immigrant study as demonstrating that such types lacked the stability the theory posited. In the published report and in *American Anthropologist* (Boas, 1912a, 1912b) he hedged his claims, qualified his conclusions, and had little to say about the kinds of environmental factors that might make a difference. But he never hesitated to interpret the findings as falsifying racial types. In any event, the U.S. Immigration Commission, which had funded the study without great enthusiasm, ultimately provided "forty volumes of justification for immigration restriction legislation," (Stocking, 1974, p. 190).

In retrospect, Boas would have been on firmer ground scientifically had he focused on the height measurements taken of the children. These showed the kinds of differences he predicted and pointed the way to future research that has since produced not only unambiguous evidence of environmental influence but also a deeper understanding of the processes through which environmental factors work. His desire to challenge racial theories led him to give primary attention to the cephalic index; yet he was already thinking about larger issues concerning environmental factors in physical growth. In 1911 he presented a paper (Boas, 1912c, reprinted in Stocking, 1974, pp. 214–218), "The Instability of Human Types," in which he made the following statements:

Observations on growth have shown that the amount of growth of the whole body depends upon more or less favorable conditions which prevail during the period of development. Unfavorable conditions retard growth; exceptionally favorable conditions accelerate it. A more detailed study of the phenomena of growth has shown that the development of different parts of the body does not proceed by any means at the same rate at a given period.... [I]f an individual is retarded by unfavorable conditions after a certain organ has obtained nearly its full development, while other organs are still in the process of rapid evolution, the former cannot be much influenced, while the latter may bear evidence of the unfavorable conditions which were controlling during a certain period of life.

It is a well-known fact that the central nervous system continues to develop in structure longer perhaps than any other part of the body, and may therefore be apt to show the most far-reaching influences of environment.

It follows from this consideration that social and geographical environment must have an influence upon the form of the body of the adult, and upon the development of the central nervous system. (Boas, 1912c, reprinted in Stocking, 1974, p. 215)

These observations [the New York study] seem to indicate a decided plasticity of human types; but I wish to repeat that the limits of this plasticity are not known to us. It follows, however, directly, that if the bodily form undergoes far-reaching changes under a new environment, concomitant changes of mind may be expected. The same reasons which led us to the conclusions that more or less favorable conditions during the period of growth will have the greater influence the longer the period of development of a particular part of the body, make it plausible that a change of environment will influence those parts of the body most thoroughly which have the longest period of growth and development. I believe, therefore, that the American observations compel us to assume that the mental makeup of a certain type of man may be considerably influenced by his social and geographical environment. It is, of course, exceedingly difficult to give an actual proof of this conclusion by observation, because we know that the mental manifestations depend to a great extent upon the social group in which each individual grows up (Boas, 1912c, reprinted in Stocking, 1974, pp. 217–218).

In these passages, written in 1911, we see Boas – within the constraints of his radical empiricism and his understanding of contemporaneous biology – attempting to lay the basis for a developmental human biology and a developmental psychobiology that have a place for (as yet unspecified) environmental influences. I believe that he was opening a door to two kinds of future research:

First, there are the studies of physical growth focusing on body size, particularly stature, as outcomes of childhood development. These have included (a) further migration research that improved on the New York study by taking longitudinal measurements and including kin who did not migrate to compare with those who did; (b) medical research on nutrition in laboratory animals and humans to identify the nutrients needed for growth and the forms of "growth faltering" and clinical symptoms in young children resulting from infectious diseases and malnutrition (e.g., protein–calorie malnutrition and micronutrient deficiencies); and (c) social research that identifies the economic, political, and other social conditions that affect the supply of nutrients and the transmission of childhood diseases in particular populations of young children. If we consider these lines of research over the past 90+ years since Boas's New York study, we see great advances in scientific understanding that are consistent with his early views on environment and growth. Without attributing these advances to his intellectual influence, we can say that Boas was on the right track concerning the importance of the environment (without denying genetic determinants) and in recognizing that the developmental immaturity of early childhood provides susceptibility to environmental factors, forming the basis for plasticity in physical growth. His failure to identify specific environmental influences was in retrospect also astute because the science for making such specifications did not exist in 1912.

The Boas legacy in anthropological research on physical growth can be seen in the contemporary work of Barry Bogin (1999, 2001; Bogin & Loucky, 1997). Bogin has studied Mayan peoples in Guatemala and the United States, showing greater height for the children of immigrants to the United States. Like Boas, he points out that in typological studies, the Mayans have been called "the pygmies of the New World," but as migrants, their increase in stature reveals a plasticity contradicting the implicit prediction of fixity. Bogin and Loucky (1997) discuss the probable causes of these differences in diet, water supply, and other public health parameters known to affect growth, and they set the quantitative findings in a contextual analysis of the political economy of Mayan peasants at home and abroad. In other publications, Bogin (1999, 2001) also perceives these environmentally induced changes in stature in the context of physical growth to be an aspect of human ontogeny evolving through natural selection. By the end of the 20th century, research on physical growth had become the kind of biosocial science Boas had imagined and hoped for eighty years earlier.

A second door that Boas opened in 1911 led to research on the mental development of children under particular environmental conditions. Here we see him attempting to find a basis in the biology of the nervous system for children's psychological development – their acquisition of a "mental makeup" influenced by the environmental setting in which they grow up. This is of course the more familiar Boas, the teacher of Sapir, Mead, and Benedict, who took his axiom of the plasticity of mental development and built on it the field of "culture and personality studies," with its emphatic developmental perspective, from the 1920s onwards. We see the Boas influence in Sapir's insistence on the individual as the bearer of culture (Sapir, 1993, p. 139) and in Mead's many contributions to the understanding of child development seen through a cross-cultural perspective. Boas wrote introductions to Mead's *Coming of Age in Samoa* (1928) and Benedict's *Patterns of Culture* (1934), but as Stocking (1992) has observed, Boas did not include the culture and personality field, then at a peak of interest among anthropologists, in his edited volume, *General Anthropology* (1938), although it contained chapters by Mead and Benedict. Nor did he leave any indication during the last five years of his life that he found anything of interest in culture and personality studies. It is not difficult to conclude that he was disappointed with what his famous students had made of his opening toward the study of psychocultural development.

Although it may remain unclear why Boas distanced himself from the emerging field of culture and personality in the late 1930s, there are some obvious facts that must have played a role: (a) his skepticism about the speculations of psychoanalysis which, in one form or another (more neo-Freudian than Freudian) was the dominant psychological influence in culture and personality studies; (b) his awareness of the division in the field between Sapir and Benedict over the issue of whether to focus on the individual (as Sapir insisted) or the culture as a collective phenomenon (in Benedict's formulations), which prevented a consensus concerning theory and method; and (c) the failure of the field to construct a coherent program for empirical research of the kind that was already evident in physical anthropology many years before. For Boas, the creative and experimental disorder of culture and personality studies in the 1930s would not have recommended it for inclusion in the anthropological science he wanted to bring to the general public in the later years of his life.

These factors aligned with Boas's long-standing ambivalence about objective, physics-like investigations and subjective, holistic studies, both of which he saw as necessary parts of anthropology (Stocking, 1992). As Stocking points out, however, his views changed over time about how the two should be distinguished and what each should consist of. It seems to me that Boas, although he foresaw a place for what we might call a cultural phenomenology and a cultural psychology that would capture the distinctive perspectives of peoples (i.e. *geisteswissenschaft*), was drawn, both by personality and by training in the laboratories of Virchow and Fechner, to a more narrow, empiricist view of mental development that prevented him from appreciating the exploratory efforts of his brilliant students.

It cannot be that Boas really expected to find the precision and consensus of anthropometrics (measuring the simplest of physical dimensions) in the domain of culture and mind. But the failure of the culture and personality field in the 1930s to establish a unified body of theory, a rigorous and vigorous critique of speculation, and above all, an ongoing research program meant that it was not ready for inclusion in his notion of anthropological science. Thus his final position seems rather close to that of the NAS committee, which concluded that cultural studies of child development, although potentially valuable, had proved "complicated" and were apparently too fraught with methodological problems for a place on the research agenda of developmental science (Shonkoff & Phillips, 2000).

The lesson I take from this excursion into the history of anthropology is that Franz Boas believed in 1911, and probably much earlier, that the field of human child development was grounded in developmental biology, involving the formation of individual characteristics, including psychological ones, statistically distributed in populations, and that these distributions were skewed in population-specific directions by the social and "geographical" environments of ontogeny in general and childhood in particular. This view anticipates in many respects that of modern population studies (population genetics, epidemiology, and demography). His major investigation of physical growth, the large and federally funded New York study of 1909–1910, brought public and scientific attention, with accompanying controversy, to issues relating a macro-level process, immigration, to the micro-level processes by which environmental factors influence the physical growth of children. Although Boas was unable to anticipate the substance of these processes, he helped set the agenda for the biomedical and biosocial research of the 20th century that would uncover the secrets of growth and its socioeconomic influences.

Boas's view of child development also provided a preliminary basis for research on the child's acquisition of cultural and mental characteristics. But theoretical disagreements among his students (Kroeber, Sapir, and Benedict) concerning the locus of culture, in addition to his own empiricist skepticism about the psychological theories and methods of his time, probably inhibited his appreciation of the psychocultural explorations that occurred prior to his death in 1942.

I believe that Boas's apparent skepticism concerning psychocultural research in his time is understandable from his empiricist perspective, particularly if it is compared with research in human biology then and throughout the 20th century. On the other hand, progress in all of the social sciences during the 20th century was far slower and less linear than that of the biological sciences, and the diverse and somewhat conflicting psychocultural approaches of the generations after Boas's formulation of 1912 can be seen in retrospect as experiments from which clarification and coherence would only later emerge. In the section that follows, I describe a coherent anthropological research agenda on child development and mental health that emerged in the work of William Caudill just after the mid-century decline of "culture and personality studies." (There were of course other anthropological projects on child development, such as the Six Cultures Study, being conducted during the same period.)

## THE CAUDILL PROJECT: CHILD DEVELOPMENT
## AND MENTAL HEALTH

In 1960, William Caudill, an anthropologist at the National Institute of Mental Health (NIMH), initiated an ambitious comparative study of Japanese and Americans that has been largely overlooked in the years since his untimely death in 1972. This project included: (a) a comparison of the symptom patterns of institutionalized mental patients in the two countries; (b) a longitudinal study of children from the first year of life onwards in 30 Japanese and 30 American middle class families; and (c) studies of parental practices, family dynamics, and culturally distinctive psychotherapies in the rapidly changing socioeconomic environment of Japanese metropolitan areas. The quantitative data collected were interpreted in terms of ethnographic material on Japanese cultural concepts and practices of family life, parent-child relationships, normal and abnormal behavior, and therapeutic intervention – material that Caudill had been collecting since the early 1950s. Although many journal articles and book chapters were published from this research, their integration was not completed at the time of Caudill's death, and much of his case material has never been published. It is nevertheless worth examining the project and its promise as an example of how anthropology can contribute to child development research and psychiatry.

Caudill had been trained in anthropology at the University of Chicago, had done pioneering work in social psychiatry at Yale Medical School, and had then taught in the Harvard Department of Social Relations before joining the NIMH. As a member of NIMH's Laboratory of Socio-Environmental Studies, he was able to devote himself to research full-time and with ample long-term funding.

During the summer of 1946, when he was a graduate student, Caudill had an apprenticeship with A. Irving Hallowell, then teaching at Northwestern University, who took a group that included Northwestern students Melford E. Spiro and Erika Bourgignon on a field trip to the Lac de Flambeau Ojibwa in Wisconsin (Caudill, 1949). Hallowell, although trained at the University of Pennsylvania, had attended Boas's seminars at Columbia in the 1920s and had worked closely with Edward Sapir in interdisciplinary seminars during the 1930s. As an influence on Caudill, Hallowell represented Sapir's interpretation of the Boas legacy (Darnell,

1986, 1990), in which the individual, as the locus of culture, should be assessed for a psychological understanding of culture. For Caudill at that time, as for Hallowell, that meant using projective personality tests.

Fourteen years later, when Caudill embarked on the Japan and America project, he structured it so as to incorporate psychiatric as well as cultural and developmental data collection, epidemiology as well as ethnography, and longitudinal child research. The Boas legacy was represented in several aspects of the project's approach: its treatment of the boundary between normal and pathological development as a question to be answered empirically rather than assumed a priori, its attempts to relate the macro level of institutions and socioeconomic change to the micro level of ontogeny, its assumption that cultural environments and developmental outcomes are statistically distributed within populations, and its use of quantitative as well as ethnographic methods of data collection and analysis.

Caudill's project was a controlled comparison that explored the boundary between normal and abnormal human development in the urban middle-class populations of two wealthy countries that resembled each other in many socioeconomic characteristics but varied dramatically in their traditional cultures. He argued that by holding technological levels and socioeconomic factors more or less constant, the Japan–America comparison was better suited to identifying the influence of cultural ideas and practices on reproduction, psychological development, and psychopathology than studies comparing peoples at disparate levels of technology and socioeconomic organization. At the same time, Caudill recognized that these two countries were undergoing socioeconomic change and that Japan in particular – in its final transformation to an urban-industrial society – presented opportunities for studying how these macro-level processes affected families and individuals.

Caudill's theoretical model can be summarized as follows: The conventional concepts and practices of child rearing in a particular population shape the child's interpersonal environment in ways that establish a culture-specific sense of self that can be observed in the prevailing patterns of interpersonal relations and in the personal preferences, strengths, and vulnerabilities of adults. Bodily routines in early childhood, including the interpersonal arrangements of sleeping and bathing, are emotionally salient contexts for the acquisition of ego boundaries and preferred self–other relationships. And not only does the eventual acquisition of a culture-specific sense of self facilitate a motivated adaptation to the norms of a particular cultural setting, it also transmits culture-specific psychological vulnerabilities that can, especially in stressful situations occasioned by socioeconomic change, result in psychopathology. Furthermore, cultural ideas and practices permeate psychiatric nosology and therapy, so that the questions of what constitutes pathological behavior and how it should be dealt with have culturally variable answers.

This theory was not unique to Caudill or his project and may even have represented a consensus among psychological anthropologists in 1960. The focus in childhood experience was on interpersonal relationships, reflecting the neo-Freudian position of the culture and personality pioneers Sapir, Mead, and Bateson (e.g., Bateson & Mead, 1942), who were influenced more by Harry Stack Sullivan and Karen Horney than by Freud's conception of psychosexual development. In Caudill's version, the interpersonal context achieves psychological depth and lasting influence through its connections with the child's early bodily experiences in sleeping and bathing as well as in emotional communication during infancy and early childhood. Thus the Freudian model of universal oral, anal, and phallic-genital (or oedipal) stages, open only to the environmental influence of gratification or frustration during each critical period set by human evolution, is replaced by a notion of culture-specific interpersonal boundaries transmitted from one generation to the next through a prolonged psychosomatic experience that is itself shaped by local conventions. The postulate of plasticity makes the meaning of this psychosomatic experience open to the influence of a culturally organized environment rather than one preformed in the evolutionary history of the human species.

It is also noteworthy that Caudill's model did not assume that the cultural sense of self always operates adaptively but rather that it also entails vulnerabilities or fragilities that can generate anxiety and lead to psychological breakdown. As he saw it, the purpose of empirical research is to find the weak points as well as strengths in a particular pattern of psychosocial ontogeny. Furthermore, as a social scientist, the anthropologist needs to investigate the macro-level processes that impose stress and convert latent vulnerability into phenotypic pathology.

The findings from Caudill's project have many implications for a developmental psychiatry. In this section, I shall offer two brief examples from his Japanese research. First, there is the analysis of sleep patterns in Japanese psychocultural development. Caudill showed that mother-child cosleeping from birth through childhood was conventional and virtually universal among middle-class families in Tokyo and Kyoto (Caudill & Plath, 1966). His observations of 30 Japanese mothers and their infants at 3–4 months of age revealed that the mothers tended more frequently than the American contrast group to initiate a sequence in which mother touches or moves her sleeping infant or rearranges his blanket, often waking him up and then comforting him to facilitate his return to sleep (Caudill & Weinstein, 1969). He interpreted this in terms of the Japanese mother's developmental goal of an interdependent child rather than an independent one, so that she treats going to sleep as something to be regulated interpersonally, rather than promoting the autoregulation preferred by Americans. In the context of a life in which the average person sleeps in the same bed as another family member until the age of 15 years and then resumes cosleeping a few years later at marriage, Caudill argued, cosleeping becomes a personal preference, the cultural meaning of which is involved with the intrapsychic equilibrium of the individual. Mother-child cobathing is another experience of bodily comfort in an interpersonal context that extends the interdependence long beyond the 3–4 month period of the infant observations. (Caudill also collected follow-up data at 30 months and 6 years, but did not live to write up those data himself; see Caudill & Schooler, 1973; Schooler, 1996.)

Given this context of normal experience and development among middle-class Japanese families in Tokyo and Kyoto in the early 1960s, Caudill turned his attention to the population of mental patients in Japan (Tokyo), rigorously compared with a similar population in the United States (Baltimore-Washington area). He found that, among hospitalized schizophrenics in the two areas, the Japanese patients were more than three times as likely to have sleep disturbance as a symptom than their American equivalents (Schooler & Caudill, 1964). He related this to the fact that the Japanese patients were far more likely to have been physically assaultive to their mothers. Because sleep and mother are associated, "sleep does not even provide physical withdrawal from the source of the conflict" (Schooler & Caudill, 1964, p. 175). Patients treated in private mental hospitals, however, were normally taken care of on a one-to-one basis by a female subprofessional nurse called a *tsukisoi*, who slept on a cot beside the patient every night and assumed responsibility for providing maternal comfort along with round-the-clock practical care (Caudill, 1961). In this case, the cosleeping of a woman who is like a mother but not the actual mother is part of a therapeutic setting to alleviate anxiety and restore the patient's psychic equilibrium.

This example shows how Caudill used multiple streams of evidence concerning the interpersonal regulation of sleep and other forms of bodily experience to track the child's acquisition of cultural meanings concerning self and other and to track the roles these meanings play in normal psycho-dynamics, conventional family life, and mental illness in Japan. Rather than suggest that the Japanese, whose typical mother-child relationship he once described as "almost symbiotic" (Caudill, 1961), were especially vulnerable to mental illness, Caudill sought to understand the particular forms their vulnerabilities – and strengths – took in the experience of children and adults, how this differed from their American counterparts, and what we can learn from the difference. This example also reveals that Caudill's approach, from ethnographic and survey research, was able to cast doubt on the ethnocentric American assumption that mother-child cosleeping is necessarily pathogenic, while exploring the psychological functions of conventionalized and culturally salient cosleeping for normal and hospitalized psychiatric populations in Japan.

The Caudill project also explored links between the socioeconomic transformation of urban Japan in the late 1950s and family dynamics that could lead to stress and mental illness. In a remarkable analysis that was never published in full, Caudill (1963) showed that, among Japanese mental patients hospitalized as "psychotic," the eldest sons and youngest unmarried daughters in families with family-run commercial or industrial firms were overrepresented to a statistically significant degree. As the tide of Japanese industrialization crested during this period, many small family firms were wiped out by competition from large corporations. The stress of business failure, Caudill reckoned, fell primarily on oldest sons, who were expected to inherit the firms, and the youngest daughters, if they remained unmarried. These young women had intense relationships with their fathers, to whom they provided practical and emotional support. (The younger sons, who could not inherit, pursued independent careers, and the married daughters moved out to live with their husbands' families.) Thus the failure of these firms was translated into impossible situations for these oldest sons and youngest unmarried daughters, precluding the successful fulfillment of their filial obligations and causing them severe emotional stress.

Questions like why stress in these situations led to hospital admission with a diagnosis as psychotic rather than neurotic and what proportion of Tokyo residents subjected to those stresses at that time were hospitalized as psychotics were not answered in the published paper. Many other questions could be raised about an analysis based on the assumptions of the early 1960s. Yet Caudill's use of ethnographic knowledge of Japanese family relationships to assess the impact of economic change on personal suffering demonstrated the potential value of another line of psychocultural research for psychiatric understanding – culturally informed epidemiology.

The value of the Caudill project as a whole was not widely recognized at the time of his death in 1972, largely because he had not yet completed the integration of its diverse quantitative findings with his ethnographic and clinical knowledge of Japanese families and the comparative data from the United States. Publications from the project were scattered across journals in psychiatry, anthropology, and sociology as well as the proceedings of international conferences. Caudill's collaborator Carmi Schooler (1973) analyzed and published follow-up data on two-thirds of the child samples at 30 months and 6 years and, with Ezra Vogel, edited two special issues of *The Journal of Nervous and Mental Disease* (Vogel & Schooler, 1973), which reprinted some of his articles. Without Caudill's interpretations in a concluding volume, the project could not fulfill its promise. Yet his attempt to formulate the psychological development of normal Japanese in terms of what his colleague Takeo Doi (1973a, 1973b) called *amae*, the active expectation of being cared for, and what Caudill called *interdependence*, was able to influence later research into the psychology of Japanese culture (e.g., Lebra, 1976; Markus & Kityama, 1991). His demonstrations of the power of cultural meanings to influence – and across cultures, diversify – psychological experience in the child, the family, and the mental patient left its mark in psychological and medical anthropology, cultural psychology, and child development research. Furthermore, his naturalistic observations of mother-infant interaction in the home – innovative for their time – inspired other cross-cultural researchers to replicate and improve on his observational methods.

The Caudill project is worthy of our attention 45 years after it was planned, primarily because we still need research on psychocultural development that is longitudinal, cross-cultural, and multifaceted in its approach to questions of individual development, adult adaptation, and psychopathology. Caudill recognized that for evidence from a non-Western culture to be taken seriously in the world of mental health research it had to be generated by research that was long-term, exacting, comparative, interdisciplinary, and sophisticated in its methodology. This kind of research is expensive and difficult to fit into the career of an investigator who is not on the intramural staff of NIMH, as he was. During the last 30 years, we have not had replications of the Caudill project in even a few culturally differing populations, although these might have provided valid estimates of how and to what extent normal child development, family life, and psychopathology fit together in a particular culture and vary across cultures.

Without such estimates we are unable to make the kind of progress in psychocultural research related to psychiatric concerns that has been possible through the large-scale, long-term projects on child survival, human nutrition, and reproduction that have been carried out in such places as Guatemala, Bangladesh, and the Philippines (the INCAP, Matlab, and Cebu projects).

The Boas and Caudill episodes, separated by fifty years within the 20th century, reveal anthropologists contributing ideas and evidence to the study of child development and conducting ambitious research projects, supported by the Federal government, designed to change the scientific thought of their times concerning the nature of environmental influence on human development. Boas's immigration study, despite or perhaps partly because of its controversial character, was successful in that it initiated a line of work that by the end of the century had clarified how environmental factors affect the physical growth of children and adults. This success, however, depended heavily on (a) biomedical research identifying the chemical agents enhancing growth and the physiological pathways through which they operate and (b) the measurability of the developmental outcomes of physical growth – namely, stature and bone growth.

Boas also opened the door conceptually to the study of environmental influence in mental (read cultural and psychological) development. But mental development proved more problematic than physical growth in ways he might not have foreseen in 1912. Psychologists disagreed among themselves about the factors, processes, pathways, and outcomes involved in mental development and on methods of assessing them. And anthropologists could not count on unequivocal progress in psychology on which to base their own cross-cultural studies. Instead they had to join, in effect, a sectlike psychological or psychiatric research community and become adherents of a theory and a methodology that was regarded as speculative by other psychologists and psychiatrists. (Boas in 1938 probably regarded all of the psychoanalytic, psychometric, behavioristic, and other experimental approaches to mental development as speculations rather than empirical science.)

This problem had not been solved by 1960, when Caudill launched his project. He tried to transcend it (a) by focusing on observable behavior and cultural meanings and abstaining from definitive psychological interpretations, (b) by using naturalistic observations rather than psychological tests in making developmental assessments, (c) by examining symptom patterns rather than psychiatric diagnoses whenever possible, and (d) by examining distributions of characteristics within samples rather than assuming homogeneity. Altogether, Caudill's project was empirically restrained and nonpartisan and built a body of evidence reasonably convincing from many perspectives, even though his psychoanalytic training and orientation shows through at many points. If its scientific impact was limited by comparison with Boas's immigration study, it was not only because of its incomplete integration at the time of his death and the lack of subsequent replications in other cultures. It was also because, even in his empiricism, Caudill could not escape the inadequate state of psychology and psychiatry at the time.

Caudill was unable to base his comparative work on a set of approaches that had been firmly validated at home and were generally held to be applicable. In fact, both psychology and psychiatry underwent revolutions during the 1960s, throwing out dominant approaches, incorporating new ideas and methods, and remaining far more divided and uncertain than biology. Thus the greater success of the Boas project concerning children's physical growth as compared to Caudill's project on the child's acquisition of culture corresponds closely to the relative progress of biology and psychology during the 20th century.

There are some lessons here for anthropologists involved in psychocultural research on normal child development and psychopathology in human populations. First of all, there is the dilemma facing Boas and Caudill and all anthropologists of child development since then: A study of environmental influence must be based on the best available knowledge of human ontogeny, especially the kinds of input or stimuli to which children are sensitive at different ages and the developmental processes through which the environmental factors operate. The anthropologist must know in detail what has been discovered by psychologists and other laboratory scientists and clinicians about human capacities for experience, learning, and the processing of experience at different ages, from early infancy onwards. Unfortunately, however, knowledge available when the anthropologist is planning the study may well be rejected by researchers a few years later, so that the data collection may turn out to have been based on false assumptions. In Boas's day there were many fallacious theories of development, including G. Stanley Hall's recapitulationism and the racial typologies of physical anthropology. When Caudill planned his study, Hullian behavior theory and other forms of stimulus-response theory were dominant in psychology, and Freudian and other forms of psychoanalysis were dominant in psychiatry.

Both Boas and Caudill decided that the "best" developmental theories of their time, with which they were thoroughly familiar, were not good enough. They expanded their observations beyond the scope of dominant paradigms. Boas measured stature as well as cephalic index, but he could not ask subjects to remove their clothes, and it had not yet been established that the wrist was a sensitive locus for measuring bone growth. In the long run, however, stature turned out to be highly appropriate for detecting the influence of environment on growth. Caudill, although trained in Freudian psychoanalysis in Boston and conversant with the theory and method of the Six Cultures Study of Socialization (as a colleague of John and Beatrice Whiting at Harvard when that study was planned and carried out in the 1950s), did not follow either of these models in his own research. In contrast with orthodox Freudian theory, he focused on the interpersonal environment of the child, and in contrast with the approach of the Whitings and their collaborators, he began his observations in early infancy. His assumptions that parents reveal their intentions for the child's future interpersonal relations in the first months after birth and begin then to shape its development represented a real step forward, reflecting the new interest in infant psychology at that time, the anthropologist's traditional interest in social relationships, and the interpersonal theory of psychiatry of Sullivan and others that had influenced Sapir, Mead, and Bateson.

Caudill, in other words, became a developmental psychologist and psychiatric researcher himself, so that he was able to contribute to the ideas and methods of those fields instead of just borrowing their approaches for his fieldwork or satisfying himself with a critique. He exemplified the point that psychological anthropologists should not wait for psychology and psychiatry to come up with theoretical formulations and methods prepackaged for use in other cultures. The anthropologist has to be a fully competent participant in the study of psychological development and psychopathology, and that is as true in these days of neuroscience as it was in previous eras.

## DEVELOPMENTAL PSYCHIATRY: GUESSWORK VS. RESEARCH

My concluding point is that developmental hypotheses in psychiatry are based in significant part on guesswork and will continue to be until they are put to the test of intensive and repeated cross-cultural investigation. This argument begins with Boas's 1902 explication of Virchow's concept of cellular plasticity in which "it is impossible to draw a sharp line between normal physiological, and abnormal or pathological, changes" (Boas, 1902, reprinted in Stocking, 1974, p. 38). Plasticity at any level affords an initial indeterminacy such that what appears in observation to be something categorically different from what the investigator has presumed as normal may turn out to be either a temporary departure from the norm or one of several variant, nonpathological, phenotypes. This means that the investigator, instead of taking his initial presumption to be correct, must make further observations to determine the range of temporary variations and of variant forms, or he will fall victim to fallacious judgments that conflate normal variations with pathology. Here we have the general principle underlying Boas's well-known antipathy to the categories and typological approaches of 19th- and early 20th-century anthropology. Without prior empirical study of their variability under different conditions, types represented no more than wild guesses about human differences, and it was the first task of empirical science to dispel the results of guesswork or speculation.

Developmental thinking in psychiatry has long been afflicted by this problem, that is, guessing at the line that distinguishes cases of pathology – or adverse experiences that give rise to psychopathology – from those of nonpathological variants, usually with the result of misclassifying the latter as the former. To illustrate this, let us return to Caudill's (1961) characterization of the normal or typical Japanese mother-child relationship as "almost symbiotic," using the term formulated by Margaret Mahler (1958) to characterize a pathogenic syndrome observed in clinical psychiatric practice. In Japan it was conventional for mothers to sleep and bathe with their children during infancy and long afterwards, never to leave the child with a babysitter, and not to confront the misbehaving child but to control her with appeals suggesting that she was inflicting emotional injury on others, including the mother (Doi, 1973; Lebra, 1976, 1994; Rothbaum, Pott, & Azuma, 2000). In American psychiatry of the 1960s and later, this profile of practices would be classified as pathogenic, interfering with the normal "separation–individuation process" essential to nonpathological development (Mahler, Pine, & Bergman, 1975) and prognostic of psychiatric disability. In fact, however, generations of Japanese were raised this way, and although as adults they did not conform to American standards of emotional maturity and interpersonal conduct, they did not on the whole suffer from the impairment of their thought processes, emotional stability, and social competence that the theories of Mahler and others would have predicted.

In this case the psychiatrist and her colleagues formulated a theory of normal development based on a psychiatric disorder observed in American clinical practice, tested it in a longitudinal study of a nonclinical, that is, "normal" New York sample (unusual in psychiatry) and claimed to have discovered a universal developmental process. It apparently did not occur to them, although it has to others, that their account of normal psychic development is heavily infused with American cultural values concerning individualism (Kirschner, 1996), and that other nonpathological variants of childhood social development are possible in cultures with differing developmental goals. In this instance, the psychiatric theory ignored or underestimated the plasticity of human social and emotional development and claimed, in effect, that deviation from American standards of child rearing would lead to psychopathology, a claim that cannot survive empirical scrutiny in diverse cultures. The evidence we have so far indicates that, on the contrary, there are multiple pathways (including the one described for the Japanese) to healthy or at least nonpathological psychic conditions in adulthood. Thus this psychiatric theory of development fails. It does not take into account variations that might have been generally expected through a postulate of developmental plasticity but can only be established through observations of parents and children in diverse cultures.

All developmental theories in psychiatry are subject to the same problem unless they engage in unethical experiments with children or, like Weisner (2001) and his colleagues, find naturally occurring child rearing experiments within the ideologically diverse population of the United States. The problem of conflating the conditions of normal or optimal development for all humans with contemporary Anglo-American cultural norms is especially acute for psychiatric clinicians, as they devote themselves to helping their patients adapt to those norms. It is unrealistic to expect them to imagine how alternative norms might support normal development elsewhere without evidence embodied in cross-cultural research. Psychiatry needs the kind of research in other cultures that Caudill began in Japan, to investigate why and how what appears to be an adverse experience for a child in the United States can lead to nonpathological outcomes elsewhere.

The fallibility of developmental psychiatry as scientific theory is thus because of the understandable, indeed unavoidable, failure of the psychiatric imagination to anticipate other cultures' developmental pathways, thereby assuming that the developmental pathways preferred by Americans (or White American middle-class Anglo-Americans, Euro-Americans, and Westerners) are optimal psychologically for humans in general. This fallacy generally takes one of two forms concerning norms of interpersonal conduct, which I call Type I and Type II errors, based on whether, to put it simply, it is excessive closeness or excessive distance in early relationships that is mistaken as pathological. The Type I error is based, like Mahler's theory, on Anglo-American norms that promote individuation or self-reliance in early childhood and classify the promotion or indulgence of childhood closeness, dependence, or passivity as a source of mental illness.

The Type II error is based, like Bowlby's formulations, on Anglo-American norms that promote warmth and affection in the child's early relationships and see the primary potentials for mental illness in distance, deprivation, and separation. As I have pointed out elsewhere (LeVine & Norman, 2001), Bowlby (1988) blurred the differences between the traumatically separated and severely neglected children of his early studies and the "insecurely attached" children of the nonpathological samples studied by Ainsworth and colleagues (1978), whose mothers may have been relatively insensitive to their communicative signals during infancy, but whose subsequent emotional problems did not amount to mental illness or psychiatric disability. Acceptance of the Bowlby-Ainsworth model in child development research has resulted in an unfortunate pathologizing of normal individual differences within Anglo-American populations and in treating populations providing less warmth and affection during infancy as anomalies beyond scientific understanding.

The Type I and Type II errors are two sides of a single tendency in American culture, the dependency conflict described by Weisner (2001). American parents and American child rearing experts favor what they consider independence, individualism, and self-reliance in children, but they also want children to be emotionally engaged with others, verbally expressive, and responsive to praise and approval. The conflict inherent in the practices inspired by this ideology has consequences in the psychodynamics of American individuals. Particular schools of thought in developmental psychiatry have tended to see the primary risks to mental health, in the form of early adverse experiences, in one type of child rearing or the other – that is, child rearing that fosters either emotional overdependence or emotional deprivation, and when they exaggerate the risks, they commit the Type I error or the Type II error, respectively. The errors are caused by connected but dialectically opposed cultural frames for conceptualizing desirable child rearing – frames inherited from Euro-American philosophical and religious traditions.

To free developmental psychiatry from its culture-bound perspectives and enable it to identify what constitutes "early adverse experience" and "early life stress" (Heim, Plotsky, & Nemeroff, 2004; Sanchez, Ladd, & Plotsky, 2001) or other forms of maltreatment resulting in psychopathology in humans, it will be necessary to examine in an ambitious, open-ended, intensive, and systematic way the variations of early experiences and normative outcomes in diverse human populations. The NAS Committee on the Science of Early Childhood Development (Shonkoff & Phillips, 2000) was right in claiming cultural research to be challenging as well as complicated, but it is a challenge that must be faced by the child development field and should assume priority in the agenda for mental health research.

REFERENCES

Ainsworth, M. D. S., Blehar, M. C., Waters, E., & Wall, S. (1978). *Patterns of attachment: A psychological study of the Strange Situation*. Hillsdale, NJ: LEA.
Bateson, G., & Mead, M. (1942). *Balinese character: A photographic analysis*. New York: New York Academy of Sciences.
Benedict, R. (1934). *Patterns of culture*. Boston: Houghton Mifflin.
Boas, F. (1892). The growth of children. *Science, 19*, 256–257, 281–282; 20, 351–352.
Boas, F. (1902). Rudolf Virchow's anthropological work. *Science, 16*, 441–445.
Boas, F. (1912a). *Changes in bodily form of descendants of immigrants*. New York: Columbia University Press.
Boas, F. (1912b). Changes in the bodily form of descendants of immigrants. *American Anthropologist, 14*, 530–562.
Boas, F. (1912c). Instability of human types. In G. Spiller (Ed.), *Papers on interracial problems communicated to the first Universal Races Congress held at the University of London, July 26–29, 1911* (pp. 99–103). Boston: Ginn & Co.
Boas, F., Ed. (1938). *General anthropology*. Boston: D.C. Heath & Co.
Bogin, B. (1999). *Patterns of human growth* (2nd ed.). Cambridge, UK: Cambridge University Press.
Bogin, B. (2001). *The growth of humanity*. New York: Wiley-Liss.
Bogin, B., & Loucky, J. (1997). Plasticity, political economy, and physical growth status of Guatemala Maya children living in the United States. *American Journal of Physical Anthropology, 102*, 17–32.
Bowlby, J. (1988). *A secure base: Parent-child attachment and healthy human development*. New York: Basic Books.
Caudill, W. (1949). Psychological characteristics of acculturated Wisconsin Ojibwa children. *American Anthropologist, 51*, 409–427.
Caudill, W. (1961). Around the clock patient care in Japanese psychiatric hospitals: The role of the Tsukisoi. *American Sociological Review, 26*, 204–214.
Caudill, W. (1963). Sibling rank and style of life among Japanese psychiatric patients. In H. Akimoto (Ed.), *Proceedings of the Joint Meeting of the Japanese Society of Psychiatry and Neurology and the American Psychiatric Association*, May 13–17, 1963, Tokyo, Japan.
Caudill, W., & Plath, D. (1966). Who sleeps by whom? Parent-child involvement in urban Japanese families. *Psychiatry, 29*, 344–366.
Caudill, W., & Schooler, C. (1973). Child behavior and child rearing in Japan and the United States: An interim report. *Journal of Nervous and Mental Disease, 157*, 323–338.
Caudill, W., & Weinstein, H. (1969). Maternal care and infant behavior in Japan and America. *Psychiatry, 32*, 12–43.

Darnell, R. (1986). Personality and culture: The fate of the Sapirian alternative. In G. Stocking (Ed.), *Malinowski, Rivers, Benedict and others: Essays on culture and personality* (pp. 156–183). Madison: University of Wisconsin Press.

Darnell, R. (1990). *Edward Sapir: Linguist, anthropologist, humanist.* Berkeley and Los Angeles: University of California Press.

Doi, T. (1973a). *The anatomy of dependence.* New York: Kodansha International.

Doi, T. (1973b). Omote and ura: Concepts derived from the Japanese two-fold structure of consciousness. *Journal of Nervous and Mental Disease, 157,* 258–261.

Gravelee, C., Bernard, H. R., & Leonard, W. R. (2003). Heredity, environment, and cranial form: A reanalysis of Boas's immigrant data. *American Anthropologist, 105,* 125–138.

Heim, C., Plotsky, P., & Nemeroff, C. (2004). Importance of studying the contributions of early adverse experience to neurobiological findings in depression. *Neuropsychopharmacology, 29,* 641–648.

Kirschner, S. (1996). *Religious and romantic origins of psychoanalysis: Individuation and integration in post-Freudian theory.* New York: Cambridge University Press.

Lebra, T. S. (1976). *Patterns of Japanese behavior.* Honolulu: University of Hawaii Press.

Lebra, T. S. (1994). Mother and child in Japanese socialization: A Japan–U.S. comparison. In P. Greenfield & R. Cocking (Eds.), *Cross-cultural roots of minority child development* (pp. 259–274). Hillsdale, NJ: LEA.

LeVine, R. A., & Norman, K. (2001). The infant's acquisition of culture: Early attachment reexamined in anthropological perspective. In C. Moore & H. Mathews (Eds.), *The psychology of cultural experience* (pp. 83–104). New York: Cambridge University Press.

Mahler, M. (1958). *On human symbiosis and the vicissitudes of individuation.* New York: International Universities Press.

Mahler, M., Pine, F., & Bergman, A. (1975). *The psychological birth of the human infant: Symbiosis and individuation.* New York: Basic Books.

Markus, H., & Kitayama, S. (1991). Culture and the self: Implications for cognition, emotion and motivation. *Psychological Review, 98,* 224–253.

Mead, M. (1928). *Coming of age in Samoa.* New York: William Morrow.

Mead, M. (1930). *Growing up in New Guinea.* New York: William Morrow.

Mead, M. (1931). Research on primitive children. In C. Murchison (Ed.), *Manual of child psychology.* Worcester, MA: Clark University Press.

Pierpont, C. (2004, March 8). The measure of America: How a rebel anthropologist waged war on racism. *The New Yorker,* pp. 48–63.

Rothbaum, F., Pott, M., & Azuma, H. (2000). The development of close relationships in Japan and the United States: Paths of symbolic harmony and generative tension. *Child Development, 71,* 1121–1142.

Sanchez, M., Ladd, C., & Plotsky, P. (2001). Early adverse experience as a developmental risk factor for later psychopathology: Evidence from rodent and primate models. *Development and Psychopathology, 13,* 419–449.

Sapir, E. (1993). *The psychology of culture: A course of lectures.* Reconstructed and edited by J. T. Irvine. New York: Mouton de Gruyter.

Schooler, C. (1996). William Caudill and the reproduction of culture: Infant, child and maternal behavior in Japan and the United States. In D. Schwalb &

B. Schwalb (Eds.), *Japanese childrearing: Two generations of scholarship*. New York: Guilford Press.

Schooler, C., & Caudill, W. (1964). Symptomatology in Japanese and American schizophrenics. *Ethnology, 3,* 172–178.

Shonkoff, J., & Phillips, D. (2000). *From neurons to neighborhoods: The science of early childhood development.* Washington: National Academy Press.

Sparks, C., & Jantz, R. (2002). A reassessment of human cranial plasticity: Boas revisited. *Proceedings of the National Academy of Sciences of the United States of America, 99*(23), pp. 14636–14639. doi: 10.1073/pnas.222389599.

Stocking, G. W. (1968). *Race, culture and evolution: Essays in the history of anthropology.* Chicago: University of Chicago Press.

Stocking, G. (1974). *A Franz Boas reader: The shaping of American anthropology* (pp. 1883–1911). New York: Basic Books.

Stocking, G. (1992). Polarity and plurality: Franz Boas as psychological anthropologist. In T. Schwartz, G. White, & C. Lutz (Eds.), *New directions in psychological anthropology* (pp. 311–323). New York: Cambridge University Press.

Tanner, J. M. (1959). Boas' contribution to knowledge of human growth and form. In W. Goldschmidt (Ed.) *The anthropology of Franz Boas. Memoir No. 89 of the American Anthropological Association, 61,* 76–111.

Vogel, E., & Schooler, C. (Eds.) (1973). In memory of William A. Caudill, Pts. I and II. *Journal of Nervous and Mental Disease, 157*(4, 5), 231–395.

Weisner, T. (2001). The American dependency conflict: Continuities and discontinuities in behavior and values of countercultural parents and their children. *Ethos, 29,* 271–295.

Whiting, J. (1954). The cross-cultural method. In G. Lindzey (Ed.), *Handbook of social psychology* (pp. 523–531). Cambridge, MA: Addison-Wesley.

Whiting, J., & Whiting, B. (1960). Contributions of anthropology to methods of studying child rearing. In P. Mussen (Ed.), *Handbook of research methods in child development* (pp. 918–944). New York: Wiley.

# TWO

# From Measurement to Meaning in Caregiving and Culture

## Current Challenges and Future Prospects

Marc H. Bornstein

It has been observed that the most significant single determiner of the future course of development may be where a child is born (Weisner, 2002); important differences in environments, emotions, and interactions characterize how different cultures shape human development. Comparisons consistently show that virtually all aspects of caregiving and human development are informed by their cultural context (Bornstein, 1980, 2009). This chapter is about the role of culture in caregiving and human development from a cross-cultural developmental science perspective. I discuss issues of both perennial and current relevance revolving around three themes: First, notions of similarity and difference across cultures; specifically, how they can be understood, measured for comparative analysis, and interpreted through the mediating role of meaning. Second, how culture can be studied; specifically, the problems of employing variables versus persons as units, the over-emphasis on cross-cultural versus cultural studies, and the abundance of cross-sectional over longitudinal studies. Third, the issue of cultural transmission; specifically, using the contextual ecological model to integrate culture into transmission, looking at the intergenerational transmission of culture, and accounting for the impact of diachronic change on cultural developmental studies. These are by no means the only topics that culture and development scholars view as important, nor are these topics always discretely different from one another. Finally, I wrap up with a discussion on current problems and future directions for the study of caregiving and human development in cultural context.

## CULTURE: SIMILARITIES AND DIFFERENCES

What is culture anyway? Is culture an ineffable emergent quality greater than the sum of its parts, or is culture an aggregation of variables that is equal to their sum? This question is of more than passing interest to developmental scientists. It is a crucial conceptual foundation that informs how culture can or should be measured in cross-cultural developmental science research. Are cultural similarities and differences somehow intrinsic and unmeasurable, or can they be categorized and quantified? Furthermore, cultures are composed of people. How do the two relate?

The *equivalence perspective* of human beings contends that cultural influences such as socialization practices, language, and opportunity structures influence constructs, structures, functions, and processes (henceforth termed *core constituents*) for all individuals in a similar fashion. In other words, if members of the same or different cultures all had access to the same cultural influences they would share the same mental constructs, structures, functions, and processes. It also possible that human beings differ intrinsically in the core constituents that make up culture. This constitutes the *variance perspective*, which posits that core constituents of culture are configured across human groups differently, and cannot be altered simply through external influences.

Similarities among cultures might be attributable to several factors, including inherent attributes of individuals (the equivalence perspective), the common press of environmental contingencies (the variance perspective), historical convergence, migration, or information dissemination via mass media. Ultimately, because caregivers must help their children experience and succeed at some similar developmental tasks, and they (presumably) wish to promote some similar general competencies in their offspring, they caregive in some manifestly similar ways. However, substantial differences also exist across cultures – as exemplified in the case studies presented by Fouts, Busch and Lieberman, Briggs, Anderson-Fye, and Lemelson in this volume – in terms of socialization practices, language, and opportunity structures, not to mention history, beliefs, and values. Central to a concept of *culture*, after all, is the expectation that different peoples possess different ideas, and behave in different ways, with respect to their caregiving.

Although we still may not agree on what culture is, how to measure it, or how it relates to the individuals who compose it, for the purposes of this chapter, we can think of culture as a unique (but not necessarily uniform) constellation of core constituents. The concept of culture can therefore be understood as a route of access to relations between environments on the one hand and individual-level or group-level core constituents on the other.

## Grounds for Comparison: Measuring Equivalence Across Cultures

Developmental scientists who conduct cross-cultural analysis normally rely on measurement of some sort. Invalid measures can inflate the risk of identifying a difference between cultures when no such difference exists or missing a true difference between cultures. Time and again, measures that have been validated in one culture have proved inappropriate with others. So-called measurement equivalence is, therefore, a crucial first step in investigating culture comparatively. Measurement equivalence means that when an informant answers a question, the chance that the informant will select a particular response is the same across all informants, regardless of their cultural membership. Legitimate comparison across cultures is assured only if measurement equivalence is first established.

The challenge is that researchers need to consider many types of measurement equivalence: configural, metric, scalar, unique variance, factor mean, factor variance, and functional (see Vandenberg & Lance, 2000). Different types of equivalence reflect increasingly restrictive levels of similarity across cultures at the level of individual items ("true measurement equivalence") and latent parameters ("structural equivalence").

Research emphasizes the first-order importance of establishing measurement equivalence; unfortunately, few cultural studies consolidate on these measurement issues. Comparative studies of cultures must test the equivalence of measures before interpreting substantive differences. Measurement inequivalence might explain some substantive differences traditionally reported between cultural groups.

## What's What? The Mediating Role of Meaning-Making

Cross-cultural comparison also engages the meaning behind local cultural practices that shape the psychological variables we seek to measure. This is because different forms normally signal different meanings in different cultures. Seeing their very young children as an extension of themselves, Japanese mothers work with their children to consolidate and strengthen mutual dependence (*amae*) consonant with collectivity and the emphasis on interpersonal sensitivity that is esteemed in their culture. By contrast, U.S. caregivers typically wish to promote autonomy in their children, organizing caregiver–child interactions to foster physical and verbal independence in children in accord with individualism and assertiveness generally valued in U.S. culture. These interactions reflect different form–different meaning relations in the different cultures.

It is also the case that a single form can have the same meaning in different cultures. For instance, mothers in both Japan and the United States respond to their infants' vocalizing distress predominantly (as would be expected) by nurturing, despite cultural differences (Bornstein et al., 1992). Such same form–same meaning relations are often thought of as cultural universals, perhaps reflective of general tendencies of the human species. Since Bowlby and Ainsworth, developmentalists have tended to regard prompt, contingent, and appropriate caregiver responsiveness as a generally good thing. Globally, caregiver responsiveness is believed to promote secure attachment, effectance, and a sense of self; it also acknowledges the integrity of the child.

However, the same form can have different meanings, depending on culture. The attribution of difficult temperament in modern individualistic societies often implies a problem in the child; a difficult temperament is associated with psychiatric risk. Some adults may find certain infant characteristics difficult, but other adults may not. In this sense, "difficult-ness" resides, not (only) in the child, but in the caregiving context, and whether temperament is difficult depends on its fit with the culture (see Nowakowski, Schmidt, & Hall; Panksepp, this volume). In an extreme example, during conditions of drought and famine in Africa, characteristics of infant "difficultness" were associated with survival – probably because such infants demanded and received more attention and nourishment than the "less difficult" infants. African infants who would be viewed by most Americans as difficult had better survival rates (deVries, 1984).

Finally, different forms can serve a single ultimate cultural meaning. To the extent that similarity exists in a given caregiving domain, it resides not necessarily in similar caregiver behaviors, but in the meaning of behaviors, patterns, or effects. Japanese and U.S. mothers are both responsive, and may be equally so, but their responsiveness differs in purpose. Japanese mothers tend to use infant eye-to-eye contact as a setting event to begin an *en face* interaction or keep one going, whereas U.S. mothers tend to use eye-to-eye contact as a setting event to introduce their infants to something in the environment outside the dyad or to label objects. Thus, caregivers may engage in different, culturally specific forms to ultimately achieve similar developmental goals and meanings.

Understanding relations between form and meaning as embedded in cultural transactions depends on context, the unit of analysis, and the level of abstraction chosen for analysis. Development in culture is the prime situation for examining how the meaning of activity is afforded, shaped, and acquired. A child's interpretation of parenting is an important source of variance (Lansford et al., 2005). Children's sense of whether the parenting they receive is typical of their culture mediates parenting's impact. Thus, cultural meaning attributed to behavior must be accounted for if we hope to understand the implications of cultural constituents for developmental outcomes.

## LEVELS OF ANALYSIS

### Where and How: Locating "Culture" in Variables and Persons

The dominant approach to assessment in biological and social science uses single variables, combinations of variables, or relations among variables as the main conceptual and analytical units (Hartmann & Pelzel, 2005). A single datum for an individual derives meaning from its position on a given dimension relative to the positions of data from other individuals. "In a variable approach... [i]ndividuals differ only quantitatively, not qualitatively, along the dimension for a certain variable" (Magnusson, 1998, pp. 45–46). The generic term "variable" is often used to describe the approach specific to analyses of individual variables.

Yet, the configuration of individual variables also has meaning, and information about an individual as a Gestalt is also of interest. The contrasting generic term "person" describes an approach to the analysis of patterns within individuals or across clusters of individuals. The person approach is based on a wholistic-interactionistic research paradigm to functioning and development. It sees the individual as an organized whole, functioning and developing as a totality (Magnusson & Allen, 1983), which derives its characteristic features and properties from interactions among its elements rather than from the effect of isolated parts of the totality or as an aggregate of variables (the whole is more than the sum of the parts). In the person approach, each datum derives its psychological meaning from its place in a pattern of data representing positions on latent dimensions, and the whole is the main conceptual and analytical unit. Like variables, patterns have been found to predict developmental outcomes; therefore, both have crucial validity.

The variable approach focuses on values on a scale; the person approach focuses on patterns of values. Cultural studies need to explore, adopt, and profit from both variable and person approaches.

### Among or Amongst: Intra-cultural and Cross-cultural Study

Cross-cultural research explores and explains similarities and differences in a culture's core constituents (Bornstein, 1980, 2009; van de Vijver & Leung, 1997). Cultural research is often conducted by developmental scientists investigating a single-culture extension of their monocultural work. Three principal reasons should motivate a more expansive cultural developmental science that embraces a variety of qualitative and quantitative approaches. One is *description*: Because core constituents attempt to include the widest diversity of human variation, they are the most inclusive and, as such, are essential to delimiting the full array of human experience. In this sense, too, they are decisive when it comes to verifying legitimate developmental standards. Knowledge of alternative manners of development through greater familiarity with cross-cultural studies in anthropology can further hone our awareness and improve our comprehension of our own culture (see Stocking, 1989–1999 for historical overview). A second reason is *explanation*: Cultural comparisons aid greatly in the quest to identify forces that determine the nature and structure of cultural constituents (see Mead, 1928; Romney & Moore, 1998; and Ember & Ember, 2003–2005, for illustrative examples from anthropology). Although the cultural view is useful to expose variables and the processes that regulate them, it may be "invisible" from behind monocultural blinders that can bias the departure point for cross-cultural research. In particular, a cross-cultural approach can contribute to understanding the parts that culture-dependent and culture-independent forces play in the nature and structure of human development. Notably, cultural inquiry increases our understanding of the processes through which biological variables fuse with environmental variables and experiences. Even behaviors that are logical candidates for a strong biological interpretation (because of their identifiable genetic roots or display of regularity in one place) are also subject to the forces of environment and experience, and often show variability when studied in other places (see Zitzer-Comfort, Reilly, Korenberg, & Bellugi, this volume). A third reason is *meaning*: Understanding human activity often depends on examining that activity in its cultural context (Shweder, 1991; Shore, 1996). Furthermore, development in culture is a prime circumstance for examining how the meaning of human activity is shaped (Harkness et al., 2007). Therefore, adding developmental trajectories to cultural elements is vital.

## Studying "Development": Cross-sectional and Longitudinal Approaches

Developmental studies typically concentrate on a particular point in the life cycle. They qualify as "developmental" because their focus falls on infants or children or (less frequently) the aged, and not because, as the term suggests, more than one point in the life span is being investigated.

Certainly, describing children at a given age serves important goals, but developmental science is interested in aspects of phenomena that implicate time and growth; thus comparative longitudinal designs are also vital to a vigorous ontogenetic science. In particular, it is crucial for analyzing two main features of ontogeny: group continuity and individual stability. In this respect, animal models have been extremely useful (see Szyf, McGowan, Turecki, & Meaney; Wiedenmayer; and Sanchez, McCormack, & Maestripieri, this volume).

The terms continuity and discontinuity refer to whether construct, structure, function, or process will display a mean level at one point in time and display that same level at a later point across time as a group average (the developmental function; Wohlwill, 1973). The terms stability or instability refer to an individual's relative standing or order in the group across time (individual differences; Baltes & Nesselroade, 1979). The predictive validity of individual variation in a particular configuration of cultural constituents at one time, a corollary of stability, tells us about the potential influence of one factor on another at a later point in development. Continuity in a group and stability in individuals are each descriptive and explanatory of development, and the two are conceptually and statistically independent (Bornstein & Suess, 2001; McCall, 1981). Group-individual patterns can be continuous-and-stable, discontinuous-and-stable, continuous-and-unstable and discontinuous-and-unstable.

Both flux and constancy are important in the course of development. Consistency helps provide basic information, meaning, and survival needs in a given context. Consistency also affects the environment: Interactants often adjust to a consistent set of cultural constituents (which may contribute to their consistency). Change arises through gene expression (see Szyf et al., this volume), cultural constituents are plastic to psychosocial experience (see Nowakowski et al.; Seraphin et al., this volume), and people engage in changing normative life tasks and roles (see Busch & Lieberman, this volume). Investigating continuity and stability informs us about possible origins, nature, norms, future, and perhaps the validity of relations between cultural constituents and development (McCall, 1981; Robinson, Emde, & Korfmacher, 1997).

To understand development in any deep sense requires understanding how its constituent phenomena present and unfold developmentally across the life course and culturally in different groups. The lifespan perspective asserts that human beings are open systems, and the plastic nature of cultural constituents ensures that people exhibit both consistency and change throughout life.

## MECHANISMS OF CULTURAL TRANSMISSION

### Integrating Culture into Transaction: The Contextual Ecological Model of Development

Development is a function of the individual and the individual's environment, and not of either alone. *Transaction* asserts that the characteristics of an individual shape his or her experiences and, reciprocally, experiences shape the characteristics of the individual through time. In the prevailing ecological contextual view, caregiver and child stand at the center of a nexus of nested systems. In all of their interactions, children participate in culturally organized activities; in this way, they gain an understanding of the world they live in.

As "apprentices" learning daily living skills, children interact with the central characters in their culture so that they can grow up and adapt successfully (Whiting & Whiting, 1979; Rogoff, 1990; Greenfield, Keller, Fuligni, & Maynard, 2003). Some forces such as parents and siblings are close at hand, but other forces are somewhat removed (extended family, peers in neighborhood, parents' workmates). Still other forces are further removed (social class, culture). Closer influences are called *proximal*, and more remote influences are called *distal*. Generally speaking, distal forces influence human development through proximal forces. Thus, culture (a distal influence) is linked to how children develop in their microsystem with caregivers, the "final common pathway" of early childhood oversight and caregiving to development, stature, adjustment, and success. Living in one or another culture may not influence the child directly; rather, parents who have themselves been enculturated in that culture (proximal influences) in turn enculturate their children in terms of life experiences. As the human case studies in this volume exemplify, the main focus of much research falls on proximal processes in caregiver-child interactions.

However, the macrosystem consists of the overarching systems characteristic of the culture, in particular the beliefs, bodies of knowledge, material resources, customs, life-styles, opportunity structures, hazards, and life course options that are embedded in each of the inner systems (Bronfenbrenner, 1994). In this framework of nested systems, the mesosystem comprises linkages and processes that take place between two or more settings containing the developing person, and the exosystem comprises linkages and processes that take place between two or more settings in which events occur that indirectly influence processes within the person's immediate setting and where at least one setting does not contain the developing person. Interactions with the environment occur at multiple levels, and all constitute effective environmental stimulants to development between the distal macrosystem and the proximal microsystem.

A challenge in the study of culture, caregiving, human development, and transaction is how parents' childrearing is culturally shaped. Parents' beliefs presumably relate to parents' behaviors and in turn to children's development. Expectations about developmental norms and milestones – for example, when a child is expected to achieve a particular developmental skill – affect parents' appraisals of their child's development and the process of development itself. Not yet well worked out are theoretical and functional connections between culture and caregiving attitudes and actions. More work is needed on linking culture to caregiving and human development, just as more work needs to link caregiving and human development to culture.

Caregivers and children are embedded in multiple contexts, and each context contributes critically to how caregivers support developing characteristics of children. Needed is a greater understanding of the processes and contents of caregivers' particular competencies and their roles as purveyors of a culture. In everyday situations, caregivers structure interactions with children using strategies geared toward actualizing socialization goals that are emphasized by their cultural value system (see Fouts, this volume). In this sense, caregivers are also culture-bearers and transmit culture across generations.

### Conveying Culture: Intergenerational Transmission

Through intergenerational transmission via interlocked genetic and experiential pathways, whether purposefully or unintentionally, one generation influences the beliefs and behaviors of the next (van IJzendoorn, 1992). A caregiver's past experiences with caregivers continue to influence his or her own caregiving (Smith & Drew, 2002; see also Busch & Lieberman and Schechter, this volume). Fraiberg and her colleagues (1975) once famously referred to such influences as "ghosts in the nursery." How does culture link to caregiving to human development to perpetuate culture?

Surprisingly, only a few empirical studies explicitly explore more than one or two links in this chain from (a) culture to (b) caregiver to (c) child back to (a) culture. The cultural and cross-cultural literatures are populated with lots of (a-b) studies, and the developmental literature is populated with lots of (b-c) studies, but (a-b-c) studies that cross the cultural-developmental literatures are few outside of anthropology (see Whiting & Whiting, 1979; Super & Harkness, 1982, 1999; Weisner, 2002; from a biological anthropological perspective, see Leonard & Thomas, 1989; Konner, 2002; Godoy et al., 2006), and (a-b-c-a) studies outside of anthropology (e.g., Bateson, 1958; Turner, 1967; and Herdt, 1981, 1982) are rare.

Moreover, unresolved tensions reside in unspoken attempts to reconcile cultural socialization with transactionist and constructivist views of child development. What are the chief processes of enculturation? Transactions occur when at least two people interact in such a way that the intentions or actions of one reciprocally affect the intentions or actions of the other. From a dynamic transactional perspective, however, both parent and child "select, edit, and refashion" cultural information. So enculturation at least involves bidirectional processes in which adult and child play transactive roles shaped by culture.

Adult culture is passed down to each new generation primarily through caregiver belief and behavior. In a larger sense, caregiving cognitions and practices contribute to the "continuity of culture" by helping to define culture and its transmission across generations. The study of intergenerational transmission instantiates a progression of ideas – from cultural systems to caregiver childrearing beliefs to caregiver childrearing behaviors to the attitudes and actions of children during childhood and later as parents.

## The Mark of History: Addressing Diachronic Change in Culture and Development

The environment of human development has both physical features (climate, nature, and designed artifacts) and social features. Instead of static entities, physical and social environments are dynamic systems that are constantly engaged in re-construction and re-negotiation as they imprint upon individual lives (see Anderson-Fye, this volume).

Worldwide changes are one example. The urbanization of traditional rural societies has produced children who have fewer interactions with their extended families and who participate less in family labor and household work (Kagitcibasi & Ataca, 2005). Seismic changes that are more local are another example. The fall of the Berlin Wall transformed the life course of East German adolescents. After German unification, adolescents tended to become financially self-supporting adults later than the preceding generations had (Silbereisen, 2000). The change in China to a market economy, beginning in the 1980s, has affected children's functional social interactions and adjustment. Chen, Cen, Li, & He (2005) suggested that extensive changes toward a market economy and the introduction of individualistic values led to a decline in the adaptive value of shy behavior; in the new, competitive environment, shy behavior that impedes self-expression and active exploration became a detriment, whereas before it was regarded as adaptive and competent.

Historical shifts toward urbanization, modernization, Westernization, and market economies produce changes in culture, caregiving, and human development. These changes have considerable implications for parenting and ontogenetic adjustment.

## MOVING FORWARD: A RENEWED RESEARCH AGENDUM FOR CULTURE, CAREGIVING, AND HUMAN DEVELOPMENT

The foregoing considerations may have some implications for the course of future study. A preliminary but necessary and frequently neglected step in cultural developmental examination is to meet measurement requirements. When constructs are comparable, then analyses can be interpreted clearly. Different analytical approaches will bear different fruit. Beyond questions of analytical unit, efforts should be mounted to conduct studies at two or more ages in the life cycle in two or more cultures, however daunting (realizing that two points in the life span or two societies are hardly representative of ontogenetic development or international variation). We must also keep in mind that caregivers operate within the larger macrosystem. Structures within this system influence caregiving, and these broader systems can be influenced by historical changes. The macro and micro are linked through transaction; child and parent bring distinctive characteristics to interactions with one another, and each person changes as a result of these interactions. The meaning attributed to action is largely a function of its ecological niche. If a given behavior is viewed as culturally desirable or acceptable, then parents (and significant others) will encourage its development. Multiple and distinctive pathways exist for socializing children to become competent adults, and optimal development is largely defined by the cultural meaning system.

These are just some issues that begin to define a future agendum of culture, caregiving, and human development. There are others, of course. If we are to fully understand the core constituents of cultural developmental processes, developmental science must go beyond the current emphasis on putative cross-cultural differences. To do so will require more nuanced approaches to culture and a thoroughgoing study of the interactions between culture and developmental psychobiology.

Finally, three different but related limitations of contemporary cultural science constrain our understanding of caregiving and human development: a narrow participant data base, a biased sampling of world cultures of authors, and a corresponding bias in the audience to which the literature is addressed. As noted by contributors Linda Richter and Jennifer Harris Requejo & Flavia Bustreo in the final section of this volume, the contemporary cultural database in caregiving and human development is less than representative. Just 10% of the world's children live in industrialized nations that can afford research; that leaves 90% under-researched. Tomlinson and Swartz (2003) reported that 93% of research studies on infants that were published from 1996–2001 originated in Northern Europe or North America. Our ready generalizations from these limited findings to caregivers or children at large are blindingly uncritical. Views of human development would demonstrably benefit from an enlarged representation of the world's caregivers and children.

The goal of cultural developmental research is to explore and explain similarities and differences in the ways individuals of different ages in different cultures think, behave, and develop. Specific experiences provided by specific caregivers to specific children at specific times exert effects in specific ways over specific aspects of human development (Bornstein, 2002, 2006). This *specificity principle* accords with a culturally informed and developmentally sensitive view of biological and social science (Bornstein, 2008). Multicultural, multiage studies allow the broadest perspective on cultural constituents and the greatest generality in addition to the specificity of empirical findings. Even though the multicultural and multiage methods necessary to study such things are demanding and complex, they are *ipso facto* the most comprehensive. Theoretically, they constitute the first step toward encompassing the full spectrum of human variation. To the extent that scientists embrace the study of multiple ages and cultures, science will enjoy more reliable and valid conclusions.

REFERENCES

Baltes, P. B., & Nesselroade, J. R. (1979). History and rationale of longitudinal research. In J. R. Nesselroade & P. B. Baltes (Eds.), *Longitudinal research in the study of behavior and development* (pp. 1–39). New York: Academic Press.

Bateson, G. (1958). *Naven: A survey of the problems suggested by a composite picture of the culture of a New Guinea tribe drawn from three points of view* (2nd ed.). Stanford: Stanford University Press.

Bornstein, M. H. (1980). Cross-cultural developmental psychology. In M. H. Bornstein (Ed.), *Comparative methods in psychology* (pp. 231–281). Hillsdale, NJ: Erlbaum.

Bornstein, M. H. (Ed.). (2002a). *Handbook of parenting: Practical issues in parenting* (2nd ed., Vol. 5). Mahwah, NJ: Erlbaum.

Bornstein, M. H. (2002b). Toward a multicultural, multiage, multimethod science. *Human Development, 45,* 257–263.

Bornstein, M. H. (2006). Parenting science and practice. In I. E. Sigel & K. A. Renninger (Eds.), W. Damon & R. M. Lerner (Series Eds.), *Handbook of child psychology: Vol. 4. Child psychology and practice* (6th ed., pp. 893–949). New York: Wiley.

Bornstein, M. H. (2008). The specificity principle in parenting and child development. Unpublished manuscript, *Eunice Kennedy Shriver* National Institute of Child Health and Human Development.

Bornstein, M. H. (Ed.). (2009). *The handbook of cross-cultural developmental science. Part 1. Domains of development across cultures. Part 2. Development in different places on earth.* New York, NY: Taylor & Francis Group.

Bornstein, M. H., & Suess, P. E. (2001). Child and mother cardiac vagal tone: Continuity, stability and concordance across the first five years. *Developmental Psychology, 36,* 54–65.

Bornstein, M. H., Tamis-LeMonda, C. S., Tal, J., Ludemann, P., Toda, S., Rahn, C. W., et al. (1992). Maternal responsiveness to infants in three societies: The United States, France, and Japan. *Child Development, 63,* 808–821.

Bronfenbrenner, U. (1994). Ecological models of human development. In T. Husen & T. N. Postlewaite (Eds.), *International encyclopedia of education* (2nd ed., Vol. 3, pp. 1643–1647). Oxford, UK: Pergamon/Eslevier Science.

Chen, X., Cen, G., Li, D., & He, Y. (2005). Social functioning and adjustment in Chinese children: The imprint of historical time. *Child Development, 76,* 182–195.

deVries, M. W. (1984). Temperament and infant mortality among the Masai of East Africa. *American Journal of Psychiatry, 141,* 10.

Ember, C. R., & Ember, M. (2003–2005). *Cross-cultural anthropology: A reference collection.* New York: Springer.

Fraiberg, S., Adelson, E., & Shapiro, V. (1975). Ghosts in the nursery. *Journal of the American Academy of Child Psychiatry, 14,* 387–421.

Godoy, R. A., Patel, A., Reyes-Garcia, V., Seyfried, C. F., Leonard, W. R., McDade, T., et al. (2006). Nutritional status and spousal empowerment among native Amazonians. *Social Science & Medicine, 63,* 1517–1530.

Greenfield, P. M., Keller, H., Fuligni, A., & Maynard, A. (2003). Cultural pathways through universal development. *Annual Review of Psychology, 54,* 461–490.

Harkness, S., Super, C. M., Moscardino, U., Rha, J.-H., Blom, M. J. M., Huitrón, B., et al. (2007). Cultural models and developmental agendas: Implications for arousal and self-regulation in early infancy. *Journal of Developmental Processes, 1*(2), 5–39.

Hartmann, D. P., & Pelzel, K. E. (2005). Design, measurement, and analysis in developmental research. In M. H. Bornstein & M. E. Lamb (Eds.), *Developmental science: An advanced textbook* (5th ed., pp. 103–84). Mahwah, NJ: Erlbaum.

Herdt, G. (1981). *Guardians of the flute: Idioms of masculinity.* New York: McGraw Hill Inc.

Herdt, G. (Ed.). (1982). *Rituals of manhood: Male initiation in Papua New Guinea.* Berkeley: University of California Press.

Kagitcibasi, & Ataca, B. (2005). Value of children and family change: A three decade portrait from Turkey. *Applied Psychology: International Review, 54*, 317–337.

Konner, M. (2002). *The tangled wing: Biological constraints on the human spirit* (2nd ed.). New York: Times Books.

Lansford, J. E., Chang, L., Dodge, K. A., Malone, P. S., Oburu, P., Palmérus, K., et al. (2005). Physical discipline and children's adjustment: Cultural normativeness as a moderator. *Child Development, 76*, 1234–1246.

Leonard, W. R., & Thomas, R. B. (1989). Biosocial responses to seasonal food stress in highland Peru. *Human Biology, 61*, 65–85.

Magnusson, D. (1998). The logic and implications of a person approach. In R. B. Cairns, L. R. Bergman, & J. Kagan (Eds.), *Methods and models for studying the individual* (pp. 33–63). Thousand Oaks, CA: Sage.

Magnusson, D., & Allen, V. L. (1983). Implications and applications of an interactional perspective for human development. In D. Magnusson & V. L. Allen (Eds.), *Human development: An interactional perspective* (pp. 369–387). New York: Academic Press.

McCall, R. B. (1981). Nature-nurture and the two realms of development: A proposed integration with respect to mental development. *Child Development, 52*, 1–12.

Mead, M. (1928). *Coming of age in Samoa: A psychological study of primitive youth for western civilization*. New York: W. Morrow & Co.

Robinson, J., Emde, R. N., & Korfmacher, J. (1997). Integrating an emotional regulation perspective in an program of prenatal and early childhood home visitation. *Journal of Community Psychology, 25*, 59–75.

Rogoff, B. (1990). *Apprenticeship in thinking: Cognitive development in social context.* New York: Oxford University Press.

Romney, A. K., & Moore, C. C. (1998). Toward a theory of culture as shared cognitive structures. *Ethos, 26*(3), 314–337.

Shore, B. (1996). *Culture in mind: Cognition, culture and the problem of meaning*. New York: Oxford University Press.

Shweder, R. (1991). *Thinking through cultures: Expeditions in cultural psychology.* Cambridge, MA: Harvard University Press.

Silbereisen, R. K. (2000). German unification and adolescents' developmental timetables: Continuities and discontinuities. In L. Crockett & R. K. Sibereisen (Eds.), *Negotiating adolescence in times of social change* (pp. 104–122). Cambridge, UK: Cambridge University Press.

Smith, P. K., & Drew, L. M. (2002). Grandparenthood. In M. H. Bornstein (Ed.), *Handbook of parenting: Vol. 3. Status and social conditions of parenting* (2nd ed., pp. 141–172). Mahwah, NJ: Erlbaum.

Stocking, G. W., Jr. (Ed.). (1989–1999). *History of anthropology series* (Vols. 1–8). Madison, WI: University of Wisconsin Press.

Super, C., & Harkness, S. (1982). The developmental niche: A conceptualization at the interface of child and culture. *International journal of Behavioral Development 9*, 1–25.

Super, C. M., & Harkness, S. (1999). The environment as culture in developmental research. In S. L. Friedman & T. D. Wachs (Eds.), *Measuring environment across the life span: Emerging methods and concepts* (pp. 279–323). Washington, DC: American Psychological Association.

Tomlinson, M., & Swartz, L. (2003). Imbalances in the knowledge about infancy: The divide between rich and poor countries. *Infant Mental Health Journal, 24,* 547–556.

Turner, V. (1967). *The forest of symbols: Aspects of Ndembu ritual.* Ithaca, NY: Cornell University Press.

Vandenberg, R. J. & Lance, C. E. (2000). A review and synthesis of the measurement invariance literature: Suggestions, practices, and recommendations for organizational research. *Organizational Research Methods, 3,* 4–69.

van de Vijver, F. J. R., & Leung, K. (1997). *Methods and data analysis for cross-cultural research.* Newbury Park, CA: Sage.

van IJzendoorn, M. H. (1992). Intergenerational transmission of parenting: A review of studies in nonclinical populations. *Developmental Review, 12,* 76–99.

Weisner, T.S. (2002). Ecocultural understanding of children's developmental pathways. *Human Development, 45*(4), 275–281.

Whiting B. B., & Whiting, J. W. M. (1979). *Children of six cultures: A psycho-cultural analysis.* Cambridge, MA: Harvard University Press.

Wohlwill, J. F. (1973). *The study of behavioral development.* Oxford, UK: Academic Press.

# HOW EXPERIENCE INTERACTS WITH BIOLOGICAL DEVELOPMENT

## Carol M. Worthman and Paul M. Plotsky

### INTRODUCTION

A recent breakthrough in developmental biology is recognition that development is a dance between nature and nurture. Once the focus turned from debates pitting nature against nurture to understanding how the two necessarily work together, whole new avenues of research opened up. In consequence, many previously intractable puzzles have been answered or reframed. By now it is clear that, by organic design, development is environment-expectant. This revelation has stimulated an explosion of work on epigenesis and greatly sharpened attention to context. Epigenetics concerns development and operation of mechanisms that regulate genetic activity without changing the DNA sequence itself. As reviewed by Szyf and colleagues in this section, the epigenome comprises the configuration of structures enveloping the genome that control its activity. A growing body of evidence details how the configuration is dynamically shaped through a suite of mechanisms sensitive to environmental circumstances. Thus, different outcomes are produced largely by differences in how the genetic message is read, not in the message itself. This work electrifies scientists who long have struggled to reconcile the manifest role of genetics with the equally manifest impact of circumstance while avoiding bioreductionism or vague contextualism.

Thus, a mantra from real estate applies to development: it's location, location, location. With regard to adaptive design, consider the expectable environments of rearing (EER), namely the range of conditions that typically developing young would reliably encounter during development. As Wiedenmayer notes, the EER represents a reliable local source of information to guide development under ambient conditions, thereby supporting adaptation to specific conditions under which the adult also must function. Thus, ecological validity of living conditions or experimental protocols can critically affect the findings from animal models and humans. Furthermore, expectable perturbations in early environment can trigger epigenetic changes with long-term psychobehavioral consequences. Szyf and colleagues review the revolutionary work revealing epigenetic mechanisms linking maternal care (amount of licking and grooming) to psychobehavioral differences among offspring in rats and connecting early abuse to suicide in humans. On a cross-cultural comparative level, Zitzer-Comfort and colleagues find that a genetic condition, Williams syndrome, is associated with a phenotype of consistently heightened social expressiveness relative to peers in the United States, France, Italy, or Japan, but that the phenotype also varies by differing levels of expressiveness among these societies. Nowakowski and colleagues invoke a goodness of fit model, pointing out that temperamental differences in reactions to the world, with their genetic underpinnings, may yield different outcomes based on their fit with sociocultural conditions.

As in common parlance, so in development: Timing is everything. Wiedenmayer reviews the literature on sensitive periods and their neurobiological substrates, and points out that there may be optimally predictive moments when early experience best anticipates future conditions. In our work on maternal separation in rodents, Plotsky and colleagues have found that the sensitive period for establishing heightened reactivity of the HPA axis is somewhere during the first week. Maternal separation in the middle week of the neo-natal period yields no differences from controls. And maternal separation during the last week actually results in a suppression of HPA-axis reactivity. Apparently, the window of sensitivity is literally closed for the HPA axis in rats by a burst of corticosterone production during the second postnatal week. Therefore, essentially the same insult timed at a different part of the developmental trajectory interacts with a changed level of plasticity to produce different outcomes. We also have observed sensitization to the maternal separation effect by subthreshold pathogen exposure (actual or biochemically simulated). Early exposures shift the developmental trajectory and thereby alter responses to later challenges.

From all these advances, we can say that the last ten years have introduced defining answers to the title of this section, namely how experience interacts with biological development. At last, the bridge between nature and nurture, genes and environment, biology and culture has been crossed. The future of the field seems limitless.

# THREE

# The Social Environment and the Epigenome

Moshe Szyf, Patrick O. McGowan, Gustavo Turecki,
and Michael J. Meaney

Early life events both before and after birth have a long-lasting impact on physical and mental health trajectories later in life. Several lines of evidence point to the early origin of adult-onset diseases and psychiatric disorders. For example, nutritional restriction or maternal stress during pregnancy has been correlated with an increased risk of developing obesity, type 2 diabetes, and coronary heart disease (Ozanne & Constancia, 2007). Postnatally, adverse socioeconomic status during early childhood has been firmly linked to a susceptibility to the same conditions, as well as autoimmune disease, whereas childhood abuse is a major risk factor in the development of mood and anxiety disorders (Heim & Nemeroff, 2001; Kendler, Kuhn, & Prescott, 2004; see also Seraphin et al.; Nater & Heim, this volume). The critical question is, what are the mechanisms that mediate the effects of the early environment on our health and mental well-being, producing stable, long-lasting changes? It is now widely believed that epigenetics may constitute the mechanism that binds nurture and nature. "Epigenetics" is a polysemous term that in the present context refers to various mechanisms in the cell's nucleus that control genetic activity without altering the DNA sequence. The "epigenome" refers to the configuration of epigenetic modifiers of gene activation around the genome. Recent data suggest that epigenetic programming of gene expression profiles represented in the epigenome is sensitive to the early-life environment and that both the chemical and social environment early in life could affect the manner by which the genome is programmed by the epigenome. In this chapter, we discuss basic epigenetic mechanisms that program the genome and how these mechanisms mediate the effects of the early environment on the genome of the offspring. We propose a mechanism to explain how experience sculpts the genome via effects on DNA demethylation. We present data from animal models, as well as recent data from human studies, supporting the hypothesis that early life adversity leaves its marks on our epigenome and affects stress responsivity, health, and mental health later in life. We also propose epigenetics as a possible biological explanation for the well-established relationship between socioeconomic status and physical health. Finally, we conclude with a brief discussion of implications based on our findings that epigenetic programming can be reversed.

Our argument runs as follows: Although epigenetic patterns are generated during cellular differentiation by a highly programmed and organized process, they are dynamic and responsive to the environment, especially during the critical periods of gestation and early life. Additionally, the epigenetic pattern is reversible by pharmacological (Szyf, 2001) and potentially other forms of intervention. Indeed, several epigenetic drugs are now at different stages of clinical trials for cancer (Kramer, Gottlicher, & Heinzel, 2001; Weidle & Grossmann, 2000) and psychiatric disease (Simonini et al., 2006). Thus in contrast to genetics, epigenetics offers hope that identifying defective epigenetic pathways will allow us to either prevent disease from occurring or therapeutically intervene to reverse deleterious epigenetic aberrations.

## INTRODUCTION: GENOTYPE, EPIGENOTYPE, AND PHENOTYPE

Human physiology and behavior are conditioned on the repertoire of proteins expressed in an individual. Differences in the repertoire or the level of expression result in phenotypic differences that could lead to pathology. It was previously believed that differences in protein abundance and their amino-acid identity were mainly caused by differences in the inherited gene sequence – in other words by genetics. In the 20th century the range of inter-individual variation in phenotype and disease vulnerability was thought to be caused by differences in the DNA sequence. The unraveling of the human genome raised hopes that genetic comparisons and genetic mapping would be able to provide an explanation for the diversity of phenotypes in humans as well as for the emergence of pathology and disease. A tremendous effort has been invested in discovering polymorphisms linked to disease. This effort has been extremely successful in the case of clear Mendelian-inherited familial diseases. Outstanding examples include discovery of the retinoblastoma gene (Neel & Falls, 1951; Sparkes et al., 1983), the breast cancer BRCA 1 gene (Bowcock, 1993; Chamberlain et al., 1993), and the genes linked to familial Alzheimer's disease (Tanzi, 1990). In 2007, five whole genome-wide association studies were published on the genetics of type 2 diabetes mellitus (T2DM) (Groop & Lyssenko, 2008). The discovery of eleven genes consistently associated with T2DM was the first successful example of cracking a complex disease that has roots in several genetic loci.

Despite these advances, it is clear that genetics cannot explain the entire gamut of chronic diseases. It would be hard to explain the recent, rapid increases in asthma and obesity solely on the basis of genetic drift. It is also quite clear that genetic variations per se cannot explain the increasingly evident relationship between variations in early life exposures and the emergence of chronic disease during adulthood.

Although the genome contains all the information required to encode the entire set of proteins needed to sustain the life of an organism, all of the proteins are not expressed in all tissues at all times. The genome is programmed to express the appropriate set of genes in specific cells at specific points in time during the life course. The programming of the genome is accomplished by the epigenome. Two elements of epigenomic control are (1) chemical modifications of the proteins knows as histones, around which DNA is wrapped (the chromatin); and (2) the introduction or removal of methyl groups on the DNA itself (primarily at the site of the dinucleotide sequence cytosine-guanine [CG]) (see Figure 3.1). Unlike the DNA sequence, which is identical in all tissues, patterns of chromatin modification and DNA methylation are tissue-specific. Thus our genome actually contains two layers of information: the DNA sequence inherited from our parents, which is fixed throughout life and identical in all the cells and tissues of our body, and the chromatin and DNA methylation patterns of the epigenome, which are cell- and tissue-specific. The epigenome delineates which genes are expressed, the level of expression, the tissue distribution, and the proper timing of expression.

It is now evident that gene function – and thus phenotype – could be influenced not only by the gene sequence but also by the epigenetic programming of the sequence. Aberrations in epigenetic programming would have an impact resembling a genetic mutation. Similar to a silencing mutation, aberrant hypermethylation of the promoter of a gene would silence it. Conversely, aberrant hypomethylation would simulate an activation mutation by activating a gene that normally should be silent. Thus human disease and aberrant behavior could be caused by either genetic or epigenetic changes. Cancer provides the best-studied example of epigenetic aberration leading to human disease. Tumor suppressor genes could be silenced by either a mutation or aberrant hypermethylation. Although either epigenetic or genetic abnormalities will have similar consequences as far as gene function is concerned, genetic and epigenetic mechanisms of pathology

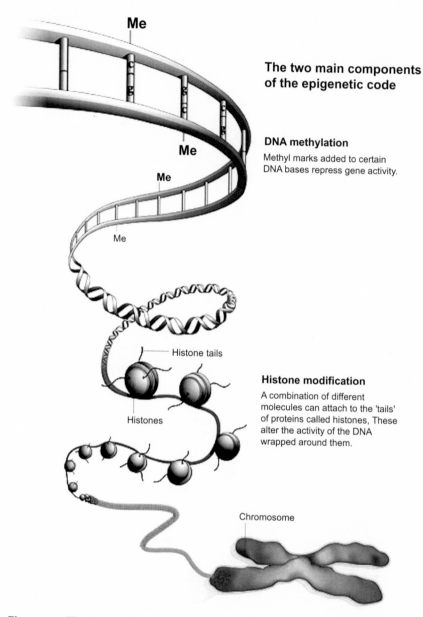

**Figure 3.1.** The two main components of the epigenetic code. Reprinted by permission from Macmillan Publishers Ltd: Qiu, J. (2006). Epigenetics: Unfinished symphony. *Nature, 441,* 143–145.

differ significantly. Such differences can illuminate the mechanisms of disease, clarify the role of the environment, and inform pharmacology and prevention. The implications will be discussed in depth in this chapter following a brief description of chromatin modification and DNA methylation.

## MECHANISMS OF EPIGENETICS: CHROMATIN MODIFICATIONS AND DNA METHYLATION

This section focuses on two mechanisms of epigenetic modification: acetylation and methylation of chromatin and methylation of the DNA molecule itself.

### Chromatin

Chromatin is composed of DNA wrapped around proteins (primarily histones), which condenses into chromosomes during cell division (see Figure 3.1). Chromatin exists in many different states, but it can primarily be thought of as either open (euchromatin) or closed (heterochromatin). This chapter focuses on mechanisms associated with open configurations of chromatin, which allow genetic transcription. In the closed state, chromatin is inactive, like spooled yarn, and the associated genes are silenced.[1]

### The Histone Code

The basic building block of chromatin is the nucleosome, which is made up of an octamer of histone proteins. There are 5 basic types of histone proteins – referred to as H1, H2A, H2, H3, and H4 (Finch et al., 1977) – as well as minor variants, which are involved in specific functions such as DNA repair or gene activation (Sarma & Reinberg, 2005). The octamer structure of the nucleosome is composed of an H3-H4 tetramer flanked on either side with an H2A-H2B dimer (Finch et al., 1977) (see Figure 3.2).

The N-terminal tails of these histones in particular are extensively modified by acetylation (Wade, Pruss, & Wolffe, 1997), methylation (Jenuwein, 2001), phosphorylation, and ubiquitination (Shilatifard, 2006). These histone modifications play an important role in defining the accessibility of

---

[1] The recent discovery of microRNAs, small non-coding RNAs that bind to messenger RNA (mRNA), has added another level of epigenetic regulation (Bergmann & Lane, 2003). microRNAs regulate gene expression in various ways, including silencing chromatin, degrading mRNA, and blocking translation. microRNAs have been found to play an important role in cancer (Zhang, Pan, Cobb, & Anderson, 2007) and could also potentially play an important role in behavioral pathologies (Vo et al., 2005).

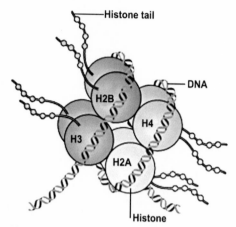

**Figure 3.2.** General scheme of chromatin remodeling. Picture of a nucleosome showing a DNA strand wrapped around a histone octamer composed of two copies each of the histones H2A, H2B, H3 and H4. The amino (N) termini of the histones face outward from the nucleosome complex. Reprinted by permission from Macmillan Publishers Ltd: Tsankova, N., Renthal, W., Kumar, A., & Nestler, E. J. (2007). Epigenetic regulation in psychiatric disorders. *Nature Reviews Neuroscience, 8,* 355–376; Levenson, J. M., & Sweatt, J. D. (2005). Epigenetic mechanisms in memory formation. *Nature Reviews Neuroscience, 6,* 108–118.

the DNA wrapped around the nucleosome core. Different histone variants, which replace the standard isoforms, also play a regulatory role and in some instances serve to mark active genes (Henikoff, McKittrick, & Ahmad, 2004). It has been proposed that the specific pattern of histone modification forms a "histone code," which delineates the parts of the genome to be expressed at a particular time in a particular cell type (Jenuwein & Allis, 2001). A change in histone modification around a gene will change its level of expression and could either convert an active gene to a silent one with consequent "loss of function," or switch a silent gene to an active one with a "gain of function."

## Histone-modifying Enzymes

The most investigated histone-modifying enzymes are histone acetyltransferases (HAT), which acetylate histone H3 at the amino acid residue K9, as well as other residues, and H4 tails at a number of residues; and histone deacetylases (HDAC), which deacetylate histone tails (Kuo & Allis, 1998). Histone acetylation is believed to be a predominant signal for an active chromatin configuration (Lee, Hayes, Pruss, & Wolffe, 1993; Perry & Chalkley, 1982). Deacetylated histones signal inactive chromatin, that is,

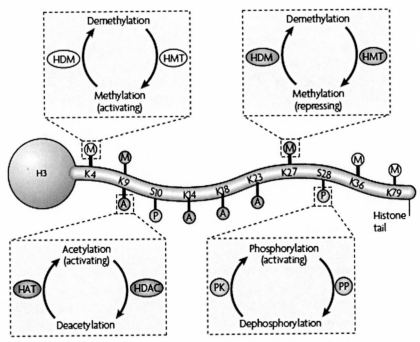

**Figure 3.3.** Summary of common covalent modifications of H3, which include acetylation, methylation (M), and phosphorylation (P) at several amino acid residues. H3 phosphoacetylation commonly involves phosphorylation of S10 and acetylation of K14. Acetylation is catalyzed by histone acetyltransferases (HATs) and reversed by histone deacetylases (HDACs); lysine methylation (which can be either activating or repressing) is catalyzed by histone methyltransferases (HMTs) and reversed by histone demethylases (HDMs); and phosphorylation is catalyzed by protein kinases (PK) and reversed by protein phosphatases (PP), which have not yet been identified with certainty. K, lysine residue; S, serine residue. Reprinted by permission from Macmillan Publishers Ltd: Tsankova, N., Renthal, W., Kumar, A., & Nestler, E. J. (2007). Epigenetic regulation in psychiatric disorders. *Nature Reviews Neuroscience, 8,* 355–376; Levenson, J. M., & Sweatt, J. D. (2005). Epigenetic mechanisms in memory formation. *Nature Reviews Neuroscience, 6,* 108–118.

chromatin associated with inactive genes. Many repressors and repressor complexes recruit HDACs to genes and consequently inactivate them (Wolffe, 1996). Histone tail acetylation is believed to enhance the accessibility of a gene to the transcription machinery, whereas deacetylated tails are highly charged and believed to be tightly associated with the DNA backbone. Consequently, accessibility of genes to transcription factors is limited (Kuo & Allis, 1998) (see Figure 3.3).

Histone modification by methylation is catalyzed by different histone methyltransfareses. Some specific methylation events are associated with gene silencing and others with gene activation. For example methylation of the K9 residue of H3-histone tails is catalyzed by histone methyltransferase SUV3–9 and is associated with silencing of the associated gene (Lachner, O'Carroll, Rea, Mechtler, & Jenuwein, 2001). Particular factors recognize histone modifications and further stabilize an inactive state. For example, the heterochromatin-associated protein HP-1 binds H3-histone tails that are methylated at the K9 residue and precipitates an inactive chromatin structure (Lachner, O'Carroll, Rea, Mechtler, & Jenuwein, 2001). Recently described histone demethylases remove the methylation mark and thereby either activate or repress gene expression (Shi et al., 2004; Tsukada et al., 2006).

## Chromatin Remodeling

Chromatin remodeling, which is dependent on ATP, involves shifting the position of nucleosomes around the transcription initiation site, thereby allowing access to the gene transcription machinery (Varga-Weisz & Becker, 2006). It is increasingly clear that there is an interrelationship between chromatin modification and chromatin remodeling. For example, BRG1, the catalytic subunit of SWI/SNF-related chromatin-remodeling complexes is required for histone acetylation and regulation of b-globin gene expression during development (Bultman, Gebuhr, & Magnuson, 2005).

## Targeting of Chromatin-modifying Enzymes to Specific Genes

Targeting is a basic principle of epigenetic regulation. Histone-modifying enzymes are generally not gene-specific. Specific transcription factors and transcription repressors recruit histone-modifying enzymes to specific genes and thus define the gene-specific profile of histone modification (Jenuwein & Allis, 2001). Specific transacting factors are responsive to cellular signaling pathways. Signal transduction pathways, which are activated by cell-surface receptors, could thus serve as conduits for epigenetic change linking the environmental trigger at cell surface receptors with gene-specific chromatin alterations and reprogramming of gene activity. For example, numerous signaling pathways including those triggered by G protein-coupled cell-surface receptors in the brain alter the concentration of cyclic AMP (cAMP), which mediates the activity of several hormones including epinephrine and adrenocorticotropin (ACTH). One of the transcription factors that respond to increased cAMP is CREB (cAMP response element-binding protein). CREB binds cAMP response elements in certain genes. CREB also recruits CBP (CREB-binding protein). CBP is a histone-modifying enzyme (HAT), which acetylates histones (Ogryzko, Schiltz, Russanova, Howard, & Nakatani, 1996). Thus, elevation of cAMP levels in response to an extracellular signal trigger a targeted change in the state of histone acetylation in specific genes. Either environmental or physiological events can interfere at any point along the signaling pathway and result in chromatin alterations. An example of one such pathway, which leads from maternal behavior to long-term programming of gene expression in the hippocampus, will be discussed in detail later in this chapter (Meaney & Szyf, 2005).

### DNA Methylation

In addition to chromatin, which is associated with DNA, the DNA molecule itself is chemically modified by methyl residues at position 5 (5') of the cytosine rings in the dinucleotide sequence CG in vertebrates (Razin, 1998) (see Figure 3.1). What distinguishes DNA methylation in vertebrate genomes is the fact that not all CGs are methylated in any given cell type (Razin, 1998). Distinct CGs are methylated in different cell types, generating cell type-specific patterns of methylation. Thus, the DNA methylation pattern confers upon the genome its cell-type identity (Razin, 1998). Because DNA methylation is part of the chemical structure of the DNA itself, it is more stable than other epigenetic marks and consequently has extremely important diagnostic potential (Beck, Olek, & Walter, 1999), which is yet to be exploited with regard to behavioral disorders.

After the DNA methylation pattern is established during development, maintenance DNA methyltransferase maintains it faithfully through life (Razin & Riggs, 1980). Because the DNA methylation reaction was once believed to be irreversible, the common consensus was that the only manner by which methyl residues could be lost was through replication (Razin & Riggs, 1980). However, later data supported the idea that, like chromatin modification, DNA methylation was also potentially reversible (Ramchandani, Bhattacharya, Cervoni, & Szyf, 1999a), even in post-mitotic tissues (Weaver et al., 2004). Recent results suggest that the DNA methylation pattern is highly dynamic in neurons and plays a critical role in memory and fear conditioning (Levenson et al., 2006; Miller & Sweatt, 2007). In vertebrates, DNA methylation patterns are distinguished by their correlation with chromatin structure. Active regions of the chromatin, which enable gene expression, are associated with hypomethylated DNA, whereas hypermethylated DNA is packaged in inactive chromatin (Razin, 1998; Razin & Cedar, 1977).

DNA methylation is now widely considered to play a key role in regulating gene expression. DNA methylation in distinct regulatory regions is believed to mark silent genes. A recent whole epigenomic screening of three human chromosomes suggests that a third of the genes analyzed show inverse correlation between gene expression and the state of DNA methylation at the 5 position regulatory regions (Eckhardt et al., 2006). Overwhelming evidence now points to aberrant silencing of tumor suppressor genes by DNA methylation as a common mechanism in the genesis of cancer (Baylin et al., 2001).

DNA methylation silences gene expression by two principal mechanisms. The first involves direct interference of a methyl residue in a recognition element for a transcription factor; blocking the binding of the transcription factor results in the silencing of gene expression (Comb & Goodman, 1990; Inamdar, Ehrlich, & Ehrlich, 1991). A second mechanism is indirect. A certain density of DNA methylation moieties in the region of the gene attracts the binding of methylated-DNA-binding proteins, such as MeCP2 (methyl CG binding protein 2) (Nan, Campoy, & Bird, 1997). MeCP2 recruits other proteins (such as SIN3A) and histone-modifying enzymes and triggers formation of a "closed" chromatin configuration that silences gene expression (Nan, Campoy, & Bird, 1997). Several methylated-DNA binding proteins such as MBD1, MBD2 and MBD3 suppress gene expression by a similar mechanism (Fujita et al., 1999; Hendrich & Bird, 1998; Ng et al., 1999).

## DNA Methylation and Demethylation Enzymes

The DNA methylation reaction is catalyzed by DNA methyltransferase(s) (DNMT) (Razin & Cedar, 1977). Methylation of DNA occurs immediately after replication by a transfer of a methyl moiety from the donor S-adenosyl-L-methionine (AdoMet) in a reaction catalyzed by DNMT. Three distinct phylogenic DNA methyltransferases (DNMT1, 2, and 3) were identified in mammals. DNMT1 shows preference for hemi-methylated DNA *in vitro*, which is consistent with its role as a maintenance DNMT, whereas DNMT3a and DNMT3b methylate unmethylated and methylated DNA at an equal rate, which is consistent with a *de novo* DNMT role (Okano, Xie, & Li, 1998). Two additional DNMT homologs were found: DNMT2, whose substrate and methylation activity is unclear (Vilain, Apiou, Dutrillaux, & Malfoy, 1998), and DNMT3L, which belongs to the DNMT3 family of DNMTs by virtue of its sequence. DNMT3L is essential for the establishment of maternal genomic imprints but lacks key methyltransferase motifs. It is possibly a regulator of methylation rather than an enzyme that methylates

DNA (Bourc'his, Xu, Lin, Bollman, & Bestor, 2001). Knock-out mouse data indicates that DNMT1 is responsible for most DNA methylation marks in the mouse (Li, Bestor, & Jaenisch, 1992) as well as the human genome (Chen et al., 2007), whereas DNMT3a and DNMT3b are responsible for some – but not all – *de novo* methylation during development (Okano, Bell, Haber, & Li, 1999).

## The DNA Methylation Pattern is Reversible;
## DNA Demethylation Enzymes

It was long believed that the pattern of DNA methylation was solely dependent on DNMTs and that the reverse reaction did not occur. Alterations in DNA methylation pattern were only thought possible during cell division when new unmethylated DNA was synthesized and served as a substrate for maintenance DNMT. If DNA methylation only occurs when DNMT is copying DNA methylation patterns during cell division, as suggested by the classic model, there would be no requirement for DNMTs in postmitotic neurons. However, DNMTs are present in postmitotic neurons (Goto et al., 1994), and some data suggest that DNMT levels in neurons change in certain pathological conditions such as schizophrenia (Veldic, Guidotti, Maloku, Davis, & Costa, 2005). Teleologically, the presence of DNMT in neurons makes sense if DNA methylation is dynamic in postmitotic tissues and is a balance of methylation and demethylation reactions (Szyf, 2001). Without active demethylation there is no need for DNA methylation activity in non-dividing neurons.

We have proposed elsewhere that the DNA methylation pattern is a balance of methylation and demethylation reactions that are responsive to physiological and environmental signals, thus forming a platform for gene-environment interactions (Ramchandani, Bhattacharya, Cervoni, & Szyf, 1999b). Accumulating evidence from both cell culture and early mouse development supports the hypothesis that active demethylation occurs in both embryonic and somatic cells. Active demethylation was reported for the *myosin* gene in differentiating myoblast cells (Lucarelli, Fuso, Strom, & Scarpa, 2001); the IL2 gene upon T cell activation (Bruniquel & Schwartz, 2003); the interferon γ gene upon antigen exposure of memory CD8 T cells (Kersh et al., 2006); and the glucocorticoid receptor gene promoter in adult rat brains upon treatment with the HDAC inhibitor TSA (Weaver et al., 2004). Recent data show that DNA methylation is indeed dynamic and reversible in neurons and that both DNA methylation and demethylation are involved in memory acquisition in fear conditioning (Levenson et al., 2006; Miller & Sweatt, 2007).

At present, identification of the enzymes responsible for demethylation poses a major challenge to the field. The biochemical properties of the enzymes responsible for active demethylation are controversial. Different demethylating mechanisms have been proposed (Jost 1993; Zhu et al., 2000), but they would concomitantly involve extensive damage to DNA, compromising genomic integrity. Very recent data suggest that active demethylation early in embryogenesis, as well as in somatic cells, is catalyzed by a nucleotide excision repair mechanism, whereby methylated cytosines are replaced by unmethylated cytosines, involving the growth arrest and damage response protein GADD45A and the DNA repair endonuclease XPG (Barreto et al., 2007). It is possible, however, that GADD45A plays a role other than repair in the demethylation process, perhaps by targeting DNA demethylases to certain sequences. Metivier et al. (2008) recently proposed another mechanism of demethylation involving deamination triggered by the DNA methyltransferases, which is followed by repair of the mismatched deaminated base. This mechanism is proposed to play a role in the dynamic and cyclical demethylation of estrogen-responsive genes. However, such a mechanism would also result in extensive damage to the integrity of the genome. For this reason, we prefer the idea that the main demethylation activity in the cell truly removes methyl groups from the methylated cytosine. Consistent with this idea, Bhattacharya and colleagues have proposed that the protein MBD2 is a demethylase that actively removes methyl groups from DNA reversing the DNA methylation reaction (Bhattacharya, Ramchandani, Cervoni, & Szyf, 1999).

Although a number of biochemical processes have been implicated in demethylation, it is unclear how and when different enzymes participate in shaping and maintaining the overall pattern of methylation and how these activities respond to different environmental exposures in the brain. The identity of the demethylase remains one of the most important unresolved questions in the field.

### Targeting DNA Methylation and Demethylation: Chromatin and DNA Methylation

In this final subsection on the epigenome, we propose a mechanism of dynamic regulation in chromatin structure and DNA demethylation that could help explain how experience sculpts the genome with long-lasting results. We outline the components of this mechanism below.

First, methylation and demethylation enzymes must be targeted to specific genes to either preserve or change their pattern of methylation. The gene-specificity of the chromatin modification state is defined by sequence-specific *trans*-acting factors that recruit chromatin-modifying enzymes to specific genes. Second, chromatin configuration then gates the accessibility of genes to either DNA methylation or demethylation machineries (Cervoni & Szyf, 2001; D'Alessio & Szyf, 2006). In support of this hypothesis we have previously shown that the histone deacetylase inhibitor (HDACi) trichostatin A, which causes histone hyperacetylation also causes active DNA demethylation (Cervoni & Szyf, 2001).

Third, histone-modification enzymes interact with DNA-methylating enzymes and participate in recruiting them to specific targets. A growing list of histone-modifying enzymes has been shown to interact with DNMT1.[2] Recently, DNMT3a was also shown to interact with EZH2 which targets the DNA methylation-histone modification multi-protein complexes to specific sequences in DNA (Vire et al., 2005).

Fourth, *trans*-acting repressors target both histone-modifying enzymes and DNMTs to specific *cis*-acting signals, such as the promyelocytic leukemia PML-RAR fusion protein, which engages histone deacetylases and DNMTs to its target binding sequences and produces *de novo* DNA methylation of adjacent genes (Di Croce et al., 2002). There are also documented interactions between proteins, which read the DNA methylation and histone methylation marks, and either histone- or DNA-modifying enzymes.[3]

Fifth, transcription factors recruit HATs to specific genes. This action causes gene-specific acetylation and thus, we propose, could facilitate gene demethylation. Examples in the literature indicate that enhancers are required for active demethylation.[4]

Our recent studies show that maternal care employs the same mechanism to program gene expression through recruitment of the nerve growth factor-inducible protein A (NGFI-A) transcription factor to the glucocorticoid recepter (GR) gene promoters in the hippocampus (Weaver

---

[2] Such enzymes include HDAC1 and HDAC2 and the histone methyltransferases SUV3–9 an EZH2, a member of the multi-protein Polycomb complex PRC2, which methylates H3 histone at the K27 residue (Fuks, Burgers, Brehm, Hughes-Davies, & Kouzarides, 2000; Fuks et al., 2003; Rountree, Bachman, & Baylin, 2000; Vire et al., 2005).

[3] The methylated DNA-binding protein MeCP2 interacts with the HMT SUV3–9 (Fuks et al., 2003); in plants it was shown that Chromomethylase3 (CMT3), a plant CNG-specific DNMT interacts with an Arabidopsis homologue of HP1, a protein that binds histone H3 methylated at Lysine 9 (Jackson, Lindroth, Cao, & Jacobsen, 2002).

[4] For example, the intronic kappa chain enhancer and the transcription factor NF-kappaB are required for B cell specific demethylation of the kappa immunoglobulin gene (Lichtenstein, Keini, Cedar, & Bergman, 1994). The demethylation of the maize Suppressor-mutator (Spm) transposon is mediated by the transposon-encoded transcriptional activator TnpA protein (Bruniquel & Schwartz, 2003).

et al., 2007). This mechanism could potentially mediate between external signals from the environment and demethylation of specific genes in neurons. Although we don't know whether transcription transactivators could physically interact with demethylases, this possibility should be considered. Another recently investigated possibility is that progression of transcription machinery triggers DNA demethylation. Our recent data suggest that DNA demethylation follows initiation of transcription by RNApolII (D'Alessio, Weaver, & Szyf, 2007). Because DNA demethylation is believed to be a requirement for transcription, this idea appears counterintuitive, unless demethylation serves to amplify the initial transcription initiated by interaction of RNA polII with a promoter. In this case, DNA demethylation would serve as a memory of a transcription signal rather than the initiating cause. If so, early life exposure resulting in enhanced gene expression could eventually be memorized through DNA demethylation long after the triggering signal is gone. Thus, the mechanism we propose would explain how experience sculpts the genome.

To summarize this section, we propose that the DNA methylation and chromatin structure are found in a dynamic balance throughout life. The direction of the balance is maintained and defined by sequence-specific factors that deliver histone modification and DNA modification enzymes to genes. These factors are responsive to signaling pathways in the cell. The state of this equilibrium is defined during development and in the process of cellular differentiation. Physiological or environmental signals, which alter signaling pathways in the cell, would tilt this balance by activating or suppressing specific *trans*-acting factors. The proposed mechanism provides a basis for understanding how the environment in early life typified by maternal care defines epigenetic programming of gene expression programs in the brain (Szyf, McGowan, & Meaney, 2007).

## EARLY LIFE EXPERIENCE AND THE EPIGENOME

The enduring effects of maternal care – the primary early-life social experience – on behavior, mental and physical state, and health of the adult offspring have long been recognized. The fundamental question has been whether early social experiences (i.e., nurture) are separate from or interact with the natural physical processes that drive human and animal physiology, including the process by which the genes we inherited from our ancestors are expressed.

It is easy to understand how early exposures to certain chemicals might affect the epigenome. Because the DNA methylation reaction is an enzymatic reaction, it stands to reason that it could be either blocked or activated by chemicals. Nutritional deficiencies appear to have a similar effect. For example, it has long been recognized that nutritional restriction can result in methylation alterations (Ke et al., 2006; MacLennan et al., 2004; Sinclair et al., 2007). Folic acid deficiency during gestation results in an array of teratogenic effects, which might be explained by reduced methyl availability in cells and reduced supply of S-adenosyl methionine (SAM) driving the DNA methylation reaction (Brunaud et al., 2003; Pogribny, Miller, & James, 1997; Wainfan, Dizik, Stender, & Christman, 1989). It is more difficult to accept that certain social "exposures," like chemical exposures, interact with the genome, resulting in changes in behavior and physiology long after the initial signals that triggered a response are have ceased.

## DNA Methylation Serves as an Interface Between the Dynamic Environment and the Static Genome

The basic hypothesis presented here is that DNA methylation might serve as a signal mediating the life-long effects of exposures to social adversity early in life. This hypothesis is based on the assumption that the DNA methylation pattern is stable on one hand (thus potentially serving as a genomic memory of social exposures), but responsive to signals from the environment on the other hand (thus sensitive to socio-environmental cues). We propose that the DNA methylation pattern represents an equilibrium of methylation and demethylation reactions, and that this equilibrium is responsive to signaling pathways that are activated by social exposure. By modulating epigenetic programming, early life experience sculpts the programming of gene expression and thus the phenotype of the offspring. Although the data supporting this hypothesis are still spotty, several lines of evidence are consistent with it.

## Epigenetic Programming by Maternal Care in the Rat

The long-term effects of maternal behavior in the rat, among other mammals, on stress responsivity and behavior of offspring during adulthood are well documented. Adult offspring of mothers that exhibited increased levels of pup licking/grooming (High LG mothers) over the first week of life show increased hippocampal GR expression, enhanced glucocorticoid feedback sensitivity, decreased expression of hypothalamic corticotrophin-releasing factor (CRF), and more modest HPA stress responses compared to animals reared by Low LG mothers (Francis, Diorio, Liu, & Meaney,

1999; Liu et al., 1997). Cross-fostering studies both suggest that maternal care has direct effects on gene expression and stress responses and exclude a genetic explanation for these long-term effects (Francis, Diorio, Liu, & Meaney, 1999; Liu et al., 1997). The cross-fostering studies therefore support an epigenetic mechanism (Francis, Diorio, Liu, & Meaney, 1999; Liu et al., 1997). In accordance with this hypothesis, differences in DNA methylation and histone acetylation in the regulatory regions of the glucocorticoid receptor (GR exon 17 promoter) gene were observed in the hippocampus of the offspring of High and Low LG mothers. These epigenetic differences correspond to differences in expression of GR in the hippocampus of adult offspring of Low and High LG mothers. Such differences in epigenetic programming emerge early in life in response to differences in maternal LG and remain stable into adulthood (Weaver et al., 2004).

## Signaling Cascade Leading from Maternal Care to Epigenetic Programming

How does maternal behavior result in epigenetic programming in the brain of the offspring? Maternal behavior triggers a signaling pathway that involves the serotonin (5HT) receptor, increase in cAMP, and recruitment of the nerve growth factor-inducible protein A (NGFI-A) transcription factor, which in turn recruits CBP (the CREB binding protein), the methylated DNA-binding protein, and candidate DNA demethylase MBD2 (Weaver et al., 2007) to the GR exon 17 promoter. We hypothesize that the increased histone acetylation triggered by CBP facilitates demethylation of the gene by MBD2 or other DNA demethylases. These data chart a route through which maternal behavior results in epigenetic modification of a specific gene in the brain (see Figure 3.4).

Recent high density-epigenome mapping of chromosome 18 in the adult rat offspring of High and Low LG mothers reveals broad differences in DNA methylation and histone acetylation that cover wide regions of chromosome 18. High LG maternal care results in hypomethylation of some regions and hypermethylation of others; an inverse picture is observed with histone acetylation. This can explain why the adult offspring of High and Low LG mothers exhibit widespread differences in gene expression (Weaver, Meaney, & Szyf, 2006).

## Reversibility of Epigenetic Programming by Maternal Care

Are early-life patterns of epigenetic modification final states or potentially reversible? The issue at stake is whether neurons in the adult brain also possess the bidirectional machinery that is known to sculpt the genome

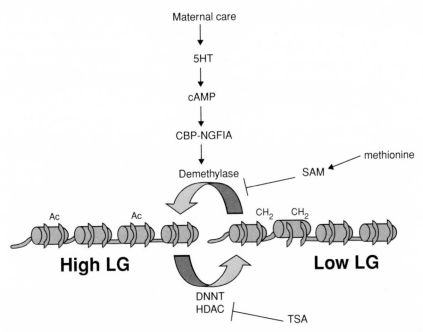

**Figure 3.4.** A model of epigenetic reprogramming by maternal care. Maternal licking/grooming (LG) in the rat triggers activation of 5HT receptor in the hippocampus leading to increase in intracellular cAMP, activation of the transcription factor NGFIA, and recruitment of the HAT CBP to the GR exon 17 promoter. Acetylation of histone tails facilitates demethylation. In offspring of Low LG mothers this process is reduced in comparison with offspring of High LG mothers leading to differential epigenetic programming of the GR promoter. In the adult rat the epigenetic state is reversible. TSA, an HDAC inhibitor, increases histone acetylation and facilitates demethylation and epigenetic activation of the gene in the offspring of the Low LG mothers. Conversely, injection of methionine to adult offspring of the High LG mothers leads to increased SAM, inhibition of demethylation, increased DNA methylation, and reduced activity of the GR exon 17 promoter gene. From Szyf, M., McGowan, P., & Meaney, M. J. (2007). The social environment and the epigenome. *Environmental and Molecular Mutagenesis, 49*(1), 46–60, Copyright © 2007 Wiley-Liss, Inc. Reprinted with permission.

during gestation and early life, or whether the early-life DNA methylation pattern is irreversible. The possibility that epigenetic states might be reversible in the adult brain has immensely important implications concerning the potential for intervention to override the effects of early life adversity.

Our studies indicate that the DNA methylation pattern remains dynamic throughout life. Injection of the histone deacetylase (HDAC) inhibitor TSA into the brains of adult offspring of Low LG maternal care reversed the epigenetic programming of the GR exon $1_7$ promoter and reestablished stress responsivity and open field behavior that was indistinguishable from the those factors in the offspring of High LG maternal care. (Although TSA is not a DNA-methylation inhibitor, we used it because we had previously shown that it could trigger a change in DNA methylation by increasing histone acetylation and facilitating the accessibility of DNA demethylases [Cervoni, Detich, Seo, Chakravarti, & Szyf, 2002; Cervoni & Szyf, 2001]). Conversely, injection of the amino acid methionine – the precursor of SAM, the donor of methyl moiety in the DNA methylation reaction, and an inhibitor of active demethylation (Detich, Hamm, Just, Knox, & Szyf, 2003) – into the brains of adult offspring of High LG mothers resulted in increased DNA methylation and downregulation of GR. It also produced heightened stress responsivity and an open field behavior that was indistinguishable from that of adult offspring of Low LG mothers (Weaver et al., 2004; Weaver et al., 2005). These data suggest that both the methylating and demethylating enzyme are present in the adult neuron.

In summary, although epigenetic programs established early in life persist throughout life, they are maintained by a dynamic equilibrium of DNA methylation and demethylation and are potentially changeable by the appropriate intervention. Our data provide an example of how pharmacological intervention might do this. A provocative possibility is that epigenetic programs established early in life could be reversed – not only by pharmacological intervention but by social and cognitive interventions as well.

## Epigenetic Programming by Early Life Events in Humans: rRNA Genes are Hypermethylated in Suicide Victims

Emerging evidence indicates that nutritional restriction and maternal stress during gestation result in health deficits in offspring that last into adulthood. For example, low birth weight is associated with development of health problems later in life. Another startling observation is the correlation of low socioeconomic status early in life with the later development of health problems. The critical question concerns mechanism. An attractive possibility is that exposure to adverse social conditions in early life results in epigenetic alterations similar to those we have observed in rats.

Bearing this in mind, we recently tested whether there is any evidence that early childhood adversity is associated with epigenetic marks later in life. We examined a cohort of suicide victims in Quebec. The first study looked at the promoter of the rRNA genes (Brown & Szyf, 2007). rRNA forms the skeleton of the ribosome, which synthesizes proteins. Protein synthesis is essential for building new memories and creating new synapses in the brain. Our genome contains around 400 copies of the genes encoding rRNA. We hypothesized that one possible way to control the protein synthesis capacity of a cell is through changing the fraction of active rRNA alleles in a cell. We had previously shown that the fraction of rRNA genes that is active and is associated with the RNA Pol1 transcription machinery is unmethylated, whereas the fraction that is inactive is methylated. Thus DNA methylation defines the level of expression of rRNA genes. In a recent study, we compared methylation of hippocampal rRNA gene promoters in victims of suicide who had experienced childhood adversity with control subjects who had not (McGowan et al., 2008). We found that the suicide victims who experienced childhood abuse had higher overall methylation of their rRNA genes and expressed less rRNA (see Figure 3.5). The difference in methylation was brain region-specific, being evident in the hippocampus and absent in the cerebellum.

Moreover, although we saw significant brain region-specific methylation differences between controls and suicide victims, no sequence differences were observed to indicate a genetic difference. This finding further strengthens our conclusion that the difference in methylation is driven by an environmental rather than a genetic variation. The tissue specificity of the epigenetic differences strikingly differentiates genetic from epigenetic variations because genetic variations occur in the germ line and are identical in all tissues. We suggest that the tissue specificity is driven by signaling pathways evoked specifically in the hippocampus in response to environmental exposures activating neuronal transmission and signaling in the hippocampus, but not in the cerebellum.

### Epigenetic Marks of Early Life Adversity in the GR Promoter in the Hippocampus of Suicide Victims

In another study, we examined whether epigenetic differences were driven by early childhood adversity or by other processes leading to suicide. We compared suicide completers who were abused as children with suicide completers who were not. This time we looked at the GR exon 1f promoter, which is homologous to the promoter affected by maternal care in the rat. This is because individuals with treatment-resistant forms of major depression show decreased GR expression and increased HPA activity. We detected site-specific differences in DNA methylation in the GR exon 1f

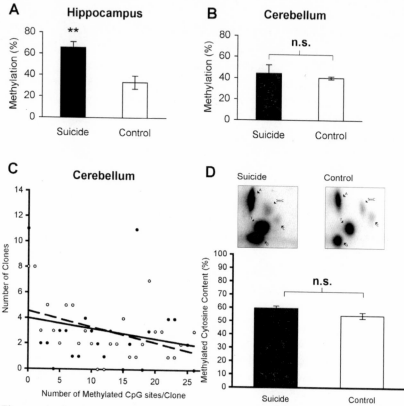

**Figure 3.5.** Anatomical and genomic specificity of rRNA hypermethylation. Average percentage of rRNA promoter methylation for selected subjects with large methylation differences in the hippocampus (A) and in the cerebellum (B) of suicide subjects (N = 4, black bars) and controls (N = 4, white bars) for the same subjects. Data are expressed as mean ± S.E.M.**, P < 0.01, measured by unpaired t-test. (C) Multiple regression analysis shows a similar negative relationship between the number of methylated CpGs per clone and the number of clones in cerebellum samples from suicide subjects (20 clones × 4 subjects, N = 80 total clones; filled circles) and controls (20 clones × 4 subjects, N = 80 total clones; open circles). There are 26 circles per group, as clones are grouped according to methylation status. (D) (above) Representative images of genome-wide methylation in the hippocampus for a suicide subject and a control, showing cytosine (C) and 5-methylcytosine (5 mC) content used for nearest neighbor analysis. (below) Quantification of the percentage of methylcytosine, following the formula: [(5-methylcytosine) × 100]/(5-methylcytosine + cytosine), shows no difference between suicide subjects (N = 13, black bar) and controls (N = 11, white bar) in genome-wide levels of methylation (P > 0.05), measured by unpaired t-test. Reprinted from McGowan, P. O., Sasaki, A., Huang, T. C., Unterberger, A., Suderman, M., Ernst, C., et al. (2008). Promoter-wide hypermethylation of the ribosomal RNA gene promoter in the suicide brain. *PLoS One, 3*(5), e2085.

promoter between suicide completers who had reported social adversity early in life and suicide completers who had not experienced early adversity. The differences in DNA methylation were associated with reduced expression of the GR gene. The site-specific methylation interfered with binding of the transcription factor NGFI-A to the human GR exon 1f promoter. Reporter-activity transfection assays indicated that this site-specific methylation inhibited GR promoter activity (McGowan et al., 2009). These data are a first demonstration that it is possible to identify the epigenetic imprints of early life exposure in the epigenome in the adult brain. These epigenetic differences have functional consequences that result in reduced expression of a key regulator of the HPA axis.

We recently performed a detailed mapping of 5 DNA megabases spanning the locus of the GR gene and identified numerous differences in DNA methylation between the suicide and control groups. These first glimpses into the epigenetic imprints of early life in the adult epigenome support the hypothesis that early life adversity might have lasting impacts on the epigenome.

### The Epigenetic Imprint of Socioeconomic Status

These preliminary data prompted us to examine whether differences in socioeconomic status early in life would also be imprinted in the epigenome and maintained into adulthood. Population studies with living people limit us to studying DNA in peripheral blood cells. Because there is documented crosstalk between the immune system and the HPA axis, and because some of the documented effects of socioeconomic status involve immune functions, we reasoned that epigenetic differences arising from early life socioeconomic status would be registered in circulating white blood cells. We therefore examined blood DNA samples from 45-year-old male subjects enrolled in a 1958 British birth cohort study. For each group, we compared 10 subjects who had experienced social adversity early in life with those who had not, along with subjects whose socioeconomic class had changed (in either direction) later in life. Our preliminary data indicate that early social adversity leaves an imprint on the epigenome that lasts into midlife. Several hundred promoters showed different levels of DNA methylation between adults who experienced social adversity early in life and those that didn't. Some of these promoters appear to be regulating genes involved in important cellular functions. The fact that we observed these differences in adult DNA support the hypothesis that DNA methylation changes in response to social adversity could last into adulthood. Although further experiments are necessary to confirm our data and to establish the functional impact on gene expression of methylation differences, our findings nevertheless provide a first glimpse of the impact of socioeconomic status on the human epigenome.

## SUMMARY AND PROSPECTUS

The relationship between nurture and nature has remained a mystery for the past several millennia. The lack of mechanisms linking the two has been the basis for a long-standing and entrenched dichotomy, which caused a rift between the social sciences and humanities and the biological and physical sciences. This rift has had an impact on all fields of biological sciences, as well as on medicine, mental health, prevention, and therapeutics. But a substantial body of evidence is now demonstrating strong linkages between social and economic status and indices of physical health such as obesity, autoimmunity, and type 2 diabetes. These data pose some fundamental questions regarding how the social environment talks to our genome. Reciprocally, how does our genome adapt its expression programs to changing social environments?

In this chapter, we have proposed that the epigenome serves as an interface between the social environment and the genome. The enzymes that sculpt chromatin states and DNA methylation patterns are proposed to be responsive to cellular signaling, which is activated in the brain in response to social stress and adversity. We proposed that the early social environment exerts long-lasting effects on mental and physical health trajectories by epigenetic marking of specific gene sets. An important corollary of the hypothesis presented here is that, although the epigenetic markings are long lasting, they are also potentially reversible. Therefore an appropriate intervention could erase adverse epigenetic markings sculpted by negative social exposures early in life. We have also suggested that pharmacological as well as cognitive and behavioral interventions might reverse adverse epigenetic markings. Social and cognitive interventions might activate signaling pathways in the brain that would result in a change in either the targeting or activity of the epigenetic machinery, and thus a change in epigenetic markings. Epigenetic drugs are now used in cancer and psychiatric therapy, and increased use of epigenetic drugs and interventions for several other health conditions is anticipated.

Understanding the serious impact of socioeconomic status early in life on health and behavioral trajectories should inform health and social policy. An important methodological question is whether peripheral blood cells could serve as appropriate read-outs of early life adversity. If social adversity is indeed registered in the epigenome of peripheral white blood cells, then the mapping of epigenomic changes associated with early life adversity will provide both important cues regarding the mechanisms involved and predictive markers of health trajectories. Knowledge of how different environmental exposures affect the epigenome could inform design of preventive strategies and enable tracking of the response to these measures. Insight into the epigenetic consequences of social exposures would not only revolutionize medicine but would also transform the social sciences and humanities. Epigenetics promises to link the social and humanistic sciences with the biological sciences and pave the way for an integrated understanding of human health and behavior.

REFERENCES

Barreto, G., Schafer, A., Marhold, J., Stach, D., Swaminathan, S. K., Handa, V., et al. (2007). Gadd45a promotes epigenetic gene activation by repair-mediated DNA demethylation. *Nature, 445*(7128), 671–675.
Baylin, S. B., Esteller, M., Rountree, M. R., Bachman, K. E., Schuebel, K., & Herman, J. G. (2001). Aberrant patterns of DNA methylation, chromatin formation and gene expression in cancer. *Human Molecular Genetics, 10*(7), 68–692.
Beck, S., Olek, A., & Walter, J. (1999). From genomics to epigenomics: A loftier view of life. *Nature Biotechnology, 17*(12), 1144.
Bergmann, A., & Lane, M. E. (2003). HIDden targets of microRNAs for growth control. *Trends in Biochemical Sciences, 28*(9), 461–463.
Bhattacharya, S. K., Ramchandani, S., Cervoni, N., & Szyf, M. (1999). A mammalian protein with specific demethylase activity for mCpG DNA [See comments]. *Nature, 397*(6720), 579–583.
Bourc'his, D., Xu, G. L., Lin, C. S., Bollman, B., & Bestor, T. H. (2001). Dnmt3L and the establishment of maternal genomic imprints. *Science, 294*(5551), 2536–2539.
Bowcock, A. M. (1993). Molecular cloning of BRCA1: A gene for early onset familial breast and ovarian cancer. *Breast Cancer Research and Treatment, 28*(2), 121–135.
Brown, S. E., & Szyf, M. (2007). Epigenetic programming of the rRNA promoter by MBD3. *Molecular and Cellular Biology, 27*(13), 4938–4952.
Brunaud, L., Alberto, J. M., Ayav, A., Gerard, P., Namour, F., Antunes, L., et al. (2003). Effects of vitamin B12 and folate deficiencies on DNA methylation and carcinogenesis in rat liver. *Clinical Chemistry and Laboratory Medicine, 41*(8), 1012–1019.
Bruniquel, D., & Schwartz, R. H. (2003). Selective, stable demethylation of the interleukin-2 gene enhances transcription by an active process. *Nature Immunology, 4*(3), 235–240.
Bultman, S. J., Gebuhr, T. C., & Magnuson, T. (2005). A Brg1 mutation that uncouples ATPase activity from chromatin remodeling reveals an essential role for SWI/SNF-related complexes in beta-globin expression and erythroid development. *Genes & Development, 19*(23), 2849–2861.
Cervoni, N., Detich, N., Seo, S. B., Chakravarti, D., & Szyf, M. (2002). The oncoprotein Set/TAF-1beta, an inhibitor of histone acetyltransferase, inhibits

active demethylation of DNA, integrating DNA methylation and transcriptional silencing. *Journal of Biological Chemistry, 277*(28), 25026–25031.

Cervoni, N., & Szyf, M. (2001). Demethylase activity is directed by histone acetylation. *Journal of Biological Chemistry, 276*(44), 40778–40787.

Chamberlain, J. S., Boehnke, M., Frank, T. S., Kiousis, S., Xu, J., Guo, S. W., et al. (1993). BRCA1 maps proximal to D17S579 on chromosome 17q21 by genetic analysis. *American Journal of Human Genetics, 52*(4), 792–798.

Chen, T., Hevi, S., Gay, F., Tsujimoto, N., He, T., Zhang, B., et al. (2007). Complete inactivation of DNMT1 leads to mitotic catastrophe in human cancer cells [Letter]. *Nature Genetics, 39*(3), 391–396.

Comb, M., & Goodman, H. M. (1990). CpG methylation inhibits proenkephalin gene expression and binding of the transcription factor AP-2. *Nucleic Acids Research, 18*(13), 3975–3982.

D'Alessio, A. C., & Szyf, M. (2006). Epigenetic tête-à-tête: The bilateral relationship between chromatin modifications and DNA methylation. *Biochemistry and Cell Biology, 84*(4), 463–476.

D'Alessio, A. C., Weaver, I. C., & Szyf, M. (2007). Acetylation-induced transcription is required for active DNA demethylation in methylation-silenced genes. *Molecular and Cellular Biology, 27*(21), 7462–7474.

Detich, N., Hamm, S., Just, G., Knox, J. D., & Szyf, M. (2003). The methyl donor S-Adenosylmethionine inhibits active demethylation of DNA: A candidate novel mechanism for the pharmacological effects of S-Adenosylmethionine. *Journal of Biological Chemistry, 278*(23), 20812–20820.

Di Croce, L., Raker, V. A., Corsaro, M., Fazi, F., Fanelli, M., Faretta, M., et al. (2002). Methyltransferase recruitment and DNA hypermethylation of target promoters by an oncogenic transcription factor. *Science, 295*(5557), 1079–1082.

Eckhardt, F., Lewin, J., Cortese, R., Rakyan, V. K., Attwood, J., Burger, M., et al. (2006). DNA methylation profiling of human chromosomes 6, 20 and 22. *Nature Genetics, 38*(12), 1378–1385.

Finch, J. T., Lutter, L. C., Rhodes, D., Brown, R. S., Rushton, B., Levitt, M., et al. (1977). Structure of nucleosome core particles of chromatin. *Nature, 269*(5623), 29–36.

Francis, D., Diorio, J., Liu, D., & Meaney, M. J. (1999). Nongenomic transmission across generations of maternal behavior and stress responses in the rat. *Science, 286*(5442), 1155–1158.

Fujita, N., Takebayashi, S., Okumura, K., Kudo, S., Chiba, T., Saya, H., et al. (1999). Methylation-mediated transcriptional silencing in euchromatin by methyl-CpG binding protein MBD1 isoforms. *Molecular and Cellular Biology, 19*(9), 6415–6426.

Fuks, F., Burgers, W. A., Brehm, A., Hughes-Davies, L., & Kouzarides, T. (2000). DNA methyltransferase Dnmt1 associates with histone deacetylase activity. *Nature Genetics, 24*(1), 88–91.

Fuks, F., Hurd, P. J., Wolf, D., Nan, X., Bird, A. P., & Kouzarides, T. (2003). The methyl-CpG-binding protein MeCP2 links DNA methylation to histone methylation. *Journal of Biological Chemistry, 278*(6), 4035–4040.

Goto, K., Numata, M., Komura, J. I., Ono, T., Bestor, T. H., & Kondo, H. (1994). Expression of DNA methyltransferase gene in mature and immature neurons as well as proliferating cells in mice. *Differentiation, 56*(1–2), 39–44.

Groop, L., & Lyssenko, V. (2008). Genes and type 2 diabetes mellitus. *Current Diabetes Reports, 8*(3), 192–197.

Heim, C., & Nemeroff, C. B. (2001). The role of childhood trauma in the neurobiology of mood and anxiety disorders: Preclinical and clinical studies. *Biological Psychiatry, 49,* 1023–1039.

Hendrich, B., & Bird, A. (1998). Identification and characterization of a family of mammalian methyl-CpG binding proteins. *Molecular and Cellular Biology, 18*(11), 6538–6547.

Henikoff, S., McKittrick, E., & Ahmad, K. (2004). Epigenetics, histone H3 variants, and the inheritance of chromatin states. *Cold Spring Harbor Symposia on Quantitative Biology, 69,* 235–243.

Inamdar, N. M., Ehrlich, K. C., & Ehrlich, M. (1991). CpG methylation inhibits binding of several sequence-specific DNA-binding proteins from pea, wheat, soybean and cauliflower. *Plant Molecular Biology, 17*(1), 111–123.

Jackson, J. P., Lindroth, A. M., Cao, X., & Jacobsen, S. E. (2002). Control of CpNpG DNA methylation by the KRYPTONITE histone H3 methyltransferase. *Nature, 416*(6880), 556–560.

Jenuwein, T. (2001). Re-SET-ting heterochromatin by histone methyltransferases. *Trends in Cell Biology, 11*(6), 266–273.

Jenuwein, T., & Allis, C. D. (2001). Translating the histone code. *Science, 293*(5532), 1074–1080.

Jost, J. P. (1993). Nuclear extracts of chicken embryos promote an active demethylation of DNA by excision repair of 5-methyldeoxycytidine. *Proceedings of the National Academy of Sciences of the United States of America, 90*(10), 4684–4688.

Ke, X., Lei, Q., James, S. J., Kelleher, S. L., Melnyk, S., Jernigan, S., et al. (2006). Uteroplacental insufficiency affects epigenetic determinants of chromatin structure in brains of neonatal and juvenile IUGR rats. *Physiological Genomics, 25*(1), 16–28.

Kendler, K. S., Kuhn, J. W., & Prescott, C. A. (2004). Childhood sexual abuse, stressful life events and risk for major depression in women. *Psychological Medicine, 34,* 1475–1482.

Kersh, E. N., Fitzpatrick, D. R., Murali-Krishna, K., Shires, J., Speck, S. H., Boss, J. M., et al. (2006). Rapid Demethylation of the IFN-{gamma}Gene Occurs in Memory but Not Naive CD8 T Cells. *Journal of Immunology, 176*(7), 4083–4093.

Kramer, O. H., Gottlicher, M., & Heinzel, T. (2001). Histone deacetylase as a therapeutic target. *Trends in Endocrinology and Metabolism, 12*(7), 294–300.

Kuo, M. H., & Allis, C. D. (1998). Roles of histone acetyltransferases and deacetylases in gene regulation. *Bioessays, 20*(8), 615–626.

Lachner, M., O'Carroll, D., Rea, S., Mechtler, K., & Jenuwein, T. (2001). Methylation of histone H3 lysine 9 creates a binding site for HP1 proteins. *Nature, 410*(6824), 116–120.

Lee, D. Y., Hayes, J. J., Pruss, D., & Wolffe, A. P. (1993). A positive role for histone acetylation in transcription factor access to nucleosomal DNA. *Cell, 72*(1), 73–84.

Levenson, J. M., & Sweatt, J. D. (2005). Epigenetic mechanisms in memory formation. *Nature Reviews Neuroscience, 6,* 108–118.

Levenson, J. M., Roth, T. L., Lubin, F. D., Miller, C. A., Huang, I. C., Desai, P., et al. (2006). Evidence that DNA (cytosine-5) methyltransferase regulates synaptic plasticity in the hippocampus. *Journal of Biological Chemistry, 281*(23), 15763–15773.

Li, E., Bestor, T. H., & Jaenisch, R. (1992). Targeted mutation of the DNA methyltransferase gene results in embryonic lethality. *Cell, 69*(6), 915–926.

Lichtenstein, M., Keini, G., Cedar, H., & Bergman, Y. (1994). B cell-specific demethylation: A novel role for the intronic kappa chain enhancer sequence. *Cell, 76*(5), 913–923.

Liu, D., Diorio, J., Tannenbaum, B., Caldji, C., Francis, D., Freedman, A., et al. (1997). Maternal care, hippocampal glucocorticoid receptors, and hypothalamic-pituitary-adrenal responses to stress. *Science, 277*(5332), 1659–1662.

Lucarelli, M., Fuso, A., Strom, R., & Scarpa, S. (2001). The dynamics of myogenin site-specific demethylation is strongly correlated with its expression and with muscle differentiation. *Journal of Biological Chemistry, 276*(10), 7500–7506.

MacLennan, N. K., James, S. J., Melnyk, S., Piroozi, A., Jernigan, S., Hsu, J. L., et al. (2004). Uteroplacental insufficiency alters DNA methylation, one-carbon metabolism, and histone acetylation in IUGR rats. *Physiological Genomics, 18*(1), 43–50.

McGowan, P. O., Sasaki, A., Huang, T. C., Unterberger, A., Suderman, M., Ernst, C., et al. (2008). Promoter-wide hypermethylation of the ribosomal RNA gene promoter in the suicide brain. *PLoS One, 3*(5), e2085.

McGowan, P. O., Sasaki, A., D'Alessio, A. C., Dymov, S., Labonté, B., Szyf, M., et al. (2009). Epigenetic regulation of the glucocorticoid receptor in human brain associates with child abuse. *Nature Neuroscience, 12*, 342–348.

Meaney, M. J., & Szyf, M. (2005). Maternal care as a model for experience-dependent chromatin plasticity? *Trends in Neurosciences, 28*(9), 456–463.

Metivier, R., Gallais, R., Tiffoche, C., Le Peron, C., Jurkowska, R. Z., Carmouche, R. P., et al. (2008). Cyclical DNA methylation of a transcriptionally active promoter. *Nature, 452*(7183), 45–50.

Miller, C. A., & Sweatt, J. D. (2007). Covalent modification of DNA regulates memory formation. *Neuron, 53*(6), 857–869.

Nan, X., Campoy, F. J., & Bird, A. (1997). MeCP2 is a transcriptional repressor with abundant binding sites in genomic chromatin. *Cell, 88*(4), 471–481.

Neel, J. V., & Falls, H. F. (1951). The rate of mutation of the gene responsible for retinoblastoma in man. *Science, 114*(2964), 419–422.

Ng, H. H., Zhang, Y., Hendrich, B., Johnson, C. A., Turner, B. M., Erdjument-Bromage, H., et al. (1999). MBD2 is a transcriptional repressor belonging to the MeCP1 histone deacetylase complex [See comments]. *Nature Genetics, 23*(1), 58–61.

Ogryzko, V. V., Schiltz, R. L., Russanova, V., Howard, B. H., & Nakatani, Y. (1996). The transcriptional coactivators p300 and CBP are histone acetyltransferases. *Cell, 87*(5), 953–959.

Okano, M., Bell, D. W., Haber, D. A., & Li, E. (1999). DNA methyltransferases Dnmt3a and Dnmt3b are essential for de novo methylation and mammalian development. *Cell, 99*(3), 247–257.

Okano, M., Xie, S., & Li, E. (1998). Cloning and characterization of a family of novel mammalian DNA (cytosine-5) methyltransferases [Letter]. *Nature Genetics, 19*(3), 219–220.

Ozanne, S. E., & Constancia, M. (2007). Mechanisms of disease: The developmental origins of disease and the role of the epigenotype. *Nature Clinical Practice Endocrinology & Metabolism, 3*(7), 539–546.

Perry, M., & Chalkley, R. (1982). Histone acetylation increases the solubility of chromatin and occurs sequentially over most of the chromatin: A novel model for the biological role of histone acetylation. *Journal of Biological Chemistry, 257*(13), 7336–7347.

Pogribny, I. P., Miller, B. J., & James, S. J. (1997). Alterations in hepatic p53 gene methylation patterns during tumor progression with folate/methyl deficiency in the rat. *Cancer Letters, 115*(1), 31–38.

Qiu, J. (2006). Epigenetics: Unfinished symphony. *Nature, 441,* 143–145.

Ramchandani, S., Bhattacharya, S. K., Cervoni, N., & Szyf, M. (1999a). DNA methylation is a reversible biological signal. *Proceedings of the National Academy of Sciences of the United States of America, 96*(11), 6107–6112.

Ramchandani, S., Bhattacharya, S. K., Cervoni, N., & Szyf, M. (1999b). DNA methylation is a reversible biological signal [See comments]. *Proceedings of the National Academy of Sciences of the United States of America, 96*(11), 6107–6112.

Razin, A. (1998). CpG methylation, chromatin structure and gene silencing: A three-way connection. *Embo Journal, 17*(17), 4905–4908.

Razin, A., & Cedar, H. (1977). Distribution of 5-methylcytosine in chromatin. *Proceedings of the National Academy of Sciences of the United States of America, 74*(7), 2725–2728.

Razin, A., & Riggs, A. D. (1980). DNA methylation and gene function. *Science, 210*(4470), 604–610.

Rountree, M. R., Bachman, K. E., & Baylin, S. B. (2000). DNMT1 binds HDAC2 and a new co-repressor, DMAP1, to form a complex at replication foci. *Nature Genetics, 25*(3), 269–277.

Sarma, K., & Reinberg, D. (2005). Histone variants meet their match. *Nature Reviews Molecular Cell Biology, 6*(2), 139–149.

Shi, Y., Lan, F., Matson, C., Mulligan, P., Whetstine, J. R., Cole, P. A., et al. (2004). Histone demethylation mediated by the nuclear amine oxidase homolog LSD1. *Cell, 119*(7), 941–953.

Shilatifard, A. (2006). Chromatin modifications by methylation and ubiquitination: Implications in the regulation of gene expression. *Annual Review of Biochemistry, 75,* 243–269.

Simonini, M. V., Camargo, L. M., Dong, E., Maloku, E., Veldic, M., Costa, E., et al. (2006). The benzamide MS-275 is a potent, long-lasting brain region-selective inhibitor of histone deacetylases. *Proceedings of the National Academy of Sciences of the United States of America, 103*(5), 1587–1592.

Sinclair, K. D., Allegrucci, C., Singh, R., Gardner, D. S., Sebastian, S., Bispham, J., et al. (2007). DNA methylation, insulin resistance, and blood pressure in offspring determined by maternal periconceptional B vitamin and methionine status. *Proceedings of the National Academy of Sciences of the United States of America, 104*(49), 19351–19356.

Sparkes, R. S., Murphree, A. L., Lingua, R. W., Sparkes, M. C., Field, L. L., Funderburk, S. J., et al. (1983). Gene for hereditary retinoblastoma assigned to human chromosome 13 by linkage to esterase D. *Science, 219*(4587), 971–973.

Szyf, M. (2001). Towards a pharmacology of DNA methylation. *Trends in Pharmacological Sciences, 22*(7), 350–354.

Szyf, M., McGowan, P., & Meaney, M. J. (2007). The social environment and the epigenome. *Environmental and Molecular Mutagenesis, 49*(1), 46–60.

Tanzi, R. E. (1990). The Alzheimer disease-associated amyloid beta protein precursor gene and familial Alzheimer disease. *Progress in Clinical Biological Research, 360,* 187–199.

Tsankova, N., Renthal, W., Kumar, A., & Nestler, E. J. (2007). Epigenetic regulation in psychiatric disorders. *Nature Reviews Neuroroscience, 8,* 355–376.

Tsukada, Y., Fang, J., Erdjument-Bromage, H., Warren, M. E., Borchers, C. H., Tempst, P., et al. (2006). Histone demethylation by a family of JmjC domain-containing proteins. *Nature, 439*(7078), 811–816.

Varga-Weisz, P. D., & Becker, P. B. (2006). Regulation of higher-order chromatin structures by nucleosome-remodelling factors. *Current Opinion in Genetics & Development, 16*(2), 151–156.

Veldic, M., Guidotti, A., Maloku, E., Davis, J. M., & Costa, E. (2005). In psychosis, cortical interneurons overexpress DNA-methyltransferase 1. *Proceedings of the National Academy of Sciences of the United States of America, 102*(6), 2152–2157.

Vilain, A., Apiou, F., Dutrillaux, B., & Malfoy, B. (1998). Assignment of candidate DNA methyltransferase gene (DNMT2) to human chromosome band 10p15.1 by in situ hybridization. *Cytogenetics and Cell Genetics, 82*(1–2), 120.

Vire, E., Brenner, C., Deplus, R., Blanchon, L., Fraga, M., Didelot, C., et al. (2005). The Polycomb group protein EZH2 directly controls DNA methylation [letter]. *Nature, 439,* 871–874.

Vo, N., Klein, M. E., Varlamova, O., Keller, D. M., Yamamoto, T., Goodman, R. H., et al. (2005). A cAMP-response element binding protein-induced microRNA regulates neuronal morphogenesis. *Proceedings of the National Academy of Sciences of the United States of America, 102*(45), 16426–16431.

Wade, P. A., Pruss, D., & Wolffe, A. P. (1997). Histone acetylation: Chromatin in action. *Trends in Biochemical Sciences, 22*(4), 128–132.

Wainfan, E., Dizik, M., Stender, M., & Christman, J. K. (1989). Rapid appearance of hypomethylated DNA in livers of rats fed cancer- promoting, methyl-deficient diets. *Cancer Research, 49*(15), 4094–4097.

Weaver, I. C., Cervoni, N., Champagne, F. A., D'Alessio, A. C., Sharma, S., Seckl, J. R., et al. (2004). Epigenetic programming by maternal behavior. *Nature Neuroscience, 7*(8), 847–854.

Weaver, I. C., Champagne, F. A., Brown, S. E., Dymov, S., Sharma, S., Meaney, M. J., et al. (2005). Reversal of maternal programming of stress responses in adult offspring through methyl supplementation: Altering epigenetic marking later in life. *Journal of Neuroscience, 25*(47), 11045–11054.

Weaver, I. C., D'Alessio, A. C., Brown, S. E., Hellstrom, I. C., Dymov, S., Sharma, S., et al. (2007). The transcription factor nerve growth factor-inducible protein a mediates epigenetic programming: Altering epigenetic marks by immediate-early genes. *Journal of Neuroscience, 27*(7), 1756–1768.

Weaver, I. C., Meaney, M. J., & Szyf, M. (2006). Maternal care effects on the hippocampal transcriptome and anxiety-mediated behaviors in the offspring that are reversible in adulthood. *Proceedings of the National Academy of Sciences of the United States of America, 103*(9), 3480–3485.

Weidle, U. H., & Grossmann, A. (2000). Inhibition of histone deacetylases: A new strategy to target epigenetic modifications for anticancer treatment. *Anticancer Research, 20*(3A), 1471–1485.

Wolffe, A. P. (1996). Histone deacetylase: A regulator of transcription. *Science, 272*(5260), 371–372.

Zhang, B., Pan, X., Cobb, G. P., & Anderson, T. A. (2007). microRNAs as oncogenes and tumor suppressors. *Developmental Biology, 302*(1), 1–12.

Zhu, B., Zheng, Y., Hess, D., Angliker, H., Schwarz, S., Siegmann, M., et al. (2000). 5-methylcytosine-DNA glycosylase activity is present in a cloned G/T mismatch DNA glycosylase associated with the chicken embryo DNA demethylation complex. *Proceedings of the National Academy of Sciences of the United States of America, 97*(10), 5135–5139.

# FOUR

# Sensitive Periods in the Behavioral Development of Mammals

## Christoph Wiedenmayer

Experience can modify the behavior of animals anytime during their life-span. Sometimes an experience is so powerful that it can alter the animal's behavior in an enduring way. It has been argued that environmental influences are particularly effective in shaping behavior when they occur in early development. This view implies that early experience differs from experience in adulthood. In other words, there are specific periods during development, windows of susceptibility, when experience has a significantly stronger impact on brain and behavior compared to other periods. In this review, I will try to answer the question, "Do particular periods exist in the early lives of mammals during which experience has long-lasting consequences in brain and behavior?" I will first describe the concept of sensitive periods, and then summarize studies that demonstrate an effect of early experience on later behavior. Examples include olfactory learning about the caregiver and the consequences of aversive stimulation on anxiety and fear. I will discuss the neural bases of experience-dependent changes in behavior during sensitive periods, and suggest, finally, that whereas early experience can result in adaptive adjustments to local environments, it can also lead to disruption and maladaptation.

## THE CONCEPT OF SENSITIVE PERIOD

The idea that experience has a more pronounced and a longer lasting effect during early development than later in life has a long history. The ethologist Konrad Lorenz introduced the concept of "critical period" into the behavioral sciences (Lorenz, 1937). He observed that young birds shortly after hatching acquire a preference for their caregiver, and that early learning also affects their behavior when they are adults. Lorenz termed this learning process "imprinting" and postulated that it requires a critical period, that is, a short, developmentally specific period during which young animals instantaneously and irreversibly learn a social preference (Lorenz, 1937). Precocial birds such as domestic chicks, goslings, and ducklings acquire a preference for their mother within hours after hatching. This preference leads to proximity-seeking behavior until the birds become independent. As adults, when they select mating partners, they respond to stimuli that they have learned during imprinting. These two preferences for the caregiver and mating partners are called filial and sexual imprinting, respectively.

Learning in early ontogeny has received considerable attention since Lorenz's pioneering work; numerous research groups have investigated the processes that underlie imprinting-like learning (Michel & Tyler, 2005). However, systematic research in various species has revealed little experimental evidence for the traditional concept of critical period. More recent studies have demonstrated that early social learning does not occur only during a single period, that periods vary in duration, and that learning is reversible (Bateson, 1990). Nevertheless, it is commonly agreed that phases indeed exist in early development when a stimulus is more effective in inducing a neurobehavioral change than during other periods (Bornstein, 1989). To account for this revised view, developmental periods during which experience is particularly effective in inducing neurobehavioral changes are called "sensitive periods" (Michel & Tyler, 2005). Even though scientists express a variety of views on them, they agree that sensitive periods share some common characteristics (Bateson, 1979; Bischof, 2007; Michel & Tyler, 2005). For example, experience has a greater impact on the individual during a sensitive period than during other phases of development. In terms of the underlying neural processes, sensitive periods are periods of enhanced plasticity, when experience has a maximal effect on brain development. The consequences of experience are stable over time and long lasting.

## EARLY LEARNING ABOUT THE CAREGIVER

Considerable evidence shows that infant animals can form long-lasting memories. One context in which early learning occurs is in the interaction with the caregiver. In mammals, the mother is typically the primary caregiver, and newborns depend heavily on her for nutrition and protection (Broad, Curley, & Keverne, 2006). Fathers rarely provide parental care and invest little in their offspring because mammalian reproductive behavior is characterized by uncertainty of paternity (Alcock, 2005). In the following pages, I will discuss mechanisms and functions of learning about the maternal environment in infant mammals. The consequences of maternal care for offspring behavior are discussed elsewhere in this volume (see Sánchez, McCormack, & Maestripieri; Szyf, McGowan, Turecki, & Meaney, this volume) and will not be covered here.

Within hours after birth, neonatal mammals have the capacity to acquire and store information about the mother and the environment provided by her. Neonatal learning seems to consist mainly of association learning (Hudson, 1993). The mother is the source of olfactory stimuli through pheromones and odorants, of tactile stimuli when she grooms and carries the newborn, and of gustatory stimuli when she nurses. A newborn that perceives these maternal cues and at the same time is exposed to other novel stimuli can form associations between the stimuli. Subsequent to the formation of associations, learned cues guide the infant animal's behaviors. Early learning has most commonly been studied using odor-conditioning paradigms because the olfactory system is well developed and highly functional at birth in mammals. To study infant olfactory learning, an arbitrary odor is paired with maternal cues; the animal's response to the odor is then assessed to determine if the animal has formed an association.

When infant rats and mice were exposed to a novel odor during suckling and milk delivery, they preferred that odor to a non-paired odor in choice tests (Armstrong, DeVito, & Cleland, 2006; Brake, 1981; Wilson, Pham, & Sullivan, 1994). Conditioning also occurs when an odor is paired with maternal saliva or tactile stimulation such as stroking (Bouslama, Durand, Chauviere, Van den Bergh, & Gallego, 2005; Sullivan, Hofer, & Brake, 1986; Sullivan & Leon, 1987). Even painful stimuli such as electric shock, when paired with an odor, induce preference for that odor (Sullivan, Landers, Yeaman, & Wilson, 2000). Painful stimuli are part of the maternal environment because the mother may step on the pups or treat them roughly in the nest (Moriceau & Sullivan, 2005).

The maternal environment of rabbit pups differs considerably from that of rodent pups. Rabbit pups are nursed only once a day when the doe returns to the nest for a couple of minutes. The pups have to be able to locate the nipple and attach during that brief period of interaction with their mother. The pups rapidly learn to associate novel odors with the presence of the mother. Two-day-old rabbits learned within 15 s an association between a maternal pheromone and a neutral odor (Coureaud et al., 2006). In addition, suckling itself can act as reinforcer. When suckling rabbits were exposed to a novel odor on the ventrum of the doe, they exhibited more nipple searching in the presence of the odor the next day (Coureaud et al., 2006). Newborn human babies also use their sense of smell to learn about odors associated with the mother immediately after birth (Winberg & Porter, 1998). Babies that had skin contact with their mother for 1 hour after delivery preferred her milk's odor to that of other mothers' milk several days later. Babies without such skin contact were not able to discriminate between the two odors (Mizuno, Mizuno, Shinohara, & Noda, 2004).

## Functions of Early Olfactory Learning

These examples demonstrate that infant mammals rapidly form memories of the maternal environment and prefer cues associated with the mother. What could be the function, or survival benefits, of early preference learning? It has been proposed that neonatal learning facilitates the infant's interactions with its mother during the nursing period and promotes the formation of a bond with her.

Young mammals are capable of attaching to the nipples and suckling within hours of birth. Chemical and tactile cues provided by the mother help a newborn locate and grasp the nipple (Hofer, Shair, & Singh, 1976; Polan, Milano, Eljuga, & Hofer, 2002; Singh, Tucker, & Hofer, 1976; Teicher & Blass, 1977; Varendi, Porter, & Winberg, 1994). For example, newborn European rabbits use pheromonal cues on the mother's ventrum to locate the nipples (Schaal et al., 2003), and this behavior is independent of previous exposure to the doe (Hudson, 1985).

Although neonatal olfactory learning does not seem to be necessary for nipple attachment, it could help the pup efficiently find the nipple. Conditioned cues are predictive for the presence of the mother, and responding to them decreases the latency period of finding the mother and suckling (Coureaud et al., 2006). The memory about maternal cues can also enable the infant to maintain proximity to the mother. Rat pups and dog puppies prefer the odor of their mother to the odor of an unfamiliar female (Hepper, 1986, 1994). Proximity-seeking mechanisms may contribute to the formation of an exclusive bond with the mother (Hofer, 2005; Moriceau & Sullivan, 2005; Romantshik, Porter, Tillmann, & Varendi, 2007). Indeed, when cues associated with the mother are removed, infant animals display signs of stress and anxiety (Hofer, 1994). Behavioral modifications that support proximity to the mother change over time, however: Memory about the maternal environment becomes weaker around weaning and disappears when young mammals become independent. Rats that grew up with a mother sprayed with aniseed odor between postnatal days 1 and 20

(P1-P20) preferred this odor on P21 but not when tested on P40 (Blais, Terkel, & Goldblatt, 2006).

On the other hand, the consequences of early learning can extend beyond the nursing period and influence behavior in adulthood. As adults, rats that grew up in a lemon-scented nest preferred that odor in a choice test (Rodriguez Echandia, Foscolo, & Broitman, 1982). In another study, rat pups nursed by mothers that had been sprinkled with aniseed odor performed better in an olfactory discrimination task using aniseed odor when tested as adults (Blais et al., 2006). One function of long-lasting odor memories related to the maternal environment is kin recognition (Hepper & Cleland, 1999), which allows animals to distinguish between related and unrelated conspecifics. Two-year-old dogs that had been separated from their mother at 8–12 weeks of age and then exposed to her odor or other females' odor exhibited a preference for the maternal odor (Hepper, 1994).

In addition to kin recognition, long-lasting memories of the maternal environment can influence reproductive behavior of the offspring. Female rat pups grew up with an artificially scented mother (Shah, Oxley, Lovic, & Fleming, 2002). When, as adults, they were exposed to pups scented with the same odor, it took them longer to become maternal. But once they expressed maternal behavior they cared more for the pups (increased licking and crouching) scented with that odor compared with unscented pups. Maternal cues seem to influence the behavior of male offspring as well. Male rat pups grew up with dams that were scented with lemon odor around their nipples and vaginal areas until weaning. When, as adults, the males were exposed to sexually receptive females, they ejaculated faster when mating with females scented with lemon odor (Fillion & Blass, 1986). In ungulates, early maternal experience affects adult sexual preferences. Male goats were cross-fostered with sheep mothers and male sheep were cross-fostered with goat mothers at birth (Kendrick, Hinton, Atkins, Haupt, & Skinner, 1998). As adults, these males preferred to mate with females of their fostered maternal species. The early maternal experience thus seems to determine sexual preferences later in life.

Early learning should result in choosing a mate that is similar to the parents to avoid mating with members of another species. At the same time, the mate has to be dissimilar enough to ensure out-breeding (Bateson, 1978). The ability of animals to chose dissimilar traits in mating partners has been demonstrated with the major histocompatibility complex (MHC). MHC genes code for proteins that play a central role in the immune system. Animals typically mate with individuals that carry a dissimilar MHC to avoid inbreeding and increase disease resistance in offspring

(Brennan & Kendrick, 2006; D. J. Penn, 2002). The ability to discriminate between MHC types seems to be acquired in early life through olfactory learning. Cross-fostering studies have shown that mice learn their parents' MHC during early life; as adults, they avoid mating with mice with their parents' HMC (D. Penn & Potts, 1998; Yamazaki et al., 1988).

Thus, learning about the maternal environment influences behavioral choices during the nursing period and later in life. If the maternal environment is predictive for the conditions the animal has to deal with during various phases of its life, this learning increases its chances of survival and reproduction. Behavioral modifications in early ontogeny can thus be considered to serve adaptive functions.

## Sensitive Periods for Learning about the Caregiver

These studies provide strong evidence that infant mammals can rapidly form memories that influence their behavior in a long-lasting and adaptive way. The most relevant question for this review is whether learning is facilitated during particular periods of development, that is, sensitive periods. In most of the summarized studies, experimental investigations and manipulations occurred during the first days and weeks of life. However, only a few studies have directly assessed the occurrence of sensitive periods. In one of these, infant or young adult rats were exposed to a novel odor with concurrent tactile stimulation (Woo & Leon, 1987). Training took place during different developmental phases, either between P1–P4, P1–P8, P8–P14, or P42–P60; testing for the infant rats was on P19 and for the young adults on P61. Rat pups that had been trained during the P1–P8 period displayed a preference for the odor, whereas the other groups did not. These findings indicate that learning the association between an odor and a tactile stimulus, which would be provided in a natural setting by the dam, is limited to the first week of life. A similar sensitive period exists in guinea pigs. They prefer an artificial odor if they are exposed to it between P1 and P6 but not anytime between P7 and P22 (Carter & Marr, 1970). A distinct time window exists for odor-shock association learning. Painful stimulation induces a preference for the odor but only until P10 in young rats. In 12-day-old rats this pairing induces an avoidance of the conditioned odor (Sullivan et al., 2000).

Sensitive periods for olfactory learning have also been found in rabbits (Kindermann, Hudson, & Distel, 1994). Rabbits were exposed to a novel odor during nursing. The next day, when they were presented with an odor-scented fur, they showed increased searching behavior, reflecting attempts to suckle. Learning, however, depended on the age of the rabbits. Highest in rabbits that were trained on their first day after birth, it then declined rapidly and was no longer evident after P5. These findings demonstrate that an odor-suckling association can only be learned during a restricted period of time (Kindermann et al., 1994).

Human babies learn preferences for odors associated with the mother, showing sensitivity to such learning a few hours immediately after birth. When babies were exposed to a fruit odor on the breast of their mother, they responded to it 2–3 days later, but only if they had smelled the odor 19 min after delivery. When first exposed to it 12 hours after birth, they did not recognize it later (Romantshik et al., 2007).

## Neural Bases of Olfactory Learning during Sensitive Period

These findings demonstrate that infant animals form associative memories more readily during particular developmental periods. During these sensitive periods, learning has to be facilitated by neural processes that do not operate during non-sensitive periods. What is known about these neural processes?

The neural bases of olfactory learning have been studied extensively in infant rodents (McLean & Harley, 2004; Wilson & Sullivan, 1994). Olfactory information is processed by a specialized neural circuit that includes the olfactory bulb, the olfactory cortex, and subcortical structures such as the amygdala. Olfactory memory is encoded within this circuit. The olfactory bulb and the olfactory cortex are activated during memory formation when rat pups learn to associate two stimuli (Roth & Sullivan, 2005). The same areas are also involved in memory retrieval. When exposed to the conditioned odor one day after training, infant rats showed increased activation of the olfactory bulb compared to untrained rats (Coopersmith & Leon, 1984; Johnson, Woo, Duong, Nguyen, & Leon, 1995). The olfactory circuit also encodes memories that last for prolonged periods of time. Rats that had been exposed to odor-stroke pairings in infancy were re-exposed to the odor at an age of 3 months (Coopersmith & Leon, 1986). Neuronal activity in the olfactory bulb was elevated compared to rats that had not experienced the odor as neonates. The neurotransmitter norepinephrine (NE) plays an important role in early associative learning. NE is synthesized by the locus ceruleus and is released in brain areas such as the olfactory bulb, where it mediates association learning (Leon, 1992; Sullivan & Wilson, 1994). Blocking of NE decreases olfactory memory formation in infant rats, and stimulation of NE increases it (Sullivan, Wilson, & Leon, 1989; Wilson et al., 1994).

Even though these findings demonstrate that we have a good understanding of the neural bases of olfactory learning, we know very little about the specific neural processes at work during sensitive periods when learning is facilitated. It has been proposed that neural plasticity is increased in early life, and that experience is thus more potent to re-organize and shape brain circuits (Hensch, 2004). There is some evidence that in the olfactory circuit maturational changes are most pronounced in early ontogeny. In one study, development of the structure and electrophysiological properties of neurons in the piriform olfactory cortex were examined in rats between P5 and P35 (Poo & Isaacson, 2007). Dendritic maturation and synaptic plasticity were highest during the first week of life, gradually declining with age. Heightened sensitivity of neurons in the olfactory cortex during this limited time window may facilitate the formation of memories in the newborn. The persistence of odor memories, in turn, appears to be mediated by glutamate receptors. The distribution of different types of glutamate receptors in the olfactory cortex changes dynamically in early ontogeny (Franks & Isaacson, 2005). Olfactory experience during the first month of life influences these developmental changes and establishes a specific combination of receptors (Franks & Isaacson, 2005). Such an experience-dependent re-arrangement could underlie the long-lasting storage of odor memories.

The only direct evidence for the neural bases of sensitive periods in olfactory learning comes from Regina Sullivan and her colleagues. In a series of elegant studies, they have examined the neural processes that terminate a sensitive period in infant rats. Learning a preference for an odor associated with a shock is limited to the early postnatal period, ending at P10 (Sullivan et al., 2000). In older pups, odor-shock parings result in avoidance of the odor. The switch from preference to avoidance is mediated by a succession of neuronal and hormonal events. Odor preference learning before P10 requires the release of NE (Moriceau & Sullivan, 2004). At the end of the sensitive period, the maturation of inhibitory autoreceptors in the locus ceruleus shuts down the release of NE in the olfactory bulb (Moriceau & Sullivan, 2004).

After this autoinhibition, the amygdala starts to support avoidance learning. The amygdala becomes functional by the action of the stress hormone corticosterone, which surges at the end of the second postnatal week (Levine, 2001). Corticosterone binds to receptors in the amygdala and thus acts as a signal to initiate olfactory association learning in the amygdala (Moriceau, Wilson, Levine, & Sullivan, 2006) (see Figure 4.1).

These studies show that infant mammals have the capacity to learn about their caregivers and that, at least in some instances, learning is limited to specific periods of development. These sensitive periods are characterized by increased neural plasticity, which facilitates the formation of long-lasting memories.

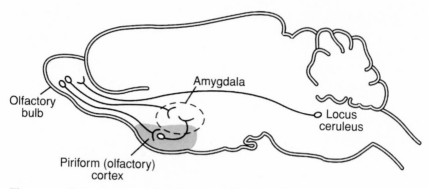

**Figure 4.1.** Neural circuits of olfactory learning in rat pups. Odor-shock pairings induce the release of norepinephrine (NE) in the olfactory bulb from ascending fibers originating in the locus ceruleus. NE is required for memory formation in the olfactory bulb when pups are younger than 10 days of age. In older pups, autoreceptors in the locus ceruleus inhibit NE release. Instead of the olfactory bulb, the amygdala is now the site of memory formation. A surge of glucocorticoid hormones at the end of the second week of life renders the amygdala functional. Odor information is passed through the olfactory system to the amygdala where odor-shock associations are encoded. From Sullivan, R. M. (2003). Developing a sense of safety: The neurobiology of neonatal attachment. *Annals New York Academy of Sciences, 1008,* 122–131. Copyright 2003 by The New York Academy of Sciences. Reprinted with permission from Wiley-Blackwell.

## EARLY EXPERIENCE AFFECTS FEAR AND ANXIETY LATER IN LIFE

When growing up, animals may be exposed to situations that can be harmful and may threaten their survival. For example, infant animals may encounter hostile conspecifics, including infanticidal adults or predators. These aversive stimuli induce emotional states such as fear and anxiety in young mammals; they respond with defensive behavior to counter the immediate threat (Mateo, 1996; Owings & Coss, 1977; Shier & Owings, 2007; Wiedenmayer & Barr, 2001). At the same time, young animals are able to learn about aversive circumstances and modify their behavior.

In some cases, exposure to a threatening stimulus has only a short-lasting effect on a young animal's behavior. When 12-day-old rats are separated from dam and littermates, they emit ultrasonic vocalizations (Hofer & Shair, 1978) that direct the dam's retrieval efforts (Brunelli, Shair, & Hofer, 1994). However, when they are separated and at the same time exposed to an unrelated adult male rat, they suppress these vocalizations, probably to avoid detection by the potentially infanticidal male (Takahashi, 1992). Suppression of vocalization continues after such an encounter, lasting only a few hours (Wiedenmayer, Lyo, & Barr, 2003). Pups thus seem to be able to remember a dangerous encounter, but this memory does not persist. Neither do memories seem to last for extended periods when mild shocks are used as aversive stimuli. Repeated mild shocks in mice between P7 and P13 had no effect on anxiety in adulthood (Carroll et al., 2007). When shocks are paired with a conditioned stimulus such as a tone, infant animals learn these associations but remember them only for a limited period of time. Juvenile rats were conditioned on P18 and they exhibited robust freezing to the conditioned stimulus the next day, but little freezing 10 days later (Kim, McNally, & Richardson, 2006).

However, under certain conditions aversive experience can have long-lasting consequences for an animal and influence its behavior throughout life (Wiedenmayer, 2004). Interactions with aggressive conspecifics can result in modifications of defensive behavior. Adolescent rats that were defeated several times by an adult male rat in a resident-intruder paradigm were tested 3 weeks later with an unfamiliar male. Defeated rats spent less time close to the unfamiliar male compared to controls, indicating that they had acquired social anxiety (Vidal et al., 2007). Encounter with a predator is a particularly dangerous experience that may induce long-term changes in behavior. The mere perception of predator cues in infancy can calibrate an animal's reactivity later in life. Juvenile rats were exposed to predator cues during a single trial by placing them on soiled cat litter or, as a control, on clean litter for 10 min. When they were tested as adults, the cat-odor exposed rats showed more anxiety and an enhanced startle response compared to control rats (Cohen et al., 2007; Tsoory, Cohen, & Richter-Levin, 2007). Predator exposure can induce similar long-term behavioral changes in adolescent rats. Adolescent rats were exposed for several days to cat odor (Wright, Hébert, & Perrot-Sinal, 2008). As adults, they exhibited elevated levels of anxiety in a novel environment and were hyperactive when exposed to cat odor compared to control rats.

In some species, young animals learn from conspecifics how to respond to dangerous stimuli. Rhesus monkeys reared in the laboratory do not exhibit fear of snakes. Nevertheless, adolescent monkeys rapidly learned to avoid snakes when they observed adult wild-born rhesus monkeys responding with fear to the presence of a snake (Mineka, Davidson, Cook, & Keir, 1984). The test monkeys still showed defensive behavior when exposed to the snake 3 months after training, indicating that they had formed long-term memories. Long-lasting effects of snake encounters were also evident in the wild-born monkeys used in this study. Before they were brought to the laboratory, the adults that served as models had grown up in the wild for at least two years (Mineka et al., 1984). When they served as models, their mean age was 22 years. Thus, they must have maintained early memories of snake encounters for approximately 20 years.

These findings indicate that young mammals modify their behavior after exposure to a predator or dangerous conspecific either in the short term or in a long-lasting way. Why do certain aversive experiences only have short-lasting effects, whereas others have a tremendous impact? There are two reasons for the transient effect of aversive experience in infancy. First, young animals differ from adult animals in learning ability, and they forget faster than adult animals (Campbell & Spear, 1972; Hayne, 2004; Pillemer, 1998). This constraint, termed "infantile amnesia," seems to be caused by immaturity in young animals of the neural processes underlying memory formation and retrieval (Bachevalier & Vargha-Khadem, 2005; Dumas, 2005b; Rudy, 1991). Secondly, from a more functional point of view, it may be adaptive to forget about an aversive experience to avoid interference of that memory with ongoing activities. Animals must make trade-offs among various behavioral activities such as predator avoidance and foraging (Lima & Dill, 1990). If threat levels are low or transient, it would be too costly for them to exhibit long-lasting fear-related and risk-assessment behaviors. On the other hand, memories can be vital if they enable the animal to successfully avoid and escape dangers. An animal can use its experience to adjust behavior to local conditions such as predatory threat, thus increasing its survival chances (Griffin, 2004; Lind & Cresswell, 2005). For example, juvenile laboratory-reared prairie dogs were trained to recognize predators in the presence or absence of an experienced adult female; then they were released in an outdoor enclosure (Shier & Owings, 2007). Survival rates after one year were higher in prairie dogs trained with a female, indicating that specific learning is required for successful dealing with predatory threat.

## Sensitive Periods for Aversive Experience

The studies discussed above did not examine directly if an aversive experience is more effective in inducing behavioral changes during specific ontogenetic periods. Only a few studies in laboratory rodents have demonstrated that sensitive periods exist for aversive experience. In one study, rats received footshocks once daily, either during the nursing period between P14 and P18 or after weaning between P21 and P25 (Konno et al., 2007). When tested as adults using standardized procedures, rats shocked after weaning were less anxious than the control rats. Rats that had been exposed to shocks before weaning did not differ from control rats. The same stimulation paradigm was used to investigate effects on fear learning (Matsumoto et al., 2005). Adult rats that had received foot shocks between P14 and P18 or P21 and P25 were subjected to contextual fear conditioning. Rats that had received footshocks before weaning exhibited less conditioned freezing than either rats shocked after weaning or control non-shock rats. Another study shows that adult learning can be influenced by aversive experience even earlier in ontogeny. Rat pups were trained with daily odor-shock pairings between P7 and P11 (Sevelinges et al., 2007), and then conditioned as adults with the same odor paired with shock. The adults exhibited less fear to the conditioned odor when compared with rats that had not been trained as infants.

Strikingly, these findings demonstrate that early aversive experience decreases adult fear and anxiety, which stands in contrast to the studies discussed above, in which conspecific and predator threat induced increased fear and anxiety. The following reasons could account for this discrepancy. First, shocks applied to rat pups during the first postnatal week induce a preference for cues associated with the shocks, and thus do not seem to relate to defensive behavior (Sullivan et al., 2000). Secondly, even though it has been proposed that the pain of electric shocks mimics an attack (Fanselow & Lester, 1988), shocks are not ecologically relevant stimuli. It is not clear whether the shocks tap into mechanisms that have evolved to predict future threats in the environment of the developing animal. At this point, we still have a limited understanding of how aversive experience during sensitive periods in early life produces long-lasting changes in fear- and anxiety-related behaviors.

**Neural Bases of Aversive Experience**

Aversive experience can clearly affect the behavior of young animals, but little is known about the underlying neural processes. Neural systems undergo substantial changes during early ontogeny, and aversive experience appears to affect those systems that are particularly sensitive to external influences (Hensch, 2004).

A few studies indicate that structures of the fear circuit, including the hippocampus and amygdala, are sensitive to aversive events in early life. Exposure to aversive odor cues affects hippocampal maturation in young rats. Five-day-old rats were placed for 30 min on bedding that had been soiled by an unfamiliar adult male rat or on unsoiled bedding (Tanapat, Galea, & Gould, 1998). The next day, cell proliferation in the hippocampus was reduced in the male odor-exposed pups. The hippocampus plays a role in defensive behavior in infant and adult rats (Pentkowski, Blanchard, Lever, Litvin, & Blanchard, 2006; Takahashi, 1995). The experience of a deadly threat could alter maturation of the hippocampus and affect the expression of defensive behaviors in encounters with a similar threat later in life. The amygdala, another brain area that plays a major role in defensive behavior, becomes functional in the second postnatal week in rats and mediates responses to social threat (Chen, Shemyakin, & Wiedenmayer, 2006; Moriceau et al., 2006). In adult animals, this forebrain structure is involved in the formation of associations between aversive and neutral stimuli, storing fear memories that can last a lifetime (Gale et al., 2004). Whether the amygdala in the infant or juvenile animal has the capacity to mediate long-lasting learning about threatening conspecifics or predators during sensitive periods remains to be investigated.

Neurotransmitter systems, which undergo rapid changes during early developmental periods (Herlenius & Lagercrantz, 2004), participate in shaping neural circuits involved in defensive behavior and emotional states. A good example is the neurotransmitter serotonin (5-HT). Through molecular manipulation, the serotonin 1 A ($5\text{-HT}_{1A}$) receptor can be deleted in mice. Mice that lack this receptor throughout life are more anxious in adulthood than mice expressing the receptor (Parks, Robinson, Sibille, Shenk, & Toth, 1998; Ramboz et al., 1998). On the other hand, deleting the $5\text{-HT}_{1A}$ receptor in the forebrain during adulthood only did not affect anxiety (Gross et al., 2002). In contrast, mice that lacked the forebrain $5\text{-HT}_{1A}$ receptor until weaning, but through pharmacological manipulation expressed it afterwards, were more anxious as adults (Gross et al., 2002). These findings indicate that the early preweaning period is critical for the development of anxiety behavior and that $5\text{-HT}_{1A}$ receptors are necessary to shape this ontogenetic process. The mechanism through which the $5\text{-HT}_{1A}$ receptor influences neural development is unknown. In young mice, it mediates the effect of a single stressful event on intracellular signaling in hippocampal neurons (Lo Iacono & Gross, 2008). Aversive experience during short windows of development can affect the 5-HT system. If rats received shocks after weaning during the fourth postnatal week, as adults they had reduced numbers of 5-HT immunoreactive cells in the midbrain (Konno et al., 2007). In contrast, shocks applied before weaning did not affect 5-HT cell number. In sum, neurotransmitters such as 5-HT participate in the construction of brain circuits during early development (Gaspar, Cases, & Maroteaux, 2003). Aversive experience can alter 5-HT function and thus the formation of circuits that mediate later defensive behavior. The possibility that periods of increased sensitivity to aversive stimulation exist, during which the 5-HT system can significantly be altered, remains to be investigated.

## GENERAL CONSIDERATIONS

The mechanisms and function of sensitive periods have been investigated mainly in birds (Bateson, 1990; Bolhuis & Honey, 1998; Horn, 1998), but, as described in this review, sensitive periods are also found in mammals. In the following pages, I will summarize some common principles regarding the neural bases and functions of sensitive periods. I then conclude by discussing how sensitive periods can make an individual more vulnerable to experience and increase the risk of abnormal development.

### Neural Processes Contributing to Sensitive Periods

Our knowledge of the neural bases of sensitive periods in mammals is still limited. Nevertheless, we can draw general conclusions when we combine findings on early olfactory learning and aversive experience, as discussed earlier, with evidence of sensitive periods in sensory systems such as vision or audition (Hensch, 2005; Knudsen, 2004). In their pioneering work, Wiesel and Hubel (1963) found that visual deprivation during a restricted post-natal period alters neuronal connectivity in the cortex and impairs visual function irreversibly. It is now well understood that during early development, sensory systems overproduce synaptic connections within and between brain areas (Katz & Shatz, 1996; Knudsen, 2004). Not all of these connections remain. Over a limited period of time, sensory input into the circuits activates a subset of synapses; these synapses are strengthened, whereas unstimulated synapses are pruned. Experience thus leads to the selective maintenance of synaptic connections: Excess synapses are eliminated and the circuit is re-organized (Knudsen, 2004). Whether similar processes relating to learning about caregivers or about aversive events operate in a similar manner remains to be investigated. Input to sensory systems is not sufficient to produce profound neural alterations because experience-induced neural changes occur throughout life, not just during sensitive periods. Adult learning, for instance, alters the structure of synapses as well (Lamprecht & LeDoux, 2004). What seems to be necessary for sensitive periods is that permissive developmental processes facilitate the effect of experience on neural organization (M. H. Johnson, 2005). Processes intrinsic to the circuit can permit experience to shape the circuit's structure and function. A sensitive period can be initiated and terminated, for instance, when neurotransmitter systems mature and provide a window of increased plasticity. The expression of neurotransmitters and their receptors changes in a dynamic way during early ontogeny (Herlenius & Lagercrantz, 2004). Maturational processes that occur postnatally increase the number of receptors, alter their molecular composition, and enhance excitatory or inhibitory function (Bottjer, 2002; Dumas, 2005a; Hensch, 2005). These transitory alterations in receptor structure and function increase plasticity and appear to facilitate the effect of experience. As discussed previously, experience during the first weeks of life organizes the serotonergic system and affects emotional behavior later in life. Levels of neuronal inhibition and excitation within local circuits determine the beginning and the end of sensitive periods. For example, receptor maturation changes the electrophysiological properties of the amygdala and thus contributes to the termination of preference learning during the second postnatal week in rats (Thompson, Sullivan, & Wilson, 2008).

Neural plasticity, high throughout early ontogeny, lasts into adolescence (Andersen, 2003; Blakemore, 2008; Spear, 2000). It is probably an overstatement to say that any experience before sexual maturity has a stronger effect on behavior than an experience during adulthood. But evidence for sensitive periods has mainly been provided for early development. The neural prerequisites are more likely to be met during the early stages of ontogeny because sensitive periods are induced when various neural processes, such as synapse formation, changes in receptor expression and hormone levels, coincide in the same brain region (Andersen & Teicher, 2008).

Environmental events that occur during periods of increased neural plasticity have a long-lasting impact on the organization of brain circuits and, consequently, on the expression of behavioral responses later in life.

## Function of Sensitive Periods

Young mammals are able to learn early and rapidly about caregivers and threats and adjust their behaviors accordingly. However, not all experience requires a sensitive period to effectively modify behavior. Why are there sensitive periods for some behaviors but not for others? The prevalence of early learning during sensitive periods in multiple species indicates an adaptive function, that is, it helps a growing animal to survive and eventually to reproduce. The fitness benefits of sensitive periods have mainly been studied in birds. Filial imprinting during sensitive periods enables recognition of parents and siblings, and helps the young animal distinguish them from other group members (Bateson, 1990). Preference for the mother and kin increases protection and decreases the risk of being harmed by other conspecifics. In sexual imprinting, the young animal acquires social preferences that enable it to recognize members of the same species. It uses this preference to select a mate that shares characteristics with the parent, but is dissimilar enough to avoid inbreeding (Bateson, 1978). More generally, sensitive periods prepare an organism for its immediate and distant future if conditions during the postnatal periods are predictive for similar conditions later in life (Bateson, 1979; Bornstein, 1989). The induction of neurobehavioral change during the sensitive period instructs the individual to successfully navigate its environment later in life by recognizing conspecifics, potential mates, and threats. But because this is true for all forms of early experience, Bateson (1979) has proposed the following functional explanation: Sensitive periods are adaptive if they facilitate learning during periods that are *most* predictive for future conditions. The growing animal is exposed to different features of its environment during different periods of development, but it is adaptive for the animal to learn during optimally predictive times. For example, features of the mother are most critical to learn very early in development, whereas features of future mates become important later in development (Bateson, 1979). Evolutionary processes thus appear to have selected for sensitive periods under conditions that necessitate rapid and effective learning. Memories acquired during optimal phases of development are stable for extended periods of time and cannot easily be overridden by subsequent experience (Bornstein, 1989).

### Sensitive Periods and Psychopathology

Early learning provides fitness benefits to animals; sensitive periods, in particular, allow them to adjust their behaviors adaptively. Clinicians, however, are interested in formative experiences because they can produce detrimental effects on brain and behavior (see Busch & Lieberman; Minde; Schechter, this volume). It is beyond the scope of this review to discuss the concept of early life stress that is associated with increased risk for developing mental disorders (see Seraphin et al., this volume). The question that can be discussed here is whether experience during sensitive periods can have maladaptive outcomes.

If sensitive periods predispose young animals to acquire information about their environment in a rapid and lasting way, then errors are possible. Most famous are Lorenz's pioneering work with goslings imprinted on humans (Lorenz, 1937). More interesting are cases when – during periods of increased neural plasticity – experience does not adjust behavior but disrupts its development. Sensitive periods have been called "windows of vulnerability," because aversive events seem particularly effective in altering the developmental trajectory of neural systems (Andersen, 2003; Bornstein, 1989; Leonardo & Hen, 2008). It has been argued that formative experiences during sensitive periods can lead to abnormal development in humans and increase the risk for psychopathology later in life (Dawson, Ashman, & Carver, 2000). Although this compelling idea has a long tradition in psychology and psychiatry, virtually nothing is known about the relationship between sensitive period, experience, and maladaptive outcome. To my knowledge, only one study has systematically compared developmental periods in humans, considering their vulnerability to adverse experience. The authors of that study demonstrate the differential effects of sexual abuse during childhood on brain development (Andersen et al., 2008). Abuse was associated with the volume of brain areas in an age-specific way. The hippocampus was smallest in young women who had been abused between 3 and 5 or 11 and 13 years of age. In contrast, the corpus callosum (CC) was reduced in women who had experienced child abuse between ages 9 and 10 and the prefrontal cortex was reduced in those with abuse between 14 and 16 years. These different periods of vulnerability seem to coincide with phases of major developmental changes in these brain areas, and the experience of abuse may have altered these processes (Andersen & Teicher, 2008; Andersen et al., 2008). Childhood abuse is a major risk factor in the development of mood and anxiety disorders (Heim & Nemeroff, 2001; Kendler, Kuhn, & Prescott, 2004; see also Seraphin et al.; Nater & Heim, this volume). How structural alterations in brain areas such as the hippocampus contribute to clinical symptoms in women with a history of sexual abuse remains to be determined (Teicher et al., 2003). These findings, nevertheless, indicate that experience during sensitive periods can have outcomes that are maladaptive.

In conclusion, the nervous system changes in a dynamic fashion throughout development. Experience is typically required for shaping neural circuits and adjusting behaviors to the local conditions in which an animal lives. But in early ontogeny, for limited periods of time, neural plasticity is enhanced and experience is particularly effective in organizing neural circuits and subsequent behaviors. These sensitive periods allow the animal to rapidly and effectively acquire information that is necessary for survival and reproduction. On the other hand, increased sensitivity makes neurobehavioral systems more vulnerable. Traumatic events have the potential to disrupt the organization of neural circuits that mediate adaptive behaviors and to result in abnormal behavior and psychopathology.

REFERENCES

Alcock, J. (2005). *Animal Behavior* (8th ed.). Sunderland, MA: Sinauer Associates.
Andersen, S. L. (2003). Trajectories of brain development: Point of vulnerability or window of opportunity? *Neuroscience and Biobehavioral Reviews, 27,* 3–18.
Andersen, S. L., & Teicher, M. H. (2008). Stress, sensitive periods and maturational events in adolescent depression. *Trends in Neurosciences, 31,* 183–191.

Andersen, S. L., Tomada, A., Vincow, E. S., Valente, E., Polcari, A., & Teicher, M. H. (2008). Preliminary evidence for sensitive periods in the effect of childhood sexual abuse on regional brain development. *Journal of Neuropsychiatry & Clinical Neurosciences, 20,* 292–301.

Armstrong, C. M., DeVito, L. M., & Cleland, T. A. (2006). One-trial associative odor learning in neonatal mice. *Chemical Senses, 31,* 343–349.

Bachevalier, J., & Vargha-Khadem, F. (2005). The primate hippocampus: Ontogeny, early insult and memory. *Current Opinion in Neurobiology, 15,* 168–174.

Bateson, P. (1978). Sexual imprinting and optimal outbreeding. *Nature, 273,* 659–660.

Bateson, P. (1979). How do sensitive periods arise and what are they for? *Animal Behaviour, 27,* 470–486.

Bateson, P. (1990). Is imprinting such a special case? *Philosophical Transactions of the Royal Society B., 329,* 125–131.

Bischof, H.-J. (2007). Behavioral and neuronal aspects of developmental sensitive periods. *NeuroReport, 18,* 461–465.

Blais, I., Terkel, J., & Goldblatt, A. (2006). Long-term impact of early olfactory experience on later olfactory conditioning. *Developmental Psychobiology, 48,* 501–507.

Blakemore, S.-J. (2008). The social brain in adolescence. *Nature Reviews Neuroscience, 9,* 267–277.

Bolhuis, J. J., & Honey, R. C. (1998). Imprinting, learning and development: From behaviour to brain and back. *Trends in Neurosciences, 21,* 306–311.

Bornstein, M. H. (1989). Sensitive periods in development: Structural characteristics and causal interpretations. *Psychological Bulletin, 105,* 179–197.

Bottjer, S. W. (2002). Neural strategies for learning during sensitive periods of development. *Journal of Comparative Physiology A, 188,* 917–928.

Bouslama, M., Durand, E., Chauviere, L., Van den Bergh, O., & Gallego, J. (2005). Olfactory classical conditioning in newborn mice. *Behavioral Brain Research, 161,* 102–106.

Brake, S. C. (1981). Suckling infant rats learn a preference for a novel olfactory stimulus paired with milk delivery. *Science, 211,* 506–508.

Brennan, P. A., & Kendrick, K. M. (2006). Mammalian social odours: Attraction and individual recognition. *Philosophical Transactions of the Royal Society B, 361,* 2061–2078.

Broad, K. D., Curley, J. P., & Keverne, E. B. (2006). Mother-infant bonding and the evolution of mammalian social relationships. *Philosophical Transactions of the Royal Society B, 361,* 2199–2214.

Brunelli, S. A., Shair, H. N., & Hofer, M. A. (1994). Hypothermic vocalizations of rat pups (Rattus norvegicus) elicit and direct maternal search behavior. *Journal of Comparative Psychology, 108,* 298–303.

Campbell, B. A., & Spear, N. E. (1972). Ontogeny of memory. *Psychological Review, 79,* 215–236.

Carroll, J. C., Boyce-Rustay, J. M., Millstein, R., Yang, R., Wiedholz, L. M., Murphy, D. L., & Holmes, A. (2007). Effects of mild early life stress on abnormal emotion-related behaviors in 5-HTT knockout mice. *Behavioral Genetics, 37,* 214–222.

Carter, C. S., & Marr, J. N. (1970). Olfactory imprinting and age variables in the guinea-pig Cavia porcellus. *Animal Behaviour, 18,* 238–244.

Chen, S. W. C., Shemyakin, A., & Wiedenmayer, C. P. (2006). The role of the amygdala and olfaction in unconditioned fear in developing rats. *Journal of Neuroscience, 26,* 233–240.

Cohen, H., Kaplan, Z., Matar, M. A., Loewenthal, U., Zohar, J., & Richter-Levin, G. (2007). Long-lasting behavioral effects of juvenile trauma in an animal model of PTSD associated with a failure of the autonomic nervous system to recover. *European Journal of Neuropsychopharmacology, 17,* 464–477.

Coopersmith, R., & Leon, M. (1984). Enhanced neural response to familiar olfactory cues. *Science, 225,* 849–851.

Coopersmith, R., & Leon, M. (1986). Enhanced neural response by adult rats to odors experienced early in life. *Brain Research, 371,* 400–403.

Coureaud, G., Moncomble, A.-S., Montigny, D., Dewas, M., Perrier, G., & Schaal, B. (2006). A pheromone that rapidly promotes learning in the newborn. *Current Biology, 16,* 1956–1961.

Dawson, G., Ashman, S. B., & Carver, L. J. (2000). The role of early experience in shaping behavioral and brain development and its implications for social policy. *Developmental Psychopathology, 12,* 695–712.

Dumas, T. C. (2005a). Developmental regulation of cognitive abilities: Modified composition of a molecular switch turns on associative learning. *Progress in Neurobiology, 76,* 189–211.

Dumas, T. C. (2005b). Late postnatal maturation of excitatory synaptic transmission permits adult-like expression of hippocampal-dependent behaviors. *Hippocampus, 15,* 562–578.

Fanselow, M. S., & Lester, L. S. (1988). A functional behavioristic approach to aversively motivated behavior: Predatory imminence as a determinant of the topography of defensive behavior. In R. C. Bolles & M. D. Beecher (Eds.), *Evolution and Learning* (pp. 185–212). Hillsdale, NJ: Lawrence Erlbaum.

Fillion, T. J., & Blass, E. M. (1986). Infantile experience with suckling odors determines adult sexual behavior in male rats. *Science, 231,* 729–731.

Franks, K. M., & Isaacson, J. S. (2005). Synapse-specific downregulation of NMDA receptors by early experience: A critical period for plasticity of sensory input to olfactory cortex. *Neuron, 47,* 101–114.

Gale, G. D., Anagnostaras, S. G., Godsil, B. P., Mitchell, S., Nozawa, T., Sage, J. R., et al. (2004). Role of the basolateral amygdala in the storage of fear memories across the adult lifetime of rats. *Journal of Neuroscience, 24,* 3810–3815.

Gaspar, P., Cases, O., & Maroteaux, L. (2003). The developmental role of serotonin: News from mouse molecular genetics. *Nature Reviews Neuroscience, 4,* 1002–1012.

Griffin, A. S. (2004). Social learning about predators: A review and prospectus. *Learning & Behavior, 32,* 131–140.

Gross, C., Zhuang, X., Stark, K., Ramboz, S., Oosting, R., Kirby, L., et al. (2002). Serotonin$_{1A}$ receptor acts during development to establish normal anxiety-like behaviour in the adult. *Nature, 416,* 396–400.

Hayne, H. (2004). Infant memory development: Implications for childhood amnesia. *Developmental Review, 24,* 33–73.

Heim, C., & Nemeroff, C. B. (2001). The role of childhood trauma in the neurobiology of mood and anxiety disorders: Preclinical and clinical studies. *Biological Psychiatry, 49*, 1023–1039.

Hensch, T. K. (2004). Critical period regulation. *Annual Review of Neuroscience, 27*, 549–579.

Hensch, T. K. (2005). Critical period plasticity in local cortical circuits. *Nature Reviews Neuroscience, 6*, 877–888.

Hepper, P. G. (1986). Parental recognition in the rat. *Quarterly Journal of Experimental Psychology, 38B*, 151–160.

Hepper, P. G. (1994). Long-term retention of kinship recognition established during infancy in the domestic dog. *Behavioral Processes, 33*, 3–14.

Hepper, P. G., & Cleland, J. (1999). Developmental aspects of kin recognition. *Genetica, 104*, 199–205.

Herlenius, E., & Lagercrantz, H. (2004). Development of neurotransmitter systems during critical periods. *Experimental Neurology, 190*, S8–S21.

Hofer, M. A. (1994). Hidden regulators in attachment, separation, and loss. *Monographs of the Society for Research in Child Development, 59*, 192–207.

Hofer, M. A. (2005). The psychobiology of early attachment. *Clinical Neuroscience Research, 4*, 291–300.

Hofer, M. A., & Shair, H. (1978). Ultrasonic vocalization during social interaction and isolation in 2-week-old rats. *Developmental Psychobiology, 11*, 495–504.

Hofer, M. A., Shair, H., & Singh, P. (1976). Evidence that maternal ventral skin substances promote suckling in infant rats. *Physiology & Behavior, 17*, 131–136.

Horn, G. (1998). Visual imprinting and the neural mechanisms of recognition memory. *Trends in Neurosciences, 21*, 300–305.

Hudson, R. (1985). Do newborn rabbits learn the odor stimuli releasing nipple-search behavior? *Developmental Psychobiology, 18*, 575–585.

Hudson, R. (1993). Olfactory imprinting. *Current Opinion in Neurobiology, 3*, 548–552.

Johnson, B. A., Woo, C. C., Duong, H., Nguyen, V., & Leon, M. (1995). A learned odor evokes an enhanced Fos-like glomerular response in the olfactory bulb of young rats. *Brain Research, 699*, 192–200.

Johnson, M. H. (2005). Sensitive periods in functional brain development: Problems and prospects. *Developmental Psychobiology, 46*, 287–292.

Katz, L. C., & Shatz, C. J. (1996). Synaptic activity and the construction of cortical circuits. *Science, 274*, 1133–1138.

Kendler, K. S., Kuhn, J. W., & Prescott, C. A. (2004). Childhood sexual abuse, stressful life events and risk for major depression in women. *Psychological Medicine, 34*, 1475–1482.

Kendrick, K. M., Hinton, M. R., Atkins, K., Haupt, M. A., & Skinner, J. D. (1998). Mothers determine sexual preferences. *Nature, 395*, 229–230.

Kim, J. H., McNally, G. P., & Richardson, R. (2006). Recovery of fear memories in rats: Role of gamma-amino butyric acid (GABA) in infantile amnesia. *Behavioral Neuroscience, 120*, 40–48.

Kindermann, U., Hudson, R., & Distel, H. (1994). Learning of suckling odors by newborn rabbits declines with age and suckling experience. *Developmental Psychobiology, 27*, 111–122.

Knudsen, E. I. (2004). Sensitive periods in the development of the brain and behavior. *Journal of Cognitive Neuroscience, 16,* 1412–1425.

Konno, K., Matsumoto, M., Togashi, H., Yamaguchi, T., Izumi, T., Watanabe, M., et al. (2007). Early postnatal stress affects the serotonergic function in the median raphe nuclei of adult rats. *Brain Research, 1172,* 60–66.

Lamprecht, R., & LeDoux, J. E. (2004). Structural plasticity and memory. *Nature Reviews Neuroscience, 5,* 45–54.

Leon, M. (1992). Neuroethology of olfactory preference development. *Journal of Neurobiology, 23,* 1557–1573.

Leonardo, E. D., & Hen, R. (2008). Anxiety as a developmental disorder. *Neuropsychopharmacology, 33,* 134–140.

Levine, S. (2001). Primary social relationships influence the development of the hypothalamic-pituitary-adrenal axis in the rat. *Physiology & Behavior, 73,* 255–260.

Lima, S. L., & Dill, L. M. (1990). Behavioral decisions made under the risk of predation: A review and prospectus. *Canadian Journal of Zoology, 68,* 619–640.

Lind, J., & Cresswell, W. (2005). Determining the fitness consequences of antipredation behavior. *Behavioral Ecology, 16,* 945–956.

Lo Iacono, L., & Gross, C. (2008). $\alpha$-$Ca^{2+}$/calmodulin-dependent protein kinase II contributes to the developmental programming of anxiety in serotonin receptor 1A knock-out mice. *Journal of Neuroscience, 28,* 6250–6257.

Lorenz, K. Z. (1937). The companion in the bird's world. *The Auk, 54,* 245–273.

Mateo, J. M. (1996). The development of alarm-call response behaviour in free-living juvenile Belding's ground squirrels. *Animal Behaviour, 52,* 489–505.

Matsumoto, M., Higuchi, K., Togashi, H., Koseki, H., Yamaguchi, T., Kanno, M., et al. (2005). Early postnatal stress alters the 5-HTergic modulation to emotional stress at postadolescent periods of rats. *Hippocampus, 15,* 775–781.

McLean, J. H., & Harley, C. W. (2004). Olfactory learning in the rat pup: A model that may permit visualization of a mammalian memory trace. *NeuroReport, 15,* 1691–1697.

Michel, G. F., & Tyler, A. N. (2005). Critical period: A history of the transition from questions of when, to what, to how. *Developmental Psychobiology, 46,* 156–162.

Mineka, S., Davidson, M., Cook, M., & Keir, R. (1984). Observational conditioning of snake fear in rhesus monkeys. *Journal of Abnormal Psychology, 93,* 355–372.

Mizuno, K., Mizuno, N., Shinohara, T., & Noda, M. (2004). Mother-infant skin-to-skin contact after delivery results in early recognition of own mother's milk odour. *Acta Paediatrica, 93,* 1640–1645.

Moriceau, S., & Sullivan, R. M. (2004). Unique neural circuitry for neonatal olfactory learning. *Journal of Neuroscience, 24,* 1182–1189.

Moriceau, S., & Sullivan, R. M. (2005). Neurobiology of infant attachment. *Developmental Psychobiology, 47,* 230–242.

Moriceau, S., Wilson, D. A., Levine, S., & Sullivan, R. M. (2006). Dual circuitry for odor-shock conditioning during infancy: Corticosterone switches between fear and attraction via amygdala. *Journal of Neuroscience, 26,* 6737–6748.

Owings, D. H., & Coss, R. G. (1977). Snake mobbing by California ground squirrels: Adaptive variation and ontogeny. *Behaviour, 62*, 50–69.

Parks, C. L., Robinson, P. S., Sibille, E., Shenk, T., & Toth, M. (1998). Increased anxiety of mice lacking the serotonin$_{1A}$ receptor. *Proceedings of the National Academy of Sciences of the United States of America, 95*, 10734–10739.

Penn, D., & Potts, W. (1998). MHC-disassortative mating preferences reversed by cross-fostering. *Proceedings of the Royal Society of London B, 265*, 1299–1306.

Penn, D. J. (2002). The scent of genetic compatibility: Sexual selection and the major histocompatibility complex. *Ethology, 108*, 1–21.

Pentkowski, N. S., Blanchard, D. C., Lever, C., Litvin, Y., & Blanchard, R. J. (2006). Effects of lesions to the dorsal and ventral hippocampus on defensive behaviors in rats. *European Journal of Neuroscience, 23*, 2185–2196.

Pillemer, D. B. (1998). What is remembered about early childhood events? *Clinical Psychology Review, 18*, 895–913.

Polan, H. J., Milano, D., Eljuga, L., & Hofer, M. A. (2002). Development of rats' maternally directed orienting behaviors from birth to day 2. *Developmental Psychobiology, 40*, 81–103.

Poo, C., & Isaacson, J. S. (2007). An early critical period for long-term plasticity and structural modification of sensory synapses in olfactory cortex. *Journal of Neuroscience, 27*, 7553–7558.

Ramboz, S., Oosting, R., Amara, D. A., Kung, H. F., Blier, P., Mendelsohn, M., et al. (1998). Serotonin receptor 1A knockout: An animal model of anxiety-related disorder. *Proceedings of the National Academy of Sciences of the United States of America, 95*, 14476–14481.

Rodriguez Echandia, E. L., Foscolo, M., & Broitman, S. T. (1982). Preferential nesting in lemon-scented environment in rats reared on lemon-scented bedding from birth to weaning. *Physiology & Behavior. Behav., 29*, 47–49.

Romantshik, O., Porter, R. H., Tillmann, V., & Varendi, H. (2007). Preliminary evidence of a sensitive period for olfactory learning by human newborns. *Acta Paediatrica, 96*, 372–376.

Roth, T. L., & Sullivan, R. M. (2005). Memory of early maltreatment: Neonatal behavioral and neural correlates of maternal maltreatment within the context of classical conditioning. *Biological Psychiatry, 57*, 823–831.

Rudy, J. W. (1991). Elemental and configural associations, the hippocampus and development. *Developmental Psychobiology, 24*, 221–236.

Schaal, B., Coureaud, G., Langlois, D., Giniès, C., Sémon, E., & Perrier, G. (2003). Chemical and behavioural characterization of the rabbit mammary pheromone. *Nature, 424*, 68–72.

Sevelinges, Y., Moriceau, S., Holman, P., Miner, C., Muzny, K., Gervais, R., Mouly, A.-M., & Sullivan, R. M. (2007). Enduring effects of infant memories: Infant odor-shock conditioning attenuates amygdala activity and adult fear conditioning. *Biological Psychiatry, 62*, 1070–1079.

Shah, A., Oxley, G., Lovic, V., & Fleming, A. S. (2002). Effects of preweaning exposure to novel maternal odors on maternal responsiveness and selectivity in adulthood. *Developmental Psychobiology, 41*, 187–196.

Shier, D. M., & Owings, D. H. (2007). Effects of social learning on predator training and postrelease survival in juvenile black-tailed prairie dogs, Cynomys ludovicianus. *Animal Behaviour, 73,* 567–577.

Singh, P. J., Tucker, A. M., & Hofer, M. A. (1976). Effects of nasal ZnSO$_4$ irrigation and olfactory bulbectomy on rat pups. *Physiology & Behavior, 17,* 373–382.

Spear, L. P. (2000). The adolescent brain and age-related behavioral manifestations. *Neuroscience and Biobehavioral Reviews, 24,* 417–463.

Sullivan, R. M. (2003). Developing a sense of safety: The neurobiology of neonatal attachment. *Annual New York Academy of Sciences, 1008,* 122–131.

Sullivan, R. M., Hofer, M. A., & Brake, S. C. (1986). Olfactory-guided orientation in neonatal rats is enhanced by a conditioned change in behavioral state. *Developmental Psychobiology, 19,* 615–623.

Sullivan, R. M., Landers, M., Yeaman, B., & Wilson, D. A. (2000). Good memories of bad events in infancy. *Nature, 407,* 38–39.

Sullivan, R. M., & Leon, M. (1987). One-trial olfactory learning enhances olfactory bulb responses to an appetitive conditioned odor in 7-day-old rats. *Developmental Brain Research, 35,* 307–311.

Sullivan, R. M., & Wilson, D. A. (1994). The locus coeruleus, norepinephrine, and memory in newborns. *Brain Research Bulletin, 35,* 467–472.

Sullivan, R. M., Wilson, D. A., & Leon, M. (1989). Norepinephrine and learning-induced plasticity in infant rat olfactory system. *Journal of Neuroscience, 9,* 3998–4006.

Takahashi, L. K. (1992). Developmental expression of defensive responses during exposure to conspecific adults in preweanling rats (Rattus norvegicus). *Journal of Comparative Psychology, 106,* 69–77.

Takahashi, L. K. (1995). Glucocorticoids, the hippocampus, and behavioral inhibition in the preweanling rat. *Journal of Neuroscience, 15,* 6023–6034.

Tanapat, P., Galea, L. A. M., & Gould, E. (1998). Stress inhibits the proliferation of granule cell percursors in the developing dentate gyrus. *International Journal of Developmental Neuroscience, 16,* 235–239.

Teicher, M. H., Andersen, S. L., Polcari, A., Anderson, C. M., Navalta, C. P., & Kim, D. M. (2003). The neurobiological consequences of early stress and childhood maltreatment. *Neuroscience and Biobehavioral Reviews, 27,* 33–44.

Teicher, M. H., & Blass, E. M. (1977). First suckling response of the newborn albino rat: The roles of olfaction and amniotic fluid. *Science, 198,* 635–636.

Thompson, J. V., Sullivan, R. M., & Wilson, D. A. (2008). Developmental emergence of fear learning corresponds with changes in amygdala synaptic plasticity. *Brain Research, 1200,* 58–65.

Tsoory, M., Cohen, H., & Richter-Levin, G. (2007). Juvenile stress induces a predisposition to either anxiety or depressive-like symptoms following stress in adulthood. *European Neuropsychopharmacology, 17,* 245–256.

Varendi, H., Porter, R. H., & Winberg, J. (1994). Does the newborn baby find the nipple by smell? *Lancet, 344,* 989–990.

Vidal, J., de Bie, J., Granneman, R. A., Wallinga, A. E., Koolhaas, J. M., & Buwalda, B. (2007). Social stress during adolescence in Wistar rats induces social anxiety in adulthood without affecting brain monoaminergic content and activity. *Physiology & Behavior, 92,* 824–830.

Wiedenmayer, C. P. (2004). Adaptations or pathologies? Long-term changes in brain and behavior after a single exposure to severe threat. *Neuroscience and Biobehavioral Reviews, 28,* 1–12.

Wiedenmayer, C. P., & Barr, G. A. (2001). Developmental changes in responsivity to threat are stimulus-specific in rats. *Developmental Psychobiology, 39,* 1–7.

Wiedenmayer, C. P., Lyo, D., & Barr, G. A. (2003). Rat pups reduce ultrasonic vocalization after exposure to an adult male rat. *Developmental Psychobiology, 42,* 386–391.

Wiesel, T. N., & Hubel, D. H. (1963). Single-cell responses in striate cortex of kittens deprived of vision in one eye. *Journal of Neurophysiology, 26,* 1003–1017.

Wilson, D. A., Pham, T.-C., & Sullivan, R. M. (1994). Norepinephrine and post-training memory consolidation in neonatal rats. *Behavioral Neuroscience, 108,* 1053–1058.

Wilson, D. A., & Sullivan, R. M. (1994). Neurobiology of associative learning in the neonate: Early olfactory learning. *Behavioral and Neural Biology, 61,* 1–18.

Winberg, J., & Porter, R. H. (1998). Olfaction and human neonatal behaviour: Clinical implications. *Acta Paediatrica, 87,* 6–10.

Woo, C. C., & Leon, M. (1987). Sensitive period for neural and behavioral response development to learned odors. *Developmental Brain Research, 36,* 309–313.

Wright, L. D., Hébert, K. E., & Perrot-Sinal, T. S. (2008). Periadolescent stress exposure exerts long-term effects on adult stress responding and expression of prefrontal dopamine receptors in male and female rats. *Psychoneuroendocrinology, 33,* 130–142.

Yamazaki, K., Beauchamp, G. K., Kupniewski, D., Bard, J., Thomas, L., & Boyse, E. A. (1988). Familial imprinting determines H-2 selective mating preferences. *Science, 240,* 1331–1332.

# FIVE

# Confluence of Individual and Caregiver Influences on Socioemotional Development in Typical and Atypical Populations

Matilda Nowakowski, Louis A. Schmidt, and Geoffrey Hall

## INTRODUCTION

Children exhibit a range of individual differences in reactions to the world at birth. Some are easily soothed, develop regular sleep-wake cycles, react positively with approach behaviors toward novel stimuli, and easily adapt to environmental changes. Other infants display high rates of negative emotions, are difficult to soothe, become easily overwhelmed by novel stimuli, react negatively to environmental changes, and have irregular sleep-wake patterns. These early individual differences make up what we call temperament. The interaction of temperament and environmental influences presumably shapes socioemotional development.

In this chapter, we illustrate how individual and caregiver differences influence socioemotional development in typical and atypical populations. The chapter comprises two major sections. The first section sets forth an overview of three models of development that can inform socioemotional development: temperament, attachment, and interactionist approaches. For each model, we give a brief historical overview and discuss definitional, conceptual, and cross-cultural issues. Section two presents how these models may shed light on socioemotional development in typical and atypical populations, using childhood shyness and childhood maltreatment and autism, respectively, as examples. We conclude with suggestions for future work examining individual and caregiver influences on socioemotional development.

## MODELS OF DEVELOPMENT

### Temperament Theories

*Historical Precedent and Definitional Issues.* The first western scientific theory of temperament was proposed in the 2nd century A.D. by Galen, a Greek physician. Galen's theory suggested that individual temperament differences could be explained by the balance between four bodily humors or fluids: *flegma, chole, melanchole,* and *sanguis* (Galen, 170 A.D.). Although contemporary research on temperament no longer relies on the balance between bodily fluids, it is still very much rooted in Galen's theory, with its focus on biological approaches to explain observable individual temperament variations.

The modern scientific study of child temperament began in the late 1950s. Previously, environment and genetics were viewed as mutually exclusive, and individual variability in behavior was largely attributed to parenting (Thomas & Chess, 1977). The New York Longitudinal Study in the 1960's and 1970's (NYLS; Thomas, Chess, Birch, Hertzig, & Korn, 1963; Thomas & Chess, 1997) shifted the focus to a more "balanced" perspective, which took both individual and caregiver factors into account.

Thomas et al. (1963) studied 141 children in 85 New York families longitudinally from 2–6 months to 16–17 years of age. They developed nine categories of temperament based on parental reports: Approach/withdrawal, activity level, rhythmicity/regularity, adaptability, threshold of stimulation, intensity of reaction, quality of mood, distractability, and attention span and persistence. Using factor analytic procedures, the researchers developed three constellations of temperament: easy, difficult, and slow-to-warm-up (Thomas et al., 1963; Thomas & Chess, 1977). According to Thomas and Chess, temperament focuses on stylistic aspects of behavior (i.e., the *how* of it) rather than actual behaviors (i.e., the *what* of it) or any motivation for particular behaviors (i.e., the *why* of it).

The New York Longitudinal Study spawned a surge of research in the field of temperament. Researchers used Thomas and Chess's theory as a starting point for definitions and views of temperament. For example, Mary Rothbart (1981, 1986) defined temperament as "individual differences in reactivity and self-regulation" (Rothbart, 1981, p. 569). In contrast, Goldsmith and Campos (1982) conceptualized temperament as emotional behavior, defined as physiological responses that motivate behavior and communicate information. Buss and Plomin (1984, 1986) viewed temperament as personality traits that were inherited and present during the first year of life. More recently, Kagan and colleagues (Kagan, Reznick, &

**Table 5.1.** *Summary of the Definitions of Temperament Proposed by Different Researchers*

| Theorist | Factors Included in Definition of Temperament |
|---|---|
| Thomas and Chess | Approach/withdrawal, activity level, rhythmicity/regularity, adaptability, threshold of stimulation, intensity of reaction, quality of mood, distractability, attention, and persistence |
| Rothbart | Activity level, smiling and laughter, fear, distress to limitations, soothability, and duration of orienting |
| Goldsmith and Campos | Motoric activity, anger, fearfulness-distress, pleasure/joy, and interest/persistence |
| Buss and Plomin | Emotionality, activity, sociability, and impulsivity |
| Kagan | Behaviorally inhibited, behaviorally uninhibited |

Snidman, 1987; Kagan & Snidman, 1991; Kagan, 1994) held that temperament comprises intensity and affect, with individual differences rooted in infant motor activity and affective responses to novelty. Kagan's work is described later in further detail.

As can be seen in Table 5.1, the different theories of temperament not only differed in their definitions but also in the dimensions/constructs included in temperament.

Rothbart and Bates (2006) recently attempted to consolidate the varying dimensions proposed to date. They developed three broad dimensions of temperament: effortful control, negative affectivity, and extraversion/surgency. Effortful control is the conscious regulation of behavior, including the extent to which one is able to focus and shift attention, plan future actions, and suppress inappropriate behaviors. Negative affectivity measures the extent to which one experiences frustration, fear, and sadness in response to the blockage of goals, the expectation of a negative situation, or the loss of an object or person, respectively, as well as the ability to self-soothe. Extraversion/surgency includes traits such as smiling and laughter, activity level, impulsivity, and behavioral inhibition. The latter is a measure of the extent to which children will express positive affect, approach behaviors, and behavioral inhibition in novel situations (Rothbart & Bates, 2006).

*Stability Issues.* Given that temperament is viewed as a precursor to personality development (Caspi & Silva, 1995), and that a difficult temperament is viewed as a risk factor for future behavioral disorders (Kaufman & Kagan, 2005), one would expect temperament to be relatively stable throughout life. Research has found significant but moderate correlations between temperament dimensions at different times of development (Matheny, Wilson, & Nuss, 1984; Worobey & Blajda, 1989). A number of theoretical and methodological reasons account for these findings.

Thomas and Chess (1977) discussed continuity and discontinuity of temperament throughout development from a theoretical perspective, finding a high level of continuity within a developmental stage, but more discontinuity across developmental stages. They hypothesized that this latter variability was largely because some temperamental characteristics are more prominent during certain stages of development, and less prominent during others. This idea was illustrated in a study by Pedlow, Sanson, Prior, and Oberklaid (1993) using structural equation modeling to test the stability of temperament measures in participants from 4 months to 8 years of age. The results showed approach and rhythmicity to be continuous and stable throughout the time of measurement. Irritability and cooperation-manageability were present during infancy and toddler years, while inflexibility, a combination of irritability and cooperation-manageability, was present only during childhood, increasing in stability as the children developed. Persistence appeared during the toddler years and showed continuity and stability throughout (Pedlow et al., 1993).

From a methodological perspective, behaviors that are part of a particular dimension of temperament present differently as children age. This issue presents a challenge because many temperament studies rely on questionnaires and different questionnaires are administered at different points in a child's development. If comparisons across time-points are based on different questionnaires, a bias is created. Thus, moderate correlations may result from actual changes in behaviors, differences in measurement methods, or a combination of both.

*Temperament and Developmental Outcomes.* With regard to developmental outcomes, children with a difficult temperament are at risk for internalizing and externalizing disorders (Kaufman & Kagan, 2005). Two main pathways may result. First, a child with a difficult temperament will have a harder time dealing with the challenges of the world and experience increased stress, which can result in psychopathology. Second, a child with a difficult temperament may evoke negative maternal reactions, producing lower quality and less frequent mother-child interactions, and consequent developmental difficulties in the child (Hetherington, Parke, & Schmuckler, 2003). To support this view, research has shown that mothers who view a child as difficult are less responsive in interactions with their infants and tend to interact with them less (Ghera, Hane, Malesa, & Fox, 2006; Goodman-Campbell, 1979).

*Temperament and Cross-Cultural Issues.* Cross-cultural studies of temperament have indicated that broad temperament dimensions are found across cultures, but with differing frequencies. A number of studies suggest that, compared to European American and Irish American infants, Chinese American mothers describe their infants as easier to soothe, better able to self-regulate, calmer, and more adaptable to new environments (Kagan, Kearsley, & Zelazo, 1978; Kagan, et al., 1994). Ahadi, Rothbart, and Ye (1993) also found that U.S. children who were high in effortful control showed less negative affect, whereas Chinese children showed lower extraversion. The authors suggested that this difference was because of different cultural values: Americans tend to place more value on controlling negative affect, whereas Chinese place more value on lower levels of extraversion (Ahadi et al., 1993). These results illustrate how temperament and environment interact, with temperament and the environment influencing behavior, whereas temperament is affected by expectations, values, and environmental perspectives.

*Summary.* Although prominent researchers disagree as to the exact dimensions of temperament, some consensus around major points has been reached. In a seminal roundtable discussion (Goldsmith et al., 1987), the following five defining features of temperament were consistent across theorists: Temperament (1) is a constellation of traits, (2) determines behavioral tendencies, (3) is present during infancy, (4) is fairly stable across time and settings (although its pure influence is seen only during infancy, with later behaviors influenced by a combination of temperament and environmental experiences), and (5) has a genetic basis. In short, temperament comprises early behavioral traits that are stable across time and place (Bates, 1986) and, although genetically determined, can be modified within limits by environmental influences (Buss & Plomin, 1984, Chess & Thomas, 1984; Goldsmith & Campos, 1982).

We know that each child has a unique temperament from birth and that temperament has major implications for psychological well-being. However, we also know that temperament does not function in isolation and does not solely determine a child's destiny. Although temperament is relatively stable throughout development, a two-way interaction involves environment influencing temperament and temperament helping shape

**Table 5.2.** *Summary of Bowlby's Attachment Stages*

| Stage | Age | Description |
|---|---|---|
| Undiscriminating social responsiveness | 0–3 months | Social responses exhibited toward adults regardless of familiarity. |
| Preferential social responsiveness | 3–6 months | Social responses exhibited only toward familiar adults. |
| Secure-based behavior | 6–24 months | Attachment behaviors toward specific individual who regularly interacts with infant. |
| Goal-corrected partnership | 24 months and onwards | Child is able to understand that social partner has his/her own goals, feelings, and motivations and is able to take these into consideration. |

socioemotional development. A major environmental influence is early mother-child attachment, which is discussed next.

**Attachment Theory**

*Historical Precedent and Definitional Issues.* John Bowlby and Mary Ainsworth jointly developed attachment theory, prompted by Bowlby's early observation that prolonged separations from the mother significantly influenced a child's personality development (Ainsworth & Bowlby, 1991). Earlier psychoanalytic and social learning theories had explained attachment as a secondary drive, resulting from primary drives such as hunger. In contrast, Bowlby postulated that attachment had a genetic basis and was advantageous from an evolutionary perspective because it increased survival and reproductive success by protecting a child from dangerous situations (Bowlby, 1973). Bowlby believed that a child was born with an attachment control system that matured throughout early development, changing from nondiscriminant to focusing specifically on the mother or other primary caregiver. This control system developed according to the child's experiences with the mother (Bowlby, 1958, 1969; see Table 5.2 for Bowlby's four-stage development process for attachment). Unlike psychoanalytic and social learning theories, which viewed an infant as passive and dependent, Bowlby saw the infant as playing an active role in developing attachment (Bowlby, 1958).

To support his theory, Bowlby used ethological studies such as Konrad Lorenz's work on imprinting in geese and Harry Harlow's work on attachment in rhesus monkeys. Lorenz (1935) showed that greylag geese chicks, which are independent from birth in terms of foraging and eating, formed a parent-offspring bond during a critical period. Harlow (Harlow & Zimmerman, 1959) studied rhesus infant monkeys separated early from their mothers and given two "surrogate" mothers: one of soft cloth, which provided no food, and another of wire that provided food from a bottle. The monkeys showed attachment toward the cloth surrogate mother, clinging to it when frightened and staying near it when not feeding. Taken together, Lorenz's (1935) and Harlow's (Harlow & Zimmerman, 1959) studies provided evidence that attachment formation did occur in the absence of the mother's meeting basic needs.

Although Bowlby provided much of the initial theoretical formulation of attachment theory, Ainsworth developed a procedure that enabled empirical testing of Bowlby's major tenets in humans. The Strange Situation is a 20-minute, 8-stage laboratory task developed by Ainsworth that is meant to elicit both exploration- and proximity-seeking behaviors in the 1-year old child (Ainsworth & Wittig, 1969). The task consists of two separation episodes, where a child is left either alone or with a stranger, and two reunion episodes, where the mother returns to her infant (Ainsworth & Wittig, 1969). The separation episode activates the attachment system, whereas the reunion episode illustrates a child's expectations in terms of the mother's availability and responsiveness. Reunion behaviors between mother and child are the strongest indicators of the quality of attachment (Ainsworth, Blehar, Waters, & Wall, 1978).

Ainsworth initially developed three attachment categories: securely attached (Type B), anxious-resistant (Type C), and anxious-avoidant (Type A) (Ainsworth et al., 1978). A fourth type, disorganized attachment, was added following further study of the Strange Situation in an attempt to categorize children who did not clearly meet the criteria for the other categories (Main & Solomon, 1990). Except for Type B, all are considered insecurely attached.

Securely attached children show a low level of attachment behaviors prior to separation. When left alone with a stranger, the children show an increase in attachment in the form of crying, searching for the mother, and protesting her departure. When reunited with their mothers, these children express high levels of proximity-seeking behaviors toward the mother. Once they have been sufficiently comforted, they will return to exploring their environment, using the mother as a secure base (Ainsworth et al., 1978). Mothers of children who are securely attached are sensitive, emotionally available, and responsive to their children's needs (Ainsworth & Bell, 1969; Ainsworth et al., 1978; Bell & Ainsworth, 1972).

In contrast, children who are insecurely attached, whether anxious-resistant, anxious avoidant, or disorganized, present very different behaviors during the Strange Situation. Anxious-resistant children show anxious behaviors prior to separation and intense distress upon separation, including high levels of crying and motor activity. Upon reunion with the mother, these children show "conflicted" behavior in that they simultaneously seek and resist contact and proximity with her (Ainsworth et al., 1978). Mothers of anxious-resistant avoidant children have been shown to be inconsistent in reacting to their infants (Cassidy & Berlin, 1994).

In contrast, anxious-avoidant children rarely show distress when the mother leaves and are indifferent to her return, often avoiding contact or proximity (Ainsworth et al., 1978). Mothers of anxious-avoidant children have been shown to be insensitive, emotionally unavailable, and unresponsive to their infants (Bates, Maslin, & Frankel, 1985; Belsky & Isabella, 1988; Isabella & Belsky, 1991).

Disorganized children show an array of confusing and perplexing behaviors, including stereotypical behaviors and freezing. They frequently simultaneously engage in contradictory behaviors, such as approaching the mother with a depressed facial expression (Main & Solomon, 1990). Research has found that maltreated or neglected children (Carlson, Cicchetti, Barnett, & Braunwald, 1989), as well as children raised by a mother suffering from depression (Egeland & Sroufe, 1981) are significantly more likely to develop a disorganized attachment style.

Such differences based on the mother's parenting style illustrate that, although all infants are born with the capacity to engage in attachment behaviors, early experiences with caregivers produce in the child internal working models of caregivers that influence the balance between attachment and exploration (Bowlby, 1958, 1969). Exploration is essential for development as it allows a child to learn about and experience the world. However, proximity-seeking and other attachment behaviors are essential for survival in novel or dangerous situations. Therefore, in a secure attachment, the child achieves a healthy balance between exploration and attachment (Goldberg, 1991). In contrast, the insecurely attached children demonstrate an imbalance in exploration and attachment; either attachment behaviors are overly activated (e.g. anxious-resistant), or attachment behaviors are underactivated (e.g. anxious-avoidant; Goldberg, 1991).

*Attachment and Developmental Outcomes.* Attachment styles are related to internalizing and externalizing disorders. Speltz (1990) found that 84% of clinically referred children who met DSM-III criteria for disruptive behavior had insecure attachments, compared with only 28% of non-clinically referred children. Furthermore, Moss, Rousseau, Parent, St-Laurent, and Saintonge (1998) found that children between ages 5 to 7 years and 7 to 9 years with an anxious-avoidant attachment style showed high rates of internalizing disorders, whereas anxious-resistant children showed high rates of externalizing disorders. The worst outcome was found for children with a disorganized attachment style; they showed high rates of both internalizing and externalizing disorders. These difficulties continue into adolescence. In interpreting these studies, it is important to remember that insecure attachment does not necessarily cause these behavioral difficulties, but rather places children at risk for such difficulties and interacts with other factors in the development of internalizing and externalizing disorders.

*Attachment and Cross-cultural Issues.* Cross-cultural studies investigating the frequency of different types of attachments have shown that cultural differences influence rates of the attachment styles across cultures by influencing how children react in the Strange Situation. For instance, more children in Sweden and Germany than in North America are classified as having anxious-avoidant attachment because those countries place greater emphasis on independence at an earlier age (Colin, 1996). On the other hand, lower rates of anxious-avoidant attachment styles are found in Japan, possibly because looking and then turning away from individuals is considered rude there, so children are socialized against those behaviors (Colin, 1996). In contrast, Japanese infants show significantly higher anxious-resistant behavior than North American infants (Colin, 1996), possibly because Japanese children and their parents experience constant close contact during the first year of life, and thus the children undergo more stressful separation stages of the Strange Situation than do North American infants.

*Summary.* The quality of the mother-child attachment plays a key role in a child's socioemotional development. An insecure mother-child attachment can set the child on a trajectory toward psychopathology. However, much like temperament, the mother-child attachment cannot be viewed as the sole determining factor in the child's socioemotional development. Rather, one must look at both the child's genetic make-up and the mother-child relationship to determine vulnerability to and resiliency in stressful situations. Accordingly, an interactionist model of the child's socioemotional development is needed.

### Interactionist Models

Many past models on development have been unidirectional, viewing genes and biological predisposition as the sole determinants of outcomes. Here we propose an interactionist model for the study of socioemotional development. Such a model is based on the concept of "goodness of fit" developed by Thomas and Chess (1977). The "goodness of fit" model states that neither temperament nor environment alone determines the developmental outcome. Rather, one must consider the interaction of the two. If demands placed on a child are compatible with ability, a "goodness of fit" is achieved and the child will progress on a normal developmental trajectory. In contrast, when demands overwhelm abilities, the resulting "poorness of fit" negatively affects the child's development (Thomas & Chess, 1977). Children come into the world with genetic blueprints, which create individual differences in styles of reacting to the world, and mothers differ in parenting styles. Interactions between these two factors influence the development of the child. Emerging empirical evidence from studies of nonhuman animals supports an interactionist model of human development.

*Nonhuman Animal Studies.* A large corpus of literature on animal subjects has examined the relation between maternal care and offspring's behavioral and neurobiological reactions to stress. The neurobiological reaction is a cascade of events in the hypothalamic-pituitary axis, which is initiated by a release of corticotropin-releasing hormone from the paraventricular nuclei of the hypothalamus and which ends with a release of cortisol from the adrenal glands (see Gunnar & Quevedo, 2007). The hippocampus, through glucocorticoid receptors, provides a negative feedback for the stress response by blocking further production of corticotropin-releasing hormone and terminating the stress response (see Gunnar & Quevedo, 2007, for a review).

In rats, mothers differ in amounts of licking, grooming, and arched-back nursing of their offspring (Caldji et al., 1998; Francis, Diorio, Liu, & Meaney, 1999). Seminal work by Meaney and colleagues (Caldji et al., 1998) found that offspring of mothers providing high licking, grooming, and arched-back nursing showed less fear and fewer neurobiological responses toward stressful situations compared to those receiving less licking, grooming, and arched-back nursing. Further, cross-fostering studies have shown that the effects of maternal licking, grooming, and arched-back nursing on the stress response are not genetically determined (Fleming, O'Day, & Kraemer, 1999; Francis et al., 1999; Meaney, 2001). Offspring with biological mothers ranked low in licking, grooming, and arched-back nursing behavior, but raised by female rats with high levels of such behaviors also had low levels of both fearfulness and corticotropin-releasing hormone. Offspring with biological mothers that showed high licking, grooming, and arched-back nursing, but raised by female rats with low levels of such behaviors showed high levels of both fearfulness and corticotropin-releasing hormone (Fleming et al., 1999; Francis et al., 1999; Meaney, 2001). These results illustrate that maternal parenting style influences the development of individual differences in the ability to regulate and terminate stress responses.

Maternal licking, grooming, and arched-back nursing appear to influence the methylation of glucocorticoid receptor genes in the hippocampus (Sapolsky, 2004; Weaver et al., 2001; Weaver et al., 2004). Methylation turns off the genes for glucocorticoid receptors, rendering them useless and producing fewer glucocorticoid receptors in the offspring's hippocampus. However, licking and grooming prevent methylation of the genes, increasing the number of glucocorticoid receptors in the hippocampus, thus increasing the efficiency of the termination of the stress response (Sapolsky, 2004; Weaver et al., 2001; Weaver et al., 2004). Thus, offspring that experience high amounts of licking and grooming during the early stages of development have a higher number of glucocorticoid receptors, which enhance the negative feedback of the stress response (Weaver et al., 2001; Weaver et al., 2004). See Figure 5.1 for a summary of findings from the work of Meaney and his colleagues.

Studies of non-human primates also have illustrated the important role of maternal parenting in stress responses. Maternal separations and poor rearing conditions, such as isolation and upbringing by peers, influence the offspring's ability to regulate and terminate the stress response (Sanchez, Ladd, & Plotsky, 2001). For instance, mothers that are placed in a variable foraging environment have offspring that as adults are more fearful and have exaggerated stress responses, compared to offspring whose mothers were in a foraging environment with a predictable food supply (Coplan et al., 1996; Rosenblum & Andrews, 1994). Thus, studies conducted with rats and non-human primates illustrate the importance of interactions between biology and the postnatal environment, especially the mother-child relationship.

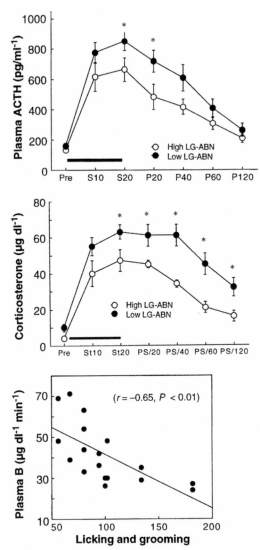

**Figure 5.1.** Mean plasma levels of adrenocorticotropin releasing hormone (ACTH; top) and corticosterone (middle) following a 20-minute stress period as a function of maternal licking and grooming (LG) and arched-back nursing (ABN). Relation between the frequency of maternal LG-ABN during the first 10-days of life and the plasma corticosterone levels in response to the stress task (bottom). From Liu, D., Diorio, J., Tannenbaum, B., Caldji, C., Francis, D., Freedman, A., et al. (1997). Maternal care, hippocampal glucocorticoid receptors, and hypothalamic-pituitary-adrenal responses to stress. *Science, 277*(5332), 1659–1662. Reprinted with permission from AAAS.

*Summary.* The studies reviewed previously illustrate that in rats and non-human primates, an interaction between genes and environment may increase the risk and may bias an individual toward a particular outcome. Environmental influence also plays a significant role in determining an individual's socioemotional outcome in humans.

## INDIVIDUAL AND CAREGIVER INFLUENCES ON SOCIOEMOTIONAL DEVELOPMENT: EXAMPLES FROM TYPICAL AND ATYPICAL DEVELOPMENT

### Typical Development: The Case of Temperamental Shyness

Kagan and the Harvard research group developed the terms *behaviorally inhibited* and *behaviorally uninhibited* to describe observed individual variations in response to novel situations (Garcia-Coll, Kagan, & Resnick, 1984). Behavioral inhibition, which is seen in about 10% of normally developing children, is characterized by fearfulness and wariness toward novel situations, objects, and individuals (Garcia-Coll et al., 1984). Children characterized as behaviorally inhibited will display long latencies to approach and communicate and high rates of crying, clinging to their mothers, and vocalizations of distress in situations involving novel objects or individuals (Garcia-Coll et al., 1984). Much overlap exists between temperamental shyness and behavioral inhibition, as both terms refer to a tendency to respond to novel situations with fear and wariness. Accordingly, the terms will be used interchangeably throughout this section.

The longitudinal work of Kagan and colleagues has shown moderate stability of temperament throughout development and into adolescence (Kagan, Reznick, Clarke, Snidman, & Garcia-Coll, 1984; Kagan, Reznick, & Snidman, 1988; Kagan, Reznick, Snidman, Gibbons, & Johnson, 1988; Reznick et al., 1986; Schwartz, Snidman, & Kagan, 1999) and twin studies have found a moderate heritability for behavioral inhibition, even when the shared environment is taken into consideration (Matheny, 1989; Robinson, Kagan, Reznick, & Corley, 1992). A number of physiological correlates for temperamental shyness have also been identified, including greater relative right frontal activity (Calkins, Fox, & Marshall, 1996; Fox et al., 1995; Fox, Henderson, Rubin, Calkins, & Schmidt, 2001), relatively higher cortisol levels (Kagan et al., 1988; Schmidt et al., 1997) and higher and less variable heart rates (Kagan et al., 1984; Kagan et al., 1987; Kagan et al., 1988; Reznick et al., 1986) at baseline. These physiological patterns have also been reported in stress-evoking situations (Schmidt, Fox, Schulkin, & Gold, 1999; Theall-Honey & Schmidt, 2006). Adults classified as temperamentally shy show similar patterns of greater relative right frontal EEG activity and high heart rate at rest and in response to stress (Beaton et al., 2008; Schmidt et al., 1999; Schmidt & Fox, 1994).

Although behavioral inhibition is stable throughout childhood and adulthood, studies show individual differences in the degree of continuity over development. Although a child may have a genetic physiological pre-disposition toward temperamental shyness, the environment interacts with this predisposition, influencing the stability and degree of temperamental shyness.

Kagan (1994) hypothesized that mothers who are highly responsive to their children's needs and distress enhance behavioral inhibition by pre-venting them from developing coping strategies and by instilling a belief that the child is not capable of handling challenges. In contrast, mothers who are firm and set limits tend to enhance their children's coping abilities and reduce behavioral inhibition (Kagan, 1994). Thus, an overprotective and intrusive parenting style can lead to increased levels of behavioral inhibition.

A number of recent studies have supported this hypothesis. Rubin, Hastings, Stewart, Henderson, and Chen (1997) found that behaviorally inhibited children of mothers who were overly intrusive showed higher levels of behavioral inhibition in a free play situation with unfamiliar peers than behaviorally inhibited children whose mothers displayed lower levels of protection. Similarly, Park, Belsky, Putnam, and Crnic (1997) found that behaviorally inhibited 2- and 3-year-old children whose mothers showed exaggerated affective, highly protective responses were even more behav-iorally inhibited at age four. Because maternal perceptions can influence the manner in which mothers react to their children, the question becomes whether maternal perceptions of behavioral inhibition, rather than objec-tive measurement, may be key in determining maternal overprotectiveness. Rubin, Nelson, Hastings, and Asendorpf (1999) found that a mother's per-ception of her child's behavioral inhibition was the determining factor for overprotectiveness, not the degree of a child's observed behavioral inhibition.

In addition to highly protective parenting, criticism has been shown to influence the development of social withdrawal in children. Parents who regularly criticize their children, especially in front of others, may evoke negative thoughts and feelings of low self-worth to develop, resulting in withdrawal from social situations (Barber, Olsen, & Shagle, 1994). Rubin and colleagues have found that children of mothers who used high rates of criticism and had an intrusive and overprotective parenting style were significantly more likely to withdraw from social situations (Mills & Rubin, 1998; Rubin et al., 1997; Rubin, Burgess, & Hastings, 2002). Thus, both degree of protectiveness and amount of criticism appear to influence the continuity or discontinuity of behavioral inhibition.

Attachment style also influences the continuity and intensity of behavioral inhibition. Behaviorally inhibited children with a secure attachment to their mothers have been shown to have lower cortisol levels in response to a novel and stressful social situation, compared to behaviorally inhibited children with insecure attachments to their mothers (Nachmias, Gunnar, Mangelsdorf, Parritz, & Buss, 1996). On the surface, these results may appear to contrast with the findings that high levels of responsiveness toward children increase behavioral inhibition. Overprotective parenting is not focused on being responsive and available to a child who needs help but rather focuses on indiscriminately responding to all of the child's cries for attention. Consequently, overprotective parenting does not provide the child with the confidence and ability to explore the environment, but rather inhibits the development of coping skills.

The influence of mother-child interactions on behavioral inhibition is also illustrated by mother-child dyads, in which mothers are experiencing internal or external stressors such as depression or a perceived lack of social support. Interactions between depressed mothers and their children tend to be characterized by decreases in shared focus of interest, positive affect, touch, and vocalizations; and increases in maternal intrusiveness and directing (Cohn, Campbell, Matias & Hopkins, 1990; Weinberg & Tronick, 1998a, 1998b). Kochanska (1991) found that children of clinically depressed mothers, whose interactions were low in affect, showed higher levels of behavioral inhibition compared to children of mothers without psychiatric illnesses. Given the heritable nature of both depression and behavioral inhibition, it is possible that children born to depressed mothers have a genetic predisposition toward behavioral inhibition. In any case, the study's results illustrate that mother-child interactions can influence the development of behavioral inhibition.

Fox et al. (2005) found that the presence of the short allele of the serotonin transporter (5-HTT) gene was not sufficient in predicting development of behavioral inhibition in middle childhood. Rather, they found the short allele of the 5-HTT gene combined with maternal perception of low social support to be predictive of behavioral inhibition in middle childhood. Children with the short allele of the 5-HTT gene and with mothers who perceived themselves as having social support were not behaviorally inhibited in middle childhood (Fox et al., 2005; see Figure 5.2). Although

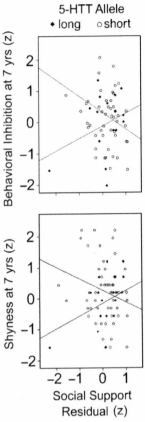

**Figure 5.2.** Behavioral inhibition (top) and shyness (bottom) at 7 years of age as a function of the 5-HTT gene and maternal perceived social support. From Fox, N. A., Nichols, K. E., Henderson, H. A., Rubin, K. H., Schmidt, L. A., Hamer, D., et al. (2005). Evidence for a gene-environment interaction in predicting behavioral inhibition in middle childhood. *Psychological Science, 16*, 921–926. Copyright 2005 by Association for Psychological Science. Reprinted with permission from Wiley-Blackwell.

children with the short allele of the 5-HTT gene may be biased toward high levels of behavioral inhibition, these results suggest that the presence of the allele is not sufficient to produce behavioral inhibition.

As can be seen from research on temperamental shyness, we cannot view temperament in isolation and as a single determinant of behavioral outcome. Although shyness appears to have a genetic basis, it interacts with environmental factors (e.g., parenting style and quality) to determine developmental outcome. We propose an interactionist model for the development of temperamental shyness whereby a biological predisposition toward temperamental shyness (e.g., greater relative right frontal activity at rest) interacts with various aspects of environment (e.g., quality of attachment and parenting style). With an appropriate parenting style that includes opportunities to interact with the world and develop coping skills, children with a biological predisposition for behavioral inhibition might not develop it. On the other hand, in an environment that promotes behavioral inhibition and prevents development of coping resources (e.g., overprotective parenting), a child develops even higher levels of behavioral inhibition.

**Atypical Development: The Case of Child Maltreatment and Abuse**

Children who experience maltreatment during development are known to have an increased risk for internalizing and externalizing problems, including increased fearfulness, anxiety, and depression (Kaufman, 1991); low self-esteem (Bolger, Patterson, & Kupersmidt, 1998); posttraumatic stress disorder (Dubner & Motta, 1999); and high levels of aggression, delinquency, and conduct disorders (Cichetti & Toth, 1995). However, not all children who experience maltreatment go on to develop these difficulties.

Some maltreated children progress through a normal trajectory of development. Research has shown that specific factors prior to, during, and after the maltreatment incident influence children's reactions. These factors include the level of social support, prior mental health problems, the degree of fear and danger experienced during maltreatment, its chronicity, and the child's relation to the perpetrator (Pynoos & Nader, 1993). Also, reaction to maltreatment is related to genetic make-up.

Caspi et al. (2002) found that males who experienced maltreatment and who had a low activity variant of the monoamine oxidase A (MAOA) gene had higher rates of antisocial behavior compared to males who experienced maltreatment and had the high activity variant of the MAOA gene. Similarly, Caspi et al. (2003) found a relation between the serotonin transporter (5-HTT) gene and the influence of stressful life events, including maltreatment, on the degree of depression experienced. Three forms of the 5-HTT gene are possible: two short alleles, two long alleles, and one long and one short allele. The authors found a positive relation between severity of maltreatment and number of major depressive episodes in participants with two short alleles and participants with one short and one long allele, with the strongest link among the former group. Participants with two long 5-HTT alleles had no such relation episodes (see Figure 5.3). These results have been independently replicated in children (Kaufman et al.,

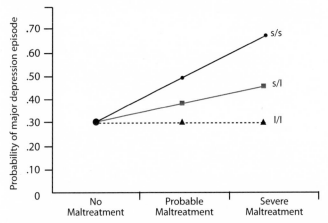

**Figure 5.3.** Probability of depression as a function of history of childhood maltreatment and the 5-HTT gene. s = short allele; l = long allele. From Caspi, A., Sugden, K., Moffitt, T. E., Taylor, A., Craig, I. W., Harrington, H. L., et al. (2003). Influence of life stress on depression: Moderation by a polymorphism in the 5-HTT gene. *Science, 301,* 386–389. Reprinted with permission from AAAS.

2004), adolescents (Eley et al., 2004), and young adults (Kendler, Khun, Vittum, Prescott, & Riley, 2005).

Recently, researchers investigating gene-by-environment interactions found an even more complex trajectory for socioemotional development in individuals with a history of childhood maltreatment. Kaufman et al. (2006) found an interaction between the brain-derived neurotrophic factor gene, the serotonin transporter gene, and maltreatment history in predicting childhood depression. Children with the methionine allele of the neurotrophic factor gene and two short alleles of the serotonin transporter gene had the highest levels of childhood depression only if they had a history of childhood maltreatment. In addition, children with high levels of social support were less likely to develop depression than those without social support. These findings illustrate that, given a genetic risk, the environment can serve either as a protective factor or as a risk factor for psychopathology.

## Atypical Development: The Case of Childhood Autism
The autism spectrum disorders are a complex group of related neurodevelopmental disorders characterized by deficits in social interaction, impaired communication, and patterns of circumscribed interests and repetitive behaviors (American Psychiatric Association, 1994). The full autism

spectrum includes autistic disorder, Asperger syndrome, and pervasive developmental disorder not otherwise specified, and has a prevalence rate of 6 in 1000 (Fombonne, 2005). Although the etiology of autism is unknown, genetic factors are currently believed to increase susceptibility by leading to aberrant patterns of neural connectivity. Neuropathological evidence (Bauman & Kemper, 2003; Rodier, 2002) indicates that autism originates prenatally, with atypical neurodevelopment continuing postnatally. By two to three years of age, children with autism show accelerated brain growth, indicated by enlarged head circumferences and heightened gray matter volumes (Courchesne et al., 2001; Courchesne, Carper, & Akshoomoff, 2003). New experiences shape a developing nervous system against the background of these early systemic brain changes. In contrast to the typically developing child, in whom experience-expectant and experience-dependant processes work to prune unused connections and to consolidate frequented pathways (Belmonte et al., 2004), a child with autism fails to produce stable changes in the neural architecture supporting social and emotional development (Johnson & Munakata, 2005).

Although autism is not typically diagnosed until a child reaches 3 or 4 years of age (Hoshino et al., 1997), marked neurodevelopmental abnormalities may be observed soon after birth. Analyses of family home movies (Adrien et al., 1992; Osterling & Dawson, 1994) and retrospective questionnaire surveys (Dahlgren & Gillberg, 1989) have revealed subtle social and communicative abnormalities that occur prior to the 1st birthday in children later diagnosed with autism. For example, very young autistic children show peculiarities of eye contact and gaze, often fail to respond to parents' voices, can be unresponsive to parental attempts to play and interact, and can appear exceptionally passive or isolated (Dahlgren & Gillberg, 1989; DeGiacomo & Fombonne, 1998). Perhaps these deficits cumulatively decrease experience with social/emotional signals, obstruct the consolidation of experiences and learning, and impede the formation of neural networks that support more complex social/emotional and communicative competencies.

*Temperament in Autism.* Relatively few studies in the extant literature have examined temperament or factors of the autistic individual, although this is changing (Garon et al., 2009; Schwartz et al., 2009). Bailey, Hatton, Mesibov, Ament, and Skinner (2000) examined temperament using the Behavioral Style Questionnaire (BSQ; McDevitt & Carey, 1978) in a group of 30 autistic children aged 3 to 7 years. Compared to a reference sample of 350 typically developed children, autistic children were rated as less intense, more distractible, and less rhythmic; they also had a higher response threshold. Kasari and Sigman (1997) collected parental ratings of temperament (BSQ) and observations of adult-child interactions for 28 autistic children (average age 3 1/2 years). They found that autistic children rated as temperamentally difficult by their caregiver spent less time engaged with that caregiver, and were less responsive to the experimenter's initiations. In a recent study, Bryson, Zwaigenbaum, McDermott, Rombough, and Brian (2007) have followed a group of 6-month old siblings of autistic children prospectively, detailing the temperament of 9 participants who later received a diagnosis of autism. They found that these participants could be separated into two distinct subgroups based largely on the onset of symptoms. Both groups showed similar temperamental characteristics, however, such as irritability, intolerance of intrusions, a tendency toward distress/negative affect, and problems with self- or other-regulation of state. Importantly, Bryson et al. (2007) noted that these temperamental characteristics may both signal and contribute to the behavioral emergence of autism. They suggest that the irritability and behavioral inflexibility seen early in the autistic child's development reflect an increasing sensitivity to environmental stimuli, and may ultimately contribute to reduced responses to others and pleasure taken in interactions.

*Attachment in Autism.* Most studies that have examined attachment behaviors in autistic children report no significant differences between them and comparison groups with respect to forming secure attachments (see Buitelaar, 1995; Rutgers et al., 2007). Autistic children seek comfort from their parents when distressed and discriminate between parent and stranger, directing more social behaviors toward their parent (Rogers, Ozonoff, & Maslin-Cole, 1993). In addition, autistic children react like control children when separated from a parent by increasing proximity-seeking behavior upon reunion (Buitelaar, 1995). However, autistic children tend to show less contact-seeking and maintaining behaviors and are less responsive than comparison children to their mothers (Rogers et al., 1993). Children whose clinical presentation is closest to the more classical definition of autism (i.e., not the broader autism spectrum) form less secure attachments, along with children who possess more significant cognitive handicaps (Rutgers et al., 2007). In these two subgroups, insecure attachments are likely caused by restricted reciprocal social exchanges and reduced capacities to form mental representations of the attachment relationship, respectively (Rutgers et al., 2007).

Dissanayake and Crossley (1996) found that autistic children who increased proximity-seeking behavior in response to a stranger also showed aberrant eye gaze, reduced positive affect, and limited reciprocal exchanges with their caregiver. Thus, it appears that attachment can occur in autism, even in the presence of behaviors that could be expected to discourage attachment. Capps, Sigman, and Mundy (1994) found that mothers of securely attached autistic children showed greater sensitivity than mothers of insecurely attached children. Thus, the effects of autistic symptomology on attachment may be offset by parental sensitivity. However, a recent study by van Ijzendoorn et al. (2007) failed to establish a clear relation between parental sensitivity and securely attached autistic children. These findings led van Ijzendoorn et al. to speculate that attachment in autism may be less influenced by parental sensitivity than by other parental inter-active factors. Parents of autistic children evidently make greater use of behavior control strategies, directives, attention-getting behaviors, nonverbal prompts, and physical proximity than other parents (Kasari, Sigman, Mundy, & Yirmiya, 1988; Lemanek, Stone, & Fishel, 1993; Sigman, Mundy, Sherman, & Ungerer, 1986). Although such strategies appear more unidirectional, diverging from the conventional sensitive reciprocal relationship important in attachment, they may reflect a unique parental response to the affective and social developmental needs of the autistic child. Indeed, such adaptations may foster greater synchrony between the child's activity and focus of attention and the caregiver's behavior, consequently promoting improved social outcomes.

*Summary.* In summary, combinations of individual and environmental factors are presumed to influence socioemotional development in typical and atypical populations. Although temperament may bias an individual toward a particular outcome, an individual's biology is not the sole determinant of socioemotional development. Rather, the environment plays an important role in conferring risk and resiliency, and two individuals with the same genotype for a particular trait can have very different developmental outcomes because of their environments. The studies discussed earlier provide strong evidence for the implementation of an interactionist model when studying development.

## CONCLUSION AND FUTURE DIRECTIONS

Throughout this chapter, we have used examples from typical (i.e., temperamental shyness) and atypical (i.e., childhood maltreatment and abuse, and autism) populations to illustrate that both genetic and environmental factors influence socioemotional development. We have shown that development is a very complex process involving integration of many factors, including genes, brain activation, parenting, culture, and society.

Although biology and genetics are present at birth, they are not destiny. Rather, throughout development, much interaction occurs among biological factors, genetics, and environmental factors to influence a child's socioemotional outcome. Consequently, only when these aspects are examined in combination will our understanding of the true complexity of development begin to emerge. Research that considers how these interactions shape development provides a more accurate picture of developmental outcome and helps to delineate the risk factors for poor developmental outcomes. Such research gives much insight into individuals' risk and resiliency, thus enhancing clinicians' ability to identify children early in life who are at risk for developmental difficulties and to provide them with effective interventions.

Currently, much research investigating the influence of gene-environment interactions has had limited longitudinal follow-ups. Longitudinal research investigating developmental outcome into adolescence and young adulthood has been lacking. Although following individuals for longer periods is costly, it will further enhance our understanding of factors that influence socioemotional development and that determine continuity of developmental outcomes.

Development is a complex puzzle that is far from being solved. Already, many genetic and environmental factors have been identified as influencing developmental outcomes, and many others will surely be added to the picture. Interdisciplinary work that brings together multiple fields of inquiry, methods, and levels of analyses to address basic questions holds particular promise, as does work involving the examination of multiple gene interactions (Schmidt, Fox, Hamer, 2007) and gene-environment interactions in which the environment is conceptualized as outside (exogeneous) of the individual (Fox et al., 2005) and inside (endogenous) of the individual (Schmidt, Fox, Perez-Edgar, & Hamer, 2009). Although the complexity of development can seem overwhelming and the research never-ending, with each finding we gain insight into risks for atypical development, and we are better able to help those at risk for developmental difficulties. Accordingly, the practical implications of such research for the well-being of our society are abundant.

REFERENCES

Adrien, J. L., Perrot, A., Sauvage, D., Leddet, I., Larmande, C., Hameury, L., et al. (1992). Early symptoms in autism from family home movies. Evaluation and comparison between 1st and 2nd year of life using I.B.S.E. scale. *Acta Paedopsychiatrica, 55,* 71–75.

Ahadi, S., Rothbart, M. K., & Ye, R. (1993). Children's temperament in the United States and China: Similarities and differences. *European Journal of Personality, 7*, 359–378.

Ainsworth, M. D. S., & Bell, S. M. (1969). Some contemporary patterns in the feeding situation. In A. Ambrose (Ed.), *Stimulation in early infancy* (pp. 133–170). London: Academic Press.

Ainsworth, M. D. S., Blehar, M. C., Waters, E., & Wall, S. (1978). *Patterns of attachment: A psychological study of the strange situation*. Hillsdale, NJ: Erlbaum.

Ainsworth, M. D. S., & Bowlby, J. (1991). An ethological approach to personality development. *American Psychologist, 46*, 333–341.

Ainsworth, M. D. S., & Wittig, B. A. (1969). Attachment and the exploratory behavior of one-year-olds in a strange situation. In B. M. Foss (Ed.), *Determinants of infant behavior* (Vol. 4, pp. 113–136). London: Methuen.

American Psychiatric Association (1994). *Diagnostic and statistical manual of mental disorders* (4th ed.). Washington, DC: Author.

Bailey, D. B. J., Hatton, D. D., Mesibov, G., Ament, N., & Skinner, M. (2000). Early development, temperament, and functional impairment in autism and fragile X syndrome. *Journal of Autism and Developmental Disorders, 30*, 49–59.

Barber, B. K., Olsen, J. E., & Shagle, S. C. (1994). Associations between parental psychological and behavioral control and youth internalized and externalized behaviors. *Child Development, 65*, 1120–1136.

Bates, J. E. (1986). The measurement of temperament. In R. Plomin & J. Dunn (Eds.), *The study of temperament: Changes, continuities and challenges* (pp. 1–11). Hillsdale, NJ: Erlbaum.

Bates, J., Maslin, C., & Frankel, K. (1985). Attachment security, mother-child interaction, and temperament as predictors of behavior problem ratings at age three years. In I. Bretherton & E. Waters (Eds.), *Monographs of the Society for Research in Child Development, 50*, 167–193.

Bauman, M. L., & Kemper, T. L. (2003). The neuropathology of the autism spectrum disorders: What have we learned? *Novartis Foundation Symposium, 251*, 112–22; discussion 122–8, 281–297.

Beaton E. A., Schmidt, L. A., Ashbaugh, A. R., Santesso, D. L., Antony, M. M., & McCabe, R. E. (2008). Resting and reactive frontal brain electrical activity (EEG) among a non-clinical sample of socially anxious adults: Does concurrent depressive mood matter? *Neuropsychiatric Disease & Treatment, 4*(1), 187–192.

Bell, S. M., & Ainsworth, M. D. S. (1972). Infant crying and maternal responsiveness. *Child Development, 43*, 1171–1190.

Belmonte, M. K., Cook, E. H. J., Anderson, G. M., Rubenstein, J. L., Greenough, W. T., Beckel-Mitchener, A., et al. (2004). Autism as a disorder of neural information processing: Directions for research and targets for therapy. *Molecular Psychiatry, 9*, 646–663.

Belsky, J., & Isabella, R. (1988). Maternal, infant and social-contextual determinants of attachment security: A process analysis. In J. Belsky & T. Nezworski (Eds.), *Clinical implications of attachment* (pp. 41–94). Hillsdale, NJ: Erlbaum.

Bolger, K. E., Patterson, C. J., & Kupersmidt, J. B. (1998). Peer relations and self-esteem among children who have been maltreated. *Child Development, 69*, 1171–1197.

Bowlby, J. (1958). The nature of the child's tie to his mother. *International Journal of Psychoanalysis, 39*, 350–373.

Bowbly, J. (1969). *Attachment and loss: Vol. 1. Attachment.* New York: Basic Books.

Bowlby, J. (1973). *Attachment and loss: Vol. 2. Separation: Anxiety and anger.* New York: Basic Books.

Bryson, S. E., Zwaigenbaum, L., McDermott, C., Rombough, V., & Brian, J. (2007). The autism observation scale for infants: Scale development and reliability data. *Journal of Autism and Developmental Disorders, 37*, 12–24.

Buitelaar, J. K. (1995). Attachment and social withdrawal in autism: Hypotheses and findings. *Behavior, 132*, 319–350.

Buss, A. H., & Plomin, R. (1984). *Temperament: Early developing personality traits.* Hillsdale, NJ: Erlbaum.

Buss, A. H., & Plomin, R. (1986). The EAS approach to temperament. In R. Plomin, & J. Dunn (Eds.), *The study of temperament: Changes, continuities and challenges* (pp. 68–80). Hillsdale, NJ: Erlbaum.

Caldji, C., Tannenbaum, B., Sharma, S., Francis, D., Plotsky, P. M., & Meaney, M. J. (1998). Maternal care during infancy regulates the development of neural systems mediating the expression of fearfulness in the rat. *Proceedings of the National Academy of Sciences of the United States of America, 95*, 5335–5340.

Calkins, S. D., Fox, N. A., & Marshall, T. R. (1996). Behavioral and physiological andtecedents of inhibited and uninhibited behavior. *Child Development, 67*, 523–540.

Capps, L., Sigman, M., & Mundy, P. (1994). Attachment security in children with autism. *Development and Psychopathology, 6*, 249–261.

Carlson, V., Cicchetti, D., Barnett, D., & Braunwald, K. (1989). Disorganized, disoriented attachment relationships in maltreated infants. *Development Psychology, 25*, 525–531.

Caspi, A., & Silva, P. A. (1995). Temperamental qualities at age three predict personality traits in young adulthood: Longitudinal evidence from a birth cohort. *Child Development, 66*, 486–498.

Caspi, A., McClay, J., Moffitt, T. E., Mill, J., Martin, J., Craig, I. W., et al. (2002). Role of genotype in the cycle of violence in maltreated children. *Science, 297*, 851–854.

Caspi, A., Sugden, K., Moffitt, T. E., Taylor, A., Craig, I. W., Harrington, H. L., et al. (2003). Influence of life stress on depression: Moderation by a polymorphism in the 5-HTT gene. *Science, 301*, 386–389.

Cassidy, J., & Berlin, L. J. (1994). The insecure/ambivalent pattern of attachment: Theory and research. *Child Development, 65*, 971–991.

Chess, S., & Thomas, A. (1984). *Origins and evolution of behavior disorders.* New York: Brunner/Mazel, Inc.

Cicchetti, D., & Toth, S. L. (1995). A developmental psychopathology perspective on child abuse and neglect. *Journal of the American Academy of Child and Adolescent Psychiatry, 34*, 541–565.

Cohn, J. F., Campbell, S. B., Matias, R., & Hopkins, J. (1990). Face-to-face interactions of postpartum depressed and nondepressed mother-infant pairs at 2 months. *Developmental Psychology, 26*, 13–23.

Colin, V. L. (1996). *Human attachment.* New York: McGraw-Hill.

Coplan, J. D., Andrews, M. W., Rosenblum, L. A., Owens, M. J., Friedman, S., Gorman, J. M., et al. (1996). Persistent elevations of cerebrospinal fluid concentrations of corticotrophin-releasing factor in adult nonhuman primates exposed to early-life stressors: Implications for the pathophysiology of mood and anxiety disorders. *Proceedings of the National Academy of Sciences of the United States of America, 93,* 1619–1623.

Courchesne, E., Carper, R., & Akshoomoff, N. (2003). Evidence of brain overgrowth in the first year of life in autism. *Journal of the American Medical Association 290,* 337–344.

Courchesne, E., Karns, C. M., Davis, H. R., Ziccardi, R., Carper, R. A., Tigue, Z. D., et al. (2001) Unusual brain growth patterns in early life in patients with autistic disorder: An MRI study. *Neurology 57,* 245–254.

Dahlgren, S. O., & Gillberg, C. (1989). Symptoms in the first two years of life. A preliminary population study of infantile autism. *European Archives of Psychiatry and Neurological Sciences 238,* 169–174.

De Giacomo, A., & Fombonne, E. (1998). Parental recognition of developmental abnormalities in autism. *European Child and Adolescent Psychiatry, 7,* 131–136.

Dissanayake, C., & Crossley, S. A. (1996). Proximity and sociable behaviors in autism: Evidence for attachment. *Journal of Child Psychology and Psychiatry, 37,* 149–156.

Dubner, A. E., & Motta, R. W. (1999). Sexually and physically abused foster care children and posttraumatic stress disorder. *Journal of Consulting & Clinical Psychology, 67,* 367–373.

Egeland, B., & Sroufe, L. A. (1981). Developmental sequelae of maltreatment in infancy. In D. Cicchetti & R. Rizle (Eds.), *Developmental approaches to child maltreatment: New directions for child development* (pp. 77–91). San Francisco, CA: Jossey-Bass.

Eley, T. C., Sugden, K., Corsico, A., Gregory, A. M., Sham, P., McGuffin, P., et al. (2004). Gene-environment interaction analysis of serotonin system markers with adolescent depression. *Molecular Psychiatry, 9,* 908–915.

Fleming, A. S., O'Day, D. H., & Kraemer, G. W. (1999). Neurobiology of mother-infant interactions: Experience and central nervous system plasticity across development and generations. *Neuroscience and Biobehavioral Reviews, 23,* 673–685.

Fombonne, E. (2005). Epidemiology of autistic disorder and other pervasive developmental disorders. *Journal of Clinical Psychiatry, 66*(Suppl. 10), 3–8.

Fox, N. A., Henderson, H. A., Rubin, K. H., Calkins, S. D., & Schmidt, L. A. (2001). Continuity and discontinuity of behavioral inhibition and exuberance: psychophysiological and behavioral influences across the first four years of life. *Child Development, 72,* 1–21.

Fox, N. A., Nichols, K. E., Henderson, H. A., Rubin, K. H., Schmidt, L. A., Hamer, D., et al. (2005). Evidence for a gene-environment interaction in predicting behavioral inhibition in middle childhood. *Psychological Science, 16,* 921–926.

Fox, N. A., Rubin, K. H., Calkins, S. D., Marshall, T. R., Coplan, R. J., Porges, S. W., et al. (1995). Frontal activation asymmetry and social competence at four years of age. *Child Development, 66,* 1770–1784.

Francis, D., Diorio, J., Liu, D., & Meaney, M. J. (1999). Nongenomic transmission across generations of maternal behavior and stress responses in the rat. *Science, 5*, 1155–1158.

Garcia-Coll, C., Kagan, J., & Reznick, S. (1984). Behavioral inhibition in young children. *Child Development, 55*, 1005–1019.

Garon, N., Bryson, S. E., Zwaigenbaum, L., Smith, I. M., Brian, J., Roberts, W., & Szatmari, P. (2009). Temperament and its relationship to autistic symptoms in a high-risk infant sib cohort. *Journal of Abnormal Child Psychology, 37*, 59–78.

Ghera, M. M., Hane, A. A., Malesa, E. E., & Fox, N. A. (2006). The role of infant soothability in the relation between infant negativity and maternal sensitivity. *Infant Behavior and Development, 29*, 289–293.

Goldberg, S. (1991). Recent development in attachment theory and research. *Canadian Journal of Psychiatry, 36*, 393–400.

Goldsmith, H. H., Buss, A. H., Plomin, R., Rothbart, M. K., Thomas, A., Chess, S., et al. (1987). Roundtable: What is temperament? Four approaches. *Child Development, 58*, 505–529.

Goldsmith, H. H., & Campos, J. J. (1982). Toward a theory of infant temperament. In R. N. Emde & R. J. Harmon (Eds.), *The development of attachment and affiliative systems*. New York: Plenum.

Goodman-Campbell, S. B. (1979). Mother-infant interaction as a function of maternal ratings of temperament. *Child Psychiatry and Human Development, 10*, 67–76.

Gunnar, M., & Quevedo, K. (2007). The neurobiology of stress and development. *Annual Review of Psychology, 58*, 145–173.

Harlow, H. F., & Zimmerman, R. R. (1959). Affectional responses in the infant monkey. *Science, 130*, 421–432.

Hetherington, M. E., Parke, R. D., & Schmuckler, M. (2003). *Child psychology: A contemporary viewpoint* (1st Canadian ed.). Toronto: McGraw-Hill Ryerson.

Hoshino, Y., Kaneko, M., Yashima, Y., Kumashiro, H., Volkmar, F. R., & Cohen, D. J. (1987). Clinical features of autistic children with setback course in their infancy. *Japanese Journal of Psychiatry and Neurology 41*, 237–245.

Isabella, R. A., & Belsky, J. (1991). Interactional synchrony and the origins of infant-mother attachments: A replication study. *Child Development, 62*, 373–384.

Johnson, M. H., & Munakata, Y. (2005). Processes of change in brain and cognitive development. *Trends in Cognitive Science, 9*, 152–158.

Kagan, J. (1994). *Galen's prophecy: Temperament in human nature*. New York: Basic Books.

Kagan, J., Arcus, D., Snidman, N., Feng, W.Y., Hendler, J., & Greene, S. (1994). Reactivity in infants: A cross-national comparison. *Developmental Psychology, 30*, 342–345.

Kagan, J., Kearsley, R. B., & Zelazo, P. R. (1978). *Infancy: Its place in human development*. Cambridge, MA: Harvard University Press.

Kagan, J., Reznick, S. J., Clarke, C., Snidman, N., & Garcia-Coll, C. (1984). Behavioral inhibition to the unfamiliar. *Child Development, 55*, 2212–2225.

Kagan, J., Reznick, J. S., & Snidman, N. (1987). The physiology and psychology of behavioral inhibition in children. *Child Development, 58*, 1459–1473.

Kagan, J., Reznick, S. J., & Snidman, N. (1988). Biological bases of childhood shyness. *Science, 240,* 167–171.

Kagan, J., Reznick, S. J., Snidman, N., Gibbons, J., Johnson, M. O. (1988). Childhood derivatives of inhibition and lack of inhibition to the unfamiliar. *Child Development, 59,* 1580–1589.

Kagan, J., & Snidman, N. (1991). Infant predictors of inhibited and uninhibited profiles. *Psychological Science, 2,* 40–44.

Kasari, C., & Sigman, M. (1997). Linking parental perceptions to interactions in young children with autism. *Journal of Autism and Developmental Disorders, 27,* 39–57.

Kasari, C., Sigman, M., Mundy, P., & Yirmiya, N. (1988). Caregiver interactions with autistic children. *Journal of Abnormal Child Psychology, 16,* 45–56.

Kaufman, J. (1991). Depressive disorders in maltreated children. *Journal of the American Academy of Child & Adolescent Psychiatry, 30,* 257–265.

Kaufman, S. E., & Kagan, J. (2005). Infant predictors of kindergarten behavior: The contribution of inhibited and uninhibited temperament styles. *Behavioral Disorders, 30,* 331–347.

Kaufman, J., Yang, B. Z., Douglas-Palumberi, H., Grasso, D., Lipschitz, D., Houshyar, S., et al. (2006). Brain-derived neurotrophic factor-5-HTTLPR gene interactions and environmental modifiers of depression in children. *Biological Psychiatry, 59,* 673–680.

Kaufman, J., Yang, B. Z., Douglas-Palumberi, H., Houshyar, S., Lipschitz, D., Krystal, J. H., et al. (2004). Social supports and serotonin transporter gene moderate depression in maltreated children. *Proceedings of the National Academy of Sciences of the United States of America, 1010,* 17316–17321.

Kendler, K. S., Kuhn, J. W., Vittum, J., Prescott, C. A., & Riley, B. (2005). The interaction of stressful life events and a serotonin transporter polymorphism in the prediction of episodes of major depression: A replication. *Archives of General Psychiatry, 62,* 529–535.

Kochanska, G. (1991). Patterns of inhibition to the unfamiliar in children of normal and affectively ill mothers. *Child Development, 62,* 250–263.

Lemanek, K. L., Stone, W. L., & Fishel, P. T. (1993). Parent-child interactions in handicapped preschoolers: The relation between parent behaviors and compliance. *Journal of Clinical Child Psychology, 22,* 68–77.

Liu, D., Diorio, J., Tannenbaum, B., Caldji, C., Francis, D., Freedman, A., et al. (1997). Maternal care, hippocampal glucocorticoid receptors, and hypothalamic-pituitary-adrenal responses to stress. *Science, 277*(5332), 1659–1662.

Lorenz, K. Z. (1935). Der Kumpan in der Umwelt des Vogels [The companion in the bird's world]. *Journal fuer Ornithologie, 83,* 137–213. (Abbreviated English translation published 1937 Auk, 54, 245–273).

Main, M., & Solomon, J. (1990). Procedures for identifying infants as disorganized/disoriented during the Ainsworth strange situation. In M. Greenberg, D. Cicchetti, & E. M. Cummings (Eds.), *Attachment in the preschool years: Theory, research, and intervention* (pp. 121–160). Chicago: University of Chicago Press.

Matheny, A. (1989). Children's behavioral inhibition over age and across situations: Genetic similarity for a trait during change. *Journal of Personality, 57,* 215–235.

Matheny, A. P., Wilson, R. S., & Nuss, S. M. (1984). Toddler temperament: Stability across setting and over ages. *Child Development, 55*, 1200–1211.

McDevitt, S. C., & Carey, W. B. (1978). The measurement of temperament in 3–7 year old children. *Journal of Child Psychology and Psychiatry, 19*, 245–253.

Meaney, M. J. (2001). Maternal care, gene expression, and the transmission of individual differences in stress reactivity across generations. *Annual Review in Neuroscience, 24*, 1161–1192.

Mills, R. S. L., & Rubin, K. H. (1998). Are behavioral and psychological control both differentially associated with childhood aggression and social withdrawal? *Canadian Journal of Behavioral Science, 30*, 132–136.

Moss, E., Rousseau, D., Parent, S., St-Laurent, D., & Saintonge, J. (1998). Correlates of attachment at school age: Maternal reported stress, mother-child interaction, and behavior problems. *Child Development, 69*, 1390–1405.

Nachmias, M., Gunnar, M., Mangelsdorf, S., Parritz, R. H., & Buss, K. (1996). Behavioral inhibition and stress reactivity: The moderating role of attachment. *Child Development, 67*, 508–522.

Osterling, J., & Dawson, G. (1994). Early recognition of children with autism: A study of first birthday home videotapes. *Journal of Autism and Developmental Disorders 24*, 247–257.

Park, S. Y., Belsky, J., Putnam, S., & Crnic, K. (1997). Infant emotionality, parenting, and 3-year inhibition: Exploring stability and lawful discontinuity in a male sample. *Developmental Psychology, 33*, 218–227.

Pedlow, R., Sanson, A., Prior, M., & Oberklaid, F. (1993). Stability of maternally reported temperament from infancy to 8 years. *Developmental Psychology, 29*, 998–1007.

Pynoos, R. S., & Nader, K. (1993). Issues in the treatment of posttraumatic stress disorder in children and adolescents. In J. Wilson & B. Raphael (Eds.), *International Handbook of Traumatic Stress Syndromes* (pp. 535–549). Washington, DC: American Psychiatric Press.

Reznick, S. J., Kagan, J., Snidman, N., Gersten, M., Baak, K., & Rosenberg, A. (1986). Inhibited and uninhibited children: A follow-up study. *Child Development, 57*, 660–680.

Robinson, J. L., Kagan, J., Reznick, J. S., & Corley, R. (1992). The heritability of inhibited and uninhibited behavior: A twin study. *Developmental Psychology, 28*, 1030–1037.

Rodier, P. M. (2002). Converging evidence for brain stem injury in autism. *Development and Psychopathology 14*, 537–557.

Rogers, S. J., Ozonoff, S., & Maslin-Cole, C. (1993). Developmental aspects of attachment behavior in young children with pervasive developmental disorders. *Journal of the American Academy of Child and Adolescent Psychiatry, 32*, 1274–1282.

Rosenblum, L. A., & Andrews, M. W. (1994). Influences of environmental demand on maternal behavior and infant development. *Acta Paediatrica Supplement, 397*, 57–63.

Rothbart, M. K. (1981). Measurement of temperament in infancy. *Child Development, 52*, 569–578.

Rothbart, M. K. (1986). Longitudinal observation of infant temperament. *Developmental Psychology, 22*, 356–365.

Rothbart, M. K., & Bates, J. E. (2006). Temperament. In W. Damon, R. Lerner. & N. Eisenberg (Eds.), *Handbook of child psychology: Vol. 3. Social, emotional, and personality development* (6th ed., pp. 99–166). New York: Wiley.

Rubin, K. H., Burgess, K. B., & Hastings, P. D. (2002). Stability and social-behavioral consequences of toddlers' inhibited temperament and parenting behaviors. *Child Development, 73*, 483–495.

Rubin, K. H., Hastings, P. D., Stewart, S. L., Henderson, H. A., & Chen, X. (1997). The consistency and concomitants of inhibition: Some of the children, all of the time. *Child Development, 68*, 467–483.

Rubin, K. H., Nelson, L. J., Hastings, P., & Asendorpf, J. (1999). Transaction between parents' perceptions of their children's shyness and their parenting styles. *International Journal of Behavioral Development, 23*, 937–957.

Rutgers, A. H., van Ijzendoorn, M. H., Bakermans-Kranenburg, M. J., Swinkels, S. H., van Daalen, E., Dietz, C., et al. (2007). Autism, attachment and parenting: A comparison of children with autism spectrum disorder, mental retardation, language disorder, and non-clinical children. *Journal of Abnormal Child Psychology, 35*, 859–870.

Sanchez, M. M., Ladd, C. O., & Plotsky, P. M. (2001). Early adverse experience as a developmental risk factor for later psychopathology: Evidence from rodent and primate models. *Development and Psychopathology, 13*, 419–450.

Sapolsky, R. M. (2004). Mothering style and methylation. *Nature Neuroscience, 7*, 791–792.

Schmidt, L. A. & Fox, N.A. (1994). Patterns of cortical electrophysiology and autonomic activity in adults' shyness and sociability. *Biological Psychology, 38*, 183–198.

Schmidt, L. A., Fox, N. A., & Hamer, D. H. (2007). Evidence for a gene-gene interaction in predicting children's behavior problems: Association of serotonin transporter short and dopamine receptor D4 long genotypes with internalizing and externalizing behaviors in typically developing 7-year-olds. *Development and Psychopathology, 19*, 1105–1116.

Schmidt, L. A., Fox, N. A., Perez-Edgar, K., & Hamer, D. H. (2009). Linking gene, brain, and behavior: DRD4, frontal asymmetry, and temperament. *Psychological Science, 20*, 831–837.

Schmidt, L. A., Fox, N. A., Rubin, K. H., Sternberg, E. M., Gold, P. W., Smith, C. C., & et al. (1997). Behavioral and neuroendocrine responses in shy children. *Developmental Psychobiology, 30*, 127–140.

Schmidt, L. A., Fox, N. A., Schulkin, J., & Gold, P. W. (1999). Behavioral and psychophysiological correlates of self-presentation in temperamentally shy children. *Developmental Psychobiology, 35*, 119–135.

Schwartz, C. B., Henderson, H. A., Inge, A. P., Zahka, N. E., Coman, D. C., Kojkowski, N. M., et al. (2009). Temperament as a predictor of symptomotology and adaptive functioning in adolescents with high-functioning autism. *Journal of Autism and Developmental Disorders, 39*, 842–855.

Schwartz, C. E., Snidman, N., & Kagan, J. (1999). Adolescent social anxiety as an outcome of inhibited temperament in childhood. *Journal of the American Academy of Child and Adolescent Psychiatry, 38,* 1008–1015.

Sigman, M., Mundy, P., Sherman, T., & Ungerer, J. (1986). Social interactions of autistic, mentally retarded and normal children and their caregivers. *Journal of Child Psychology and Psychiatry, 27,* 647–655.

Speltz, M. L. (1990). The treatment of preschool conduct problems: An integration of behavioral and attachment concepts. In M. Greenberg, D. Cicchetti, & E. M. Cummings (Eds.), *Attachment in the preschool years: Theory, research and intervention* (pp. 399–426). Chicago, IL: University Press.

Theall-Honey, L. A., & Schmidt, L. A. (2006). Do temperamentally shy children process emotion differently than non-shy children? Behavioral, psychophysiological, and gender differences in reticent preschoolers. *Developmental Psychobiology, 48,* 187–196.

Thomas, A., & Chess, S. (1977). *Temperament and development.* New York: Brunner/Mazel.

Thomas, A., Chess, S., Birch, H. G., Hertzig, M. E., & Korn, S. (1963). *Behavioral inhibition in early childhood.* New York: New York University Press.

van Ijzendoorn, M. H., Rutgers, A. H., Bakermans-Kranenburg, M. J., Swinkels, S. H., van Daalen, E., Dietz, C., et al. (2007). Parental sensitivity and attachment in children with autism spectrum disorder: comparison with children with mental retardation, with language delays, and with typical development. *Child Development, 78,* 597–608.

Weaver, I. C. G., Cervoni, N., Champagne, F. A., D'Alessio, A. C., Sharma, S., Seckl, J. R., et al. (2004). Epigenetic programming by maternal behavior. *Nature Neuroscience, 7,* 847–854.

Weaver, I. C., La Plante, P., Weaver, S., Parent, A., Sharma, S., Diorio, J., et al. (2001). Early environmental regulation of hippocampal glucocorticoid receptor gene expression: Characterization of intracellular mediators and potential genomic target sites. *Molecular and Cellular Endocrinology, 185,* 205–218.

Weinberg, M. K., & Tronick, E. Z. (1998a). Emotional characteristics of infants associated with maternal depression and anxiety. *Pediatrics, 102,* 1298–1304.

Weinberg, M. K., & Tronick, E. Z. (1998b). The impact of maternal psychiatric illness on infant development. *Journal of Clinical Psychiatry, 59,* 53–61.

Worobey, J., & Blajda, V. M. (1989). Temperament ratings at 2 weeks, 2 months, and 1 year: Differential stability of activity and emotionality. *Developmental Psychology, 25,* 257–263.

# SIX

# We Are Social – Therefore We Are

*The Interplay of Mind, Culture, and Genetics
in Williams Syndrome*

Carol Zitzer-Comfort, Judy Reilly, Julie R. Korenberg, and
Ursula Bellugi

## INTRODUCTION

Williams syndrome (WS) is a rare neurodevelopmental disorder arising
from a hemideletion in chromosome band 7q11.23, including the gene for
elastin (ELN) and approximately 20 surrounding genes (Ewart et al., 1993;
Korenberg, Chen, et al., 2000; Korenberg, Bellugi, Salandanan, Mills, &
Reiss, 2003; and Korenberg et al., 2008). More than 95% of individuals clinically diagnosed with WS are estimated to have deletions that fall within
the same breakpoints (Perez-Jurado, Peoples, Kaplan, Hamel, & Franke,
1996; Korenberg et al., 2003) (see Figure 6.1). Physical characteristics of WS
include specific facial and physical anomalies; a variety of cardiovascu-
lar difficulties, commonly supravalvular aortic stenosis; mild to moderate
mental retardation; failure to thrive in infancy; and small stature (Bellugi,
Lichtenberger, Jones, Lai, & St. George, 2000; Morris & Mervis, 1999, 2000;
and Korenberg et al., 2008).

## CHARACTERISTIC FEATURES OF WILLIAMS SYNDROME

The basic anatomy of the brain in people with WS is normal, but the total
volume is somewhat reduced. The areas that seem to be best preserved
include the frontal lobes and a part of the cerebellum called the neocere-
bellum, as well as parts of the temporal lobes known as the limbic area,
the primary auditory area, and the planum temporale (Lenhoff, Wang,
Greenberg, & Bellugi, 1997).

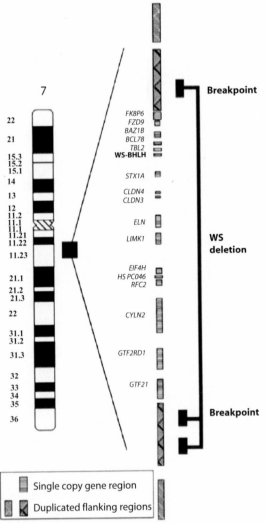

**Figure 6.1.** The ideogram represents the region of chromosome 7, band 7q11.23, which is commonly deleted in WS. This region is expanded at the right to illustrate its genomic organization, a region of largely single-copy genes flanked by a series of genomic duplications. Bars at the end of the bracket indicate the regions used in the common breakpoints. From Järvinen-Pasley, A., Bellugi, U., Reilly, J., Mills, D. L., Galaburda, A., Reiss, A. L., et al. (2008). Defining the social phenotype in Williams syndrome: a model of linking gene, the brain, and cognition. *Development and Psychopathology, 20*(1), 1–35. Copyright 2008 by Cambridge University Press. Reprinted with permission.

**Figure 6.2.** Photographs of children with Williams syndrome (WS). Reproduced with parental permission.

Lenhoff et al.'s (1997) widely circulated overview of the syndrome noted that:

The Salk group's examination of brains by magnetic resonance imaging and by autopsy supports the probability that the chromosomal deletion responsible for Williams syndrome alters the brain in a more complicated way. The deletion seems to produce anatomical changes (such as abnormal clustering of neurons in visual areas) that yield deficits in visual-spatial abilities. But the chromosomal defect appears to spare a network that includes structures in the frontal lobes, the temporal lobe and the cerebellum. This preserved network, then, may serve as a neuroanatomical scaffolding for the unexpectedly strong language abilities of Williams people. (p. 72)

This research is, indeed, exciting and yields new insight into the complexity of the relationship among the brain, genes, and the environment. Neuroanatomical studies, alone, cannot account for the variability nor for the uniqueness of WS; thus, these types of studies must be combined with the newly emerging cross-cultural research.

In addition to the physical characteristics (Figure 6.2), adults with WS often display characteristic patterns of cognitive strengths and weaknesses, that is, comparatively strong language abilities coupled with profound deficits in visuospatial construction (Bellugi et al., 2000). Williams syndrome thus presents a compelling model for the investigation of the impact of genetics on behavior because its genetic basis is well defined and circumscribed and results in an uneven cognitive profile phenotypic of the syndrome.

A consistent behavioral characteristic of WS is the heightened affiliative behavior (see Jones et al., 2000; Bellugi, Järvinen-Pasley, Doyle, Reilly, Reiss, & Korenberg, 2007; Järvinen-Pasley et al., 2008; and Mervis & Klein-Tasman, 2000, for reviews). Almost since it was characterized as a syndrome, anecdotal observations have held that persons with WS are outgoing (Von Arnin & Engel, 1964). Descriptions of hypersociability in adults and children with WS, such as "gregarious personality" and "indiscriminate friendliness" have been reported around the world (Udwin, Yule, & Martin, 1987; Gosch & Pankau, 1994; Bjornstad, 1994; Kotzot et al., 1995; Einfeld, Tonge, & Florio, 1997; Ruangdaraganon, Tocharoentanaphol, Kotchabhakdi, & Khowsathit,1999; Battin, Lancombe, Taine, & Goizet, 2000; Nakaji, Kawame, Nagai, & Iwata, 2001).

One salient phenotypic feature of the syndrome, evident from infancy and extending into adulthood, is increased interest in social interactions (Mervis & Klein-Tasman, 2000; Jones et al., 2000; Meyer-Lindenberg, Mervis, & Berman, 2006; Järvinen-Pasley et al., 2008). In individuals with WS, gregariousness is accompanied by social disinhibition, even toward people not considered approachable (Bellugi, Adolphs, Cassady, & Chiles, 1999; Järvinen-Pasley et al., 2008; Frigerio et al., 2006). In spite of this exuberant sociability, WS individuals may have pronounced difficulty in making lasting friendships, as well as pragmatic difficulties (Tager-Flusberg & Sullivan, 2000; Laws & Bishop, 2004). Despite widespread reports of an unusually intense social drive among these subjects and a growing literature of studies of social behavior in WS, almost no studies to date have examined the effects of different cultural settings on the social behavior of people with WS. In this chapter, we present two studies investigating the sociability of individuals with WS across different cultures. The first focuses on the social use of language in narratives of American, French, and Italian children, and adolescents with WS. The second explores social behavior in American and Japanese children with WS.

## THE SOCIAL USE OF LANGUAGE IN WS ACROSS CULTURES

In our past studies, we investigated the narratives of English-speaking children and adolescents with WS (Losh, Bellugi, Reilly, & Anderson, 2000;

Reilly, Klima, & Bellugi, 1990; Reilly, Losh, Bellugi, & Wulfeck, 2004; Kreiter et al., 2002). The developmental profile is one of prolific talkers who have a somewhat delayed but continuing mastery of English morphology and syntax in the face of more impoverished narrative structure (Losh et al., 2000; Reilly et al., 2004). Here, we present a summary of our narrative studies with American children and adolescents with WS.

## Language as an Index of Sociability in Williams Syndrome

We presented individuals with WS and their typically developing peers with the same wordless picture book: *Frog, Where Are You?* (Mayer, 1969). The subjects were asked to tell the story to the experimenter. Because this picture book contains no words and provides a rich context for language production, it has been used extensively in cross-linguistic work (Berman & Slobin, 1994) and across typically and atypically developing populations (Reilly et al., 2004; Losh et al., 2000). After the stories were told, they were coded using a scheme designed to assess both grammatical proficiency and use of evaluative language (Reilly et al., 1990; Reilly et al., 2004).

The stories were first coded for length as measured by the number of propositions presented; a proposition is defined as a verb and its arguments, roughly corresponding semantically to a single event. Each clause in a complex sentence was considered to represent one event, and therefore one proposition. Morphological errors were tallied and categorized by type, as were the frequency and types of complex syntax recruited. Proportions were created for all measures.

To capture the social aspects of the narration, we coded the stories for the use of social evaluative language, using a definition of evaluation that draws from William Labov's work on narratives. Evaluation is language that reflects the narrator's attitude or perspective (Labov & Waletzky, 1967). Specifically, evaluative devices are linguistic tools used to attribute emotions or motivations to characters in a story, build suspense, and maintain audience involvement and interest. Examples include emphatics, intensifiers (e.g., *really, very,* and *so*), character speech, direct quotes, and sound effects. Because the language of WS appeared so extensively colorful and attention-getting, we added to our coding schemes a special category of evaluative devices termed "audience hookers," which are intended to capture and maintain the listener's attention. For indices of both language structure (grammatically correct clauses) and language use (evaluative language), proportions were created using story length, as measured by the number of propositions, as the denominator. Two independently trained researchers conducted transcription and coding, and reliability was at or above 90%.

## The Social Use of Language in Adolescents with WS

In one of the first language studies on WS (Reilly et al., 1990), we asked adolescents with WS, aged 10–18 years, to narrate the *Frog* story; control groups included age- and IQ-matched adolescents with Down syndrome (DS), and mental-age-matched typically developing (TD) children. The stories were then analyzed for grammar and evaluative language. The adolescents with WS were relatively proficient, specifically in their use of grammar. Also, the WS group used evaluative language significantly more frequently than did the TD controls or the adolescents with DS. Table 6.1 provides examples of evaluative language in WS and Figure 6.3 shows the enriched linguistic affect in WS, as compared to DS and mental-age matched controls. Both the figure and the table provide a taste of the richness of social language among those with WS.

## The Social Use of Language in Children With WS
## in the United States

Because the adolescents in our early study had mastered English grammar by and large, we wanted to know if their excessive use of evaluative language was characteristic of the WS group as a whole, and if so, when and how it developed. To address these questions, our next studies included larger and younger samples of children and adolescents. For example, data from 35 children with WS ages 4–12 years, and 70 chronologically age-matched TD children are shown later (Losh et al., 2000; Reilly et al., 2004). Using the coding scheme described earlier, Figure 6.4a shows the mastery of morphosyntax in the narratives of children with WS, compared with age-matched controls. Unlike the adolescents, children with WS are consistently impaired in the proportion of grammatically correct clauses, compared with controls.

In contrast to this developmental lag vis-à-vis the acquisition and use of morphosyntax, one of the most striking aspects of narratives told by WS children is the frequent and pervasive use of what we have termed social evaluation. That is, evaluative devices designed to engage and maintain the listener's attention, such as the use of character voice, intensifiers, and what we have called "audience hookers" (e.g., exclamations, sound effects, and rhetorical questions). As we have found across studies, the WS group recruits these social evaluative devices significantly more frequently than their TD peers (see Figure 6.4b). Thus, whereas morphosyntactic development in this younger group varies, with some children in the normal range and others significantly below (Reilly et al., 2004), the use of social evaluation in their narratives is significantly higher for every single subject that we have studied, compared with controls (Losh et al., 2000, Reilly et al., 2004).

**Table 6.1.** *Examples from WS of Evaluative Language*

| | |
|---|---|
| **AFFECTIVE STATES** | WS: -And ah! he was <u>amazed</u>! |
| | WS: -The boy looks <u>suspicious</u>. |
| | WS: -And then he was <u>happy</u> because he had a big family. |
| | WS: -The dog gets <u>worried</u> and the boy gets <u>mad.</u> |
| | WS: -And the poor dog was just <u>tired</u>, walking slowly. |
| | WS: -The next morning, he was <u>sad</u> because the frog left. |
| **CHARACTER SPEECH** | WS: -He goes, 'Ouch! oh uh get outta here bumblebees!' |
| | WS: -And the dog licked him and said, 'Thank you for saving me.' |
| | WS: -And then the frogs all sat up and the frog goes 'ribbit.' |
| | WS: -And the boy said, 'Goodbye, Mrs. Frog. Goodbye, Mr. Frog. Goodbye, many frogs. I might see you if I come around again.' |
| | WS: -He said, 'Wow!, look at these, a female and a male frog and also lots of baby frogs.' |
| | WS: And the dog licked him and said: "Thank you for saving my life." |
| **SOUND EFFECTS** | WS: -And the light goes 'ching.' |
| | WS: -And 'boom,' millions of bees came out and tried to sting him. |
| | WS: -Suddenly splash! The water came up. |
| | WS: -He was looking for the frog, and 'boom,' he broke it. |
| **AUDIENCE HOOKERS** | WS: -Suddenly, the frog jumped out! |
| | WS: -Ouch! that hurt! |
| | WS: -<u>Gadzooks</u>! The boy and the dog start flipping over. |
| | WS: -And <u>ah</u>! he was amazed! |
| | WS: -<u>Lo and behold</u>! they find him . . . with a lady. |
| | WS: -And all of a sudden, the boy saw a <u>female</u> frog with the frog <u>that he lost</u>. |
| | WS: -Well, what do you know? A frog family! Two lovers. END |
| | WS: -And when the frog went out. . .the boy and the dog were still sleeping. Next morning it was beautiful in the morning. It was bright and the sun was. . .really bright and was nice and warm. |

Consistent with our previous findings, these results demonstrate the excessively social use of language in WS. Whereas structural language proficiency varies across individuals, as soon as children with WS are able to produce simple narratives, they exploit their linguistic abilities maximally for social purposes. This, perhaps, is one of the most striking characteristics of WS. Talking with a person with WS is an experience one does not soon forget.

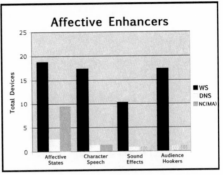

**Enriched Linguistic Affect in WS**

**Affective Enhancers**

**WMS Age 17, IQ 50:** Once upon a time when it was dark at night...the boy had a frog. The boy was looking at the frog...sitting on the chair, on the table, and the dog was looking through...looking up to the frog in a jar. That night he sleeped and slept for a long time, the dog did. But, the frog was not gonna go to sleep. The frog went out from the jar. And when the frog went out...the boy and the dog were still sleeping. Next morning it was beautiful in the morning. It was bright and the sun was nice and warm. Then suddenly when he opened his eyes...he looked at the jar and then suddenly the frog was not there. The jar was empty. There was no frog to be found.

**DNS Age 18, IQ 55:** The frog is in the jar. The jar is on the floor. The jar on the floor. That's it. The stool is broke. The clothes is laying there.

**Figure 6.3.** (1) Enriched linguistic affect in Williams syndrome (WS), as compared to Down syndrome (DS) and mental-age matched controls. (2) Story openings by WS and DS children. (1) and (2) adapted from Reilly, J., Klima, E. S., & Bellugi, U. (1990). Once more with feeling: Affect and language in atypical populations. *Development and Psychopathology, 2,* 367–391. Copyright 1990 by Cambridge University Press. Illustrations reprinted from *Frog, Where Are You?* by Mercer Mayer, copyright ©1969 by Mercer Mayer. Used by permission of Dial Books for Young Readers, A Division of Penguin Young Reader Group, A Member of Penguin Group (USA) Inc., 345 Hudson Street, New York, NY 10014. All rights reserved.

## NATURAL BORN STORYTELLERS

### Individuals with WS Are Unrivaled in Their Use of Social Language

We recently extended our studies to investigate the specificity of excessive social language use across different populations, including individuals with neurodevelopmental disorders other than WS. We compared and contrasted age-matched WS children and adolescents with three groups, individuals with language impairment (LI), with early focal lesions (FL), and with high functioning autism (HFA), as well as a group of TD children. Whereas the neurodevelopmentally disabled

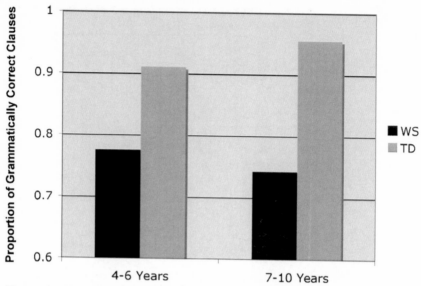

**Figure 6.4a.** Language structure: Grammatically correct clauses. The mastery of morphosyntax in the narratives of children with Williams syndrome (WS) compared with their age-matched typically developing (TD) controls. Note that at both developmental ages shown, the WS are impaired compared to the controls in the proportion of grammatically correct clauses. From Järvinen-Pasley, A., Bellugi, U., Reilly, J., Mills, D. L. Galaburda, A, Reiss, A. L., et al. (2008). Defining the social phenotype in Williams syndrome: A model of linking gene, the brain, and cognition. *Development and Psychopathology, 20*(1), 1–35. Copyright 2008 by Cambridge University Press. Reprinted with permission.

groups showed differentially impaired acquisition of grammatical structure, individuals with WS far exceeded any other group, including TD individuals, in their overabundance of social evaluative language (Reilly et al., 2004). As Figure 6.5 demonstrates, our findings strongly suggest that excessively social evaluative language may indeed be uniquely characteristic of WS, in contrast with other populations.

### Comparisons Across Genres

Our narrative analyses have drawn from the characterization of narratives by Labov and Waletzky (1967), who described different functions of narrative as *referential* (information pertaining to plot) and *evaluative* (the narrator's perspective and attitude toward events). The latter is largely related to the story's significance to the narrator. Given this theoretical perspective, it is possible that the particular genre used in the studies, that is, narrative,

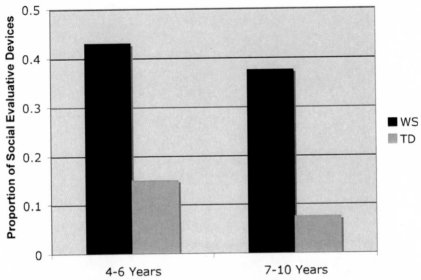

**Figure 6.4b.** Language use: Social-evaluative language in narratives. The use of social evaluation in the narratives of children with WS and typically developing children (TD). Contrasted with the mastery of morphosyntax, where children with WS lag behind, in the proportion of social evaluative devices, the WS are significantly higher than their matched normal controls. From Järvinen-Pasley, A., Bellugi, U., Reilly, J., Mills, D. L. Galaburda, A, Reiss, A. L., et al. (2008). Defining the social phenotype in Williams syndrome: A model of linking gene, the brain, and cognition. *Development and Psychopathology, 20*(1), 1–35. Copyright 2008 by Cambridge University Press. Reprinted with permission.

was responsible for the distinctive profile of WS. To control for this possibility, we coded and analyzed biographical "warm-up" interviews from adolescents with WS, DS, and mental-age-typical controls. In these warm-up interviews, conducted at the beginning of testing sessions, experimenters asked questions about the individual's family, friends, school, siblings and pets (Harrison, Reilly, & Klima, 1995). Interviews, as a genre, display a certain structure: The interviewer asks questions and the interviewee responds. Individuals with WS were the only group to *turn the tables* on the experimenter, often reversing the normal roles of interviewer and interviewee by asking questions, making evaluative comments, and even using personal flattery. For example, when asked about family, a WS adolescent said, "I have a sister. Do you have a sister? How old is she?" Another child with WS said to the examiner, "Where do you live? What do you like to eat for dinner? Do you have a boyfriend? I think you are beautiful." Similar

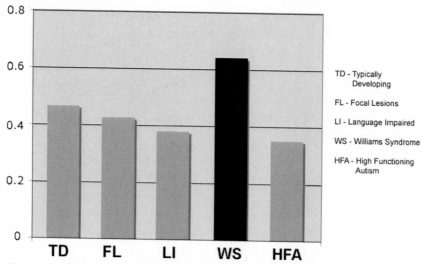

**Figure 6.5.** Uniqueness of WS language evaluation across groups. In a separate study, we have examined the use of grammatical structure and the social use of language devices from the same narrative across different populations. Shown here are the proportions of social evaluative language in stories from typically developing children (TD) at the far left, followed by those from children with early focal lesions (FL), language impaired children (LI), children with Williams syndrome (WS) in black, and finally individuals with high functioning autism (HFA). Note that the proportion of social language in WS is significantly higher than any other population, including normal controls.

to social evaluative devices, such personal questions and comments function to "hook" an audience, engaging the interlocutor's attention. These complementary data suggest that the social use of language, apparent in the narratives of WS individuals, is not genre-specific, but is a much more pervasive and general phenomenon in this group.

## THE INTERSECTION OF GENETICS, CULTURE, AND SOCIAL LANGUAGE IN WS

The studies of language structure and the social use of language in WS described above, which were conducted in the United States, led us to critically important questions that we address in this paper. We have seen that the extensive use of social evaluation, the intersection of language and affect, is pervasive in WS at all ages and across genres, as contrasted with other developmental disorders as well as with age- and mental-age-matched controls. An important issue, not heretofore addressed, is the degree to which this quality, noted in various studies with WS, appears in different cultures and linguistic environments. Thus, our current research focuses on the following questions: "How do different cultures and languages influence the social use of language in WS?" "Given significant differences in languages and cultures, is this WS profile of exuberant sociability consistent outside of the United States?" "What is the effect of different cultural settings on the social language of this genetically based syndrome?" We know from anecdotes, personal experiences, stories, and studies that cultures can vary widely in the socialization of children, the expression of emotion, the use of gestures, the manner of greeting strangers, and the structure of spoken language. Cross-linguistic and cross-cultural studies would provide opportunities to separate some effects of the genetic basis for WS from environmental and cultural effects.

These questions led us to our current study, in which we chose cultures and environments that contrast with American culture in noteworthy ways. We chose Italy and France, using our contacts in those two countries to initiate the studies (Reilly, Bernicot, Vicari, Lacroix, & Bellugi, 2005). Both Italy and France are romance cultures, yet they contrast in their display rules for emotion: The French are considered rather reserved, whereas the Italians are more effusive. In fact, comparative studies found American mothers to be more expressive than French mothers with infants (Suizzo, 2004; Bril, Dasen, Sabatier, & Krewer, 1999). French children are taught to control their emotional expressions, to be quiet and discreet in public, and to express their emotions appropriately and correctly. This discretion is nicely reflected in the French proverb, "Vivre heureux, vivons cachés" (To live happily, we live hidden). In contrast, Italian is categorized as a "high-gesture" language (Kendon, 1995a, 1995b), reflecting the overall increased expressivity of Italian culture. This expressivity has also been documented in a comparative study of children's story books (Shatz, Dyer, Marchetti, & Massaro, 2006), in which the authors found that Italian translations differed from the English version in three ways: heightened emotional intensity, more specific expression of mental states, and more explicit expression of social awareness or responsibility. Such findings reflect not only an increased expressivity, but also a higher value placed on sociability in Italian culture.

## Social Use of Language in Children and Adolescents with WS in Italy

The first non-U.S. group of individuals we studied were 17 Italian children with WS aged 10–16 years, and their mental-age-matched TD peers. As noted above, Italian has been categorized as "high-gesture" (Kendon, 1995) in that speakers frequently recruit gestures in their social interactions.

As in other languages, evaluation can be conveyed lexically and paralinguistically in Italian (i.e., by gestures and intonation); however, an Italian speaker also can use suffixes that convey evaluative content. For example, a boy is *un ragazzo*, a nasty boy is *un ragazzaccio*, a little boy is *un ragazzino* and a nasty little boy is *un ragazzinaccio*.

Given the richness of Italian forms and the frequency of gesture, one might ask whether Italian children with WS use social evaluation or affective language in a manner similar to that of TD Italian children, that is, whether all Italian children rely heavily on social evaluation, with little difference in the WS group. To address this question, we again collected, transcribed, and coded narratives from the Italian version of *Frog, Where Are You?* Looking at morphology and syntax, we found that Italian children with WS, like their American counterparts, made more errors and used less complex syntax than age-matched controls, but they also used significantly more social evaluation than did the TD Italian children.

## Social Use of Language in Children and Adolescents with WS in France

Our second non-U.S. group is composed of 12 children and adolescents with WS aged 6–16 years who live in France, along with chronological age-matched TD peers. When we examined the use of evaluation in the French group, (Reilly, Bernicot, et al., 2005; Reilly, LaCroix, et al., 2005), we again found significantly more social evaluation in the WS group than in the control group. The findings for French subjects are consistent with the findings in English and Italian subjects with respect to the effect of the genetic basis of WS. That is, French children with WS use significantly more social evaluation than their typically developing peers, just as American and Italian WS children do. To give a taste of the rich and unique nature of children's use of social evaluation, Table 6.2 below includes examples from the *Frog* stories, highlighting the use of evaluative language among subjects with WS in the three countries.

Thus, all three groups of WS children and adolescents from different linguistic and cultural backgrounds are significantly more socially expressive than their respective control groups. Importantly, however, the results also show a significant effect of culture: Typically developing Italian children show the highest social evaluation, whereas the French are lowest in that parameter and the Americans are in between (Reilly, Bernicot, et al., 2005).

These comparative results suggest that in spite of the clear propensity of individuals with WS to recruit high levels of social evaluation, the nature of each culture and its conventions for demonstrating sociability and

**Table 6.2.** *Evaluative Language in English, Italian, and French*

---

**Examples of Evaluative Language in English**

But, phew! (signaling relief), it was just a little bit swampy

He said "wow, look at these . . . a female and a male frog and also lots of baby frogs

And lo and behold . . . Some frogs came out of the bushes

Here's the frog and he's in love! And he says "Hooray! Hooray! Hooray! I found my froggie!" And then he "Byeeee!"

**Examples of Evaluative Language in Italian**

| | |
|---|---|
| "Rana, . . . (ride) raaana dove sei?" | *"Frog . . . (laughs) frooog, where are you?"* |
| "Bow wow". | *"Bow wow". The dog fell with that thing Boom! And then "Where did you get to?"* |
| | |
| Il cane cadeva con questa cosa Bum! | |
| E poi "dove sei finita?" | |
| Questo rana simpatiche! | *What a funny frog!* |
| Trovano un piccolino | *They found a little bitty one* |
| E poi c'e il gufo che sta cosi triste | *And then there is the owl that is so sad* |

**Examples of Evaluative Language in French**

| | |
|---|---|
| Le garcon dit "mince le bocal va etre casse" | *The boy said: Darn! The jar is gonna break* |
| Et puis il s'enerve finalment et le chien il est content | *and then he gets upset finally and the dog's happy* |

---

conveying emotion also help determine how the social behavior of WS children and adolescents is expressed in language.

## DISCUSSION: THE INTERPLAY OF MIND, GENETICS, CULTURE, AND SOCIAL LANGUAGE IN WS ACROSS CULTURES

In this first section of the chapter, we have used narratives as a context to explore the intersection of affect and language in children and adolescents with WS to better understand the phenotype and how cultural conventions might modulate its expression. It appears that in spite of the culture and the resources of the language, or lack thereof, children and adolescents with WS are characterized by their frequent and extensive use of social evaluation in their stories. Although language studies are one avenue for investigating the impact of culture on a genetically based syndrome, we continued to seek additional avenues to investigate the interplay of nature and nurture in WS across cultures. We turn now to the use of a different measurement tool, parental questionnaires, to assess the social drive in WS in contrasting cultures, the United States, and Japan.

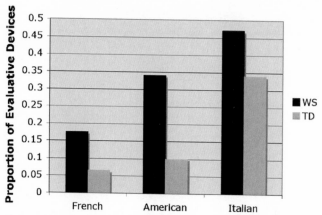

**Figure 6.6.** The effect on social evaluative language in Williams syndrome (WS) and typically developing (TD) controls. Note that in both the figure and the table, WS individuals use significantly higher social language than controls, but at the same time, the culture has an effect as well. From Järvinen-Pasley, A., Bellugi, U., Reilly, J., Mills, D. L. Galaburda, A, Reiss, A. L., et al. (2008). Defining the social phenotype in Williams syndrome: A model of linking gene, the brain, and cognition. *Development and Psychopathology, 20*(1), 1–35. Copyright 2008 by Cambridge University Press. Reprinted with permission.

## THE SOCIAL DRIVE OF WILLIAMS SYNDROME ACROSS CULTURES

The French, Italian, and American language studies discussed earlier led to more questions about the impact of "nurture" on the expression of a genetic syndrome. We were particularly interested in the expression of hypersociability in WS among various cultural groups in the United States and abroad. As with language studies, which had been conducted in the United States only, the affiliative drive that is typical of WS had not been examined across cultures.

Nobody questions that the color of our eyes is encoded in our genes. When it comes to behavior, however, the concept of "DNA as fate" quickly breaks down. It has long been accepted that both genes and the environment shape human behavior. But just how much sway the environment holds over our genetic destiny has been difficult to untangle. By comparing the social behavior of WS children – known for their innate drive to interact with people – across cultures that have differing social mores, we are beginning to learn the answer. Overall, a consistent result has emerged: Regardless of age, language, or cultural background, the social phenotype of individuals with WS is shaped by both genes and gene-environment interactions.

## Assessing the Social Drive in WS and TD Controls Using the SISQ

In a previous study (Doyle, Bellugi, Korenberg, & Graham, 2004), we assessed sociability among a large group of children in the United States using a parental report questionnaire, the Salk Institute Sociability Questionnaire (SISQ). SISQ is designed to ask parents to rate their child's tendencies to approach others, to remember names and faces, to please other people, and to empathize with or comment on others' emotional states. It also asks about the child's general behavior in social situations and the tendency for other people to approach their child.

The questionnaire was completed by 64 parents of WS children aged 2–12 years; control groups included 31 parents of children with Down syndrome (DS) and 27 parents of typically developing (TD) age-matched controls. Results showed that children with WS were rated overall as significantly more social than DS children or TD subjects. In addition, children with WS were rated significantly higher in approaching strangers than the other two groups, and higher with respect to social-emotional behaviors than DS children (but not different when compared with age-matched TD subjects). Significant differences in social behavior were reported from the earliest ages assessed, with WS children exceeding both comparison groups.

These findings provide initial evidence that differences in hypersociability, particularly an attraction to strangers, cannot be attributed simply to cognitive impairment, resulting in a lack of understanding of the social conventions governing others (both WS and DS children are cognitively impaired); nor can they be attributed to developmental factors (see also Jones et al., 2000).


### SOCIAL BEINGS BY NATURE

Our previous studies suggest the involvement of genetic predisposition in the expression of hypersociability in WS; thus, exploring sociability across cultures can provide keen insight into the interplay of temperament (in a disorder with a known genetic basis) and culture. This study examines the ways in which social behavior in WS, which is thought to have a genetic predisposition, might be mediated by cultural expectations in both Japan and the United States. Because both the genetic phenotype of WS and the presence of excessive friendliness toward strangers or overly social behavior in that syndrome are well documented within the United States, it is of great interest to know whether the expression of hypersociability is influenced by cultural and societal mores, particularly by the factors that

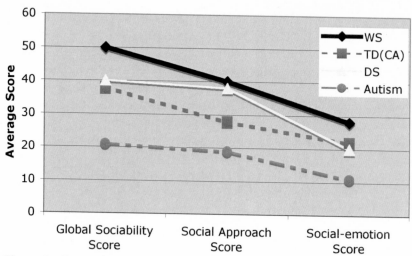

**Figure 6.7.** Parental characterization of sociability contrasting WS, DS, Autism, and TDs (SISQ). Individuals WS are consistently rated higher by their parents in social behaviors using the Salk Institute Sociability Questionnaire than chronological age (CA)-matched individuals with autism, DS, or TD. From Järvinen-Pasley, A., Bellugi, U., Reilly, J., Mills, D. L. Galaburda, A, Reiss, A. L., et al. (2008). Defining the social phenotype in Williams syndrome: A model of linking gene, the brain, and cognition. *Development and Psychopathology, 20*(1), 1–35. Copyright 2008 by Cambridge University Press. Reprinted with permission.

prescribe appropriate social behavior. It is intriguing to explore ways in which children with developmental disorders – especially those disorders with a known genetic basis – might be affected by social mores of two vastly differing cultures.

## THE SOCIAL DRIVE OF WS IN THE UNITED STATES AND JAPAN

### Genetics and Culture at Play

To determine the extent to which the affiliative drive in individuals with WS is universal, we settled on two countries with markedly contrasting cultures for this research study: the United States and Japan. These two cultures, respectively, have often been contrasted as exemplars of "individualistic" and "collectivist" societies. Differences between them can be summed up by the following distinctive proverbs: In America, "The squeaky wheel gets the grease." In Japan, "The nail that stands out gets pounded down" (Markus & Kitayama, 1991). In their landmark paper examining culture and the self, Markus and Kitayama further note that "People in Japan and America may hold strikingly divergent construals of the self, others, and the interdependence of the two. American examples stress attending to the self, the appreciation of one's difference from others, and the importance of asserting the self. The Japanese examples emphasize attending to and fitting in with others and the importance of harmonious interdependence with them" (p. 224).

This "individualistic" self-view in western cultures leads to defining one's self in terms of one's own feelings and actions, placing emphasis on the ways in which the individual is unique. Asian cultures emphasize more of a "collectivistic" self-view in which one defines oneself in terms of relationships with others (see Triandis, 1989, 1995).

Because of the contrasting viewpoints of "self" in the two countries, such differences could be expected to lead to variations in socialization of children in the two countries. Hess et al. (1986) note that "In Japan, a child is thought to be good if he or she is 'obedient' (*sunao*), 'mild and gentle' (*otonasii*), and 'self-controlled' (*jiseishin ga aru*). In the United States, the good child is assertive, socially competent with peers, and courteous" (p. 158). Moreover, parental reports in these countries have shown that mothers in Japan rate their children as shyer and less sociable than comparable ratings by mothers in the United States (Stevenson et al., 1990). (For further discussion on differences between United States and Japanese socialization and child rearing practices, see Conroy, Hess, Azuma, & Kashiwagi, 1980; LaFreniere et al., 2002; Lebra, 1994; Masataka, 2002; White, 1993; Zahn-Waxler, Friedman, Cole, Mizuta, & Hiruma, 1996.)

It is, therefore, of great interest to know how the expression of hypersociability is also influenced by cultural and societal mores, particularly the factors prescribing appropriate social behavior. Although a number of research groups have been studying the strengths and weaknesses of the cognitive profiles of individuals with WS in various countries, little or nothing is known about the effects of different cultures and environments on people with WS. For example, how does genetics influence the expression of sociability in these subjects across cultures that have varying expectations for appropriate behavior?

## ASSESSING SOCIABILITY IN WS USING A PARENTAL QUESTIONNAIRE

### Across Cultures and Languages

Participants included the parents of 24 children living in Japan and 24 in the United States. Twelve of the children in each sample had WS and 12 were TD. The children ranged in age from 3 years to 13 years; males and females were equally represented. We studied age-matched and gender-matched pairs, with one American and one Japanese child in each pair. The study was conducted via questionnaires given to the parents of the 48 children. In the United States, participants included parents of WS children who were attending a meeting of the Williams Syndrome Association and parents of TD children who attend school near the Salk Institute in California. In Japan, the Japanese Williams Syndrome Foundation collected the WS data, whereas TD data were collected through the laboratory of co-author Dr. Nobuo Masataka (Zitzer-Comfort, Doyle, Masataka, Korenberg, & Bellugi, 2007). To ensure consistency between the English and Japanese versions of the SISQ for cross-cultural comparison, two individuals, fluent and literate in both English and Japanese, independently translated the SISQ from English into Japanese and then back-translated from Japanese to English.

## Evaluating Sociability in WS Children in the East and West

The Salk Institute Sociability Questionnaire (SISQ) was developed to assess specific aspects of social behavior commonly reported among people with WS; results from the SISQ were first reported in Jones et al. (2000). The SISQ has been used in a variety of different contexts and across age groups. Moreover, the Salk Institute's Laboratory for Cognitive Neuroscience (LCN) has collected data on over 80 adolescent and adult individuals with WS; parents of 44 of these individuals had completed both the SISQ and another standardized parent report instrument, the Multidimensional Personality Questionnaire (MPQ) (Tellegen, 1985). LCN studies find that the SISQ overall scores show high correlations with the MPQ in the WS cohort on social dimensions such as Social Potency and Social Closeness, but no correlation with either other MPQ measures or IQ. Bonnie Klein-Tasman has also used the MPQ with a different cohort of individuals with WS (Klein-Tasman & Mervis, 2003) and found that, like the Salk Institute team, the distinctiveness of the WS personality appears to lie in focusing on others, a pattern characterized by an eagerness to interact with others as well as high levels of tension and sensitivity. This distinctiveness of the WS social phenotype provides the groundwork for the present study of cross-cultural influences upon social behavior.

## DISCUSSION: NATURE AND NURTURE OF SOCIABILITY AMONG INDIVIDUALS WITH WS

The SISQ consists of both quantitative and qualitative items. Quantitative items ask parents to rate their child's specific social behavior on a 7-point

Likert scale. Qualitative items ask the parents to provide a descriptive response. These items assess Global Sociability by yielding three subscales: a tendency to approach strangers, a tendency to approach familiars, and social emotional behavior (such as tendency to empathize with others, accuracy of emotional evaluations of others, eagerness to please others, and ability to remember names and faces of others).

Items assessing social approach behavior ("Social-Emotional") consist of statements such as "How would you compare your child's tendency to approach strangers with an average child of the same age?" or "How would you describe your child's general behavior in social situations?" Results for the first question are rated on a scale ranging from 1 ("approaches much less") to 7 ("approaches much more"), whereas the scale for the second question ranges from 1 ("very shy and inhibited") to 7 ("extremely outgoing"). Qualitative items include "Describe your child's typical reactions when meeting someone for the first time (please give examples)"; or "Give some examples of your child's socializing with strangers." The social approach items were grouped for analysis into two types. Those that assess a child's tendency to approach family members or others who are encountered frequently ("Approach Familiars") and those that assess a child's tendency to approach people unknown to them ("Approach Strangers"). The Social-Emotional score was the sum of four items; the Approach Familiars score was the sum of three items; the Approach Strangers score was the sum of five items; and all 12 items added up to the Global Sociability score.

### Quantitative Data Analysis

The quantitative data were analyzed by a 2 × 2 analysis of variance (ANOVA) with Diagnostic Category (WS children versus TD children) and Culture (American versus Japanese) as independent variables, and Global Sociability as the dependent variable. Wilks' Lambda criterion was used to assess significance. Figure 6.8 shows the data distribution for the Global Sociability score, combining all questionnaire items, and the data for each of the three subscales.

As Figure 6.8 shows, both American and Japanese WS children rated significantly higher on Global Sociability than did the TD children; thus, there was a very strong effect for Diagnostic Category (WS or TD). At the same time, however, there was a significant effect of Culture, in that parents of U.S. children tended to rate their children higher in Global Sociability than did parents of Japanese children, regardless of the diagnostic category (WS or TD).

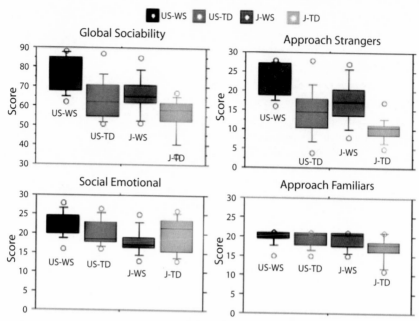

**Figure 6.8.** Summary of comparisons across Diagnostic Category (Williams vs. typically developing) and Culture (Japanese vs. U.S.) for the quantitative analysis of the SISQ. Graphs display horizontal lines at the 10th, 25th, 50th, 75th, and 90th percentiles. The top box shows Global Sociability, encompassing all parts of the SISQ combined. The Japanese WS mean scores are significantly higher than the Japanese TD means; and the U.S.-WS means are significantly higher than the U.S.-TD means, a major effect of Diagnostic Category. Whereas the U.S.-WS means are significantly higher than all other means, the Japanese-WS are almost on a par with the U.S.-TD, and there is also a significant effect of Culture (U.S. vs. Japanese) as well. These patterns do not hold for Social-Emotional items. Note that on Approach Familiar items, the four groups are almost indistinguishable, at near ceiling. On the Approach Strangers items, the significant effects of both Diagnostic Category and Culture are strongly observed. From Zitzer-Comfort, C., Doyle, T., Masataka, N., Korenberg, J., & Bellugi, U. (2007). Nature and nurture: Williams syndrome across cultures. *Developmental Science*, 10(6):755–762.

Comparison of scores across Cultures indicates a major difference for Approach Strangers, but not for Approach Familiars (scores for Approach Familiars were consistent across groups and cultures) or Social-Emotional items. Similarly, comparison of scores across Diagnostic Category indicates a major difference for Approach Strangers, but not for the other two subscales. Overall, the significant between-group differences in Global Sociability resulted primarily from higher Approach Strangers ratings for both Diagnosis and Culture.

## Qualitative Analysis of Sociability Data

The SISQ also asks parents for qualitative descriptions of their child in various social situations, e.g., "Describe your child's typical reactions when meeting someone for the first time (please give examples)." Table 6.3 presents samples of qualitative responses from the various age groups across the cultural and diagnostic groups discussed in this study.

The examples presented in Table 6.3 demonstrate that specific behaviors described by parents of children with WS to illustrate approaching strangers and socializing with them are very similar in both cultures. Nevertheless, Japanese parents rated their children lower on the 7-point scale than did U.S. parents.

The differences in quantitative scores for Japanese WS children may more accurately reflect parental attitudes or sensitivities than the actual behaviors of the children: Perhaps cultural influence is exerted more on parents' *ratings* than on the expression of the behavior, or perhaps the stigma of having a "different" child in Japan affects how parents rank their child's degree of sociability. Yet this explanation does not account for the lower Global Sociability and Approaching Strangers scores for Japanese TD children. To resolve possible discrepancies caused by reliance on parental reports, with the objective of understanding the interplay of phenotype and culture in WS, further cross-cultural observational studies are needed that involve more participants and a deeper look at interactions with strangers.

## CONCLUSION AND FUTURE RESEARCH DIRECTIONS: THE SOCIAL NATURE OF WS – WHERE GENETICS AND CULTURE MEET AND CONVERGE IN THE EAST AND WEST

Williams syndrome provides a compelling model for investigating the effects of genotype, phenotype, and environmental interactions. The genetic basis of WS is by now well known and has been documented in great detail (unlike, for example, the basis of autism). The genetic phenotype thus involves the absence of one copy of a small set of genes on chromosome 7, an absence that occurs in nearly all those clinically identified with WS (Korenberg et al., 2003; Korenberg et al., 2008). Currently members of our research group (Korenberg, Reiss, Reilly, Bellugi, et al.) are working together to begin to link genotype and phenotype in WS, and the hunt is on to link specific genes within the WS region with brain development and behavioral functions. An initial yet powerful approach involves intensive examination of some specific cases of individuals with specific smaller deletions (see Doyle, Bellugi, Korenberg, et al., 2004; Doyle, Bellugi,

**Table 6.3.** *Sample Responses to Qualitative Item 5: "Describe your child's typical reactions on meeting a stranger for the first time"*

| Age Range | J TD | J WS | US TD | US WS |
|---|---|---|---|---|
| (3–4 years) | She flinches and comes to parents | He says words that are used in greeting like "hello" and "what are you doing?" It happened frequently when he just learned the words. Although it is not happening as frequently as before, when he wants to brag about something, he still approaches strangers and starts talking to them. | Shy. Makes only minimal eye contact. Tries to hide behind familiar people | Searches them out to attain eye contact. Reaches for their hands o pull them down to his level. Big, happy smiles. |
| (5–8 years) | She often holds my hand tightly, stays behind me, and observes the person. She will greet if told to do so. She observes how I, her mother, respond to the person and tries to correspond the situation | She always greets them by saying "Hi! I'm M___" energetically. If someone talks to her, she happily starts to talk about different things | Warms up to children but not to adults for some time. | Introduces self with, "Hi, I'm J . . . May I ask a question or two?" |
| (9–13 years) | She more likely watches the person from a distance rather than talking to him/her. She has a little difficulty greeting even after she is introduced to the person. She tries to minimize her words when she has to answer | He starts talking about himself by looking straight into a person's eyes. He says, "What are you doing." Or "I'm K.___" He still greets people by saying "hello" to strangers passing by. | Sometimes shy with adults and/or disinterested. With friends, she will introduce herself and is very friendly | 13, is always engaging. She asks numerous questions and inquires as to a person's living arrangements. She has invited strangers to our home for dinner. |

Reiss, Galaburda, Mills, & Korenberg, 2004; Korenberg et al., 2003; Hirota et al., 2003; Dai et al., 2008 for examples). The approach already has led to the hypothesis that specific genes near the end of the deletion in WS may be related to expression of social behavior (Korenberg et al., 2007; Bellugi, Järvinen-Pasley, Reilly, et al., 2007; Salk Press Release, 2007).

The focus on both consistency and variability of sociability in WS children permits consideration of the expression of sociability not only in WS individuals with typically sized deletions but also in those with atypical deletions. For example, the large-scale study of development of sociability in young WS, DS, and TD subjects described earlier included data from a young WS child. This child had a smaller-than-typical deletion that retained between one to three genes in the telomeric region that are almost invariably deleted in the "classic" allele. This child had typical medical and cognitive diagnostic characteristics for WS; however, her sociability scores, most significantly, those for approaching strangers, were significantly lower than the mean of the WS group, implicating specific genes in the emergence of this behavior in WS (Doyle, Bellugi, Reiss, et al., 2004; Korenberg et al., 2007).

The relative lack of variability in hypersociability among WS children, which can be gleaned both from parental reports and experimental as well as observational measures, suggests that the behavioral feature of hypersociability in approaching strangers may be strongly influenced by the genetic deletion (see also Klein-Tasman & Mervis, 2003), tempered by environmental factors. The early age of onset of WS and the case of the child with the atypical deletion further support this conclusion.

The results of the comparative Japan–U.S. study support a genetic "proportional stamp" on the expression of social behavior in WS across cultures; children with WS in both cultures showed more affinity for approaching strangers and rated higher in Global Sociability than TD children in their respective countries. That study, using a common instrument, aimed to examine social behavior among WS children in the two countries to investigate how cultural expectations or mores influence social behavior. Our results suggest that the WS social and genetic phenotype may influence affiliative behavior toward strangers, even among children who are subject to a cultural expectation of cautiousness towards strangers. Despite differences in upbringing and cultural expectations regarding social interaction, both Japanese and Americans with WS were rated significantly higher in Global Sociability and in tending to approach strangers than their TD counterparts. However, the sociability of American TD children was on par with Japanese WS children – whose social behavior is considered out of bounds by Japanese standards – a sign that cultural expectations clearly influence social behavior. By both quantitative and qualitative measures, these differences are evidence of nature's stamp on culture's milieus, and the reverse.

The same can be said of the use of social evaluation in language in WS. Because social language use varies across cultures in TD individuals, language studies also provide a glimpse of the exciting interaction of culture and genetics in WS. As demonstrated in the first section of this chapter, WS children across cultures consistently engage their listeners with "audience hookers," turn the tables on interviewers, and outperform their respective control groups in using social evaluative language. Given this persistent profile, the atypical expressive use of language in narratives may well be a "marker" of the WS phenotype; it is also intriguing with respect to the contribution of genes to neural systems that underlie social behavior (Doyle, Bellugi, Korenberg, et al., 2004). Most importantly, it becomes clear that the form and intensity of social behavior in WS is influenced by an individual culture's display rules and social conventions for *expressing* sociability. Thus language in a genetically based syndrome, in particular its structure and social uses, proves a productive tool in studying the complex interplay between our genes and our environment.

The expression of sociability in WS and the inimitable nature of social language in WS may not be "either/or" phenotype/culture; they are, rather, "both/and." The particular features of WS allow us to investigate the dual influences of nature and nurture; thus, continuing to examine WS across cultures and across domains will be an important avenue for further exploration.

## ACKNOWLEDGMENTS

This is a review chapter that borrows heavily from our work and writing from several papers (Doyle, Bellugi, Korenberg, et al., 2004; Zitzer-Comfort et al., 2007; and Järvinen-Pasley et al., 2008). All illustrations are the copyright of Dr. Ursula Bellugi and the Laboratory for Cognitive Neuroscience.

We thank Dr. Anna Järvinen-Pasley and Yvonne Searcy for their contributions to the analyses. We also would like to thank the many families who contributed to this research in four countries. Without the continuing support of families living with Williams syndrome, our understanding of the interplay of nature, nurture, and the human condition would not be nearly as advanced as it is today. In Japan, Mr. Sugimoto of the Japanese Williams Syndrome Association, was particularly helpful as he translated many of the materials into Japanese and acted as a liaison for the Japanese families who chose to participate. In Italy, the data were gathered by Stefano Vicari in collaboration with the Ospedale Bambino Gesù in Santa Marinella (Rome); and in France, data were gathered by A. Lacroix in children's homes through the Williams Syndrome Family Associations and the Laboratoire, Langage et Cognition (LaCo, Université de Poitiers-CNRS).

The research was supported in part by NICHD HD 33113 to UB, JRK and NIND NS 22323 to UB, JR.

REFERENCES

Battin, J., Lacombe, D., Taine, L., & Goizet, C. (2000). Williams syndrome (microdeletion 7q11.23), model of behavioral phenotype. *Bulletin de l Academie Nationale de Medecine* (Paris), *184*(1), 105–15; discussion 115–6.

Bellugi, U., Adolphs, R., Cassady, C., & Chiles, M. (1999). Towards the neural basis for hypersociability in a genetic syndrome. *Neuroreport, 10*(8), 1653–1657.

Bellugi, U., Järvinen-Pasley, A., Doyle, T., Reilly, J. Reiss, A. L. & Korenberg, J. (2007). Affect, social behavior and brain in Williams syndrome. *Current Directions in Psychological Science 16*, 99–104.

Bellugi, U., Järvinen-Pasley, A., Reilly, J., Searcy, Y. M., Mills, D., Galaburda, A., et al. (2007). Genes, neural systems, and social behavior: Defining the social phenotype in Williams syndrome [Abstract/Poster]. Program No. 696.1. 2007 Neuroscience Meeting Planner. San Diego, CA: Society for Neuroscience.

Bellugi, U., Lichtenberger, L., Jones, W., Lai, Z., & St. George, M. (2000). The neurocognitive profile of Williams syndrome: A complex pattern of strengths and weaknesses. *Journal of Cognitive Neuroscience, 1*(Suppl. 1), 7–29.

Berman, R., & Slobin, D. (1994). *Relating events in narrative: A crosslinguistic developmental study* (pp. xiv, 748). Hillsdale, NJ: Erlbaum.

Bjornstad, P. (1994, January 10). Williams–Beuren syndrome in Norway. *Tidsskr Nor Laegeforen, 114*(1), 25–28. (Article in Norwegian.)

Bril, B., Dasen, P., Sabatier, C. & Krewer, B. (Eds.) (1999). *Propos sur l'enfant et l'adolescent – Quels enfants pour quelles cultures ?* Paris: L'Harmattan.

Conroy, M., Hess, R., Azuma, H., & Kashiwagi, K. (1980). Maternal strategies for regulating children's behavior: Japanese and American families. *Journal of Cross-Cultural Psychology, 11*, 153–172.

Dai, L., Bellugi, U., Chen, X. N., Pulst-Korenberg, A. M., Järvinen-Pasley, A., Tirosh-Wagner, T., et al. (2008). Is it Williams syndrome? GTF21 implicated in sociability and GTF21RD1 in visual–spatial construction revealed by high resolution arrays. Poster presented at the 12th International Professional Conference on Williams Syndrome Garden Grove, CA.

Doyle, T. F., Bellugi, U., Korenberg, J. R., & Graham, J. (2004). "Everybody in the world is my friend": Hypersociability in young children with Williams Syndrome. *American Journal of Medical Genetics, 124A*, 263–273. (PMID: 14708099)

Doyle, T. F., Bellugi, U., Reiss, A. L., Galaburda, A. M, Mills, D. L., & Korenberg, J. R. (2004). Genes, neural systems, and cognition: Social behavior of children with Williams syndrome: Observing genes at play? [Abstract/Poster]. Program No. 666.11. 2004 Neuroscience Meeting Planner. San Diego, CA: Society for Neuroscience.

Einfeld, S. L., Tonge, B. J., & Florio, T. (1997). Behavioral and emotional disturbance in individuals with Williams syndrome. *American Journal of Mental Retardation, 102*, 45–53.

Ewart, A. K., Morris, C. A., Atkinson, D., Jin, W., Sternes, K., Spallone, P., et al. (1993). Hemizygosity at the elastin locus in a developmental disorder, Williams syndrome. *Nature Genetics, 5*, 11–16.

Frigerio, E., Burt, D. M., Gagliardi, C., Cioffi, G., Martelli, S., Perrett, D.I., & et al. (2006). Is everybody always my friend? Perception of approachability in Williams syndrome. *Neuropsychologia, 44*, 254–259.

Gosch, A., & Pankau, R. (1994). Social-emotional and behavioral adjustment in children with Williams–Beuren syndrome. *American Journal of Medical Genetics, 53*, 335–339.

Harrison, D., Reilly, J. S., & Klima, E. S. (1995). Unusual social behavior in Williams syndrome: Evidence from biographical interviews. *Genetic Counseling, 6*, 181–183.

Hess, R., Azuma, H., Kashiwagi, K., Dickson, W P., Nagano, S., Holloway, S., et al. (1986). Family influences on school readiness and achievement in Japan and the United States: An overview of a longitudinal study. In H. Stevenson, H. Azuma, & K. Hakuta (Eds.), *Child development and education in Japan* (pp. 147–166). New York: Freeman.

Hirota, H., Matsuoka, R., Chen, X.-N., Salandanan, L. S., Lincoln, A., Rose, F. E., et al. (2003). Williams syndrome deficits in visual spatial processing linked to GTF2IRD1 and GTF2I on chromosome 7q11.23. *Genetics in Medicine, 5*(4), 311–321. (PMID: 12865760).

Järvinen-Pasley, A., Bellugi, U., Reilly, J., Mills, D. L. Galaburda, A, Reiss, A. L., et al. (2008). Defining the social phenotype in Williams syndrome: A model of linking gene, the brain, and cognition. *Development and Psychopathology, 20*(1), 1–35.

Jones, W., Bellugi, U., Lai, Z., Chiles, M., Reilly, J., Lincoln, A., et al. (2000). Hypersociability in Williams syndrome. In U. Bellugi & M. St. George (Eds.), *Linking cognitive neuroscience and molecular genetics: New perspectives from Williams syndrome. Journal of Cognitive Neuroscience, 12*(Suppl. 1), 30–46.

Kendon, A. (1995a). Gestures as illocutionary and discourse structure markers in southern Italian conversation. *Journal of Pragmatics, 23*, 247–279.

Kendon, A. (1995b, July). *The open hand: Observations for a study of compositionality in gesture.* Paper presented at the conference "Gesture," Albuquerque, NM.

Klein-Tasman, B. P., & Mervis, C. B. (2003). Distinctive personality characteristics of 8-, 9-, and 10-year-olds with Williams syndrome. *Developmental Neurospychology, 23*(1&2), 269–290.

Korenberg, J. R., Bellugi, U., Chen, X.-N., Salandanan, L. S., Tirosh-Wagner, T., Galaburda, A., et al. (2007). Genetic origins of sociability in Williams syndrome [Abstract/Poster]. Program No. 696.2. 2007 Neuroscience Meeting Planner. San Diego, CA: Society for Neuroscience.

Korenberg, J. R., Bellugi, U., Salandanan, L. S., Mills, D. L., & Reiss, A. L. (2003). *Williams syndrome : A neurogenetic model of human behavior.* In *Encyclopedia of the human genome* (pp. 757–766). London: The Nature Publishing Group.

Korenberg, J. R., Chen, X.-N., Hirota, H., Lai, Z., Bellugi, U., Burian, D., et al. (2000). VI. Genome structure and cognitive map of Williams syndrome. *Journal of Cognitive Neuroscience, 12*(Suppl, 1), 89–107.

Korenberg, J. R., Dai, L., Bellugi, U., Jarvinen-Pasley, A., Mills, D., Galaburda, A., et al. (2008). Deletion of 7q11.23 genes and Williams syndrome. In C. J. Epstein, R. P. Erickson & A. Wynshaw-Boris (Eds.), *Inborn Errors of Development: The molecular basis of clinical disorders of morphogenesis* (2nd ed.). New York: Oxford University Press.

Kotzot, D., Bernasconi, F., Brecevic, L., Robinson, W. P., Kiss, P., Kosztolanyi, G., et al. (1995). Phenotype of the Williams-Beuren syndrome associated with hemizygosity at the elastin locus. *European Journal of Pediatrics, 154,* 477–82.

Kreiter, J., Bellugi, U., Lichtenberger, E.O., Klima, E., Reilly, J., & Kikuchi, D.K. (2002). *Gregarious language in narratives by adolescents Williams syndrome.* Poster presented at the American Speech-Language-Hearing Association Conference, Atlanta, GA.

Labov, W., & Waletzky, J. (1967). Narrative analysis: Oral versions of personal experience. In J. Helm (Ed.), *Essays on the verbal and visual arts* (pp. 12–44). Seattle: University of Washington Press.

LaFreniere, P., Masataka, N., Butovskaya, M., Chen, Q., Auxiliadora-Dessen, M., Atwanger, K., et al. (2002). Cross-cultural analysis of social competence and behavior problems in preschoolers. *Early Education and Development, 13*(2), 187–199.

Laws, G., & Bishop, D. M. V. (2004). Pragmatic language impairment and social deficits in Williams syndrome: A comparison with Down's syndrome and specific language impairment. *International Journal of Language and Communication Disorders, 39,* 45–64.

Lebra, T. S. (1994). Mother and child in Japanese socialization: A Japan–US comparison. In P. Greenfield & R. Cocking (Eds.), *Cross-cultural roots of minority child development* (pp. 259–274). Hillsdale, NJ: Erlbaum.

Lenhoff, H., Wang, P., Greenberg, F., & Bellugi, U. (1997). Williams syndrome and the brain. *Scientific American, 277*(6), 68–73.

Losh, M., Bellugi, U., Reilly, J., & Anderson, D. (2000). Narrative as a social engagement tool: The excessive use of evaluation in narratives from children with Williams syndrome. *Narrative Inquiry, 10,* 1–26.

Markus, H., & Kitayama, S. (1991). Culture and the self implications for cognition, emotion, and motivation. *Psychological Review, 98*(2), 224–253.

Masataka, N. (2002). Low anger-aggression and anxiety-withdrawal characteristic to preschoolers in Japanese society where 'Hikkikomori' is becoming a major social problem. *Early Education and Development, 13*(2), 187–199.

Mayer, M. (1969). *Frog, where are you?* New York: Dial Press.

Mervis, C. B., & Klein-Tasman, B. P. (2000). Williams syndrome: Cognition, personality, and adaptive behavior. *Mental Retardation and Developmental Disabilities Research Reviews, 6,* 148–158.

Meyer-Lindenberg, A., Mervis, C. B., & Berman, K. F. (2006). Neural mechanisms in Williams syndrome: A unique window to genetic influences on cognition and behaviour. *Nature Reviews Neuroscience, 7,* 380–393.

Morris, C., & Mervis, C. (1999). Williams syndrome. In S. Goldstein & C. Reynolds (Eds.), *Handbook of neurodevelopmental and genetic disorders in children* (pp. 555–590). New York: Guilford Press.

Morris, C. A., & Mervis, C. B. (2000). Williams syndrome and related disorders. *Annual Review of Genomics and Human Genetics, 1,* 461–484.

Nakaji, A., Kawame, Y., Nagai C., & Iwata M. (2001). Clinical features of a senior patient with Williams syndrome. *Rinsho Shinkeigaku, 41,* 592–8.

Perez-Jurado, L. A., Peoples, R., Kaplan, P., Hamel, B. C., & Franke, U. (1996). Molecular definition of the chromosome 7 deletion in Williams syndrome and parent-of-origin effects on growth. *American Journal of Human Genetics, 59,* 781–792.

Reilly, J., Bernicot, J., Vicari, S., LaCroix, A., & Bellugi, U. (2005). Narratives in children with Williams syndrome: A cross linguistic perspective. In D. Ravid & H. B. Z. Shyldkrot (Eds.), *Perspectives on language and language development: Essays in honor of Ruth A. Berman* (pp. 303–312). Dordrecht, the Netherlands: Kluwer.

Reilly, J., Klima, E. S., & Bellugi, U. (1990). Once more with feeling: Affect and language in atypical populations. *Development and Psychopathology, 2,* 367–391.

Reilly, J., LaCroix, A., Poirier, J., Bernicot, J., Bellugi, U., & Klima, E. (2005). Narratives in French and American children with Williams syndrome. In a Special Issue of *Le langage et l'homme,* in memory of Elizabeth A. Bates, *40*(2), 111–125.

Reilly, J., Losh, M., Bellugi, U., & Wulfeck, B. (2004). Frog, where are you? Narratives in children with specific language impairment, early focal brain injury, and Williams syndrome [Special issue]. *Brain and Language, 88,* 229–247.

Ruangdaraganon, N., Tocharoentanaphol, C., Kotchabhakdi, N., & Khowsathit, P. (1999, November). Williams syndrome and the elastin gene in Thai patients. *Journal of the Medical Association of Thailand, 82*(Suppl. 1), S174–S178.

Salk Institute for Biological Studies (1997, January 25). *Beyond nature and nurture: Williams syndrome across cultures* [Press release]. Retrieved from http://www.salk.edu/news/pressrelease_details.php?press_id=275

Shatz, M., Dyer, J., Marchetti, A., & Massaro, D. (2006). Culture and mental states: A comparison of English and Italian versions of chidlren's books. In A. Antonietti, O. Liverta-Sempio, & A. Marchetti (Eds.), *Theory of mind and language in developmental contexts* (pp. 93–106). New York: Springer.

Stevenson, H. W., Lee, S.-Y., Chen, C., Stigler, J. W., Hsu, C.-C., Kitamura, S., et al. (1990). *Contexts of achievement: A study of American, Chinese, and Japanese children. Monograph of the Society for Research in Child Development,* Vol. *55,* pp. 80–81.

Suizzo, M.-A. (2004). French and American mothers' childrearing beliefs: Stimulating, responding and long-term goals. *Journal of Cross-Cultural Psychology, 35*(5), 606–626.

Tager-Flusberg, H., & Sullivan, K. (2000). A componential view of theory of mind: Evidence from Williams syndrome. *Cognition, 76,* 59–89.

Tellegen, A. (1985). Structures of mood and personality and their relevance to assessing anxiety, with an emphasis on self–report. In A. H. Tuma & J. D. Maser (Eds.), *Anxiety and the anxiety disorders* (pp. 681–716). Hillsdale, NJ: Lawrence Erlbaum Associates, Inc.

Triandis, H. C. (1995). *Individualism and collectivism (New Directions in Social Psychology)*. Oxford, UK: Westview Press.

Triandis, H.C. (1989). The self and social behavior in differing cultural contexts. *Psychological Review, 96* (3), 506–520.

Udwin, O., Yule, W., & Martin, N. 1987. Cognitive abilities and behavioural characteristics of children with idiopathic infantile hypercalcemia. *Journal of Child Psychology and Psychiatry, 28,* 297–309.

von Arnim, G., & Engel, P. (1964). Mental retardation related to hypercalcaemia. *Developmental Medicine and Child Neurology, 6,* 366–377.

White, M. (1993). *The material child: Coming of age in Japan and America.* New York: Free Press.

Zahn-Waxler, C., Friedman, R. J., Cole, P. M., Mizuta, I., & Hiruma, N. (1996). Japanese and United States preschool children's responses to conflict and stress. *Child Development, 67,* 2462–2477.

Zitzer-Comfort, C., Doyle, T., Masataka, N., Korenberg, J., & Bellugi, U. (2007). Nature and Nurture: Williams syndrome across cultures. *Developmental Science, 10*(6):755–62.

# FORMATIVE RELATIONSHIPS WITHIN AND ACROSS GENERATIONS

Daniel S. Schechter

## INTRODUCTION

This section focuses on the interaction of attachment and intergenerational transmission of aggressive behavior. Each of the case studies and commentaries that follow explores how, in the context of human development, the caregiving environment shapes the infant's experience, understanding, and expression of aggression. One of these case studies (Fouts) compares approaches to parenting that affect the very young child's understanding and expression of aggression in a hunter-gatherer society versus a neighboring agrarian society in the Congo Basin rainforest. Among other questions, this ethnographic case study raises the question of how culture potentially constrains caregivers' behavior and childrearing goals with outcomes that may or may not prove adaptive for a given society over time.

The remaining case studies describe formative violent experiences whose effects on the organism, in human (i.e., Busch & Lieberman and Schechter) and primate studies (i.e., Sánchez, McCormack, & Maestripieri), ripple across generations in biological and psychological domains that we are only now beginning to understand. The child's potential to become parent-victim and/or perpetrator of violence may have many determinants, not the least of which are the following: the developmental window of exposure (Moriceau & Sullivan, 2006), genetic and epigenetic vulnerability (Binder et al., 2008), the quality of infant-parent attachment, the larger caregiving system's attunement to the child's developmental needs, as well as the child's ever-evolving narrative construction of his or her own experience as influenced by family relationships, community, and cultural contexts (Madigan, Moran, Schuengel, Pederson, & Otten, 2007; Tremblay et al., 2004; Schechter et al., 2007).

Since adversity breeds adversity, we hold in mind that 26,500–30,000 children die each day due to poverty (UNICEF, 2008). Moreover, in addition to malnutrition (e.g., one half of all rural children in India are underweight for their age), infectious diseases continue to blight the lives of the poor across the world. Most readers will not be surprised to note that much of the world's violence occurs precisely in those areas of the globe already hit hardest by poverty, hunger, and disease.

So, for the majority of the world's population who are "lucky enough" to survive early childhood long enough to suffer the consequences of early adverse events, how might the cases presented in this section be useful in thinking about how interdisciplinary efforts could potentially aid the interruption of cycles of violence and abuse?

Some answers:

1. In the clinical cases described, concrete community outreach (i.e., obtaining support and protective services) and symbolic psychotherapeutic work (i.e., language, video-feedback, and play in psychotherapy) are both used to support the family's resources (i.e., links to family, community, and culture). In order for any symbolic psychotherapeutic work to take place, it is necessary to ensure a sense of safety and stability, as well as a trusting alliance with the therapist. This may require helping the family gain access to an array of concrete supportive services.

2. Both community-based and specialized institution-based interventions are presented to demonstrate principles by which systemic environmental and intrapsychic change can be effected towards the goal of interrupting cycles of family violence.

3. Although these principles are demonstrated in what for the majority of the world's families-in-need would be exceedingly rare (i.e., in North American models), the case-authors share the belief that these principles, in whole or in part, likely can be applied across cultures, while bearing in mind that both individual and individual-cultural variation likely will inform the specific nature of the actual intervention.

REFERENCES

Binder, E. B., Bradley, R. G., Liu, W., Epstein, M. P., Deveau, T. C., Mercer, K. B., et al. (2008). Association of FKBP5 polymorphisms and childhood abuse with risk of posttraumatic stress disorder symptoms in adults. *Journal of the American Medical Association, 299*(11), 1291–1305.

Madigan, S., Moran, G., Schuengel, C., Pederson, D. R., & Otten, R. (2007). Unresolved maternal attachment representations, disrupted maternal behavior and disorganized attachment in infancy: Links to toddler behavior problems. *Journal of Child Psychology & Psychiatry, 48*(10), 1042–1080.

Moriceau, S., & Sullivan, R. M. (2006). Maternal presence serves as a switch between learning fear and attraction in infancy. *Nature Neuroscience, 9*(8), 1004–1006.

Schechter, D. S., Zygmunt, A., Coates, S. W., Davies, M., Trabka, K. A., McCaw, J., et al. (2007). Caregiver traumatisation adversely impacts young children's mental representations on the MacArthur Story Stem Battery. *Attachment & Human Development, 9*(3), 187–205.

Tremblay, R. E., Nagin, D. S., Séguin, J. R., Zoccolillo, M., Zelazo, P. D., Boivin, M., et al. (2004). Physical aggression during early childhood: Trajectories and predictors. *Pediatrics, 104*(1), 43–50.

United Nations Children's Fund (2007). *State of the world's children, 2008: Child survival.* Retrieved from http://www.unicef.org/sowc08/

# SEVEN

# Ethnographic Case Study

*Bofi Foragers and Farmers: Case Studies on the Determinants of Parenting Behavior and Early Childhood Experiences*

Hillary N. Fouts

The literature on early experience and child development emphasizes the role of the immediate social environment, in particular the parental and sociocultural factors that shape parents' caregiving behaviors. But another, less prominent literature considers adaptive-evolutionary factors that inform and modify the behaviors of parent and child to achieve optimal reproductive and survival outcomes for each (e.g., Blurton Jones, 1993; Chisholm, 1996; Hewlett & Lamb, 2002). LeVine (1989) has noted that these cultural and adaptive-evolutionary contexts of caregiving may conflict, and that even though parents strive to provide children with competencies that are fitted to their specific culture, environments with a high risk of child morbidity may prompt them to prioritize child survival over socialization. As human behavioral ecologists have pointed out, parents are further constrained by the finite resources of time and energy that they must carefully allocate among parenting and other critical activities, such as subsistence (Hill & Hurtado, 1996). Thus their care of any given child, or children in general, cannot be understood without reference to the limits of and competing claims on their resources.

In view of these considerations, complete understanding of parenting behavior should integrate dynamics among biology, evolutionary ecology, and culture. From a bioevolutionary perspective, reproductively significant behaviors such as parenting should represent solutions to adaptive problems posed by recurring conditions that have influenced reproductive fitness. An example of such an adaptive solution is the capacity of infant distress signals (fussing and crying) to evoke a response from caregivers. Attachment theorists have suggested that crying is an adaptation that enhanced the survival of infants in the environment of evolutionary adaptation (EEA), by promoting proximity and attachment to caregivers, and signaling need for care (Bowlby, 1969). In addition, ecological contexts determine the costs and benefits of certain behaviors in particular environments. For example, there may be fertility and mortality consequences of certain childrearing practices under specific living conditions. Or individuals may have evolved ways to maximize their reproductive fitness in particular environments. A final consideration is the constraint of culture on parent behaviors and childrearing goals. Cultural practices and goals that may or may not be adaptive to survival may well be fitted to the attributes valued by the specific culture in which the parent is operating and in which the child must become competent. Thus, diverse cultural and adaptationist evolutionary priorities may interact or even collide in shaping parent caregiving and its effects on child outcomes.

In this chapter I describe the care of two individual children in two small-scale cultures in order to illustrate the complex tension and intersection between evolutionary and cultural contexts as parents presumably provide children with the best chance to survive as well as to gain competencies valued in their particular culture. The case study of each child is based on data from a larger multimethod study on cultural variation in early childhood experiences and caregiving (Fouts, 2008; Fouts, 2004; Fouts, Hewlett, & Lamb, 2005). The multimethod approach in the study included quantitative observations of focal children and their caregivers, demographic interviews with families, and qualitative parental ideology interviews. The two case studies are presented together for illustrative purposes rather than as substantive bases for broad cross-cultural comparisons or generalizations. Nevertheless, these case studies provide an opportunity to detail individual experiences that are often omitted from larger studies.

## ETHNOGRAPHIC BACKGROUND

The Bofi foragers and farmers live in the northwestern regions of the Congo Basin rainforest in the Central African Republic and both speak the same Oubanguian language (*Bofi*). The data presented in this chapter are from one Bofi farmer village, with approximately 250 Bofi farmer inhabitants and 190 Bofi foragers living on the outskirts of the village and in the surrounding forests. The village is located on a dirt logging road and is approximately 155 miles by road from the capital city of Bangui. Very few of the Bofi farmers and foragers near this village have ever been to Bangui, because of the long distance, which can span seven or more hours by vehicle on predominantly dirt roads. The majority of the population in the study region self-identified as either Bofi farmer or Bofi forager, with very few individuals from other ethnic groups.

Distinct Bofi speaking groups that subsist largely from foraging or from farming interact with each other in social, spiritual, and economic settings. Such extensive contact means that each is aware of the other's caregiving patterns. Even though the Bofi farmers and foragers have long lived in this pattern of association, they identify themselves as culturally and ethnically distinct from one another.[1] The Bofi foragers are locally referred to as "pygmies." The Bofi farmer-forager sympatric relationship is similar to other farmer-forager relationships in the Congo Basin rainforest region like those of the Efe foragers and Lese farmers (Bailey & DeVore, 1989) and the Aka foragers and Ngandu farmers (Hewlett, 1991b).

## The Bofi Farmers

The Bofi farmers live in permanent villages on the outskirts of the rainforest. The villages are comprised of mud and wood houses with palm thatched roofs. Typically, a single nuclear family occupies each house, sometimes with the addition of one or two extended kin (e.g., grandparent, cousin). Houses are grouped by patrilineal clan, so that close neighbors are mostly members of the same clan.

The Bofi farmers subsist primarily through slash-and-burn horticulture. Although Bofi farmer men hunt periodically in the forest using shotguns and snares, the farmers obtain most forest products by trading with the Bofi foragers. The Bofi farmers maintain a distinct sexual division of labor. Women perform most of the farming, and men spend most of their time engaged in intervillage trade or politicking within the village. Farmer men and women thus spend their days apart – women and children in or near the fields and men in the village. Consistent with this sexual division of labor, the Bofi farmers emphasize gender and age hierarchy and organize villages and clans under male chiefs. Bofi farmers stress the value of communalism (putting the interests of the clan before individual interests), and children are expected to obey their older siblings as well as adults. Sanctions for child disobedience include corporal punishment.

---

[1] The Bofi foragers are known as Bofi "pygmies," although they prefer to simply call themselves "Bofi." The Bofi farmers do not refer to the Bofi foragers as "Bofi"; they instead refer to them *yidi*, a derogatory term that indicates that the foragers are "pygmies." The Bofi farmers refer to themselves as "Bofi" or *wi moli* which is the Bofi term for villager. The Bofi foragers generally call the Bofi farmers *wi moli* or "Bofi." To respect the wishes of both groups to be called "Bofi" and to distinguish between the two groups, this essay uses the terms Bofi farmer and Bofi forager.

## The Bofi Foragers

The Bofi foragers live part of the year in semipermanent camps on the outskirts of Bofi farmer villages and part of the year in temporary camps in the forest. But even these camps are typically within 10 kilometers of the villages. Bofi forager camps usually include 50 to 100 individuals who are predominantly members of the same patrilineal clan, although many families also choose to live matrilocally. Bofi forager houses are dome-shaped, constructed by interweaving branches and covering the dome with large leaves. This one-room hut is usually inhabited by one nuclear family.

The Bofi foragers principally hunt using large nets. Men, women, and children participate in the net-hunt, and both men and women gather edible plants in the forest, although the foragers obtain most of their carbohydrates through trade with the nearby Bofi farmers. Bofi forager husband-and-wife dyads spend most days together in the forest or in camp, thus passing substantial portions of the day with their children. Infants and toddlers up to 3 or 4 years of age are carried by their mother or father into the forest on most days. Children between the ages of 4 and 8 years typically stay in camp with adults who are not hunting or gathering that day. Consistent with their cooperative style of work and child care, the Bofi foragers place high value on age and gender egalitarianism, respect for personal autonomy, and high levels of cooperation and sharing. The emphasis on personal autonomy extends to the Bofi foragers' treatment of their children. Children are not punished and are rarely scolded or told what to do.

## EARLY CHILDHOOD EXPERIENCES AMONG THE BOFI FORAGERS AND FARMERS

The distinctive childrearing techniques practiced by Bofi farmers and for-agers reflect their respective cultural and subsistence patterns, and they consequently yield very different experiences for children.

## The Bofi Farmers

The Bofi farmers have a 2- to 3-year interbirth interval related to the typical weaning age of 2 years. The child mortality rate (birth to 15 years) is relatively high (31%) and is comparable to that of other horticulturalist groups (see Hewlett, 1991a).

Bofi farmer children are carried with their mothers to the fields each day until they are weaned from breast-feeding. Thereafter, they are left with older siblings, commonly aged 5 to 7 years, whereas siblings over the age of

7 years usually go to the fields. Bofi farmer parents reported that although they would prefer adult caregivers to child caregivers, adults are unavailable because all of them, including the elderly women, work in the fields. Thus during the day, many men are present in the village, drinking or politicking, whereas some men have gone to the forest to procure palm wine or hunt; but the village is primarily occupied by children between the ages of 2 and 7 years.

Mothers act as the primary caregivers for Bofi farmer children. Older siblings or cousins are secondary providers, and fathers have little direct involvement. Fathers verbally endorse their responsibility for taking care of children by providing them with food, clothing, medicine, and school supplies, but very rarely provide direct care to children (e.g., holding, cleaning, or soothing). Direct observational studies have found that after the age of 2 years, Bofi farmer children receive very little direct care from anyone (Fouts et al., 2005). Instead, Bofi farmer children are expected to stay close to older siblings during the day and to help with their own care (e.g., bathing themselves). Moreover, after weaning, Bofi farmer children are rarely soothed in response to their fussing and crying.

## The Bofi Foragers

The Bofi foragers have a longer interbirth interval (4–5 years) than the Bofi farmers, as Bofi forager parents allow children to stop nursing on their own. This usually happens between the ages of 3 and 4 years. Child mortality rates (birth to 15 years) are higher among the Bofi foragers (41%), perhaps because the foragers are less likely than the farmers to make use of local health clinics that offer western-style medicine. The Bofi forager high child–mortality rate is similar to that of other active forager groups (see Hewlett, 1991a).

In addition to later weaning, Bofi forager children are carried to the forest with their parents on most days until they are around the age of 3 or 4 years. Fully weaned children between the ages of 3 and 4 years who stay in camp are still held frequently (nearly 30% of the day, see Fouts et al., 2005), often by grandparents, aunts, and uncles. Bofi forager parents prefer adult surrogate caregivers when possible, and often commented that leaving children with older children (e.g., adolescents) puts them at risk for being hit, dropped, or left on the ground all day. Adult caregivers are usually available because not every Bofi forager adult travels to the forest every day. Younger as well as older individuals stay in camp periodically: Food sharing within and between families is extensive, so that individuals who remain in camp nevertheless receive food from those who forage.

Among the Bofi foragers direct care decreases with age but does not decline or cease abruptly as among the Bofi farmers (Fouts et al., 2005). In fact, children continue to be held and to receive caregiving (e.g., cleaning, grooming) primarily from adult caregivers. Even after weaning, the fussing and crying of children will elicit soothing responses by adults (Fouts & Lamb, 2005). Sources of nonmaternal care vary widely. Previous studies have found that the level of father involvement with young children was predicted by kin resources, residence patterns, and the age of the children (Fouts, 2008). Fathers' likelihood of involvement and availability to children was greater when living patrilocally and lower when grandparents lived in the same camp. Fathers were more likely to be available to older children (3–4 years) than to younger children (1–2 years). Overall, father-involvement patterns were related to biological, cultural, and ecological contexts, in that Bofi forager fathers were most involved with children at a time of increased risk for mortality (i.e., during and immediately after weaning). Such paternal involvement was influenced by the social ecology (e.g., availability of grandparents, and maternal kin) and cultural schema that promote gender egalitarianism and cooperation between husband and wife in work and child care (Fouts, 2008).

## Case Studies of Early Childhood Experiences

The two children described in the case studies represent typical experiences in their respective cultures, as neither was an outlier in any of the analyses of child or caregiver behaviors (Fouts, 2008; Fouts et al., 2005; Fouts & Lamb, 2005). Both are two-year-old later-born boys. Descriptions of the treatment of each child are based on quantitative observations[2] across daylight hours (6 a.m.–6 p.m.). Qualitative interviews with parents provide descriptions of how parents regarded caregiving and interpreted children's behavior. Names of children and their caregivers are fictitious.

---

[2] Quantitative behavioral observations were taken using a focal child sampling technique, which involved observing one child at a time, and recording child and caregiver behaviors onto a detailed checklist of behavioral codes. The behaviors were recorded on-the-mark, as indicated by a tape recording with a verbal message of "observe" to begin 20 seconds of observation, followed by "record" to mark down the current behaviors on a detailed checklist in 10 seconds. Signaling of the observe/record regimen took place through a small earphone worn by the observer. Each child was observed for 4 hours on 3 different days (6:00–10:00 a.m., 10:00 a.m.–2:00 p.m. and 2:00–6:00 p.m.) covering 12 daytime hours. Each 4-hour observation block contained four 45-minute observation sessions followed by a 15-minute rest to prevent observer fatigue. In sum, this procedure yielded 1080 observation points per child.

**Table 7.1.** *Data from Behavioral Observations*

| Behaviors[a] | Anbo | Dema |
|---|---|---|
| Proximity to Mother | 89.2 | 4.4 |
| Proximity to Juvenile Siblings and Cousins | 38.2 | 57.2 |
| Proximity to Grandparents | 22.5 | n/a |
| Held by Mother | 61.6 | 0.9 |
| Held by Adult Sister | n/a | 0.3 |
| Held by Grandfather | 2.7 | n/a |
| Play by himself or with objects | 33.5 | 64.9 |
| Interactive play with other children | 2.8 | 4.5 |
| Fussing and Crying | 4.4 | 6.9 |
| Percent of fussing and crying for which the child was soothed | 88.0 | 13.6 |

[a] Behaviors are presented as the percent of total observations, except for soothing, which is presented as the percent of fussing and crying for which the child was soothed.

*Anbo.* Anbo, a 2-year-old Bofi forager boy, is the fourth child of his parents, although his two eldest siblings died before he was born. Anbo lives in a small hut with his mother, Whina; his father, Kopay; and his 6-year-old brother, Keti. The family lives in the same camp as Whina's clan (matrilocally), while Kopay performs bride-service.[3] Whina's parents live in an adjacent hut with three of Whina's younger siblings; the youngest is 4 years old and, like Anbo, still nurses. Anbo periodically travels to the forest during the day with his parents; at other times he stays in camp with his grandfather or grandmother.

Quantitative summaries of Anbo's behavior and caregiving are presented in Table 7.1.

During observations Anbo was predominantly in close proximity (i.e., within an arm's reach) to his mother, his siblings and cousins, and his grandparents. Anbo's father often left early in the morning for the forest to perform tasks for his in-laws and was rarely present in camp during the rest of the day. Anbo was held in his mother's lap or arms for the majority of the day, but was also held by his grandfather. Anbo's mother provided most of his physical care, such as grooming and cleaning. When Anbo fussed or cried, his mother usually responded with physical and verbal soothing. He was not observed being scolded by adults; nor was he hit by other children.

---

[3] For the first 2–7 years of marriage Bofi forager husbands conduct bride-service. During this time the family lives matrilocally and the husband performs subsistence-related services for their wives' families. These services are often difficult and dangerous (i.e., collecting honey), and often bride-service men avoid such tasks by leaving for the forest early in the morning or taking extended trips to other forager camps.

Anbo spent much of the day playing by himself or with objects and seldom played interactively with his sibling or a cousin. These conditions closely resemble those of other Bofi forager children who were living matrilocally and had one or more grandparents living in camp. As previously noted, fathers were most likely to be involved with children when grandmothers were not living in camp and when the family lived patrilocally.

Consistent with observations, Whina and Kopay reported that Whina carries Anbo to the forest almost everyday and that she intends to continue to do so until Anbo is the size of her 4-year-old sister. Although Anbo's grandfather was more likely than his grandmother to take care of Anbo during observations, Whina and Kopay's stated preference was to leave him in the care of Whina's mother when they were away from camp. Whina described a typical leavetaking: "Anbo cries when he see us (parents) leave. He wants me to take him with me. Then Dekay (Whina's mother) picks him up and comforts him." When asked why they prefer to leave Anbo in Dekay's care, Whina spoke of both her mother and father, explaining that:

Dekay can make him all kinds of food, like *sokoba* (boiled manioc leaves) and *poto* (koko leaf stew). She takes care of him very well. Other people have large families, but our family is just my parents. Grandparents must take care of children because everyone else goes to the forest. If another person (Bofi forager) comes through camp they will not comfort your child because it is not their family.

Furthermore, Whina and Kopay explained that they bring collected food back from the forest to give to Whina's parents when Anbo's grandparents stay in camp. Whina and Kopay both regarded adults as better caregivers than children or adolescents. Whina explained:

Adults take care of children better because they watch them closely. Adolescents (*points to an adolescent girl*) do not watch children very well, they watch other things and then other children will hit our child but an adult will tell children not to hit our child.

The regularity of grandparental care and the closeness of the grandparent-child relationship were exemplified during one of the four-hour behavioral observation sessions of Anbo. During this particular observation, Whina, Kopay, and Dekay were all in the forest. When I arrived in camp, Anbo was sitting approximately 3 feet from Banga, his grandfather, quietly playing with a stick. Within 10 minutes of the start of the observation, a heavy rain began. Immediately, every adult and child in camp quickly headed for cover. Banga did not verbally call or overtly signal Anbo, but quickly ducked into a hut. I stood in the rain carefully watching to see which shelter Anbo would enter, thinking that he might follow either his cousins, his great-aunt, or his grandfather. Anbo followed his grandfather into a hut and climbed directly into Banga's lap. For the next hour of the rainstorm, Anbo and Banga sat together or near each other in the hut. On several occasions, Banga cuddled Anbo when he shivered, but mostly they just spent time together in quiet and close proximity.

Both Whina and Kopay explained that they want to have more children, although they do not know how many; nor did they provide a reason for wanting more children. Their explanations about choices for nonparental care providers, implied that such decisions might be easier for larger families. Likewise, larger patriclans have more nets and families to participate in cooperative net-hunts, and larger net-hunts have been found to yield more game per family (Hewlett, 1991b).

Whina thought that sometimes village women stop having children after only one or two births, because:

A *wimoli* (farmer woman) has one or two children and then they see that their husband does not help with the children (direct care). The woman then sleeps with other men and wears a cord (i.e., magical charm) to stop having children.

## Dema

Dema, a 2-year-old Bofi farmer boy, is the tenth child of his parents, although 2 of his older siblings are deceased. Dema lives with his mother, Senbola, his father, Botongo, and his seven siblings in a house with four rooms. Dema's siblings range from 23 to 5 years of age. Dema's family lives in a patrilineal clan centered around his father and his father's three younger brothers. Both of Dema's grandfathers are deceased; his maternal grandmother lives in his mother's natal village and his blind paternal grandmother lives next door.

Dema is weaned and during most observations[2] was near his home in the presence of several of his brothers and sisters. In fact, Dema was observed in close proximity (within an arm's reach) to his siblings for the majority of observations and infrequently in proximity to his mother (see Table 7.1). Dema was rarely held or given direct care such as grooming and cleaning; the direct care he did receive was mainly from his 5-year-old sister (0.6% of observations). When Dema fussed or cried, others seldom responded and he was left to recover on his own (see Table 7.1). Sometimes his mother and siblings responded by physically or verbally soothing him, but notably, they responded with soothing only when their own teasing had caused him to fuss or cry.

Dema spent most of his day playing on his own or with objects, and periodically played interactively with other children (see Table 7.1). Although he was not regularly observed either being hit or acting aggressively, a notable exception occurred during an in-home interview with his parents, who encouraged his aggression toward an elder sibling. Here is a vignette of the incident from my fieldnotes:

*Dema seems very fussy this morning; crying and fussing in almost any circumstance. His sister walks over to him and plops herself down onto the sand next to him. Dema angrily screams and lunges over to the small camp fire and grabs a large stick from the fire. Dema's sister jumps up and flees while Dema chases her, trying to hit her or touch her with the hot coals at the end of the stick. Dema's mother is sitting nearby and laughs at the situation, clapping her hands and encouraging Dema to "get her."*

Senbola and Botongo designated Dema's 5-year-old sister (Anne) as his daytime caregiver. Senbola explained that "I cook food and leave it in the house and tell Anne to give it Dema during the day." Senbola explained that Anne knows how to feed and take care of Dema; also Senbola noted that "if Dema hits Anne, I tell her to hit him back." Dema's parents explained that the reason they chose Anne as Dema's caregiver is that she is too young to go the fields to work, and all older children and adults are busy working during the day. A year later, when Dema was 3 years old, Senbola informed me that Dema no longer needed a guardian during the day and instead was able to "walk around the village on his own all day and get his food from the house." I also noticed that Anne had started going to the fields with her mother.

In addition to Anne, Senbola and Botongo opined that a grandparent would be a good caregiver, but the blindness of the only one available, Botongo's mother, prevented her from caring for Dema. Botongo noted the importance of older siblings, stating that if there are no siblings then . . .

mothers must be like the pygmies (foragers) and carry them (children) to work. Among the pygmies they continue to carry children everyday to the forest . . . it is not good. They (forager children) do not play with children their own age. Then when they do play with children they are scared, so the parents must keep carrying them because it is impossible for them (forager children) to play with other children.

Bofi Farmer children do tend to spend more time playing with other children, but also spend more time fussing and crying, especially in the second year, perhaps because of the Bofi farmers' lower rates of soothing responses to fussing and to their practice of weaning children at around the age of 2 years (Fouts et al., 2005). Furthermore, it is noteworthy that practices that are perceived by the foragers to be somewhat neglectful (i.e., see Whina's comments on how juvenile alloparents are not good), are interpreted by the Bofi farmers as beneficial, reflecting their priority to socialize children with other children.

## CONTEXTS OF EARLY CHILDHOOD EXPERIENCES

The case studies, along with data from the larger studies, illustrate two distinct patterns in terms of caregiving style and parental choice of caregivers. Furthermore, the Bofi foragers and farmers have distinct socialization patterns that shape identities and promote social competencies that are valued in their particular cultural contexts. The styles of caregiving, choice of caregivers, and socialization patterns reflect the intersection between cultural and evolutionary contexts.

LeVine (2005) has noted that the cultural practice of sibling care among the Gusii of Western Kenya (which resembles that of the Bofi farmers), whereby toddlers are left with 5- or 6-year-old children, would be considered neglectful by current U.S. standards. But he also found no evidence to suggest that their caregiving patterns led to any "flagrant abnormalities in later development" (LeVine, 2005, p. 159). The same may be true of Bofi farmers. Their lack of sensitivity to fussing and crying and the rough teasing to instigate fussing and crying contradicts western child development standards for promoting healthy attachment and social and emotional development.

Bowlby (1969) posited that attachment to the primary caregiver is an adaptive mechanism that protected infants and children from predators in the EEA. However, infant and child mortality among the Bofi farmers and foragers relate largely to infectious diseases, not predators. Whether or not protection specifically from predators was the primary instigator of the adaptation, it is a likely candidate because contemporary hunter-gatherers, such as the Bofi foragers, suffer high child mortality rates (Hewlett, 1991a). Bofi farmers have lower child mortality rates, but 31% still represents substantial risk to infants and children. Proximity to caregivers in both cultures is likely protective in their current ecologies, as close proximity to caregivers would provide the ability for caregivers to monitor children's health and provide resources (food). Bofi foragers and farmers exhibit different caregiver–child proximity patterns, illustrated by how often Anbo was held compared to the infrequent holding of Dema. This may be related to both the higher child mortality rate among Bofi foragers and their desire to monitor and respond to children's emotional needs.

Bofi forager children are held and carried by adult caregivers even beyond Anbo's age; in fact 4-year-olds spend much of their day in the lap or arms of a caregiver. The nature of holding entails close physical contact, and caregiver and child are likely to learn much about each other by spending extended time together in this manner. Likewise, during holding, caregivers can easily provide for children's emotional needs (e.g., responding when children fuss or cry). Such close contact may promote strong emotional bonds between caregiver and child. These patterns of close physical contact – holding and frequent soothing beyond toddlerhood and into early childhood – are consistent with the Bofi forager cultural schema of defining relationships based on social and emotional bonds and mutual cooperation. Like most Bofi foragers, Whina and Kopay characterized the ideal caregiver as someone who would protect their child from being harmed emotionally. For example, Whina and Kopy considered the risk of Anbo's being hit by another child if left with a child caregiver, even though being hit by another child does not present a great physical risk, because it would likely cause a child to cry.

Protecting children's emotional and physical welfare are intertwined in Bofi forager cultural schemas, because emotional harm or mild physical discomfort (e.g., child being left on the ground and not held) are associated with a risk of illness. For example, in previous studies of weaning from breast-feeding, Bofi forager parents often described how children were physically kicked or pushed by their unborn sibling (i.e., through mother's abdomen) and how this caused the child to become ill with diarrhea. Another common story is that as children see their mother's growing belly during pregnancy, they become afraid and then fall ill. Thus, the choice of caregivers among the foragers appears to be precipitated by the desire to protect children from emotional distress and from illness but it is also mediated by the social ecology, including who is available, perceived kin resources (e.g., grandparents living in camp), and the age of the children. This configuration exemplifies how frequent holding and use of adult caregivers may optimize both the physical monitoring and protection of children and the emotional security valued in this culture, with the tradeoff that some adults do not participate in net-hunts to provide care to children.

In contrast to the Bofi forager emphasis on protection from emotional harm, Bofi farmer parents like Senbo and Botongo characterized an able caregiver as someone who could provide food to their child during the day. Furthermore, caregivers become unnecessary once the child is capable of obtaining food from the house. Bofi farmer relationships emphasize resource exchange (e.g., food or goods). For example, a good husband is one who provides food, medicine, and clothing to his wife and children, rather than one who provides direct care to children. In addition, patriclans are exceptionally important to Bofi farmers because they produce and protect resources for the group. The larger patriclans have more members available for protection and farm labor.

Bofi farmer parents generally agree that although 5-year-olds are not ideal caregivers, they are capable of providing food (left by mother) to a younger sibling. The choice of juvenile caregivers apparently also relates to the value placed on cultivating peer relationships. This theme is exemplified by Botongo's opinion of Bofi forager socialization; the Bofi farmers say one should leave children with other children so that they can learn to play well with each other. The encouragement of physical conflict may be a method by which Bofi farmer parents assist children to learn about resolving conflicts with other children on their own and reduce their fear of playing with other children.

Emotional security versus material security is a tradeoff that permeates the comparison between Bofi forager and Bofi farmer parenting patterns. Bofi farmers emphasize material security (cultivation and protection of farming) over emotional security, as all capable children and women provide work on the farms, leaving only the very fragile elderly (e.g., Demo's blind grandmother) or very young siblings (e.g., 5-year-olds) to tend weaned toddlers. In contrast, the Bofi foragers emphasize emotional over material security for children; consequently, adults who are capable of hunting and gathering often stay in camp to care for young children. In Anbo's case, the caregivers were his grandparents, although oftentimes the adult caregiver may be an aunt or uncle. Among both Bofi foragers and Bofi farmers, it appears difficult or perhaps impossible to maximize both emotional security and material security because the ideal resources for nurturance, adults, are the very same resources for subsistence work. The emphasis on emotional security over material resources among the Bofi foragers may seem maladaptive, but in fact, to be successful on large, cooperative net-hunts, individuals must know each other very well and trust that each member will share the meat with the entire group. Thus emphasis on emotional security appears to enhance the cooperative and extensive sharing involved in the subsistence patterns of the Bofi foragers. For the Bofi farmers, mostly women and children conduct farming work while men focus more on political discussions related to resource defense (e.g., protecting farm land and cultivated goods). Emotional security among the members of one's group may not be necessary for successful farming cultivation. In consequence, the Bofi farmers allocate resources toward subsistence work at a cost to nurturance.

## REFERENCES

Bailey, R. C., & DeVore, I. (1989). Research on the Efe and Lese populations of the Ituri forest, Zaire. *American Journal of Physical Anthropology, 78*, 459–471.

Blurton Jones, N. (1993). The lives of hunter-gatherer children: Effects of parental behavior and parental reproductive strategy. In M. E. Pereira and L. A. Fairbanks (Eds.), *Juvenile Primates* (pp. 309–326). New York: Oxford University Press.

Bowlby, J. (1969). *Attachment and loss.* New York: Basic Books.

Chisholm, J. (1996). The evolutionary ecology of attachment organization. *Human Nature, 7*, 1–38.

Fouts, H. N. (2004). Social and emotional contexts of weaning among Bofi farmers and foragers. *Ethnology, 43*, 65–81.

Fouts, H. N. (2008). Father involvement with young children among the Aka and Bofi foragers. *Cross-Cultural Research, 42*(3), 290–312.

Fouts, H. N., Hewlett, B. S., & Lamb, M. E. (2005). Parent-offspring weaning conflicts among the Bofi farmers and foragers of Central Africa. *Current Anthropology, 46*, 29–50.

Fouts, H. N., & Lamb, M. E. (2005). Weanling emotional patterns among the Bofi foragers of Central Africa: The role of maternal availability and sensitivity, In B. S. Hewlett & M. E. Lamb (Eds.), *Hunter-gatherer childhoods* (pp. 309–321). Hawthorne, NY: Aldine De Gruyter.

Hewlett, B. S. (1991a). Demography and childcare in preindustrial societies. *Journal of Anthropological Research, 47*, 1–37.

Hewlett, B. S. (1991b). *Intimate fathers: The nature and context of Aka Pygmy paternal infant care.* Ann Arbor: The University of Michigan Press.

Hewlett, B. S., & Lamb, M. E. (2002). Integrating evolution, culture and developmental psychology: Explaining caregiver-infant proximity and responsiveness in central Africa and the USA. In H. Keller, Y. H. Poortinga, & A. Schölmerich (Eds.), *Between culture and biology: Perspectives on ontogenetic development* (pp. 241–269). New York: Cambridge University Press.

Hill, K., & Hurtado, A. M. (1996). *Ache life history.* Hawthorne, NY: Aldine De Gruyter.

LeVine, R. A. (1989). Human parental care: Universal goals, cultural strategies, individual behavior. In R. A. LeVine, P. M. Miller, & M. M. West (Eds.), *Parental behavior in diverse societies* (pp. 3–12). San Francisco: Jossey Bass.

LeVine, R. A. (2005). Challenging expert knowledge: Findings from an African study of infant care and development. In U. P. Gielen & J. L. Roopnarine (Eds.), *Childhood and adolescence: Cross-cultural perspectives and applications* (pp. 149–165). Westport, CT: Praeger.

# Commentary on

*"Bofi Foragers and Farmers: Case Studies on the Determinants of Parenting Behavior and Early Childhood Experiences"*

Myron A. Hofer

## INTRODUCTION

This study illustrates, in a very convincing way, that widely different parent-infant interaction patterns can evolve to become stable and adaptive components of two different but equally successful sub-cultures, existing within the same geographical and linguistic context. When I recall Fouts's observations that in the Bofi farmer tribe it is routine for parents to leave their 2- to 4-year-old toddlers with their 5- to 7-year-old siblings all day without adult supervision, I realized that such practices in our culture are likely to be grounds for removal of children from parental custody by child welfare agencies.

The implications of Fouts's paper are far-reaching. Those of us in the health care and social welfare professions must not simply assume that certain forms of mother-child interactions are "healthy" and other practices are "pathological." Furthermore, it strongly suggests that we review our ideas of "resilience" and "vulnerability," as well as our efforts to design interventions, in the light of a broader context of biological and social evolution.

## COMMENTS

The results of these studies lead to a number of further questions. Ideally, we would like to know, in some detail, how the cultural, psychological, and biological components of the two Bofi tribes' different early caregiving patterns interact in preparing their children for the different kinds of lives they will lead when they are adolescents and adults. But we know a

**Table 7.2.** *Summary of data on Bofi tribes showing different percentage times observed in parenting behavior, measures of reproductive outcome, and tribal cultural characteristics*

|                              | Forager      | Farmer      |
| ---------------------------- | ------------ | ----------- |
| Parenting Data:              |              |             |
| proximity to mother          | 89.2%        | 4.2%        |
| held by mother               | 61.6%        | 0.9%        |
| play by self or sibs         | 36.9%        | 63.1%       |
| weaning age                  | 4 yrs        | 2 yrs       |
| interbirth interval          | 3-5 yrs      | 2-3 yrs     |
| no. live births/woman        | 5.5          | 5.3         |
| child mortality to 15 yrs.   | 41%          | 31%         |
| Work Patterns                | Cooperative  | Individual  |
| Social Organization          | Egalitarian  | Hierarchy   |

great deal less about biological than about cultural or psychological components of early parenting effects on the developing young. So we must first ask, what biological processes could underlie and interact with the more familiar psychological and cultural processes in the development of Bofi tribesmen and women.

In Table 7.2 above, I have summarized (and over-simplified) the data presented by Fouts on the two Bofi tribes. Apparently, long, close, and interactive early parenting prepares the Bofi foragers for their highly cooperative hunting and food gathering strategies and generates an egalitarian adult society. In contrast, the abbreviated period of dependence on parents before weaning within the farming tribe, and subsequent erratic caregiving interactions with siblings, seem to encourage early self reliance and independence; this parenting pattern prepares individuals, then, for relatively solitary roles in the work of farming within a hierarchal adult society. From an evolutionary point of view, it is interesting that reproductive rates, as measured by the number of live children per woman, are identical in the 2 tribes, despite the much shorter interbirth intervals in the farmer tribe. The mortality rates between birth and 15 years of age seem quite high in both groups and higher in foragers – the group that receives the most intense and protective parenting. Whether the mortality difference is a cause or an effect of the different parenting patterns is not clear, but by these measures the evolutionary reproductive fitness of the two groups is about equal.

To understand how biological processes might contribute to these two equally adaptive living patterns, we first need to know what biological mechanisms are likely to exist within the observable parent-infant interactions of the two Bofi tribes. This question can be divided into three parts: (1) what biological processes mediate the "bond" that keep the infants close to their mother or older sibling caregivers; (2) what mechanisms underlie the responses to separation of Bofi farmer infants from their caregivers; and (3) how are the long-term effects of different patterns of caregiving in the two Bofi tribes translated biologically into altered developmental paths – and even extended to offspring in the next generation? To begin to answer these questions of biological mechanism, we must turn to analytic experiments that are only feasible in simpler laboratory animals than primates, such as rats. We have reason to believe that these mechanisms will have been conserved in evolution, allowing us to use them as hypotheses to explore more indirectly in humans.

First, in a series of studies, Regina Sullivan and her colleagues have found that underlying the psychological construct of the "bond" between infant rat and its mother are very early and rapid associative learning processes that enable a newborn rat to recognize its own mother and keep close to her (Sullivan, Brake, Hofer, & Williams, 1986). They found that if a specific odor was associated several times with some reinforcement that mimics maternal behavior, such as stroking with a small brush to mimic maternal licking, the pup would rapidly learn to recognize that specific odor and stay close to any object with that odor on it. It seems that the infant rat's psychological "bond" is made up of memories, established by a familiar simple learning process.

Regina went on to discover that, early in development, a similar bond was formed in rat pups, even when painful stimulation (by tailpinch or mild electric shock) was used to reinforce the association (Moriceau, Wilson, Levine, & Sullivan, 2006). A sensitive period for this early "traumatic bond formation" lasted from birth to mid-infancy, although this sensitive period could be extended by daily repetition of the association. Interestingly, the brain and hormonal systems mediating this early aversive learning are different from those mediating a positive association learning. These findings seem to provide a biological basis for strong early attachments in Bofi farmer infants exposed to less-than-optimal parenting and elder sibling caregiver interactions.

In pursuing the second question posed earlier, we found the separation responses of infant rats equally surprising. Having expected infant rats to be incapable of so complex a psychological response, we found that following removal of the mother from the home cage, 2-week-old rats, capable of living alone, nevertheless showed widespread responses in behavior, physiology, brain chemistry, and sleep organization. To our surprise, we found that this was not simply a psychophysiological stress response to "rupture of an emotional bond," but instead resulted from removal, or loss, of the pups' physical interactions with their mother prior to separation. We found that different behavioral and physiological systems of the infant were regulated by different components of the mother-infant interaction prior to separation – that is, by the mother's licking, warmth, fur scent, nursing position, and periodic milk letdown – and by the timing or rhythm with which these interactions occurred (Hofer, 1995). We called these components "hidden maternal regulators" because they were not apparent just by observing the mother with her litter. The biological responses to early separation and their dependence on multiple maternal regulators seemed to have implications for understanding the effects of different interaction patterns in parenting behavior on development, and this finding may provide a new mechanism for the effects of early maternal deprivation in humans (Hofer, 1984).

We, and others since, have found that these hidden maternal regulators control and shape the levels of hormones, blood pressure, and sleep over extended periods of development. For example, Saul Schanberg's finding that levels of growth hormone in rat pups were regulated by vigorous tactile stimulation led to the discovery of a brain mechanism for this effect, involving serotonin 2A and 2C receptor regulation of pituitary release of growth hormone (Katz, Nathan, Kuhn, & Schanberg, 1996). Schanberg and Tiffany Field (Field et al., 1986) translated the implications of this basic research to a clinical setting in which human premature infants with very low birth weights were studied. They found that weight gain and overall growth in preemies that were isolated in an intensive care unit could be significantly increased over a period of days with an intervention of stroking and limb movement three times a day, just 15 minutes at a time – and this intervention allowed the infants to leave the intensive care unit six days earlier than a control group of infants that received traditional care.

The third kind of biological mechanism, one that could mediate some of the long-term effects of early parenting involved in the adult behavioral differences between the two Bofi tribes, would require some form of change originating early in development that would persist far beyond the period of the early mother-infant relationship. Several psychological and cultural processes have been conceived to explain this kind of extended effect, but no biological process was identified until a few years ago. Michael Meaney and his group at McGill (Cameron et al., 2005) produced evidence that naturally occurring or stress-induced differences in levels of maternal behavioral regulators, like licking and grooming of the young, could permanently change the long-term expression of genes regulating the development and adult functioning of certain groups of cells within the pups' brains, through a novel "epigenetic" mechanism. As a result, in adulthood these animals were different in important behaviors, such as anxiety and reproductive behavior, as well as in hormonal stress responses. Furthermore, the adult daughter's maternal behavior toward her own pups closely resembled what had been the patterns of her mother's maternal behavior toward her, thus extending these long-term effects across generations. This provides evidence of biological support for the psychological and cultural processes known to mediate transgenerational effects.

Taken together, these examples of results from experimental laboratory research show an unexpected plasticity in the biological developmental systems involved in parenting interactions. In addition, the kinds of behavioral parenting interactions that are effective are similar to those thought to influence psychological development in humans and to be involved in the paths by which cultural influences shape development. Thus, a kind of synergy seems to exist among the influences acting at these different levels of organization.

## CONCLUDING REMARKS

In thinking about Hillary Fouts's fascinating paper, and in trying to answer the three questions I raised at the outset, I have found myself asking why the parent-infant interaction in particular should have been selected as a major source of variation in biological development. As a result of reading in the new field of Evolutionary Developmental Biology or "Evo Devo" (Carroll, 2005), I have grown to think of development not just as an interconnected set of processes for constructing an organism and its repertoire of behavior, but as a participant in the evolutionary process, as well as one of its creations.

The evolution of multicellular development created a major transition in the capacity of life to evolve (similar to the evolution of sexual recombination of genes during the evolution of single-celled organisms). Development evolved as a novel means of increasing the production of variation in traits for selection to act upon, as well as providing new forms of developmental inheritance that ensured that successful variants could be reproduced in the next generation. It has become apparent that, even at the cellular/molecular level, the roles of certain environmental features on the course of development have evolved in specific ways that are related to the adaptive advantage provided by such developmental plasticity (Kirschner & Gerhart, 2005).

There is good reason to suppose that the mother-infant interaction offers a number of adaptive opportunities that other environments do not. In mammals, the mother is the complete first environment, and because she is part of the pup's inheritance, an "inherited environment." The mother-infant interaction thus functions as a matrix and template to guide and shape the transgenerational inheritance of successful variations in developmental patterns into the next generation. Changes in the mother-infant interaction can produce useful long-term changes in the development of the young – variations that are potentially heritable, in that altered maternal behavior can be passed on to the next generation, as described in this commentary.

I have come to think of the evolution of animal and human development as having been driven by four interlocking selection pressures (1) to construct more complex organisms capable of exploiting new ecological niches; (2) to shape these construction processes to the special needs of immature forms as they pass through their unique micro-environments (for example, the unique form of learning adapted only to the early postnatal period, as described previously, is an "ontogenetic adaptation"); (3) to create potentially useful variations in these processes; and (4) to create new ways by which successful variants in developmental processes can be inherited by subsequent generations (Hofer, 2009). These four components make up what I have called "Developmental Selection" – construction, ontogenetic adaptation, variation, and inheritance. Developmental processes selected primarily for their contribution to construction and ontogenetic adaptation will have also been shaped to a considerable degree by their capacity for variation and by selection for heritability. Thus, these components should be considered to have been co-selected.

Thinking about development in terms of its evolution in this way gives new meaning to the embedding of embryos and fetuses in the internal environment of their mothers and the sustained close physical interactions of newborns and infants with parents. It seems to me that the concept of Developmental Selection is useful because it defines a set of functions that developmental processes are organized to carry out. Knowing the evolutionary functions of developmental processes should be a source of new hypotheses about how a given developmental process works, in much the same way that understanding the evolutionary function of stress responses enabled us to ask new questions about the mechanisms involved. In relation to the findings in Hillary Fouts's paper, we can increase our understanding of the developmental processes involved beyond their contribution to maturation by thinking of them as functioning to provide ontogenetic adaptation, and as contributing not only to variation but also to inheritance of useful variations in the next generation.

## REFERENCES

Cameron, N., Parent, C., Champagne, F., Fish, E., Kuroda, K., & Meaney, M. (2005). The programming of individual differences in defensive responses and reproductive strategies in the rat through variations in maternal care. *Neuroscience and Biobehavioral Review, 29,* 843–865.

Carroll, S. (2005). *Endless forms most beautiful: The new science of Evo-Devo.* New York: W. W. Norton & Company.

Field, T. M., Schanberg, S. M., Scafidi, F., Bauer, C. R., Vega-Lahr, N., Garcia, R., et al. (1986). Tactile/kinesthetic stimulation effects on preterm neonates. *Pediatrics, 77*(5), 654–658.

Hofer, M. A. (1984). Relationships as regulators: A psychobiological perspective on bereavement. *Psychosomatic Medicine, 46*(3), 183–187.

Hofer, M. A. (1995). Hidden regulators: Implications for a new understanding of attachment, separation and loss. In S. Goldberg, R. Muir, & J. Kerr (Eds.), *Attachment theory: Social development and clinical perspectives* (pp. 203–217). Hillsdale, NJ: Analytic Press.

Hofer, M. A. (2009). Developmental neuroscience. In G. C. Berntson & J. T. Cacioppo (Eds.), *Handbook of neuroscience for the behavioral sciences* (Vol. 1, pp. 12–31). Hoboken, NJ: John Wiley.

Katz, L. M., Nathan, L., Kuhn, C. M., & Schanberg, S. M. (1996). Inhibition of GH in maternal separation may be mediated through altered serotonergic activity at 5-HT2A and 5-HT2C receptors. *Psychoneuroendocrinology, 21*(2), 219–235.

Kirschner, M. W., & Gerhart, J. C. (2005). *The plausibility of life: Resolving Darwin's dilemma.* New Haven, CT: Yale University Press.

Moriceau, S., Wilson, D. A., Levine, S., & Sullivan, R. M. (2006). Dual circuitry for odor-shock conditioning during infancy: Corticosterone switches between fear and attraction via amygdala. *Journal of Neuroscience, 26*(25), 6737–6748.

Sullivan, R. M., Brake, S. C., Hofer, M. A., & Williams, C. L. (1986). Huddling and independent feeding of neonatal rats can be facilitated by a conditioned change in behavioral state. *Developmental Psychobiology, 19*(6), 625–635.

# Commentary on

## "Bofi Foragers and Farmers: Case Studies on the Determinants of Parenting Behavior and Early Childhood Experiences"

### Klaus K. Minde

In this chapter, Dr. Fouts presents observational data on two boys, Anbo and Dema, aged 2 years, who live in the Congo Basin rainforest in the Central African Republic. The children are members of two different subgroups of the Bofi speaking people who are exposed to different rearing conditions: Anbo's parents primarily hunt in the forest whereas Dema's family lives in a nearby farming community.

The author presents these two case studies to detail the individual parenting these boys experience and to illustrate the "tension" between evolutionary and cultural contexts as they are reflected in the children's lives. Although the author discusses her case examples primarily from an anthropological and social and ecological point of view, I will discuss this "tension" from the point of view of my experience as an academic infant and child psychiatrist who also lived and practiced for some years in sub-Saharan Africa. Thus my comments will use an ecocultural perspective that is based on two assumptions: (a) the "universalist" assumption, which implies that human societies exhibit significant commonalities and that children have universal biological and emotional developmental needs; and (b) the "adaptive" assumption, which views behavior as differentially developed and expressed in response to ecological and cultural contexts (Berry, Poortinga, Segall, & Dasen, 2002). Under the adaptive assumption, individual parents or small groups may use their universal ability, for example, e.g., speech or the provision of physical punishment in a variety of culturally determined ways. In addition, as a child psychiatrist I deal with parents anywhere in the world whose personal upbringing or life experiences have created a private "family" or even an individual "mother" or "father" culture that potentially compromises the "universalist" developmental needs of their children.

Dr. Fouts begins her chapter by stating that there are adaptive evolutionary factors that inform and modify parent-child interactions to achieve optimal reproductive and survival outcome. This is a somewhat different understanding of adaptation than the previously mentioned statement by Berry and colleagues, who see adaptation as the outcome rather than the origin of a needed change. However, there is also good evidence that present day socio-cultural pressures demand adaptations in parenting behaviors that may require more rapid changes than regular evolution provides and most individuals can biologically manage. For example, an increasing amount of literature has examined multigenerational problematic and maladaptive behaviors of children and families with symptoms such as attention deficit hyperactivity disorder (ADHD) in an evolutionary context and suggests that the persistence of such behaviors, despite general societal disapproval today, may be at least partly because of their adaptive function 3000 years ago (Jensen et al., 2006). Specifically, ADHD in children is associated with inattention, hyperactivity, and impulsivity that result, among other things, in poor learning styles, a lack of long-term planning, and frequently oppositional or even antisocial behaviors. Jensen and colleagues hypothesize that the reason for the persistence of this disorder may be that each of the symptoms can be adaptive in certain circumstances. For example, in the past, human survival depended on being hypervigilant, including the ability to retrieve information through all senses at once; scan it rapidly; pounce quickly or flee; and be motorically very active (Jensen et al., 2006, p. 99). Hence for Jensen and colleagues the readiness for action, quick responsiveness, and a tendency to take on risks or challenges may have been advantageous in an environment where one had to depend on hunting for survival and guard against dangerous animals. The continuing high incidence of ADHD, despite its lack of present-day survival advantage, suggests that natural evolution and its associated cultural traditions can be extremely slow in responding to changing socio-cultural circumstances.

The slow process of evolutionary change with its associated cultural practices, therefore, can become an obstacle to competent behavioral adaptation in a rapidly changing society. Moreover, because parents are important mediators of culture and their rearing strategies aim to translate traditional cultural values into present day adaptive child behaviors, they are at the frontline of this tension between the more "hard-wired" traditions and the required responses to a changing society. However, parents rear children through modeling and verbal exchanges within the context of an emotional relationship. Both of these strategies – reflections of cognitive thought processes – are potentially more easily changed than more biologically based behavior patterns. Modifying parenting routines would therefore be expected to be the first step in providing a mediating link between the demands of contemporary society, traditional culture, and biology.

How do these reflections relate to the stories of Anbo and Dema, the 2-year-old children from a Bofi forager and a Bofi farming family? They have some experiences in common. Both are growing up speaking the same language and both live in societies where about one third of children die before age 15. Fouts suggests that this extraordinary high death rate reflects the hesitation of both foragers and farmers to make sufficient use of local health clinics when their children become ill. This is certainly an example of the tension between adaptation and traditional belief systems. Both children live in extended family groups, are exposed to the same climate, and have similar diets. The educational level of their parents is not mentioned, but presumably in both cases it is low. Yet there are major differences in the children's experiences. (1) Anbo has one sibling whereas Dema is one of 10 children. (2) Fathers from the farming community are mainly occupied with trading and politics and less directly involved with their families and in child care than the forager fathers, leaving most of the farming work to women. (3) Therefore, the forager child, Anbo, is near his mother almost 90% of the time, whereas Dema is in proximity to his mother less than 5% of the time. (4) Other adults act as substitute caretakers among the foragers, whereas in the farming community rather young children take on this role. As a result, Dema plays alone a lot (65% of the time) whereas Anbo experiences more adult supervision and is held by his mother 62% of the time. The question becomes to what degree are these toddlers' universal developmental needs met in the two environments described by Dr. Fouts?

In general, investigators agree that sound physical and mental development in toddlers must be built on the foundation of parental protection, which gives children internal security and external safety (Bowlby, 1982). This protection facilitates their biologically programmed developmental drive for exploring their environment, having been assured that their caretakers will prevent them from getting into trouble by taking risks that they are not yet ready to manage, risks that could subsequently lead them to develop fears and anxieties. A young child's innate capacities can best unfold within an individualized nurturing environment.

Although parents are the primary caretakers of toddlers in many cultures, this parental role is not an essential requirement for adequate developmental care. However, the observations of the lives of Anbo and Dema provide interesting data. Anbo is said to stay with his mother Whina most days as she considers that "adults take care of children better" (p. 177). If she cannot care for him, she leaves him with her parents because "other people have large families, but our family is just my parents," implying that her parents will be more readily available to him should he need them. On the other hand, his grandfather did not pick him up to take him to a shelter when, during one observation, a sudden downpour began that sent the adults running for cover. Anbo was left in the rain until he found his way into his grandfather's hut. The grandfather is said to have cuddled the shivering, wet child, but the protective aspect of early caretaking did not become activated soon enough to prevent Anbo from potentially feeling miserable. If this interpretation is not correct, and if, in fact, Anbo's grandfather modeled an appropriate response that was designed to promote independence, one must remember that children's perceptions of stressful or traumatic life events are primarily determined by their developmental status. Because a 12-month-old child may experience a sudden rainstorm as an exceedingly real danger, that event must be taken seriously by the caretaker. The same event may be far less traumatic when the child is 24 months old, although being teased or laughed at may be far more traumatic at 24 months than at 12 months because the older child has developed basic receptive and expressive language abilities.

Dema, on the other hand, received little individualized care from anyone and is described as "crying and fussing a lot" and even engaging in an aggressive act against his older sister. In fact, his mother Senbola seemed to support aggressive behavior by roughly teasing and making fun of her children. One could speculate that Anbo's mother behaves in ways overall that are more likely to foster a "secure attachment," whereas Dema's mother trains her son to "dismiss" emotional warmth as irrelevant and to prepare himself to live without depending on the availability of trustworthy adults. It is not clear whether this distinction is truly culturally based or related to the individual history of these two mothers. One could argue that Dema's mother may feel rather overwhelmed after having given birth to ten and raising eight children, whereas Anbo's mother has had to concern herself with only two. It is also said that Dema's maternal grandmother had left the village, depriving her daughter and grandchildren of additional support. It is possible that she raised Dema's mother in a manner that also ignored the need for emotional closeness, that is, an insecure attachment working model, and that model may determine how Senbola parents her son.

It should be stressed that parental strategies leading to a "secure attachment pattern" are seen as "best" by the great majority of adults in 80 evaluated cultures (Waters 1995; Van Ijzendoorn & Sagi, 1999). This suggests that the associated benefits of a secure attachment for the emotional and cognitive life of children is a universal phenomenon. One important difference between the data obtained from observing Anbo and Dema may therefore be related to the different attachment patterns shown by their respective mothers toward their children. This implication would agree with results of recent work by K. Minde, R. Minde, and Vogel (2006) that confirmed the worldwide rate of secure (about 65%) vs. insecure (about 35%) attachment patterns in African populations; other data show a high degree (about 80%) of intergenerational transmission of identical attachment patterns, at least in western cultures (Benoit & Parker, 1994). This substantiates the ongoing effects parenting strategies have on the behavior of children.

In summary, the present paper provides an interesting view into the life of two families and their respective 2-year-old toddlers. Past work would suggest that "achievement," "self-reliance," and "independence" would be encouraged in hunter and gatherer families, whereas agricultural societies train their children for "responsibility" and "obedience" (Barry, Child, & Bacon, 1959). The presented data lack the long-range perspective needed to confirm a relationship between the subsistence pattern and socialization. Both children are encouraged to be self-reliant (surviving despite very limited time with mother vs. finding your own way into the hut during a rainstorm), but there are few comments dealing with obedience, independence, or achievement-oriented training, possibly because of the young ages of the children.

Because the families are not well matched, it is not clear whether the observed parenting differences are based on culturally sanctioned rearing patterns, the number of children the mothers are parenting, or the different attachment parameters the mothers display. To clarify the role of attachment, it would be interesting to have home observations, using a methodology like the Q-sort developed by Waters (1995) to control for attachment category before comparing single case caretaker-child observations. Clearly, foragers and farmers have different child care priorities because of their respective lifestyles; furthermore, the availability of food, which Fouts identifies as the major developmental necessity for Dema's family, is most likely a priority for both groups. It is possible that Anbo's mother did not refer to food because for her it did not even need to be mentioned that adult caretakers provide appropriate food for a toddler and recognize when the child needs to eat. The primary cultural difference between the two group may therefore be that the men are active providers in the foraging groups but have no active role in the farming community, where the women do the work in the fields. Dema's mother most likely would not have encouraged a 2-year-old *girl* to chase after a bigger brother with a glowing piece of wood; this assumed difference may reflect different adult expectations of male vs. female children. Perhaps a more securely attached farming mother would have tried to find an especially reliable youngster to care for her toddler in her absence and would not have supported openly aggressive behavior on the part of children toward family members or alternative caretakers. It will require a modified methodology in future case reports to provide more informed answers to these important questions.

REFERENCES

Barry, H. H., Child, I. L., & Bacon, M. K. (1959). Relations of child training to subsistence economy. *American Anthropologist*, *61*, 51–63.

Benoit, D., & Parker, K. C. H. (1994). Stability and transmission of attachment across three generations, *Child Development*, *65*, 1444–1456.

Berry, J. W., Poortinga, Y. H., Segall, M. H., & Dasen, P.R. (2002). *Cross-cultural psychology: Research and applications* (2nd ed.). New York: Cambridge University Press.

Bowlby, (1982). *Attachment and loss: Attachment* (2nd ed.). New York: Basic Books.

Jensen, P. S., Mrazek, D. A., Knapp. P., Steinberg, L., Pfeffer, C. R., Schowalter, J., et al. (2006). Application of evolutionary models to Attention-Deficit/Hyperactivity Disorder. In P. S. Jensen, P. Knapp, & D. A. Mrazek (Eds.), *Toward a new diagnostic system for child psychopathology: Moving beyond the DSM* (pp. 96–110). New York: Guilford Press.

Minde, K., Minde, R., & Vogel, W. (2006). Culturally sensitive assessment of attachment in children aged 18–40 months in a South African township. *Infant Mental Health Journal*, *27*, 544–558.

Van IJzendoorn, M. H., & Sagi, A. (1999). Cross-cultural patterns of attachment: Universal and contextual dimensions. In J. Cassidy, P. R. Shaver (Eds.), *Handbook of attachment* (pp.713–735). New York: Guilford Press.

Waters, E. (1995). The attachment Q-Set. In E. Waters, B. E. Vaughn, G. Posada, & K. Kondo-Ikemura (Eds.), *Caregiving, cultural and cognitive perspectives on secure-base behavior and working models* (pp. 247–254). Monographs of the Society for Research in Child Development, 60 (2–3, Serial No. 244).

# EIGHT

# Clinical Case Study

*Good Expectations: A Case Study of Perinatal Child-Parent Psychotherapy to Prevent the Intergenerational Transmission of Trauma*

## Amy L. Busch and Alicia F. Lieberman

The intimate interconnections linking biological, psychological, and social processes often are most apparent under conditions of environmental adversity, when the risk factors are so salient that their impact on personality functioning can be readily measured. In this case study, we present the treatment of a young pregnant woman whose childhood history of chronic and severe trauma, deprivation, and abuse was enacted in the present through violent and self-destructive behavior that endangered her well-being and her unborn child's healthy development. The treatment aimed at increasing the mother's safety, preventing abuse after the baby's birth, and interrupting the intergenerational transmission of psychopathology, which is well documented in the clinical and research literature (Fraiberg, Adelson, & Shapiro, 1975; Doumas, Margolin, & John, 1994).

Pregnancy is a time of profound transformation for women physically, psychologically, and interpersonally. The impending birth of the baby may be anticipated as the fulfillment of a cherished wish, but it may also elicit fear of body damage, resentment about loss of autonomy, and anxiety about the capacity to fulfill the new role expectations. For some women, the resulting stresses can result in anxiety, depression, and increased risk of domestic violence and child abuse (Gazmararian et al., 1996; O'Hara, 1995). At the same time, this developmental transition offers an opportunity for the improvement of long-standing maladaptive patterns (Benedek, 1959; Bibring, 1959). The "psychic plasticity" that accompanies pregnancy and the perinatal period reawakens unresolved conflicts originating in infancy and early childhood and offers the opportunity of a new and more mature resolution (Blos, 2003). For these reasons, pregnancy and the months following the birth comprise an important window for therapeutic intervention. Perinatal Child-Parent Psychotherapy is a treatment approach designed to maximize the potential for psychological growth during this developmental stage by helping the pregnant woman reflect on the links between her past and present emotional experiences and on the implications of these connections for her mothering of her baby. When the father is also available for treatment, the treatment focuses on the impact of expecting a baby on each parent, as well as on their relationship as a couple. Treatment continues for six months after the baby's birth, or longer if clinically necessary, to enable the parents to implement in their caregiving practices the insights they acquired during the pregnancy. Treatment outcome studies currently are underway regarding the effectiveness of child-parent psychotherapy during the perinatal period (Lieberman, Van Horn, & Diaz, 2008), but this relationship-based model has been shown effective with at-risk young children and their mothers, including maltreated infants and preschoolers exposed to domestic violence (Cicchetti, Rogosch, & Toth, 2006; Cicchetti, Toth, & Rogosch, 1999; Lieberman, Van Horn, & Gosh Ippen, 2005; Lieberman, Weston, & Pawl, 1991; Toth, Maughan, Manly, Spagnola, & Cicchetti, 2002; Toth, Rogosch, Cicchetti, & Manly, 2006).

## BACKGROUND AND PRESENTING PROBLEMS

Letisha[1] was an unemployed 21-year-old African American woman who began treatment when she was seven months pregnant with her first baby. She was expecting to have a son. She was referred to our clinic by her obstetrician, who was concerned that Letisha's severe trauma and substance abuse history posed a danger to her unborn baby's future safety. Letisha's life history revealed overwhelming hardship and fear. Letisha's father left the family when she was 6 months old, and shortly after, her mother became severely depressed and began abusing alcohol and heroin. During her childhood, Letisha witnessed her mother being physically abused by many male partners. Her mother hit her often, leaving bruises and welts on her body. She was locked in a closet while her mother received male visitors, and she often fell asleep lying on the heroin needles strewn on the closet's floor. At age 9, Letisha was first sexually fondled by an uncle, but her mother laughed when she reported this incident and took no measures to protect her from the uncle's continued abuse. She responded to these situations by "going somewhere else" in her mind, an early indication

---

[1] We have changed names and identifying information to protect client confidentiality.

of dissociation. Her mother was jailed several times for drug crimes, but Letisha reported this as normal within the context of her family's history – her father, brother, and cousins all had been incarcerated repeatedly for violent and drug-related crimes.

Letisha reported that her most difficult life experience occurred at age 10, when her cousin was shot in the head in a drive-by shooting while Letisha was standing next to him. She showed the therapist a scar on her cheek that she received from a piece of her cousin's skull, but appeared matter-of-fact while telling these events. The therapist asked if she had been frightened. Letisha replied, "No, that's the strange thing. I don't ever remember being afraid, even when my cousin was shot. I just watched it happen. I don't think I'm normal."

The absence of appropriate fear described by Letisha is consistent with the emotional numbing and dissociation that are common features of post-traumatic stress disorder (PTSD; APA, 2004). At age 21, 11 years after her cousin's murder, Letisha also was experiencing other features of PTSD, including flashbacks, difficulty sleeping, sudden rage, memory lapses, and avoidance of the place where the murder had occurred. Many of these symptoms likely predated her cousin's murder because Letisha had experienced multiple traumatic events from her first years of life. In addition to her PTSD symptoms, Letisha had had several episodes of major depression and tried to commit suicide once as a teenager. She had used methamphetamine for several years but said that she stopped after discovering her pregnancy. However, she still smoked marijuana daily. She reported that for the past few months she had been taking antidepressants prescribed by a psychiatrist and found that the medication alleviated her depressive symptoms. In addition to her psychological problems, she also suffered from obesity and hypertension.

Letisha's relationships were marked by a great deal of violence. Nearly all of her male partners had physically abused her and she, in turn, had been violent towards them. She also hurt other women in street fights and whenever she felt provoked. However, Letisha denied any violence in her current relationship with her baby's father. They had been together for one year, and Letisha reported that it was one of the first relationships that felt good to her. "We don't fight – we don't even argue. I've been there, done that. He knows that I'll just walk out if he ever hit me, because I don't need that for my baby." Letisha explained that, now that she was pregnant, she didn't want to fight others anymore. She saw her pregnancy as a turning point. "I want things to be different, now that I'm going to have this child," she said.

## CASE CONCEPTUALIZATION AND TREATMENT PLAN

Letisha had experienced chronic, unremitting trauma starting in her early childhood, in the context of her closest relationships. Traumatic experiences are unpredictable and generate helplessness and terror. As a young child, Letisha had to mobilize herself constantly to face new dangers, and she turned inwards for protection because she was helpless to gain age-appropriate protection from her parents or other caregivers. She did not allow herself to notice what was happening to her – she fell asleep in the drug-strewn closet, she dissociated when sexually molested, and she felt nothing in response to her cousin's murder. She also transformed her fear into anger, taking on the role of the aggressor as a way of defending herself against potential victimization. This aggressive coping strategy created a high risk that her baby might become the object of her rage if he evoked early experiences of abuse, continuing the intergenerational cycle of violence and trauma (Fraiberg et al., 1975). For this reason, an important component of the treatment plan was to help Letisha remember the feelings of terror and helplessness associated with her childhood experiences, and to use these memories as a basis for understanding her present aggression as an effort to cope with early fear by making herself feel strong and in control.

The therapist and Letisha collaborated in setting two treatment goals: reducing Letisha's aggressive behavior and reducing her substance use. Both goals would involve a focus on behavior change as well as a focus on the feelings that led to the behavior. Rediscovering early feelings of helplessness as a means to change aggressive behavior can be a useful clinical strategy when the client lives in safe surroundings, but it may have unforeseen iatrogenic effects when danger remains a part of the person's life. Letisha continued to live in a violent community where drugs, domestic violence, and gang violence were prevalent, and where others could exploit or hurt her if they perceived her as weak. For this reason, treatment was aimed at helping Letisha examine the difference between protective self-assertion and self-endangering violent outbursts. Although Letisha denied that she was worried about hurting her baby, her comment that she wanted to stop fighting suggested that she was motivated to change her aggressive behavior as she prepared to become a mother.

The prenatal period was an important window of opportunity to help Letisha develop the tools to manage her strong negative emotions before the baby arrived. This was a daunting goal to work towards in the 3 months that remained before the due date given Letisha's extensive history of violence, but she was a very motivated partner. She had witnessed child protective services remove many of her friends' children because of violence, drug use, or neglect, and she was determined that this would not happen to her child.

The intergenerational transmission of mental health problems from parent to child has traditionally focused on helping the parent retrieve painful early memories as a way of exorcising the "ghosts in the nursery" that lead to distorted parental perceptions of the child (Fraiberg et al., 1975). In the treatment of parents who have experienced severe trauma, it is important to balance this approach with a sustained encouragement to retrieve and recreate memories of having been protected, accepted and loved (Lieberman, Padron, Van Horn, & Harris, 2005). These benevolent experiences shore up the parent's self-esteem and instill hope in the possibility of creating a happier future. This approach had a positive effect on Letisha's treatment. In the following sections, we describe highlights of how treatment was conducted, with particular emphasis on how the therapist addressed the overlap between the external dangers facing Letisha and her child and the physical and psychological threats to safety and well-being represented by Letisha's use of violence as a form of self-defense.

## INSTILLING HOPE IN THE FUTURE: IDENTIFYING A BENEVOLENT FIGURE FROM THE PAST

As she was learning about Letisha's extensive trauma history, the therapist asked her what motivated her to change.

LETISHA: For every bad thing or person that's happened to me, there's been a good one. But the person who was really there for me was my aunt. I think if I had stayed with my aunt, if she had raised me, things would have been different for me. But my mom kept coming back to get me, and the hell would start all over again.

The therapist commented that Letisha had someone in her life who had wanted to protect her, even though she couldn't always do so.

LETISHA: ((*agreeing*)) She called me every week while I was in prison. She never forgot about me. Even when I went to visit her recently, after being away for a few years, she didn't say anything about all my scars and tattoos. She just hugged me and made me my favorite foods.

After Letisha described in detail what her aunt did for her, the therapist made the link to Letisha's baby.

THERAPIST: It sounds as though your aunt acted like the kind of mom you'd like to be for your son. She made you feel cared for, she tried to protect you, and she was there for you, even when you didn't always do what she hoped you would.

LETISHA: *((smiling))* Yeah, she was definitely all that, and she believes that I can be a good mom. I guess that helps me believe it, too.

The identification of a loving role model was pivotal in establishing for Letisha the concrete possibility of raising her child as she wished she had been raised herself. Throughout the treatment, the therapist often asked Letisha how her memories of her aunt might guide her in making decisions regarding her son. In one session, Letisha was able to reflect on how her aunt was able to inspire good behavior from her by showing disapproval for bad behavior rather than by giving her "a beating." She came to the conclusion that she wanted to have the same kind of relationship with her son. This aspiration served as an organizing theme for the treatment.

## RECOGNIZING ANGER AS A RESPONSE TO FEAR

One month into treatment, Letisha arrived at a session angry because she had to wait more than an hour for her routine prenatal exam. The therapist asked how she had dealt with her anger, and Letisha answered that she had yelled at the receptionist.

THERAPIST: I know you were angry, but I'm concerned about the fact that these are the people who will be helping you deliver your child. We all want to make sure that you and your baby get the best possible care. But it can be hard for people to care for you if you yell at them.

LETISHA: I don't worry about getting care for myself. I just want to make sure my son gets good care.

THERAPIST: But your son will depend on you being well – your health and safety are key to his well-being.

LETISHA: I guess I'm just scared of hospitals, and I hate going there for my appointments. No one I know who's gone into a hospital has ever come back out alive.

This was an important revelation. For Letisha, the hospital was a traumatic reminder of death and loss. As the therapist explored this connection, Letisha's disclosed her fear of dying in the hospital. The therapist explained that fear often leads to one of two responses – flight or fight.

LETISHA: I'm all fight. That's me.

THERAPIST: Fighting had been your reaction up until now, and it makes sense, because when you were young, you needed to protect yourself. There was no one to run to for protection when you were scared, so fighting became your way of surviving. But now, fighting can lead to other outcomes that you don't want. If your goal is to get the best care for you and your baby in the hospital, let's think together about how you can do that.

After some thought, Letisha suggested that she would talk to the hospital social worker, who could then inform the medical staff of Letisha's worries to make the delivery go more smoothly.

In this session, the therapist helped Letisha trace her anger at the hospital staff to her fear of harm, and she interpreted Letisha's fight response as something that may have helped her as a small child but could now be harmful to her and her baby. After this session, Letisha began to identify situations when her anger was a signal that she was actually feeling frightened and vulnerable. Her changed demeanor resulted in her receiving kinder care from her medical providers and more support from the baby's father. Letisha's insight and the pronounced behavioral change that followed gave the therapist hope that after the baby's birth she would seek out support instead of responding angrily towards the baby.

## ADDRESSING SUBSTANCE ABUSE AS A RESPONSE TO STRESS

Letisha continued to use marijuana daily, although the therapist had discussed with her the potential negative effects on the fetus. After Letisha reported that she had gotten into an argument with her mother on the phone, the therapist engaged in a sustained exploration of how she felt after the argument. Letisha eventually acknowledged that she had felt a little stressed, and that the tension resided in her back and neck. She added, "I can always tell I'm angry when my neck starts to hurt like that." When the therapist asked what she had done after her neck started hurting, Letisha said that she had wanted to smoke some marijuana but did not, because she feared her baby would be born with a positive toxicology test. The therapist talked about how hard it must be to stop using drugs, because smoking marijuana must have provided her with something. Letisha said that it helped her to relax. The therapist asked her what she had done instead to relax after the conflict with her mother, and Letisha responded that she had talked with a friend on the phone and she had listened to some of her favorite music. As she described these behaviors, she seemed genuinely surprised that they had made her feel better and showed interest in continuing to think with the therapist about other behaviors that she could resort to instead of using drugs.

This intervention was successful for several reasons. First, Letisha was already highly motivated to stop using illegal substances, primarily because she was worried that her baby would test positive for drugs at birth and would be taken away from her. She also had gained some understanding of the negative effects of drugs on the developing fetus. In addition, Letisha was able to identify some of the warning signs – anger and physical tension – that usually led to her drug use. The therapist encouraged Letisha's use of alternative coping strategies that she had found helpful. With each week that passed, Letisha seemed less interested in using substances and more confident that she could cope effectively without them. Within two months of treatment, Letisha was able to stop using marijuana, and to stay clean and sober throughout the rest of her pregnancy and after the baby's birth. This was a remarkable achievement for a young woman who had used drugs for much of her life, and spoke to her will power and motivation to become a good mother to her child.

## BECOMING A PROTECTIVE MOTHER

Adverse events were prevalent in Letisha's life in spite of her efforts to change. During one session she told the therapist that her brother had returned to prison for selling drugs. She said that she was disappointed because her young nephew wouldn't see his father for a long time. The therapist took this as an opportunity to talk about Letisha's feelings about her own child's future.

THERAPIST: So many people in your life have been in jail. I wonder how you think about your son's future in that way. We know that the statistics say that many black men go to jail at some point in their lives, and knowing that you're going to have a boy, do you worry about that?

LETISHA: ((*nodding forcefully*)) I'm going to be right on top of him, making sure he's doing good. There's a teenage boy who lives next door to me. He has a good job, works hard, and treats people well. His mother wouldn't let him play with the other kids in the neighborhood, the ones who always got in trouble. She kept him busy in after school programs and he came home just to sleep. If that's what it's going to take, I'll do it. Because I don't want my son to die before I do.

Here again, the presence of a good role model to guide Letisha's efforts offered hope that the kind of life she wanted to achieve was within her reach.

## STRUGGLING IN THE PRESENT WITH GHOSTS FROM THE PAST

Letisha continued to maintain a relationship with her mother, hoping that the mother would change despite her continued drug use, her repeated demands on Letisha for money, and her ongoing verbal abuse. At the same time, Letisha was often angry at her mother. A few weeks before her expected delivery, Letisha reported that she and her mother had fought again and said she was finished with her mother once and for all. Addressing the mixed feelings, the therapist responded that part of Letisha did seem finished with her mother, but part of her still seemed to call and visit the mother.

LETISHA: It's because I'm going to have a baby. I want my mom to act more like a mom, because I'm about to become a mom myself. I want her to do her job! *((laughing))*

THERAPIST: You're looking for a role model right now in your mom, wanting her to be a positive guide for how you should parent your son. But she keeps disappointing you.

LETISHA: *((becoming serious))* Here's the thing. Kids need stability from their parents. And I didn't have that. If you're sitting in school, and you're wondering what you'll wear the next day because you're wearing your only clothes, or you don't have any food at home, you'll have a hard timing paying attention.

Letisha went on to describe how her mother's drug use and neglect kept her from feeling secure enough to focus on learning.

THERAPIST: I can picture that little girl sitting in class, and I just feel so sad for her. *((Letisha suddenly begins to cry))* You've told me before that you haven't felt sadness in a long time – just anger. It seems you might be feeling sad right now, and that would be a normal feeling to have when you think of those memories. You needed something from your mom that you didn't get, and that's so sad. You have to find your own path to becoming a different kind of mother for your own child.

Although Letisha's mother had been both abusive and neglectful, Letisha still loved her and hoped that she might change. As she made the transition to parenthood, Letisha began to grieve her own childhood losses and to use the feelings of fear and sadness associated with those memories to prepare herself to mother her child.

Yet even with signs of progress, there also were indications that Letisha's experiences of violence and abuse might be coloring her views of her unborn child. Later in the same session, Letisha put her hand on her stomach and grimaced. "You're pushing against me, you're a mean baby," she said in a somewhat joking tone. In spite of her conscious efforts to change, Letisha's anger at her mother was being displaced towards her unborn baby, who was perceived as being "mean" and hurting her in the way her mother had done in the past. This episode made clear that Letisha was far from "finished" with her mother. The therapist's intervention consisted of legitimizing Letisha's discomfort while upholding the reality of the unborn baby's developmental needs to make a clear differentiation between the baby and Letisha's mother.

THERAPIST: Pregnancy can be a hard time for mothers. There can be a lot of celebration about the new life you are creating, but this time also can be exhausting and painful for the mother.

Letisha said she was ready to deliver her child because she was so tired of carrying around the extra weight.

THERAPIST: Your baby is growing so big inside you, moving around a lot now. It seems as though he's also getting ready to come out.

LETISHA: ((smiling)) He's an active baby, that's for sure. I can't wait to meet him.

It was reassuring that Letisha could incorporate the therapist's comment into a more developmentally accurate perception of her baby.

### THE NEXT CHAPTER: LETISHA AND HER BABY

A week later, Letisha called her therapist to say that she was in labor and asked the therapist to come to the hospital to support her and her boyfriend. "I'm scared," she said. The therapist arrived to find Letisha's boyfriend, James, holding her hand as Letisha tried to breathe through her painful contractions. James said proudly, "She's been so good. She's been really calm and hasn't yelled or screamed at anyone." The therapist smiled and said, "It sounds, Letisha, like you are really doing great, even though this must feel scary for you." Letisha said she was scared, but she was also excited for the baby to come. Letisha's son Justin was born later that day, healthy and welcomed by both of his parents.

Two weeks after Justin's birth, the therapist visited Letisha and her baby at her sister's apartment, where the new family was staying. Letisha reported that she felt good because Justin was eating and sleeping well.

LETISHA: I don't seem to care about the things I used to care about – I don't really want to talk to my friends on the phone or go out partying. I just want to look at him all day.

THERAPIST: *((smiling))* You love him so much. And it's clear he's completely focused on you, too.

A few minutes later, Letisha said it was time to change his diaper. She put him on the bed.

LETISHA: It's going to be cold, now, so don't cry.

BABY: *((cries in protest when his diaper is removed))*

LETISHA: *((in a teasing voice))* Do you want a spanking, little boy? Is that what you want?

THERAPIST: *((speaking for the baby))* No mamma, I don't want a spanking! I'm cold, just like you knew I would be.

LETISHA: *((smiles))*

THERAPIST: But it seems hard for you to hear him cry like that.

LETISHA: *((nodding))* Yeah, I hate hearing him cry. I want to protect him from feeling bad.

The therapist talked with Letisha about how very young children communicate their basic needs by crying, but that it can be hard for parents to hear those cries, especially parents who weren't comforted when they cried as children. Letisha and the therapist agreed that they would continue to work together on helping her hear her baby's cries without feeling overwhelmed.

This session highlights the mixture of "ghosts" and "angels" that continued to populate Letisha's psychic world as she made the transition to parenthood. On the one hand, she had strong protective urges toward her child, but she also had moments in which the negative influences of her abusive past resurfaced, and her immediate response to feelings of helplessness was to threaten violence toward her child, albeit jokingly. The interplay between Letisha's positive changes and her longstanding negative patterns suggested she would need continued support in learning how to foster her child's security as he grew up.

## CONCLUSION

Letisha's story is one of tremendous childhood trauma, but also of potential resilience and recovery. Individuals like Letisha, growing up in social conditions of violence and deprivation, may protect themselves from the ever-present danger of victimization through violence. They push out of consciousness feelings of helplessness and terror that would immobilize them, but these feelings live on in the mind and the body through PTSD, depression, substance abuse, violence, hypertension, and other medical conditions (Felitti et al., 1998). For Letisha, these emotional, physical, and relational problems put her at risk for an early death, and they put her child at risk for a continuing cycle of violence and trauma. Yet Letisha's pregnancy became a turning point for her. With the therapist's help, Letisha harnessed a positive influence from her past – her aunt's love and protection – to guide her in her transition to parenthood. Letisha and her therapist were able to identify this protective and nurturing figure from Letisha's childhood and use these memories to inspire positive parenting of her baby even before his birth. At the same time, the therapist helped Letisha to identify the sadness and anger she felt towards her mother's abuse and neglect and to find safer ways to cope with her strong feelings than becoming violent or using illegal substances. Letisha has just begun the transition to parenthood, and although her increased insightfulness, support from her partner, and strong motivation to care for her baby are hopeful signs, we know that she will need more than long-term psychotherapy to succeed as a young parent. Women such as Letisha need better housing, childcare, job training, and medical care than are currently available to them (Harris, Lieberman, & Marans, 2007). To stop the intergenerational cycle of violence, society will need to move beyond the individual mother and child and improve community support for our most vulnerable families.

REFERENCES

American Psychiatric Association (1994). *Diagnostic and statistical manual of mental disorders* (4th ed). Washington, DC: Author.
Benedek, T. (1959). Parenthood as a developmental phase: A contribution to the libido theory. *Journal of the American Psychoanalytic Association*, 389–417.
Bibring, G. (1959). Some considerations of the psychological processes in pregnancy. *Psychoanalytic Study of the Child*, 14, 113–121.

Blos, P. J. (2003). The maternal experience: A contribution from clinical work. In D. Mendell & P. Turrini (Eds.), *The inner world of the mother* (pp. 1–17). Madison, CT: Psychosocial Press.

Cicchetti, D., Rogosch, F. A., & Toth, S. L. (2006). Fostering secure attachment in infants in maltreating families through preventive interventions. *Development and Psychopathology, 18*, 623–650.

Cicchetti D., Toth, S. L., & Rogosch, F. A. (1999). The efficacy of toddler-parent psychotherapy to increase attachment security in offspring of depressed mothers. *Attachment and Human Development 1*, 34–66.

Doumas, D., Margolin, G., & John, R. (1994). The intergenerational transmission of aggression across three generations. *Journal of Family Violence, 9*(2), 157–175.

Felitti, V. J., Anda, R., F., Nordenberg, D., Williamson, D. F., Spitz, A. M., Edwards, V., et al. (1998). Relationship of childhood abuse and household dysfunction to many of the leading causes of death in adults: The adverse childhood experiences (ACES) study. *American Journal of Preventive Medicine 14*(4), 245–258.

Fraiberg, S., Adelson, E., & Shapiro, V. (1975). Ghosts in the nursery. *Journal of the American Academy of Child Psychiatry, 14*, 387–421.

Gazmararian, J. A., Lazorick, S., Spitz, A. M., Ballard, T. J., Saltzman, L. E., & Marks, J. S. (1996). Prevalence of violence during pregnancy: A review of the literature. *Journal of the American Medical Association, 275*(24), 1915–1920.

Harris, W. W., Lieberman, A. F., Marans, S. (2007). In the best interests of society. *Journal of Child Psychology and Psychiatry, 48*(3–4), 392–411.

Lieberman, A. F., Padron, E., Van Horn, P., & Harris, W. (2005). Angels in the nursery: The intergenerational transmission of benevolent parental influences. *Infant Mental Health Journal, 26*(6), 504–520.

Lieberman, A. F., Van Horn, P., & Diaz, M. A. (2008). *Preventing abuse with young mothers and their babies: Child-Parent Psychotherapy with pregnant women exposed to domestic violence.* Unpublished manuscript, University of California, San Francisco.

Lieberman, A.F., Van Horn, P., & Ghosh Ippen, C. (2005). Toward evidence-based treatment: Child-parent psychotherapy with preschoolers exposed to marital violence. *Journal of the American Academy of Child and Adolescent Psychiatry, 44*(12), 1241–1248.

Lieberman, A. F., Weston, D., & Pawl, J. (1991). Preventive intervention and outcome with anxiously attached dyads. *Child Development, 62*, 199–209.

O'Hara, M. W. (1995). Childbearing. In M. W. O'Hara, R. Reiter, S. Johnson, Milburn, & J. Engeldinger (Eds.), *Psychological aspects of women's reproductive health* (pp. 26–48). New York: Springer Publishing.

Toth S. L., Maughan A., Manly J. T., Spagnola M., & Cicchetti D. (2002). The relative efficacy of two interventions in altering maltreated preschool children's representational models: Implications for attachment theory. *Developmental Psychopathology, 14*, 877–908.

Toth, S. L., Rogosch, F. A., Cicchetti, D, & Manly, J. T. (2006). The efficacy of Toddler-Parent Psychotherapy to reorganize attachment in young offspring of mothers with major depressive disorder: A randomized trial. *Journal of Consulting & Clinical Psychology, 74*(6), 1006–1016.

# Commentary on

## "Good Expectations: A Case Study of Perinatal Child-Parent Psychotherapy to Prevent the Intergenerational Transmission of Trauma"

### Jill E. Korbin

The case study presented by Busch and Lieberman highlights the multi-faceted and complex nature of the intergenerational transmission of abusive and neglectful parenting. Whereas this case study's focal interest is the resolution of intrapsychic and relationship issues, Busch and Lieberman also point to the importance of the context of poverty and violence in which these dynamics occur, noting at the very end of their case study: "In order to stop the intergenerational cycle of violence, society will need to move beyond the individual mother and child and improve community support for our most vulnerable families." Even in light of Letisha's remarkable insights and progress, guided by perinatal child parent psychotherapy, she still must live and raise her child in an environment rife with poverty, violence, and danger. This commentary will focus on contextual influences on child maltreatment, although this is not meant to exclude the individual and psychological factors that Letisha's case so powerfully illustrates.

Intergenerational transmission of abusive parenting has been among the most frequently and consistently offered etiological explanations in the child maltreatment literature. However, the intergenerational transmission of abusive or neglectful parenting is not inevitable, posing a challenge and an opportunity for understanding the etiology and sequelae of child maltreatment. The case presented by Busch and Lieberman speaks powerfully to one pathway to avert intergenerational transmission. Despite the positive gains made in therapeutic intervention with Letisha, Busch and Lieberman acknowledge that this path of remediating individual dynamics will not suffice unless contextual factors also are considered, and that Letisha and women like her also need "better housing, childcare, job training, and medical care than are currently available to them."

The National Research Council's (1993) review of child maltreatment research promoted an ecological-transactional approach that also considered developmental factors. Building on Bronfenbrenner's (1979) ecological model of child development, an ecological-transactional model is interested not only in multiple ecological levels, but more specifically in the transactions across those levels. For example, research in urban Cleveland, Ohio, found that neighborhood conditions seemed to influence the effects of known risk factors such as violence in the family of origin (Coulton, Korbin, & Su, 1999). In the case presented by Busch and Lieberman, Letisha's vulnerabilities stemming from her own childhood occur in the context of a high poverty and high violence context. What might have been Letisha's outlook for her first child if she had instead been in a more positive environment? Busch and Leiberman comment that this kind of therapeutic intervention "can be a useful clinical strategy when the client lives in safe surroundings, but it may have unforeseen iatrogenic effects when danger remains a part of the person's life. Letisha continued to live in a violent community."

Anthropology's interest in the fit between the individual and culture, between the person and the social and physical environment has been expressed in ideas of the developmental niche (Super & Harkness, 1986) and the ecocultural niche (Weisner, 1984). The impact of culture was recognized in *From Neurons to Neighborhoods*, a recent review by the National Academy for Sciences Committee on Integrating the Science of Early Childhood Development (Shonkoff & Phillips, 2000). Culture was identified as the second of ten core concepts, noting that "culture influences every aspect of human development and is reflected in childrearing beliefs and practices designed to promote healthy adaptation" (Shonkoff & Phillips, 2000, p. 3). Despite this centrality of culture, however, "given the magnitude of its influence on the daily experience of children, the relative disregard for cultural influences in traditional child development research is striking" (Shonkoff & Phillips 2000, p. 25). Rogoff's (2003, p. 3) view that culture is expressed in context, that "people develop as participants in cultural communities," suggests that communities and neighborhoods are a fruitful ecological level to elucidate the transactions among individual, family, and contextual factors.

The association between neighborhood conditions and reported child maltreatment rates has been well documented, but the precise mechanisms and processes by which neighborhood conditions of disadvantage result in child maltreatment have been more elusive. Aggregate analyses using large samples can be powerful in demonstrating statistically significant associations between neighborhood conditions and child maltreatment. Ethnography can yield insights on the processes behind these associations. For example, in our study in Cleveland, Ohio, aggregate analyses of administrative data and neighborhood structural conditions yielded a factor we termed child care burden, reflecting the proportion of young children and the lack of adult males and elders in neighborhoods. The explanation one would expect is that single young mothers are simply overburdened by too many children. In addition to this possible explanation, neighborhood ethnography yielded the finding that were impacted by neighborhood fears of intervention with other people's children conditions for children (Korbin & Coulton, 1997).

Neighborhood effects on child maltreatment can result from multiple pathways (Coulton, Crampton, Irwin, Spilsbury, & Korbin, 2007) First, neighborhood structural conditions such as poverty, employment, and instability may act to increase the likelihood of child maltreatment behaviors. Second, it is possible that there are neighborhood differences in how child maltreatment is defined, recognized, and reported. This may lead to variation in child maltreatment reports, but not necessarily differences in rates of actual child maltreatment. And third, neighborhood research always has to consider that families choose neighborhoods for a variety of reasons and troubled families may simply end up in troubled neighborhoods.

As an African American living in a poor neighborhood, Letisha is at heightened risk of being reported for child maltreatment, not only because of her own background and individual risk factors, but also because of potential disparities in the reporting of child maltreatment. Child maltreatment reports are subject to multiple levels of bias. Estimates are that less than half of reportable child maltreatment events are actually reported, and that there are racial and economic disparities in child maltreatment reporting statistics. The debate has persisted as to whether disproportionality of child maltreatment reports by race and class is due to the stresses of poverty that result in abusive or neglectful behaviors, or to scrutiny of such populations through multiple public welfare systems that results in increased likelihood of being reported.

Disparities in child maltreatment reporting are even more pronounced when using a life table rather than a cross-sectional approach. Approximately one-third of African American children, as compared with approximately 12% of white children in Cleveland, Ohio, had a substantiated or indicated case of child maltreatment by the time they were 10 years of age, and reports were three times higher for urban than suburban children

(Sabol, Coulton, & Polousky, 2004). The impact of these disparities is even more striking in that close to half of all African American children will be investigated at least once for a report of child maltreatment before their tenth birthday.

Little is known about how disproportionality in reporting of child maltreatment may affect neighborhood residents. However, Letisha recognized the risk of child protective services involvement that she witnessed among her friends. As reported in this case study, she viewed child protective services as a risk to losing her child and therapeutic intervention as a way to protect against this happening.

Neighborhoods also impact the social networks of children and families. Networks are not exclusively linked to neighborhoods, but neighborhood is a powerful influence on the day-to-day context of other individuals available to children and families. In this case study, Letisha recognized the same dynamics as those found in social science research in her discussions of the need to protect her son from the adverse conditions and bad influences in her neighborhood. Letisha planned to emulate a neighbor who did not allow her child to play with other neighborhood children, who could be bad influences, and to try and guide her son towards other activities.

The presence of social networks is not sufficient to protect against child maltreatment. The social networks of abusive parents can be problematic. In an ethnographic study of women incarcerated for fatal child maltreatment, social network members often acted to buttress women's views of themselves as good mothers even though they were known by network members to be maltreating their children. Children were portrayed as difficult to raise, and network members engaged in similarly harsh childrearing strategies themselves. Thus, although maltreating mothers perceived their social support to be high, the actions of social networks did not act to protect their children (Korbin, 1998). In this case study, Letisha is beginning to more effectively employ social networks and social support. Nevertheless, her social networks continue to encompass a number of problematic relatives. She must continue to be vigilant about network members and the content of her interactions with others in relation to her parenting.

Letisha offers a poignant case study of how an individual who has experienced a multitude of assaults on her development and well-being can enhance her potential to break the intergenerational cycle of abusive parenting. Her case study illustrates the importance of transactions across ecological levels. With the aid of effective therapeutic intervention, she is striving to do better for her child than was done for her, to take the example of her aunt, a loving and supportive "significant other," and to find positive influences and models in her neighborhood. Still, as Busch and Lieberman caution, Letisha lives in a dangerous and unsupportive context, surrounded by poverty, violence, and problematic neighbors and relatives. Against this backdrop Letisha will continue to strive to bring her good intentions for her child to fruition.

REFERENCES

Bronfenbrenner, U. (1979). *The ecology of human development. Experiments by nature and design.* Cambridge, MA: Harvard University Press.

Coulton, C. J., Korbin, J. E., & Su, M. (1999). Neighborhoods and child maltreatment: A multi-level analysis. *Child Abuse & Neglect, 23*(11), 1019–1040.

Coulton, C. J., Crampton, D. S., Irwin, M., Spilsbury, J. C., & Korbin, J. E. (2007). How neighborhoods influence child maltreatment: A review of the literature and alternative pathways. *Child Abuse & Neglect, 31*(11–12), 1117–1142.

Korbin, J. E. (1998). "Good mothers," "babykillers," and fatal child maltreatment. In N. Scheper-Hughes & C. Sargent (Eds.), *Small wars: The cultural politics of childhood* (pp. 253–276). Berkeley: University of California Press.

Korbin, J. E., & Coulton, C. J. (1997). Understanding the neighborhood context for children and families: Epidemiological and ethnographic approaches. In J. Brooks-Gunn, L. Aber, & G. Duncan (Eds.), *Neighborhood poverty: Context and consequences for children* (pp. 77–91). New York: Russell Sage Foundation.

National Research Council (1993). *Understanding child abuse and neglect.* Washington DC: National Academy Press.

Rogoff, B. (2003). *The cultural nature of human development.* Oxford, UK: Oxford University Press.

Sabol, W., Coulton, C. J., & Polousky, E. (2004). Measuring child maltreatment risk: A life table approach. *Child Abuse & Neglect, 28*(9), 967–983.

Shonkoff, J., & Phillips, D. (Eds.). (2000). *From neurons to neighborhoods: The science of early childhood development.* Washington, DC: National Academy Press.

Super, C. M., & Harkness, S. (1986). The developmental niche: A conceptualization at the interface of child and culture. *International Journal of Behavior Development, 9*, 1–25.

Weisner, T. (1984). Ecocultural niches of middle childhood: A cross-cultural perspective. In W. A. Collins (Ed.), *Development during middle childhood. The years from six to twelve* (pp. 335–369). Washington, DC: National Academy Press.

# Commentary on

## *"Good Expectations: A Case Study of Perinatal Child-Parent Psychotherapy to Prevent the Intergenerational Transmission of Trauma"*

Emeran A. Mayer and Stefan Brunnhuber

## INTRODUCTION

The case study by Busch and Lieberman describes a young pregnant woman who had experienced multiple forms of severe trauma while growing up. Her experiences ranged from severe, adverse early life events (loss of father and severe mental illness with substance abuse in mother); to traumatic events she witnessed as a child (including physical abuse of her mother, her uncle's sexual abuse of his patients, and death of a cousin from a gunshot); to persistent adult trauma (abuse by her male partners). Psychologically, she had responded to these experiences by (1) dissociating from memories of the actual events, and (2) developing serious psychiatric and behavioral disorders. The latter included depression, substance abuse, attempted suicide, and aggressive behaviors. In addition, she became a victim of violence by male partners.

The Busch and Lieberman study reveals insights into the transgenerational transmission of psychopathology initiated by early life trauma and explores the potential of perinatal child–parent psychotherapy to break the cycle of intergenerational perpetuation. Although clinical knowledge of relationships between childhood trauma and adult psychopathology dates back to the insights of Freud (1986) and Bowlby (1940), neurobiological mechanisms underlying these behavioral changes have been described only in the last 20 years.

Based on extensive clinical experience, Freud and others first postulated that adverse early childhood experiences can influence adult mental states, distorting interactional bonding patterns and ultimately producing distinctive clinical signs and psychopathological symptoms in the affected

individual. These groundbreaking clinical observations were the beginning of an important aspect of research in clinical psychology, with major
implications for a better understanding of the psychopathology associated
with traumatic stress (Nemeroff et al., 2006). Moreover, the re-enactment of
salient, abusive, and depriving experiences within the doctor–patient relationship, so-called "transference," plays an important role in identifying
transgenerational mechanisms that reach beyond the present individual
complaints (Racker, 2001).

In contrast to the well-established clinical knowledge of the transgenerational transmission of violence and psychopathology, only in the last two
decades have neurobiological substrates for these clinical manifestations
been identified. An extensive literature on animal studies has clearly established the close interaction between genetic and early environmental factors
in shaping the adult brain and its responsiveness to environment perturbations (Szyf, McGowan, & Meaney, 2008; see also Szyf, McGowan, Turecki,
& Meaney, this volume). For example in rats, deficiencies in specific maternal postnatal behaviors have been shown to influence DNA methylation,
which has long-term effects on gene expression and behaviors, including
maternal behavior in offspring (Meaney & Szyf, 2005). Thus, variations
in the quality of maternal care (expressed in the rat as specific stereotypical behaviors) produce long-lasting effects on several neurobiological
systems (Charney, 2004), resulting in alterations in adult stress responsiveness, pain sensitivity, anxiety, and depression-like behaviors (Foa, Stein, &
McFarlane, 2006). Pre- or postnatal environmental stress experienced by
the mother can also have profound effects on her own behavior (ranging
from eating newborn pups to inappropriate mothering), and a biological
cycle can perpetuate compromised mother-infant interactions across generations. Particularly pertinent to the case under discussion, such potentially
life-long detrimental effects in the perinatal period of rodents is potentially
reversible through cross-fostering with a non-stressed mother, i.e., with
the re-introduction of a nurturing environment (Champagne & Meaney,
2007).

## THE EFFECT OF MATERNAL STRESS ON OFFSPRING

A number of empirical observations have identified distinctive parameters
for the transgenerational transmission of interpersonal violence (Dixon,
Browne, & Hamilton-Giachritsis, 2005). The mental representations and
psychic transformations of traumatic experiences in the human caregiver
and the impact of these representations on their off-spring represent a

**Table 8.1.** *Three Different Stages and Examples to Investigate the Clinical Impact of the Transgenerational Transmission*

| Stages | Examples |
|---|---|
| 1. Doctor-patient relation | Transference and counter-transference |
| 2. Individual psychopathology | Education, role model, conditioning |
| 3. Dyads | Life events |

major component in revealing this "chain-reaction" (Burke, 2007; Lieberman, Van Horn, & Ippen, 2005; Main, 2000). The caregiver's experience of interpersonal violence is considered an important risk factor in misbehaviors directed toward the child (Huth-Bocks, Levendovsky, Theran, & Bogat, 2004). For example, studies have demonstrated that a child's internalized images of self and others depend to a large extent on the severity of the mother's traumatic experience (Schechter et al., 2007). Besides findings of long-term transmission effects in the second and third generations (Scharf, 2007), and the impact of in-utero exposure to stress in the next generation (Brand, Engel, Canfield, & Yehuda, 2006), this mechanism also holds true for the dissociation mechanism often found in traumatized patients: Children of traumatized caregivers use dissociation far more often then children of non-traumatized parents in critical situations (Chu & Deprince, 2006). Adverse traumatic experiences can predict future neurological and psychological patterns in infants. When studying the impact on infants in utero of trauma associated with an earthquake, researchers found that affected offspring showed increased depression and cognitive dysfunction, compared with children born one year later (Watson, Mednick, Huttunen, & Wang, 1999). More common traumatic experiences like death of the father, job loss, or divorce have also been shown to significantly influence behavioral patterns in infants (King et al., 2000).

From a conceptual perspective, the impact of any transgenerational transmission can be identified in a clinical context at least at three levels, as shown in Table 8.1. The levels are: (1) within the doctor-patient relationship, where aspects of the intergenerational component of any conflict or adverse experience are reenacted "in situ"; (2) at the individual psychopathology level, where signs and symptoms are modulated by transgenerational experiences via education, role model identifications, or conditioning, including individual risk and resilience factors; and (3) within different dyads (e.g. caregiver and child, or couples), where life events such as pregnancies or marriages can reveal the pivotal role of developmental transition periods and intergenerational components of recovery and relapse.

## THE IMPORTANCE OF EARLY ENVIRONMENT IN SHAPING ADULT VULNERABILITY TO PSYCHOPATHOLOGY

Recent evidence from studies in both animals and humans strongly suggests that a number of genes ("susceptibility genes") are active in establishing brain circuits that mediate symptoms and behaviors in the adult early in life (Leonardo & Hen, 2006). However, these findings predict that genetic variability alone is not sufficient to produce distinct adult phenotypic traits (including human psychopathology), and that environmental influences at the time of circuit formation are of critical importance. For example, the influence of a genetic polymorphism affecting the expression of the serotonin transporter (SERT) on behaviors in monkeys is dependent on the environment the monkeys grow up in (Spinelli et al., 2007). Thus, the polymorphism encoding the low SERT expression is associated with reduced control of aggression in monkeys brought up with peers alone, rather than peers *and* the mother. In contrast, animals without this low SERT polymorphism demonstrated normal behaviors regardless of early environmental experiences.

Two independent landmark studies reported that a functional polymorphism in the human SERT gene moderates the effect of life stress on the later development of affective and mood disorders (Caspi et al., 2003; Kendler, Kuhn, Vittum, Prescott, & Riley, 2005). The greater probability of s allele carriers of the serotonin transporter polymorphism (5-HTTLPR) (resulting in lower SERT expression) for developing depression was seen only in individuals with a history of early life stressors. The same SERT polymorphism was found to increase the risk of PTSD under the conditions of high stress exposure *including* low social support (Kilpatrick et al., 2007). In the case of PTSD, recent twin studies further support the prominent role that early environmental influences play in the development of PTSD. Beyond a threshold of 3–4 traumatic situations, genetic factors seemed to decrease in importance, whereas the environmental impact appeared to overrule genetic disposition (Jang, Taylor, Stein, & Yamagata, 2007).

## WHY DOES EARLY LIFE (PERINATAL AND POSTNATAL) STRESS PRODUCE PSYCHOPATHOLOGY?

Although human psychopathology, violence, and suffering are the tragic consequences of adverse early life events, the substrates underlying this psychopathology have evolved because of their considerable adaptive value for non-human animals. The plasticity of developing brain circuits in responding to environmental influences in the pre- and postnatal periods represents a sophisticated mechanism by which an organism's behavior is programmed for the most likely future environmental conditions for the offspring (Kaffman & Meaney, 2007). This programming is largely affected through the influence of the environment on maternal behavior and maternal homeostasis. More severe environmental influences have an increasingly greater role in this process, when compared to genetically determined vulnerabilities. In the rodent, this future-oriented programming occurs in multiple forms: (1) The most drastic maternal behavior of eating her own pups under the most severe stress (cases of human infanticide by mothers under severe distress have also been reported) represents the evolutionary wisdom that it may be better for a mother's reproductive success in a future, more secure environment to optimize her own nutritional status, rather than investing valuable mothering efforts in a generation without a future. (2) The development of brain circuits hyperresponsive to environmental stressors, and of hypervigilance to all types of environmental stimuli, in offspring enhances their chances for survival in a dangerous and hostile world. (3) Intergenerational programming of the same maternal behaviors and the effects on offspring extends the time span of the "stress-adapted" phenotype even further. From a pessimistic viewpoint (and commenting on the final paragraph in the Busch and Lieberman study), one may say that the powerful, and presumably "hardwired," neurobiological mechanisms described continue to send an ancient evolutionary message to the mother-infant dyad: Considering persistent poor socioeconomic conditions and an expected harsh environment, the best behavioral strategy for the future is one of hypervigilance, aggression, violence, and ultimately self-destruction. From an optimistic viewpoint, the described perinatal child–parent psychotherapeutic intervention may help interrupt this vicious circle and allow the patient to pursue a more "salutogenic" behavioral strategy. The same plasticity of the developing human brain that we share with our non-human relatives, and which is mediating behavioral programming for a less than optimal future, may be used by such a unique human intervention as psychotherapy at the time of pregnancy, with the goal of changing evolutionary strategy, making possible a future of hope and possibilities.

## RESILIENCE FACTORS PROTECT FROM DEVELOPMENT OF ADULT PSYCHOPATHOLOGY

Even though animal studies have focused on the role of adverse early life events and genetics as vulnerability factors for the development of CNS changes explaining psychopathology, the positive effect on brain

development of resilience factors have been studied less frequently (Davidson, 2000). Letisha demonstrates important resilience factors, including her
capacity to generate humor, her acknowledgement of previous abusive
experiences, changes in her affect regulation, her ability to recall positive
identifications with her aunt, her overall belief system about posttraumatic
growth (Zoellner & Maercker, 2006), an awareness of her own fragility, her
sense of coherence, and her capability to distance the self. Whereas mild
stress promotes resilience (Parker et al., 2007), it is assumed that the relative importance of an individual's resilience and risk factors can account
for many differences among those who develop PTSD under stress exposure (Yehuda & Flory, 2007). Some of the best-documented resilience factors
are male gender, age (adults are more resilient then children), fewer past
life stressors, less frequent chronic diseases, a higher level of education,
higher socioeconomic status, and better social support (Bonanno, Galea,
Bucciarelli, & Vlahov, 2007).

Figure 8.1 illustrates the most common clinical predictors and resilience
factors along the clinical course. Most of these have an intergenerational
component.

## CONCLUSION AND FURTHER PERSPECTIVES

Letisha's case reveals in a beautiful way the tragic dilemma that we humans
find ourselves in: Endowed with the wisdom of millions of years of evolution, our brains respond to the dark side of human civilization in a way that
becomes maladaptive and destructive. Yet, these same biological mechanisms of neuroplasticity and brain development provide us with the hope

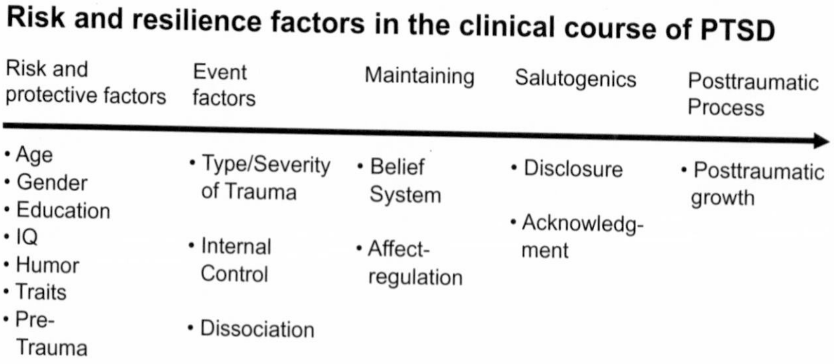

## Risk and resilience factors in the clinical course of PTSD

| Risk and protective factors | Event factors | Maintaining | Salutogenics | Posttraumatic Process |
|---|---|---|---|---|
| • Age<br>• Gender<br>• Education<br>• IQ<br>• Humor<br>• Traits<br>• Pre-Trauma | • Type/Severity of Trauma<br>• Internal Control<br>• Dissociation | • Belief System<br>• Affect-regulation | • Disclosure<br>• Acknowledgment | • Posttraumatic growth |

**Figure 8.1.** Risk and resilience in the clinical course of PTSD.

of being able to program a newborn's life for a more positive future, using psychotherapeutic intervention during pregnancy.

The emerging integrated view of Letisha's case reconciles the historical clinical findings of early 20th-century psychoanalytic pioneers with recent breakthroughs in neurobiology and psychology, confirming that adverse early childhood experiences – although long neglected by victim, parents, and society – do play a major role in transmitting psychopathology to future generations, with a tremendous cost in terms of both individual human suffering and an economic burden on society.

REFERENCES

Bonanno, G. A., Galea, S., Bucciarelli, A., & Vlahov, D. (2007). What predicts psychological resilience after disaster? The role of demographics, resources, and life stress. *Journal of Consulting and Clinical Psychology, 75*(5), 671–682.

Bowlby, J. (1940). The influence of early environment in the development of neurosis and neurotic character. *International Journal of Psycho-Analysis, 21*, 1–25.

Brand, S. R., Engel, S. M., Canfield, R. L., & Yehuda, R. (2006). The effect of maternal PTSD following in utero trauma exposure on behavior and temperament in the 9-month-old infant. *Annals of the New York Academy of Sciences, 1071*, 454–458.

Burke, D. (2007, July/August). Chain reaction? *Mental Health Today*, 8–9.

Caspi, A., Sugden, K., Moffitt, T. E., Taylor, A., Craig, I. W., Harrington, H., et al. (2003/July 18). Influence of life stress on depression: Moderation by a polymorphism in the 5-HTT gene. *Science, 301*, 386–389.

Champagne, F. A., & Meaney, M. J. (2007). Transgenerational effects of social environment on variations in maternal care and behavioral response to novelty. *Behavioral Neuroscience, 121*(6), 1353–1363.

Charney, D. S. (2004). Psychobiological mechanisms of resilience and vulnerability: Implications for successful adaptation to extreme stress. *American Journal of Psychiatry, 161*(2), 195–216.

Chu, A, & Deprince, A. P. (2006). Development of dissociation: Examining the relationship between parenting, maternal trauma and child dissociation. *Journal of Trauma and Dissociation, 7*(4), 75–89.

Davidson, R. J. (2000). Affective style, psychopathology, and resilience: Brain mechanisms and plasticity. *American Psychologist, 55*(11), 1196–1214.

Dixon, L., Browne, K., & Hamilton-Giachritsis, C. (2005). Risk factors of parents abused as children: A meditational analysis of the intergenerational continuity of child maltreatment (Pt., 1). *Journal of Child Psychology and Psychiatry, 46*(1), 47–57.

Foa, E. B., Stein, D. J., & McFarlane, A. C. (2006). Symptomatology and psychopathology of mental health problems after disaster [Review]. *Journal of Clinical Psychiatry, 67*(Suppl. 2), 15–25.

Freud, S. (1986). *Gesamtwerk* [Complete works]: 18 Bände. London, Frankfurt/Main: Fischer.

Huth-Bocks, A. C., Levendovsky, A. A., Theran, S. A., & Bogat, G. A. (2004). The impact of domestic violence on mothers' prenatal representations of their infants. *Infant Mental Health Journal, 25*(2), 79–98.

Jang, K. L., Taylor, S., Stein, M. B., & Yamagata, S. (2007). Trauma exposure and stress response: Exploration of mechanisms of cause and effect. *Twin Research and Human Genetics, 10*(4), 564–72.

Kaffman, A., & Meaney, M. J. (2007). Neurodevelopmental sequelae of postnatal maternal care in rodents: Clinical and research implications of molecular insights [Review]. *Journal of Child Psychology and Psychiatry, 48*(3–4), 224–44.

Kendler, K. S., Kuhn, J. W., Vittum J, Prescott, C. A., & Riley, B. (2005). The interaction of stressful life events and a serotonin transporter polymorphism in the prediction of episodes of major depression: A replication. *Archives of General Psychiatry, 62*, 529–535.

Kilpatrick, D. G., Koenen, K. C., Ruggiero, K. J., Acierno, R., Galea, S., Resnick, H. S., et al. (2007). The serotonin transporter genotype and social support and moderation of posttraumatic stress disorder and depression in hurricane-exposed adults. *American Journal of Psychiatry, 164*(11), 1693–1699.

King, S., Barr, R. G., Brunet, A., Saucier, J. F., Meaney, M., Woo, S., et al. (2000). The ice storm: An opportunity to study the effects of prenatal stress on the baby and the mother. *Santé Mentale au Québec, 25*(1), 163–185.

Leonardo, E. D., & Hen, R. (2006). Genetics of affective anxiety disorders. *Annual Review of Psychology, 57*, 117–137.

Lieberman, A. F., Van Horn, P., Ippen, C. G. (2005). Towards evidence-based treatment: Child-parent psychotherapy with preschoolers exposed to marital violence. *Journal of the American Academy of Child & Adolescent Psychiatry, 44*, 1241–1248.

Main M. (2000). The organized categories of infant, child, and adult attachment. *Journal of the American Psychoanalytic Association, 48*, 1055–1095.

Meaney, M. J., & Szyf, M. (2005). Environmental programming of stress responses through DNA methylation: Life at the interface between a dynamic environment and a fixed genome. *Dialogues in Clinical Neuroscience, 7*(2), 103–123.

Nemeroff, C. B., Bremner, J. D., Foa, E. B., Mayberg, H. S., North, C. S., & Stein, M. B. (2006). Posttraumatic stress disorder: A state-of-the-science review. *Journal of Psychiatric Research, 40*(1), 1–21.

Parker, K. J., Rainwater, K. L., Buckmaster, C. L., Schatzberg, A. F., Lindley, S. E., & Lyons, D. M. (2007). Early life stress and novelty seeking behavior in adolescent monkeys. *Psychoneuroendocrinology, 32*(7), 785–92.

Racker, H. (2001). *Transference and counter-transference.* Madison, CT: International Universities Press.

Scharf, M. (2007). Long-term effects of trauma: Psychosocial functioning of the second and third generation of Holocaust survivors. *Developmental Psychopathology, 19*(2), 603–622.

Schechter, D. S., Zygmunt, A., Coates, S. W., Davies, M., Trabka, K., McCaw, J., et al. (2007). Caregiver traumatization adversely impacts young children's mental representations on the MacArthur Story Stem Battery. *Attachment & Human Development, 9*(3), 187–205.

Spinelli, S., Schwandt, M. L., Lindell, S. G., Newman, T. K., Heilig, M., Suomi, S. J., et al. (2007). Association between the recombinant human serotonin transporter linked promoter region polymorphism and behavior in rhesus macaques during a separation paradigm. *Developmental Psychopathology, 19*(4), 977–987.

Szyf, M., McGowan, P., & Meaney, M. J. (2008). The social environment and the epigenome. *Environmental and Molecular Mutagenesis, 49*(1), 46–60.

Watson, J. B., Mednick, S. A., Huttunen, M., & Wang, X. (1999). Prenatal teratogens and the development of adult mental illness [Review]. *Developmental Psychopathology, 11*(3), 457–466.

Yehuda, R., & Flory, J. D. (2007). Differentiating biological correlates of risk, PTSD, and resilience following trauma exposure. *Journal of Traumatic Stress, 20*(4), 435–447.

Zoellner, T., & Maercker, A. (2006). Posttraumatic growth in clinical psychology: A critical review and introduction of a two component model. *Clinical Psychology Review, 26*(5), 626–653.

# NINE

# Ethological Case Study
*Infant Abuse in Rhesus Macaques*

M. Mar Sánchez, Kai M. McCormack, and
Dario Maestripieri

## INTRODUCTION

The use of animal models figures prominently in mental health research
and can play an especially important role in our efforts to understand
developmental psychopathologies. The vast majority of animal research is
conducted with rodents, and a typical approach involves experimentally
re-creating behavioral, psychological, or neurobiological conditions that
share some similarities with human psychopathologies or their biological
substrates. For example, human depression can be experimentally modeled as learned helplessness in rodents, and tested in a forced swimming
paradigm. In this task, a rat is placed in a water tank for a given period of
time. After the rat's efforts at escaping from the tank through swimming
have failed, some animals stop struggling, exhibiting behavioral passivity and neuroendocrine changes that share some similarities with those
observed in people who suffer from clinical depression.

A different approach to modeling human psychopathologies involves
identifying similar pathologies that occur naturally in animals. This
approach is particularly powerful if conditions similar to human mental
disorders are identified in animals that are closest and most similar to us,
such as the anthropomorphic primates (i.e., the Old World monkeys and
apes). In this chapter, we illustrate this approach by reviewing research
on the natural occurrence of infant abuse in nonhuman primate populations, and by discussing how this research can help us understand the
causes and developmental consequences of child maltreatment in humans
(see also Maestripieri, 1999; Maestripieri & Carroll, 1998a; Sanchez, 2006).
Using prospective, longitudinal techniques that are difficult with humans,

such animal studies permit us to identify critical factors that affect individual variability in the effects of early adversity, as well as the time course of biobehavioral alterations.

## NATURALLY OCCURRING INFANT MALTREATMENT IN
## NONHUMAN PRIMATES: GENERAL CHARACTERISTICS

Childhood maltreatment is a significant public health problem. In addition to the risk of physical injury or death, the emotional distress associated with acts of maltreatment negatively affects child development. Thus, childhood maltreatment is associated with social, emotional, and cognitive problems, and increased risk of developing anxiety, mood, conduct, and addiction disorders later in life (e.g. Glaser, 2000; Gunnar & Vazquez, 2006).

Not just a human problem, maltreatment also occurs spontaneously in nonhuman primate species. Studies of large populations of rhesus macaques (*Macaca mulatta*), pigtail macaques (*Macaca nemestrina*), and sooty mangabeys (*Cercocebus atys*) at the Field Station of the Yerkes National Primate Research Center have shown that 2%–10% of all infants born in a given year are physically abused by their mothers (Maestripieri, Wallen, & Carroll, 1997a, 1997b; Maestripieri & Carroll, 1998b). These primates live in semi-naturalistic social environments and have species-typical rearing histories (i.e., they are reared by their biological mothers and are exposed to male and female conspecifics of varying ages during development, as they would be in a natural environment). Therefore, abusive parenting is not a by-product of artificial housing conditions or aberrant rearing histories, as reported in other studies (e.g., Nadler, 1980; Ruppenthal, Arling, Harlow, Sackett, & Suomi, 1976). Naturally occurring infant abuse has also been observed in free-ranging rhesus macaques (D. Maestripieri, pers. obs.), as well as in captive groups of other Old World monkeys such as Japanese macaques, *Macaca fuscata* (Troisi, D'Amato, Fuccillo, Scucchi, 1982; Troisi & D'Amato, 1983); baboons, *Papio anubis* (e.g., Brent, Koban, & Ramirez, 2002); and New World monkey species such as common marmosets, *Callithrix Callithrix jacchus* (Johnson, Kamilaris, Calogero, Gold, & Chrousos, 1996).

Abusive maternal behavior is characterized by violent behaviors such as dragging, crushing, throwing, stepping on or sitting on the infant (Maestripieri, 1998; Troisi & D'Amato, 1984). These behaviors are clearly distinguishable from those in the species-typical maternal and aggressive repertoire. Abusive mothers, however, also exhibit competent and nurturing caregiving behaviors, and, in fact, alternate long periods of appropriate

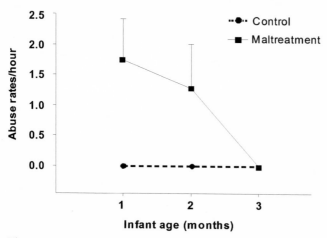

**Figure 9.1.** Average rates of abuse per hour, received by the infants. Rates of abuse were highest during month 1, and nonexistent by month 3. From McCormack, K., Sanchez, M. M., Bardi, M., & Maestripieri, D. (2006). Maternal care patterns and behavioral development of rhesus macaque abused infants in the first six months. *Developmental Psychobiology, 48,* 537–550. Copyright 2006 by Wiley Periodicals, Inc., A Wiley Company. Reprinted with permission of John Wiley & Sons, Inc.

maternal care with short bouts of abuse. Abusive parenting causes intense infant distress and, occasionally, serious injury or death.

Macaque females produce an infant every year, or every other year. In this species, infant abuse is most frequent in the first month postpartum and typically terminates after the end of third month of infant life (Maestripieri, 1998; McCormack, Sanchez, Bardi, & Maestripieri, 2006) (see Figure 9.1). Abusive parenting is a stable maternal characteristic, in that abusive mothers typically abuse all of their infants with very similar patterns and rates (Maestripieri, 1999). Abusive mothers that are induced to adopt unrelated infants shortly after giving birth abuse their adopted infants with patterns and rates very similar to those exhibited with their previous biological offspring (Maestripieri, Megna, & Jovanovic, 2000), suggesting that the infant's contributions to the occurrence of abuse are minimal.

Data spanning 5–7 generations have indicated that infant abuse runs in families, being frequent in some matrilines and absent in others (Maestripieri et al., 1997a, 1997b; Maestripieri & Carroll, 1998b). Moreover, within the families in which it occurs, closely related females such as mothers, daughters, or sisters are especially likely to abuse their offspring, suggesting that abusive parenting may be transmitted across generations along the maternal line. This was recently confirmed by a prospective longitudinal study showing that approximately half of the rhesus macaque females who were abused by their mothers in infancy exhibited abusive behavior toward their first-born offspring (Maestripieri, 2005). Data from cross-fostered females indicated that early experience plays an important role in the intergenerational transmission of abuse (Maestripieri, 2005).

In humans, child physical abuse frequently co-occurs with neglect, and neglect has been shown to have consequences for development as detrimental as physical abuse (Cicchetti, 1998; Glaser 2000; 2002). Obtaining an operational definition of neglect in nonhuman primates has proved difficult. Like humans, non-human primate mothers exhibit a broad spectrum of caregiving styles toward their infants. Some mothers spend relatively little time in ventro-ventral contact with their infants, frequently reject their infants' attempts to make nipple contact and nurse, and show low levels of vigilance and protective behaviors. Labeling these behaviors neglectful, however, is controversial because in some cases, "rejecting" or "laissez-faire" parenting styles have been shown to encourage infant independence, and therefore have beneficial consequences for both mothers and infants (Fairbanks, 1996). However, maternal involvement in caregiving varies along a continuum and it is difficult to identify when rejectfulness and uninvolvement cease to be beneficial and become harmful to the infant (Fairbanks, 1996; Fairbanks & McGuire, 1995).

An extreme and more straightforward example of maternal neglect in primates involves the complete abandonment of the infant by the mother, typically shortly after birth. In macaques, infant abandonment is exhibited almost exclusively by primiparous mothers (Maestripieri et al., 1997a; Maestripieri & Carroll, 1998b; Schino & Troisi, 2005). In other words, a certain percentage (between 1%–15%) of first-time mothers are likely to abandon their infants after giving birth, but typically they successfully rear their second-born offspring. Infant abandonment may have some adaptive significance and is clearly a different phenomenon from physical abuse; for example, abusive mothers do not show a higher probability of abandoning their first-born infants than nonabusive mothers (Maestripieri & Carroll, 1998b). Abusive mothers, however, often display higher rates of infant rejection than nonabusive mothers (Maestripieri, 1998; McCormack et al., 2006) (see Figure 9.2). Abusive mothers also begin rejecting their infants shortly after birth, whereas nonabusive mothers tend to show maternal rejection when infants are 3–4 weeks old. Early and intense maternal rejection, a significant correlate of abusive parenting, may be an important driver of developmental and transgenerational effects of infant abuse on behavior; affective responsiveness; and neuroendocrine, neurochemical, and immune function (Maestripieri, Higley, et al., 2006; Maestripieri, McCormack, Higley, Lindell, & Sanchez, 2006; McCormack et al., 2006; Sanchez et al., 2007).

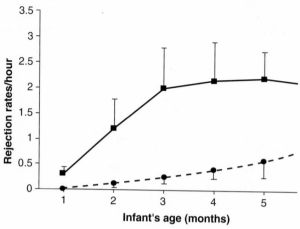

**Figure 9.2.** Average rates of rejections per hour, received by the infants. Abused infants received a greater frequency of rejections across the first 6 months of life compared to control infants (F(1,16)=6.96, *p=.02). From McCormack, K., Sanchez, M. M., Bardi, M., & Maestripieri, D. (2006). Maternal care patterns and behavioral development of rhesus macaque abused infants in the first six months. *Developmental Psychobiology, 48,* 537–550. Copyright 2006 by Wiley Periodicals, Inc., A Wiley Company. Reprinted with permission of John Wiley & Sons, Inc.

From a behavioral standpoint, developmental outcomes of infant maltreatment in nonhuman primates compare with those in maltreated children. For example, maltreated rhesus macaque infants exhibit delayed social development, frequent behavioral signs of distress, heightened anxiety and fearfulness, and impulsive aggression (Maestripieri & Carroll, 1998c; McCormack et al., 2006; Grand, McCormack, Maestripieri, & Sanchez, 2005). Similar social, affective, and emotional deficits have been observed in maltreated human children (Cicchetti, 1998; Crittenden & Ainsworth, 1997). Until recently little was known about the physiological and neural substrates of these behavioral alterations, but significant progress has been made lately in the study of the neuroendocrine, neurochemical, and neuroanatomical consequences of maltreatment in human and nonhuman primates.

## PHYSIOLOGICAL CONSEQUENCES OF INFANT ABUSE IN RHESUS MACAQUES

### Effects on Stress Neuroendocrine Systems

Studies of rodents, monkeys, and humans show compelling evidence that the hypothalamic-pituitary-adrenal (HPA) axis is particularly vulnerable to the effects of adverse early experience, including disruption of the mother-infant bond and exposure to poor parenting (Sanchez, Ladd, & Plotsky, 2001). However, the developmental time course of experience-induced neuroendocrine alterations leading to pathophysiology in adulthood is not fully understood.

The HPA axis mediates neuroendocrine responses to stress, triggering the release of glucocorticoids (GCs) from the adrenal cortex (see Figure 9.3). These highly catabolic steroid hormones affect multiple bodily functions, including energy mobilization, immune and reproductive functions, behavior, and cognition. Altered cortisol secretion (either higher or lower than normal) has been associated with psychiatric and somatic illnesses, including depression, posttraumatic stress disorder (PTSD), fibromyalgia, hypertension, immunosuppression, and sexual dysfunction, among others. Superimposed upon its circadian pattern of activity, stress activates stressor-specific pathways that converge in the hypothalamus, where the stressor-specific information is integrated in the paraventricular nucleus (PVN) by parvocellular neurons expressing corticotropin releasing-factor (CRF). CRF is released from nerve endings in the median eminence in response to metabolic, psychological, or physical threats and stimulates the release of adrenocorticotrophic hormone (ACTH) from the anterior pituitary. ACTH, in turn, stimulates the release of GCs (mainly cortisol in primates) from the adrenal cortex.

Research by our group has shown that the effects of infant maltreatment on HPA axis function are similar to those following exposure to other stressful and traumatic events. Abused infants showed elevated cortisol levels in their first month of life, the period of most intense physical abuse by the mother, and low cortisol levels in subsequent months, particularly in the early a.m. hours (McCormack et al., 2003). A similar effect has been reported in institutionalized children and children in foster care (see Gunnar & Vazquez, 2006). Pharmacological studies to analyze pituitary and adrenal function in abused and nonabused subjects revealed blunted ACTH responses to CRF administration later in life (Sanchez et al., unpublished data). These findings suggest a downregulation of CRF receptors in the pituitary and are consistent with the effects of harsh parenting reported in another nonhuman primate, the common marmoset (*C. jacchus*) (Johnson et al., 1996); they also correlate with neuroendocrine alterations detected in girls with a history of childhood abuse (De Bellis et al., 1994). This downregulation of pituitary CRF receptors may be the result of central CRF hyperactivity due to sustained emotional and/or physical stress in infancy.

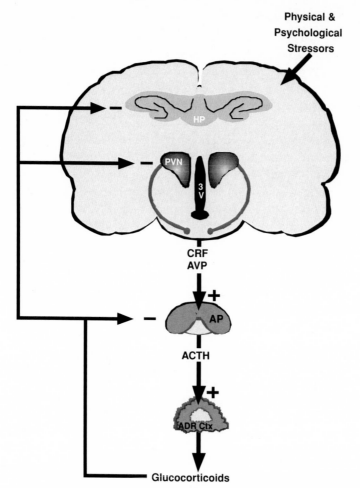

**Figure 9.3.** Schematic illustrating the hypothalamic-pituitary-adrenal (HPA) axis. Stressful stimuli of different kinds (systemic, psychogenic) are encoded within different regions in the CNS and funneled to the hypothalamic paraventricular nucleus (PVN), adjacent to the third ventricle (3V), where they stimulate the secretion of corticotropin-releasing factor (CRF) and vasopressin (AVP) from nerve terminals in the median eminence into the hypophyseal-portal vascular system. These neuropeptides are carried to the anterior pituitary (AP), where they stimulate the secretion of ACTH from corticotropes into the systemic circulation. ACTH, in turn, stimulates the de novo synthesis and secretion of glucocorticoids (corticosterone in the rat, cortisol in primates) from the adrenal cortex (ADR Ctx) into the systemic circulation. These circulating glucocorticoids complete a negative feedback loop to shut off the current HPA axis activity and modulate HPA axis activation through their actions at cytoplasmic glucocorticoid receptors (GR) distributed at different levels of the axis. HP: hippocampus. From Sanchez, M. M., Ladd, C. O., & Plotsky, P. M. (2001). Early adverse experience as a developmental risk factor for later psychopathology: Evidence from rodent and primate models. *Development and Psychopathology, 13,* 419–449. Copyright 2001 by Cambridge University Press. Reprinted with permission.

## Effects on Brain Serotonergic Function

Brain serotonergic systems are involved in controlling many physiological, affective, and behavioral functions such as sleep, emotionality, aggression, and locomotor activity; children and adolescents with histories of childhood maltreatment exhibit dysregulation in these core functions. Reduced serotonergic function has been reported in maltreated children (Kaufman et al., 1998). Alterations in brain serotonin (5-HT) neurotransmission contribute to different forms of adult psychopathology, including anxiety and mood disorders (Krystal, D'Souza, Sanacora, Goddard, & Charney, 2001; Manji, Drevets, & Charney, 2001) and some pathophysiological states associated with those disorders, such as HPA axis dysregulation.

Previous studies of monkeys have demonstrated that early adverse experiences (e.g., maternal deprivation and peer-rearing) affect brain serotonergic function, as reflected by lower CSF levels of the 5-HT metabolite 5-hydroxyindoleacetic acid (5-HIAA) in deprived infants relative to controls (e.g., Higley, Suomi, & Linnoila 1996). Similarly, our studies have demonstrated that infants who experienced more stressful interactions with their mothers early in life exhibited reduced CSF levels of 5-HT and 5-HIAA in subsequent years. Developmental alterations in brain serotonergic function, however, were associated with exposure to high rates of maternal rejection, which co-occur with abusive parenting, rather than with physical abuse in itself (Maestripieri, McCormack, et al., 2006; Sanchez et al., 2007). Data from cross-fostered females indicate that the association between high rates of maternal rejection and low CSF levels of 5-HIAA in offspring reflected the effects of early experience rather than underlying genetic similarities between mothers and daughters (Maestripieri, Higley, et al., 2006).

Individual differences in CSF concentrations of 5-HIAA were highly stable across the first 3 years of life and were associated with anxious behavior (Maestripieri, Higley, et al., 2006; Maestripieri, McCormack, et al., 2006). Moreover, long-term alterations in brain serotonergic function induced by maternal rejection appeared to affect the expression of maternal behavior when female offspring reached adulthood. Cross-fostered females exhibited rates of maternal rejection similar to those of their foster mothers, as well as correlations between CSF 5-HIAA levels and maternal rejection, such that adult offspring with low CSF 5-HIAA exhibited higher rejection rates than adult offspring with high CSF 5-HIAA (Maestripieri, Lindell, & Higley, 2007). Abusive parenting was also transmitted across generations through experiential mechanisms. Approximately half of the cross-fostered and non-cross-fostered females reared by abusive mothers exhibited abusive behavior toward their first-born offspring, but none of the females reared by nonabusive mothers did (Maestripieri, 2005). Moreover, the abused females who became abusive mothers had lower CSF levels of 5-HIAA than the abused females who did not become abusive (Maestripieri, Higley, et al., 2006), suggesting that low serotonergic function induced by high maternal rejection may contribute to the transmission of abusive parenting from mothers to daughters. These findings underscore the importance of early maternal care in determining adaptive behavioral and neurobiological development in primates. They also elucidate possible neurobiological mechanisms underlying the development of psychopathologies and their transmission across generations.

### Effects on Immune Function

In addition to the activation of the HPA axis, stress is associated with innate immune responses, including the release of proinflammatory cytokines and activation of proinflammatory cytokine signaling cascades (Raison, Capuron, & Miller, 2006). Interestingly, cytokine release can affect serotonergic function; recent data indicate that activation of the p38 mitogen-activated protein kinase (MAPK) signaling cascade by cytokines – including interleukin (IL)-1 and tumor necrosis factor (TNF)-alpha – increases the expression and activity of the serotonin transporter (SERT) in the brain (Zhu, Carneriro, Dostmann, Hewlett, & Blakely, 2005). This increase triggers an increase in 5-HT reuptake, resulting in reduced levels of 5-HT available at the synapse.

Given the interactions between stress, proinflammatory cytokines, and brain 5-HT systems, we examined the relationship between activation (phosphorylation) of p38 MAPK in peripheral blood monocytes and central 5-HT function in juvenile rhesus monkeys that had experienced infant maltreatment (Sanchez et al., 2007). Our data showed activation of inflammatory signaling pathways in the maltreated individuals (as reflected by increased % of monocytes staining positive for p-p38). In addition, this activation was associated with levels of maternal rejection early in life, as well as with CSF concentrations of 5-HIAA: specifically, the higher the maternal rejection, the higher the inflammatory markers, and the higher the inflammatory markers, the lower the CSF 5-HIAA.

These data provide the first evidence in a maltreated infant animal model of an *in vivo* relationship between activation of p38 MAPK signaling pathways in monocytes and reduced brain serotonin function. We would expect that increasing SERT expression and/or activity and activating p-38 pathways would decrease synaptic availability of serotonin and reduce serotonin metabolites, just as was found in our study. Of note, proinflammatory cytokines, including IL-1 and TNF-alpha, are also capable of influencing the activity of the enzyme indolamine 2,3 dioxygenase, which metabolizes tryptophan (TRP) to kynurenine and quinolinic acid, thereby shunting TRP from the synthesis of serotonin (Raison et al., 2006). Thus, in addition to directly influencing the expression of the SERT, proinflammatory cytokines may influence serotonin metabolism by altering the availability of TRP, the primary precursor of serotonin. Taken together, these data suggest that increased activity in p-38 MAPK pathways resulting from infant maltreatment may represent a novel mechanism by which early life stress is translated into risk for psychopathology and illness. Moreover, p38 pathways may serve as a unique target for reversing the impact of early life stress on relevant pathophysiologic endpoints, including depression and anxiety.

## CONCLUDING REMARKS

Naturally occurring infant abuse in large populations of nonhuman primates is similar in several respects to human child maltreatment, including the prevalence of the phenomenon in the population and its transmission across generations. Although abusive parenting in monkeys and humans clearly involves different patterns of behavior, the two phenomena may have similar determinants and similar developmental outcomes. Research with this animal model of child maltreatment can provide unique opportunities to investigate the contribution of genetic and environmental factors to pathological parenting, to characterize the developmental time course of biobehavioral and neurobiological alterations induced by infant abuse and neglect, and to test the effectiveness of intervention and treatment strategies.

Given the evidence of a possible role of brain serotonergic systems in intergenerational transmission of rejection and abuse behaviors in rhesus macaques, we recently began investigating complex gene by environment interactions: the relation between polymorphisms in the serotonin transporter gene, neuroendocrine alterations in monkey infants reared by rejecting and abusive mothers, and the manifestation of abusive parenting in adulthood. Preliminary results suggest that such interactions may play a role in both the expression of abusive parenting and its transmission across generations (McCormack, Newman, Higley, Maestripieri, & Sanchez, 2009). Genotype also appears to modulate the effects of early stressful experience on development of emotional behavior, the HPA axis and other stress-sensitive physiological systems.

In addition to expanding the investigation of experiential and genetic aspects of infant abuse in primates, more research is needed on the possible long-term effects of maltreatment on the anatomy and function of particular areas of the brain, especially those areas involved in affect regulation and cognition such as the amygdala, hippocampus, and prefrontal cortex. These studies can be conducted with brain-imaging techniques already used in human research, and also with *post-mortem* brain studies that would be difficult in humans.

Elucidating the environmental and biological mechanisms underlying infant abuse in nonhuman primate populations can help us identify at-risk individuals in the human population, and develop strategies for intervention. Some strategies may involve environmental modification, whereas others can be aimed at reversing or reducing abuse-associated neu-roendocrine and neurochemical alterations, using pharmacological tools. Although nonhuman primate research can be difficult because of costs, logistical constraints, and ethical considerations, these animals provide excellent models for our study of developmental human psychopathology. Therefore, primate research is an important component of the compara-tive, interdisciplinary, and integrative approach necessary to understand the complexities of human development and its pathologies.

REFERENCES

Brent, L., Koban, T., & Ramirez, S. (2002). Abnormal, abusive and stress-related behaviors in baboon mothers. *Biological Psychiatry, 52*, 1047–1056.
Cicchetti, D. (1998). Child abuse and neglect – Usefulness of the animal data: Comment on Maestripieri and Carroll (1998). *Psychological Bulletin, 123*, 224–230.
Crittenden, P. M. & Ainsworth, M. D. S. (1997). Child maltreatment and attach-ment theory. In D. Cicchetti & V. Carlson (Eds.), *Child maltreatment: Theory and research on the causes and consequences of child abuse and neglect* (pp. 432–463). Cambridge, UK: Cambridge University Press.
De Bellis, M. D., Chrousos, G. P., Dorn, L. D., Burke, L., Helmers, K., Kling, M. A., et al. (1994). Hypothalamic-pituitary-adrenal axis dysregulation in sex-ually abused girls. *Journal of Clinical Endocrinolgy and Metabolism, 78*, 249–255.
Fairbanks, L. A. (1996). Individual differences in maternal styles: Causes and consequences for mothers and offspring. *Advances in the Study of Behavior, 25*, 579–611.
Fairbanks, L. A., & McGuire, M. T. (1995). Maternal condition and the quality of maternal care in vervet monkeys. *Behavior, 132*, 733–754.
Glaser, D. (2000). Child abuse and neglect and the brain – a review. *Journal of Child Psychology & Psychiatry & Allied Disciplines, 41*, 97–116.
Glaser, D. (2002). Emotional abuse and neglect (psychological maltreatment): A conceptual framework. *Child Abuse & Neglect, 26*, 697–714.

Grand, A., McCormack, K. M., Maestripieri, D., & Sanchez, M. M. (2005, November). Effects of infant maltreatment on emotional and HPA axis reactivity in juvenile rhesus macaques. Annual Meeting of the Society for Neuroscience, Washington, DC.

Gunnar, M. R. & Vazquez, D. M. (2006). Stress neurobiology and developmental psychopathology. In D. Cicchetti & D. Cohen (Eds.), *Developmental Psychopathology: Developmental Neuroscience* (2nd ed., pp. 533–577). New York: Wiley Press.

Higley, J. D., Suomi, S. J., & Linnoila, M. (1996). A nonhuman primate model of type II alcoholism? Part 2. Diminished social competence and excessive aggression correlates with low cerebrospinal fluid 5-hydroxyindoleacetic acid concentrations. *Alcoholism: Clinical and Experimental Research, 20,* 643–650.

Johnson, E. O., Kamilaris, T. C., Calogero, A. E., Gold, P. W., & Chrousos, G. P. (1996). Effects of early parenting on growth and development in a small primate. *Pediatric Research, 39,* 999–1005.

Kaufman, J., Birmaher, B., Perel, J., Dahl, R. E., Stull, S., Brent, D. et al. (1998). Serotonergic functioning in depressed abused children: Clinical and familial correlates. *Biological Psychiatry, 44,* 973–981.

Krystal, J. H., D'Souza, D. C., Sanacora, G., Goddard, A. W., & Charney, D. S. (2001). Current perspectives on the pathophysiology of schizophrenia, depression and anxiety disorders. *Medical Clinics of North America, 85,* 559–577.

Maestripieri, D. (1998). Parenting styles of abusive mothers in group-living rhesus macaques. *Animal Behavior, 55,* 1–11.

Maestripieri, D. (1999). The biology of human parenting: Insights from nonhuman primates. *Neuroscience & Biobehavioral Reviews, 23,* 411–422.

Maestripieri, D. (2005). Early experience affects the intergenerational transmission of infant abuse in rhesus monkeys. *Proceedings of the National Academy of Sciences of the United States of America, 102,* 9726–9729.

Maestripieri, D., & Carroll, K. A. (1998a). Child abuse and neglect: usefulness of the animal data. *Psychological Bulletin, 123,* 211–223.

Maestripieri, D. & Carroll, K. A. (1998b). Risk factors for infant abuse and neglect in group-living rhesus monkeys. *Psychological Science, 9,* 143–145.

Maestripieri, D., & Carroll, K. A. (1998c). Behavioral and environmental correlates of infant abuse in group-living pigtail macaques. *Infant Behavior and Development, 21*(4), 603–612.

Maestripieri, D., Higley, J. D., Lindell, J. D., McCormack, K. M., Sanchez, M. M., & Newman, T. K. (2006). Early maternal rejection affects the development of monoaminergic systems and adult abusive parenting in rhesus macaques. *Behavioral Neuroscience, 120*(5), 1017–1024.

Maestripieri, D., McCormack, K. M., Higley, J. D., Lindell, S. G., & Sanchez, M. M. (2006). Influence of parenting style on the offspring's behavior and CSF monoamine metabolites in cross-fostered and noncrossfostered rhesus macaques. *Behavioral Brain Research, 175,* 90–95.

Maestripieri, D., Megna, N. L., & Jovanovic, T. (2000). Adoption and maltreatment of foster infants by rhesus macaque abusive mothers. *Developmental Science, 3,* 287–293.

Maestripieri, D., Wallen, K., & Carroll, K. A. (1997a). Infant abuse runs in families of group-living pigtail macaques. *Child Abuse & Neglect, 21*, 465–471.

Maestripieri, D., K. Wallen, K., & Carroll, K. A. (1997b). Genealogical and demographic influences on infant abuse and neglect in group-living sooty mangabeys (Cercocebus atys). *Developmental Psychobiology, 31*, 175–180.

Maestripieri, D., Lindell, S. G., & Higley, J. D. (2007). Intergenerational transmission of maternal behavior in rhesus macaques and its underlying mechanisms. *Developmental Psychobiology, 49*, 165–171.

Manji, H. K., Drevets, W. C., & Charney, D. S. (2001). The cellular neurobiology of depression. *Nature Medicine, 7*, 541–547.

McCormack, K. M., Grand, A., LaPrairie, J., Fulks, R., Graff, A., Maestripieri, D. et al. (2003). Behavioral and neuroendocrine outcomes of infant maltreatment in rhesus monkeys: The first four months. Program No.641.14.2003 Abstract Viewer/Itinerary Planner.Washington, DC: Society for Neuroscience.

McCormack, K., Sanchez, M. M., Bardi, M., & Maestripieri, D. (2006). Maternal care patterns and behavioral development of rhesus macaque abused infants in the first six months. *Developmental Psychobiology, 48*, 537–550.

McCormack, K., Newman, T. K., Higley, J. D., Maestripieri, D., Sanchez, M. M. (2009). Serotonin transporter gene variation, infant abuse, and responsiveness to stress in rhesus macaque mothers and infants. *Hormones & Behavior, 55*(4), 538–547.

McEwen, B. S. (1998). Protective and damaging effects of stress mediators. *New England Journal of Medicine, 338*, 171–179.

Nadler, R. D. (1980). Child abuse: Evidence from nonhuman primates. *Developmental Psychobiology, 13*(5), 507–512.

Raison, C. L., Capuron, C., & Miller, A. H. (2006). Cytokines sing the blues: Inflammation and the pathogenesis of depression. *Trends in Immunology, 227*, 24–31.

Ruppenthal. G. C., Arling, G. L., Harlow, H. F., Sackett, G. P., & Suomi, S. J. (1976). A 10-year perspective of motherless mother monkey behavior. *Journal of Abnormal Psychology, 85*, 341–349.

Sanchez, M. M. (2006). The impact of early adverse care on HPA axis development: Nonhuman primate models. *Hormones & Behavior, 50*, 623–631.

Sanchez, M. M., Alagbe, O., Felger, J. C., Zhang, J., Graff, A. E., Grand, A. P., et al. (2007). Activated p38 MAPK is associated with decreased CSF 5-HIAA and increased maternal rejection during infancy in rhesus monkeys. *Molecular Psychiatry, 12*(10), 895–897.

Sanchez, M. M., Ladd, C. O., & Plotsky, P. M. (2001). Early adverse experience as a developmental risk factor for later psychopathology: Evidence from rodent and primate models. *Development and Psychopathology, 13*, 419–449.

Schino, G. & Troisi, A. (2005). Neonatal abandonment in Japanese macaques. *American Journal of Physical Anthropology, 126*, 447–452.

Troisi, A. & D'Amato, F. R. (1983). Is monkey maternal abuse of offspring aggressive behavior? *Aggressive Behavior, 9*, 173.

Troisi, A. & D'Amato, F. R. (1984). Ambivalence in monkey mothering: Infant abuse combined with maternal possessiveness. *The Journal of Nervous and Mental Disease, 172*, 105–108.

Troisi, A., D'Amato, F. R., Fuccillo, R., & Scucchi, S. (1982). Infant abuse by a wild-born group-living Japanese macaque mother. *Journal of Abnormal Psychology, 91,* 451–456.

Zhu, C. B., Carneriro, A. M., Dostmann, W. R., Hewlett, W. A., & Blakely, R. D. (2005). p38 MAPK activation elevates serotonin transport activity via a trafficking-independent, protein phosphatase 2A-dependent process. *Journal of Biological Chemistry, 280,* 15649–15658.

# Commentary

## Infant Abuse in Rhesus Macaques as an Example of Early Experience "Getting Under the Skin"

### Ronald G. Barr

**INTRODUCTION**

The case study on infant abuse in rhesus macaques by M. Mar Sánchez, Kai McCormack, and Dario Maestripieri is particularly germane to a work about the effects of early life experiences on later outcomes. As the authors point out, behavioral similarities between nonhuman primate abuse and human abuse are very close, if not identical, given what we know at this time. Furthermore, studying the neuroendocrine, neurochemical, and neuroanatomical consequences in nonhuman primates, although challenging, can be especially helpful.

The work of Sánchez and colleagues has particular resonance and meaning for my field and my research. Three aspects in particular are intriguing points of convergence: (1) the nicely documented multi-system consequences (that is, the hypothalamic-pituitary-adrenal [HPA], serotonergic, and neuroimmune systems) and interactions of abuse and/or rejection, including intergenerational transmission; (2) the dimensional continuum approach to quality of early maternal care seen in natural observations; and (3) the age or developmental specificity of the time course of abuse and rejection. I will discuss each of these further in this commentary.

My connections with this case study intersect both at a general and a specific level. On a general level, my "field" is the very young subspecialty of Developmental and Behavioral Pediatrics. For this field, the influences of early life experiences on later functioning are absolutely central (Barr, 2004). However, in these exciting days of "consilience" among the sciences (Wilson, 1998), this issue is even more general, and transcends many disciplinary boundaries. As but one example, the Canadian Institute for

238

Advanced Research (CIFAR) supports an international, interdisciplinary network called the Experience-based Brain and Biological Development (EBBD) program that I direct. Its focal question is: "How do differential social experiences 'get under the skin' to affect early human development and inform health, learning, and behavior throughout life?" The work in this ethological case study is right on target for that question.

On a specific level, my research examines how the caregiver–infant dyad (as opposed to the infant itself) allows the infant to "get a good start in life," through dyadic influences on three important early challenges: regulation of infant behavioral state (in particular, crying); regulation of infant pain-stress experiences (in particular, minor medical procedures like immunizations); and memory for spoken words (in particular, feeding effects on memory). It turns out that the first of these challenges (managing early infant crying) is directly relevant to abuse, because normal, early increased crying is the principal stimulus for shaken baby syndrome, a particularly damaging form of infant maltreatment, and probably of maltreatment generally. I will expand on this challenge further on.

As Keating and Hertzman argued in *Developmental Health and the Wealth of Nations* (1999), differential early caregiving effects become "embedded" in human biology, and result in later life trajectory differences not only in regard to health, but also in regard to virtually all learning and behavioral outcomes. It seems likely that, because of the complicated interacting net of pathways that are developing, differential early caregiving (reflected in this case by maternal rejection and/or abuse) will have far reaching effects in many domains (health, learning, and behavior), and be mediated by effects in many systems (HPA axis, serotonergic, and immune, among others).

## MULTI-SYSTEM CONSEQUENCES AND INTERACTIONS OF ABUSE AND/OR REJECTION

As Sánchez and colleagues argue, one advantage to studying nonhuman primate models is the ability to elucidate the time course of biobehavioral alterations that are the developmental consequences of maltreatment. In the third section of their chapter, they demonstrate that early maltreatment and/or rejection in rhesus macaques affects three systems: (1) the stress-sensitive hypothalamic-pituitary-adrenal (HPA) axis by elevating cortisol levels in the first month during physical abuse and lowering it in subsequent months, especially by "flattening" the early morning peak; this flattening likely results from central downregulation of corticotropin-releasing factor (CRF) receptors; (2) cerebral spinal fluid (CSF) levels of serotonin and its metabolites, producing stable early life individual differences and the subsequent rejection of offspring by the now-adult females, who maintained lowered serotonin indicators in their CSF; and (3) activation of inflammatory signaling pathways (particularly p38 mitogen activated protein kinase [MAPK]). The MAPK signaling cascade increases the expression and activity of the serotonin transporter (SERT), thereby reducing CSF serotonin metabolites directly; also, via proinflammatory cytokines, it reduces serotonin synthesis by shunting tryptophan metabolism away from serotonin synthesis. Of these three "systems" that are affected, at least two of them interact.

Why is this important? As Sánchez and colleagues argue, the increased activity in p-38 MAPK pathways may represent a novel mechanism for translating early life stress into psychopathology and illness, as well as a possible target for reversing these effects. In addition, however, the authors clearly show that this pathway is one of a "net" of such mechanisms that appear to underlie the early life experience effects on later outcomes. Sánchez and colleagues, CIFAR's EBBD program, Suomi and colleagues in mother- vs. peer-reared infant rhesus macaques, and others are reporting a similar multiplicity of the pathways that are implicated by differences in early caregiving experiences of infants.

## THE DIMENSIONAL CONTINUUM OF THE QUALITY OF EARLY MATERNAL CARE IN NATURAL OBSERVATIONS

When discussing the interesting challenge of making the concept of neglect operational in nonhuman primates, Sánchez and colleagues indicate that there are individual maternal variations in the behaviors of time spent in ventro-ventral contact, rejection of infant attempts at nipple contact, and low levels of vigilance and protective behaviors that are seen in natural observations. However, it is unclear whether any particular amounts of these behaviors should be labeled "neglect," as they may also contribute to appropriate and perhaps beneficial independence. Furthermore, it seems clear that *Protectiveness* (making contact with and restraining infants) clusters differently from *Rejection* (breaking contact and rejecting infant approaches) and that *Rejection* has stronger associations than *Protectiveness* with serotonin, dopamine, and norepinephrine metabolites in the CSF (Maestripieri et al., 2006). The Sánchez case was the first demonstration that naturally occurring variations in maternal behavior in nonhuman primates are associated with differences in neurobiological development of offspring (Maestripieri et al., 2006).

Another interesting development is that not the abuse itself, but *Rejection*, is associated with different levels of metabolites in the offspring (Maestripieri et al., 2006). This observation is important for a couple of reasons. First, it begins to help us understand not just whether early caregiving experiences may be important for the hypothesized "biological embedding" to occur, but which experiences might be involved. We can begin to "parse" the dimensions of early caregiving that might make a difference.

Secondly, this approach reinforces the value of looking at behaviors that occur in a continuum, and that make up part of the behaviors of species in a relatively normal habitat. Meaney and colleagues have taken a similar approach to measuring maternal caregiving of infant rats. They documented a clear bell-shaped curve within a normal range of licking, grooming, and arched-back nursing behaviors by mothers separated from their infants. The researchers compared "high" licking and grooming with "low" licking and grooming and arched-back nursing, and found clear differences in later stress responsivity among these infants as adults; the mechanism can be tracked to epigenetic programming of a glucocorticoid receptor gene promoter in the hippocampus (Weaver et al., 2004). One interesting challenge will be to identify maternal behaviors that are components of the normal range of infant caregiving in humans that might be important for similar biological embedding processes to occur.

Using detailed diary recordings of infant and caregiver behaviors in humans, we have found a remarkable spread in "contact time" (i.e., holding and carrying, including during feeding) in human caregivers and a likewise clear normal-range "bell-shaped" distribution. Following Meaney, we consider "high" and "low" contact time caregivers to be those whose contact time is greater than one standard deviation above and below the mean respectively. The high contact caregivers have greater than 12 hours per day of contact, whereas the low contact caregivers have fewer than 6.25 hours of contact – a difference of almost 6 hours a day (Barr, Kobor, Boyce, & Robinson, 2008).

Determining the effects on infants of variations in normal caregiving is clearly an important question for study in humans. Normal human caregiving has considerable range in some caregiving parameters. However, whether hours of contact or some other caregiving parameter is related to analogous biological embedding processes has yet to be documented. Perhaps it will have no effect (analogous to *Protection* behaviors in the nonhuman primates) or have an important effect (analogous to licking, grooming, and arch-back nursing among rodents). The parameters being documented by Sánchez and colleagues are beginning to point to some likely candidate caregiving behaviors.

## AGE OR DEVELOPMENTAL SPECIFICITY OF THE TIME COURSE OF ABUSE AND REJECTION

Because abusive non-human mothers that adopt infants abuse them in accordance with patterns and rates similar to those previously exhibited with their biological offspring, Sánchez and colleagues understandably suggest that the infant's contributions to abuse incidents are minimal. However, they also describe some interesting *timing* characteristics of infant abuse: (1) it is most frequent in the first month, terminating by the end of the third month; (2) abusive mothers begin rejecting their infants shortly after birth, whereas non-abusive mothers begin rejecting their infants at 3–4 weeks of age; and (3) it may be this early, intense rejection that correlates with abuse and drives the subsequent neurodevelopmental consequences.

In humans, there is increasing evidence that at least the timing of abuse, if not which infants are abused, is related to normal developmental characteristics in humans. This relationship comes from an increasing recognition of a developmentally normal behavioral universal during infancy that is usually referred to as the "normal crying curve" (Barr, 2006).

In the first four months, the overall amount of infant distress per day (fussing, crying, and unsoothable crying) increases, generally peaking during the second month and declining afterward. A number of features of this increased crying add to the parent's frustration: Some of the crying bouts are unsoothable, unpredictable, and unrelated to anything in the environment. They seem to resist any manner of soothing, making caregivers think that the infant is in pain. They are long-lasting (averaging 35–40 minutes per bout), and tend to cluster in the late afternoon and evening hours. Although previously thought to result from some abnormality or illness, this pattern of crying has now been recognized as a "behavioral universal of infancy," occurring in all samples of human infants, even though overall amounts of crying vary significantly from infant to infant. For years, anecdotal accounts of physical abuse and shaken baby syndrome have described this unexpected and frustrating infant crying as a trigger. More recently, indirect but convergent evidence of the time courses of abuse, neglect, and shaken baby syndrome has strengthened the apparent relationships among these phenomena.

In a seminal article, Phyllis Agran and her colleagues looked at age-specific indices of a number of infant and childhood injuries using hospital

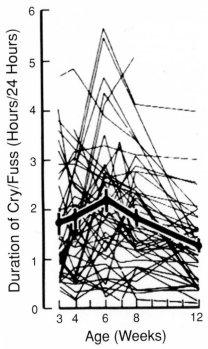

**Figure 9.4.** Cry/fuss duration by week of age of 50 infants, with superimposed mean and SEM values for whole group. Reprinted from Barr, R. G. (1990). The normal crying curve: What do we really know? *Developmental Medicine and Child Neurology, 32*(4), 356–362, with permission from Wiley-Blackwell.

discharge data from California hospitals (Agran et al., 2003). For the "cause of injury" codes of Assault and Neglect, the rate of hospitalization was highest in first three months, next highest between 3–5 months, and declined significantly thereafter. In two other studies, we used a similar strategy, but reduced the age range to 4-week brackets, and looked at the age-specific pattern of shaken baby syndrome cases. In the first study using the same California database (Barr, Trent, & Cross, 2006), the incidence of SBS cases began to increase at about 2 weeks, peaked at 10–13 weeks, and subsequently declined. In a second study using the Victim Database from the National Center for Shaken Baby Syndrome (Lee, Barr, Catherine, & Wicks, 2007), a virtually identical age-specific pattern was found.

In addition, however, the subgroup of infants in whom crying was identified as a trigger had the same peak pattern, making the relationship between the frustrating characteristics of infant crying and shaken baby syndrome more direct. The discrepancy between the usual peak age of

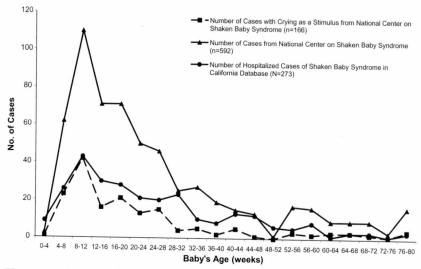

**Figure 9.5.** Age-specific number of reported cases of shaken baby syndrome from the National Center on Shaken Baby Syndrome (NCSBS) and California Hospitals (CH). Data from NCSBS reprinted from Lee, C., Barr, R. G., Catherine, N., & Wicks, A. (2007). Age-related incidence curve of publicly reported shaken baby syndrome cases: Is crying a trigger for shaking? *Journal of Developmental & Behavioral Pediatrics 28*(4), 288–293, with permission from Wolters Kluwer Health. Data from CH reprinted from Barr, R. G., Trent, R. B., & Cross, J. (2006). Age-related incidence curve of hospitalized shaken baby syndrome cases: Convergent evidence for crying as a trigger to shaking. *Child Abuse & Neglect, 30*(1), 7–16, with permission from Elsevier.

crying (about 6 weeks) and abuse, neglect, or shaken baby syndrome (10–13 weeks) is probably due to the recurrent nature of abuse and the well-documented missed diagnosis on first presentation (Barr et al., 2006; Lee et al., 2007).

Interestingly, in our investigations of early distress characteristics in other mammalian species, we reported preliminarily a distress peak in free-living rhesus macaque infants using focal subject behavioral observations (Barr, Warfield, & Catherine, 2005). The peak pattern is a bit more attenuated, with the peak distress vocalizations occurring between 13 and 24 weeks of age. However, it has the same individual variability seen in human infants. Bard has reported a similar distress curve in captive infant chimpanzees, but with a peak at 2 months (Bard, 2000). However, in neither rhesus nor chimpanzee infants have prolonged crying bouts been documented. From the description of Sánchez and colleagues, it does not appear that infant crying shares the same role as a stimulus for abuse or rejection, since the peak pattern in rhesus infants appears to occur after the abuse has stopped at 3 months, and rates of *Rejection* behaviors appear to remain stable through at least 6 months (Maestripieri et al., 2006). So, although distress behavior is a strong compelling trigger for abuse and shaking in human infants, it may not have the same role in nonhuman primate abuse.

## CONCLUDING REMARKS

As might be expected when species are compared, in some respects findings can be generalized and in other respects, they cannot. With regard to the points of convergence I have focused on the following: (1) the neurobiological consequences of abuse and/or rejection appear to be a specific case of pathways and mechanisms that are also being documented in early human experiences; (2) the dimensional approach to describing normal caregiver parameters is proving productive in animal models, may provide an important and specific caregiving dimension (*Rejection*), and may contribute to understanding early caregiving effects in humans; and (3) current information suggests that, despite some parallels in developmental patterning and timing of distress vocalizations, infant behaviors play a slight role in stimulating abuse in infant rhesus macaques, but a more significant role in leading to abuse and shaken baby syndrome in human infants.

Interestingly, just at the point of *divergence* between the nonhuman primate and human abuse story, a window of opportunity may occur for introducing a prevention program to reduce abuse and shaken baby syndrome in humans. Currently, the awareness of the dangers of shaking an infant is quite high, but this awareness has not appeared to reduce the incidence of this tragic outcome. In fact, as an acceptable behavior for discipline and/or soothing, shaking is endorsed by 2.6% of Carolinians in the United States, about 5 % of the Dutch in Holland, and by 20%–50% of people in a number of other countries around the world (Runyan, 2008). Awareness that the properties of crying in human infants that are frustrating to mothers are a manifestation of *normal* behavioral development is much less widely known. Because of the close connection in humans between abuse and shaking and infant crying, the National Center on Shaken Baby Syndrome (NCSBS) has developed a program called the *Period of PURPLE Crying*, which is designed to be attractive to, and to educate, all parents of newborn infants about the normality of the frustrating properties of early crying (Barr, 2006). Its aim – to bring about a sustained reduction in abuse and shaken baby syndrome cases by effecting a societal change in our understanding of normative early increased crying – is a tall challenge for public policy, public health, and societal education, but one that is in the process of being addressed.

REFERENCES

Agran, P. F., Anderson, C., Winn, D., Trent, R., Walton-Haynes, L., & Thayer, S. (2003). Rates of pediatric injuries by 3-month intervals for children 0 to 3 years of age. *Pediatrics, 111*(6), e683–e692.

Bard, K. A. (2000). Crying in infant primates: insights into the development of crying in chimpanzees. In R. G. Barr, B. Hopkins, & J. A. Green (Eds.), *Crying as a sign, a symptom, and a signal: Clinical, emotional and developmental aspects of infant and toddler crying* (pp. 157–175). London: Mac Keith Press.

Barr, R. G. (1990). The normal crying curve: What do we really know? *Developmental Medicine and Child Neurology, 32*(4), 356–362.

Barr, R. G. (2004). From infant crying to political action: What is the basic science of developmental-behavioral pediatrics? *Journal of Developmental and Behavioral Pediatrics, 25*(2), 123–130.

Barr, R. G. (2006). Crying behavior and its importance for psychosocial development in children. In R. E. Tremblay, R. D. Peters, M. Boivin, & R. G. Barr (Eds.), *Encyclopedia on early childhood development* [Internet] (pp. 1–10). Montreal: Centre of Excellence for Early Childhood Development. Retrieved from http://www.child-encyclopedia.com/en-ca/home.html

Barr, R. G., Kobor, M., Boyce, W. T., & Robinson, W. (2008). Hours of contact in a sample of mothers and infants during the fifth week of life. Unpublished raw data.

Barr, R. G., Trent, R. B., & Cross, J. (2006). Age-related incidence curve of hospitalized shaken baby syndrome cases: convergent evidence for crying as a trigger to shaking. *Child Abuse & Neglect, 30*(1), 7–16.

Barr, R. G., Warfield, J. J., & Catherine, N. L. A. (2005). Is there an 'early distress peak' in free ranging rhesus macaque monkeys? Poster presented at the Society for Research in Child Development, Atlanta, GA.

Keating, D. P., & Hertzman, C. (1999). *Developmental health and the wealth of nations: Social, biological, and educational dynamics*. New York: Guilford Press.

Lee, C., Barr, R. G., Catherine, N., & Wicks, A. (2007). Age-related incidence curve of publicly reported shaken baby syndrome cases: Is crying a trigger for shaking? *Journal of Developmental & Behavioral Pediatrics 28*(4), 288–293.

Maestripieri, D., Higley, J. D., Lindell, S. G., McCormack, K., Sanchez, M. M., & Newman, T. K. (2006). Early maternal rejection affects the development of monoaminergic systems and adult abusive parenting in rhesus macaques. *Behavioral Neuroscience, 120*(5), 1017–1024.

Runyan, D. K. (2008). The challenges of assessing the incidence of inflicted traumatic brain injury: A world perspective. *American Journal of Preventive Medicine*, 34(4), S112–S115.

Weaver, I. C. G., Cervoni, N., Champagne, F. A., D'Alessio, A. C., Sharma, S., Seckl, J. R., et al. (2004). Epigenetic programming by maternal behavior. *Nature Neuroscience*, 7(8), 847–854.

Wilson, E. O. (1998). *Consilience: The unity of knowledge*. New York: Knopf.

# Commentary on
## *"Infant Abuse in Rhesus Macaques"*

### Dante Cicchetti

Developmental psychopathology is an integrative scientific discipline that strives to unify contributions from multiple fields of inquiry with the goal of understanding the mutual interplay between the study of normative adaptation and mental illness (Cicchetti, 2006). Whereas traditional viewpoints portray maladaptation and mental disorder as inherent to the individual, the developmental psychopathology framework places them in the dynamic relation between the individual and his/her internal and external contexts. An examination of the historical roots of the discipline of developmental psychopathology reveals that ethology and experimental and physiological psychology, three fields where scientists predominantly conduct their research with a variety of animal species, including monkeys, were seminal in its evolution into a mature science (Cicchetti, 1990). The influence of diverse disciplines on the field of developmental psychopathology illustrates the manner in which advances in our knowledge of the operation of developmental processes within particular scientific domains mutually inform each other. As such, the ethological case study on infant abuse in rhesus macaques, co-authored by M. Mar Sánchez, Kai McCormack, and Dario Maestripieri, addresses a highly significant topic in developmental psychopathology. Through their research on infant abuse, a naturally occurring problem in nonhuman primates, the authors make important contributions to understanding the etiology and developmental sequelae of human child maltreatment.

The notion of an average expectable environment for promoting development proposes that there are species-specific ranges of environmental conditions that elicit normative developmental processes. Human and nonhuman primates develop within a "normal range" when presented with such an average expectable environment (Dobzhansky, 1972). For human and non-human infants, the expectable environment includes protective, nurturant caregivers and a larger social group to which the child will be socialized. When environments fall outside the expectable range, normal development is impeded and often goes awry.

## THE IMPACT OF MALTREATMENT ON DEVELOPING BIOLOGICAL AND PSYCHOLOGICAL SYSTEMS

Child maltreatment is a pathogenic relational experience that represents one of the most adverse and stressful challenges that confront children. Through the examination of child abuse and neglect, we can begin to identify the range of conditions that encompass the average-expectable environment and to discern how serious deviations from this range may affect biological, behavioral, and psychological development. Without adequate environmental supports, the probabilistic path of individual development for maltreated children is characterized by an increased risk for unsuccessful resolution of the stage salient issues of development, as well as for alterations of functioning across a number of biological systems and a heightened risk for the emergence of psychopathology and mental disorders across the life course. Specifically, maltreated children are likely to exhibit atypicalities in neurobiological processes, physiological responsiveness, emotion regulation, attachment relationships, self-development, and peer relationships, resulting in a profile of relatively enduring vulnerability factors that increase the probability of the future development of maladaptation and psychopathology (Cicchetti & Valentino, 2006). Because the vast majority of children are adversely affected by their maltreatment experiences, child abuse and neglect may exemplify the greatest failure of the caregiving environment to provide opportunities for normal biological and psychological development.

The scientific investigations reviewed and conducted by Sánchez et al. reveal that the developmental outcomes of infant monkeys who are abused and neglected are comparable to those of human infants who have been maltreated. Most of the extant knowledge about the causes, correlates, pathways, and consequences of child maltreatment has been gleaned from studies that focused on relatively narrow domains of variables. It has become increasingly critical for scientists striving to obtain a process-level understanding of the developmental sequelae of child maltreatment to implement research designs that assess multiple domains of variables at multiple-levels-of-analysis. The interdisciplinary research characteristic of investigations of non-human primates can make important contributions to the development of the integrative multi-domain and multi-system knowledge necessary to comprehend the complexities inherent to the study of human child abuse and neglect.

Adverse life stresses, exemplified by the experience of child abuse and neglect, affect neurobiological and psychological processes. Physiological and behavioral responses to maltreatment are interrelated and contribute to children's making choices and responding to experiences in ways that generally produce pathological development. Numerous interconnected neurobiological systems are affected by the various stressors associated with child maltreatment. Moreover, each of these neurobiological systems influences and is influenced by multiple domains of biological and psychological development. Research with nonhuman primates has revealed that social experiences, such as abuse and neglect, affect gene expression as well as aspects of brain structure and function (Sanchez, Ladd, & Plotsky, 2001). It is likely that child maltreatment affects the expression of genes that impact brain structure and function as well as basic regulatory processes.

Until the past several decades, there was a paucity of information on how the experience of child maltreatment affected physiological, neurobiological, and neurochemical processes in both human and non-human primates (Cicchetti & Valentino, 2006). Consistent with the recent calls for multiple-levels approaches in the field of developmental psychopathology (Cicchetti & Curtis, 2007), Sánchez et al. investigated several genetic, physiological, and biochemical systems that provide potential insights into putative mechanisms undergirding the links between child maltreatment and developmental outcomes.

Investigations of hypothalamic-pituitary-adrenal (HPA) axis functioning in abused monkey infants revealed elevated levels of cortisol during the first month of life, the developmental period during which infant monkeys are most likely to receive the harshest treatment from their mothers. Over time, these abused infants displayed low levels of cortisol, especially during the early morning. These cortisol findings with infant monkeys experiencing abuse are congruent with studies conducted with human infants reared in institutions, maltreated youngsters in foster care, and abused/neglected children residing in their natural homes (Cicchetti & Valentino, 2006). Similarly, the administration of corticotropin-releasing-factor (CRF) challenge tests to abused infant monkeys was associated with blunted adrenocorticotropic hormone (ACTH) later in life; these results, suggestive of downregulation of CRF receptors in the pituitary, are consistent with neuroendocrine alterations in girls who have been sexually abused. Furthermore, because sexual abuse in humans is often accompanied by additional co-morbid subtypes of maltreatment, it is conceivable that chronic co-occurring emotional, physical, and sexual abuse may also contribute significantly to these multiply abused children's constructing their worlds as marked by fear and a hypersensitivity to future maltreatment.

Sánchez et al. also reported the results of several investigations that demonstrate how early adverse and stressful experiences, such as maternal rejection and harsh parenting, exert deleterious effects on the functioning of the serotonergic system. Furthermore, the authors suggest that the low serotonergic functioning in infant monkeys who experience high maternal rejection may be a risk factor for these monkeys abusing and neglecting their offspring. The impairments in serotonergic functioning, as well as the increased probability that the experience of prior abuse exerts on maltreating one's own offspring, converge with findings in the human child maltreatment literature.

## A MULTI-LEVEL PERSPECTIVE ON RESILIENCE

In addition to research documenting the deleterious impact that child abuse and neglect exert on human and non-human primates, there is multifinality in developmental processes such that the manner in which the individual responds to and interacts with vulnerability and protective factors, both within and outside the developing organism, allows for a diversity of outcomes. Just as deviations from the average expectable environment potentiate some individuals toward the development of maladaptation and psychopathology, others evidence adaptation in the face of the same challenges. Although maltreatment represents an adverse and stressful experience, not all maltreated children demonstrate maladaptive outcomes.

Indeed, some abused and neglected youngsters function in a competent fashion despite the pernicious experiences they have encountered. Consequently, the investigation of pathways to resilience among children who have been maltreated seeks to uncover the dynamic processes, both extra- and intra-organismic, that eventuate in multiplicity in developmental outcomes (Cicchetti & Curtis, 2007).

Resilience has been conceptualized as the individual's capacity for adapting successfully and functioning competently, despite experiencing chronic stress or adversity following exposure to prolonged or severe trauma (Cicchetti, 2006). Discovering the processes underlying the development of psychopathology and resilience offers considerable promise for translating these findings to prevention, intervention, and social policy initiatives.

The empirical study of resilience has focused primarily on detecting its psychosocial determinants. For the field of resilience to grow in ways that are commensurate with the complexity inherent to the construct, efforts to understand underlying processes would be facilitated by the increased implementation of interdisciplinary, multiple-levels-of-analysis research. Investigations from the fields of genetics, psychophysiology, neuroendocrinology, and emotion regulatory processes are just beginning to elucidate how neurobiological and physiological mechanisms might contribute to the development of resilient adaptation in humans (Cicchetti & Curtis, 2007).

In one of the first multi-level investigations of resilience in maltreated and nonmaltreated children, Cicchetti and Rogosch (2007) found that lower morning cortisol was related to higher resilient functioning, but only in nonmaltreated youngsters. In contrast, among physically abused children, who typically exhibit lower morning cortisol, high morning cortisol was related to higher resilient functioning. Moreover, maltreated children who manifested high resilience revealed an atypical rise in dehydroepiandrosterone (DHEA) from morning to afternoon. Additionally, morning and afternoon cortisol/DHEA ratios were positively related to resilient functioning, but did not interact with maltreatment status. The regulation of these two stress-responsive adrenal steroid hormones, as well as the personality constructs of ego resiliency and ego control, maintained independent contributions to predicting resilience among these high-risk youth. These results highlight the contributions that a multi-level approach can make to elucidating resilience.

Advances in molecular genetics also have helped to engender growing interest in the contribution that studies on gene-environment interaction (GxE) can make to unraveling the complex pathways to maladaptation and resilience (Cicchetti, 2007). In GxE, environmental experiences moderate genetic effects (or vice-versa) on psychopathological and resilient outcomes. For example, genetic effects on functioning outcomes may be observed only under certain environmental contexts or in conjunction with different histories of experience; conversely, experience may only relate to outcomes among individuals with specific genetic characteristics. Progress in molecular genetics raises hope of increasing our understanding not only of psychopathology and resilience, but also of developing interventions to prevent and remediate mental disorder and to promote resilience.

In our laboratory, we examined child maltreatment and polymorphisms of the serotonin transporter (5-HTT) and monoamine oxidase A (MAOA) genes in relation to depressive symptomatology. Heightened depressive symptoms were found only among children who had experienced multiple maltreatment subtypes with low MAOA activity. Among comparably maltreated youth with high MAOA activity, self-coping strategies related to lower symptoms. Sexual abuse and the 5-HTT s/s genotype predicted higher depression, anxiety, and somatic symptoms. This GxE interaction was moderated by MAOA activity level. These results highlight the protective functions of genetic polymorphisms and coping strategies in high-risk youth and suggest directions for understanding resilience and its promotion from a multiple-levels-of-analysis perspective (Cicchetti, Rogosch, & Sturge-Apple, 2007).

Current technology does not permit us to comprehend how genetic polymorphisms influence molecular change in human developmental processes. Hence, in the future, it would be opportune if animal and human researchers conducted interdisciplinary multiple-levels-of-analysis collaborations that addressed critical topics in developmental psychology and psychopathology. Parallel animal and human investigations conducted by scientists examining questions of major developmental import have the potential to contribute to the acquisition of a more precise understanding of the mechanisms and pathways to normality, psychopathology, and resilience. Multiple-level research conducted on nonhuman primates who are residing in their naturally occurring contexts also would permit the identification of critical factors that contribute to individual variability in the effects of adverse early experiences. The discovery of the respective roles of genetics, biology, caregiving, and peer relations will enable researchers investigating nonhuman primates to discern the varying developmental pathways to resilience.

## CONCLUSION

Child maltreatment is a complex, insidious problem that cuts across all sectors of society. The economic and human costs of maltreatment in American society are astronomical. It has been estimated that billions of dollars are spent in psychiatric treatment and social services costs and lost in lessened productivity for a generation of maltreated children. The human costs are a litany of biological and psychological tragedies. To improve the health and well-being of maltreated individuals, it is clear that the scientific discoveries of human and non-human primate research on child abuse and neglect must be translated into practical applications. The chasm that now exists between what has been learned through careful research with human and non-human primates and the application of this evidence-based knowledge to intervening with maltreated children and their families must be bridged.

In efforts to minimize the research to practice gap, a randomized clinical trial (RCT) preventive intervention was conducted with maltreated youngsters. This RCT, informed by research on attachment and the determinants of successful parenting, revealed that child-parent psychotherapy and psychoeducational parenting interventions were successful in reducing insecure attachment organization in abused and neglected infants. Maltreated babies randomly assigned to the treatments usually available in the community did not improve their attachment insecurity (Cicchetti, Rogosch, & Toth, 2006).

The results of this RCT are both gratifying and sobering. The fact that insecure attachment is modifiable in extremely dysfunctional mother-infant dyads offers significant hope for thousands of young children and their families. By fostering secure attachment, costlier interventions such as foster care placement, special education services, residential treatment, and incarceration can be averted. Unfortunately, the results of our RCT also highlight the harsh reality of the ineffectiveness of the services currently being provided for many abused and neglected children.

The ultimate goal of science is to benefit from the generation of a knowledge base. Through developing relationships and fostering collaborations between researchers studying maltreatment in human and non-human primates, and through disseminating such information to policy makers, initiatives can be built upon empirical evidence rather than myth. Furthermore, the translation of basic multiple-levels-of-analysis investigations on child maltreatment conducted with human and non-human primates into the development of preventive interventions will be helpful in reducing the burden of mental illness associated with this grave individual and societal ill.

REFERENCES

Cicchetti, D. (1990). A historical perspective on the discipline of developmental psychopathology. In J. Rolf, A. Masten, D. Cicchetti, K. Nuechterlein & S. Weintraub (Eds.), *Risk and protective factors in the development of psychopathology* (pp. 2–28). New York: Cambridge University Press.
Cicchetti, D. (2006). Development and psychopathology. In D. Cicchetti & D. J. Cohen (Eds.), *Developmental psychopathology* (2nd ed.), *Vol. 1: Theory and method* (pp. 1–23). New York: Wiley.
Cicchetti, D. (Ed.). (2007). GxE interactions and developmental psychopathology [Special Issue]. *Development and Psychopathology, 19*(4), 957–1208.

Cicchetti, D., & Curtis, W. J. (Eds.). (2007). A multi-level approach to resilience [Special Issue]. *Development and Psychopathology, 19*(3), 627–955.

Cicchetti, D., & Rogosch, F. A. (2007). Personality, adrenal steroid hormones, and resilience in maltreated children: A Multilevel perspective. *Development and Psychopathology, 19*(3), 787–809.

Cicchetti, D., Rogosch, F. A., & Sturge-Apple, M. L. (2007). Interactions of child maltreatment and 5-HTT and monoamine oxidase A polymorphisms: Depressive symptomatology among adolescents from low-socioeconomic status backgrounds. *Development and Psychopathology, 19*(4), 1161–1180.

Cicchetti, D., Rogosch, F. A., & Toth, S. L. (2006). Fostering secure attachment in infants in maltreating families through preventive interventions. *Development and Psychopathology, 18*(3), 623–650.

Cicchetti, D., & Valentino, K. (2006). An ecological transactional perspective on child maltreatment: Failure of the average expectable environment and its influence upon child development. In D. Cicchetti & D. J. Cohen (Eds.), *Developmental psychopathology (2nd ed.), Vol. 3: Risk, disorder, and adaptation* (pp. 129–201). New York: Wiley.

Dobzhansky, T. (1972). Genetics and the diversity of behavior. *American Psychologist, 27*, 523–530.

Sanchez, M. M., Ladd, C. O., & Plotsky, P. M. (2001). Early adverse experience as a developmental risk factor for later psychopathology: Evidence from rodent and primate models. *Development and Psychopathology, 13*, 419–449.

# TEN

# Clinical Case Study

## Multigenerational Ataques de Nervios *in a Dominican American Family: A Form of Intergenerational Transmission of Violent Trauma?*

Daniel S. Schechter

This case study describes a mother and daughter who participated in a clinical research study of the psychological and communicative processes involved in the intergenerational transmission of violent trauma. The research study is described in greater detail in previous publications (Schechter, Kaminer, Grienenberger, & Amat, 2003; Schechter, 2003). The version of the case presented in this chapter provides additional follow-up through the child's seventh year of life, some of which has been described in previous papers (Schechter et al., 2007; Hatzor, 2005).

Posttraumatic stress disorder (PTSD) and commonly comorbid psychopathology associated with the intergenerational transmission of violent trauma (i.e. dissociative, somatoform, affective, personality, and substance use disorders) are serious public health problems. We know from epidemiologic research that at least one-third of abused children will abuse their children when they become parents themselves. A similar number of male children who witness partner violence will become violent with their partners beginning in adolescence and continuing through adulthood. Abused, violence-exposed, and neglected children show an astonishingly high rate of PTSD and associated comorbid psychopathology – in particular, dissociative phenomena – that have been linked to intergenerational transmission (Oliver, 1993; Widom, 1999; Egeland & Susman-Stillman, 1996).

However, the specific psychological mechanisms by which perpetuation of violence (i.e., hostile stance), repeated victimization (i.e., helpless stance), and psychopathology associated with both (e.g., PTSD, dissociative phenomena) are transmitted remain largely unknown: hence our research study.

The original research study in which the particular mother-daughter pair described below participated involved 41 clinically referred inner-city Latino and African-American mothers who survived interpersonal violent trauma during childhood and adulthood, physical and sexual abuse and assault, and domestic violence. Although psychological processes at play in one case cannot serve as representative for all 41 cases, let alone the larger problem of intergenerational transmission, it is our hope that a detailed understanding of this case will provide a window through which the reader can view the complexity involved in intergenerational transmission of violent trauma and PTSD in a broader sense.

## THE CASE

Nancy was a 29-year-old married Dominican American mother of two girls – Alisa, age 5 years, and Libby, age 8 months – when she brought Libby to the Pediatric Emergency Room (ER) with the complaint that Libby was having multiple, prolonged tonic-clonic seizures following a flu-like illness.

Fluent in English, Nancy described Libby's seizures in vivid detail with understandable terror and uncertainty about what would happen next. Her descriptions convinced the pediatricians and neurologist that her young daughter had developed a form of epilepsy. This was despite the fact that no medical staff had witnessed any seizure activity, the neurological exam was unremarkable, and an EEG had significant motion artifact, making the EEG readings difficult to interpret. The neurologist could not rule out the presence of epileptiform activity.

These data, plus a family history that she and her older daughter Alisa suffered from a seizure disorder and took antiseizure medications, convinced the pediatric neurologist to prescribe the sedative Phenobarbital for the infant.

The medication seemed to help for a few months. But then Nancy and Libby returned to the ER at age 13, then 15, months of age. Nancy said that despite compliance with the regimen, the seizures had increased in frequency and severity. Only after the Phenobarbital dose had been increased and Valium suppositories had been added, did one neurologist recommend an inpatient 24-hour video-monitored EEG.

Libby, who had been born as the healthy product of a full-term, uncomplicated pregnancy and normal delivery, and who had unremarkably unfolding milestones, turned out to show no evidence of a seizure disorder during the continuous EEG monitoring. MRI and CT scans of the brain were unremarkable. The hospital staff described Libby as "alert, awake, and delightful." Her blood–phenobarbital level remained at a nontoxic value. The staff held Libby on the pediatrics ward while her medications were tapered and stopped.

Meanwhile, concerned that Nancy had fictitiously reported seizure activity or taken the sedatives herself, the medical team reported Nancy to Child Protective Services for possible medical neglect and physical mal-treatment. When the report was disclosed in the conference room of the pediatrics ward, Nancy was horrified and ran out of the meeting crying. She burst into Libby and Alisa's hospital room shouting, "I'm not going to let them take my children!"

As she was restrained by hospital staff in front of her children, Nancy rolled her eyes back, fell to the floor, and displayed whole-body convulsive movements and headbanging. Nancy was strapped to a stretcher while her daughters cried inconsolably and was brought downstairs to the Psychi-atric Emergency Room.

## THE EMERGENCY ROOM EVALUATION

Nancy told the ER staff calmly and cooperatively, "I had a kind of seizure . . . I felt like punching out the pediatrician who reported me and the next thing I knew, I was on the floor having an *ataque*" (*Ataque de nervios* is the Spanish term for 'fit' and is often used as a cultural idiom for trauma-linked distress that can be confused with neurological symptoms) (Interian et al., 2005).

The staff found her to be likable. They felt for her. Nancy asked the staff to imagine what it would be like for her – as a mother who was terrified to leave her children with a relative even for a half hour – to contemplate the possibility that her children could be taken from her and put in the care of a stranger.

She described, in addition to depressive symptoms, the following chronic symptoms: intrusive memories of violence, nightmares, night-time hypervigilance, pervasive mistrust, multiple somatic symptoms, hyperstartle response, severe early and middle insomnia, and compulsive checking of locks and windows. These symptoms of full-blown PTSD were exacerbated by an amalgam of present stressors (i.e., the staff report to Child Protective Services) as well as a past history of severe violent trauma: maltreatment; neglect; domestic violence exposure; and sudden, unresolved losses.

She recounted that she had been frequently hit with a belt and shoes by her father up to age 4. Her mother left her stormy marriage and family behind to seek employment in the United States when Nancy was 8 years old. After her mother left the family in the care of Nancy's father and his family, Nancy's paternal uncle not only smothered and battered her but forced her to perform fellatio and forced her to perform intercourse repeatedly over the next 3 to 4 years, until Nancy was nearly 13 years old. Of note, this uncle, like Nancy's father, was an alcoholic. Before her fourteenth birthday, Nancy had already given birth to the first of two children fathered by this uncle. After their birth, when she was about 15 years old, she was sent away to New York to join her mother. Nancy never saw those children again and says that she has difficulty even thinking about them.

At age 24, while on a visit to her native country, Nancy was raped again by this uncle. He broke into her bedroom in the middle of the night, struck her as she tried to flee, and covered her face with a pillow as he had done during the childhood molestation. It may not be chance that Nancy has an intense aversion to pillows and will not keep any in her home.

The rape by her uncle at age 24, she said, precipitated the onset of her "seizures." (Nancy used the Latino idiom of distress, *ataques*, when asked what she would call these events in Spanish.) She described a cardinal sensation accompanying the *ataque*: feeling suffocated before she falls to the floor and writhes convulsively. On further history, Nancy stated that her mother, maternal grandmother, and great-grandmother also had these fits (see Figure 10.1).

Although Nancy had no formal past psychiatric history, she had been diagnosed with Conversion Disorder (Psychogenic Seizures) and PTSD by a consult–liaison psychiatrist, after her inpatient video-EEG monitoring on the neurology ward four years prior. But instead of following recommendations for psychotherapy, Nancy found a non-Hispanic community internist who prescribed antiseizure medications.

By the end of the emergency room evaluation, Nancy agreed to pursue mental health treatment for herself and her children. After a 24-hour observation period in the ER, Nancy was referred to the adult psychiatry clinic for treatment. Alisa was referred to the Pediatric Psychiatry Clinic for individual child psychotherapy. And Libby and Nancy were referred to our Infant–Family Service for an infant–mother intervention. After an initial screening and informed consent from Nancy, she and Libby – then age 16 months, returned two weeks after her discharge from the ER to participate in the aforementioned research protocol, including three videotaped visits: (1) an in-depth interview of Nancy about Libby and Nancy's own history, (2) a parent-child play paradigm one week later, and (3) a video–feedback intervention visit with Nancy alone two weeks after that.

**Figure 10.1.** Paul Richer. A depiction of a severe hysterical attack. #153, Pencil/
Paper, 28.5 × 20 cm. Private collection of the Richer family. As described by
Charcot in Paris during the latter half of the 19th century, the "hysterical attack"
that one sees rendered in this drawing of a woman tearing her clothing and
screaming in a profoundly dysregulated state closely resembles what is presently
described by many Caribbean Hispanic individuals who experience "ataques de
nervios."

During the first research visit, when asked on one item to choose five adjectives describing Libby's personality, Nancy said the following: "She's grouchy ... she always has to take charge ... she loves to hit and fight, but she's really not such a bad thing. Well, she is mean!" On another item, Nancy associated these attributions with her labile, abandoning mother and physically abusive father. She saw nothing of herself in Libby. And she stated that she did not believe that her own behavior could have any impact on her relationship with Libby.

At this time, Nancy reported significant posttraumatic stress symptoms. Diagnoses of current and past PTSD were confirmed on a semistructured psychiatric interview.

One week later, Nancy and Libby were videotaped during the play procedure. Although showing the capacity for warm relatedness and contingent sensitivity to Libby's needs, the mother–daughter interaction reflected a predominance of frightening and frightened maternal behavior with frequent hostile intrusions, incongruence of affect, and self-referencing, all of which have been associated with intergenerational transmission of trauma and its effects, such as dissociative phenomena (Lyons-Ruth, Dutra, Schuder, & Bianchi, 2006).

## LIBBY'S SYMPTOMS AT HOME: WHAT TO MAKE OF THEM?

We know from Nancy's report, as corroborated by Libby's sister Alisa, that Libby would frequently wake up during the night, crying as if she had had a nightmare. She would then sit up in bed vigilantly with her mother – who also suffers from chronic insomnia – and, according to Nancy, the two would watch the window and door for any signs of an intruder until exhausted and no longer able to stay awake. Nancy said that Libby was easily startled by loud noises at home, as had also been observed in the clinic. Moreover, Libby had been noted during the assessment to be apprehensive, with a restricted range of affect, sparse vocalization, and constricted exploration and play. We know that Libby had the capacity for a brighter engagement and greater interest in her environment because of her interaction with the staff, with whom she readily engaged. Of note, Nancy denied that Libby had been exposed to any domestic violence, physical or sexual abuse, accidents, or medical trauma.

So, although Libby did indeed seem traumatized, she could not tell others directly what had been traumatic to her.

After a single session of videofeedback in a nonstressed, supportive therapeutic framework, during which an optimal interactive moment was shown, Nancy showed a dramatic change in her perception of Libby. As distinguished from the five terms initially used to describe Libby's personality, "Grouchy . . . takes charge . . . likes to hit and fight . . . not such a bad thing . . . Well she is mean!," Nancy, following videofeedback, stated that Libby was "more sweet . . . lovable . . . wants to bond more . . . still hits . . . but is not mean . . . "

Nancy, like many of the more than 30 traumatized mothers who returned for a videofeedback session two to four weeks after the play procedure, showed a significant reduction in the degree of negativity and distortion of her attributions toward her child on a rating scale coded blindly by four developmental specialists.

When shown her child's distress during the separation sequence in the containing company of a reflective observer, Nancy was able to respond more reflectively and sensitively to her daughter's and her own distress.

The following is a verbatim excerpt transcribed from this part of the feedback session, during which Nancy views with the author her child's separation response and then responds to items probing for what she sees, thinks, and feels.

### Videofeedback Excerpt Midway Through Videofeedback Session

*Nancy sees separation reaction: Child cries and looks toward door. Nancy watches intently and smiles. Her face grows concerned as Libby throws down the toy puppet that Nancy had been playing with.*

Dr. S:  *Okay so what happened there?*
   N:  *You broke her heart. You broke my daughter's heart in pieces!*
Dr. S:  *What broke her heart?*
   N:  *That I left. I never leave her! Never . . .*
Dr. S:  *Most mothers don't like to leave the room. . . . What do you think was going on in her mind?*
   N:  *Mommy left . . . Mommy never do that. Why she do that now?*
Dr. S:  *Do you remember what was going on in your mind when you left?*
   N:  *I was going to come in. I was going to come in and tell you something: "Don't ever do that again!" [ask me to leave without daughter]*
Dr. S:  *How were you feeling then?*
   N:  *That I was leaving her behind. That I wasn't protecting her.*
Dr. S:  *Mm . . . What do think she was feeling? What emotions?*
   N:  *Real sad and angry?*
Dr. S:  *Tell me about each – what makes you say those feelings: sad and then angry.*
   N:  *Sad because I left and angry because I never did that before. And I always . . . That's the first time I did that . . .*

Dr. S: *How did you know she was angry?*

   N: *Because she threw the puppet.*

Dr. S: *Why do you think I showed you this moment?*

   N: *I don't know . . . to see how I react when my daughter cries?*

Dr. S: *Why would I want to do that?*

   N: *I don't know.*

Dr. S: *Well, I was wondering if we could think together about what she was feeling when you left the room. I was wondering what was going on in her mind when she threw the puppet down. And I think you're onto something when you say that she was angry because you left.*

   N: *Yeah because I left, she was angry.*

Dr. S: *Who does she remind you of there?*

   N: *Me!*

Dr. S: *How so?*

   N: *That I would get angry when I would ask anything of my father and he would just leave me there crying; he wouldn't even give me a quarter. (stares and seems to focus inwardly)*

Dr. S: *Are you thinking of a particular memory right now?*

   N: *Yeah . . . I would get hit. My father would lock me in the bathroom and I would throw things. She gets her angry attitude from me like when she throws things. I would throw the soap . . . anything that I could get my hands on. And then he would come back and hit me harder . . . No kid deserves to be locked in the room and be hit for nothing . . . No kid deserves that . . .*

Dr. S: *How old were you then?*

   N: *. . . I was 7 or 8 . . . (before mother abandoned family)*

Dr. S: *Mm . . . And when you saw yourself leaving – did that image remind you of anyone?*

   N: *It reminded me of my father . . . he'd leave me there for hours.*

Dr. S: *Tell me about your father: What was he like?*

   N: *I don't like to talk about my father. I'm not going to say that I'll forget him but I don't like what he did to me or my sister or my mother.*

Dr. S: *What words would you use to describe his personality?*

   N: *Mean . . . I never knew if my father loved me or hated me because he never told me. Cheap! Oh my god was he cheap!*

Following this videotaped research assessment with a single videofeed-back intervention (Schechter et al., 2003; Schechter et al., 2006), the dyad entered child–parent psychotherapy (Hatzor, 2005). Despite many missed visits and a limited course of fewer than ten sessions in six months as described by Hatzor (2005), the following changes were noted: Within one month, Nancy's trauma-related distress moved from somatic memory and symptoms (pseudoseizures) to declarative memory and a verbalized/symbolized emotional domain. She suffered no further somatoform relapses. An empathic focus on Nancy's traumatic life experiences, with (a) gentle confrontation of avoidance of painful affects, and (b) concommitant support and stimulation of reflective functioning, enabled Nancy to engage and maintain phone contact with the therapist despite missed visits.

A substantial portion of the therapeutic work involved helping Nancy to follow Libby's lead, attend to her interests with her, and maintain joint attention long enough to reflect upon Libby's perspective. A telling moment in the treatment occurred when the therapist, Dr. Hatzor, suggested that Nancy and Libby read a picture book together before bedtime. Nancy returned the next day and said that they had "read together" for an hour! When Dr. Hatzor asked her to tell more about the experience, it became clear that Nancy had chosen to read a violent crime novel by herself while seated next to Libby, to whom Nancy had given a board book. It was some days later that the mother and daughter would actually be looking at the same children's book from cover to cover. Only gradually could Nancy begin to take on Libby's developmental and individual perspective.

In a parallel, simultaneous process, Libby's play, which had for weeks involved being the caregiver while playing with dolls or animal figures, reached a turning point. Libby turned over her precious dolls to the therapist for care during the last session and hugged the therapist, as if to say she could give up her reversed caregiver role and be the child. Overall, Libby's play became more reciprocal with both her therapist and her mother and involved less time spent reading her own book to the exclusion of the therapist.

Efforts were made to explore the meaning of the missed visits and to reach out to the family. However, Nancy would not accept that her ambivalence towards the treatment and what it might bring up contributed to her avoidance of the sessions. And when in session, Nancy often avoided making connections between her own and her daughter's memories, affects, and actions, and in turn, reactions at many levels, which we also understood as defensive (Bion, 1959). Of note, Libby's father never came into treatment, despite many invitations and outreach. Although we suspected a stormy marriage bordering on domestic violence by both partners, physical violence was never confirmed.

Despite the family's elusiveness, Nancy responded to our recruitment call for a follow-up study two years later, when Libby was 4 years old.

**Figure 10.2.** Follow-up study: Libby's family drawing at age 4.

Nancy denied any new traumatic life events in the family with the possible exception of increased marital tension since her husband's unemployment had begun.

The following material from the videotaped assessment of Libby at age 4 consists of a MacArthur Story Stem Battery (MSSB) narrative that completes the story stem entitled "Hot Gravy." This story highlights Libby's mental representation of the caregiving relationship and the child's vulnerable self-representation:

MSSB Story-Stem Completion: "Hot Gravy"

(Ok, well here's the story. Mom and Susan are at the stove. Ok?)

And mom says, "Ow! I burned myself."

(Oh! Wait a minute, wait a minute. You almost . . . you, you, you have a good, uh, imagination . . . So, here's what happens. You ready? Hands on your lap, and we're going to start! Mom says, "We're going to have a good supper, but it's not ready yet, so don't get too close to the stove. And Susan says, "mmmm . . . that looks good. I don't want to wait, I want some now!" *(I. has doll reach for pan on stove and drop it)* "Ow, ow. Ow, I burned my hand, it hurts, it hurts!")

Now I go?

(Yes.)

And then, Susan says, she put her arm up and she say, "Ow!"

(She puts her arm up and says "ow.")

And then she says, "Ok mommy, I go sit at the table."

(I'm going to the table.)

And they say, "What happened Susan?"

(They say what happened Susan.)

So, Susan says, "I, I burned myself"

. . . And then mommy said, "I will pick this up."

... And she says, "I, I will clean it."

... So she had to put more sauces inside.

... And then she turned on the grill, with that button and that button hot.

... And then she said, "I cooking, I cooking."

... And then she hold it. There.

... And then she says, "supper time!"

... And then, Susan, says, "great." *(C. has mom putting sauce from pan into plates on the table.)*

(What about Susan's burned hand? What did they do about her burned hand, her hurt hand?)

*(sighs)* Dad, Mom says, "Susan, we're going to take you to the doctor."

... And Susan says, "oh mommy, watch out for my mom."

(And she says what?)

Watch out for my arm.

And then she says, "Oh no, I burnt my head."

(Who? Mommy burnt her head? What about Susan's hand. What did they do with Susan's hand?)

Oh... Oh. George said, "Whoa. I better cook." *(In aggressive voice) (has George (brother) kick down Mommy and Susan dolls to the floor)* And then he said, "thank you."

(George is kicking everybody?)

Uh huh. But, but, George and daddy gotta cook.

(Everybody's on the floor?)

Uh huh.

(Why, why is George kicking everybody?)

Cause, cause you say *(whispers)* "be a good girl."

(What?)

*(looks around)* "I wanna be a girl." *(still whispering)*

(he says, I wanna be a girl?)

Uh huh. But a magic girl came.

(What?)

A magic girl came.

... And then George said, "Eat your food. Let me make you a girl."

... And then he said "Ahh!" *(screams)*

(How does the story end?)

The mom says, "Ahhhh.... That was hot."

(Mommy burned her head. So, mommy has a burned head and Susan has a burned hand...)

So, he has to burn hair.

... The dad go like that *(puts father doll near stove)*. Ah! I burned my foot!

(So, everybody's a little bit burned.)

Uh huh. So they says, "oh, wah, wah, wah." And they like this *(has them all laying down on the ground)*.


CONCLUSION

Within weeks to months of implementing a comprehensive culturally sensitive mental health intervention, the cycle of locating distress in the body had been understood to be, in Caribbean Hispanic terms, *ataques de nervios* and was thus broken. This case study attests to the fact that the effects of that intervention endured, with reinforcement and greater psychological depth, over the two to four years of follow-up prior to this publication. In this sense, a relatively brief, targeted intervention, which was aimed at helping Nancy and – via Nancy's improved understanding as well as narrative-formation (i.e., meaning-making) with Libby during and after her play therapy – Libby to understand the ways in which they communicated traumatic experience, had been able to reassociate their previously dissociated physical and mental suffering and affect and the content of trauma-associated memories – hostile and helpless aspects of the self that had been fragmented in both time and space. The effect overall was to increase the likelihood of verbal self-reflection and effective communication, as opposed to unreflected – in this case, medicalized – action and consequent disruption of psychological meaning.

Equally or more important, Nancy and Libby were seeking help for very real human suffering and dysfunction as sequelae of Nancy's and the dyad's traumatic experiences. An important resilience factor in this case is therefore their tenacity. They made repeated efforts to seek help, even as their culturally informed communication of *ataques* was misunderstood in the North American medical culture – with a few important exceptions. Nancy's persistence resulted in the eventual interruption of intergenerational transmission of violent trauma. This is not to say that the already exacted toll on Libby's formative development of emotion regulation is magically reversible.

Nevertheless, Libby by age four, was able to engage fully in the story–completion task, and to complete rich verbal narratives. Four years after the initial intervention, Nancy and Libby remained in weekly psychotherapy without further relapse of somatoform symptoms leading to unnecessary medical procedures or treatments. Libby, to this day, continues to attend a regular school where she is performing at grade level. Nancy has obtained a position as a medical office assistant and functions more confidently and independently.

Within this overall positive outcome, as mentioned, we still noted in Libby's play narratives a fair amount of role reversal and narcissistic defensiveness. In other words, the narratives feature a helpless parent(s) or hostile parent(s) or both, who imposed their needs on the child. The child, in turn, took on the burden, with exaggerated, if not grandiose or omnipotent, and unrealistic expectations. The story–stem completion showed prominent dysregulated hostile aggression between family members. In the story-stem completion, the little girl ("Susan") was left with a burn, unattended, only to tolerate the father figure's aggression. When the interviewer reminded Libby about the injury to the child, she had the father say that she should see a doctor. But soon, father and mother themselves were burned and rendered helpless, and Susan never did receive medical attention.

In the absence of any competent, available caregiver, a deus-ex-machina figure, a "magic girl" came in to rescue the little girl. This concretization of Libby's narcissistic defenses as the magic girl seemed to allow Libby to finish the story even as she began to become disorganized, as noted by her making suddenly random sounds. Everyone in the story ended up "a little bit burned." And so, we can feel sadness and frustration for Libby, given that she feels so unprotected and so misunderstood in the world. But we can also feel hope, given our knowledge that she continues to receive help in considering what she and others around her are thinking and feeling, and in so doing, can work towards better self-regulation and integration.

REFERENCES

Bion, W. R. (1959). Attacks on linking. *International Journal of Psycho-Analysis*, 40(5/6), 308–315.

Egeland, B., & Susman-Stillman, A. (1996). Dissociation as a mediator of child abuse across generations. *Child Abuse & Neglect, 20*(11), 1123–1132.

Hatzor, T. (2005, June). *Anywhere I go, it's me and my girls: A parent-infant psychotherapy case of a severly traumatized mother and her 18-month old daughter.* Paper presented at the meeting of the Fifth International Congress of Psychic Trauma and Traumatic Stress, Argentine Society for Psychotrauma. Buenos Aires, Argentina.

Interian, A., Guarnaccia, P. J., Vega, W. A., Gara, M. A., Like, R. C., Escobar, J. I., et al. (2005). The relationship between ataque de nervios and unexplained neurological symptoms: a preliminary analysis. *Journal of Nervous and Mental Disorder, 193*(1), 32–39.

Lyons-Ruth, K., Dutra, L., Schuder, M. R., & Bianchi, I. (2006). From infant attachment disorganization to adult dissociation: relational adaptations or traumatic experiences? *Psychiatric Clinics of North America, 29*(1), 63–86.

Oliver, J. E. (1993). Intergenerational transmission of child abuse: rates, research, and clinical implications. *American Journal of Psychiatry, 150*(9), 1315–1324.

Schechter, D. S. (2003). Intergenerational communication of maternal violent trauma: Understanding the interplay of reflective functioning and posttraumatic psychopathology. In S. W. Coates, J. L. Rosenthal, & D. S. Schechter (Eds.), *September 11: Trauma and human bonds* (pp. 115–142). Hillside, NJ: Analytic Press, Inc.

Schechter, D. S., Kaminer, T., Grienenberger, J. F., & Amat, J. (2003). Fits and starts: A mother-infant case study involving pseudoseizures across three generations in the context of violent trauma history (with Commentaries by R. D. Marshall, C. H. Zeanah, & T. Gaensbauer). *Infant Mental Health Journal, 24*(5), 510–528.

Schechter, D. S., Myers, M. M., Brunelli, S. A., Coates, S. W., Zeanah, C. H., Davies, M., et al. (2006). Traumatized mothers can change their minds about their toddlers: Understanding how a novel use of videofeedback supports positive change of maternal attributions. *Infant Mental Health Journal, 27*(5), 429–448.

Schechter, D. S., Zygmunt, A., Coates, S. W., Davies, M., Trabka, K. A., McCaw, J., et al. (2007). Caregiver traumatization adversely impacts young children's mental representations on the MacArthur Story Stem Battery. *Attachment & Human Development, 9*(3), 187–205.

Widom, C.S. (1999). Posttraumatic stress disorder in abused and neglected children grown up. *American Journal of Psychiatry, 156*(8), 1223–1229.

# Commentary

## Childhood Trauma and Functional Somatic Syndromes

Urs M. Nater and Christine M. Heim

### INTRODUCTION

The case study by Dr. Schechter presents a fascinating account of a 29-year-old mother presenting in a hospital with her two children (5 years and 8 months, respectively), with the younger child exhibiting seizure-like symptoms at arrival. As the case study unfolds, the reader learns that the mother and her older child also suffer from seizure-like symptoms. Despite efforts by the doctors to identify a medical cause for these seizures, no medical explanation for these symptoms can be found. Over the course of her life, the mother had been diagnosed with a variety of psychiatric conditions, including posttraumatic stress disorder (PTSD) and conversion disorder (non-epileptic seizures). It becomes evident that she had suffered repeated and severe physical, sexual, and emotional abuse during her early childhood and adolescence. Although she reports that her children have not been exposed to any severe trauma, the children exhibit similar symptoms, including PTSD-like symptoms and non-epileptic seizures. Mother and children seem to have benefitted from psychotherapeutic intervention. In summary, two interesting phenomena have occurred: (1) after being exposed to severe stress early in her life, the mother developed a variety of psychiatric and medically unexplained somatic symptoms; and (2) these symptoms have been passed on from one generation to the next. The mechanisms underlying these phenomena are unclear and difficult to illuminate. The author of the case study thoroughly examines the potential psychological mechanisms translating trauma experienced early in life into somatic symptoms and the subsequent transmission of these symptoms from mother to child. In our commentary, we would like to focus on potential neurobiological mechanisms involved in mediating the manifestation of functional somatic symptoms after childhood trauma.

## MEDICALLY UNEXPLAINED SYMPTOMS

The symptoms exhibited by the mother and her young daughter are part of the larger spectrum of symptoms that can manifest without known medical cause, termed "medically unexplained" symptoms. In some instances, these symptoms form specific, reproducible clusters and are thus grouped as "functional somatic syndromes" (Henningsen, Zipfel, & Herzog, 2007). These syndromes are defined by the co-occurrence of several physical symptoms that manifest without identifiable physical signs or medical abnormalities. Specific symptom patterns are used to define syndromal disorders. Typical examples for these syndromal disorders are chronic fatigue syndrome (CFS), fibromyalgia, irritable bowel syndrome (IBS), chronic pelvic pain, and, as is the case in the current case study, pseudoseizures.

Pseudoseizures are "epileptic-like spells not due to a medical cause" (Nash, 1993). In recent years, the neurological literature has replaced the term pseudoseizures with the term "psychogenic nonepileptic seizure" (PNES). PNES are relatively common, with incidence rates ranging from 1 to 3 per 100,000 (Fiszman, Alves-Leon, Nunes, D'Andrea, & Figueira, 2004). ICD-10 includes PNES under the spectrum of dissociative disorders, and DSM-IV uses the terms *conversion* or *dissociation* to describe this phenomenon.

Not much is known about the etiology of PNES. There is, however, increasing evidence that childhood trauma might be associated with increased risk of developing PNES. Interestingly, in her account of two PNES case studies, Harden (1997) mentions that the Greek physician Galen "taught that seizures were a result of premature intercourse," and the Navajo thought that "a person who has a seizure is assumed to have experienced incest." Notably, in a review of published studies on PNES, Fiszman and colleagues (2004) report rates of trauma in PNES of 76%–100%, with the prevalence of lifetime physical and/or sexual abuse ranging between 50% and 77%. As observed in the mother described in the current case study, a comorbid diagnosis of PTSD in PNES is common.

Traditional explanations of the development of pseudoseizures or PNES are rooted in psychodynamic theory: an unspeakable level of trauma or distress is translated into distorted bodily functions. We will next discuss potential complementary explanations based on a psychobiological approach and try to answer the question what (neuro-) biological mechanisms might link traumatic *experiences* early in life with long-lived *somatic* manifestation of symptoms, as is the case in PNES.

## A PSYCHOBIOLOGICAL APPROACH

It is well established that adverse experiences during early development, particularly during vulnerable stages of heightened brain plasticity, permanently shape the development of brain regions involved in the mediation of stress and emotion. This environmental programming, in interaction with genetic factors, determines how a given individual responds to the environment, including stress, later in life. Specifically, in animal models, it has been shown that early adversity leads to structural, functional, and even epigenetic changes in the hippocampus, the amygdala, the prefrontal cortex, and brain stem regions, which converge into increased endocrine, autonomic, and behavioral responsiveness to stress (Plotsky, Sanchez, & Levine, 2001; Meaney & Szyf, 2005). Such changes may decrease a person's threshold to develop stress-related disorders. Of note, results from clinical studies have provided convincing support for stress sensitization in adult humans after childhood sexual or physical abuse (see Heim, Plotsky, & Nemeroff, 2004).

Several of the neurobiological effects of early adverse experience, as observed in animal models and human studies, could plausibly contribute to the development of PNES. Two brain regions – the hippocampus and the amygdala –are particularly affected by early adverse experience and may be implicated in the development of seizure-like symptoms:

1. The hippocampus has long been known to play a critical role in memory storage and retrieval, as well as contextual fear conditioning. It has also been postulated that the hippocampus is a critical locus for the generation of dissociative states. The hippocampus is densely packed with receptors for the stress hormone cortisol, which has toxic effects on the hippocampus. Early adversity has been associated with structural and functional changes, including impaired neurogenesis, in the hippocampus. Repeated surges of cortisol in individuals with childhood trauma may adversely impact the hippocampus, causing further structural and functional impairment, promoting dissociation, and facilitating the development of PNES.

2. The amygdala, a critical structure involved in the processing of emotion, is activated even by subtle or subliminally presented emotionally

threatening stimuli. Of note, the amygdaloid nuclei are among the most sensitive structures for the occurrence of "kindling," an important phenomenon in which repeated intermittent stimulation produces increased alteration and neuronal excitability that may eventually result in seizures. Early adversity has been associated with structural, functional, and neurochemical changes in the amygdala. Thus, childhood trauma may be causally related to excessive neuronal irritability and vulnerability to seizure-like symptoms, particularly upon further stress. The kindling phenomenon might also explain the overlap of PTSD and PNES.

The neurobiological consequences of childhood trauma may have similar effects on the pathophysiology of other functional somatic syndromes, such as CFS or IBS. Childhood trauma dramatically increases the risk for CFS (Heim et al., 2006), and has been identified as a major risk factor for IBS and other functional gastrointestinal disorders (Ringel, Sperber, & Drossman, 2001). Thus, the common denominator of these functional somatic syndromes seems to be an insult or a destructive experience at an early developmental stage. This insult might lead to sensitization of the brain's stress response system and failure to compensate in regulatory systems in response to challenge. As a result, there might be inadequate responses in regulatory outflow systems of the brain, leading to reduced thresholds for development of bodily symptoms. The neuroendocrine, autonomic, and immune consequences of childhood trauma may plausibly induce risk for developing these symptoms. A variety of studies have reported decreased cortisol secretion in both CFS and IBS patients; basal hypocortisolism has also been described after childhood adversity. Upon additional challenge, low cortisol availability might lead to disinhibition of central nervous and peripheral immune and autonomic responses, and such maladaptive physiological responses might ultimately evolve into the symptom patterns of CFS or IBS.

Taken together, early adverse experience seems to induce a vulnerable phenotype with changes in cortical-limbic-brainstem systems, particularly in genetically predisposed individuals. This neurobiological phenotype seems to be sensitized to additional challenge, leading to altered behavioral and physiological responsiveness and ultimately the clinical picture of PNES, CFS, or IBS. These disorders can therefore be considered part of a spectrum of adaptation disorders, given that stress plays an important role in triggering functional somatic symptoms. It is likely that stress interacts with other vulnerability factors in people who go on to develop these disorders, although it should be noted that gene-environment interactions in functional somatic disorders are only poorly understood.

## TRANSMISSION ACROSS GENERATIONS

Little is known about biological mechanisms that might explain the apparent intergenerational transmission of functional somatic symptoms from mother to child in the current case study. One hypothesis is that in a mother with childhood trauma, high vulnerability to stress and impaired emotional regulation promotes inadequate parenting and thus the transmission of early adverse experience (and its neurobiological consequences) in the offspring. Interestingly, animal research has shown that variations in maternal behavior and stress responsiveness are transmitted from one generation to the next in a non-genomic fashion (Meaney, 2001). In this cross-fostering study, lack of caretaking behavior in stressed rat mothers produced increased behavioral and physiological stress reactivity in offspring, and the affected offspring subsequently exhibited low care-giving behavior. However, our understanding of these complex interactions is still limited to the animal model and awaits further elucidation in human research.

## CONCLUSION

One of the most important health consequences of childhood trauma is an increased prevalence of functional somatic syndromes, characterized by chronic pain, fatigue, and related symptoms in adulthood. PNES is part of this spectrum of syndromes. Core features of all of these syndromes appear to be altered stress-responsiveness and failure of the brain to adapt different regulatory systems that are implicated in the pathophysiology of these syndromes. Childhood trauma, during vulnerable phases of high plasticity, might interfere with the development of such critical brain regions. The precise mechanisms that translate childhood trauma into specific brain changes involved in functional symptom patterns are clearly complex and need to be elucidated in future studies. Such studies will also allow for deriving direct targets for the prevention and treatment of these disorders.

Case studies such as the one presented by Dr. Schechter are invaluable in helping us understand the intricate associations between traumatic experiences and somatic manifestations, inasmuch as they offer insight into specific associations in the individual, often lost in quantitative studies. Certainly, future research needs to integrate both the individual and the group approach to facilitate understanding of the pathophysiology of functional somatic syndromes. Special attention should be directed towards buffering factors that might mediate resilience against illness after childhood trauma, such as genotype, social support, protective caregiver characteristics, and others.

As impressively demonstrated in the present case study, psychotherapeutic interventions are beneficial in resolving functional somatic syndromes. It is possible that persons with an acquired illness might also be disposed to resolve such illness using environmental interventions such as psychotherapy. Psychotherapy might be able to alter or even reverse certain neurobiological consequences of childhood trauma. These possibilities should be addressed in future studies.

In adults, psychotherapy is focused on identifying dysfunctional attributions and illness behavior and reframing symptoms within a biopsychosocial framework. Clearly, an efficient therapeutic strategy can be chosen only when adequate information on the patient has been gathered. Childhood trauma, if present, may be an important factor. A thorough investigation of previous traumas, maintaining factors (such as ongoing stress), psychosocial factors (such as maladaptive coping strategies), and potential resilience factors (such as social support), along with a detailed medical history and examination, will help determine whether presenting symptoms are functional or caused by a medical disease.

## DISCLOSURES

Dr. Nater receives or has received funding or grants from the Swiss National Science Foundation and the CDC. Dr. Heim receives or has received funding or grant support from NIMH, NARSAD, ADAA, Eli Lilly, Novartis, Center for Behavioral Neuroscience, CDC. The authors do not report any conflict of interest.

REFERENCES

Fiszman, A., Alves-Leon, S. V., Nunes, R. G., D'Andrea, I., & Figueira, I. (2004). Traumatic events and posttraumatic stress disorder in patients with psychogenic nonepileptic seizures: a critical review. *Epilepsy & Behavior, 5*(6), 818–825.

Harden, C. L. (1997). Pseudoseizures and dissociative disorders: A common mechanism involving traumatic experiences. *Seizure, 6*(2), 151–155.

Heim, C., Plotsky, P. M., & Nemeroff, C. B. (2004). Importance of studying the contributions of early adverse experience to neurobiological findings in depression. *Neuropsychopharmacology, 29*(4), 641–648.

Heim, C., Wagner, D., Maloney, E., Papanicolaou, D. A., Solomon, L., Jones, J. F., et al. (2006). Early adverse experience and risk for chronic fatigue syndrome: Results from a population-based study. *Archives of General Psychiatry, 63*(11), 1258–1266.

Henningsen, P., Zipfel, S., & Herzog, W. (2007). Management of functional somatic syndromes. *Lancet, 369*(9565), 946–955.

Meaney, M. J. (2001). Maternal care, gene expression, and the transmission of individual differences in stress reactivity across generations. *Annual Review of Neuroscience, 24*, 1161–1192.

Meaney, M. J., & Szyf, M. (2005). Environmental programming of stress responses through DNA methylation: Life at the interface between a dynamic environment and a fixed genome. *Dialogues in Clinical Neuroscience, 7*(2), 103–123.

Nash, J. L. (1993). Pseudoseizures: Etiologic and psychotherapeutic considerations. *Southern Medical Journal, 86*(11), 1248–1252.

Plotsky, P. M., Sánchez, M. M., & Levine, S. (2001). Intrinsic and extrinsic factors modulating physiological coping systems during development. In D. M. Broom (Ed.), *Coping with challenge* (pp. 169–196). Berlin: Dahlem University Press.

Ringel, Y., Sperber, A. D., & Drossman, D. A. (2001). Irritable bowel syndrome. *Annual Review of Medicine, 52*, 319–338.

# Commentary on

## *"Multigenerational* Ataques de Nervios *in a Dominican American Family: A Form of Intergenerational Transmission of Violent Trauma?"*

Thomas S. Weisner

### INTRODUCTION

Schechter and colleagues offer us a sensitive, empathic report of their engagement with Nancy, the mother of Alisa (5 years) and Libby (8 months), from the time of the first encounter in the emergency room to discoveries about their lives and traumatic experiences, through therapy and follow-up.

The case study reports a history of trauma and abuse in Nancy's life, a complex psychiatric history, and a hopefully successful series of interventions, including individual psychotherapy for Libby's older sister, for Nancy, and for Libby and Nancy together for an infant-mother intervention. This included "three videotaped visits: (1) an in-depth interview of Nancy about Libby and Nancy's own history, (2) a parent-child play paradigm one week later, and (3) a videofeedback intervention with Nancy alone two weeks after that." The goal of these interventions included increasing "the likelihood of verbal self-reflection and effective communication, as opposed to unreflected – in this case, medicalized – action [e.g. somatic *ataques,* and PTSD physical symptoms] and consequent disruption of psychological meaning."

The pathway through which Nancy encounters professionals who may be able to help her is via the emergency room (ER), and other medical care situations. Nancy returned to the ER two more times after an initial visit, and some staff began to question the previous diagnosis of epilepsy and medications given to treat epilepsy. Only after staff reported the possibility of medical neglect and physical maltreatment of her children by Nancy did she have the *ataque* that then led to further referrals, including referrals to the infant-mother intervention program. Schechter emphasizes the resilience shown by Nancy in persisting to seek medical help for her suffering,

...even as their culturally informed communication of *ataques* was misunderstood in the North American medical culture – with a few important
exceptions. Nancy's persistence resulted in the eventual interruption of intergenerational transmission of violent trauma. This is not to say that the already
exacted toll on Libby's formative development of emotion regulation is magically reversible.

   Libby and Nancy were fortunate to become connected with Schechter
and his research team, but the vast majority of parents and children in
circumstances like Nancy's (in Santo Domingo, where Nancy grew up, as
well as in the United States or elsewhere) would be very unlikely to find
a support service like the one they found in New York. I am sure that
Schechter, and all the colleagues and collaborators in the research program
designed to interrupt the transmission of violent and traumatic parenting
across generations, would agree: Community programs and public health
interventions with proven effectiveness will have to be an essential part of
any scalable attempt to intervene and disrupt the intergenerational transmission of violent trauma.

   More generally, are there changes possible in the *settings* Nancy and
Libby are engaged in that could improve their situations, including the
violence and traumatic responses that Schechter and his team have identified? The medical settings Nancy went to would be one set of places to
start with. What interventions in those settings would put in place ways to
identify and better treat patients like Nancy?

   The Schechter et al. intervention was psychological and clinic-based.
The goals of the interventions are individual psychotherapeutic insights
and "interruptions" of Nancy and Libby's responses to and interpretations
of trauma and violence. Treatment goals include inducing and affirming
insights by Nancy that increase her verbal self-reflection, more positive
beliefs about her children and connections with them, and a reappraisal of
negative meanings and feelings – hers and those she attributed to Libby
and Alisa. No family home visits are reported; nor are other intervention
efforts that may have been situated in the family and neighborhood ecology
of Nancy and her children. Here again, I am sure that Schechter and his
team would agree that a complementary intervention – one that brought a
home visitor to work with Nancy and her children in the everyday world in
which they are embedded – could likely have enhanced the clinic services
described in this case.

   There is strong research evidence that such home visit interventions
have a greater likelihood of producing positive and sustainable changes in
subsequent children's behavior problems, maternal life course, and child

neglect (e.g. Olds et al., 1997; Olds et al., 1998). There is no question about the value of the insights from the video sessions for interrupting transmission of violence by Nancy and others in this study. However, such insights have to be taken up by clients and function in the everyday world parents and children live in. Those new personal insights must continually compete with other insights and ideas and cultural beliefs in the world – and, hopefully, survive in that competition. Home, neighborhood, classroom, and other kinds of setting-focused interventions and changes could not only assist Nancy and Libby, but also (if they can be sustained) help all the other parents and children with trauma who will come after them.

The Schechter infant–mother treatment program focused on Nancy's personal experience and trauma, and the treatment was for her as an individual, and for the mother-infant dyad as well. The mother-infant attachment relationship and ways to reframe Nancy and Libby's interactions and beliefs were the key. However, a social-relational, ecocultural approach to understanding working models of close relationships provide a complementary model for the study of such relationships over time and in cultural context (LeVine & Norman, 2001; Lewis & Takahashi, 2005). Patterned expectations for close relationships vary across age, class, purposes, contexts, and local cultural communities' goals for those relationships (Weisner, 2005). Children are involved in sibling attachments, peer friendships, the worlds of preschool and school, fantasy- and story-based relationships from media, then romantic partners, then weaker but nonetheless very important acquaintance networks and work affiliations over time. Each of these relationships and roles has its own varied cultural norms and expectations, and its own functions and emotional scripts. There are multiple contexts and opportunities for flexibility in relationship models and settings available for intervention, in addition to the mother-infant dyad, important as that dyad is.

Nancy is a working poor single mother, as well as a victim of trauma, abuse, and family tragedies. There are tested and effective interventions that can assist her in managing her daily routine, finding a job, providing health care, and finding appropriate child care for Libby and Alisa (Duncan, Huston, & Weisner, 2007; Yoshikawa, Weisner, & Lowe, 2006). Such work-based supports for parents can assist working poor parents with troubled children (Bernheimer, Weisner, & Lowe, 2003). Nancy would most likely benefit from assistance and intervention in helping her sustain a daily routine of family life that had meaning for her and for her children. There are ways to ask parents about this ongoing project of sustaining their family routines of life, as well as ways to assess that project (Weisner, Matheson, Coots, & Bernheimer, 2005; Weisner, 2008). More sustainable family routines have characteristics in common: They fit with available resources, have lower levels of conflict and disagreement among family members, provide meaningful activities that fit with parental goals, and are reasonably predictable and consistent over time (Weisner, 2002). A family-level setting intervention that assisted parents in their project of creating these kinds of family activities and routines would in turn support individual and dyadic therapeutic interventions such as those Schechter et al. have developed.

### REFERENCES

Bernheimer, L., Weisner, T. S., & Lowe, T. (2003). Impacts of children with troubles on working poor families: Experimental and mixed-method evidence. *Mental Retardation, 41*(6), 403–419.

Duncan, G., Huston, A., & Weisner, T.S. (2007). *Higher ground: New hope for the working poor and their children*. New York: Russell Sage Foundation.

LeVine, R. A., & Norman, K. (2001). The infant's acquisition of culture: Early attachment reexamined in anthropological perspective. In C. C. Moore & H. F. Mathews (Eds.), *The psychology of cultural experience* (pp. 83–104). New York: Cambridge University Press.

Lewis, M., & Takahashi K. (Eds.). (2005). Beyond the dyad: Conceptualization of social networks. *Human Development, 48*(1–2), 1–113.

Olds, D., Eckenrode, J., Henderson, C.R., Jr., Kitzman, H., Powers, J., Cole, R., et al. (1997). Long-term effects of home visitation on maternal life course and child abuse and neglect: 15-year follow-up of a randomized trial. *Journal of the American Medical Association, 278*(8), 637–643.

Olds, D., Henderson, C.R., Jr., Cole, R., Eckenrode, J., Kitzman, H., Luckey, D., et al. (1998). Long-term effects of nurse home visitation on children's criminal and antisocial behavior: 15-year follow-up of a randomized trial. *Journal of the American Medical Association, 280*(14), 1238–1244.

Weisner, T. S. (2002). Ecocultural understanding of children's developmental pathways. *Human Development 45*(4), 275–281.

Weisner, T. S. (2005). Commentary: Attachment as a cultural and ecological problem with pluralistic solutions. *Human Development, 48* (1–2), 89–94.

Weisner, T. S. (2008). Well being and sustainability of the daily routine of life. In G. Mathews & C. Izquerdo (Eds.), *The good life: Well-being in anthropological perspective*, (pp. 349–380). New York: Berghahn Press.

Weisner, T. S., Matheson, C., Coots, J., & Bernheimer, L. (2005). Sustainability of daily routines as a family outcome. In A. Maynard & M. Martini (Eds.), *The psychology of learning in cultural context* (pp. 41–73). New York: Kluwer/Plenum.

Yoshikawa, H., Weisner, T. S., & Lowe, E. (Eds.). (2006). *Making it work: Low-wage employment, family life, and child development*. New York: Russell Sage Foundation.

# SOCIAL AND CULTURAL CONTEXTS OF CHILDHOOD DEVELOPMENT: NORMATIVE SETTINGS, PRACTICES, AND CONSEQUENCES

## Carol M. Worthman

The material in this section leads to encounters with the old anthropological problem of how to evaluate culturally normative conditions and practices. Concerning pathways in human development, how many roads lead to Rome? What makes a practice "good" or "right" for a child? Hence, Glover responds to Briggs's case study about Inuit use of teasing and shaming for early child socialization by asking "whether the type of upbringing described will really help young Inuit children adapt successfully to their future life." Similarly, Kirmayer notes the "urgency to understand cultural variations in parenting practices and healthy developmental trajectories."

But how do we define "success" and "healthy"? Such questions spring to mind when we are confronted with normative practices of other cultures that jar against our own. We start to wonder about what childcare practices really do, as opposed to what culturally received views suggest they do, although we may not be so quick to ask the same critical question about our own society. Through its engagement with other cultures, anthropology has cultivated unsettling epistemological moments to cast into relief preconceptions about the "natural order" of things and permit us to see our and others' worlds in a new light.

Now with globalization and media, all of us are anthropologists. Encounters with unfamiliar cultural logics and meanings may catch us up at any moment, with unexpected and enduring effects. Thus, the Anderson-Fye case study: An apparently well-adjusted teen with culturally unexceptionable parenting in Belize sees American women on *Oprah* discussing domestic violence and sexual abuse, and the experience catalyzes a thoroughgoing reframing of her life experiences as a moral outrage of "I have *abuse!*" Similarly, in commenting on this case, Becker notes that eating disorders emerged among young Fijian girls after the introduction of TV into a society that valued plumpness led to dissemination of thinness as an ideal body image. In a different but related vein, Herdt discusses the possible role of subconscious biobehavioral cues transmitted in the daily intimacies of family life for organizing parent socialization of child sexuality. His analysis evokes questions about the impact of culture change and transformations in daily family life on the socialization and economy of sexuality in the family. Certainly, in the case of Maria, the Belizean teenager, the entire family consequently went into therapy and was "reformed."

Thus, both the goals and rubrics for evaluating the social and cultural conditions for child development rest upon criteria for personhood, or what Inuit call a "full-human being" (Jessen Williamson and Kirmayer, p. 301). In her appreciation of Briggs's case study, Jessen Williamson points to the depth of contrast between Inuit and Anglo views of personhood, with particular implications for education, in that, for Inuit, a full-human being comprises pro-social and pro-cosmic qualities of the body, soul, and spirit rather than individuated autonomous materialist qualities that many contemporary western societies cultivate.

Although recognizing the range of human differences nourished by cultural diversity in normative settings and practices during development (and adulthood), many would draw limits to cultural relativity for defining best practices or even good-enough care for the young. Often those limits are identified as the suffering of long-term harm or impairment. By definition, abuse and neglect transgress those limits. But defining them is complicated, because what is normative in one society (putting babies to sleep alone) can be regarded as abuse in another. Yet a society's definitions may also be open to question on its own terms. Seraphin and colleagues' richly detailed examination of the effects of child abuse and neglect on psychopathology and their neurobiological underpinnings in the United States demonstrate an enduring harm and thence argue the appropriateness of judging such conditions of rearing as wrong. Yet their analysis also challenges normative tolerance of circumstances that prove to be as harmful as those regarded as abusive or neglectful in the United States. Specifically, they find that parental verbal abuse and perceived financial distress exact psychopathological costs that exceed those of child physical abuse or actual poverty, respectively. The findings refute cultural norms sensitive to harm from physical or sexual abuse but insensitive to mere talk as well as those that foster a materialism that inculcates perceived poverty among youth in the face of basic sufficiency or even great material wealth.

Hence, the case studies, reflections, and extended analyses in this section amply illustrate the power of biocultural approaches to child development and well-being, and indeed the necessity of this approach if we are to understand what drives important human differences and difficulties within and between societies.

# ELEVEN

# Ethnographic Case Study

*Inuit Morality Play and the Danish Medical Officer*

Jean L. Briggs

This case study was inspired – or perhaps provoked – by the Chief Medical Officer of Greenland, who told me after hearing me lecture that he thought all Inuit children ought to be removed from their parents for their own protection. Inuit, of course, consider *our* childrearing abusive, not theirs. By and large, Inuit love their children dearly, and in their own eyes, they treat them extremely benignly. They just create strengths and vulnerabilities that are different from the ones we create. I want to show you the morality in the kind of interaction that shocked the medical officer and how it is conveyed to the child.

Imagine the following scene[1]: Aqnaqjuaq, a woman in her late 50s, comes into the home of her married daughter, Liila, to pay a late-evening visit. She is carrying Liila's youngest daughter, Aita, a baby less than a year old, whom Aqnaqjuaq has adopted. Liila tenderly holds Aita on her lap and feeds her bits of bread. Meanwhile, Liila's three-year-old daughter, Chubby Maata, now the youngest in the family, is sitting beside her mother, playing with an empty cigarette package. Nobody else is present. The women's affectionate attention focuses on Aita, who is crying, and they're trying to figure out why.

Suddenly, Aqnaqjuaq, without any reason that I can see, begins chanting over and over again to Chubby Maata, "Your father is very bad!" Her eyes are smiling, but her voice is vigorous and emphatic. Chubby Maata does

---

[1] Extended versions of parts of this paper were previously published in Briggs (1998). A complete version of this incident is recorded in that work on pages 127–129. The fieldwork on which this case study is based took place in 1979.

**Figure 11.1.** One of the winter camps where Chubby Maata lived during her childhood. Photograph by the author.

*not* smile. I see no expression on her face and her body is perfectly still. She watches her grandmother.

After a while, Aqnaqjuaq changes the words of her chant, but her tone remains the same and her eyes are still smiling, "Your father is very bad! Your mother is very bad! My dear little granddaughter is very bad! Isn't that so? You *are* bad, aren't you? Your father is bad, isn't that so? I've heard that my dear little granddaughter is bad, yes indeed. Your mother is very bad!" And so on. The stream of words is unremitting and inexorable.

At some point during Aqnaqjuaq's speech, Chubby Maata covers her face with her cigarette package. Aqnaqjuaq says imperatively, "Look at me." Chubby Maata doesn't move, but Liila removes the wrapper from her daughter's face and begins to watch her with an amused smile, while Aqnaqjuaq continues to rain "bads" on Chubby Maata. Chubby Maata sits motionless for a while, then suddenly she leans over and kisses Aita, who is still sitting on Liila's lap. The kiss doesn't seem, to me, particularly rough, but Aqnaqjuaq says in a cautionary tone, "Don't bite her!" Then she comments to Liila, "She's trying to bite! She's beginning to *attack* the baby!"

Chubby Maata says to her grandmother, "My father cut his finger, isn't that so?" She turns to her mother for confirmation and then says something else about her father, which I don't understand. Her tone is conversational, as though she is conveying perfectly ordinary information to her grandmother, but Aqnaqjuaq says rejectingly, "Never mind," and she resumes her chant, "Your father is bad!"

Then, all at once, she begins a new theme, "Your genitals are bad! Aaq! They stink!" She comes over to Chubby Maata, who is sitting with knees raised, and pokes a finger between the little girl's legs. "Are you aware of your horrid little genitals? *There* they are!" And she pretends to pull down Chubby Maata's trousers from behind. Chubby Maata bursts into loud tears, but they only last a short minute and stop as abruptly as they began. The two women laugh, and Aqnaqjuaq says to Liila, "She took it seriously!" Her voice and eyes are amused. Then, in a different tone, she says to Chubby Maata, "Did you cry because you felt shy?" Chubby Maata doesn't answer. Her grandmother continues her chant for a bit, with less intensity, and then stops when Chubby Maata doesn't react.

Chubby Maata begins to tease Aita with the cigarette package, repeatedly brushing it against Aita's fingers, while Aita tries in vain to catch hold of it and whimpers in frustration. Liila comments, "She's angry. She wants to boss." At this, Chubby Maata begins a chant of her own, directed at Aita, "Crybaby, crybaby!" Eventually Aqnaqjuaq gets up to carry Aita home to bed, but before she takes the baby from Liila, Liila holds Aita towards Chubby Maata, and says in a tender, persuasive voice, "Give her a little kiss." And Chubby Maata kisses her.

Well, are you shocked like the Danish medical officer? What searing consequences do you imagine Chubby Maata will suffer from this treatment? The obvious answer is that she will feel demeaned, defeated, utterly powerless, and alone – vulnerable to attack from a hostile world, which includes her nearest and dearest. Because she doesn't know her grandmother is joking, she will believe that she, her parents, and her genitals are all bad, and that there is no help for her. Perhaps the Chief Medical Officer was right in judging that Inuit children ought to be rescued from their parents.

But let's look at the drama in the context of Chubby Maata's life situation. Chubby Maata is a well-loved child, a favorite of her parents and grandparents. The world revolves around her. Like other much-loved Inuit children, she is fed when she is hungry, comforted when she is unhappy, often given baby bottles of milk on demand, and put to bed when she is sleepy. Moreover, she is almost always within touching distance of a loving caretaker: an aunt, a cousin, an uncle, her father, her mother's parents, and most often, her mother.

But Chubby Maata is almost three years old, and her loving parents know it would be dangerous for her to go on expecting to be the center of her world, unaware of the requirements of the larger social world. She has to learn what the rules of interaction are, what she is allowed and not allowed to do. But that's not enough. To interpret other people's behavior, to respond appropriately and keep herself out of trouble, she has to learn how to recognize the plots of everyday life: people's goals, their strategies and motives, their probable reactions to her behavior, and the likely consequences. Most important of all, Chubby Maata has to acquire feelings and sensitivities that help her to make intuitive sense of the plots and motivate her to respond appropriately.

These are not easy lessons. Life in any society is full of pushes and pulls, currents, countercurrents, and undercurrents, rules that contradict each other, and feelings that are not consonant with behavioral dictates. Chubby Maata will have to learn both a surface plot and hidden plots. The surface plot, which paints an ideal situation and governs the rhetoric of everyday life, is that if Maata likes everybody and treats them well, they will like *her* and treat *her* well; she will never have to fear. The hidden plots, which can't be spoken, are less savory. Chubby Maata has to learn that people are not entirely trustworthy. They – and she, too – can be vengeful, hostile, greedy, possessive, or just self-interested. And because these motives can provoke people to do unpleasant things, Maata has to learn to be a little suspicious, both of other people's intentions and of her own. She has to be a little fearful, and more than a little alert to hidden dangers. She also has to learn culturally appropriate ways of defusing or avoiding the dangers: giving people what they want before they know they want it; joking with them so they'll know she's friendly; even, on occasion, temporarily retreating.

But how can small children learn to see turbulent potentials under calm surfaces? To distrust people who always treat them benignly? To fear people without being driven away from the people they fear? And how can they learn to deal with difficult situations if they never have opportunity to practice?

I think a good part of the answer lies in dramas like the one I've just introduced you to. But before I tell you how I think the dramas work, I want to show you another playful exchange, this time between Chubby Maata and her mother. This one happened ten days before the "bad" drama (Briggs, 1998, p. 117).

Chubby Maata was sitting cozily on Liila's lap. An uncle and an aunt were watching. Liila asked her daughter, "Do you consider your father good?" (That word could also have been translated as 'do you like him?')

**Figure 11.2.** Interior of a winter dwelling in Chubby Maata's camp. Photograph by the author.

Chubby Maata wrinkled her nose, "No." "Do you consider your mother's mother good?" "No." "Your mother's father?" "No." One by one, Liila listed all Chubby Maata's relatives, then me, and finally Liila herself. Chubby Maata rejected every name, one by one. Liila, waiting for a response after each question, asked her: "Are you the only good one? Have you no nurturant, loving feelings? Why don't you consider [so-and-so] good? Because he doesn't nurturantly love you? Who considers you good?"

Here, we have the "sunny side" plot I told you about. Liila is telling Chubby Maata that she should like and nurture everybody, not just herself. She also implies that Chubby Maata has no reason to dislike anybody, because everybody likes *her*. Even in the one case when she seems to suggest that somebody dislikes Chubby Maata, she's really telling her daughter that appearances are deceiving and that Chubby Maata should doubt her first impressions and look beneath the surface. She is teaching Chubby Maata to be alert but, at the same time, leading her to expect that the world is benign.

That's the moral framework of the "good" interrogation. What about the moral world of the "bad" drama? Now, all of a sudden, nobody is good, not Chubby Maata, not any of the people who ordinarily cherish and coddle her, and nobody in the surrounding world, either, as all those people seem to be passing critical judgment on Chubby Maata and her parents. A sudden upside-down flip that must surely catch Chubby Maata's attention, because the "bad" attack is so grossly out of keeping with many of her other experiences.

Let's look more closely at Chubby Maata's problem, what she might learn from it, and how she might learn it. Both episodes direct Chubby Maata's attention to issues of goodness and badness, and both make her aware that she is an actor in the cosmic drama. In the "good" interrogation, Liila is exploring her daughter's mind; she doesn't contradict Chubby Maata or close off her options. She asks questions that can make Chubby Maata think autonomously about the feelings she has for her fellows, questions that suggest to her that she is responsible for her own fate. The lesson is delivered in a convivial atmosphere. Liila is not scolding her daughter for her improper attitudes. On the contrary, she is showing Chubby Maata that she, her mother, and others, too, consider her good, regardless of her childish failure to live up to the ideal of liking everybody in return; so Chubby Maata can feel appreciated, prosocial, not alienated.

The "bad" drama is a beast of another character. This time, Chubby Maata is at the mercy of others, who are evaluating very uncharitably indeed both her three-year-old self and the people she depends on. And when Aqnaqjuaq asks Chubby Maata what she thinks of herself, it doesn't sound like an egalitarian consultation. Aqnaqjuaq is demanding assent. Moreover, this time, Chubby Maata is not allowed to escape, either by hiding behind her cigarette wrapper or by representing herself as good, kissing her sister, expressing concern for her father. She is not allowed to enlist support, either: Her mother seems to be on her grandmother's side. She is all alone. She must feel weak and vulnerable when she reads the surface messages of *this* drama, especially as Aqnaqjuaq acts out her criticisms very vividly. But is it an experience that might alienate Chubby Maata from herself, or make her turn against her elders and resist the prosocial lessons they want to teach her? I think not.

Why not? Well, for one thing, the motivation of the adult players is important. The confrontation between grandmother and granddaughter is not punitive. It isn't even real. Aqnaqjuaq is testing, teaching, cautioning, and – surprise! – celebrating, in a backhanded Inuit way, her cherished granddaughter. She is curious about Chubby Maata's state of social and moral development. Will Chubby Maata defend her beleaguered parents, as she should? Will she protect her genitals, as she should? Will she take the attack seriously, as she should *not*? And in the process of testing – and satisfying her curiosity – Aqnaqjuaq is laying the emotional foundations for all of these essential moral attitudes.

That's the same thing Liila was doing when she questioned Chubby Maata about whom she liked: laying the foundations for moral behavior. It's only the strategies that are different. Aqnaqjuaq's is the inverse of Liila's. Aqnaqjuaq turns the moral rules inside out and shows Chubby Maata the unacceptable backside of the scenario that Liila sketched for her in the "good" interrogation. When she threatens what is, and should be, important to Chubby Maata – her good parents, her good self, her good body – there is a good chance that she will attach Chubby Maata more firmly to those values and motivate her to defend them. At the same time, she unsettles Chubby Maata's innocent and dangerous belief in her own perfection and her parents' perfection, a belief she has to outgrow if she is to be a social person, a person who is vulnerable to criticism and open to sanction.

Another important factor is that the dramas are only partly serious. To the extent that Chubby Maata sees playfulness in the inversion, she can feel safe. Both mother and grandmother give her a number of clues that could show her that she is safe. Aqnaqjuaq's smiling eyes, her exaggerated voice, Liila's equanimity when Aqnaqjuaq attacks her, and her failure to leap to the defense of her daughter are all signs that Chubby Maata is not in danger. Aqnaqjuaq even tells Chubby Maata explicitly that she shouldn't take her attacks seriously, although she addresses her amused remark to Chubby Maata's mother. A final clue is that Aqnaqjuaq attributes to Chubby Maata's tears a socially approved cause: shyness. In doing so, she tells Chubby Maata, in effect, that she is growing up appropriately.

But to the extent that Chubby Maata feels serious truth in her grandmother's accusations, when she wonders, "Maybe I *am* bad," she will see herself dangerously exposed – all the more so because the accusations are not attached to specific sins. Chubby Maata is free to call to mind whatever misdemeanors are capable of troubling her. The awareness that there is a potentially critical audience out there, watching her, will motivate Chubby Maata to be alert to her antisocial inclinations and to govern them carefully. And the fact that she doesn't know in what direction to look for critics, must heighten her sense of vulnerability and her vigilance. At the same time, she is prevented from turning against individuals, as she might if Aqnaqjuaq had identified specific people who thought Chubby Maata was bad. So the lesson of the "bad" drama, like the lesson of the "good" interrogation, is to turn *toward* people, not away.

Chubby Maata will learn from dramas like these, not to dislike herself and her genitals, but to be modest and cautious, sensitive to the meanings and intentions of others, and prompt to respond nurturantly. She will become aware of criticism and of the force behind criticism, that of injury and death. She will become aware that she is personally vulnerable to sanction, because – the doubt is sown – she is not quite perfect. At the same time, she'll know that she herself is responsible for the fate of her relationships.

And she will learn all this without punishment. Punishing wrongdoing, from an Inuit point of view, models the wrong sort of relationship, by setting one person against another in serious confrontation. When Chubby Maata grows up, a joke will be all that's necessary to control unwanted behavior – a joke that resonates with the emotionally powerful dramas that she experienced in childhood.

The medical officer made several mistakes when he judged Inuit socialization dramas and interrogations abusive.

First, he assumed that words and tones of voice that were familiar to him had the same meanings and were motivated in the same way in a different cultural context. In his way of thinking, "Bad!" is bad and an accusation is always an accusation.

Second, he lifted a single episode out of the context of Chubby Maata's whole experience. Being told that you're "bad" when no one ever tells you you're "good" is not at all the same thing as being told you're "bad" when everybody, including the "bad" speaker, 99 out of a hundred times, makes perfectly clear that you're a jewel.

Third, he assumed that *our* ideas about the social and emotional capacities and incapacities of three-year-olds are universally valid. He didn't give Chubby Maata credit for having the experience and the acquired sensitivities to at least suspect that she might not be in danger.

Fourth, he didn't allow for the possibility that children might need to develop different sensitivities and learn different interpersonal skills in different social worlds. I've suggested that Chubby Maata will need: finely honed powers of observation and a sharp awareness of being observed; a strong sense of responsibility for being nurturant to everybody all the time; and a pervasive but vague – and therefore powerful – anxiety about the possible consequences of failing to fulfill her obligations. She will need to feel a horror of confrontation and conflict and to have a subliminal suspicion that everybody is dangerously capable of confrontation if scratched the wrong way. I hope I've persuaded you that all these qualities can be very effectively taught in dramas like the ones I've described.

Finally, the good doctor didn't know that *how* one learns affects *what* one learns and how one can use one's knowledge. Eleanor Duckworth, in a cogent Piagetian criticism of our own system of education, tells us that children who are taught Facts with a capital "f" and given Answers with a capital "a" aren't very inclined to extrapolate to other situations the specific facts or procedures they were taught. They aren't very inclined to experiment, and they tend to mistrust their own judgment. Chubby Maata's elders believe that if you ask children enough difficult and dangerous questions and dramatize the consequences of their answers, sooner or later the children will figure things out for themselves. More, they will develop confidence in their ability to observe and figure things out. I'm sure you can see how essential this skill will be for Chubby Maata, who must analyze situations and solve complicated social problems all by herself, without relying on "expert" advice.

I could end here, but I want to show you that Chubby Maata *is* learning, and lighten the atmosphere a bit. So I will leave you with this charming incident, which happened a few weeks after the "bad" drama (Briggs, 1998, p. 143). Chubby Maata and her mother were visiting me, and Chubby Maata, sitting on her mother's lap, had picked up some of my note slips to play with. Liila, in the mildest of tones, said, "Don't do that." Chubby Maata put the slips down and began to chant over and over in a happy-sounding sing-song, "Because I'm not good, I'm not good."

Liila cooed tenderly at Chubby Maata, "Because you're not a baby?" Chubby Maata raised her brows, agreeing that she was not a baby. But her mother, nevertheless, snuffed her warmly and in the same tender voice assured her, "You're a darling little good one." In response, Chubby Maata began to chant in a happy-sounding sing-song, "I am good, I am not good, I am good, I am not good." Then, after a number of repetitions, she changed the words, and in the same happy tone, chanted over and over again, "Because I don't consider my chubby cousin good, I do consider him good, I don't consider him good, I do consider him good."

Liila made tender sounds to her daughter.

REFERENCE

Briggs, J. (1998). *Inuit morality play: The emotional education of a three-year-old*. New Haven: Yale University Press; St. Johns, NL: ISER Books

# Commentary on
## *"Inuit Morality Play and the Danish Medical Officer"*

Vivette Glover

This case study is very intriguing, and raises interesting questions about cultural differences in childrearing, their impact on the child, and what criteria one should use to evaluate these things. From a modern Western perspective the story does seem shocking and one can understand the response of the Chief Medical Officer of Greenland, although one might think it much more appropriate to offer help with parenting, rather than remove all the children. The description of the case provides no information on many relevant factors. Is this case typical? Are the family members in their traditional environment? It is asserted that the mother loves her child, but support for this is mainly good physical care. How is this love shown? But the main question is whether the type of upbringing described will really help young Inuit children adapt successfully to their future life. And what is success? This can be approached from both a biological and psychological perspective.

There is certainly good evidence that the very early environment, both in utero and postnatally, can affect long-term vulnerability or resilience to a range of diseases and disorders including the psychological. The concept of fetal programming posits that during critical periods, the uterine milieu can alter the development of the fetus, with a permanent effect on the phenotype (Barker, 2003). Gluckman and Hanson (2005) have proposed the idea of the "predictive adaptive response" to explain the evolutionary purpose of such adaptations, and suggest that they prepare the offspring for the particular postnatal environment in which it will find itself. They suggest that the plasticity underlying such early life changes increases the chance of survival of the individual to maturity and thus enhances reproductive fitness. Such epigenetic changes affect the phenotype without a permanent effect on the genotype, and at the molecular level, involve changes in gene function that do not involve changes in DNA sequence. Predictive adaptive responses represent much more rapid adjustments to a changing environment than natural selection based on genetic variation, which can take very many generations and hundreds of years.

Gluckman and Hanson discuss the example of the large fluctuations in population numbers of snowshoe hares in North America. When food is scarce, for example after a late spring, the population declines and many die of starvation. The fewer numbers mean that the remaining animals are more likely to be killed by their natural predators such as the lynx or coyote. The remaining hares must be extremely vigilant. Stress in female hares produces high cortisol levels during pregnancy; this in turn heightens cortisol responsivity in the offspring, making them more vigilant and sensitive to threat from potential predators. Such adjustments will help offspring to survive until food supplies replenish and population numbers can increase, whereupon hares who have lower stress responses will be able to reproduce in greater numbers. Thus the type of early programming that is most effective for appropriate later physiological responses and behavior depends on the environment in which the offspring will live.

Animal studies also have found that different mothering styles can exert long-term effects on both the behavior and the physiology of the offspring. Michael Meaney and his colleagues have demonstrated that mother rats who carry out more nursing and licking have adult offspring who are less anxious in behavioral tests and also have smaller and briefer corticosterone (the equivalent of cortisol in rats) responses to a novel stressor (Caldji, Diorio, & Meaney, 2000). They have also shown that such increased nurturing is associated with epigenetic changes in a gene in the hippocampus of the rat offspring brain, the glucocorticoid receptor, which exerts feedback control of the stress system (see Figure 11.3). Such changes can persist through several succeeding generations. Thus more nurturant mothering can reduce the stress responses in the grandchild generation, and conversely the offspring of less nurturant mothers will have stronger stress responses, and more anxious behavior. In a dangerous or stressful environment the mother may have less time, or be less able, to be nurturant and this may produce changes in offspring which will help them to survive and reproduce themselves.

This type of early adaptive response to stressful surroundings has developed in primates, including humans, also. Strong evidence now indicates that if the mother is stressed while she is pregnant, her child is more likely to be anxious, and to have symptoms of attention deficit/hyperactivity and

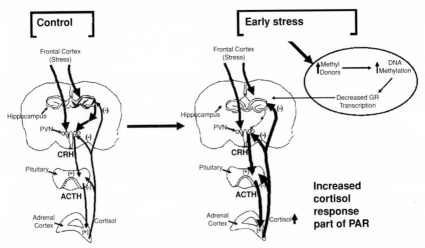

**Figure 11.3.** The figure shows how early stress (either prenatal or early postnatal) may modify the cortisol stress response. Epigenetic changes (increased methylation) of the promoter region of the glucocorticoid receptor (GR), leads to less expression of the receptor in the hippocampus, which in turn leads to less feedback control onto the paraventricular nucleus (PVN) and so increased production of CRH, ACTH, and the stress hormone cortisol, in response to a new stressor. This may be part of the mechanism of the predictive adaptive response (PAR), which helps the child survive in a stressful environment. Adapted from Talge, N. M., Neal, C., & Glover, V. (2007). Antenatal maternal stress and long-term effects on child neurodevelopment: How and why? *Journal of Child Psychology and Psychiatry, 48*(3–4), 245–261, with permission from Wiley-Blackwell.

higher cortisol levels (Talge, Neal, & Glover, 2007). We can speculate that the anxiety in the child is associated with extra vigilance, and this together with rapid shifts in attention, was adaptive in an environment full of danger or predators, which had stressed the mother. In postindustrial societies, with few non-human predators, and in which a high premium is placed on education with demands for focus and concentration, heightened vigilance and rapid shifts in attention can be maladaptive. Consequently, maternal stress during pregnancy can yield unnecessary anxiety and attention problems for the child.

Thus different *in utero* environments and parenting styles can cause biological changes in the child that will be adaptive for the specific situation in which they will grow up. It has been suggested that there may be analogous psychological adaptive responses whereby, if the environment is going to be harsh, the child will need to be toughened up. However it does not follow that any specific harsh parenting style will necessarily be helpful.

Sebastian Kraemer, in an article on promoting resilience and changing concepts of parenting and child care, discusses changes in parenting styles over the last few centuries in England. He quotes this eighteenth century advice:

I insist on conquering the wills of children... the parent who studies to subdue self-will in his children, works together with God in the saving of a soul: the parent who indulges it does the devil's work... break their wills betimes... let a child from a year old be taught to fear the rod and to cry softly... at all events from that age make him do as he is bid if you whip him ten times running to effect it. Let none persuade you that it is cruelty to do this; it is cruelty not to. (Susanna Wesley, as cited in Newson & Newson 1974, p. 56)

In the early to mid twentieth century, the New Zealander, Truby King, was a very influential guide to new mothers. Kraemer says that the key to the Truby King method was to:

Feed your baby by the clock every four hours and never at night. If you gave in to him he would become spoiled and spineless and, by implication, no use as a soldier when he grew up. To toughen them up, babies were to spend much of the day on their own outside in the fresh air, and should not be cuddled or comforted even when in distress. Mothers were not encouraged to play with babies, because it would excite them too much. Fathers had no role except earning money. (Kraemer, 1999)

Thus it is not just in other countries that rearing practices that we would now find abusive, have been used. They were employed in the U.K. not very long ago. It is an interesting question as to whether these childrearing practices did result in preparing children in a helpful way for their future life. For example if the boys were going to have to fight in wars, Kraemer suggests that "resilience would then be defined in terms of acts of courage on the battlefield, and its opposite as cowardice." Sensitivity and empathy towards others might make it harder to function as a soldier. One may wonder what the benefit would be to the girls, who were presumably brought up the same way, but perhaps it made them less nurturing towards their own sons, which in turn helped their survival. Even though not all males became soldiers, this type of upbringing could also have helped to develop other characteristics that were valued by society at the time, such as a "stiff upper lip." In our present culture we have different values that we would like to encourage in our children apart from, or indeed, instead of, being able to succeed in battle.

However, there are some values and behaviors that are universal across cultures. We all smile and laugh when we are happy, and cry when we are sad, and we all think the former is better than the latter. I imagine that in most societies domestic violence and suicide are thought of as best avoided.

So, to return to the case study described by Jean Briggs. It is suggested that Chubby Maata "has to learn culturally appropriate ways of defusing or avoiding the dangers: giving people what they want before they know they want it; joking with them so they'll know she's friendly; even, on occasion, temporarily retreating"; and that the upbringing described will help her with this. However, it is not obvious how the type of chanting described in the article, as practiced by Aqnaqjuaq with Chubby Maata, would help her with all this. Indeed hearing: "Your father is very bad! Your mother is very bad! My dear little granddaughter is very bad! Isn't that so? You *are* bad, aren't you? Your father is bad, isn't that so? I've heard that my dear little granddaughter is bad, yes indeed. Your mother is very bad!" and "Your genitals are bad! Aaq! They stink!"might be quite disturbing and would not be expected to raise self esteem.

One relevant type of evidence as to the benefit or harm of the Inuit upbringing described, assuming it is representative, is whether Inuit children are indeed resilient to difficulties they encounter in their own environment, with robust mental health outcomes. There is some evidence to the contrary, with several studies showing high levels of violence and suicide in Inuit populations. For example Curtis and colleagues analyzed the lifetime prevalence of violence and sexual abuse among the Inuit in Greenland, from a large cross-sectional health interview survey conducted during 1993–1994, and found very high levels (Curtis, Larsen, Helweg-Larsen, & Bjerregaard, 2002). The prevalence of ever having been a victim of violence was 47% among women and 48% among men. Women more often than men had been sexually abused, and more often had been sexually abused in childhood. Having been the victim of violence or sexual abuse was significantly associated with a number of health problems such as chronic disease, recent illness, poor self-rated health, and mental health problems. Tester and McNicoll found that Inuit suicide is very high, with rates in the Inuit Nunavut Territory of Canada's eastern Arctic being six times those of Canada's southern provinces (Tester & McNicoll, 2004). They suggest that low Inuit *inuusittiaqarniq* (self-esteem) is an important factor in Inuit suicide, although they also state that the causes of this low self esteem are several and complex. Of course, one cannot interpret much from one case history, nor from a few studies showing high levels of Inuit mental ill health, which may have many causes, but these things put together do give some cause for concern.

In conclusion, it is clear from the literature that appropriate mechanisms have evolved to prepare the child, from before birth, for the environment in which s/he is going to live. These include different patterns of early mothering. What is an optimal pattern of growth or behavior in one environment may not be in another. The same can be true for different human cultures, with different values, or attitudes to religion. An appropriate upbringing for a son to be a successful hunter-gatherer or warrior may not be optimal for a future psychoanalyst. However it does not follow that all upbringing patterns used in different cultures are adaptive. The methods described here for the Inuit are disturbing from our perspective, and it would be of great interest to have more evidence about if and why they are actually helpful for the child.

REFERENCES

Barker, D. J. (2003). Coronary heart disease: A disorder of growth. *Hormone Research, 59* (Suppl. 1), 35–41.

Caldji, C., Diorio, J., & Meaney, M. J. (2000). Variations in maternal care in infancy regulate the development of stress reactivity. *Biological Psychiatry, 48*(12), 1164–1174.

Curtis, T., Larsen, F. B., Helweg-Larsen, K., & Bjerregaard, P. (2002). Violence, sexual abuse and health in Greenland. *International Journal of Circumpolar Health, 61*(2), 110–122.

Gluckman, P. & Hanson, M. (2005). *The fetal matrix: Evolution, development and disease.* Cambridge, UK: Cambridge University Press.

Kraemer, S. (1999). Promoting resilience: Changing concepts of parenting and child care. *International Journal of Child and Family Welfare, 3*, 273–287.

Newson, J., & Newson E. (1974). Cultural aspects of childrearing in the English-speaking world. In M. Richards (Ed.), *The integration of a child into a social world* (pp. 53–68). Cambridge, UK: Cambridge University Press.

Talge, N. M., Neal, C., & Glover, V. (2007). Antenatal maternal stress and long-term effects on child neurodevelopment: How and why? *Journal of Child Psychology and Psychiatry, 48*(3–4), 245–261.

Tester, F. J., & McNicoll, P. (2004). Isumagijaksaq: Mindful of the state: Social constructions of Inuit suicide. *Social Science and Medicine, 58*(12), 2625–2636.

# Commentary

## Inuit Ways of Knowing: Cosmocentrism and the Role of Teasing in Child Development

### Karla Jessen Williamson and Laurence J. Kirmayer

As colleagues with different personal and professional backgrounds working together on Inuit mental health research, we found that Jean Briggs's chapter evoked quite different responses. Karla Jessen Williamson is an Inuk anthropologist, Laurence Kirmayer a Euro-Canadian psychiatrist. Our contrasting responses illuminate both the richness and the controversies inherent in Briggs's insightful work and touch on persistent dilemmas in cross-cultural research. In this commentary, we will present some of our respective reflections separately and conclude with some points of convergence.

### JESSEN WILLIAMSON: COSMOCENTRISM AND INUIT CHILDREARING

*"Naak silavit qeqqa?"* This question roughly translates into "Where is the middle of your universe?" My youngest paternal aunt asked me that question in a demanding tone. A totally dumbfounded, awe-struck six-year-old, I was hit by waves of sensation at the prospect of having to locate in my body the very part that housed my intellect, the air that I breathe, and my universe. I looked around at the air surrounding us, seeking the middle of my universe and my intellect; in desperation, I slowly pointed between my eyes! My aunt laughed and laughed. I was never sure whether she took my response seriously, or whether it merely satisfied her need for joking and teasing me.

*Sila* is the root of the word *silavit*, and Inuit use it to refer to air, weather, intellect, knowledge, integratedness, wisdom, and the external. MacDonald (1998, p. 35) describes *sila* as "an indicator of environment, an indicator of locality, and an indicator of intelligence or spirit." He quotes Spalding, who correlates *sila* and *silarsuaq*:

In a word like [*silarsua*] . . . we have a synthesis, one might say, of all these: that which supports life and physical being, that which defines horizons and limits, that which regulates and clarifies mind and spirit. In this concept, one feels a unity of microcosm and macrocosm, near and far, inner and outer, that is one living physical and spiritual unity of being. These are the outlooks and values of all peoples who are wise from their contact with the air, earth and water." (1972, p. 102, as cited in MacDonald 1998, p. 35)

I have described *sila* as a "force that gives all the living beings air to breathe, and intelligence. With every breath people and animals take, air becomes transformed into energy to be used for intelligence, because as much as there is no life without air, without it there is no intelligence either" (Jessen Williamson, 1992, p. 24).

Over the years, as I was growing up in Greenland, my aunt continued asking me about the center of my universe and each time it filled me with wonder – I felt waves of awe. In my physicality, there were cosmic and spiritual aspects that I needed to tend to. These pro-cosmic values that the Inuit inculcate in the process of bringing up their children come to mind when Briggs talks about "pro-social" values in Inuit childrearing. The two types of values are never really disconnected.

Briggs's observations on the Inuit and her subsequent discussion and analyses are rarities in intellectual circles. She makes an effort to anchor these analyses to her estimation of Inuit thinking, extending and applying her capacities for imagination and sympathy to Inuit thought. This effort is commendable because Inuit and academic modes of thought are significantly different. Her effort to understand the Inuit on their own terms represents a tremendous contribution to other academic efforts to gather knowledge in cross-cultural settings. Given the structural power relations between the Inuit and the institutions of academia, Briggs's stance must have been difficult to arrive at and maintain. Many of her colleagues tend to merge their newly gained knowledge about the Inuit into academic discourse that reflects their own mindset, as poignantly illustrated by Briggs's story of the Danish medical officer. Were Briggs to share the Danish officer's mindset, she would have lost most of the new meaning she acquired, and her insights would have little value.

In my own research on Inuit gender relations in Greenland, I realized that the majority of Inuit there (we call ourselves *kalaallit*) continue to use pan-Inuit methods in bringing up children. Kalaallit freely combine teachings that originated with the Inuit and teachings of the Lutheran church in such a way that the two complement one another. Inuit in Canada – and, for that matter, in Alaska and Siberia – experience different religious influences. Each group negotiates original Inuit values with the group's particular church. In Greenland, the education system is the most obvious place where Inuit-originated practices conflict with those of *Qallunaat* (non-Inuit) culture. This is an arena where kalaallit exercise their equality with the Qallunaat (the Danes). Unfortunately, this competition does not promote Inuit traditions of instilling pro-social aspirations (and therefore the pro-cosmic ones) into their children. Inuit thought on what constitutes a "full human being" is based on three aspects: *timikkut, tarnikkut,* and *anersaakkullu* (the body, the soul, and the spirit) (Jessen Williamson, 2006). But within the educational system, an antagonism arises based on individuals competing over aspects of the Western emphasis on "body and mind." Our educational system therefore shortchanges the modern Inuit learner in that only two learning environs (body and mind) are addressed, rather than three. Questions develop, such as whether one set of teachings is better than the other. Whose motivation and framework should be used to make decisions on these questions?

Returning to recollections of my own upbringing and that of Briggs's subject, Chubby Maata, it becomes obvious that she and I have experienced the same phenomenon, namely teasing. In my instance, the teasing immediately positioned me as having to extend exponentially my understanding that as a human being I am part of the cosmos, the universe, and the air, and to use my intellect to contextualize and materialize my own potential. This sort of teasing helps a learner understand that human beings are just a small fraction of the whole, considering the vast extent of the universe. Inuit reject the anthropomorphic worldview of European tradition, aiming instead to understand the importance of the relationships between humans and the nonhuman beings of the Arctic. Apprehending this cosmic web of relations is a humbling experience; when I reflect on it, I feel incredibly grateful that as a child I was given an awe-inspiring question to think through by myself.

Of course, both Chubby Maata and I were also given many oral stories to extend our cognitive and mental capacities, and teasing was just one aspect of childrearing. In my own estimation, teasing continues to be well utilized in Inuit homes and in general society across the Arctic.

## A VIEW FROM CULTURAL PSYCHIATRY

Kirmayer comes to this chapter as a clinician-researcher who has worked with the Inuit for 20 years. For Kirmayer, Jean Briggs's close observation of this Inuit play with morality raises basic methodological and conceptual questions about the cross-cultural study of childrearing and its impacts on personality and psychological dynamics.

Teasing is a common form of interaction between people who may have deep attachments, affection, and mutual trust (Keltner, Capps, Kring, Young, & Heerey, 2001). It plays with experiences of self-consciousness, exposure, shame, and criticism – or even ridicule and humiliation – and so may express aggression even as it conveys strong social norms and expectations. Briggs describes a teasing interaction that seems quite intense – so intense that the Danish medical officer, a cultural outsider, views the interaction as abusive and worries about the child's fate. This cross-cultural disagreement is important not only because it raises basic questions about how to judge behavior against divergent norms, but also because such judgments have been used to justify interventions. There is a long history of state intervention in the lives of Inuit and other indigenous peoples, with well-meaning social workers and other agencies taking children from their homes in the belief that indigenous modes of childrearing were destructive (Kirmayer, Tait, & Simpson, 2008). Understanding how diverse cultural systems of childrearing work is therefore of great practical and political importance.

Briggs's work is provocative in presenting a different mode of childrearing and insisting that its logic be understood in terms of larger cultural frames that enable a child to become a certain kind of social person. Her efforts to relate the microdynamics of interaction to cultural concepts of personhood and emotion show the unique contribution ethnography can make to our understanding of human development. Methodologically, however, significant epistemological problems are posed by using a single case vignette or even a more extended ethnographic study to reflect on child development.

One basic problem concerns the limits of observation and interpretation of actions and interactions. We do not have privileged access to the perspectives of the several participants and can only conjecture their motivations and what their behaviors mean. Even the participants cannot tell us all of the meanings at play in their own actions and experience, because many influences or associations either are non-conscious (automatic or implicit) or unconscious (actively defended against or denied). We must infer the meaning of another's actions by applying a psychological theory, and so our interpretations presume the theories they are meant to demonstrate. Nor is this problem simply a matter of understanding individual psychological dynamics. Ultimately, meaning resides not only in conscious or explicit self-depiction, but also in the discursive systems in which we are embedded, so that actions have irreducible social dimensions, which vary across cultures.

For Briggs the encounter between Chubby Maata and her grandmother is play, but the signs of play seem not to be immediately obvious to Chubby Maata. Her actions suggest that she is confused and distressed by her grandmother's words. Eventually her grandmother and mother make explicit the message "this is play" (Bateson, 1972), but only after she has felt the full impact of their provocations. From psychodynamic and interactional perspectives, Chubby Maata's efforts to deal with her grandmother's teasing seem to involve a succession of defensive maneuvers or rhetorical strategies:

1) She directly counters her grandmother's negative ascriptions by saying "I am good," suppressing her own antagonism toward the baby and demonstrating her goodness, or perhaps trying to get to the root of her grandmother's attack and eliminate its justification.
2) She introduces a story about the vulnerability of her father ("my father cut his finger"). This story may express her own anxiety about being attacked, but it also serves to displace or diffuse some of the attention directed to her and perhaps evoke her grandmother's protectiveness and concern.
3) She turns to her mother for confirmation and in doing so, tries to elicit her mother's support.
4) She bursts into tears – surely a sign that this is not play – but quickly contains and suppresses her emotional response.
5) She teases the baby and, when her mother comments on this, she begins chanting "crybaby" at the baby, thus mirroring the pattern of teasing and ridicule she has just experienced. In this way, she identifies with the aggressor and asserts her own competence or mastery, in contrast to her baby sister's immaturity.

Of course, these interpretations of Chubby Maata's actions depend on a set of assumptions about her experiences. But there is ample evidence to build a case for the distressing impact of this interaction and the challenges it presents to the child's capacity for self-regulation and dealing with interpersonal provocation. The question that remains is what long-term effects such interactions may have on the child's sense of self, modes of interaction with others (human and nonhuman), resilience in the face of future challenges, and eventually her own ways of parenting.

A second key methodological issue concerns the basis of claims about the outcome of this type of interaction on the child's ultimate functioning and adaptation. From the examples presented in this chapter, we have no evidence of the outcome of the socialization process. Neither the brief vignette Briggs presents here nor her more extended ethnographic analysis of Inuit childrearing (Briggs, 1998) give us any certainty about the long-term consequences of specific elements of Inuit childrearing. Does such teasing lead to a positive, pro-social outcome or does it leave the child anxious and insecure? Can teasing help the developing mind acquire the eco-centric and pro-cosmic values of Inuit personhood? If so, how does this developmental process work? Resolving these questions would require a longitudinal study, ideally including experimental or observational controls.

The third issue raised by using a single case to illustrate a mode of childrearing concerns generalizability. Is this vignette representative of wider cultural practices, or does it reflect local influences or the idiosyncrasies of one family or a few individuals? If the latter, we cannot appeal to norms but must understand individual personality styles and agendas. Jessen Williams believes this pattern is, indeed, prevalent across the Arctic. Teasing is frequently used to correct an anthropocentric emphasis and challenge excessive self-importance.

In interviews Kirmayer's research team conducted in Nunavik (the Inuit region of arctic Quebec) in the early 1990s, when Inuit were asked explicitly about teasing, most participants did not report it as an intentional or conscious aspect of childrearing. Some Inuit saw teasing as a playful form of exchange, and some also mentioned the emotionally damaging effects of unfair or excessive teasing. One excerpt from these interviews illustrates the common response:

Generally speaking, people only tease children; more often, if it's your brother's child, let's say. You might tease the kid. You're the uncle, the child is the nephew, you might tease the kid in a friendly way. Without making them feel bad. Without undermining their sense of self worth. A lot of the time, children were named after immediate family members, and particular traits of the senior person, were used as a way of teasing the kid. If your uncle tended to sneeze a lot and you carried his name, chances are, "You're going to sneeze again are you?" That kind of thing would come out. "Let's have something to eat here. Don't you sneeze." You know, that kind of stuff. But that's, sneezing is not, ah, not a usual thing that happens. It's mostly the way they speak. The way they carry themselves. (Kirmayer, Fletcher, Corin, & Boothroyd, 1994)

Like the example provided by Jessen Williamson from her own life experience, this account seems quite benign compared to the intense challenge presented to Chubby Maata. The association with the Inuit naming practice of *saunik* (Guemple, 1965), which links the child's behavior to the personality of the deceased person whose name-soul they have received, suggests another way of shaping identity to reinforce social ties.

Finally, it is important to recognize that much of Briggs's fieldwork took place 30 years ago, which is a whole epoch in the rapidly changing world of Inuit in Canada, as elsewhere. Inuit strategies for social control were developed in and made sense in a very small-scale society, comprised of groups with one or a few extended families. In this context, the use of modeling for teaching and the threat of social censure, shaming, or ridicule were effective strategies to maintain social control in an environment in which survival depended on the solidarity and support of the group. Teasing conveys overarching lessons about the importance of sharing and controlling one's impulses, and about the risks of social rejection; but, because Inuit see fundamental continuities between the human environment, the natural environment, and the cosmos, teasing can also provoke profound reflections on one's place in the world.

## CONCLUSION: TEASING, COSMOCENTRISM, AND RESILIENCE

Briggs's earlier work contributed greatly to an anthropological shift toward a deeper understanding and appreciation of the power and coherence of emotional worldviews and paradigms that exist in the world beyond academia (Briggs, 1970). In this case study, she directs our attention to the importance of normative judgments both within and across cultures and encourages us to better understand the use and role of teasing in contemporary Inuit contexts. The Danish medical officer in her story stands for all of us who reason about others in ways that are based on ethnocentric assumptions about human nature and development.

Social norms define standards of minimal, acceptable, or optimal care in childrearing. In situations of unequal power, norms derived from one culture may be imposed on another and used to justify interventions by health and social services, the law, and other agents of social control. In the case of the Inuit and other Aboriginal peoples in Canada this attitude has sometimes led to high levels of intervention by social welfare and child protection systems. Thus, it becomes a matter of some urgency to understand cultural variations in parenting practices and healthy developmental trajectories. As Briggs's account shows, our interpretation of parent-child interactions may be skewed by implicit norms that remain unexamined. Further, to consider the impact of childrearing practices only in terms of a narrow set of outcomes is to ignore their broader significance for a way of life with its own affective logic and system of values (Quinn, 2005).

Inuit approaches to childrearing reflect a particular concept of person-hood that may be termed *relational, ecocentric,* and *cosmocentric* (Kirmayer, 2007; Kirmayer, Fletcher, & Watt, 2008). As described in the first part of this commentary, Inuit understand the self as being in constant transaction with larger forces in the environment. This ecocentric and cosmocentric view gives different meaning to the challenges described by Briggs in her portrait of Inuit childrearing. It suggests that teasing has more than one goal. One objective is to impress on the child the importance of adhering to norms of interpersonal behavior (while tacitly acknowledging the com-plexity of our conflicting desires and emotions as human beings). Another objective of teasing is to encourage the child to engage in an active pro-cess of searching for the right way to think and act pro-socially in everyday encounters. A third objective is to reduce anthropocentrism and instill a cos-mocentric view. Within Inuit culture, teasing communicates social norms in a powerful way that the child is unlikely to forget. Rather than setting out clear rules to follow, however, it serves to create anxiety or concern about a whole domain of behavior. This focus encourages an active engagement with questions of the child's place in the social world and the cosmos.

Traditional childrearing, therefore, can be seen to encourage a distinc-tively Inuit way of being-in-the-world. Inuit today face elevated rates of mental health problems that can be traced, in part, to the dilemmas and disjunctures of forced culture change and political disempowerment that came with colonization and engulfment by Euro-Canadian institutions (Kirmayer, Fletcher, & Boothroyd, 1997; Hicks, 2007; Williamson, 1974). In recent years, Inuit in Greenland and Canada have established new forms of self-government within their own territories, requiring that they engage with bureaucratic ways of thinking and Euro-American concepts of person-hood that emphasize individual autonomy and achievement. The challenge the Inuit face lies in forging a new individual and collective identity within the nation-state that would allow them to enjoy the fruits of modernity and globalization without losing the wisdom of their traditions. The Inuit sense of connectedness and respect for the modest place of human beings in a large and awe-inspiring natural and cosmic environment may provide an important ethical and aesthetic sensibility with which to address the most urgent problems facing our world.

REFERENCES

Bateson, G. (1972). A theory of play and fantasy. In G. Bateson, *Steps to an ecology of mind* (pp. 177–193). New York: Ballantine Books.

Briggs, J. L. (1970). *Never in anger: Portrait of an Eskimo family.* Cambridge, MA: Harvard University Press.

Briggs, J. L. (1998). *Inuit morality play: The emotional education of a three-year-old.* New Haven, CT: Yale University Press.

Guemple, D. L. (1965). *Saunik*: Name sharing as a factor governing Eskimo kinship terms. *Ethnology, 4,* 323–335.

Hicks, J. (2007). The social determinants of elevated rates of suicide among Inuit youth. *Indigenous Affairs, 4,* 1–37.

Jessen Williamson, K. (1992). *The cultural ecological perspectives of Canadian Inuit: Implications for child rearing and education.* (Unpublished master's thesis). University of Saskatchewan, Saskatoon, Saskatchewan, Canada.

Jessen Williamson, K. (2006). *Inuit post-colonial gender relations in Greenland.* (Unpublished doctoral dissertation). University of Aberdeen, Aberdeen, Scotland.

Keltner, D., Capps, L., Kring, A. M., Young, R. C., & Heerey, E. A. (2001). Just teasing: A conceptual analysis and empirical review. *Psychological Bulletin, 127*(2), 229–248.

Kirmayer, L. J. (2007). Psychotherapy and the cultural concept of the person. *Transcultural Psychiatry, 44*(2), 232–257.

Kirmayer, L. J., Fletcher, C., & Boothroyd, L. J. (1997). Suicide among the Inuit of Canada. In A. Leenaars, S. Wenckstern, I. Sakinofsky, R. J. Dyck, M. J. Kral & R. C. Bland (Eds.), *Suicide in Canada* (pp. 189–211). Toronto: University of Toronto Press.

Kirmayer, L. J., Fletcher, C., Corin, E., & Boothroyd, L. (1994). Inuit concepts of mental health and illness: An ethnographic study (Working Paper No. 4). Montreal: Culture & Mental Health Research Unit, Institute of Community & Family Psychiatry, Jewish General Hospital.

Kirmayer, L. J., Fletcher, C., & Watt, R. (2008). Locating the ecocentric self: Inuit concepts of mental health and illness. In L. J. Kirmayer & G. Valaskakis (Eds.), *Healing traditions: The mental health of Aboriginal peoples in Canada* (pp. 289–314). Vancouver: University of British Columbia Press.

Kirmayer, L. J., Tait, C. L., & Simpson, C. (2008). The mental health of Aboriginal peoples in Canada: Transformations of identity and community. In L. J. Kirmayer & G. Valaskakis (Eds.), *Healing traditions: The mental health of Aboriginal peoples in Canada* (pp. 3–35). Vancouver: University of British Columbia Press.

MacDonald, J. (1998). *The Arctic sky: Inuit astronomy, star lore and legend.* Toronto: the Royal Ontario Museum and Nunavut Research Institute.

Quinn, N. (2005). Universals of child rearing. *Anthropological Theory, 5*(4), 477–516.

Williamson, R. (1974). *Eskimo underground: Socio-cultural change in the Central Arctic.* Uppsala: Institutionen for allman och jamforende etnografi Uppsala Universitet.

# TWELVE

# Ontogenetic Perspectives on the Neurobiological Basis of Psychopathology Following Abuse and Neglect

Sally B. Seraphin, Martin H. Teicher, Keren Rabi, Yi-Shin Sheu, Susan L. Andersen, Carl M. Anderson, Jeewook Choi, and Akemi Tomoda

## INTRODUCTION

The US Federal Child Abuse Prevention and Treatment Act defines child abuse and neglect as the recent act or failure of parents and caretakers resulting in physical or emotional injury, sexual exploitation, and/or death. According to national statistics on the prevalence of childhood abuse and neglect in the United States, 905,000 people under 18 years of age were victimized during 2006. Of these, 64.1% were neglected; 16.0% were physically abused; and 15.1% suffered abandonment, threats of harm, congenital drug addiction, or other forms of maltreatment. Furthermore, 8.8% were sexually abused; 6.6% were either emotionally or psychologically maltreated; and 2.2% were medically neglected.

Childhood maltreatment is a major risk factor for the development of depression, drug and alcohol abuse, posttraumatic stress disorder (PTSD), bipolar disorder (BPD), personality disorders, and aggression. Depending on an individual's sex, genetic makeup, and age at insult, chronic childhood traumatic stress (CTS) alters the endocrine profile and gene-expression pattern, as well as the functional activity, hemispheric integration, and morphology of the brain. In this chapter, we offer a holistic portrayal of the pathways between maltreatment and adverse psychiatric outcomes, arguing that the impact of abuse and neglect is best understood in the context of normal ontogenetic processes relating to trajectories of brain development.

## NEUROPSYCHIATRIC EFFECTS OF TRAUMA

Several studies have documented the consequences of exposure to CTS. One of the most compelling is the Adverse Childhood Experience (ACE)

Study, led by Vincent Felitti and Robert Anda (Felitti et al., 1998). Briefly, adult members of the Kaiser-Permanente Health Plan in San Diego, California, were invited to participate in a study examining the relationship between childhood events and health outcomes. A total of 17,337 adults provided complete information. An ACE score was derived by ascertaining how many different categories of adversity (0 – 8) an individual was exposed to during the first 18 years of life. Categories included: childhood emotional abuse; childhood physical abuse (CPA); contact sexual abuse (CSA); witnessing domestic violence (WDV); parental loss; and household rearing in the presence of mentally ill, substance abusing, or criminal people. Exposure to ACEs was associated with attributable risk for depression, suicide attempts, drug abuse, and alcoholism in 50%–75% of the population (Anda et al., 2006).

One limitation of the ACE study is that data available are cross-sectional and exposure was retrospectively ascertained. However, comparable findings have emerged from longitudinal investigations. For example, to assess the impacts of CPA and CSA on mental health, Fergusson, Boden, and Horwood (2008) analyzed data from a birth cohort of over 1,000 New Zealand young adults who were studied to the age of 25 years. These forms of abuse were associated with increased vulnerability to substance dependence, suicidal ideation and suicide attempts, anxiety, depression, conduct disorder, and antisocial behaviors (ASB) (Fergusson et al., 2008). When the overall family context was controlled, individuals experiencing persistent CSA or CPA were 2.4 and 1.5 times more likely, respectively, to develop mental illness than those unexposed to CSA or CPA (Fergusson et al., 2008).

***Other Significant Types of Early Maltreatment or Adversity:*** Childhood maltreatment research has focused primarily on the effects of CPA, CSA, and WDV. By contrast, parental verbal abuse (PVA) has received little attention as a specific form of abuse. We compared the impacts upon psychiatric symptoms of exposure to PVA versus WDV, CPA, and CSA (Teicher, Samson, Polcari, & McGreenery, 2006). Symptoms and exposure ratings were collected from 554 18–22 year-old subjects (68% female) who responded to study advertisements; exposure to PVA was assessed using the Verbal Abuse Scale. Outcome measures included dissociation and symptoms of limbic irritability, depression, anxiety, and anger-hostility. PVA was associated with moderate to large statistical effects, comparable to those associated with WDV or non-familial CSA, and greater than those associated with CPA. Exposure to multiple forms of maltreatment had an effect size that was often greater than the component sum. These findings proved PVA to be a potent form of maltreatment (Teicher, Samson, et al., 2006).

Poverty is generally regarded as an important developmental risk factor for psychopathology and substance abuse. However, a recent longitudinal study, Spence, Najman, Bor, O'Callaghan, and Williams, (2002) found that the effects of poverty were small, although significant. We reasoned that a major driving force linking low socioeconomic status (SES) to psychopathology would be the extent of perceived financial distress (PFS), which can diverge from real income. Hence, in addition to collecting information from subjects regarding their parents' finances, we also had them rate on a scale of 1–5 their degree of PFS: 1 = much less than enough money to meet their family's needs; 2 = less than enough . . . ; 3 = enough . . . ; 4 = more than enough . . . ; 5 = much more than enough. . . . Financial data were available from 1,201 subjects in the Memories of Childhood Study. Analyses assessed whether PFS was associated with psychopathology, controlling for parental income and education, along with exposures to CPA, CSA, WDV, and PVA. We found that PFS was strongly associated with symptoms of depression ($F_{4,1151} = 6.00$, $p < 0.0001$) and dissociation ($F_{4,1156} = 6.25$, $p < 0.0001$). Although neither actual income levels nor levels of parental education were associated with psychopathology, parental education was significantly and inversely linked with ratings of anger–hostility ($F_{1,1144} = 11.725$, $p < 0.001$). These findings suggest that it may be useful to assess PFS, rather than mere parental income, as a developmental risk factor. Also, finances and education should be viewed as separate determinants, rather than components of a composite SES score (Duncan & Magnuson, 2003).

*Developmental Considerations:* Ontogeny is a key factor often omitted in discussions of the relationship between exposure to adversity and psychopathology. We believe it to be critical in two ways. First, the timing of exposure is important. Neurobiologically, the effects of abuse at age 3–5 years may be very different than those from abuse at age 14–16 years (Andersen & Teicher, 2008a, 2008b; Andersen et al., 2008). Second, the consequences of exposure unfold over the course of development and may manifest in dissimilar ways at different stages. For example, although the most common adult sequela of exposure to CSA is depression, sexualized behavior is its most common manifestation in childhood (Putnam, 2003).

A number of studies have examined the association between age of maltreatment exposure and subsequent sequelae. For instance, Kaplow and Widom (2007) reported that symptoms of anxiety and depression were particularly associated with documented early (0–5 years of age) developmental exposure to CSA or CPA. In contrast, later-onset (ages 6–11 years) maltreatment tended to present in adulthood as behavioral problems. We have recently published the first study delineating the time lag between exposure to CSA and emergence of major depression (Teicher, Samson, Polcari, & Andersen, 2009). Briefly, an average of 9.2 ± 3.6 years lapsed between first exposure and onset of depression in young women. Initial episodes of major depression frequently emerged between 12–15 years of age, suggesting that exposure to CSA not only markedly increases risk for depression, but also accelerates its onset (Teicher et al., 2009).

The emergence of provoking disorders (or risky behaviors) at atypically young ages appears to be associated with exposure to adversity (Andersen & Teicher, 2008a, 2008b). Experiencing CSA or CPA leads to an earlier age of onset for BPD (Post, Leverich, Xing, & Weiss, 2001) and substance abuse disorders (Dube et al., 2003). Earlier onset of major psychiatric disorders is typically associated with a more difficult course and a poorer prognosis (Post et al., 2001).

It is important to delineate developmental windows of vulnerability – when exposure to adversity is most strongly linked to depression or other forms of psychopathology – because such windows of vulnerability intersect with sensitive periods in which specific brain regions are more susceptible to the effects of maltreatment (Andersen & Teicher, 2008a, 2008b). We believe that there are two sensitive developmental periods wherein exposure to abuse is strongly associated with increased risk for depression in adulthood. The first period occurs relatively early in childhood (ca. 5–7 years of age) and the second during adolescence (ca. 15–17 years of age) (Andersen & Teicher, 2008b).

Figure 12.1 presents the results of a preliminary study assessing symptoms of depression in 18–22 year old women with exposure to CSA during different stages of development (n = 29) versus 17 matched controls. The graph shows the eta-squared effect size associated with a presence or absence of CSA at each age. A positive history of depression documented in the structured diagnostic interview was associated with relatively early abuse (peak ages 5–6 years). Current symptoms elicited by the Adult Suicidal Ideation Questionnaire appeared to be strongly associated with CSA at age 6. Contrastingly, current depressive symptoms on the Hopkins Symptom Checklist-90 were associated with CSA peaks during both childhood and adolescence. The period between those two peaks may represent a time when the consequences of exposure to violence tend to manifest in other ways. For example, Sternberg, Lamb, Guterman, and Abbott (2006) reported that 7–14 year olds (but not 4–6 year olds)

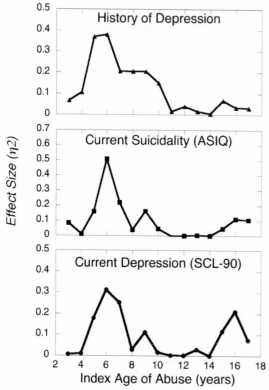

**Figure 12.1.** Depression symptoms in young adult women (n = 29) with childhood sexual abuse (CSA) at various developmental stages. History of depression and current suicidality on the Adult Suicidal Ideation Questionnaire (ASIQ) are associated with abuse that peaks between ages 4–8. Contrastingly, current depression on the Hopkins Symptom Checklist-90 (SCL-90) is associated with both early and later abuse during adolescence.

exposed to violence showed an elevated potential for clinically significant externalizing behaviors, compared with children who have neither experienced nor witnessed violence. These findings are largely compatible with the observation that exposure to abuse during latency (6–11 years) is primarily associated with behavioral problems in adulthood (Kaplow & Widom, 2007).

*Cognitive and Behavioral Problems:* Early maltreatment has the potential to thwart achievement of important developmental milestones (Kaplow & Widom, 2007). For instance, WDV can negatively affect children's cognitive development. In a study of 1,116 monozygotic and dizygotic 5-year-old British twin pairs, domestic violence was associated with

IQ suppression, with WDV children having IQs 8 points lower than controls (Koenen, Moffitt, Caspi, Taylor, & Purcell, 2003). In a study of 110 African-American boys and girls, Farah and colleagues found that early environmental stimulation significantly predicts language ability in middle school. Also, the degree of parental nurturance experienced earlier in childhood significantly predicted variance in memory ability (Farah et al., 2008). We recently reported that the duration of exposure to CSA was inversely related to measures of global memory (Navalta, Polcari, Webster, Boghossian, & Teicher, 2006). It has been our observation that collegiate women who were exposed to CSA had math SAT scores 74 points lower than those of non-abused subjects (Navalta et al., 2006).

## NEUROPHYSIOLOGICAL EFFECTS OF TRAUMA

Early maltreatment results in a cascade of physical and neurohumoral responses characterized by the stress-induced programming of glucocorticoid, noradrenergic, and vasopressin-oxytocin stress response systems (Teicher, Andersen, Polcari, Anderson, & Navalta, 2002). These responses affect neurogenesis, synaptic overproduction and pruning, as well as myelination during sensitive periods. Brain regions differ in sensitivity, as determined by their developmental rate, genetics, glucocorticoid receptor density, and the timing of insult (Teicher, Tomoda, & Andersen, 2006).

*Stress Response Systems:* The hypothalamic-pituitary-adrenal axis (HPA) and autonomic nervous system (ANS) are particularly affected by CTS (De Bellis, 2002; Nemeroff, 2004). Early stress is associated with a lasting sensitization of the HPA and ANS stress response, which may later culminate in increased risks for psychopathology in adulthood (Nemeroff, 2004). Both a blunted response of adrenocorticotropic hormone (ACTH) to corticotropin releasing hormone (CRH) and hypercortisolemia have been observed in sexually abused girls (Bremner & Vermetten, 2001; Nemeroff, 2004). In women, increased neuroendocrine stress reactivity is associated with a history of childhood abuse and further exacerbated by trauma experience in adulthood (Heim & Nemeroff, 2002). Severe childhood abuse also results in some degree of later CRH hyperactivity among women (Heim, Newport, Mletzko, Miller, & Nemeroff, 2008).

*Neurotransmitters:* Early traumatic experience can potentially alter monoaminergic and neuropeptide functioning. For instance, CNS dopaminergic responses to a stressful arithmetic task are evident among healthy subjects with poor parental care (Heim et al., 2008). Elevated urinary norepinephrine and dopamine have been observed in abused children with

PTSD (De Bellis, Baum et al., 1999; Nemeroff, 2004). Urinary catecholamine and free cortisol were both positively correlated with PTSD symptom severity and duration of past trauma (De Bellis, Baum, et al., 1999). Family-reared and orphanage-reared children significantly differ with respect to levels of the neuropeptides oxytocin and vasopressin (Carter, 2005; Fries, Ziegler, Kurian, Jacoris, & Pollak, 2005). Finally, women with recurrent major depression and childhood physical neglect have dramatically reduced plasma levels of brain-derived neurotrophic factor (Grassi-Oliveira, Stein, Lopes, Teixeira, & Bauer, 2008).

*Gene Expression:* Exposure to violence in childhood is strongly associated with subsequent risk for violent behavior. This was most powerfully reflected in the studies of Dorothy O. Lewis, for instance, which examined 14 American adolescents condemned to death for murder. Lewis discovered that 12 of the subjects had been brutally physically abused and five had been sodomized by relatives (Lewis et al., 1988). In a landmark study, Caspi et al. (2002) found that a polymorphism in the gene for monoamine oxidase A (MAO-A), which metabolizes dopamine, serotonin, norepinephrine, and epinephrine (adrenaline), moderates the risk for developing aggressive behaviors in individuals exposed to childhood abuse. Male subjects who experienced childhood maltreatment and possessed a functional polymorphism in the MAO-A-linked promotor region (MAOA-LPR), which is associated with low levels of MAO-A expression, were more likely to develop ASB than abused males with a polymorphism associated with high levels of MAO-A expression. That only a relative degree of protection is conferred by high-expression polymorphisms is supported by Weder et al. (2009), who recently reported that such a relationship is only seen in children exposed to moderate levels of trauma. By contrast, children experiencing extreme levels of trauma had high aggression scores, regardless of their genotype.

Several studies have identified genetic links between early maltreatment and the development of behavioral disorders. Ducci et al. (2008) recently extended the MAOA-LPR findings to substance abuse and women. They tested whether this functional polymorphism moderated the effects of childhood maltreatment on ASB and alcoholism in women exposed to CSA. The MAOA-LPR low-activity allele was associated with alcoholism ($P = 0.005$), particularly antisocial alcoholism ($P = 0.00009$), but only among CSA subjects. Depression, in particular, may frequently result from the confluence of CTS occurring during a sensitive period in genetically susceptible individuals (Andersen & Teicher, 2008b). A critical factor modulating the influence of life stress upon later depression is a functional polymorphism in the promoter region of the serotonin transporter (5-HTT) gene. Severe childhood maltreatment between ages 3–11 years doubles the risk of major depression in people with the 5-HTT "short" allele (Caspi et al., 2003). Kaufman et al. (2004) found that maltreated children who were homozygous for the short allele and had no positive social supports had the highest depression ratings. However, the presence of positive social supports reduced the risk in such children to the extent that maltreatment was associated with only a minimal increase in depression scores.

Not all studies have reported a strong association between maltreatment and ASB. Huizinga et al. (2006) found adolescent maltreatment to be a risk factor for the development of ASB, but could not conclude that MAO-A moderated the relationship. Furthermore, Caspi et al. (2002) indicated that MAO-A expression only moderated the interaction between early (prepubertal) adversity and subsequent aggression because developing levels of MAO-B compensate for the reduced expression of MAO-A. Similarly, a prospective study of 31–51-year-old men and women revealed a significant relationship between the MAO-A genotype and violent and antisocial behavior in white subjects but not in non-white individuals (Widom & Brzustowicz, 2006). The lack of association in non-white individuals may be a consequence of greater exposure to early adversity among non-whites, which could overcome the protective effect of the high-expression polymorphism (Weder et al., 2009).

## NORMAL BRAIN DEVELOPMENT AND THE NEUROANATOMICAL EFFECTS OF TRAUMA

In the last decade, researchers have identified a host of structural and functional neurobiological abnormalities associated with exposure to CTS. These alterations, which depend on the timing and severity of exposure, likely reflect the impacts of stress on trajectories of brain development. Assuming that these effects are stress-mediated, we hypothesized that different forms of abuse would exert comparable effects on brain structures. However, different types of abuse could have unique effects, because the growing brain may endeavor to attenuate the development of sensory systems and pathways relaying these adverse experiences (Teicher, Tomoda, et al., 2006).

Two major processes shape the developing brain during the postnatal period. The first process leads to a progressive wave of dendritic branching and synaptogenesis that occurs early in childhood and results in synaptic densities and metabolic requirements substantially exceeding adult levels. A subsequent stage of this process consists of a competitive elimination of excessive dendrites, synapses and receptors, which occurs primarily during the transition between puberty and adulthood. Together, these stages are known as activity-dependent synapse formation (Fields & Nelson, 1992), which has eight important features. First, neuronal connections not specified by the environment are genetically generated. Second, exposure to the environment produces inputs to systems that guide and determine the reduction of connections in such a way as to produce a nervous system optimally tuned to the characteristics of the environment. Third, synaptic connections initially formed during development cover a diffuse region of appropriate targets. Fourth, electrical activity within neuronal circuits is necessary for remodeling these initially diffuse synaptic connections. Fifth, the pattern of activation is an important factor in the remodeling process. Sixth, postsynaptic neurons often regulate activity-dependent plasticity. Seventh, in some neurons the coincidental occurrence of synaptic activity and the firing of the postsynaptic neuron serves to stabilize and preserve the synaptic connection. Finally, a critical period typically occurs relatively early in postnatal life wherein synaptic connections are particularly or exclusively sensitive to alterations initiated by electrical activity (Fields & Nelson, 1992).

The second postnatal process is myelination, in which glial cells wrap axons in a fatty sheath that facilitates rapid conduction of nerve impulses. Myelination proceeds regionally between 29 weeks and early childhood, starting with the brain stem and progressing along inferior to superior and posterior to anterior pathways (Lenroot & Giedd, 2006). Some pathways, including corpus callosum (CC) and cortical association pathways interconnecting the prefrontal, temporal, and parietal cortices, can continue myelinating into the second and third decades of life.

*White Matter (WM), Corpus Callosum (CC), and other Fiber Tracts:* Named for its color, WM comprises myelinated axon bundles and modulates the speed of signal transmission as well as the timing and synchrony of neuronal firing. WM volume shows an approximately linear pattern of increase from childhood to adulthood (Giedd, 2008). Myelinated regions, such as the CC, are potentially vulnerable to the effects of early exposure to excessive levels of stress hormones, which suppress the glial cell division that is critical for myelination (Lauder, 1983). The CC has about 200 million axons. Its roles include merging the sensory fields that support attention, arousal, language, and auditory functions, as well as the storage and retrieval of memories (Giedd, 2008).

Reduced size of the CC has been associated with diminished communication between brain hemispheres. Schiffer, Teicher, and Papanicolaou (1995) studied laterality and hemispheric integration of memory in adults who had a history of childhood maltreatment. Maltreatment was associated with increased hemispheric laterality and decreased hemispheric integration.

Pioneering studies by Denenberg showed that CC size was markedly affected by early experience, and that the effects were gender-dependent (Berrebi et al., 1988). Sanchez, Young, Plotsky, and Insel (2000) found that rearing male monkeys in an isolating environment attenuated the development of the CC and created deficits in learning tasks. We provided the first indication that the CC may be adversely affected by childhood trauma (Teicher et al., 1997). This observation was replicated and extended by De Bellis, Keshavan, et al. (1999), who later showed that reduced CC size was the most prominent anatomical finding in children with a history of abuse and PTSD. Males may be more affected than females. We have observed the CC of boys to be particularly vulnerable to the effects of neglect. The CC of girls appears to be more vulnerable to CSA (Teicher et al., 2000). Using diffusion tensor imaging (DTI), Jackowski et al. (2008) reported a reduction of WM integrity in middle and posterior portions of the CC in 17 maltreated children with PTSD versus 15 demographically matched normal controls. We recently reported that the CC of females was particularly susceptible to the effects of CSA occurring between 9–10 years of age (Andersen et al., 2008).

We also recently reported the results of the first study to use global analytical techniques (versus region-of-interest approaches) to delineate WM effects of exposure to maltreatment such as parental verbal abuse (PVA). We screened 1,271 healthy young adults to select an ideal set of subjects who had been exposed to PVA but to no other forms of maltreatment. Although PVA exposure is relatively common (around 10% of sample), it is quite rare to find PVA-exposed subjects who have no exposure to other forms of maltreatment or adversity, which could confound results. The sample consisted of 16 unmedicated subjects with a history of high-level exposure to PVA but no other form of maltreatment (4M/12F, mean age 21.9 ± 2.4 years) and 16 healthy controls (5M/11F, 21.0 ± 1.6 yrs) (Choi, Jeong, Rohan, Polcari, & Teicher, 2009). DTI data were analyzed using Tract-Based Spatial Statistics (TBSS), covaried by parental education and income. Three WM tracts had significantly reduced measures of fractional anisotropy (FA), an indicator of fiber tract integrity. These were the (1) *arcuate fasciculus* in left superior temporal gyrus, (2) *cingulum bundle* in the fusiform gyrus by the posterior tail of the left hippocampus, and (3) left body of *fornix*. The *arcuate fasciculus* connects Wernicke's and Broca's area. The *cingulum bundle* is a major pathway between limbic system and neocortex, particularly cingulate cortex. The *fornix* interconnects the hippocampus to the mammillary bodies and septal nuclei. FA in the arcuate fasciculus correlated with verbal IQ ($r_s = 0.411, p = 0.024$). FA in the cingulum bundle was inversely correlated with ratings of dissociation ($r_s = -0.373$), depression ($r_s = -0.504$), and limbic irritability ($r_s = -0.602$). FA in the fornix was inversely correlated with ratings of anxiety ($r_s = -0.311$) and somatization ($r_s = -0.389$). Interestingly, the hippocampus receives serotonin fibers from the midbrain raphe through two pathways: the fornix, which innervates all portions, and the cingulum bundle, which predominantly innervates dorsal hippocampus (Giedd, 2008; Patel, Azmitia, & Zhou, 1996).

We also discovered WM tract abnormalities in young adults with a history of witnessing domestic violence (WDV). 1,402 right-handed, healthy, unmedicated young adult volunteers recruited from the community were screened for a history of WDV without exposure to other forms of trauma or adversity. Twenty subjects with a history of WDV (16F/4M, 22.4 ± 2.48 years old) and 27 healthy control subjects without trauma exposure or Axis-I disorders (19F/8M, 21.9 ± 1.97 years old) were recruited. FA in the left inferior longitudinal fasciculus (ILF) was markedly reduced in the WDV group ($p < 0.05$ corrected). The degree of reduction in FA significantly correlated with ratings of depression, anxiety, somatization, dissociation, and limbic irritability. The ILF connects occipital and temporal cortex, and is the main component of the visual-limbic pathway that subserves modality-specific emotional, learning, and memory functions of vision.

*Hippocampus:* The WM region most strongly associated with stress-related alterations is the hippocampus. Exposure to corticosteroids can markedly alter pyramidal cell morphology, and can even produce pyramidal cell death (Sapolsky, Uno, Rebert, & Finch, 1990). Stress also suppresses production of new granule cells (Gould & Tanapat, 1999). We have found that early stress prevents the normal peripubertal overproduction of synapses in CA1 and CA3 of rats, but does not prevent pruning; these effects lead to an enduring deficit in synaptic numbers (Andersen & Teicher, 2004).

In our initial studies on the impact of childhood abuse, we reasoned that early stress could kindle the developing amygdala or hippocampus, producing seizure-like psychomotor phenomena without seizures. We therefore created the Limbic System Checklist-33 (LSCL-33) to rate the occurrence of symptoms often emerging during temporal lobe seizures (e.g., perceptual distortions, brief hallucinatory events, motor automatisms, and dissociative phenomena). This checklist enabled us to ascertain whether symptoms we refer to as "limbic irritability," were associated with exposure to early abuse (Teicher, Glod, Surrey, & Swett, 1993). We found that adult outpatients with a self-reported history of CPA or CSA had increased LSCL-33 scores, and that these were dramatically elevated in patients with combined abuse histories (Teicher et al., 1993). We have also observed that psychiatrically hospitalized children with histories of abuse have a two-fold increased incidence of clinically significant EEG abnormalities (Ito et al., 1993). These abnormalities were frontotemporal in origin; consisted of spikes, sharp waves or paroxysmal slowing; and were strongly associated with a history of self-destructive or violent behavior.

Bremner et al. (1997) and Stein (1997) reported a reduction in left hippocampal volume in adults with childhood trauma and a current diagnosis of PTSD or dissociative identity disorder (DID). Driessen et al. (2000) reported a 16% reduction in hippocampal volume bilaterally in women with BPD and a history of childhood abuse. More recently, Vythilingam et al. (2002) reported a 15%–18% reduction of left hippocampal volume in women with histories of prepubertal CPA and/or CSA plus depression, compared with either healthy or depressed female controls who had never been exposed to childhood abuse. Vermetten, Schmahl, Lindner, Loewenstein, and Bremner (2006) reported a 19.2% reduction bilaterally in women with childhood abuse and DID. On the other hand, De Bellis, Keshavan, et al. (1999) conducted detailed volumetric analysis of the hippocampus in 44 maltreated children with PTSD and 61 controls. They failed to observe a significant difference in hippocampal volume. Carrion et al. (2001) also failed to find a significant reduction in hippocampal volume in abused children with PTSD, as did De Bellis et al. (2002) in a separate sociodemographically matched sample. We conducted a complete volumetric analysis of the hippocampus in 18–22 year old women with repeated CSA (n = 26) and healthy controls (n = 17) (Andersen et al., 2008). Unlike participants in previous studies, these were not patients, but a nonclinical community sample. Only 6 of the 26 abused subjects met current criteria for PTSD and no subject had a history of significant drug or alcohol use. Hippocampal volume was reduced bilaterally (6.8%); this finding was most apparent in young adult females who indicated that they had been sexually abused between ages 3–5 years or 11–13 years (Andersen et al., 2008).

There are several potential reasons why six studies detected reduced hippocampal volume in adults with a history of childhood abuse and three studies failed to find any differences in such children (Andersen & Teicher, 2004; Teicher, Tomoda, et al., 2006). We proposed that the most likely explanation is a delayed effect that stress exerts on hippocampal development, which becomes manifest in early adulthood, as we have observed in rats exposed to maternal isolation stress (Andersen & Teicher, 2004). This delay may occur through stress-induced programming of neurotrophic factors.

Early abuse is also associated with increased brain transverse magnetization relaxation time (T2-RT), which is a surrogate marker for cerebral perfusion. Our laboratory has observed T2-signal strength abnormalities in young adults exposed to PVA. Voxel-based relaxometry (VBR) was performed on T2-RT scans (Anderson et al., 2005) from 22 unmedicated subjects with PVA (7M/15F) and 22 matched controls of equivalent age and SES, but without trauma history. VBR identified regional clusters of T2-RT differing between those exposed to PVA and controls. Exposure to PVA was associated with increased T2-signal strength in the parahippocampal gyrus ($p < 0.017$, corrected), anterior cingulate cortex ($p < 0.01$, corrected), and cerebellar vermis ($p < 0.001$, uncorrected). We previously found increased T2-RT in the cerebellar vermis of subjects exposed to CSA (Anderson, Teicher, Polcari, & Renshaw, 2002). VBR analysis of subjects exposed to CSA also revealed increased T2-RT in parahippocampal gyrus, which correlated strongly with LSCL-33 scores. Hence, VBR analyses revealed similar effects of early stress exposure in subjects with CSA and subjects exposed to PVA; these findings suggest that symptoms of limbic irritability may have a parahippocampal source.

*Gray Matter:* Named for its color, gray matter comprises nerve cells, dendritic processes, capillaries, glial cells and short axons. Its density peaks during development in primary sensorimotor brain regions before higher-order association areas. Although WM increases throughout childhood and adolescence, cortical gray matter development between ages 7 and 19 years follows an inverted U-shaped trajectory (Giedd, 2008). Motor and sensory systems develop before higher order association areas.

*Cerebral Cortex:* The cerebral cortex slowly matures through cyclical processes of reorganization. Delayed myelination of the CC enables the two hemispheres to develop relatively independently. We investigated the effects of childhood trauma on left versus right hemisphere development, using EEG coherence, which provides information on the quality of the brain's wiring and circuitry (Thatcher, Walker, & Giudice, 1987). We compared normal children aged 10.1 ± 3.1 years with hospitalized children of

10.7 ± 2.5 years who had severe CPA or CSA (Ito, Teicher, Glod, & Ackerman, 1998). We found that the abused children had reversed asymmetry marked by relatively greater left hemispheric coherence and deficient left cortical differentiation (Ito et al., 1998). Overall, EEG coherence measures indicated that left hemisphere development of abused subjects lagged substantially behind that of healthy controls (Ito et al., 1998).

The PFC has the most delayed functional ontogeny of any brain region. Major projections to the PFC scarcely begin to myelinate until adolescence, and this process continues into the third decade of life. With its protracted development, the PFC may have later or prolonged vulnerability to insult (Andersen et al., 2008). The PFC attains a progressively more regulatory role in cognitive and affective behavior. It develops in parallel with skills such as attention shifting, abstract reasoning, response inhibition, and processing speed (Yurgelun-Todd, 2007).

In a comparison of children and adolescents with histories of maltreatment-related PTSD and their healthy counterparts, De Bellis, Keshavan, et al. (1999) observed reduced cerebral and intracranial volumes in subjects with PTSD and maltreatment exposure. Brain volume negatively correlated with duration of abuse and positively correlated with the age at which PTSD trauma occurred.

These researchers also used single voxel proton magnetic resonance spectroscopy to measure the relative concentration of N-acetylaspartate (NAA) and creatine (Cr) in the anterior cingulate cortex of 11 children and adolescents who met DSM-IV criteria for PTSD secondary to maltreatment and 11 healthy matched comparison subjects (De Bellis, Keshavan, Spencer, & Hall, 2000). They found a significant reduction in the ratio of NAA/Cr in the abused subjects with PTSD. NAA is located primarily within neurons, and reduction of NAA/Cr is a marker of neuronal loss or dysfunction. Carrion et al. (2001) quantified cortical volumes in 24 children exposed to trauma (50% with PTSD) versus 24 matched archived controls. They found significant reductions in total brain and cerebral GMV, and most strikingly a loss of normal left-right asymmetry in the frontal lobes of children exposed to trauma (Carrion et al., 2001). More refined analysis showed that children with PTSD symptoms had significantly larger GMV in the delineated middle-inferior and ventral regions of the PFC than did controls (Richert, Carrion, Karchemskiy, & Reiss, 2006). Decreased GMV in the dorsal PFC correlates with increased impairment scores (Richert et al., 2006).

Voxel-based morphometry (VBM) is a fully automated, whole-brain morphometric technique for detecting group regional differences in grey matter volume (GMV) in an even-handed, unbiased manner. Using VBM, we recently discovered the most significant effect of exposure to repeated episodes of sexual abuse (SA) to be a reduction in GMV of the visual cortex. We recruited 30 subjects with SA and 30 controls for MRI after screening 723 volunteers. We observed an 18.1% lower average GMV reduction in the left primary visual (V-1) and visual association cortices (V-2) (Brodmann's Area [BA] 17 to 18; $p < 0.0001$, corrected cluster level) of abused subjects. The degree of GMV reduction in the left V-1 was associated with the duration of abuse occurring prior to 12 years of age ($r = -0.559, p = 0.0003$), but not later ($r = 0.088, p > 0.5$).

Positron emission tomography (PET) studies have shown that women with CSA-related PTSD also showed increased activation of the left middle frontal gyrus, posterior cingulate, visual association cortex, motor cortex, and left inferior parietal cortex; and decreased activation of the anterior cingulate, orbitofrontal cortex, medial prefrontal cortex, fusiform gyrus/inferior temporal gyrus, and left hippocampus. These findings were measured while subjects performed a retrieval task for emotionally valenced word pairs (Bremner et al., 2003).

Given their variable rates of maturation, we hypothesized that brain regions should have different periods of sensitivity to the effects of abuse (Andersen et al., 2008). In a study of right-handed women aged 18–22 years with CSA occurring during different developmental stages (n = 26) or without CSA (n = 17), we provided the first preliminary evidence in humans that brain regions have different windows of vulnerability to the effects of exposure to CTS. Hippocampal volume was reduced when CSA occurred at 3–5 and 11–13 years. CC was reduced with CSA occurring at 9–10 years, and frontal cortex GMV was attenuated in subjects with CSA present at ages 14–16 years (Andersen et al., 2008).

***Cerebellum and Cerebellar Vermis (CV):*** The CV shows the greatest degree of growth in humans during the postnatal period (Giedd et al., 1999). It also has the highest density of glucocorticoid receptors during development (Lawson, Ahima, Krozowski, & Harlan, 1992) and is a portion of the brain whose size is least strongly dictated by heredity (Wallace et al., 2006). Hence, the CV may be particularly vulnerable to the effects of stress (Ferguson & Holson, 1999). Abnormalities in the CV appear to be involved in a wide array of psychiatric disorders, including bipolar and unipolar depression, schizophrenia, autism, and ADHD. We have come to suspect that the CV may serve an important role in drug and alcohol abuse. Through its fastigial projections to the ventral tegmental area, it exerts strong effects on the turnover of dopamine in the caudate and nucleus accumbens (Snider & Snider, 1982). The CV is affected by drugs of abuse and methylphenidate exerts robust effects on blood flow in this region (Volkow et al., 2003). The putative anti-addictive agent ibogaine exerts profound and possibly selective effects on the vermis. ADHD is a significant risk factor for development of substance abuse (Wilens, Biederman, & Mick, 1998), and the most consistent anatomical finding in ADHD is reduced CV size (Castellanos et al., 2001). Hence, it is plausible that the CV may be affected by early stress, and it may be a component of a neural circuit that modulates risk for substance abuse.

The importance of the CV in moderating the effects of exposure to adversity came to our attention through the work of Harlow and colleagues. Briefly, H. F. Harlow and M. Harlow (1966) demonstrated the deleterious effects of maternal separation and early isolation on primates. Heath (1972) found that these monkeys had epileptiform EEG patterns in their hippocampus and fastigial nuclei. Mason and Berkson (1975) showed that a swinging wire surrogate mother greatly diminished the degree of psychopathology (aggression, self-stimulation), and Prescott (1980) and Berman (1997) suggested that vestibular stimulation projecting to the CV was protective against adversity. These findings together suggest that the CV is an important region for the maintenance of psychiatric health and it may mediate some of the neurobehavioral consequences of early stress or neglect.

We found that exposure to CSA was associated with increased T2 signal strength, which is indicative of reduced blood flow in the CV (Anderson et al., 2005); Anderson et al., 2002). T2 relaxation time in the CV correlated inversely with symptoms of limbic irritability, which in turn correlated strongly with the degree of substance use in a community sample (n = 553). This link between vermal blood flow and limbic irritability makes sense, because the vermis connects with the limbic system through its projections from the intrinsic fastigial nucleus. Also, activation of this pathway suppresses electrical excitability and seizure activity within the limbic system (Cooper & Upton, 1985).

De Bellis and Kuchibhatla (2006) reported a reduction in the left, right, and total cerebellar volume in maltreated children with PTSD. Cerebellar volume positively correlated with age of onset of the trauma that led to PTSD and negatively correlated with the duration of the trauma.

## CONCLUSIONS

Normal development and maturation rely upon the introduction of appropriate exogenous stimulation (Andersen, 2003). Conversely, early insult may lead to abnormal developmental outcomes (Teicher et al., 2003). We suggest that witnessing domestic violence and experiencing parental verbal abuse, childhood physical abuse, neglect, and contact sexual abuse may affect gene expression, neuroendocrine functions and brain development differently, culminating in specific neuropsychological and neurocognitive changes. There are different developmental trajectories for cognitive and emotional domains of brain functioning during childhood, adolescence, and adulthood. Thus, it is important to consider early adversity in the context of sensitive developmental periods, as well as family environment.

The sheer number of adverse events in childhood significantly determines risk for negative outcomes. Boys and girls may differ in their sensitivity to verbal abuse, emotional maltreatment, corporal punishment, and peer bullying. Financial stress may magnify the deleterious effects of early stressors. Certain genes may offer a neuroprotective advantage to those suffering early abuse and neglect. Finally, differences in myelination, neurogenesis, synaptogenesis, and neurochemistry may shape the vulnerability of particular brain regions to child traumatic stress because critical developmental periods determine the potential impacts of formative experience.

## ACKNOWLEDGMENT

This work was supported, in part, by National Institute of Mental Health RO1 grants MH53636 and MH-66222, and National Institute of Drug Abuse RO1 grants DA-016934 and DA-017846 to MHT, and by the Joanne B. Simches Research Endowment. We thank Dr. Ann Polcari, Dr. Carryl Navalta, as well as Katherine Flagg, Cynthia McGreenery, and Elizabeth Bolger for their diligent efforts in recruitment, assessment and evaluation of subjects.

### REFERENCES

Anda, R. F., Felitti, V. J., Bremner, J. D., Walker, J. D., Whitfield, C., Perry, B. D., et al. (2006). The enduring effects of abuse and related adverse experiences in childhood: A convergence of evidence from neurobiology and epidemiology. *European Archives of Psychiatry and Clinical Neuroscience, 256*(3), 174–186.

Andersen, S. L. (2003). Trajectories of brain development: Point of vulnerability or window of opportunity? *Neuroscience and Biobehavioral Reviews, 27*(1–2), 3–18.

Andersen, S. L., & Teicher, M. H. (2004). Delayed effects of early stress on hippocampal development. *Neuropsychopharmacology, 29*(11), 1988–1993.

Andersen, S. L., & Teicher, M. H. (2008a). Desperately driven and no brakes: Developmental stress exposure and subsequent risk for substance abuse. *Neuroscience and Biobehavioral Reviews, 33*(4), 516–524.

Andersen, S. L., & Teicher, M. H. (2008b). Stress, sensitive periods and maturational events in adolescent depression. *Trends in Neuroscience, 31*(4), 183–191.

Andersen, S. L., Tomoda, A., Vincow, E. S., Valente, E., Polcari, A., & Teicher, M. H. (2008). Preliminary evidence for sensitive periods in the effect of childhood sexual abuse on regional brain development. *Journal of Neuropsychiatry and Clinical Neurosciences, 20*(3), 292–301.

Anderson, C. M., Kaufman, M. J., Lowen, S. B., Rohan, M., Renshaw, P. F., & Teicher, M. H. (2005). Brain T2 relaxation times correlate with regional cerebral blood volume. *Magma, 18*(1), 3–6.

Anderson, C. M., Teicher, M. H., Polcari, A., & Renshaw, P. F. (2002). Abnormal T2 relaxation time in the cerebellar vermis of adults sexually abused in childhood: Potential role of the vermis in stress-enhanced risk for drug abuse. *Psychoneuroendocrinology, 27*(1–2), 231–244.

Berman, A. J. (1997). Amelioration of aggression: Response to selective cerebellar lesions in the rhesus monkey. *International Review of Neurobiology, 41*, 111–119.

Berrebi, A. S., Fitch, R. H., Ralphe, D. L., Denenberg, J. O., Friedrich, V. L., Jr., & Denenberg, V. H. (1988). Corpus callosum: Region-specific effects of sex, early experience and age. *Brain Research, 438*(1–2), 216–224.

Bremner, J. D., Randall, P., Vermetten, E., Staib, L., Bronen, R. A., Mazure, C., et al. (1997). Magnetic resonance imaging-based measurement of hippocampal volume in posttraumatic stress disorder related to childhood physical and sexual abuse – a preliminary report. *Biological Psychiatry, 41*(1), 23–32.

Bremner, J. D., & Vermetten, E. (2001). Stress and development: Behavioral and biological consequences. *Development and Psychopathology, 13*(3), 473–489.

Bremner, J. D., Vythilingam, M., Vermetten, E., Southwick, S. M., McGlashan, T., Staib, L. H., et al. (2003). Neural correlates of declarative memory for emotionally valenced words in women with posttraumatic stress disorder related to early childhood sexual abuse. *Biological Psychiatry, 53*(10), 879–889.

Carrion, V. G., Weems, C. F., Eliez, S., Patwardhan, A., Brown, W., Ray, R. D., et al. (2001). Attenuation of frontal asymmetry in pediatric posttraumatic stress disorder. *Biological Psychiatry, 50*(12), 943–951.

Carter, C. S. (2005). The chemistry of child neglect: Do oxytocin and vasopressin mediate the effects of early experience? *Proceedings of the National Academy of Sciences of the United States of America, 102*(51), 18247–18248.

Caspi, A., McClay, J., Moffitt, T. E., Mill, J., Martin, J., Craig, I. W., et al. (2002). Role of genotype in the cycle of violence in maltreated children. *Science, 297*(5582), 851–854.

Caspi, A., Sugden, K., Moffitt, T. E., Taylor, A., Craig, I. W., Harrington, H., et al. (2003). Influence of life stress on depression: Moderation by a polymorphism in the 5-HTT gene. *Science, 301*(5631), 386–389.

Castellanos, F. X., Giedd, J. N., Berquin, P. C., Walter, J. M., Sharp, W., Tran, T., et al. (2001). Quantitative brain magnetic resonance imaging in girls with attention-deficit/hyperactivity disorder. *Archives of General Psychiatry, 58*(3), 289–295.

Choi, J., Jeong, B., Rohan, M. L., Polcari, A. M., & Teicher, M. H. (2009). Preliminary evidence for white matter tract abnormalities in young adults exposed to parental verbal abuse. *Biological Psychiatry, 65*(3), 227–234.

Cooper, I. S., & Upton, A. R. (1985). Therapeutic implications of modulation of metabolism and functional activity of cerebral cortex by chronic stimulation of cerebellum and thalamus. *Biological Psychiatry, 20*(7), 811–813.

De Bellis, M. D. (2002). Developmental traumatology: A contributory mechanism for alcohol and substance use disorders. *Psychoneuroendocrinology, 27*(1–2), 155–170.

De Bellis, M. D., Baum, A. S., Birmaher, B., Keshavan, M. S., Eccard, C. H., Boring, A. M., et al. (1999). Developmental traumatology. Part I: Biological stress systems. *Biological Psychiatry, 45*(10), 1259–1270.

De Bellis, M. D., Keshavan, M. S., Clark, D. B., Casey, B. J., Giedd, J. N., Boring, A. M., et al. (1999). Developmental traumatology. Part II: Brain development. *Biological Psychiatry, 45*(10), 1271–1284.

De Bellis, M. D., Keshavan, M. S., Shifflett, H., Iyengar, S., Beers, S. R., Hall, J., et al. (2002). Brain structures in pediatric maltreatment-related posttraumatic stress disorder: A sociodemographically matched study. *Biological Psychiatry, 52*(11), 1066–1078.

De Bellis, M. D., Keshavan, M. S., Spencer, S., & Hall, J. (2000). N-Acetylaspartate concentration in the anterior cingulate of maltreated children and adolescents with PTSD. *American Journal of Psychiatry, 157*(7), 1175–1177.

De Bellis, M. D., & Kuchibhatla, M. (2006). Cerebellar volumes in pediatric maltreatment-related posttraumatic stress disorder. *Biological Psychiatry, 60*(7), 697–703.

Driessen, M., Herrmann, J., Stahl, K., Zwaan, M., Meier, S., Hill, A., et al. (2000). Magnetic resonance imaging volumes of the hippocampus and the amygdala in women with borderline personality disorder and early traumatization. *Archives of General Psychiatry, 57*(12), 1115–1122.

Dube, S. R., Felitti, V. J., Dong, M., Chapman, D. P., Giles, W. H., & Anda, R. F. (2003). Childhood abuse, neglect, and household dysfunction and the risk of illicit drug use: The adverse childhood experiences study. *Pediatrics, 111*(3), 564–572.

Ducci, F., Enoch, M. A., Hodgkinson, C., Xu, K., Catena, M., Robin, R. W., et al. (2008). Interaction between a functional MAOA locus and childhood sexual abuse predicts alcoholism and antisocial personality disorder in adult women. *Molecular Psychiatry, 13*(3), 334–347.

Duncan, G. L., & Magnuson, K. A. (2003). Off with Hollingshead: Socioeconomic resources, parenting, and child development. In M. H. Bornstein & R. H. Bradley (Eds.), *Socioeconomic status, parenting, and child development* (pp. 83–106). Mahwah, NJ: Lawrence Erlbaum.

Farah, M. J., Betancourt, L., Shera, D. M., Savage, J. H., Giannetta, J. M., Brodsky, N. L., et al. (2008). Environmental stimulation, parental nurturance and cognitive development in humans. *Developmental Science, 11*(5), 793–801.

Felitti, V. J., Anda, R. F., Nordenberg, D., Williamson, D. F., Spitz, A. M., Edwards, V., et al. (1998). Relationship of childhood abuse and household dysfunction to many of the leading causes of death in adults. The Adverse Childhood Experiences (ACE) Study. *American Journal of Preventive Medicine, 14*(4), 245–258.

Ferguson, S. A., & Holson, R. R. (1999). Neonatal dexamethasone on day 7 in rats causes mild hyperactivity and cerebellar stunting. *Neurotoxicology and Teratology, 21,* 71–76.

Fergusson, D. M., Boden, J. M., & Horwood, L. J. (2008). Exposure to childhood sexual and physical abuse and adjustment in early adulthood. *Child Abuse and Neglect, 32*(6), 607–619.

Fields, R. D., & Nelson, P. G. (1992). Activity-dependent development of the vertebrate nervous system. *International Review of Neurobiology, 34,* 133–214.

Fries, A. B., Ziegler, T. E., Kurian, J. R., Jacoris, S., & Pollak, S. D. (2005). Early experience in humans is associated with changes in neuropeptides critical for regulating social behavior. *Proceedings of the National Academy of Sciences of the United States of America, 102*(47), 17237–17240.

Giedd, J. N. (2008). The teen brain: Insights from neuroimaging. *Journal of Adolescent Health, 42*(4), 335–343.

Giedd, J. N., Blumenthal, J., Jeffries, N. O., Rajapakse, J. C., Vaituzis, A. C., Liu, H., et al. (1999). Development of the human corpus callosum during childhood and adolescence: A longitudinal MRI study. *Progress in Neuropsychopharmacology & Biological Psychiatry, 23*(4), 571–588.

Gould, E., & Tanapat, P. (1999). Stress and hippocampal neurogenesis. *Biological Psychiatry, 46*(11), 1472–1479.

Grassi-Oliveira, R., Stein, L. M., Lopes, R. P., Teixeira, A. L., & Bauer, M. E. (2008). Low plasma brain-derived neurotrophic factor and childhood physical neglect are associated with verbal memory impairment in major depression – a preliminary report. *Biological Psychiatry, 64*(4), 281–285.

Harlow, H. F., & Harlow, M. (1966). Learning to love. *American Scientist, 54*(3), 244–272.

Heath, R. G. (1972). Electroencephalographic studies in isolation-raised monkeys with behavioral impairment. *Diseases of the Nervous System, 33*(3), 157–163.

Heim, C., & Nemeroff, C. B. (2002). Neurobiology of early life stress: Clinical studies. *Seminars in Clinical Neuropsychiatry, 7*(2), 147–159.

Heim, C., Newport, D. J., Mletzko, T., Miller, A. H., & Nemeroff, C. B. (2008). The link between childhood trauma and depression: Insights from HPA axis studies in humans. *Psychoneuroendocrinology, 33*(6), 693–710.

Huizinga, D., Haberstick, B. C., Smolen, A., Menard, S., Young, S. E., Corley, R. P., et al. (2006). Childhood maltreatment, subsequent antisocial behavior, and the role of monoamine oxidase A genotype. *Biological Psychiatry, 60*(7), 677–683.

Ito, Y., Teicher, M. H., Glod, C. A., & Ackerman, E. (1998). Preliminary evidence for aberrant cortical development in abused children: A quantitative EEG study. *Journal of Neuropsychiatry and Clinical Neurosciences, 10,* 298–307.

Ito, Y., Teicher, M. H., Glod, C. A., Harper, D., Magnus, E., & Gelbard, H. A. (1993). Increased prevalence of electrophysiological abnormalities in children with psychological, physical, and sexual abuse. *Journal of Neuropsychiatry and Clinical Neurosciences, 5,* 401–408.

Jackowski, A. P., Douglas-Palumberi, H., Jackowski, M., Win, L., Schultz, R. T., Staib, L. W., et al. (2008). Corpus callosum in maltreated children with posttraumatic stress disorder: A diffusion tensor imaging study. *Psychiatry Research, 162*(3), 256–261.

Kaplow, J. B., & Widom, C. S. (2007). Age of onset of child maltreatment predicts long-term mental health outcomes. *Journal of Abnormal Psychology, 116*(1), 176–187.

Kaufman, J., Yang, B. Z., Douglas-Palumberi, H., Houshyar, S., Lipschitz, D., Krystal, J. H., et al. (2004). Social supports and serotonin transporter gene moderate depression in maltreated children. *Proceedings of the National Academy of Sciences of the United States of America, 101*(49), 17316–17321.

Koenen, K. C., Moffitt, T. E., Caspi, A., Taylor, A., & Purcell, S. (2003). Domestic violence is associated with environmental suppression of IQ in young children. *Development and Psychopathology, 15*(2), 297–311.

Lauder, J. M. (1983). Hormonal and humoral influences on brain development. *Psychoneuroendocrinology, 8*(2), 121–155.

Lawson, A., Ahima, R. S., Krozowski, Z., & Harlan, R. E. (1992). Postnatal development of corticosteroid receptor immunoreactivity in the rat cerebellum and brain stem. *Neuroendocrinology, 55*, 695–707.

Lenroot, R. K., & Giedd, J. N. (2006). Brain development in children and adolescents: Insights from anatomical magnetic resonance imaging. *Neuroscience and Biobehavioral Reviews, 30*(6), 718–729.

Lewis, D. O., Pincus, J. H., Bard, B., Richardson, E., Prichep, L. S., Feldman, M., et al. (1988). Neuropsychiatric, psychoeducational, and family characteristics of 14 juveniles condemned to death in the United States. *American Journal of Psychiatry, 145*(5), 584–589.

Mason, W. A., & Berkson, G. (1975). Effects of maternal mobility on the development of rocking and other behaviors in rhesus monkeys: A study with artificial mothers. *Developmental Psychobiology, 8*(3), 197–211.

Navalta, C. P., Polcari, A., Webster, D. M., Boghossian, A., & Teicher, M. H. (2006). Effects of childhood sexual abuse on neuropsychological and cognitive function in college women. *Journal of Neuropsychiatry and Clinical Neurosciences, 18*(1), 45–53.

Nemeroff, C. B. (2004). Neurobiblogical consequences of childhood trauma. *Journal of Clinical Psychiatry, 65*, 18–28.

Patel, T. D., Azmitia, E. C., & Zhou, F. C. (1996). Increased 5-HT1A receptor immunoreactivity in the rat hippocampus following 5,7-dihydroxytryptamine lesions in the cingulum bundle and fimbria-fornix. *Behavioural Brain Research, 73*(1–2), 319–323.

Post, R. M., Leverich, G. S., Xing, G., & Weiss, R. B. (2001). Developmental vulnerabilities to the onset and course of bipolar disorder. *Development and Psychopathology, 13*(3), 581–598.

Prescott, J. W. (1980). Somatosensory affectional deprivation (SAD) theory of drug and alcohol use. *NIDA Research Monograph, 30*, 286–296.

Putnam, F. W. (2003). Ten-year research update review: Child sexual abuse. *Journal of the American Academy of Child and Adolescent Psychiatry, 42*(3), 269–278.

Richert, K. A., Carrion, V. G., Karchemskiy, A., & Reiss, A. L. (2006). Regional differences of the prefrontal cortex in pediatric PTSD: An MRI study. *Depression and Anxiety, 23*(1), 17–25.

Sanchez, M. M., Young, L. J., Plotsky, P. M., & Insel, T. R. (2000). Distribution of corticosteroid receptors in the rhesus brain: Relative absence of glucocorticoid receptors in the hippocampal formation. *Journal of Neuroscience, 20*(12), 4657–4668.

Sapolsky, R. M., Uno, H., Rebert, C. S., & Finch, C. E. (1990). Hippocampal damage associated with prolonged glucocorticoid exposure in primates. *Journal of Neuroscience, 10*, 2897–2902.

Schiffer, F., Teicher, M. H., & Papanicolaou, A. C. (1995). Evoked potential evidence for right brain activity during the recall of traumatic memories. *Journal of Neuropsychiatry and Clinical Neurosciences, 7*, 169–175.

Snider, S. R., & Snider, R. S. (1982). Structural and functional relationships betwen cerebellum and catecholamine systems: An overview. *Experimental Brain Research* (Suppl 6).

Spence, S. H., Najman, J. M., Bor, W., O'Callaghan, M. J., & Williams, G. M. (2002). Maternal anxiety and depression, poverty and marital relationship factors during early childhood as predictors of anxiety and depressive symptoms in adolescence. *Journal of Child Psychology and Psychiatry, 43*(4), 457–469.

Stein, M. B. (1997). Hippocampal volume in women victimized by childhood sexual abuse. *Psychological Medicine, 27*(4), 951–959.

Sternberg, K. J., Lamb, M. E., Guterman, E., & Abbott, C. B. (2006). Effects of early and later family violence on children's behavior problems and depression: A longitudinal, multi-informant perspective. *Child Abuse and Neglect, 30*(3), 283–306.

Teicher, M. H., Andersen, S. L., Dumont, N. L., Ito, Y., Glod, C. A., Vaituzis, C., et al. (2000). Childhood neglect attentuates development of the corpus callosum. *Society for Neuroscience Abstract, 26*, 549.

Teicher, M. H., Andersen, S. L., Polcari, A., Anderson, C. M., & Navalta, C. P. (2002). Developmental neurobiology of childhood stress and trauma. *Psychiatric Clinics of North America, 25*(2), 397–426.

Teicher, M. H., Andersen, S. L., Polcari, A., Anderson, C. M., Navalta, C. P., & Kim, D. M. (2003). The neurobiological consequences of early stress and childhood maltreatment. *Neuroscience and Biobehavioral Reviews, 27*(1–2), 33–44.

Teicher, M. H., Glod, C. A., Surrey, J., & Swett, C., Jr. (1993). Early childhood abuse and limbic system ratings in adult psychiatric outpatients. *Journal of Neuropsychiatry & Clinical Neurosciences, 5*(3), 301–306.

Teicher, M. H., Ito, Y., Glod, C. A., Andersen, S. L., Dumont, N., & Ackerman, E. (1997). Preliminary evidence for abnormal cortical development in physically and sexually abused children using EEG coherence and MRI. *Annals of the New York Academy of Sciences, 821*, 160–175.

Teicher, M. H., Samson, J. A., Polcari, A., & Andersen, S. L. (2009). Length of time between onset of childhood sexual abuse and emergence of depression in a young adult sample. *Journal of Clinical Psychiatry, 70*(5), 684–691.

Teicher, M. H., Samson, J. A., Polcari, A., & McGreenery, C. E. (2006). Sticks, stones, and hurtful words: Relative effects of various forms of childhood maltreatment. *American Journal of Psychiatry, 163*(6), 993–1000.

Teicher, M. H., Tomoda, A., & Andersen, S. L. (2006). Neurobiological consequences of early stress and childhood maltreatment: Are results from human and animal studies comparable? *Annals of the New York Academy of Sciences, 1071*, 313–323.

Thatcher, R. W., Walker, R. A., & Giudice, S. (1987). Human cerebral hemispheric development at different rates and ages. *Science, 236,* 1110–1113.

Vermetten, E., Schmahl, C., Lindner, S., Loewenstein, R. J., & Bremner, J. D. (2006). Hippocampal and amygdalar volumes in dissociative identity disorder. *American Journal of Psychiatry, 163*(4), 630–636.

Volkow, N. D., Wang, G. J., Ma, Y., Fowler, J. S., Zhu, W., Maynard, L., et al. (2003). Expectation enhances the regional brain metabolic and the reinforcing effects of stimulants in cocaine abusers. *Journal of Neuroscience, 23*(36), 11461–11468.

Vythilingam, M., Heim, C., Newport, J., Miller, A. H., Anderson, E., Bronen, R., et al. (2002). Childhood trauma associated with smaller hippocampal volume in women with major depression. *American Journal of Psychiatry, 159*(12), 2072–2080.

Wallace, G. L., Eric Schmitt, J., Lenroot, R., Viding, E., Ordaz, S., Rosenthal, M. A., et al. (2006). A pediatric twin study of brain morphometry. *Journal of Child Psychology and Psychiatry, 47*(10), 987–993.

Weder, N., Yang, B. Z., Douglas-Palumberi, H., Massey, J., Krystal, J. H., Gelernter, J., et al. (2008). MAOA genotype, maltreatment, and aggressive behavior: The changing impact of genotype at varying levels of trauma. *Biological Psychiatry, 65*(5), 417–424.

Widom, C. S., & Brzustowicz, L. M. (2006). MAOA and the "cycle of violence": Childhood abuse and neglect, MAOA genotype, and risk for violent and anti-social behavior. *Biological Psychiatry, 60*(7), 684–689.

Wilens, T. E., Biederman, J., & Mick, E. (1998). Does ADHD affect the course of substance abuse? Findings from a sample of adults with and without ADHD. *American Journal of Addictions, 7*(2), 156–163.

Yurgelun-Todd, D. (2007). Emotional and cognitive changes during adolescence. *Current Opinion in Neurobiology, 17*(2), 251–257.

# THIRTEEN

# Ethnographic Case Study

*Maria: Cultural Change and Posttraumatic Stress
in the Life of a Belizean Adolescent Girl*

Eileen Anderson-Fye

I can feel the pain inside me and joy
Yes, it makes me think God's a woman too.
*Chorus of song by Maria, 12 years old*

Twenty percent of the world's children and adolescents suffer from a disabling mental illness, and this percentage is thought to be increasing (WHO,
2003). Moreover, subclinical mental illness is thought to compromise quality of life for thousands more children. Globalization and cultural change
also appear to play a role in the worldwide increase of diagnosed mental
illness among children and adolescents (WHO, 2003). One of the psychiatric illnesses linked to cultural change is posttraumatic stress disorder
(PTSD). Although the sociocultural and psychological pathways that lead
to an increase in diagnoses of PTSD under conditions of change such as war
have been well studied, these pathways have been less carefully examined
in more normative situations such as economic and cultural globalization.

One cause of PTSD is child maltreatment. Korbin (1987) has suggested a
relationship between cultural change and an increase in child maltreatment,
though the exact way this increase affects PTSD prevalence is unknown.
Following is a well-accepted definition of child maltreatment containing
three tiers:

(1) cultural practices that are viewed as abusive or neglectful by other cultures, but not by the culture in question; (2) idiosyncratic departure from
one's cultural continuum of acceptable behavior; and (3) societally induced
harm to children beyond the control of individual parents and caretakers.
(Korbin, 1980, 1981; 1987, p. 34)

**Figure 13.1.** A residential neighborhood in San Andrés (Belize). Photograph by the author.

In the case of cultural change, the first and second levels of this definition may be in flux, as is the situation in the case presented here. Individual experiences within these situations have not been well documented, and it is unknown how experiencing maltreatment in the context of globalizing cultural change affects a child's traumatic stress responses.

Moreover, medical anthropologists and cultural psychiatrists have questioned the universality of psychiatric diagnoses, categories of experience, and symptom profiles of PTSD and other disorders. Are these illnesses really increasing, or are they just being diagnosed more frequently? Are the diagnostic criteria valid cross-culturally? Are the symptoms only culturally shaped in their content or in their very constitution?

The case study presented here examines some of the microprocesses by which ideas and images from transnational media – in particular, television – impact the well-being of a young woman in a community undergoing rapid sociocultural change in Belize (Figures 13.1 and 13.2). The young woman, Maria,[1] reinterpreted prior experiences of maltreatment as

---

[1] This young woman's name has been changed and her identity disguised to protect her anonymity.

**Figure 13.2.** A key commercial harbor in San Andrés (Belize). Photograph by the author.

*abuse* in the context of U.S.-based media and had subsequent posttraumatic stress symptoms. She ultimately received a PTSD diagnosis, making her one of the first documented cases with the disorder in her country of origin. Maria's case is interesting not only regarding the precipitating events of her diagnosis related to globalizing cultural change, but also in that it highlights the importance of the *interpretation* of traumatic events, something which is always culturally shaped.

Maria's case emerged out of a larger five-year longitudinal ethnography from 1996 to 2001 investigating the impact of rapid sociocultural change on the well-being of adolescent girls in San Andrés,[2] Belize. Belize is a multicultural Central American and Caribbean nation that was a British colony until 1981. The economic base of the country has been shifting from agriculture to ecotourism as increasing numbers come to visit the world's second largest reef as well as rain forest areas. San Andrés, located on the largest offshore cay, is visited by 85% of the nation's tourists, most of whom are from the United States and Canada. Once a quiet fishing village, San Andrés has had a population explosion as people from other regions of

---

[2] Name of the community has been changed.

the country and from neighboring countries come for employment in the tourism industry.

The high school girls with whom I worked had relatively high levels of interaction with transnational ideas and images in their lives. The major sources of this interaction were media, including cable television, print magazines, and the Internet; tourists; and return migrants. U.S.-based television programming was a regular part of most girls' lives. The young women from all class and ethnic backgrounds reported watching talk shows more than any other type of programming. Of the talk shows, *Oprah* was by far the girls' favorite. Girls reported trusting and being able to relate to Oprah Winfrey, who could pass as Belizean physically. Many girls talked about identifying with Oprah's guests as well, forgetting that, "they're in America, and I'm here in Belize," as one 16 year old put it. Maria rushed home from school every day just in time to sit down in front of *Oprah*.

I met Maria in 1996 when I began to conduct ethnographic research in her school. One arm of this ethnography included in-depth longitudinal interviews with a sample of 16 young women across all five years of the project. In Maria's case, I met with her weekly for about an hour for approximately six months of the first year and then met with her for several hours of interviews each year following. After I had been in her school for several months, Maria approached me and asked if I could "interview" her once per week, "because I need to talk." Although a number of other young women had also approached me, Maria was unique in clearly wanting to meet "once per week" as opposed to, "when I feel like it," or "when I can." She said she had been watching me for a while and decided I was "nice" and "wouldn't gossip."[3] Her mother, her teachers, and the school administrators were supportive of this idea. Although I was concerned that this setup was suspiciously like therapy – a construct not available in this community – I decided to proceed cautiously with Maria's request in consultation with the caring adults in her life as well as my own advisors in Belize and the United States.

Maria was 12 years old when I met her. She lived with her mother, step-father, and three young half sisters. Her biological father lived in a neighboring town, although she rarely saw him. She was born out of wedlock,[4]

---

[3] Gossip was a significant concern among the girls in San Andrés as in many island communities. I was well aware of the irony that the girls were relieved I did not gossip in the community, even though I explained that the research was aimed at group-level community dispersal as well as publication. Most girls responded like Maria, who said, "I want my story heard. I hope other people can learn from it."

[4] In this case, "wedlock" includes marriage and common law marriage, both of which were widespread and accepted in the community.

and her parents parted ways shortly after her birth. She was fluent in English, Spanish, and Creole, as were most of the young women in the community, and her home language was Spanish, with a strong mix of the other two. Her mother and stepfather were both well employed in the tourism industry, so they were relatively comfortable though not wealthy. Maria's grandparents were of Spanish, Creole, Anglo, and Mayan heritage. Multicultural heritage is the norm in Belize, although most girls reported fewer than four distinct cultural backgrounds.

When we began to meet, Maria was an exemplary student. She held close to a perfect grade point average and was known among her teachers for being bright and inquisitive. She was often described as "fiery," a characteristic attributed to her mother's side of the family. She told me that she wanted to be a lawyer when she grew up, and she had concrete ideas about how to achieve this goal, although her own parents had not completed high school. Though she was well liked by her peers, she was occasionally considered mean and did not have a "best friend" as some other girls did. "I guess my mom is my best friend," she said, "but I can't stand her sometimes too." She reported a loneliness that she felt was unfillable because she had so much to share but felt that no one could understand. In particular, she wished her father could be the listener she wanted.

Because Maria was clear in her request to begin our relationship, I let her take the lead in the structure of our weekly meetings. In addition to sharing narrative, Maria began to bring artwork, poetry, song lyrics, and stories she had created to our meetings. I found her wide range of talents notable and in particular her mastery of English written language. Not infrequently, she would tell me about an event or experience one week and bring a poem about it the next. In both her narrative and creative work, she emphasized her emotional responses to what happened to her. One week she spontaneously brought a several-page, single-spaced autobiography that began at her birth and went up to and included her description and feelings about our meetings together.

The theme of the vast majority of her words and pictures was the difficult interpersonal events she had faced in her life, and her feelings about and responses to them. Without ever using the term "abuse," a term I was careful not to introduce to her or to others, Maria described very difficult experiences of physical, sexual, and emotional brutality. Many of these experiences came at the hands of her stepfather "over and over again." She described how he had beaten her and regularly beat her mother until she was bleeding and unconscious, sometimes using tools such as knives. Maria described how he attempted to molest her sexually, although she was able to escape the worst of it. She also discussed her sadness because

he "didn't want to get to know me as a person and support me." She also
reported sexual molestation by two of her uncles and her stepfather's father
over the course of about six years. In addition, she reported neglect from
her biological father, making her the only young woman in the study to
discuss that concept. Maria usually appeared to me sad but matter-of-fact
when discussing these types of "hard things" that had happened to her.
Her mother, teachers, and neighbors discussed and corroborated a number
of these events.

Maria reported her strongest negative feelings over being forced to
watch a beating of her mother that was so severe she was terrified that
her mother would die. She reported "hating" watching her mother's pain.
Despite being unusually articulate, she shared limited feeling words for
these hard experiences saying that she felt "annoyed," "mad," and "sad,"
about her own beatings and sexual molestation. She called the situations
"unpleasant" and sometimes "awful" or "bad." She described the bodily
sensations of her experiences such as, "sometimes [after witnessing beat-
ings], I felt like my head would explode. I could see my head so red like
catsup." She incorporated these words into her poetry as well, as in the
following first stanza of a poem about her mother's beating:

> She's gone, I feel pain, I feel hunger.
> My head is spinning
> And I'm wondering if she'll make it.
> I'm almost out of breath.

She also reported having regular headaches, though "probably not more
than other girls." In describing her relationships with her stepfather and
father, she used a number of nature metaphors, for example, describing
these men as being dark clouds cutting out needed sunlight to a beautiful
flower.

However, Maria also indicated that none of these experiences was surprising or unusual. She said, "that's just how men are," a sentiment echoed
in a majority of girls' narratives. She told me that she "expected" such
behavior as "part of life" for girls and women, herself included. She was
hoping that she could shelter her younger sisters from the worst of it, but
she fully expected that they would have their own "hard times" at the
hands of men.

Her interpretation of her stepfather's and other men's harmful behaviors
as "normal" helped to explain why she still claimed to "love" her stepfather,
"though I don't like him," she was careful to add. A number of other girls
in the study who discussed similar difficult experiences expressed feeling

considerably more anger toward their mothers, who condoned "horrible" behavior by men, than toward the men themselves, under a similar logic holding that "you can't expect more from men... that's just how they are," as another 15-year-old young woman put it. So, even though she "hated" the pain they caused and their actions, Maria never claimed to "hate" her stepfather or the other men who hurt her. And although she generalized about "how men are," she seemed to judge each relationship with a man individually, continuing to "long for a relationship" with her dad, and beginning to have crushes on boys in the community. Despite the many difficult experiences she had had by the time she was 13 years old, she appeared to be functioning relatively well in school and in other relationships.

After several months of our meetings, Maria underwent a dramatic change in interpretation of what had happened to her and began referring to the events as "abuse." The pivotal interpretive moment reportedly occurred after school one day while Maria was watching her usual daily *Oprah* program. I walked or biked home from the school around the same time every day, which was about an hour after school ended. This day, as I made my usual trek, Maria came running full speed toward me shouting my name. I was surprised by the intensity I saw in her face and moved her out of the street to a quieter corner. She began immediately in rapid-fire speech: "I was watching *Oprah* and these girls, they were discussing like exactly what happened to me... and I, I thought, 'That's me! That's me!' And I couldn't believe it. Tears came spilling out of my eyes as I realized I have *abuse*! And I had to come find you."

From this day on, Maria's life appeared to change. Maria began to have trouble in school and began to exhibit posttraumatic stress symptomatology that was absent previously. She began to contemplate suicide, became prone to sudden outbursts, had sleeping difficulties and intrusive thoughts, and showed hyperstartle, among other changes. Her mother, familiar with psychiatric concepts, decided to pursue intervention. Maria was taken to the only practicing psychiatrist in Belize as well as to psychiatrists in Mexico and ultimately the United States. Her family went into significant debt as her mother pursued her treatment. Maria was diagnosed with PTSD and treated with both medication and family therapy. In fact, she was able to persuade her entire nuclear family to attend "treatments," and her mother and stepfather were also treated with antidepressant medications. The younger children were taught about psychiatric concepts such as neurotransmitters ("neuros") as well as how a family should function (i.e., the father should not harm anyone).

Later, in discussing her Oprah moment, Maria spoke of it as a turning point in her life.

> I never heard anyone talk about that [abuse] like that before. They were talking about their stepfathers and stuff . . . I couldn't believe when they said their feelings, how they felt, because I've felt like that – so scared and sad – and they were angry and confused. I felt that too. . . . I knew I wasn't the only one . . . it changed me.

Maria had her feelings validated and, in fact, appeared to learn a number of feeling-related words that she began to use in conversation with me. Maria recognized herself in the young women discussing abuse, identified with them, and reinterpreted her own experiences with the concepts and words from the television show. According to Maria, the powerful cultural script on the talk show "made me see my real feelings," and ultimately became "the most important day in my life." Although certainly Maria had interacted with similar ideas through school curricula,[5] other television programs, and family members who moved back and forth between Belize and the United States, there was something about the presentation on this show at that moment of her life that caused a strong identification.

The key factor in Maria's reinterpretation of her experiences appeared to be the distinction between her perception of the events as "normal" and thinking of them as "something that should never happen." The moral outrage created in this shift – where men went from uncontrollable to conscious actors who should "know better" – seemed to be the trigger for Maria. Just acknowledging that her maltreatment "didn't have to be that way" repeatedly sent Maria into tears. The shift from her experiences as reality and the only way the world operates to imagined possibilities where norms were different and individual men could make different choices brought her into a world where she then experienced what was labeled as posttraumatic stress. This reinterpretation was immediately applied to her past, present, and future, changing her sense of the relational world forever.

In comparison with the psychiatric literature on child-abuse-related PTSD, I found several absences in Maria's case notable. Maria never used

---

[5] Primary school curricula included a standardized lesson on the definitions of physical, emotional, and sexual abuse found throughout the Caribbean. This sort of "top-down" teaching about abuse has increased over the past decade as a new national campaign and hotline for the prevention of "child abuse" were begun. I found it interesting that at the time of this study, these notions and words did not appear in girls' personal narratives about maltreatment.

the term "victim" in our interviews, which was consistent with interviews with her peers. A victim in the community seemed only to be someone who had suffered an accident such as drowning or being hit by a car. The word "perpetrator" was also absent from her vocabulary, although it was a term taught in primary school. Maria – again consistent with her peers – did not blame herself for her stepfather's or other men's hurtful behaviors. Even after her reinterpretation, she never ruminated or wondered if there was something *she* could have done differently. She, along with her peers, put the responsibility squarely on the men themselves and wondered why *they* did not behave differently. Moreover, she seemed to reconcile quickly with her stepfather once he also began treatment and lessened the behaviors. She appeared to genuinely welcome him back into her life and to value the relationship. In part due to Maria's diligence, her entire family reported being "helped" by this experience. Maria was sure the environment would be better for her younger sisters.

Maria herself continued to struggle off and on over the next five years. She entered into a romantic relationship she later termed abusive and ended up dropping out of school. Her peers also gossiped about her as sexually promiscuous and abusing alcohol. However, she reentered high school the next year and ultimately graduated with a 3.8 grade-point average. She had changed her professional goals to work at a "good office job," which she began after graduation. She stopped her medications and her therapies and felt she was "on a good path . . . just living my life and trying to be happy."

This experience – of young women reinterpreting events in their own lives based on how they saw others doing so in digital and print media – was so common among the girls that I began to call it, the "Oprah effect" (Anderson-Fye, 2003). Elsewhere, I have made the argument that this powerful reinterpretation was not random but rather was mediated by ethnopsychology and occurred primarily in areas where the girls had the most to gain, namely gender equity (Anderson-Fye, 2003). Maria's case is an unusually crystallized example that raises a number of questions about the role of cultural context in psychiatric illness. Could a different thought and judgment have thrown Maria into a traumatic stress response?

What is the mechanism by which this could happen and her life could change literally overnight? A psychiatric hypothesis of what happened to Maria is that this particular viewing of the young women discussing their lives on television *triggered* long dormant trauma and symptom sequelae, whereas a cultural phenomenological hypothesis is that the traumatic stress was *created* at the moment of identification, thus giving rise to a PTSD response in the interpretation of events. Was the trauma prior, new, or perhaps both? Was the trauma located in the events, the experience of the events, or in the interpretation of the events?

As an observer of Maria and her peers, I believe the situation is complicated and multilayered. Maltreatment of girls and women is surprisingly common in Belize, as it is in many parts of the world, especially in post-colonial situations. In fact, the three books written to date about Belizean women in different regions of the country have all focused on domestic violence (Henderson & Houghton, 1993; McClaurin, 1996; McCluskey, 2001) and have gone so far as to call "acceptance of domestic violence" part of "Belize's culture of gender" (McClaurin, 1996, p. 81). A government report on girls' health suggested that physical, sexual, and emotional abuse are "disturbingly widespread" but did not quantify that impression (Cameron, 1997). In my study, about one-third of the girls enrolled in the high school reported physical maltreatment, sexual maltreatment, or both (Anderson-Fye, 2002). If the psychiatric hypothesis is true and it is the case that gender-based maltreatment is common in young women's lives, then posttraumatic stress disorder and symptoms should be extant or even common in Belize. In fact, they do not appear to be, although other girls in this study also started to show symptoms after undergoing similar, albeit more gradual, processes of reinterpretation in the context of television, magazines, the Internet, and transnational relationships (Anderson-Fye, 2002). None of the girls in this study with what could be called trauma histories who had not made this sort of interpretive shift showed posttraumatic stress symptoms. These data suggest that something directly related to a new sense of this maltreatment as not only "bad" but actually "wrong" is present, as is suggested by the cultural hypothesis.

On the other hand, a number of girls made this same interpretive shift and did not display posttraumatic stress symptoms, irrespective of a history of maltreatment. There was something specific to Maria's experiences or psychology that made a trigger possible. Her symptoms were easily recognizable to psychiatrists as related to posttraumatic stress, suggesting the importance of a biological response that has been found to be relatively consistent around the world. In her case, the flashbacks and intrusive thoughts were centered on two experiences that she reported to be the worst, and it is likely that the trauma of these overwhelming moments was reelicited. Interestingly, although both of these moments included harm to her, she was primarily focused on having witnessed her mother's pain.

There also appear to be important developmental and generational effects to the onset of symptoms in Maria's life. Maria and a number of her peers reinterpreted gender-based maltreatment in early to mid adolescence. Not only is this a time when hypothetical thought emerges, but it is also a time of immense neurological plasticity. In typical development, the neurons are pared down during this time, allowing more efficient brain communication. One of the focal areas of the rapid development includes increasing communication between the frontal cortex and the limbic system (Spear, 2000). It makes sense that this would be a prime developmental time for abstract thoughts to profoundly affect deep emotional experiences and memories. Moreover, this life cycle period is known to be important to mental health outcomes. A number of mental illnesses have their onset or worsen in adolescence (Walker, 2002), and in the case of child-abuse-related PTSD, adult outcomes are predicted by adolescent experiences. In some ways, adolescents like Maria are wired to take in and consider novel information around them (Spear, 2000) better than at any other time in the life cycle.

Maria and her peers are also living in a unique historical period that may allow them to see things in a way that generations before them could not. Maria's cohort is the first to grow up with widespread access to both jobs that are better than subsistence and educational opportunities including high school.[6] In short, it is the first generation of young women who can fully support themselves without being dependent on a man. The feminized service sector jobs that the tourism industry introduced, such as hotel receptionist or gift shop clerk, pay enough to allow a woman to support herself and her children if necessary. The prior generations did not have that opportunity, as men were the major players in agriculture, fishing, and logging. Interpreting a domestic violence situation as "wrong" when there was no alternative would have been an impossible situation. Maria and her peers have an alternative – to support themselves in a new class of jobs not available to their predecessors.

Finally, I do not think it was coincidental that Maria sought out an American citizen with whom to share this experience. This Belizean community is home to the largest concentration of U.S. expatriates in the country, and a number of local San Andranos had dual citizenship. Almost every family knows someone who immigrated to the United States or who moves back and forth between the two countries. The tourists are also integrated into the community space rather than being separated as

---

[6] School is only mandatory through primary school. A high school education is increasingly needed to gain access to good jobs in the tourism industry. Most women of Maria's mother's generation do not have high school degrees.

in other Caribbean areas. Therefore, interacting with someone from the United States was not a particularly novel experience; it was one with which most young women appeared comfortable. Although there were still clear insider–outsider lines drawn in terms of sharing information deemed "authentic," in my case, I had passed through some major gate-keepers over time and was welcomed into the school and other areas where girls could then choose how to negotiate a relationship with me. In Maria's case, she expressed that I was a trusted adult in her life, approved of by her family. I am confident that she knew I would be sympathetic to her situation and hold beliefs consistent with those she had just seen without being embroiled in local politics.[7]

Maria's case brings up a number of questions about the role of changing cultural context and interpretation in traumatic experience, and in PTSD specifically, and about the role of culture and cognition in psychiatric disorders more generally. In Maria's case, not only was her individual interpretation relevant in the context of powerful media, but also the changing economic situation potentially opened up interpretative possibilities too dangerous to entertain previously for individual women in the community. Obviously, condoning gender-based abuse, as appears to have been the case historically in this community, is not an acceptable or desirable measure to reduce posttraumatic stress symptoms. In Maria's case, her symptoms and personal suffering ultimately provided reason for an intervention for her entire family that they report as positive. Although her family was probably unusually receptive and resourceful in responding to her distress, her symptoms ironically led to increased social health by local and international standards. In this community, there is promise that these individual girls who are experiencing individual reinterpretations of gendered violence are actually causing social change by increasing their motivation for education and "good" jobs as well as by enabling them to seek partners for themselves who do not hurt them (Anderson-Fye, 2002). Such findings provide further support for the mutual roles of individual and social well-being.

Maria's case also flags the role of adolescence specifically in the interaction of cultural change and mental health. Other research has found that the introduction of U.S. television programming into previously media-naïve

---

[7] Maria had tried to tell a primary school teacher about some of her sexual molestation as it was occurring, but because of complicated family business relationships, the teacher – who might otherwise have tried to help or at least listen – did not even allow Maria to finish talking.

communities can have profound and rapid effects on adolescent mental health (Becker, Burwell, Gilman, Herzog, & Hamburg, 2002). Developmentally, adolescents may be especially poised to interpret and use ideas, images, and technologies salient in specific instances of cultural change in ways that affect their mental health and well-being.

REFERENCES

Anderson-Fye, E. P. (2002). *Never leave yourself: Belizean schoolgirls' psychological development in cultural context.* (Unpublished doctoral dissertation). Harvard University, Cambridge, Massachusetts.

Anderson-Fye, E. P. (2003). Never leave yourself: Ethnopsychology as mediator of psychological globalization among Belizean schoolgirls. *Ethos, 31*(1), 77–112.

Becker, A. E., Burwell, R. A., Gilman, S. E., Herzog, D. B., Hamburg, P. (2002). Eating behaviours and attitudes following prolonged exposure to television among ethnic Fijian adolescent girls. *British Journal of Psychiatry, 180,* 509–514.

Cameron, S. (1997). *From girls to women: Growing up healthy in Belize.* Belize City: Government of Belize.

Henderson, P., & Houghton, A. (Eds.). (1993). *Rising up: Life stories of Belizean women.* Toronto: Sister Vision.

Korbin, J. (1987). Child maltreatment in cross-cultural perspective: Vulnerable children and circumstances. In R. J. Gelles & J. B. Lancaster (Eds.), *Child abuse and neglect: Biosocial dimensions* (pp. 31–56). Hawthorne, NY: Aldine de Gruyter.

Korbin J. (Ed.). (1981). *Child abuse and neglect Cross-cultural perspectives.* Berkeley, CA: University of California Press.

Korbin, J. (1980). The cultural context of child abuse and neglect. In C. H. Kempe & R. E. Helfer (Eds.), *The battered child* (3rd ed., pp. 21–35). Chicago, IL: University of Chicago Press.

McClaurin, I. (1996). *Women of Belize: Gender and change in Central America.* New Brunswick, NJ: Rutgers University Press.

McCluskey, L. (2001). *Here, our culture is hard: Stories of domestic violence from a Mayan community in Belize.* Austin, TX: University of Texas.

Spear L. (2000). Neurobehavioral Changes in Adolescence. *Current Directions in Psychological Science, 9*(4), 111–114.

Walker, E. (2002). Adolescent neurodevelopment and psychopathology. *Current Directions in Psychological Science, 11*(1), 24–28.

World Health Organization (2003). *Caring for children and adolescents with mental disorders: Setting WHO directions.* Geneva: Author.

# Commentary on

## "Maria: Cultural Change and Posttraumatic Stress in the Life of a Belizean Adolescent Girl"

Anne E. Becker

Dr. Anderson-Fye's presentation of the case of emergent posttraumatic stress symptoms in a Belizean adolescent girl provides a textured ethnographic and clinical account of resilience in the setting of personal and social turbulence. This case describes the identification of, elaboration of, and social response to symptoms generated in the context of traumatic experience in a young adolescent girl. In doing so, it suggests the complex dimensions whereby the transformation of the cultural landscape both results in extraordinary need and presents opportunities for large-scale public health interventions that mobilize community and family-based resources for prevention, education, and enhanced access to care.

Dr. Anderson-Fye notes in her introduction that social and economic changes associated with globalization have been associated with an increase in diagnosed mental illness among adolescents. The social turbulence that frequently accompanies globalization augments the vulnerability of this age group, a group that is not only in the midst of a rather perilous developmental crossing, but that also has limited access to and visibility in health services across many settings.

The case involves an adolescent Belizean girl – Maria, a pseudonym – who eventually receives a diagnosis of posttraumatic stress disorder (PTSD). This young adolescent, Maria, participated in a series of ethnographic interviews begun at her school in 1996 when she was 12 years old. She was apparently well-liked, yet socially isolated inasmuch as she described a "loneliness that she felt was unfillable because she had so much to share but felt no one could understand." She was a motivated student with ambitious professional and academic goals that would place her well beyond what either of her parents had achieved academically. This must have alienated her even further from her parents – apart from their neglect and abuse – but may represent conflict widely shared by her peers.

Navigation of rapid social and economic change during adolescence presents unique developmental challenges inherent in the unfamiliar and uncertain social landscape. Culturally established reference points for identity, social status, and brokering social capital may transform much more quickly than traditional resources for guidance can adapt. Generational differences in perspective may become marked, compounded by newly introduced transnational ideas and values, as well as economic opportunities, that disrupt expectations about gender relations, youth autonomy and agency, and social hierarchies. Traditional expectations may impose unrealistic constraints on behavior just as strategies for resolving inherent conflicts in obligations to community, family, and self may abruptly enter obsolescence. This intergenerational conflict may become especially polarized as adolescents tap new cultural resources – such as mass media and other technologies of communication – that either provide pragmatic guidance in the absence of informed traditional role models, or shortcut traditional pathways to social capital or other resources. Previously established means of developing social competencies through transgenerational role modeling or participation in cultural milestones may become defunct and thereby lose their utility.

This case raises many interesting questions about how social norms frame experience, how local patterning of symptoms may relate to "universal" or core biology, and how a legitimated rhetoric of distress promotes or impedes resolution. Some of the issues raised about psychiatric nosology and suffering in this case are situated in a robust literature addressing the cross-cultural validity of this particular diagnostic entity, PTSD. For example, both the universality and cultural specificity of features of this illness have been asserted (Jones et al., 2003; Sack, Seeley, & Clarke, 1997). Central to this debate is the potential political agenda related to medicalization of suffering in addressing social injustice associated with the emergence of prevalent PTSD (for example, in populations facing persecution, displacement, or violence) (Breslau, 2004). The possibilities for remedying a particular social injustice – the apparently widespread maltreatment of children in Belize – are alluded to in the presentation of this case as well. Dr. Anderson-Fye focuses her discussion on how "ideas and images from transnational media" became a strategic resource for one young woman and may, by extrapolation, motivate revision of local socio-moral norms on a larger scale.

Some noteworthy features of the case deserve comment. Maria's hybrid ethnic identity, reflected in a tri-lingual household and a heritage of Spanish, Creole, Anglo, and Mayan cultures, is normative in her community. Perhaps this multi-cultural identity provided a readiness to absorb novel perspectives as well as a template for eclectic use of ideas from transnational media. Maria distinguished herself among key informants for this ethnographic study by revealing a personal agenda for interview sessions. Indeed, she set the frame which, if not "suspiciously like therapy," as Dr. Anderson-Fye observed, at least grounded her with a safe, consistent, non-judgmental, and sympathetic sounding board for processing her experience. However, Maria's expectations that girls endure abusive behavior as "part of life," as well as a cultural lexicon that limits adequate expression of feelings, reveal elements of the social milieu that collectively silence Belizean adolescent girls. Maria may have been uniquely posed to seek redress for her experience through a novel medical idiom of distress, but the details of her narrative appear to resonate with collective capacities as well as pervasive suffering among Belizean adolescent girls. These details also outline a potential strategy for resilience.

Viewing a discussion about abuse on an episode of the serial television talk show, *Oprah*, appeared to transform Maria's experience of suffering into illness. It also recast it from a private, personal experience to her family's – if not her society's – problem. The discussion catalyzed her identification with others who had suffered *"abuse"* and also offered an alternative frame for her experience – a clinical one. The clinical idiom also authorized a rhetoric of complaint, drawing from *Oprah*'s local cachet. This reframe (as both clinical problem and social injustice) and legitimization of her complaint mobilized critical medical and social resources for Maria.

For all the benefits that a clinical reframe afforded Maria, her story also suggests serious drawbacks of medicalization. In her case, her entire family is enjoined to enter treatment. We gather that medical care and medical reframing may have rescued Maria, but strained the family's finances by introducing therapies of questionable benefit in this cultural context. We also learn about a perplexing and disturbing escalation in symptoms after Maria identifies her experience as PTSD following the *Oprah* episode. The strong possibility that the televised discussion of PTSD triggered this exacerbation – possibly by presenting discussion that was retraumatizing – is suggested by the temporal sequence of events.

It is also plausible that the symptoms represent an amplification intended to reinforce the urgency for relief and reconfiguration of the family and social dynamics contributing to Maria's suffering. It is plausible that her exacerbation of symptoms was necessary to reach a threshold of visibility essential for mobilizing family participation in treatment. Even if the symptoms were consciously contrived for secondary gain, it was a brilliantly adaptive strategy. In doing so, she has managed to vividly and effectively convey to her family and community her distress and request for treatment. Although PTSD is not a locally understood idiom, in borrowing it from *Oprah*, she has leveraged her gravitas and apparent credibility to claim redress for her suffering. This is a remarkable achievement within the local context of gender inequity and low expectations of protections for young women.

A *de novo* and effective idiom of distress that borrows legitimacy and form from an American television icon is probably unusual. However, the process by which adolescents glean novel perspectives from mass media may be more widespread. Notwithstanding abundant evidence of the adverse effects of television viewing on youth with respect to health risk behaviors (Anderson-Fye, this volume; Becker, Burwell, Gilman, Herzog, & Hamburg 2002), other data support that television offers information and role models that assist in navigating the social transition associated with globalization (Barker, 1997; Becker, 2004; Miller, 1998; Varan, 1998). Insofar as Western-based mass media suggest social possibilities beyond the previously imaginable range, they offer a creative resource for consumers. However, in confusing information with entertainment, in presenting highly contrived and idealized vistas of others' lives, and in stimulating consumerism even in the absence of need and resources, imported mass media also mislead and foster discontent among young viewers. Likewise, the reification of experience as illness in this case illustrates the paradoxical nature of television – and specifically *Oprah* – as a source of information that may have been as crippling as it was empowering for this young woman. For example, whether Maria is traversing a period of elevated risk for suicidal behavior and social isolation on her way to recovery remains uncertain. Moreover, how she will wear this illness identity when encountering future social opportunities and how it may stigmatize her are unclear.

Does Maria's case unmask an evolving social crisis among Belizean girls? Is it a harbinger of an unfortunate trend in mental illness? Can lessons be extrapolated to other social contexts? Specific characterologic or family attributes may have allowed events to unfold in ways that limit generalizability to other Belizean teens. For example, on Maria's initiative, the ethnographic research interviews are reset to a frame of weekly meetings and exploration of her emotional experience. Perhaps she had a therapeutic agenda in doing this. Her rapid transformation after viewing an episode of *Oprah* may have reflected a readiness for insight, a resonance with a particular scenario of abuse, or a reformulation of her experience that turned into an excellent pragmatic strategy. Even so, her remarkable trajectory during which she was able to channel information and legitimacy from mass media may be instructive in envisioning opportunities for young women to circumvent traditional constraints as part of the double-edged fall-out of globalization. The low cost of access to print, televised, and electronic media results in wide distribution to disenfranchised populations. Both mental illness and trauma can be highly stigmatizing and socially isolating. The experience is often kept secret and private. In this case, Oprah's candid discussion of PTSD allowed Maria to relocate private experience to a collective one and to join a virtual community of co-sufferers.

This case, situated in a rich ethnographic study, suggests many possible interpretations about how adolescents import and exploit cultural products to transcend traditional social constraints. This case also augments mounting evidence that mass media can and does have a profound impact on adolescents. Moreover, Maria's remarkable story supports the intriguing possibility that television programming can have pro-social impact. Even if this positive impact were inadvertent in Maria's case, it is intriguing to imagine how the appeal and reach of the mass media could be engineered to advance public health objectives. These objectives may be attained indirectly by legitimizing agency, autonomy, and educational opportunities for girls and women through the portrayal of cultural settings that support gender equity. They may also be approached more directly through presentation of health information that is otherwise not accessible. However, we must be aware that even as the mass media may stimulate reformulation of social norms, it may also provoke renewed dedication to these norms or even further suppression of threats to destabilize them, particularly by those with a stake in maintaining them.

There are other disturbing implications of this case, namely that viewing emotionally charged material in the "safe" decontextualized, time-delimited, highly contrived, world of a television set can be harmful in triggering symptoms. Understanding behaviors and feelings as illness is of questionable value in resource-poor settings when access to appropriate care is not feasible. Presentation of information that agitates trauma victims without offering a solution may even be regarded as irresponsible and morally corrupt. Although Maria effectively exploits the episode to resolve her own problem, the television industry also exploits its audience in providing entertainment in the guise of education.

The clinical reframe of suffering resulting from violence and sexual trauma as PTSD is a pragmatic response to a social injustice in this particular individual's case. However, medicalization of trauma can also undermine humanitarian concerns in addressing its source. Arthur Kleinman has decried the "superficial and soulless model of the person" created when political and social violence is reformulated as medical illness (Kleinman, 2006). Relocating the sequelae in Maria's symptoms and experience and addressing the perpetrator's outrageous behavior as a clinical problem obscures the social dynamics underlying this particular story, and likely many others. It leaves the social norm unchallenged. On the other hand, as Dr. Anderson-Fye suggests, identification with a community of sufferers – even a virtual one – has assisted in re-experiencing distress as a symptom and has provided a legitimized rhetoric of complaint in this case. It would be unfortunate – and indeed, unconscionable – if response to the sexual abuse and violence against young women in Belize were limited to the clinical realm.

Although we do not know what clinical trajectory Maria's illness followed, her case reflects her resourcefulness and resilience in constructing an illness identity that so effectively mobilized clinical resources. In what must be both an extraordinary and double-edged story of buy-in to a Western biomedical model, both personal experience and family perspective were reconfigured with undeniable benefits to this young woman. She was able to use both the credibility of scientific discourse and the wide popularity and accessibility of a television icon to invert the authority structure in her family. Her story also reflects potentially broader opportunities for strategic and eclectic use of new cultural resources. Dr. Anderson-Fye's nuanced discussion of this case also suggests intriguing possibilities for re-engineering social norms for parenting behaviors and responsibilities, as well as for augmenting female agency and authority in populations undergoing rapid social and economic transition.

REFERENCES

Barker, C. (1997). Television and the reflexive project of the self: Soaps, teenage talk and hybrid identities. *British Journal of Sociology, 48*, 611–628.

Becker, A. E. (2004). Television, disordered eating, and young women in Fiji: Negotiating body image and identity during rapid social change. *Culture, Medicine & Psychiatry, 28*, 533–559.

Becker, A. E., Burwell, R. A., Gilman, S. E., Herzog, D. B., & Hamburg, P. (2002). Eating behaviours and attitudes following prolonged television exposure among ethnic Fijian adolescent girls. *The British Journal of Psychiatry, 180*, 509–514.

Breslau, J. (2004). Cultures of trauma: Anthropological views of posttraumatic stress disorder in international health. *Culture, Medicine & Psychiatry, 28*(2), 113–126; discussion 211–220.

Jones, E., Vermaas, R. H., McCartney, H., Beech, C., Palmer, I., Hyams, K., & Wessely S. (2003). Flashbacks and post-traumatic stress disorder: The genesis of a 20th-century diagnosis. *British Journal of Psychiatry, 182*, 158–63.

Kleinman, A. (2006). *What really matters: Living a moral life amidst uncertainty and danger*. Oxford, UK: Oxford University Press.

Miller, C. J. (1998). The social impacts of televised media among the Yucatec Maya. *Human Organization, 57*, 307–14.

Sack, W. H., Seeley, J. R., & Clarke G. N. (1997). Does PTSD transcend cultural barriers? A study from the Khmer Adolescent Refugee Project. *Journal of the American Academy of Child & Adolescent Psychiatry, 36*(1), 49–54.

Varan, D. (1998). The cultural erosion metaphor and the transcultural impact of media systems. *Journal of Communication, 48*, 58–85.

# Commentary
## Can Watching Oprah Cause PTSD?

Frank W. Putnam

Perhaps the starkest interpretation of Eileen Anderson-Fye's case study, "Maria: Cultural Change and Posttraumatic Stress in the Life of a Belizean Adolescent Girl," is that simply to bestow a psychiatric diagnosis such as posttraumatic stress disorder (PTSD) upon an impressionable young adolescent girl like Maria is to condemn her to suffer from that disorder. There are some who would draw such a conclusion from this chapter. Indeed, there is a litany of professional and public statements to the effect that merely asking about possible child abuse or about certain symptoms associated with child abuse actually causes patients to falsely believe that they were abused – so called false memory syndrome – when, in fact, they were not. For some reason, those who believe in this syndrome regard young female patients as especially susceptible to being influenced into making false allegations of sexual abuse against their fathers.

A more nuanced interpretation would be that by providing a special language with which to talk about troubling experiences one can shape an individual's perception of the experience and, perhaps, even the way in which they symptomatically express the pain that those experiences have caused in them. Just as a doctor's diagnosis of cancer does not actually cause the cancer, it can, nonetheless, completely change how patients think about themselves and how they relate to others.

A diagnosis can also change the way in which doctors and psychotherapists perceive their patients. I am reminded of my training at the West Haven Veterans Hospital in the late 1970s, before the diagnosis of PTSD was even coined. We had many young Vietnam veterans as psychiatric patients. Most were admitted to a ward that specialized in treating schizophrenia, while others were given pejorative diagnoses such as borderline personality disorder (then much in vogue) or antisocial personality disorder. Virtually all were considered difficult or impossible to treat successfully.

Fortunately, one of the Yale faculty psychiatrists, Arthur Blank, had served in Vietnam and understood that what we were seeing clinically was a result of their combat experiences. Art Blank, Robert J. Lifton, and others drafted the diagnostic criteria for PTSD, which were first published in the third revision of the *Diagnostic and Statistical Manual of Mental Disorders* (DSM-III) in 1980. Before that, there was no PTSD – only very troubled young Vietnam veterans carrying diagnoses of schizophrenia and pernicious personality disorders. The larger effect of this new way of understanding patients was remarkable, and many who were previously considered psychotic or seriously antisocial could now be redefined in ways that helped both doctors and patients to seek new remedies. We now have highly effective therapies for these kinds of cases as a direct result of defining the diagnosis of PTSD. That definitional process continues, however, as experts work on the DSM-V, scheduled to be published in 2012, and debate the merits of adding a more developmentally sensitive trauma diagnosis for cases such as Maria's. After all, Art Blank and his colleagues first defined PTSD to describe what they saw in Vietnam combat veterans, not sexually abused adolescent girls.

From the description of Maria before the transformative *Oprah* episode, it is clear that this young girl was in pain. And her therapy-like request to meet weekly with Anderson-Fye is evidence that she felt a strong need to talk about this pain with someone who could help her make sense of it. Anderson-Fye notes that "the theme of the vast majority of her words and pictures was the difficult interpersonal events she had faced in her life and her feelings about and responses to them." These difficult experiences include her own physical, sexual, and emotional abuse as well as witnessing near-lethal violence repeatedly inflicted on her mother. While her affect appeared to Anderson-Fye as "sad but matter-of-fact when discussing these types of 'hard things' that happened to her," this should not be construed as evidence that she was not seriously disturbed by these experiences. Indeed, one of the hallmarks of chronic PTSD is the flat, unemotional manner in which the person relates horrible experiences. This can also be partly a developmental process, in that it is well documented that children often talk about awful experiences in an emotionless manner, despite the fact that they may exhibit florid somatic and behavioral PTSD symptoms.

Maria's revelation watching *Oprah* is not that she has PTSD. That diagnosis actually came later – after she was taken by her mother to see several psychiatrists because of her now overtly troubled behavior. It would be interesting to know what the girls on *Oprah* actually said and whether any of them even used the term PTSD to describe their experiences. More likely, they simply spoke about their abuse. Maria says, "I was watching *Oprah* and these girls, they were discussing like exactly what happened to . . . and I, I thought, 'That's me! That's me!'" Maria's revelation is that there is someone else who has had similar experiences and that these experiences are regarded as abusive – at least in the context of all that *Oprah* represents for her.[8]

This revelation triggers a strong affective response in Maria. She says, "Tears came spilling out of my eyes as I realized I have abuse!" From this point forward, Anderson-Fye feels that Maria changed. That her posttraumatic symptoms – sudden angry outbursts, sleeping difficulties, intrusive thoughts, hyperstartle reactions, and suicidal ideation – suddenly erupted where none had existed before. But Maria doesn't talk about these symptoms; she talks about her feelings – about being scared, sad, angry, and confused. She doesn't see these as new feelings either; she says that she too has felt what the girls were describing. What changes for Maria is the realization that "I wasn't the only one . . . it changed me." Maria says that the show "made me see my real feelings." The recognition of her real feelings is the driving force for the change in her, which she regards as having happened on "the most important day in my life."

Very soon after this revelation, Maria appears much worse to Anderson-Fye. She has PTSD symptoms sufficiently severe to mobilize her family, particularly her mother, who takes her to see a series of psychiatrists, first in Belize and then in Mexico, and ultimately in the United States. At some point in this series of evaluations, she acquires the diagnosis of PTSD. All this comes at great financial and most likely at enormous emotional cost to all involved. Maria is put on medication, and its purpose or therapeutic mechanism is explained to the family in some fashion that includes invoking concepts like *neurotransmitters*, which are believed to be sites of action for the drugs commonly used to treat PTSD.

But something else important is also happening. Maria's whole family is getting family therapy. And among the things that they are learning in

---

[8] I have watched Oprah on TV talk with young women about their abusive experiences – she is a remarkably sensitive interviewer and is able to elicit their feelings without being exploitive or sensationalistic.

therapy is that the father should not harm anyone. Maria repairs her relationship with her stepfather, and her entire family reports being "helped" by this therapy. Maria seems confident that the family environment will be better for her younger sisters than it was for her. Several more troubled years pass, but Maria eventually graduates from high school with high grades, acquires a good job, and ends her treatment saying that she "felt that she was on a good path. . . . " May all such treatments end so well!

In many respects, the course of Maria's symptoms was classic for a sexually abused young woman in the United States, although her hopeful outcome is not always typical. In cases of incest, where ongoing, long-term sexual abuse is suddenly discovered, acknowledged, remembered, or otherwise publicly validated in some fashion that now and forever changes the way that it is regarded, there is often an explosion of symptoms and an apparent rapid deterioration in function. The world has changed totally. Janoff-Bulman (1992) characterized this moment as a shattering of all of the person's assumptions about the nature of the world. Not surprisingly, those who cannot appreciate the way the person's internal world was before see this as an enormous setback. And although it is not easy to see a person become so painfully symptomatic, it is expectable and perhaps even necessary in many instances.

But this florid display of symptoms accomplishes something for Maria that she was not able to achieve previously. She gets treatment – which she seemed to have been seeking in some fashion from Anderson-Fye. Her family gets treatment. Her stepfather is told not to harm his family, and presumably, some or all of his wife-beating stops. Her sisters are better protected. Everyone expresses a sense of having been helped. It is a remarkable story, especially given the lack of local mental health resources.

Did watching *Oprah* cause Maria's PTSD? No, although what she heard discussed on *Oprah* may have helped to shape the expressive form that her PTSD took. But we must be cautious in even attributing this much influence to *Oprah*. Children and adolescents exhibit a wide range of trauma responses, many of which are sufficiently different from classic PTSD to warrant their own developmentally anchored diagnostic criteria (see, e.g., Scheeringa, Zeanah, Myers, & Putnam, 2003). *Oprah* aside, what role does Maria's own culture play in shaping her symptoms? Cross-cultural psychiatric research by Arthur Kleinman and colleagues document that even so seemingly universal a condition as depression has, in fact, many cultural variations (Kleinman & Good, 1986). I doubt that we will ever be able to parse which part of the symptomatic expression of a mental disorder is exclusively a result of culture, which is purely developmental, which is a result of temperament, and which is unique to each person's history and layered environments. That is why we must rely on admittedly crude diagnoses such as PTSD, which are periodically revised as a result of changes in our ability to identify and code salient variables and as a result of our growing experience with the many ways in which humans react to overwhelming and damaging life experiences.

REFERENCES

Janoff-Bulman, R. (1992). *Shattered assumptions: Towards a new psychology of trauma.* New York: Free Press.
Kleinman, A. & Good, B. (Eds.) (1986). *Culture and depression: Studies in the anthropology and cross-cultural psychiatry of affect and disorder.* Berkeley, CA: University of California Press.
Scheeringa, M., Zeanah, C., Myers, L., & Putnam, F. W. (2003). New findings on alternative criteria for PTSD in pre-school children. *Journal of the American Academy of Child and Adolescent Psychiatry, 42,* 561–570.

# FOURTEEN

# Sex/Gender, Culture, and Development

*Issues in the Emergence of Puberty and Attraction*[1]

Gilbert Herdt

## INTRODUCTION

In the great arc of human development across time and space, sexuality and gender play a special role in thinking about the interaction between caregiving, culture, and developmental factors leading from childhood into adolescence. Such interaction was observed long ago in that great classic of cultural anthropology, Ruth Benedict's *Patterns of Culture* (1934), in which cultural relativism artfully accepted the central role of the "push" and "pull" factors of individual and society to be of equal importance in the production of what was then called "sexual temperament" and personality. Today we understand that development is not only a "shared project" in the Boasian sense (as used by Benedict and Margaret Mead), but that it also has subtle interactional components that have been documented by Robert A. LeVine and colleagues (1994). Seeing social tasks as part of the developmental competence and emotional support for caretaker/child interactions has helped to create a sharper way of understanding the "work" culture does in developmental experience. Researchers now recognize that sexuality and gender play a vital role earlier in life than had been believed (Money & Ehrhardt, 1972; Herdt & McClintock, 2000). Examples of the form this role takes include gender attitudes toward very young offspring, sexual and gender socialization that subtly guides development in particular

[1] This chapter has drawn heavily upon three prior publications, McClintock and Herdt (1996), Herdt and McClintock (2000), and Herdt (2006), in which the hormonal and cultural model is more fully developed. I am grateful to the Ford Foundation for its support of my writing and thinking through issues of sex/gender and caretaking, as argued here.

356

directions, and in task assignments that match culture to experience (see also Whiting & Edwards, 1988).

These factors condition the extent to which significant developmental antecedents of adult life are set in motion through the combined effect of sexual knowledge, sexual subjectivity, and gender norms and roles (Tolman, 2005). The pubertal process is a classic and in some ways still fertile ground for understanding these dynamics (McClintock & Herdt, 1996). Prior studies have focused upon the late childhood/early adolescence ages of 9–10 years and the emergence of attraction as a marker in the pubertal process (Herdt & McClintock, 2000). This chapter reviews this research but also extends our thinking about how the development of attraction creates a dynamic interaction between the young person and caretakers with respect to their ideas and attitudes about appropriate socialization in the cultural surround (Hruschka, Lende, & Worthman, 2005).

Puberty, in this view, becomes a particular lens for understanding how and why caretakers interact with young people during the emergence of what we would today call the "sex–gender package" (Gagnon, 1990). Attitudes exist in communities around the world about the development of sexuality, and caretakers in particular feel a singular responsibility to monitor and guide this process. I have focused on the role that the development of sexual attraction plays in this process because I believe that it holds a key to our thinking about the interaction of nature and culture in human development. The upsurge in interest in the development of attraction from both the biological and cultural sides (Bem, 1996; Diamond, 2008; Herdt & McClintock, 2000) suggests that complementary perspectives will ultimately provide a fuller understanding of this aspect of human development. However, little consideration has been given to the role that caretakers play in responding to and/or mediating intrapsychic and interpersonal events during puberty, which I view as a lengthy process. This chapter addresses these issues.

## CULTURE AND SEXUAL DEVELOPMENT

Cultures around the world are concerned with the regulation of sexuality and the structure and content of gender roles. In the formative period of the adolescent transition, related social pressures may achieve their zenith (Herdt & Stolpe, 2005). Male-centered societies that perpetuate ideologies of patrilineal kinship – in the context of what French anthropologist Maurice Godelier (1986) has called the domination of women and children among the the Sambia of Papua and their neighbors the Baruya, in Papua

New Guinea (Herdt, 2003) – are especially attuned to the regulation of sexual conduct and moral norms in adolescence. Cross-cultural reviews have shown the patterning of such domination in Melanesia (Strathern, 1988) as well as in other societies in the developing world (Wieringa, 2009). The socializing role of caretakers becomes not only a problem of surveillance with respect to sexual and gender development, but also one of determining an appropriate behavioral response to subtle cues that emerge in the intimate context of daily cohabitation and sleeping and eating arrangements. During the adolescent transition, then, there may be a "compression" of subjective development interacting with hormonal development that is related to gender norms; restrictions on interaction may impinge upon the adolescent's mating and marriage expectations because parents, families, and communities regulate intimacy and sexual relations, especially when relationships may lead to reproductive unions (Herdt & Leavitt, 1998). Additionally, a transition to adult moral attitudes occurs as the child's body changes morphologically into an adult's. Individuals experiencing desire and attraction toward others may lack the cultural means either to recognize their feelings or to express them in public.

In fact, I have come to believe that this lack of awareness of attraction and its biopsychosocial feedback in subjective development until early adulthood is common, perhaps the norm, in human cultures (Herdt, 2006). As attraction becomes genitally arousing in the course of time, such arousal must be reconciled with customary arrangements in sex-object choice, sexual selection, and marriage proscriptions as recognized in the local culture (Herdt & Stolpe, 2005). Concomitantly, as Margaret Mead (1961) pointed out long ago, there is a central tendency to secrecy in sexual encounters across cultures, an issue that complicates the monitoring and caretaking responsibilities of adults. Hence, in some societies, secrecy not only becomes an ideology with which men create solidarity in the patrilineal group; it also protects individuals from public scrutiny when they stray from the norm in sexual encounters between men and women (Herdt, 2003; Tuzin, 1997). In maturational terms, this psychosexual transition also depends upon the achievement of gonadal puberty in males and menarche in females, as explained later, though neither achievement should be reduced to the presence or absence of orgasm or menstrual flow, as was once thought.[2]

Western tradition historically treated children as sexually naive; indeed, despite a huge change in the accessibility of television, print, and new

---

[2] See the discussion of preadolescent orgasm in Kinsey, Pomeroy, and Martin (1948/1953, pp. 175–180).

media such as the Internet, caretakers remain conservative in believing that the young are sexually naive (Irvine, 2000). Because of the taboo on sexual research in childhood, as John Money warned long ago, actual empirical data on childhood sexual development and behavior are scarce outside of selected Western European countries, such as Denmark and Germany, which complicates the process of understanding precisely what develops, at what pace, and in what contexts of caretaking (Herdt, 2009).

Freud (1905/1962) famously challenged the late Victorian idea that children were sexually innocent, effectively turning the folk notion on its head through his notoriously flawed seduction theory. Freud's discovery of unconscious sexual motivations and the Oedipus complex, beginning at around the age of 5 years, led to the emergence of a developmental theory of the erogenous zones. According to this theory, subjectivity in an infant's body begins with nursing (oral sensation) and bowel control (anal sensation), followed by a long latency period in which sexuality disappears and then an active genital period in adolescence. As the child's intrinsic drives inevitably clash with the surrounding social mores and parental moral systems (later internalized as Superego in Freud's lingo), each erogenous zone is symbolically associated with sensations and emotional expressions that may entail frustration or conflict. Freudian-versed caretakers responded to a child's budding reactions with fear and suppression; for example, childhood masturbation was widely treated as a disease, perhaps even symptomatic of later mental illness. These biopsychosocial dynamics came to be considered formative of the middle class in turn-of-the-century Vienna (Gay, 1984). Nevertheless, Freud originated what Foucault (1980) has called the "repressive hypothesis," the interpretation of subjective childhood developmental experiences not as history or cultural convention, but rather as timeless psychic universals, a view largely rejected by theorists today (Weeks, 1985). This canonical discussion of sex/gender, development, and repression has taken many forms but remains central to our understanding of sexuality and adolescence today.

The Freudian model treated both caretakers and children as simultaneously reactive and passive when it came to sexual development, which was thought to end around the age of 5 years. Even adolescence just continued what came before, contributing little to the development of sexual subjectivity. Sexual expression falling short of the expectations of middle-class timing and violating that period's norms, such as mid-teen dating, was believed harmful in the medicalized paradigm of the times (Irvine, 2000). Freud (1905/1962) argued that biopsychosocial development, including sexual temperament and "gendered" traits, was uniform, unconsciously determined by early childhood conflict, and therefore universal. His assertion – that the biopsychosocial building blocks of "sex" and "temperament" were more or less identical for all humans – reflected the so-called "replication of uniformity" model of human nature (Wallace, 1969). Most anthropologists have rejected this simple, static, developmental model as far too simplified (LeVine, 1973).

Of special interest in the context of this chapter is Freud's central concept of the latent period of sexual development in middle childhood, roughly the ages of 6 to 9 years or so, as being quiescent and lacking in conscious sexual feelings or wishes. While Anna Freud subsequently revised the theory of sexuality to encompass adolescence as a second phase of sexual development (Erick Erickson followed in this line), she did not revise the idea of latency. We shall return to this problem later.

Clearly these factors play a prominent role in the evolution of discourses and studies about sexuality, as argued by David Buss (1994) and others. Social-difference theories from the time of Malinowski's work with Trobriand islanders (1929) and Margaret Mead's with New Guinea peoples (1935/1968) view sexuality primarily as a product of social environment across the course of life. Most behavioral research in the developmental psychology of children in the ensuing years has focused on gender (e.g., Maccoby & Jacklin, 1974) rather than sexual development, except in clinical sexology (reviewed in Herdt & Boxer, 1993; Money & Ehrhardt, 1972). American and European studies of childhood sexuality have remained captive to individual-difference theories, having been typically conducted within experimental and developmental psychology contexts that left out local culture and models of intentionality (Schweder, 1989). When it came to the study of socialization, however, social psychologists (Whiting & Edwards, 1988) turned to more complementary perspectives, envisioning the conduct of sexual relations in adulthood to be mediated through parents, family caretakers, peers, communities, and major institutions of a society such as business, religion, and schools during development.

Since the time of Freud (1905/1962) and with pioneers like Margaret Mead (1927), Alfred Kinsey and colleagues (1948/1953), and Gagnon and Simon (1973), sexuality has become an interdisciplinary field in its own right, and a more creative approach has emerged in which master narratives are invented about what sexuality is and what it does to society. This intellectual history helps us understand current trends that compel an interactionist view, which credits both individual development and cultural context as factors in key developmental outcomes such as sexual attraction. Evolutionary psychology today, for example, tends to provide a master narrative of genetic motivations that produce sexual and gender outcomes in adulthood – outcomes that are strongly dualistic in seeing individuals pitted against society (Buss, 1994). As primatologist Martin Pavelka (1995) has lamented regarding this dualism, "Perhaps more than any other area of human behavior, sexuality spans the gap between what is normally perceived as biological and what is regarded as cultural" (p. 17). An interactive paradigm would be more productive (Worthman, 1999).

## PUBERTY, CONTEXT, AND DEVELOPMENTAL PROCESS

Following the seminal work of Van Gennep (1909/1960), anthropologists long have suggested that puberty in humans is primarily a social, not a biological, event. By this they have meant that whatever internal changes happen to the individual through menarche or spermadarche, the cultural response of the community in recognizing status change and new roles is by far the greater event. Cross-cultural study of adolescence began, of course, with Malinowski (1929) and Margaret Mead (1935/1968), fanning out to a range of other societies as explicit examination of adolescence became more prominent (reviewed in Whiting & Edwards, 1988; Herdt & Leavitt, 1998). Indeed, whether in late childhood or adolescence, ritual initiation ceremonies are so common as a framework for "coming of age" in moral, social, economic, and political terms that these rituals might be called the very foundation of nonwestern societies.

Historically, by contrast, western popular culture and science largely have shared a view of puberty as a single event or developmental milestone that normatively occurs around age 11–12. But over the last century, timing of puberty has declined markedly in these populations to increasingly earlier ages of onset; age of onset moreover varies substantially within populations (Herdt & McClintock, 2000). Thus, the phenomenon that has been called puberty ("gonadal puberty") and is denoted by the onset of secondary "sex characteristics" in adolescence, now is known to vary considerably by chronological biological age (McClintock & Herdt, 1996). Part of the difficulty concerns the epistemology of puberty in historical western science.

As Kinsey et al. (1948/1953) noted long ago, pinning the onset of maturation on first orgasm, or in males ejaculation, is complicated. The structural trend in Kinsey's evidence was for younger maturing males to have sex earlier and to have it more frequently compared with peers, and this intriguing difference carried on into adulthood. Indeed, Kinsey described the maturational difference in its early developmental effects as "astounding" in how it shaped later adult sexual behavior (Kinsey et al., 1948/1954, p. 307; see also Bem, 1996; and Martinson, 1981). Although no definitive study of this phenomenon exists, comparisons of the Kinsey data and those of the National Health and Social Life Survey conducted at the University of Chicago suggest significant age-cohort differences, related to the emergence of early sexual attraction (Laumann, Gagnon, Michael, & Michaels, 1994; Michaels, 1996). The relationship of timing variations in physical maturation to the organization of sexuality remains poorly understood; nevertheless, such cohort differences are especially striking and early among minority young people, particularly among African Americans seen in clinics today (Herdt & McClintock, 2000). The changes in social attraction and behavior associated with puberty and adolescence play out against a developmental background of gender-differentiated sociality. Notably, gender segregation steadily increases during middle childhood. Some time ago, Maccoby and Jacklin (1974) demonstrated the preference of nursery school children for their same-gendered peers. By age 4.5 years, children spent three times as much social time with the same gender. By age 6.5 years, this ratio had increased to 11 to 1. As Ehrhardt and Meyer-Bahlburg (1981) suggested early on, gender differences in social grouping may signal important developmental trends that continue throughout the lives of adult men and women in terms of, for example, how relationships are narrated, and how desires are experienced as for or against the self (Tolman, 2005).

These research trends unfortunately cause puberty to be overly identified – in the minds of both researchers and the public – with the emergence of morphological changes (incorrectly labeled "secondary sex changes" at puberty, as noted by Money & Erhardt, 1972; see also Money, 1987). Classic reviews of the literature (Money & Lewis, 1990, pp. 241–242) on the evidence for gonadal pubertal onset provide benchmarks. For males, the first visible evidence of puberty is in the enlargement of the testes, scrotum, and penis, with a mean onset of these changes at the age of 11.5 years. However, these changes may begin as early as 9 or as late as 15 years, and still be considered within the normal range. The process of completion typically takes 2–4.5 years, culminating in growth and distribution of pubic hair. For females, the changes, including pubic hair and breast growth, begin between the ages of 9 and 13 years. The average age of the growth spurt is just past 12, with the average first menstruation between 13 and 13.5 years and a range of 11.5 to 15.5 years. In females, these changes may take as little as 1.5 years or as long as 6 years.

Our work has suggested the developmental hypothesis that in cultures around the world sexual attraction begins in middle to late childhood and reaches subjective awareness at around the age of 10 years. This view counters the notion that sexual attraction awaits the onset of psychophysiological "puberty" following the onset of gonadarche. In prior models of developmental sexual psychology, gonadarche is typically seen as a kind of "timer" or internal "switch," which turns on desire and attraction, triggering the developmental sequelae of adult sexuality. As previously argued (McClintock & Herdt, 1996), puberty may now be viewed more broadly as also encompassing the process of adrenarche that begins developmentally prior to gonadarche. Rather than viewing sexual attraction as following upon gonadarche, we see the subjectivity of attraction as forming a much longer sequence of intertwined erotic and gendered psychobehavioral trends that begin in childhood, achieve conscious awareness typically between the ages of 9 and 10 years, and fan out into adolescence. Eventually these trends will include adult gender roles and romantic and sexual performances as scripted by community and culture (Gagnon, 1990). Thus, we may distinguish between two distinct but overlapping processes of puberty: adrenal puberty and gonadal puberty. They apparently are independent of each other and are temporally processed by different development mechanisms (Hopper & Yen, 1975; Korth-Schütz, 1989; argued in McClintock & Herdt, 1996).

In this model, each sex begins development in early infancy with adult levels of testosterone and estrogen. Within the first year, sex hormone levels decline sharply and remain low until ages 6 to 8, when the adrenal glands increase production of adrenal androgens (weak androgenic hormones), primarily dehydroepiandrosterone (DHEA), a precursor for testosterone and estrogen. At this point, the onset and hormone levels are similar in both sexes until gonadarche. DHEA levels increase significantly around age 10 and continue to increase strongly and linearly until they peak by age 25 in both men and women. While the levels at age 10 are low compared with normal adult levels, they are still many (10 to 20) times those of typical young children. Hormone levels required for an organizational (long-term, permanent) effect are unknown; the levels experienced between ages 6 and 10 years are within an activational (short-term, temporary) range. It is highly probable that the levels of hormones secreted during that period have an organizing effect on preadolescent brains (see Diamond, 2008, pp. 34–38). The effect may be to heighten awareness of the body and sensations related to attraction, and hence to produce the experience of arousal known as sexual and romantic attraction – even before gonadal puberty.

Adrenarche is thus a key source of first erotic attraction in this hypothetical model. In addition to the factors already outlined, we would note four general trends that influence the development of attraction. First, the adrenals release hormones that have been identified as relevant for sexual attraction in adults. Second, girls and boys do not appear to show an age difference in adrenal pubertal development. Third, the same hormones continue to rise in concentration during gonadarche. Thus, if the gonads constitute the structure for biological "priming" in sexual attraction development, then it intuitively follows that the same hormones have a similar effect at earlier ages. Finally, DHEA – the primary androgen released by the adrenals – is only two metabolic steps away from testosterone, and three steps from estradiol, the major adult sex hormones. Current research continues to examine the behavioral effects of these adrenal hormones (Angold, 2003).

With these clues in mind, McClintock and Herdt (1996) argued for a conceptualization of puberty that would include a continuum of internal hormonal development extending from adrenarche to gonadarche. We suggested that in the United States, children between grades 4 and 5 reach a new way of thinking about their bodies, gender roles, sexual feelings, and intimacies with their playmates. Studies of sex typing in play and popularity also support the importance of gender changes occurring around grade 4 (Moller, Hymel, & Rubin, 1992).

## THE SAMBIA CASE STUDY

In previous publications I have suggested that the Sambia of Papua New Guinea respond to these issues in their culture and the local developmental folk model with an implicit understanding of the role played by the pubertal process and the early onset of attraction (Herdt, 2002, 2006). The Sambia feel an urgent need to initiate boys **before age 10** as a means of monitoring, controlling, and ultimately implementing behavioral mechanisms of caretaking in modifying sexual and gender development in their society.

In this view, the development of a boy's desires and sexual behavior are governed not by the intrinsic elements that we would label "sexual orientation," but rather by cultural institutions and roles, as well as by material forces and constraints, including technology and warfare. Thus, while it is often assumed in western society that "sexual orientation" is intrinsic to the individual, whether by genes, hormones, brain symmetry, or some other factor, the Sambia do not share this view. Indeed, they lack a construct of "sexual orientation," instead assuming that it is possible – through changes in social and material relationships – to alter a boy's desires, teach him new desires, and direct subsequent developmental energy into these new desires.

The Sambia express an intense belief that a boy must be initiated before he is "too old" or "too big" for the rite of passage to have its necessary and desired effect. That process, in brief, is: (1) to separate the boy from his mother; (2) to "defeminize" the boy's physical body through ritual practices such as blood-letting; (3) to "masculinize the boy's body," through other ritual practices such as insemination; and thus (4) to socialize him into the role of being a warrior/hunter in preparation for warfare and the perceived dangers of marriage. In fact, the Sambia set the absolute threshold of this necessary change at the age of 10 years. Clearly, something prior to puberty is transforming the child's body and psyche in the direction of sexual arousal.

## PUBERTAL PROCESS AND HORMONAL DEVELOPMENT

What might be the precursor of this development? Clearly, neuroendocrine changes in mid-late childhood and early adolescence are critical elements in theorizing about the development of sexuality. The previously described process of adrenarche is a good candidate for being the primary (if not the sole) source of the first erotic attraction at around the age of 10 years. Simple learning theory has been unable to explain changes in subjectivity (McClintock & Herdt, 1996). A combination of internal and external factors are thought to create the adult forms of sexuality; but presumably this transformation cannot happen without earlier and later hormonal changes. In the United States, simple learning theory clearly does not apply because for most children there is no unusual prompt at age 10 years, an age that typically finds children in 4th grade. No overt change in socialization is apparent between grades 3 and 4, or between grades 4 and 5. So-called rites of passage typically occur between ages 12 and 13 years, when the adolescent becomes a teenager, or around ages 15 to 16 years, when the driver's license is issued. Perhaps between grades 5 and 6 (or 6 and 7, depending on the school system), we might identify a critical change for the transition from elementary to middle school. Yet all of these culturally more prominent transitions are later than age 10 years and fail to yield differences (McClintock & Herdt, 1996). Other subtle changes, such as the wearing of makeup for girls or the formation of preteen groups for boys, may occur at around the age of 10 years as well, but these social factors seem insufficient to explain the sudden appearance of sexual attraction before anatomical changes are noteworthy.

A new picture of these processes has emerged from recent research involving samples of heterosexuals and homosexuals in the United States (McClintock & Herdt, 1996; Herdt & McClintock, 2000). Participant recall elicited in separate studies of gay-identified males and lesbians conducted by different investigators from different fields in different parts of the country, has pinpointed age 10 as the onset of first attraction to the same sex. The uniformity of responses is all the more remarkable in that it seems impervious to cultural and historical change. For example, the mean age of participants in one study was 37 years (Hamer, S. Hu, Magnuson, N. Hu, & Pattutucci, 1993), while the mean age in another was 17.9 years (Herdt & Boxer, 1993); nevertheless, same-sex attraction emerged in both populations around 9.5–10 years of age. Such a difference (approximately one generation) suggests that the developmental onset of awareness of first attraction to the same sex may be independent of simple social learning or of the social/historical influences that would show up in age-cohort differences. One might have predicted that the intervention of the 1960s "sexual revolution" and/or the AIDS epidemic in the 1980s and '90s would have altered the age of first attraction (Gagnon, 1990). What is even more remarkable is that both heterosexuals and homosexuals report the beginning of sexual attraction at the age of 9.5 to 10 years. A comparable age (10.4 years) has recently been found by Bailey and Oberschneider (1997) in a smaller sample of males. Sexual orientation is thus independent of the mechanisms governing the onset and manifestation of erotic desire and attraction.

In short, normative boys and girls in the United States begin to experience liking and affection directed typically to same-aged peers sometime around grades 4 or 5. At the time, they may think of these feelings as "friendship" or "puppy love" – or the idealization of a much admired sports celebrity or movie star – but in retrospect, many interpreted that experience as their first sexual attraction.

Although we have found that boys report experiencing their first remembered attraction at a slightly younger age than girls, this difference may itself be significant for understanding subtle but very powerful micromechanisms of the cultural environment that influence the emergence of attraction (Herdt & Boxer, 1993, chap. 5). In fact, sexual attraction before gonadal puberty, as well as erotic fantasy, sexual desire, and perhaps generalized arousability linked to gender differences (Bem, 1996), all suggest that these elements do not depend upon the biosocial components of the pubertal process in any simple sense. While the precise identification of pubertal onset has not been established for either males or females (McClintock & Herdt, 1996), erotic and social precocity may be linked to adrenal pubertal development. On the other hand, precocity as a distinctive feature of sexual or sexual-identity development in gay men has long been questioned or denied (Meyer-Bahlburg, 1984). Indeed, there are plenty of reasons to believe that, in developmental and cultural terms, the age of 9.5 to 10 years is a critical transition point in cognitive, emotional, and social adjustment (Herdt & McClinctock, 2000; Diamond 2008, 34ff.) despite our culture's lack of a specific ritual or social marker for this critical transition.

As McClintock and Herdt (1996) argue, androgens have developmental effects on multiple adult outcomes, including aggression, emotions, and sexual development. This theory certainly agrees with Bem's (1996) important argument that biosocial variables do not "code" for sexual orientation as such, but rather for the childhood temperaments that influence a child's preferences. Such effects have not been demonstrated in children although children presumably have the same micro areas in their developmental systems. Thus, androgenization has been regarded as a key effect of sexual development in a continuous sequence from childhood through adulthood, with gonadarche as the apex. Previous sexual developmental research has attributed changes in adolescent behavior to changes in hormone levels accompanied by gonadarche.

However, if gonadarche were responsible for first sexual attractions, then the mean age of its occurrence should be later – around age 12 years for girls and 13 years for boys. Clearly, as shown repeatedly, the mean age of first sexual attraction is younger than 12 or 13 years. Since girls experience gonadarche at earlier ages than boys, we could expect that this sex difference would also be manifested in the mean ages of first attraction (with women recalling an earlier first attraction), but studies attempting to illuminate the sources of sexual orientation have produced surprising answers. Herdt and Boxer (1993) studied a group of self-identified gay and lesbian teenagers (aged 14–20 years, with a mean age of 17.9 years). This cohort revealed a sequence of first same-sex attraction, first same-sex fantasy, and first same-sex behavior: The mean age for same-sex attraction was around 10 years for both males and females and sexual behavior came earlier for boys than for girls. In short, although a robust onset of attraction may appear at around the age of 10 years, social and psychological pressures, especially those associated with gender roles, may influence the subtleties of first desires; certainly such pressures strongly influence the emergence of sexual behavior later, as Lisa Diamond (2008) has suggested in her longitudinal study of young women whose sexual identity and behavior change over time.

## RETHINKING PUBERTY

Understanding the neuroendocrine changes in children between the ages of 5 and 12 years, particularly the increase in adrenal activity, is critical for understanding both the physical bodies and the psychological (interpersonal and intrapsychic) development of preadolescents (Money & Ehrhardt, 1972). Given the strong possibility that the current popular model is incorrect, puberty needs to be rethought as a more complex and protracted maturational process. The new models require testing in a wide range of fields. Adrenarche clearly increases the presence of androgens to significant levels, and if those hormones are responsible for the effects seen in sexual attraction, then adrenarche should also affect a wide range of behaviors, including aggression, cognition, perception, attention, arousal, emotions, and – of course – sexual identity and attraction development. Even if hormones released from the adrenal glands are not responsible for changes in sexual attraction (Angold, 2003), the concept of puberty must be greatly enlarged and reconsidered. Current work suggests that puberty encompasses two apparently separate maturational processes: Adrenarche and gonadarche (Havelock, Auchus, & Rainey, 2004). Any social research that includes puberty as a stage in development ought to distinguish the relevant developmental and social behaviors involved in these two stages of pubertal formation and maturation. Researchers will need to consider that normal adrenarche puberty starts as early as ages 6 to 8 years, whereas gonadal puberty does not end until around ages 15 to 17 years. In between, the age threshold of 10 may mark the average onset of sexual attraction in human populations.

If the onset of sexual attraction is indeed strongly motivated internally by these hormonal developments, and especially the adrenal puberty that seems to reach its peak before adolescence, then it is no surprise that non-western peoples such as the Sambia have hit upon customs that institutionalize the significant life-course changes that occur at around the age of 10 years. In this view, over generations, cultures such as the Sambia may have inferred that the developmental events and processes leading to male sexual arousal, attraction, and behavior development require formal recognition before gonadal puberty occurs. The efforts of such cultures to impose separation from the mother and siblings, as well as gender segregation, followed by powerful identity changes in the boy through forcible ritual initiations, thus prepare for and anticipate the changes that will occur at age 10 years. By placing the child in a new context for learning and perceiving, the Sambia have actively engaged the internal and cultural processes of sex and gender development.

## CONCLUSION

This chapter has considered cross-cultural and U.S. studies of adolescence and the pubertal process, including hormonal factors affecting the development of attraction and related developmental sequelae. For caretakers, the idea of attraction developing earlier than previously thought might have implications for playgroup formation, gender roles, and sexual development, especially with regard to issues of gender segregation. Gender segregation in many nonwestern societies is common (Whiting & Edwards, 1988; Worthman, 1996). Developmental studies in the United States of "spontaneous" gender segregation observed on primary school playgrounds are certainly common (Gelman, Collman, & Maccoby, 1986; Maccoby, 1998). It is often remarked that gender segregation in playgroups changes the experience and direction of attraction and arousal, and the homosocial environment certainly may infuse the fantasies and desires that surround arousal (Bem, 1996; Gagnon, 1972).

Does the development of attraction change if young people are in segregated groups? According to Knoth, Boyd, and Singer (1988), the modal age of boys' first arousal across all samples was between ages 11 and 12. The modal age for girls was between 13 and 15, usually "occurring during physical contact with a male" (Knoth et al., 1988, p. 79). Perhaps even more important for the present discussion of adrenal puberty, Knoth et al. (1988) found that 40% of males reported having their first sexual arousal by age 8, while the aggregate of 60% reported that event by age 10. Surely, the effects upon sexual subjectivity are discernible. As Gagnon (1972) insightfully noted with respect to patterns of gender difference in sexual scripts, white working and middle-class boys in the United States typically experience their first sexual attractions and fantasies in homosocial environments, sometimes resulting in masturbation and sexual play, including same-gender masturbatory play.

For caretakers, the implications suggest new ways of thinking about the pubertal process and sex/gender development. Cultures and caretakers may create barriers to the expression of internal desires and subjectivities. In the case of non-normative or diverse sexualities, some people may postpone the expression of their feelings until they leave home or go to college (Herdt, 1996), while others may never reveal these feelings, and instead marry and live a secret life (Herdt, 2000). Given the social context, one would expect that the difference in social experience and the person's proximity to the developmental marker would have resulted in different reported outcomes. Since, as we saw earlier, the reported age for same-sex attraction is the same for both generations in two independent studies, this makes the findings even more compelling. Apparently a subjective process continues to develop in spite of social oppression and even stigma. In Norway, for example, masturbation in childhood seems common, and 8- to 12-year-old males engage in sexual relations as a normal part of growing up (Langfeldt, 1981). If early maturation and sexuality are positively regarded in countries such as Norway, we might then predict that the expression of both early sexual attraction and sexual feelings will develop relatively unimpeded. There will be less of a hiatus – less of what I have elsewhere referred to as "developmental discontinuity" (Herdt, 1999) – in the emergence of sexuality and sexual subjectivity.

What roles do power, domination, and social oppression play in this developmental regime? Obviously, power structures strongly influence the conditions of caretaking, causing inhibition, poor attachment, and the lack of socialization into affectionate and robust gender and sexual roles. Caretakers may themselves bear the brunt of such power systems and in turn be little empowered to help maintain a more positive part in development (Herdt & Stolpe, 2005). When a society worries about the effects of early gender development, when it institutionalizes misogyny and gender segregation and fails to acknowledge the expression of sexual attraction before adulthood, its folk psychology and institutions will implement controls on the child's sexuality well before gonadarche. Such were the conditions in precolonial Papua New Guinea. It is remarkable that our own postindustrial society continues to exert similar powerful controls over childhood sexuality in the face of enormous change and access to sexual knowledge and the media (Herdt, 2004).

This chapter suggests that we take a different look at pubertal development, seeing it as a "push" and "pull" between individual and society in the emergence of sexuality and gender in the young person. When care is not taken to support the child's transition into adulthood, acknowledging the sexual crisis that sometimes accompanies puberty, a variety of societal contradictions, including gender role and double standards (Tolman, 2006), may affect the process, seriously undermining the heart and spirit of the young. A child becoming aware of sexual feelings may feel the swift and heavy hand of cultural restrictions that effectively thwart personal development and bring turmoil into the young person's life. Recognizing the impact of this interaction will be central to progress in childhood sexual study in the coming years. We urgently need social policy to inform the many social and ethical questions that will emerge from this kind of study. We also need a new paradigm for the study of sexual development in childhood that sensitively reconsiders the dynamics between what is inside the person and what is outside in the culture – the complex contributions of hormones on one hand and caretakers and culture on the other.

REFERENCES

Angold, A. (2003). Adolescent depression, cortisol and DHEA. *Psychological Medicine, 33,* 573–581.

Bailey, J. M., & Oberschneider, M. (1997). Sexual orientation professional dance. *Archives of Sexual Behavior, 26,* 433–444.

Bem, D. (1996). Exotic becomes erotic: A developmental theory of sexual orientation. *Psychological Review, 103,* 320–335.

Benedict, R. (1934). *Patterns of culture.* New York: Houghton Mifflin.

Buss, D. (1994). *Evolution of desire.* New York City: Basic Books.

Diamond, L. (2008). *Sexual fluidity.* Cambridge, MA: Harvard University Press.

Ehrhardt, A. A., & Meyer-Bahlburg, H. F. (1981, March 20). Effects of prenatal sex hormones on gender-related behavior. *Science, 211*(4488), 1312–1318.

Foucault, M. (1980). *The history of sexuality: An introduction* (Vol. 1) (R. Hurley, Trans.). New York: Vintage Books.

Freud, S. (1962). *Three essays on the theory of sexuality.* (J. Strachey, Trans.). New York: Norton. (Original work published 1905)

Gagnon, J. (1990). The explicit and implicit use of the scripting perspective in sex research. *Annual Review of Sex Research, 1,* 1–44.

Gagnon, J. H., & Simon, W. (1973). *Sexual conduct: The social sources of human sexuality.* London: Hutchinson.

Gay, P. (1984). *The bourgeois experience.* New York: Oxford University Press.

Gelman, S. A., Collman, P., & Maccoby, E. E. (1986). Inferring properties from categories versus inferring categories from properties: The case of gender. *Child Development, 57,* 396–404.

Godelier, Maurice. (1986). *The making of great men: Male domination and power among the New Guinea Baruya.* (R. Swyer, Trans.). New York: Cambridge University Press.

Hamer, D. H., Hu, S., Magnuson, V. L., Hu, N., & Pattutucci, A. M. (1993/July 16). A linkage between DNA markers on the X chromosome and male sexual orientation. *Science, 261*(5119), 321–327.

Havelock, J. C., Auchus, R. J., & Rainey, W. E. (2004). The rise in adrenal androgen biosynthesis: Adrenarche. *Seminars in Reproductive Medicine, 22*(4), 337–347.

Herdt, G. *Sambia Sexual Culture.* Chicago: University of Chicago Press.

Herdt, G. (2000). Why the Sambia initiate boys before age 10. In J. Bancroft (Ed.), *The role of theory in sex research* (pp. 82–109). Bloomington: Indiana University Press.

Herdt, G. (2002). Social change, sexual diversity, and tolerance for bisexuality in the United States. In A. D'Augelli & C. Patterson (Eds.), *Gay, lesbian and bisexual youth: Research and intervention* (pp. 267–283). New York: Oxford University Press.

Herdt, G. (2003). *Secrecy and cultural reality.* Ann Arbor, MI: University of Michigan Press.

Herdt, G. (2004). Sambia women's positionality and men's rituals. In P. Bonnemerre (Ed.), *Women in men's rituals* (pp. 16–43). Philadelphia: University of Pennsylvania Press.

Herdt, G. (2006). *The Sambia: Ritual, sexuality and gender* (Rev. 2nd ed.). New York: Wadsworth/Thompson Learning.

Herdt, G. (Ed.), (2009). *Moral panics, sex panics: Fear and the fight over sexual rights.* New York: NYU Press.

Herdt, G., & Boxer, A. (1993). Milestones of sexual identity development. In *Children of horizons: How gay and lesbian youth are forging a new way out of the closet* (Chap. 5, pp. 173–202). Boston: Beacon Press.

Herdt, G., & Leavitt, S. C. (Eds.). (1998). *Adolescence in Pacific Island societies.* Pittsburgh: University of Pittsburgh Press.

Herdt, G., & McClintock, M. (2000). The magical age of 10. *Archives of Sexual Behavior, 29* (6), 587–606.

Herdt, G., & Stolpe, B. (2005). Sambia sexuality, gender and social change. In J. Stockard & G. Spindler (Eds.), *Cultures through case studies: Continuity, change, and challenge.* New York: Thompson.

Hopper, B. R., & Yen, S. S. (1975). Circulating concentrations of dehydro-epiandrosterone and dehydroepiandrosterone sulfate during puberty. *Journal of Clinical Endocrinology and Metabolism, 40*(3), 458–461.

Hruschka, D. J., Lende, D. H., & Worthman, C. M. (2005). Biocultural dialogues: Biology and culture in psychological anthropology [Special issue: Biocultural anthropology]. *Ethos, 33*(1), 1–19.

Irvine, J. (2000). *Disorders of desire.* Philadelphia: Temple.

Kinsey, A. C., Pomeroy, W. B., & Martin, C. E. (1953). *Sexual behavior in the human male* (pp. 175–180, 307). Philadelphia: W. B. Saunders. (Original work published 1948)

Knoth, R., Boyd, K., & Singer, B. (1988). Empirical tests of sexual selection theory: Predictions of sex difference in onset, intensity, and time course of sexual arousal. *Journal of Sex Research, 24,* 73–89.

Korth-Schütz, S. (1989). Precocious adrenarche. *Pediatric Adolescent Endocrinology, 19,* 226–235.

Langfeldt, T. (1981). Childhood masturbation: Individual and social organization. In L. L. Constantine & F. M Martinson (Eds.), *Children and sex* (pp. 63–74). Boston: Little, Brown and Co.

Langfeldt, T. (1990). Early childhood and juvenile sexuality, development and problems. In J. Money & H. Musaph (Series Eds.) & M. E. Perry (Ed.), *Handbook of sexology:* Vol. 7. *Child and adolescent sexology* (pp. 179–200). Amsterdam: Elsevier Science Publishers.

Laumann, E. O., Gagnon, J. H., Michael, R. T., & Michaels, S. (1994). *The social organization of sexuality: Sexual practices in the United States.* Chicago: University of Chicago Press.

LeVine, R. A. (1973). *Culture, behavior and personality.* Chicago: Aldine.

LeVine, R. A., Dixon, S., LeVine, S., Richman, A., Leiderman, P. H., Keefer, C. H., et al. (1994). *Child care and culture: Lessons from Africa.* Cambridge, UK: Cambridge University Press.

McClintock, M., & Herdt, G. (1996). Rethinking puberty: The development of sexual attraction. *Current Directions in Psychological Science, 5,* 178–183.

Maccoby, E. E. (1988). Gender as a social category. *Developmental Psychology, 24,* 755–765.

Maccoby, E. E., & Jacklin, C. (1974). *The psychology of sex differences*. Stanford: Stanford University Press.

Malcolm, L. A. (1968). Determination of the growth curve of the Kukukuku people of New Guinea from dental eruption in children and adult height. *Archeology and Physical Anthropology in Oceania, 4*, 72–78.

Malinowski, B. (1929). *The sexual life of savages*. New York: Liveright.

Martinson, F. M. (1981). Eroticism in infancy and childhood. In L. L. Constantine & F. M. Martinson (Eds.), *Children and sex: New findings, new perspectives* (pp. 23–36). Boston: Little Brown.

McClintock, M., & Herdt, G. (1996). Rethinking puberty: The development of sexual attraction. *Current Directions in Psychological Science, 5*, 178–183.

Mead, M. (1927). *Coming of age in Samoa*. New York: Norton.

Mead, M. (1968). *Sex and temperament in three primitive societies*. New York: Dell Publishing Co., Inc. (Original work published in 1935)

Mead, M. (1961). *Cultural determinants of sexual behavior*. In W. C. Young (Ed.), *Sex and internal secretions* (pp. 1433–1479). Baltimore, MD: Williams and Wilkins.

Meyer-Bahlburg, H. (1984). Psychoendocrine research on sexual orientation. Current status and future options. *Progress in Brain Research, 61*, 375–398.

Michaels, S. 1996. The prevalence of homosexuality in the United States. In R. P. Cabaj & T. S. Stein (Eds.), *Textbook of homosexuality and mental health* (pp. 43–65). Washington, DC: American Psychiatric Press.

Moller, L. C., Hymel, S., & Rubin, K. H. (1992). Sex typing in play and popularity in middle childhood. *Sex Roles, 26*, 331–353.

Money, J. (1987). Sin, sickness, or society? *American Psychologist, 42*, 384–399.

Money, J., & Ehrhardt, A. (1972). *Man and woman, boy and girl*. Baltimore: Johns Hopkins University Press.

Money, J., & Lewis, V. G. (1990). Puberty: Precocious, delayed and incongruous. In J. Money & H. Musaph (Series Eds.) & M. E. Perry (Ed.), *Handbook of sexology: Vol. 7. Child and adolescent sexology* (pp. 236–262). Amsterdam: Elsevier Science Publishers.

Pavelka, M. S. (1995). Sexual nature: What can we learn form a cross-species perspective? In P. R. Abramson & S. D. Pinkerton (Eds.), *Sexual nature, sexual culture* (pp. 17–36). Chicago: University of Chicago Press.

Shweder, R. (1989). Cultural psychology, what is it? In J. Stigler, R. Schweder, & G. Herdt (Eds.), *Cultural psychology: The Chicago Symposia in Culture and Human Development*. New York: Cambridge University Press.

Strathern, M. (1988). *The gender of the gift*. Berkeley: University of California Press.

Tolman, D. (2005). *Dilemmas of desire*. Cambridge, MA: Harvard University Press.

Tuzin, D. (1997). *The Cassowary's revenge*. Chicago: University of Chicago Press.

Van Gennep, A. (1960). *The rites of passage*. Chicago: University of Chicago Press. (Original work published in 1909)

Wallace, A. F. C. (1969). *Culture and personality* (2nd. ed.). New York: Random House.

Weeks, J. (1985). *Sexuality and its discontents*. London: Routledge and Kegan Paul.

Weiranga, S. (2009). Postcolonial amnesia in Indonesia and South Africa. In G. Herdt, (Ed.), *Moral panics, sex panics: Fear and the fight over sexual rights* (pp. 205–233). New York: New York University Press.

Whiting, B., & Edwards, C. (1988). *Children of different worlds.* Cambridge, MA: Harvard University Press.

Worthman, C. (1999). Faster, farther, and higher: Biology and the discourses on human sexuality. In D. N. Suggs & A. W. Miracle (Eds.), *Culture, biology and sexuality* (pp. 64–75). Athens, GA: University of Georgia Press.

# FEAR, FUN, AND THE BOUNDARIES OF SOCIAL EXPERIENCE

Carol M. Worthman

## INTRODUCTION

The material in this section reflects the growing recognition that a complete account of development involves concerted attention not only to emotional as well as cognitive and physical needs of any individual child, but also to the larger social conditions under which children grow up. Six arresting observations from this section illustrate the point:

**Cycles of violence:** A boy afflicted by PTSD from social violence, including violence inflicted by his brother, recounts as his most traumatic memory, the public beating and humiliation of that same brother (Lemelson et al., p. 379–380, this volume).

**Sensitive periods:** Brain maturation in puberty and adolescence opens a window of developmental sensitivity to particular experiences (De Bellis, p. 394–396, this volume), exemplified by a reversal at puberty of the effect of defeat in hamsters (Huhman, p. 436–437, this volume).

**Pervasiveness of trauma:** In a clinic population of an inner city population of Atlanta, 50% of clients counted a murder victim among their relatives (Jasnow & Ressler, p. 452, this volume).

**Adaptation and survival:** The consistent associations of early experience of violence and hostile environments with risk for later violence might be considered in light of their evolved survival value rather than as pathology (Koolhaas, p. 402, this volume). At another level, social emotions such as shame and defeat may be experienced at the collective rather than individual level (Wilce, p. 467–468).

**Cultural epidemiology:** Both the "epidemic" of diagnosed attentional disorders and the consequent psychotropic medication of children may represent products of cultural practices that generate both the initial condition and the developmental outcome via their impact on contextual conditions and demands, and on neurocognitive functioning (Panksepp, pp. 470–471).

**Need for play:** Rodent work showing the importance of play for development of reciprocity and social skills suggests that loss of play opportunities may contribute to difficulties of emotional development in bullied and ostracized children (Pellis, pp. 412–420, this volume).

The state of developmental science reflects a struggle to reassemble elements that had been sundered in western thought and inquiry, via a mind-body split that also pitted emotion against rationality. The case studies and chapters explore the impact of social relationships and interactions on the formation of social competence and its emotional foundations. Social competence involves not only capacity for positive engagement, but also for self protection, avoidance of harm, and coping with adversity. The world is a changeable and potentially inimical place, and abundant evidence suggests that developmental systems reflect this enduring adaptive challenge in the sensitivity to early and ongoing cues of environmental quality (predictability, security). Such cues include the quality and stability of family relationships, positionality within the community and society, and the nature and meaning of social experiences, all of which have been implicated in neurodevelopmental processes that ground emotion, social cognition, and behavior. Thus, play-fighting emerges as a context for species-specific formation of neural bases, behavioral competencies, and social cognitions required for titrating reciprocity and partner manipulation or self defense.

On the down side, developmental openness to and reliance on context opens a window of psychobehavioral vulnerability to disrupted relationships, trauma, and social discrimination, oppression, and hostility. Thus, Lemelson's case study of social ostracism and violence against the Javanese boy, Joko, and Jasnow and Ressler's data from a heavily traumatized inner city population in Atlanta, link social conditions that produce early trauma to later emotional and behavioral difficulties. As De Bellis also points out, the developmental importance of caregiver nurturance creates a pathway for intergenerational transmission of psychobehavioral patterns, strengths, and vulnerabilities.

Yet against an adaptive background one may ask whose problem it is when abused or marginalized youth respond with violence and hostility. Similarly, commentators on Huhman's case study of social defeat in hamsters wrestle with the problem of whether the behavior makes adaptive sense and hence, what it "means" and whether it should be considered a protective rather than pathological response. Wilce also draws attention to the value of attending to meaning and identity, and their extension well beyond the level of the individual. In all the materials in this section, we note the need to observe creatures in place, whether they are hamsters, rats, rhesus, or humans.

# FIFTEEN

# Ethnographic Case Study

*Anak PKI: A Longitudinal Case Study of the Effects of Social Ostracism, Political Violence, and Bullying on an Adolescent Javanese Boy*

Robert Lemelson, Ninik Supartini, and Emily Ng

I am told not to think about the past, but I still do, and (when I do), my emotions intensify... I was a quiet person before, so many people picked fights with me. Now (that I am different), the voices tell me to go back (and face) that past world.  (Joko, 2006 interview)

What is a "healthy" psychological response to long-term discrimination, oppression, social ostracism, and discriminatory violence, enacted not only by a state apparatus but also through the agency of local community members? How should notions of revenge and retribution be viewed in this context? And how does such a cultural environment affect a child's neurobiological and developmental changes?

These are some of the questions explored in the following case study of a central Javanese boy named Joko and his transition from childhood to early adulthood.[1]

---

[1] This case study is drawn from the author's visual ethnography project on the long-term psychosocial outcomes of Indonesian families who survived the executions, disappearances, and political imprisonments following former president Suharto's rise to power and his "New Order" regime (1965–1998). An abbreviated version of the same case study is discussed in Lemelson, Kirmayer, and Barad (2007). Longitudinal studies of all three families form the basis of an ethnographic film (Lemelson, 2009).

The interviews with Joko used in this chapter occurred between 2002 and early 2007 in and around Yogyakarta, a city of approximately 1 million in Central Java. All participants gave informed consent for their participation in this study. Consent for filming was obtained at the time of the interviews and recorded on film. The interviews were undertaken with the understanding that this material would be used for documentary, educational, and research purposes. In this chapter, we have used pseudonyms for the interviewees in order to protect their identity.

## CASE STUDY

Joko was a patient of Dr. Mahar Agusno (MA), a Javanese psychiatrist with whom one of the authors, Robert Lemelson (RL), has been conducting ongoing research on neuropsychiatric disorders in Indonesia. Joko was referred to MA by the staff of the Catholic orphanage where his parents had placed him at age 12. The clinical interviews with Joko were initially conducted by MA, his wife Ninik Supartini (NS), and RL and were recorded on video. As the research progressed, RL, usually accompanied by NS (who also became Joko's counselor), conducted ethnographic person-centered interviews with Joko, his family, social workers, and the orphanage staff, as well as children from Joko's home village and other members of his community.

RL initially spoke to Joko in a rather stark, drab, but clean meeting room in the orphanage. At that time, Joko was a slight, somewhat gaunt 12-year-old who often had a distant or lost expression on his face. He spoke calmly and articulately during the interview, but often in a low voice. Joko talked quietly about his life in the orphanage and politely answered our questions.

> JOKO: I came to this home because I had a problem. It was a rather complicated problem, you know. My family was unjustly maltreated, slandered, terrorized (*keluarga saya dianiaya, difitnah, gitu, diteror*). It was like that. (2002)[2]

When MA asked Joko how he felt during the specific incidents of injustice he had experienced, Joko's face tightened up. He bent over in his chair, clenched his fists, and began to sob silently while rocking back and forth. One of the memories that disturbed him most was from from age 9, when Joko witnessed his 17-year-old brother Paidjo "unjustly maltreated" by his fellow villagers. Paidjo was so severely beaten and stoned that he bled and experienced uncontrolled defecation, and was forced to walk naked on his hands. Joko himself was dragged away by youngsters who started to beat him as well, but he was able to escape and find refuge and help.

> JOKO: When (Paidjo) was tortured he screamed, cried, you know. Eerr . . . he called my name. I wanted to run, wanted to run to help him. I was dragged by the youngsters and they wanted to hit me. Then I cried. "Why . . . why did you guys beat my brother?" Suddenly I was slapped

---

[2] Throughout this chapter, each quote from an interviewee will be followed by the year in which the interview was conducted, as one of the goals of this chapter is to highlight the interactions between developmental changes, clinical symptoms, and familial and sociopolitical contexts.

by the (military) officer. "You little child, you know nothing but you dare (to argue) with older ones," he said. Then I cried. I went home crying. (2002)

This incident was one of numerous violent experiences this family had at the hands of fellow villagers. Throughout the years, Joko himself was ganged up on and beaten by peers repeatedly. In addition to the ongoing violence, Joko was mocked regularly by youth in the community. They would say, "Look, the thief's brother is walking by." Then another person would say, "Hey, the commie kid... the commie kid is passing by. Step back, step back, step back" (2002). Joko explained that repetitive memories of such experiences, which he said began when he was seven, led to much distress and suffering. The unusual political circumstances that had led to his placement in the orphanage made him feel "worthless." And Joko's memories of these numerous traumatic events were associated with autonomic nervous-system symptoms of arousal and anxiety.

> JOKO: I feel my body temperature increase. It becomes hot. There is a stabbing pain in my chest as if it were pricked with needles. Then I feel short-winded. Then my heart beats quickly, and after that I feel tense... and I want to punch whoever is around me. And suddenly I pass out, I faint. (2002)

Joko's teachers reported that he often daydreamed in class, or sometimes simply fell asleep at his desk. The nuns at the orphanage noted that he often awoke in the middle of the night calling his brother's name, which sometimes resulted in physical paroxysms that caused the sisters to bring him to the emergency room at the local hospital. Whenever Joko remembered the unrecognizable appearance of his brother's face after one particularly severe beating, he experienced severe, debilitating stomach cramps. Additionally, Joko had frequent suicidal thoughts, and the nuns at the orphanage said they intercepted several times when they found him standing at the edge of a nearby well.

MA's initial psychiatric assessment documented Joko's frequent flashbacks and intrusive thoughts, involving images from past maltreatment, re-experiencing of these traumatic events during arguments with peers or discussion of the past, and recurrent nightmares of his brother being tortured and killed. Joko had also made multiple suicide attempts and experienced repeated fantasies of revenge. Given this profile, Joko was diagnosed with posttraumatic stress disorder (PTSD), depression with psychotic features, and conversion disorder. He was administered Amitriptyline and

Haloperidol, followed by Fluoxetine, to reduce his depressive and psychotic symptoms. In addition to pharmacotherapy, five counseling sessions were arranged with MA and NS to address his feelings of worthlessness, his desire for vengeance, and the danger of a foreshortened future. Unfortunately for Joko, MA received a fellowship that caused him to leave the country for one year with his family. Although MA and NS referred Joko to a local psychiatrist for follow-up care, further treatment was not continued.

Although Joko was seriously troubled, RL did not initially understand why he had been placed in an orphanage; both parents were alive and lived within ten miles of the facility. In the first meeting with the research team Joko's family framed his placement in the orphanage as an educational decision based on their inability to afford public school (in Indonesia, there is a fee for public schools, which keeps many of the poorest children from attending). Later interviews revealed that this decision had involved many other members of the community, and was also based on the domestic violence rampant within the family, particularly Paidjo's frequent violence toward Joko.

Interviews with Joko's family and members of the community revealed layers of violence and hardship impacting Joko's everyday life. However, to understand why the villagers had scapegoated and tortured Joko and his family, one needs to unravel Joko's father's life story, including the broader historical and political contexts of his experiences.

## A CAGE OF LIONS: G-30-S AND ITS IMPACTS ON FAMILY HISTORY

Sukiman, Joko's father, is a short, thin man with skin wizened and darkened by many years of working in the open sun. Sukiman grew up in a poor village outside of Yogyakarta. He said that he was known as a troublemaker as a youngster, often getting into fights because he had a difficult time controlling his temper. As a young man he worked as a salesman at a coffee factory. There he fell in love with a young woman from his village and planned to marry her. At the time, the son of the village headman was also in love with the same young woman.

In 1965, a political incident occurred involving the death of six generals and one high-ranking official. Colonel – later General – Suharto framed the incident as a coup by the Indonesian Communist Party (*Partai Komunis Indonesia* [PKI]), which, it is important to note, was a legal political party at the time. Using these assassinations as a pretext, Suharto organized a purge of suspected members of the PKI. In less than a year, upward of a million Indonesians were summarily executed or disappeared, usually because of an alleged PKI affiliation (Robinson, 1995). This bloodbath was the worst in Indonesian history and ranks as the 11th largest genocide of the twentieth century. In addition to massacres, anyone accused of being a PKI member or affiliate risked arrest. As a result, hundreds of thousands were held in local jails, and later, on remote prison islands. In 1967, Suharto took power as president of Indonesia and began his "New Order" regime, which was characterized by continued attempts to punish and purge alleged communists over the next three decades.

As the events following G-30-S (short for *Gerakan 30 September*, or the September 30th Movement, the Indonesian state's official title for the assassination incident) unfolded, the son of Sukiman's village headman reported to the authorities that Sukiman was a prominent PKI member and activist. Sukiman stated that although he socialized with PKI members, he had never been a member himself. Nonetheless, he was taken away with no notification to his family. After his initial arrest in 1965, Sukiman was sent to a prison for four months, then to Nusakambangan – a top-security island prison designated for first-class criminals. He was imprisoned there for five years and then sent to Buru Island – the most infamous prison island of that period – for nine years. The conditions in these prisons were terrible, and gross human rights violations occurred on a daily basis.

> SUKIMAN: Nusakambangan was . . . the cage of lions, that is what people say. . . . For me, my life was full of suffering, full of strikes of the whip and beatings until my head got multiple fractures . . . they treated us like animals.

Upon his release in 1979, Sukiman found out that the young woman he had been in love with years earlier had married the man who had initially reported him to the authorities. He also realized that he now frequently lost emotional control and often flew into violent rages, which he attributed to the maltreatment he had experienced.

## "CHILD OF THE COMMUNIST PARTY" AND AN "UNCLEAN ENVIRONMENT": SOCIOPOLITICAL STIGMATIZATION AND FAMILY LIFE POST-1965

The world Sukiman returned to was very different from the one he had known prior to his imprisonment 14 years earlier. The Suharto regime had instituted numerous legal restrictions and regulations for anyone thought to be associated with the now-banned PKI. Those accused of affiliation with the PKI had different identity papers, which classified them as having an "unclean environment" (*lingkungan tidak bersih*). Having this status, which was often assigned unpredictably and arbitrarily, meant that many kinds of jobs were prohibited, such as working in the civil service or military, or in occupations as variable as education or journalism, or even being a *dalang* ("puppet master") in traditional leather puppetry. Moreover, their movements and ability to travel were highly restricted, and their daily activities were monitored by local police, other political apparatchiks, and local community members. In addition, family members were also considered suspect under these laws, and similar restrictions were placed upon their activities, movements, and career opportunities. Thus, after his release, Sukiman faced numerous difficulties. With his spoiled identity as an alleged ex-PKI, finding a spouse was very difficult. Eventually, through a family member's matchmaking, Sukiman was introduced to Giyarti, whose father had also been accused of being a PKI member. Giyarti's mother quickly agreed to the marriage and forced Giyarti to accept Sukiman as her husband, threatening to disown her if she refused to marry him.

The start of married life was terrible for Giyarti. Sukiman's parents treated her poorly, and Sukiman was frequently violent toward her and their young sons. In addition to troubles at home, the family was continuously subjected to harassment, intimidation, and discrimination from the local community because of Sukiman's political status. Giyarti was often sexually harassed by village men when Sukiman was away at work. When she tried to report these incidents to local leaders, they threatened to send her husband back to jail if she did "anything stupid."

In 2000, Giyarti filed a lawsuit against the military police officers who tortured Joko's brother. Because the military officers threatened to publicize her case in the newspaper, which would endanger the entire family, the family moved to Yogyakarta – approximately 10 kilometers from their former village – the very next day. Joko and Sukiman continued to visit and maintain the house occasionally, but in 2002, they were told that villagers had destroyed the house. Thus ceased their visits.

## "MY FUTURE IS DISAPPEARING FROM MY SIGHT. I NOW WANT TO DO EVIL THINGS": TRAUMA, REVENGE, AND JUSTICE IN LONGITUDINAL PERSPECTIVE

From our initial interviews with Joko in 2002, to our most recent in 2007, the theme of revenge has recurred consistently. Indeed, revenge fantasies have played a prominent role in his everyday preoccupations throughout the years and have constituted a salient narrative arc linking his past, present, and future.

> MA: How do you see your future, Joko?
> JOKO: I think my future is complicated. I think it is disappearing from my sight.... Because after I got the problems I do not know who I am anymore.... I now want to do evil things. For example, I want to assassinate, to torture them the way they did to my family members....

Then another thought from Joko:

If I want to fight them, then I have to have a bottle and chemical substance, gasoline, and a match. What I wanted to do was blow up their houses so that they experience the grief and pain that my family members and I have been suffering from. (2002)

Caretakers and counselors surrounding Joko have constantly tried to deter his vengeful thoughts. However, he may well have thought he was receiving mixed messages due to the domestic and community violence surrounding him. And the means of coping deemed appropriate by caretakers might not have seemed accessible from Joko's standpoint, in light of his past experiences and his awareness of his own status in the community. Although he apparently perceived violence as a more fulfilling response, he felt very ambivalent about its potential consequences for himself and his family if he were to act on his urges. Despite this ambivalence, Joko has been learning to assemble bombs and formulate poisons since 2002. He at first denied that these interests were connected to his desire for revenge. When pressed during later interviews, however, the linkages in motivation became clearer.

> NS: Do you really want to take revenge on the people who hurt you? Do you think that this feeling has encouraged you to make real bombs (and think) "Ah, when I run into them, watch out, I will blow them up."
> JOKO: Well, frankly speaking, if that intention emerged, and if I could not control it, it might happen like that, Bu (ma'am). Yes. (2006)

Joko was quite proud of his knowledge and skills, which seemed to give him a sense of identity, mastery, and dignity that he could not achieve as an adolescent through the conventional framework of schooling.

> JOKO: My former school principal called me the "insane professor" because of my vast knowledge in the field of explosives, and because of (my knowledge of) poisons. I was satisfied because none of the children

my age at that time was able to do that.... I admit that I was slow in schoolwork, but outside of classrooms ... (2006)

Beyond the sense of accomplishment and esteem gained from these pursuits, another motivation for revenge became increasingly salient for Joko in our later interviews: justice. This component of his revenge schema is most evident in his fascination with Ninjutsu, a Japanese form of martial arts that emphasizes secret or hidden skills. Although Joko's understanding of them is filtered through *manga* (Japanese *anime* comics) and movies, the essential understanding of ninjas as heroes who seek revenge and justice through covert means seems isomorphic with Joko's experience. Joko's notions about the role of ninjas helped to provide a broader moral framework for his more recent discussions of revenge.

> JOKO: It is like what I saw in (the movie) *American Ninja*. It is about someone living an area occupied by another nation. The people there were suffering very much.... Eventually there were a couple of ninjas who succeeded in freeing the area. (2005)

Joko's concurrent yearnings for empowerment, revenge, and justice are apparent in his story of a recent encounter in his former village with someone who had tortured Paidjo in the past.

> JOKO: I told him, "I am Joko." He said, "Oh, you are Paidjo' brother? Why don't we just kill you altogether?" And I said, "There are many Jokos (out there). How many do you need?" (2006)

This notion of representing fellow marginalized "Jokos" also emerged when Joko was asked recently about his future. He named peace and safety as the ultimate purpose of life, and characterized himself as a potential agent of justice.

> JOKO: I sincerely want to help people. I will see what kind of problems they have, and if the problems are like mine, then I will use my own experiences to help them without any reservation. (2006)

## "MY FACE THEN WAS THAT OF CLAY. NOW I AM A ROCK": DEVELOPMENT, COPING, AND SOCIAL CHANGE

In early 2006, Joko began training in *pencak silat*, a broad term for Indonesian, particularly Javanese, forms of martial arts. The combination of breathing exercises, meditation, and free fight created a bodily, spiritual, and psychological outlet for coping with his emotions at times of difficulty.

JOKO: When I was (back at the orphanage), every time I remembered people who tortured my brother, my temper would rise right away . . . From
martial arts practice I can release my emotion during free fight . . . I felt
that my emotions could be channeled. (2007)

Also, a growing sense of trust in close relationships has helped in facing
new problems.

MA: Can you apply the knowledge you have gained from martial arts (e.g.,
calming oneself, controlling emotions) to encounters with enemies?
JOKO: Yes. . . . Before I could not, but now I can, because I now also remember that there are people who love me. (2006)

In the autumn of 2006, RL, NS, and the film crew showed the edited ethnographic film of Joko's family (2002–2005) to Joko, Giyarti, and Sukiman.[3]
Throughout the viewing, Sukiman watched the screen intently, Giyarti
chuckled at some moments and dabbed away tears at others, and Joko
nestled himself next to Giyarti, looking away from the screen for some of
the film, particularly during the footage of himself as a young boy recalling those who had hurt or persecuted his family. Although Joko seemed
moved, even disturbed at times, by what he saw, he claimed that the film
had no emotional impact on him.

JOKO: It (the film) does not affect me. Even if it was played a thousand
times, it would still have no effects on me. I do not feel sad or happy. I
just feel normal. The past is the past. (2006)

At the same time, Joko voiced embarrassment and disgust at seeing his
younger self, saying, "My face at that time was that of a coward. Ugh. . . .
The face then was that of clay. But (to NS) now I am a rock" (2006).

Joko said that he was now able to return to his old village without
fear and face his past tormentors. Overall, by early 2007 Joko seemed to
present and narrate a sense of self that was much more stable, *berani* (brave
and confident), and in control compared to what he was like during our
interviews in 2002. While cognitive and moral transitions accompanying
development were likely one source of these shifts, changes in sociopolitical circumstances also play a crucial role. It is no surprise that many
of the events in the early 2000s that initially traumatized Joko and his
family occurred during the period of civil unrest following the Asian economic crisis and Suharto's fall in 1998 – for example, the beating of Joko

---

[3] The process of participating in this ethnographic research project has doubtlessly been
another source of influence for Joko and his family. Unfortunately, due to the limited
scope of this paper, this issue will not discussed at length here.

and his brother and the destruction of the family's house in their former village. Throughout Indonesia there was an upsurge of local violence across numerous ethnic and religious divides. Ex-PKI members formed one among many convenient scapegoats targeted for violence in communities devastated by an economic downturn and influenced by years of propaganda that dehumanized and demonized those associated with the now-banned Communist Party.

By the time of our later interviews, the widespread political turmoil had eased slightly. Joko's growing sense of psychological empowerment cannot be divorced from systematic changes in his environment that now provide previously nonexistent possibilities for support. This can be seen in Joko's narrative of a recent confrontation with someone from his former village who used to torment his brother, in which Joko said to him, "If you want to continue torturing me right now, that is fine, but it will be added to my brother's (legal) case. . . . Now there is law" (2006).

Legal recourse has also been a source of relief and empowerment for Giyarti. After her house was destroyed in 2002, she gave up hope of ever regaining the land. However, with the aid of the research team, Giyarti was introduced in December 2006, to a Muslim Indonesian organization geared toward seeking justice for those who had survived the political violence of 1965. This provided the possibility of reestablishing her ownership. She noted that contacting such an organization made her feel that she was no longer "trash," because her opinions and desires were finally being heard and accounted for.

However, despite some notable changes in the political climate since the Suharto era, the realities and fears of continued community violence and political persecution are far from over.[4] Although space has gradually begun to open for critical discourses problematizing the state-sanctioned narrative of 1965 and its aftermath, such discussions remain risky and tend to occur on a small scale. Thus, the relative peace experienced by the family during our most recent interviews cannot be taken for granted. Nonetheless, the longitudinal approach of this case study has allowed for a view of vulnerability and resilience in Joko and his family, which would have been impossible to capture with a mere snapshot of their lives in 2002.

---

[4] As Robinson (1995) argues, outbreaks of aggression such as that surrounding G-30-S should not be viewed as an anomaly, but rather seen in the context of the cycles of violence that have affected Indonesia throughout its history. Robinson notes that one source of violence in Indonesia involves the central government's periodic endorsements of local violence when they perceive a potential threat to the regime. Of course, local politics then play into how this state-sanctioned violence is carried out and against whom it is enacted.

## DISCUSSION

The origins and consequences of bullying in a child's life cannot be grasped without addressing the layers of context that provide particular conditions of possibility that permit the noxious and destructive acts of bullying. In Joko's case, the course of Indonesian national politics and the existence of hierarchical systems at the national, local, and family levels all render him an easy target for bullying, social ostracism, and interpersonal and political violence. He is the youngest in a violence-laden family; he is poor and lacks extensive formal education; his family is Catholic in a predominantly Muslim region; and, perhaps most important, he is *anak PKI* (a child of a PKI member). In consequence, many of the social and interpersonal restrictions that normally would have prevented a child from being stigmatized and bullied were lifted. In addition, dependable social and legal avenues for confronting those who bullied Joko and his brother were unavailable to his family until recently.

After accounting for Joko's socioeconomic position, the longitudinal trajectory of his development within the context of both family and community violence, and his sociomoral framework for justice, we can see that there are problems with trying to categorize his recurrent revenge fantasies as a psychiatric symptom. In light of the multiple layers of oppression and domestic violence he has endured, are norm-based scales or the categorical strictures of the Diagnostic and Statistical Manual of Mental Disorders (DSM) useful for defining Joko's levels of developmental pathology and resilience? What factors should be considered, and how much relative weight should the cultural, historical, developmental, psychological, and neurobiological factors be given? Although epidemiological data indeed show that the vast majority of those who encounter trauma do not experience clinically defined clusters of biological and psychological PTSD responses such as Joko's (Yehuda & McFarlane, 1995), these data cannot address the moral and political implications of defining Joko's reactions to the physical, emotional, structural, and symbolic violence in his family, community, and nation as mere pathology.

Developmental contexts of fear, oppression, and ostracism should be the exception in life rather than the norm. Unfortunately, as social scientists, we know that many children inhabit worlds filled with such trauma. And we know that this topic has been downplayed or ignored in many previous accounts of children's lives. But the current explosion of research in the neurobiology of fear, in the ethology of social domination, and in affective neuroscience makes this a good time for social scientists to reach out to the neurosciences. Constructive dialogue about how the contexts in which children like Joko live may affect their current lives and relationships can help scientists to evaluate these experiences and determine what they portend for children's future development and their ability to engage as full participants in their respective societies. A good first step, before invoking a clinical or neuroscientific integration, would be to understand and address the various historical, political, sociocultural, and local community factors that intermesh to build one child's life.

REFERENCES

Lemelson, R. (Producer & Director). (2009). *40 years of silence: An Indonesian trajedy.* (Information available from http://www.40yearsofsilence.com)

Lemelson, R., Kirmayer, L. J., & Barad, M. (2007). Trauma in context: Integrating biological, clinical, and cultural perspectives. In L. Kirmayer, R. Lemelson, & M. Barad (Eds.), *Understanding trauma: Integrating biological, clinical, and cultural perspectives* (pp. 451–474). New York: Cambridge University Press.

Robinson, G. B. (1995). *The dark side of paradise: Political violence in Bali.* New York: Cornell University Press.

Yehuda, R., & McFarlane, A. C. (1995). Conflict between current knowledge about post-traumatic stress disorder and its original conceptual basis. *American Journal of Psychiatry, 152*(12), 1705–1713.

# Commentary

*Developmental Traumatology: A Commentary on the Factors for Risk and Resiliency in the Case of an Adolescent Javanese Boy*

Michael D. De Bellis

## INTRODUCTION

The case of Joko, a Javanese boy who suffered from repeated traumas of interpersonal origins, illustrates the principles of developmental traumatology (De Bellis, 2001). Developmental traumatology is the systematic investigation of the neurobiological impact of chronic interpersonal violence on the developing child. It is a relatively new area of study that synthesizes knowledge from developmental psychopathology, developmental neuroscience, and stress and trauma research. In the emerging field of developmental traumatology, measures of trauma (type, age of onset, and duration of trauma), as well as other mediating factors such as social support, are regarded as independent variables. Behavioral, cognitive, emotional, and neurobiological measures are considered dependent variables (De Bellis et al., 1999).

Joko was interviewed while living at a Catholic orphanage, and following a horrific experience of being bullied, assaulted, all while witnessing the torture and public humiliation of his older brother, Paidjo. Joko was suffering from posttraumatic stress disorder (PTSD). He had significant symptoms of PTSD cluster B intrusions of the trauma; PTSD cluster C symptoms of dissociation, hopelessness, depression, and numbing; and PTSD cluster D symptoms of hyperarrousal (American Psychiatric Association, 2000, pp. 424–432).

Neurobiological sequelae of child maltreatment may be regarded as an environmentally induced complex developmental disorder, which may lead to an array of outcomes through these clusters of symptoms (De Bellis, 2001). During adolescence, the healthy development of prefrontal cortex leads to inhibitory pathways that quiet the brain's amygdala and biological stress systems, complex structures that register the emotional rage of injustice. Dysfunction of these systems leads to PTSD and depression. Considering PTSD a dimensional diagnosis that encompasses a range of reactions to severe stress (rather than as a dichotomous diagnosis) leads to a better understanding of the neurobiological consequences of this condition.

For an adolescent such as Joko, major developmental issues include detachment, shame, guilt, acting out, life-threatening reenactment behaviors, desire for revenge, intense anger, and changes in attitudes about life (Pynoos & Nader, 1993). His struggle with cluster C symptoms, which represent both avoidant and dissociative behaviors, can be thought of as ways to control painful and distressing re-experiencing of intrusive symptoms. These include efforts to avoid thoughts, feelings, activities, places, people, and memories associated with the trauma; diminished interest in others; feelings of detachment from others; a restricted range of affect; and a sense of a foreshortened future. Emotional numbing and diminished interest in others, particularly during development, may result in lack of empathy and antisocial behaviors (De Bellis, 2001). These issues were particularly compelling for Joko as he struggled with intrusive thoughts of his traumas and his intense desire for revenge.

Some of the understudied protective factors illustrated in the case of Joko are cultural (religion, early psychiatric treatment, social support, and structure). Joko's resiliency during his adolescent years and his choice to "sincerely want to help people" instead of "to assassinate" may be linked to his being Catholic, living in a structured and safe Catholic orphanage, and receiving psychiatric treatment along with mind-body therapy and psychotropic medications following his worst experiences of being bullied and assaulted.

## THE EFFECT OF CHRONIC TRAUMA ON JOKO'S BIOLOGICAL STRESS SYSTEMS

One of the major principles of developmental traumatology is that while an infinite number of stressors can cause a subjective sense of overwhelming stress and distress, the brain and the body (i.e., biological stress systems) can respond to those stressors in finite ways (for review see De Bellis, 2001). In Joko's case, the nature of his chronic stressors comprises a series of dysfunctional and traumatized interpersonal relationships, first with his father, then his brother, and finally with society. Joko experienced social ostracism, political violence, bullying, and multiple assaults because his father, Sukiman, was an alleged member of the *Partai Komunis* (Indonesia's Communist Party). Sukiman was a victim of political torture, and may have also suffered from PTSD; he perpetrated domestic violence on his sons and on their mother. Joko's brother Paidjo was also frequently violent toward Joko. These chronic stressors preceded Joko's most disturbing memory of witnessing, at the age of 9, the stoning of Paidjo.

The second developmental traumatology principle involves the nature of the chronic stressors – dysfunctional and traumatized interpersonal relationships. Interpersonal stressors usually involve a child losing faith and trust in authority figures, and building a therapeutic alliance con-sists of a lengthy process of desensitizing the maltreated individual to distrust so that he can reestablish trust and empathy with others. Joko experienced chronic stress throughout his life from these kinds of stres-sors, although spending his adolescent years in the Catholic orphanage where he received a formal education may have helped him reestablish this trust.

The third principle of developmental traumatology is that interpersonal stressors in childhood may be more detrimental than trauma experienced in adulthood because of the interactions that take place between trauma and neurodevelopment. The results from this research suggest that traumatic childhood experiences are associated with alterations of biological stress response systems and subsequent adverse influences on brain development (De Bellis et al., 1999).

Traumatic experiences are perceived through the five senses as fear. In preclinical studies, electrical stimulation of the amygdala of animals is asso-ciated with fearful behaviors, including increases in heart rate, blood pres-sure, freezing, activation of fear-related motor movements, and increases in cortisol levels. (Amygdala lesions reduce fearful behaviors and emotional reactivity and interfere with the acquisition of conditioned fear and the rise in cortisol levels.) This intense fear or anxiety activates the amygdala and the locus ceruleus, an ancient brain area, which, in turn, stimulates the hypothalamus and the release of corticotropin-releasing hormone (CRH) or factor (CRF). CRH cell bodies and receptors are located in the amygdala and throughout the brain. CRH causes the pituitary to secrete adrenocor-ticotropin (ACTH), but CRH also stimulates brain cortical regions. CRH promotes hypercortisolism and stimulates the sympathetic nervous system (SNS), causing high blood pressure, increased arousal, and a "fight or flight or freeze reaction." ACTH results in release of cortisol from the adrenal gland, with feedback to the SNS, causing further activation and the "fight or flight reaction" important for survival. This sequence of events results in tachycardia, hypertension, increased metabolic rate, hypervigilance, and

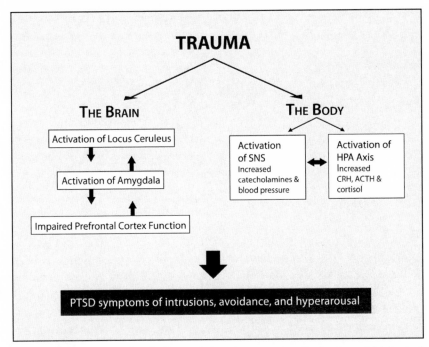

**Figure 15.1.** The cascade of effects of chronic trauma on the brain and biological stress systems.

increased levels of stress chemicals including catecholamines. Prolonged exposure to stress leads individuals to display increased stress levels at rest and enhanced stress responsiveness. This stress response is characterized by elevations in catecholamines and cortisol levels, which are likely to adversely affect brain development. Catecholamines contribute to dilation of the pupils, diaphoresis, renal inhibition, and decrease in peripheral blood flow. Activation of the locus ceruleus/SNS/catecholamine system and CRH results in animal behaviors consistent with anxiety, hyperarousal, and hypervigilance, which are the symptoms of PTSD. These stress chemicals impair the brain's prefrontal cortex and executive functions (see Figure 15.1). Maltreated children with PTSD show greater levels of cortisol and catecholamines at baseline than children who have not been maltreated, as well as evidence of adverse brain development and psychopathology (De Bellis et al., 1999).

The fourth principle of developmental traumatology is that the responses of biological stress systems are influenced by environmental and individual differences. Variables include the nature of the stressor, its frequency and chronicity, and genetic vulnerabilities in regulating biological stress systems, which relate to how these systems respond to the stressor: Do they become permanently dysregulated or can they adopt a new homeostasis in the face of chronic and severe stress? Birth to adulthood is marked by progressive physical, behavioral, cognitive, and emotional development, with changes in brain maturation paralleling these stages. Biological stress response systems are interconnected at many levels to coordinate an individual's responses and adaptations to acute and chronic environmental stressors, and these interconnections influence brain development. In the developing brain, elevated levels of catecholamines and cortisol may lead to adverse brain development through a variety of mechanisms (De Bellis et al., 1999).

The fifth principle of developmental traumatology is that PTSD-like symptoms in childhood are common human responses to severe stressors. These symptoms are usually short-lived. However, if trauma is chronic and severe, most individuals will suffer from PTSD (for review see De Bellis, 2001), as did Joko. In PTSD, areas of the prefrontal cortex that inhibit amygdala activation are dysfunctional. Studies have shown that when confronted with traumatic reminders, individuals with PTSD show decreased activity of medial prefrontal brain regions and increased activity of the amygdala, while traumatized individuals without PTSD did not show the same degree of amygdala activation (Shin et al., 2004). Thus, treatment of PTSD symptoms involves strengthening prefrontal inhibitory pathways and down-regulating locus ceruleus and amygdala activity, which leads to increased SNS activity. These types of biological stress activity are believed to lead to anxiety, panic attacks, nightmares, poor concentration, and hypervigilence, symptoms that Joko experienced. Cognitive behavioral therapy, social support, and the normal prefrontal brain maturation seen in adolescence may strengthen these prefrontal systems. One of the most important stress chemicals is serotonin, a neurotransmitter that regulates mood and intrusive, suicidal, and violent thoughts. Antidepressants such as fluoxetine (Prozac) (which was given to Joko) can down-regulate biological stress systems and decrease trauma intrusions. Fluoxetine may cause a decrease in PTSD symptoms because it down-regulates locus ceruleus and amygdala activity, and increases serotonin levels in brain synapses.

## PSYCHOLOGICAL DEVELOPMENT IN ADOLESCENCE AND PTSD CLUSTER C SYMPTOMS

As puberty begins, cortical white matter is maturing, particularly in the prefrontal areas of the brain, which house executive functions, planning,

**Healthy Child**          **Child with PTSD**

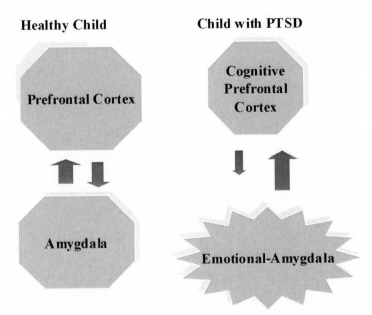

**Figure 15.2.** The comparison of the functional activity and interconnections of the medial prefrontal brain regions and the amygdala in an individual without PTSD and one with PTSD.

moral decisions, and problem solving. Subcortical areas of the brain linked to emotion, including the amygdala, are also nearing maturity. As connections of inhibitory neurons from prefrontal areas to the amygdala mature, the ability to control thoughts and impulses develops. Healthy adolescents develop internal standards of behavior, a sense of right and wrong, and self-control. They begin to form a permanent sense of identity, understand others' motivations and behavior, and think abstractly. For the traumatized adolescent, major issues include detachment, shame, acting out, life-threatening reenactment behaviors (e.g, suicidal behaviors), desire for revenge, intense anger, and changes in attitudes about life (e.g., hopelessness) (for review see Pynoos & Nader, 1993). Joko experienced repeated fantasies of revenge, a cluster B intrusive symptom. He experienced intense cluster C symptoms of being in a daze (i.e., having a lost expression on his face, daydreaming), regression ("rocking back and forth"), and a sense of a foreshortened future. The cluster B intrusive desire for revenge, coupled with cluster C symptoms of dissociation and numbing, can lead to a lack of empathy with consequent antisocial and violent behaviors (see Figure 15.2).

When he said, "My future is disappearing from my sight. I now want to do evil things." Joko was losing his sense of self. He also said, "I do not know who I am anymore. I want to assassinate, to torture them the way they did my family members." He learned to assemble bombs and formulate poisons, and was preoccupied with Ninjutsu, a Japanese form of martial arts, which emphasizes secret skills. Joko was able to learn mastery of self and regain his dignity through these violent pursuits, and he also learned that he had a choice, a discovery that empowered him. Joko ultimately decided to pursue justice, peace, and safety, and was able to put the past into perspective.

## THE ROLE OF SOCIAL SUPPORT IN JOKO'S RESILIENCY

Biological stress systems are down-regulated when an individual experiences social support (for review see De Bellis, 2001). Joko received early intervention through his placement in the Catholic orphanage. The nuns frequently monitored him for suicidal ideation, intercepting him several times when they found him standing at the edge of a nearby well. The tenets of Catholic teachings, the teachings of Jesus, are to uphold life, discourage vengeful actions, and encourage forgiveness and justice for the oppressed. It is likely that the structure of the orphanage decreased the ongoing stressors from Joko's family and the community, while giving him a safe and supportive structure. This placement also provided an opportunity for Joko to receive psychiatric treatment and medications, which may have led to down-regulation of his biological stress systems. Martial arts provided him with an alternative type of therapy via mind-body mechanism, which emphasized breathing exercises and meditation. These treatments strengthen prefrontal inhibitory connections and down-regulate the amygdala. Furthermore, Joko was cared for and was able to grieve in a supportive environment, which alleviated his numbness. He regained an ability to trust others and form relationships, and he gained empathy. Lastly, legal recourse became available to the family and Joko's mother was able to seek justice. The law, when followed and delivered by just individuals, is a powerful form of social support. These factors likely led Joko, a victim of PTSD, away from life of violence to a future in which he could use his ability to plan a legal means to deal with the injustice in his life rather than reacting to that injustice.

## CONCLUDING REMARKS

The case of Joko outlines the severe effects of trauma on biological stress systems and prefrontal brain development. It demonstrates that a variety of social supports and alternative treatments can free victims to grieve and heal from their traumas and aim for a life of resilience. The alternative – a lack of empathy and a life of dissociation, numbing, and restricted affect – can lead to severe antisocial behaviors, including terrorism, and the continuation of an intergenerational cycle of violence. The negative effects of biological stress system dysregulation can be reversed to some degree by political justice, outside interventions, treatment, nonviolent religious teachings, alternative mind-body medical treatments (Osuch & Engel, 2004), and evidence-based treatments (Cohen, Kelleher, & Mannarino, 2008) for PTSD symptoms. By lessening the potential harmful effects of cluster C symptoms to an individual and a society, such interventions can decrease the intergenerational transmission of PTSD and violence.

REFERENCES

American Psychiatric Association. (2000). *Diagnostic and statistical manual of mental disorders* (Rev. 4th ed.). Washington, DC: Author.

Cohen, J. A., Kelleher, K. K., & Mannarino, A. P. (2008). Identifying, treating, and referring traumatized children: The role of pediatric providers. *Archives of Pediatric and Adolescent Medicine, 162*(5), 447–452.

De Bellis, M. D. (2001). Developmental traumatology: The psychobiological development of maltreated children and its implications for research, treatment, and policy. *Development and Psychopathology, 13*, 537–561.

De Bellis, M. D., Keshavan, M., Baum, A., Birmaher, B., Clark, D. B., Casey, B. J., et al. (1999). A. E. Bennett Research Award. Developmental traumatology (Pt. 1 & 2): Biological stress systems and brain development. *Biological Psychiatry, 45*(10), 1259–1284.

Osuch, E., & Engel, C. C. (2004). Research on the treatment of trauma spectrum responses: the role of the optimal healing environment and neurobiology. *Journal of Alternative & Complementary Medicine, 10*(Suppl. 1), S211–S221.

Pynoos, R. S., & Nader, K. (Eds.). (1993). *Issues in the treatment of posttraumatic stress disorder in children and adolescents.* Washington, DC: American Psychiatric Press, Inc.

Shin, L. M., Orr, S. P., Carson, M. A., Rauch, S. L., Macklin, M. L., Lasko, N. B., et al. (2004). Regional cerebral blood flow in the amygdala and medial prefrontal cortex during traumatic imagery in male and female Vietnam veterans with PTSD. *Archives of General Psychiatry, 61*, 168–176.

# Commentary

## The Lemelson Case Study Considered from a Biological Point of View

### Jaap M. Koolhaas

The sad story of Joko and his family fortunately has a hopeful end. After being treated as a social outcast in the community of his parents during childhood, as a young adult Joko seems to have found a way to cope with his traumatic past. The hopeful perspective of this case study is without any doubt from the early psychiatric intervention and care Joko has received during the most difficult episodes of his life. This treatment and care is based on the extensive practical experience of the staff and the application of best practices. However, as an empirically oriented biologist specializing in the neuroscience of social behavior, I wonder what the causal relationship might be between life events, treatment, and development. Obviously, causality cannot be derived from a case study such as the present one and is very hard to ascertain in humans. Therefore, I consider the case report as a rich source of inspiration for experimental work using animal models. The case study emphasizes our lack of knowledge and provides empirical support for evidence-based treatment. It strengthens my view that much more progress can be made when clinicians work together more closely with preclinical researchers using translational animal models. Ideally, both approaches should inspire and complement each other. Consequently, I will analyze the Lemelson case study to see where clinical studies need to be supported by preclinical experimental cause-effect studies. I would like to address four main issues: the stressor, the developmental period, the symptomatology, and the treatment.

### STRESSOR

The main characteristic of Joko's life history is having experienced numerous traumatic experiences during childhood. Joko and his family were treated as outcasts in their social community. Consequently, Joko witnessed violent attacks on his brother and also was regularly the target of violent assaults. It is important to notice the social nature of these traumatic events. Animal studies have shown that social stress is by far the strongest stressor in terms of the magnitude of the physiological and neuroendocrine stress response. In adult rats and mice, even one social defeat induces behavioral, neuroendocrine, and neurobiological changes that may last for weeks and months (Koolhaas, Meerlo, De Boer, & Strubbe, 1996). Loss of control and lack of predictability of the environment are the driving forces in the development of stress pathology. Given the magnitude of the neuroendocrine stress response to social defeat, it seems that an uncontrollable social environment is one of the worst things that might happen to socially living animals. Recent experiments with rats and hamsters show that adolescence is a sensitive period in the development of adult social behavior and resilience (Wommack, Salinas, Melloni, & Delville, 2004). Also, studies in humans have suggested that exposure to uncontrollable stress during adolescence may contribute to an individual's vulnerability to various mental disorders later in life (Rutter, 2006), whereas controllable stress may enhance resilience. Characterized by major biological, psychological, and social challenges and opportunities, adolescence is a time of dynamic synaptic organization and formation of the neural circuitry underlying stress reactivity (Fergusson, Lynskey, & Horwood, 1996). Understandably, stress during this period can affect neural processes and eventually have enduring consequences on mental health.

Social life is not only a major source of severe stressors; it can also serve as a buffer against the adverse effects of stressors. Studies in adult humans and animals show the importance of social support in preventing and reducing stress pathology (Devries, Craft, Glasper, Neigh, & Alexander, 2007). From that point of view, Joko's parents seem to have wisely decided to send him at the age of 12 to the relatively safe haven of an orphanage. This dualistic function of the social environment of mammals is fascinating but has not been explored very well. To the best of my knowledge, there are no systematic experimental studies on the relationship between social stress and social support. It is conceivable that the nature of social support is somehow related to the process of social bonding. Despite the considerable body of experimental literature on the neurobiology of social bonding (Lim & Young, 2006), connections to the social stress literature have not been explored systematically. Fortunately, an increasing number of animal studies focus on social factors such as the quality of nursing by the mother on the developing offspring (Heim, Plotsky, & Nemeroff, 2004), and these studies should be expanded to include the social environment during later development.

## DEVELOPMENTAL PERIOD

The traumatic social experiences of Joko ranged from early childhood to puberty and adolescence, periods that are generally characterized by rapid and extensive neuronal growth and maturation. The period until the age of 7 is characterized by neuronal growth, whereas puberty and adolescence involve neuronal pruning and a strong decline in number of neurons. Compared to the large body of experiments aimed at the causal relationship between neonatal stress on adult behavior and stress vulnerability (Cushing & Kramer, 2005), there is a paucity of experimental research aimed at environmental influences during later developmental stages. In the case of Joko, it is difficult to disentangle the relative contributions of traumatic life events during various developmental stages, treatment received during those periods, and the normal developmental trajectory. One cannot exclude the possibility that his more rational behavior at 17 is simply due to normal maturation of the brain.

## SYMPTOMATOLOGY

As a teenager, i.e., during puberty and adolescence, Joko's behavior was characterized by depressive symptoms, suicide attempts, violence, and thoughts of revenge. The development of violence is an intriguing aspect of the case study. Joko is a victim of repeated violence, and as he grows older he becomes violent himself. His father had episodes of violent rage after being severely maltreated during several years as a political prisoner; he presumably did not receive any psychiatric care and he has apparently remained violent. Joko, on the other hand, has developed some skills that help him control his thoughts of revenge and his tendency to become violent.

The fact that both father and son became violent emphasizes our need for much more knowledge of environmental factors that might affect adult aggression and violence during development and adulthood. Preclinical animal model research aimed at the developmental modulation of adult stress vulnerability has focused almost exclusively on behavioral, neuroendocrinal, and neurobiological symptoms of depression as the adult consequences of early life stress. Very few studies have considered the influence of the social environment during the various stages of development on aggressive behavior and violence. The distinction between aggression and violence is important in this context. Animal studies have begun to recognize the fact that aggression is a highly functional form of social communication. Escalation of aggression is heavily controlled by a range of inhibitory mechanisms. Violence, on the other hand, should be considered as a pathological form of aggression, which has gone beyond inhibitory control and lost its function in social communication. Recent animal studies have started to unravel the role of serotonin in the transition of aggression into violence (De Boer & Koolhaas, 2005). Serotonin is a common mediator in both adolescent depression and violence, which tend to occur together; it is important to understand the causal nature of this interrelationship, both with respect to its etiology and underlying neurobiology.

## TREATMENT

Joko received not only psychiatric treatment, but also medication including a tricyclic antidepressant (Amitriptyline), a non-selective dopamine receptor antagonist (Haloperidol) and a selective serotonin reuptake inhibitor (Fluoxetine) in dose regimes that are not further specified. Although the medication is understandable from the point of view of Joko's acute psychiatric condition, these compounds are likely to interfere with the brain's normal development. This consideration has led to a warning in Europe and the United States, against the use of selective serotonin reuptake inhibitors in adolescents (Cohen, 2007). Few experimental studies address the long-term behavioral and physiological consequences of pharmacotherapy during development in animal models, and they are limited to the prenatal and early nursing periods. Clearly, we need more knowledge on the long-term behavioral and neurobiological effects of pharmacotherapy that is given during phases of rapid brain development.

## CONCLUDING REMARKS

I cannot resist the temptation to consider the fundamental questions in stress research that relate to the adaptive or maladaptive nature of stress-induced changes in behavior and physiology. Numerous experimental studies in a variety of animal species demonstrate the effects of early life stress on adult stress reactivity (Heim et al., 2004). Generally, these effects are interpreted as maladaptive, i.e., as creating an increased vulnerability to stress-related disease and even as early signs of psychopathology. Recently however, this view seems to be changing. Several biological studies suggest that behavioral and physiological changes induced by stress during early life might in fact be adaptive in the sense that they prepare the organism for environmental conditions that it is likely to meet in adult life. In the case study of Joko, both depression and occasional assertive or aggressive behavior can be interpreted as adaptive responses to a hostile environment. Obviously, the suicidal tendencies and psychotic symptoms that Joko expressed reflect a state of disease and are, by definition, maladaptive. Nevertheless, the discussion on the adaptive or maladaptive nature of the stress response is important. An evolutionary view can provide an important antidote against the growing tendency in psychiatry and preclinical research to medicalize the stress response (Korte, Koolhaas, Wingfield, & McEwen, 2005; Nesse, 2000).

REFERENCES

Cohen, D. (2007). Should the use of selective serotonin reuptake inhibitors in child and adolescent depression be banned? *Psychotherapy and Psychosomatics, 76*, 5–14.

Cushing, B. S., & Kramer, K. M. (2005). Mechanisms underlying epigenetic effects of early social experience: The role of neuropeptides and steroids. *Neuroscience & Biobehavioral Reviews, 29*, 1089–1105.

De Boer, S. F., & Koolhaas, J. M. (2005). 5-HT1A and 5-HT1B receptor agonists and aggression: A pharmacological challenge of the serotonin deficiency hypothesis. *European Journal of Pharmacology, 526*, 125–139.

Devries, A. C., Craft, T. K., Glasper, E. R., Neigh, G. N., & Alexander, J. K. (2007). 2006 Curt P. Richter award winner: Social influences on stress responses and health. *Psychoneuroendocrinology, 32*, 587–603.

Fergusson, D. M., Lynskey, M. T., & Horwood, L. J. (1996). Factors associated with continuity and changes in disruptive behavior patterns between childhood and adolescence. *Journal of Abnormal Child Psychology, 24*, 533–553.

Heim, C., Plotsky, P. M., & Nemeroff, C. B. (2004). Importance of studying the contributions of early adverse experience to neurobiological findings in depression. *Neuropsychopharmacology, 29*, 641–648.

Koolhaas J. M., Meerlo, P., De Boer, S. F., & Strubbe, J. H. (1996). Temporal dynamics of the stress response [Abstract]. International Society for Research on Aggression, XII World Meeting, Strasbourg, France.

Korte, S. M., Koolhaas, J. M., Wingfield, J. C., & McEwen, B. S. (2005). The Darwinian concept of stress: Benefits of allostasis and costs of allostatic load and the trade-offs in health and disease. *Neuroscience & Biobehavioral Reviews, 29*, 3–38.

Lim, M. M., & Young, L. J. (2006). Neuropeptidergic regulation of affiliative behavior and social bonding in animals. *Hormones and Behavior, 50*, 506–517.

Nesse, R. M. (2000). Is depression an adaptation? *Archives of General Psychiatry, 57*, 14–20.

Rutter, M. (2006). *Genes and behavior: Nature-nurture interplay explained*. Malden, MA: Blackwell Publishing.

Wommack, J. C., Salinas, A., Melloni, R. H., Jr., & Delville, Y. (2004). Behavioural and neuroendocrine adaptations to repeated stress during puberty in male golden hamsters. *Journal of Neuroendocrinology, 16,* 767–775.

# SIXTEEN

# The Evolution of Social Play

Sergio M. Pellis, Vivien C. Pellis, and
Christine J. Reinhart

## INTRODUCTION

Voric runs up to Victor from behind. As he runs past him, he grabs Victor by the tuft of hair on the crown of his head. Victor jerks his body back, bracing against being pulled forward; this brings Voric to a standstill facing Victor. After looking at each other for a moment, Victor turns his head and lunges, with his mouth wide open, and attempts to bite Voric's hand, which is still grasping Victor's hair. As Voric releases his grip and withdraws his hand, he simultaneously lunges forward, grabbing Victor by both shoulders, and tries to bite the side of his neck. Victor ducks and rolls onto his side. Voric follows, falling on top of him. They then grapple, and, when possible, gently deliver bites at each other. After a few seconds, Voric jumps up. He begins to run away, but then slows down, and with a wide-open mouth, looks back over his shoulder at Victor. While slow to rise at first, Victor now bolts upright and chases after Voric, who disappears into the bushes.

This description of play-fighting in two Tonkean macaques (*Macaca tonkeana*) taken from our research videotapes (Primate Research Centre, Strasbourg, 1996) could well represent almost any mammal. Intriguingly, two researchers who watched young rhesus macaques (*Macaca mulatta*) play like this drew fundamentally different conclusions about why they played. One claimed that the monkeys were rehearsing skills they would need as adults to be effective in combat (Symons, 1978). The other claimed that such play provided the participants with the opportunity to learn skills necessary for social cohesion in their complex society (Levy, 1979). To this day, researchers, both in human and non-human animal literature, continue to argue over the functions served by the rough-and-tumble play known as play-fighting (Power, 2000). This example of rhesus macaque play is especially poignant; even when observing similar behavior in the same species, two researchers can draw differing conclusions. It becomes more problematic when researchers are studying different species. Some commonalities are evident across species that do assure us that whatever the benefits of such play, we are comparing similar behavior.

During play-fighting, as one animal attacks another, the recipient may defend itself and then launch its own counterattack. The first attacker may then defend itself, and so on (Figure 16.1). The body targets contested can be derived from species-typical agonistic, predatory or socio-sexual behavior (Pellis, 1988, 1993). Play-fighting is the most common form of play reported in non-human mammals (Pellis & Pellis, 1998a). In children freely interacting in the schoolyard or home, this type of play accounts for about 10% of all play (Smith, 2005), and, despite some minor cultural variations, has a basic theme that appears universal (Fry, 2005). Although play-fighting resembles serious fighting, a number of differences exist (Smith, 1997). In play-fighting, (1) a resource is not gained or protected; (2) the contact is restrained, or, at least, combat-induced injuries do not typically result; (3) the sequence of attack, defense, and counterattack can be repeated many times, with the partners reversing roles; (4) such contact can lead to further affiliation between participants; and (5) for many species, including humans, special facial and bodily gestures signal that the interaction is play.

But given that play-fighting can be distinguished from serious fighting, why do researchers emphasize different facets of the behavior and hence its potential to serve very different functions? In this chapter, we contend that to fully understand play-fighting, species differences must be taken seriously, and that this diversity can help unravel how play-fighting has evolved. Such an understanding can further our analysis of the functions play-fighting may serve.

## PLAY-FIGHTING AND RECIPROCITY

Casual observation suggests that for play-fighting to remain playful, animals have to follow the 50:50 rule, in that each partner wins about 50% of the fights (Altmann, 1962). This conclusion is supported by a study using game theory, in which a mathematical simulation of play-fighting has shown that only when each partner wins about 50% of the bouts is playful fighting stable. Other win-loss ratios tend to lead to a cessation of further interaction or to an escalation into serious fighting. That is, playing must be fair (Dugatkin & Bekoff, 2003). In several rodent and primate species studied in detail, such reciprocity is achieved by the manner in which attack and

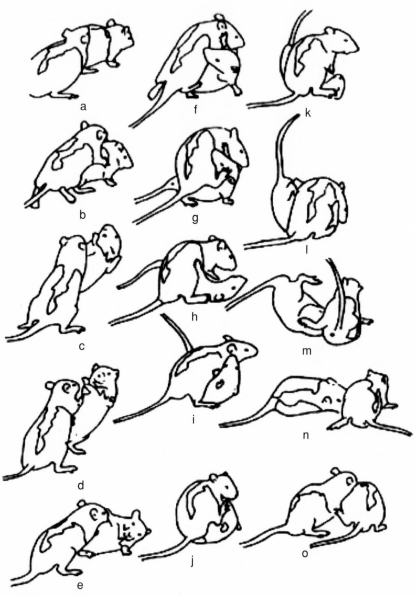

**Figure 16.1.** A sequence of play fighting is shown for a pair of juvenile rats. The rat on the left approaches (a), and then pounces, from the rear, on the other (b), but before contact is made the defender rotates around its longitudinal axis (c) to face the attacker (d). By moving forward, the attacker pushes the defender onto its side (e). The defender then rolls over onto its back as the attacker continues to reach for its nape (f–h). Once in the supine position, the defender launches an

defense is organized in play-fighting, as compared to how it is organized in serious fighting. In serious fighting, an attacker incorporates a defensive maneuver into its attack. By doing so, the attacker reduces the risk of a counterattack (Pellis, 1997). In contrast, in play-fighting, the attacker does not typically include such a protective action, which facilitates the defender's ability to counterattack. Furthermore, in serious fighting, defenders move as quickly as possible to block the attacker, whereas in playful fighting, the defense is slower (Pellis & Pellis, 1998b). Thus, during play-fighting, both attacker and defender curtail their advantage, which gives their partner an opportunity to gain the advantage. But although such failure to use the most advantageous tactics have been reported in some rodents and primates (Biben, 1998; Foroud & Pellis, 2003; Pellis & Pellis, 1987, 1988, 1997a), other researchers report that their species play to win (Thompson, 1998). Such a lack of restraint would be counter to the 50:50 rule (Bauer & Smuts, 2007). Either the 50:50 rule is not a universal feature of play-fighting or there is more than one path to fairness. A detailed description of a test case will illustrate our solution to this quandary.

Videotapes of playful and serious fighting in degus (*Octodon degus*) – a South American rodent related to the punaré (*Trichomys apereoides*) studied by Thompson (1998) – were compared using subjects from six litters, born from and reared by two pairs of adult degus. Each litter remained with the parents for 8 weeks and then same-sex littermates were separated. Each enclosure had a Plexiglas floor and four walls (123.5 cm length × 55.8 cm width × 61 cm height), a metal mesh ceiling, and two mesh panels on the two short sides of the cage, from which water bottles were hung. The floor had a 2–3cm layer of processed corn cobs, with food (Purina Guinea Pig Chow and dried alfalfa) provided *ad libitum*. The separately vented room was kept at 23°C on a 12:12 light/dark cycle, lights on at 0700 hours. In degus, both sociosexual and aggressive sequences appear to be involved in play-fighting. Sociosexual sequences involve one partner approaching

---

**Figure 16.1 (*continued*)** attack to its partner's nape (i), but fails because of its partner's use of its hind foot (j, k). Eventually, the rat on top (l) is pushed off by the supine animal (m), which regains its footing (n). The original defender then lunges towards its partner's nape (o). The whole sequence involves repeated attack and defense of the nape and frequent role reversals between the partners with regard to which one attacks and which one defends. Pellis, S. M., & Pellis, V. C. (1987). Play-fighting differs from serious fighting in both target of attack and tactics of fighting in the laboratory rat *Rattus norvegicus. Aggressive Behavior, 13,* 227–242. Copyright 1987 by Wiley-Liss, Inc., A Wiley Company. Reprinted with permission of John Wiley & Sons, Inc.

another and then nuzzling and grooming its shoulders, neck, and head on the side. Aggressive sequences involve mutual rearing, boxing, and pushing with the front paws and kicking with the hind legs (Wilson & Kleiman, 1974). During development, different elements of behavior gradually emerge, with gentler, sexual components appearing first, followed by rougher, aggressive components. By 6–8 weeks after birth, all components of play-fighting are present (Wilson, 1981).

For play-fighting, groups of young males from each litter (3 pups in the smallest and 5 pups in the largest) were placed for 15 minutes in neutral cages with Plexiglas walls (46 cm × 25 cm × 20 cm) and processed corncob bedding, and were videotaped. For serious fighting, 12 pairs of adult males – from different litters and thus unfamiliar with each other – were placed for 15 minutes in neutral cages (76 cm × 30 cm × 30 cm), and were videotaped. The main focus of comparison between the two types of fighting was hind-leg kicking from an upright position; this involves the degus holding its partner's arms with forepaws and jumping up, rotating its body around the longitudinal axis and delivering a two-legged kick to its partner's ventrum. This action typically pushes the opponent backwards by several body lengths onto its back on the ground. The animal that delivers the kick typically lands on all fours with its rump facing its partner (Figure 16.2). This kicking occurs, with the same destabilizing consequences, in both playful and serious fighting. This indication that degus fail to exhibit restraint during play-fighting seemingly supports Thompson's (1998) conclusion that animals play to win. However, closer inspection of such kicking suggests that degus show restraint during play-fighting in a manner that differs from the restraint shown by rats and monkeys.

In serious fighting, a degus that approaches and attacks its opponent will deliver bites. In each of the 12 pairings described above, one or more successful bites were delivered. Of these, 76.9% of 26 bites were directed at the shoulders, with the majority (84.6%) landing on the lateral aspect. The remaining bites were either slightly posterior (19.2%) or slightly anterior (3.9%) to the shoulders. Thus, a primary objective of serious fighting in degus is to bite and avoid being bitten on the shoulders.

As the encounters were in a neutral arena, after some exploratory sniffing both animals went on the offensive. Once one delivered a successful bite, the recipient attempted to avoid the attacker, engaging in defense only when attacked. The targeting of the shoulder caused the other animal to protect that body area. For example, if the attacker approached its opponent obliquely from the front, the defender turned to face it, juxtaposing its teeth between its shoulders and the opponent's teeth. Conversely, if the

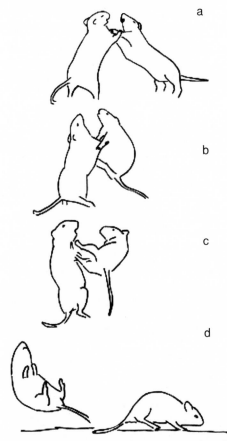

**Figure 16.2.** Two adult male degus, introduced as strangers, are shown engaged in combat in a neutral arena. Initially, they rear onto their hind feet and grapple with each other's forelimbs (a). After maneuvering for several seconds, the degu on the right manages to gain the footing needed to launch a hind leg kick to its opponent's ventrum (b, c). The kick is then successfully delivered, which sends the opponent flying backwards. The degu that delivered the kick then turns to land on all four of its paws (d).

attacker approached its opponent obliquely from the rear, the defender turned, placing its rump between its mid-body and the opponent's teeth. By doing so, it blocked bites to its shoulders. When the attacker approached directly from the rear, moving its head over the rump and lower back of its opponent, the defender pushed its hind legs upward, raising its rump. This maneuver kept the attacker away from the mid-back area, even though it made the rump more vulnerable. Instead of biting the exposed rump, the

**Table 16.1.** *The Percentage Distribution of Actions Following Hind Leg Kicking*

| Actions | Serious Fighting ($n = 90$) | Play Fighting ($n = 70$) |
|---|---|---|
| Deliver bite | 12.2 | 7.1 |
| Attack/defense orientation | 84.7 | 5.7 |
| End fighting | 1.1 | 57.2 |
| Engage amicable encounter | 0 | 30.0 |

attacker attempted to move along the flank toward the shoulder, but the defender would pivot around its mid-body, keeping the rump closer to the attacker's face. The attacker was, at times, successful in breaching its opponent's defenses.

Of all bites recorded, 80% accompanied the hind-leg kick tactic. If the recipient of the kick fell onto its side or back while within a body length or so of its opponent, the opponent quickly turned and directed a bite to the exposed shoulder. In 70% of these cases, the kicking animal successfully delivered a bite, but in the other cases, the recipient of the kick delivered the bite. When an adjacent wall helped the recipient of a kick remain on its feet, and if the animal delivering the kick landed on its side, the standing animal was able to leap and bite the shoulder of its opponent as it was righting itself. Hence, the tactic of kicking with the hind legs is a high-risk maneuver, not only for the defender, but also for the attacker; and both animals couple the maneuver with the immediate adoption of a defensive tactic. The kicking animal attempts to land on all fours, turning its rump toward the opponent and makes small scanning movements of its head to identify the other animal's location. In contrast, the animal receiving the kick attempts to regain its feet as quickly as possible, turning and moving toward its opponent, apparently to ward off a biting attack.

In serious fighting, quantitative comparison of the behavior most likely to follow hind-leg kicking shows that some form of agonistic maneuvering is most likely, with both partners simultaneously moving to gain an advantage or offset their opponent's advantage (Table 16.1). The most common form of agonistic maneuvering was for the attacker to land on all fours with its rump facing the opponent, while the defender regained a four-footed stance and faced, or moved toward, the other animal (78.2%). Alternatively, the kicking animal regained its footing and ran toward its opponent, which also regained its footing and fled; this led to a chase (10.3%). The critical issue in these behaviors was that both animals simultaneously maneuvered agonistically, thus producing a low frequency of successfully delivered bites (Table 16.1). In only one case after the kick did the animals move off and explore the enclosure, ending the agonistic encounter. However, in play fighting, the situation is very different.

In play-fighting, biting is rare, but like serious fighting, when it does occur it is also directed at the shoulders. When the hind-leg kick tactic is used during play-fighting, the behavior appears to be the same as in serious fighting up to the point when the kick is delivered; at that point, differences between the two types of fighting emerge (Table 16.1). In play-fighting, neither the recipient of the kick nor the kicking animal move quickly to establish a defensive posture and orientation; furthermore, neither animal is likely to take advantage of the other's destabilized position to deliver a bite. Indeed, even when bites did occur, most of them appeared gentle, with the recipient failing to perform defensive maneuvers. Vigorous defensive movements by the recipient indicated that only two of the recorded five bites appeared to be forcefully delivered. In most cases, one or both partners moved away and explored the enclosure, thus ending the encounter. The second most frequent outcome was for the pair to resume an amicable interaction. Most often (66.7%), play-fighting followed hind leg kicks, involving either "sexual" nuzzling of upper flanks or "agonistic" boxing. Even more at variance with serious fighting, some amicable encounters (14.3%) involved the kicking animal resuming a four-footed stance, turning laterally or obliquely to face its partner, and then rotating its head gently to one side, partially closing its eyes and remaining immobile. After having regained a standing position, the defender walked to its motionless partner and nuzzled and groomed its shoulders, neck, and face. Thus, unlike serious fighting, in play-fighting animals do not take advantage of their destabilized partner, nor do they adopt tactics to offset their partner's advantage (Table 16.1) – indeed, they may sometimes even "offer" their play targets to their partner!

These observations suggest that unlike rats, degus "play to win," combining attack and defense maneuvers in a manner typical of serious fighting in that they show a lack of restraint. However, play-fighting can persist without escalating to serious fighting because in play-fighting degus tend *not* to take advantage of the situation once their partner has been knocked over. By failing to adopt defensive measures and even relinquishing the advantage, degus may clearly signal that the foregoing action was a playful one and that the opportunity to initiate and win a play fight has now been turned over to the loser. Thus, in the degus, this strategy of taking turns preserves the 50:50 rule. Other species may use different behavioral

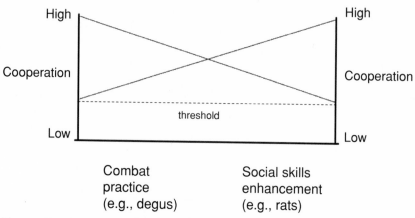

| Combat | Social skills |
| practice | enhancement |
| (e.g., degus) | (e.g., rats) |

**Figure 16.3.** A representational graphic illustrating the interaction of competition and cooperation during play fighting. Note that there is a threshold level of both needed for play to remain playful and enjoyable. As illustrated for the rat and degu, depending on whether the cooperative or competitive pattern of attack and defense is emphasized, different modes of solving the fairness problem become available.

strategies to maintain fairness during play-fighting, but the underlying theme seems to be that for play-fighting to remain playful, animals should not take advantage of their success.

Play-fighting involves both competition and cooperation. Without competition play-fighting becomes excessively predictable and loses its pleasurable quality, and without cooperation play-fighting escalates into serious aggression and will cease. Thus, for play-fighting to be playful, it must have some minimum level of both competition and cooperation. As shown by comparing rats and degus, the balance between competition and cooperation may differ across species (Figure 16.3). But how animals solve the fairness problem affords them different opportunities to use play-fighting for functional ends. When the fairness solution permits the use of unrestrained tactics of attack and defense, such a performance can enhance fighting skills. When the fairness solution involves curtailing the tactics of attack and defense – as it does in rats – play-fighting will be a poor vehicle for practicing fighting skills (Pellis & Pellis, 1998b); on the other hand, it can afford the opportunity for developing nuanced social skills (Pellis, Pellis, & Foroud, 2005). The opposing views of Symons (1978) and Levy (1979) regarding the function of play-fighting in rhesus monkeys give rise to an empirical question: Is the play of this species closer to the left or the right of the model shown in Figure 16.3?

The most detailed analyses of the structure and function of play-fighting are for rats, and we will use the data on rats to illustrate how a species-typical solution to the reciprocity problem constrains the kinds of benefits that can be gained from play-fighting. But first we will explore the possible neural underpinnings of reciprocity, irrespective of whether it is rat-typical or degu-typical, to provide a baseline upon which play behavior can be modified and so further honed to better serve its proposed functions.

## THE NEURAL BASIS FOR RECIPROCITY

Ablation of the cortex shortly after birth does not prevent juvenile rats from play-fighting; indeed, decorticated rats exhibit the normal pattern of increasing the frequency of play at around the mid-juvenile period (30–40 days) and then decreasing the frequency with the approach of puberty (50–60 days) (Pellis, Pellis, & Whishaw, 1992). Decorticated rats not only play at the typical frequency, but also use all behavior patterns typically incorporated into play sequences (Pellis et al., 1992). These findings suggest that the basic neural equipment needed to motivate and generate play involves subcortical systems (Panksepp, 1998; Siviy, 1998). Most importantly, decorticated rats are able to sustain repeated and prolonged play fights without escalating to serious aggression – that is, regulating reciprocal exchanges during play-fighting must involve a subcortical circuit.

The amygdala, a subcortical structure in the medial temporal lobes, has been strongly implicated in the regulation of social behavior (Aggelton, 2000). Indeed, in rats, damage to the amygdala disrupts social recognition (Maaswinkel, Baars, Gispen, & Spruijt, 1996) and play-fighting (Daenaen, Wolterink, Gerrits, & van Ree, 2002). Similarly, genetic selection for lines of rats with different amygdala properties leads to differences in the organization and frequency of play-fighting (Reinhart, Pellis, & McIntyre, 2004; Reinhart, McIntyre, Metz, & Pellis, 2006). Comparative studies of adult sexual play (Pellis & Iwaniuk, 2002) and juvenile social play (Lewis & Barton, 2006) in primates have shown that the prevalence of these play behaviors are significantly predicted by the size of the amygdala: The species that play the most tend to have a larger amygdala. Finally, altered function of the amygdala has been implicated in autism (Baron-Cohen et al., 2000), a key symptom of which is an inability to reciprocate during social encounters, leading to impoverished social play (Jordan, 2003).

The amygdala may be involved in play-fighting either through its role in learning and modulating fear (Adolphs, 1999) or in providing a mechanism for impulse control (Emery et al., 2001). Excessive fear can prevent an animal from accepting playful overtures (Pellis & Pellis, 1993) or other amicable social contact (Prather et al., 2001). Furthermore, animals with too little impulse control quickly become unattractive play partners (Suomi, 2005). Either way, monkeys with amygdala lesions engage in atypical play compared to intact animals in that they seem to misinterpret playful contacts (Meunier, Bachevalier, Murray, Malkova, & Mishkin, 1999). Thus, for several reasons, the amygdala is likely an important part of the subcortical neural system regulating the reciprocity crucial to the maintenance of play fights. However, rats and monkeys apparently differ, and the differences may provide a clue to the evolution of more complex patterns of reciprocity.

In rats, damage to the amygdala has been reported to affect only the frequency of play. These disruptions to play-fighting are present whether the damage occurs shortly after birth or at around weaning, although disruptions in animals with the earlier lesions also involve other affiliative social behavior (Daenen et al., 2002; Diergaarde, Gerrits, Stuy, Spruijt, & van Ree, 2004). None of these studies in rats with damage to the amygdala examined patterns of defense, however, and because complex play-fighting involves a combination of attack and defense (see Figure 16.1), it is possible that monkey-like distortions to the manner of play, not just frequency, are also present in rats. To understand the relevance of the data, it is necessary to provide some descriptive detail of defense tactics rats use during play-fighting.

During play-fighting, rats launch playful attacks to their partner's nape, nuzzling it with the snout, if contacted (Pellis & Pellis, 1987). The recipient can prevent such contact by adopting one of several defensive tactics. The simplest is evasive defense involving the defender distancing its nape from the attacker by leaping, running or swerving. A more complex defense involves blocking nape contact by turning to face the attacker, but this tactic involves extensive bodily contact between partners as they wrestle for each other's napes (Figure 16.1). Three forms of blocking tactics involve a facing defense. In the first tactic, the defender performs a cephalocaudal rotation around its longitudinal axis, ending up on its back with all four paws in the air, thus attempting to hold its partner at bay. In the second method, the defender partially rotates around its longitudinal axis, keeping one or both hind feet on the ground; from this position, it can push its partner with forepaws or hip. In the final tactic, the defender continues to face its approaching partner by rotating around a vertical axis, perpendicular to the ground, while standing either on all four paws or on hind paws. From this position, the defender can block its partner's movements with forepaws or teeth (Pellis & Pellis, 1987; Pellis, Pellis, & McKenna, 1994; Pellis et al., 1992).

At all ages, evasion accounts for 20–30% of defensive responses and rotation around the vertical axis for about 5–10%. For both males and females, prior to the juvenile period around weaning when play-fighting first emerges, the partial rotation tactic is most frequently used, but during the juvenile period, the complete rotation tactic becomes more common. With the onset of puberty, males begin to use the partial rotation tactic most frequently, while females prefer complete rotation (Pellis, 2002b; Pellis & Pellis, 1990, 1997b; Pellis, Field, Smith, & Pellis, 1997).

To test whether amygdala damage affects playful defense, four quadrads of male post-weaning rats were established. Two rats per group received an amygdala lesion and one rat per group was sham-treated (see Daenen et al., 2002, for details on the surgery). In the peak juvenile period (30–40 days), and then again in early adulthood (80–90 days), one rat from each quadrad with the amygdala lesion and the sham-treated rat were each tested twice in the play-fighting paradigm – once with another animal with amygdala damage and once with an intact partner. Both the frequency of launching playful attacks and the types of defensive tactics used were scored from the videotaped records (see Pellis & Pellis, 1990; Pellis et al., 1992; Reinhart et al., 2004, for details).

No significant group differences were shown in frequency of launching playful attacks ($p > 0.05$), but there were significant age ($F (1, 56) = 88.74$, $p < 0.0001$) and partner ($F (1, 56) = 14.80$, $p < 0.001$) effects. The age effect reflects the normal age-related decline in play-fighting, but the partner effect results from both rats with lesions and sham-treated rats initiating more playful attacks when partnered with a rat that had an amygdala lesion (Figure 16.4A). Also, there was an age effect for complete rotation ($F (1, 56) = 4.56$, $p < 0.05$) but no group effect ($p > 0.05$), showing that both rats with and without amygdala lesions exhibited the normal age-related decline in this form of facing defense. Similarly, no other group effects occurred for other measures of playful defense ($p > 0.05$). Our findings suggest that the overall pattern of play and age-related changes in the play patterns are not disrupted when the amygdala is damaged around the time of weaning. Nevertheless, the greater frequency of playful attacks initiated by intact rats against partners with amygdala damage suggests that rats with such damage are not treated as normal partners by other rats.

Following the procedure of Diergaarde et al. (2004) and using the testing paradigm described earlier, except that pairs of males were used rather than quadrads, three rats with amygdala lesions made at seven days of age were

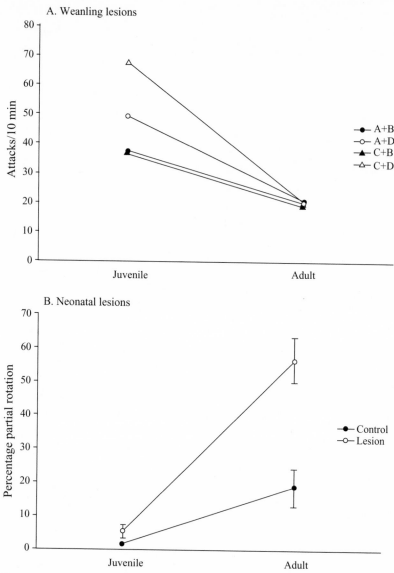

**Figure 16.4.** Two features of play-fighting behavior are shown for rats playing with partners with lesions to the amygdala. A. A comparison of the frequency of launching playful attacks on rats with lesions made just after weaning. When either intact or lesion rats interacted with a partner that had a lesion (A+D, C+D), they initiated more playful attacks than when they interacted with an intact partner (A+B, C+B). However, this partner effect was transitory, – present in the juvenile period, but then disappearing in adulthood. B. A comparison of the use of the partial rotation tactic by intact partners interacting with either an intact control or a partner with an amygdala lesion made shortly after birth. With age, the increase in the use of the partial rotation tactic was much greater for intact animals that played with animals with lesions.

compared with seven sham-treated animals. Each rat with a lesion or sham treatment was paired with an untreated control. These preliminary data showed no significant group effects for either launching playful attacks or any type of defensive tactic ($p > 0.05$). Furthermore, there were significant age effects for both attack ($F_{(1, 8)} = 9.41$, $p < 0.05$) and complete rotation ($F_{(1, 8)} = 13.84$, $p < 0.01$), the normally occurring age-related changes in both attack and defense. For partial rotation, there were significant age ($F_{(1, 8)} = 25.55$, $p < 0.01$), partner ($F_{(1, 8)} = 11.12$, $p < 0.01$) and age by partner interaction ($F_{(1, 8)} = 5.84$, $p < 0.05$) effects. That is, partners of animals with lesions were more likely to use the partial rotation tactic with increasing age (Figure 16.4B). Greater use of this tactic often suggests that an animal is agonistic toward playful contact by a partner (Pellis et al., 2006), indicating that the intact partners of animals with amygdala lesions find playful contact by those animals aversive.

Although our data are not fully consistent with earlier reports (Daenen et al., 2002; Diergaarde et al., 2004), it would seem that, in rats, damage to the amygdala either early or late in the pre-weaning developmental period has only a minor effect on play-fighting. But the changed behavior of the partners of rats with amygdala lesions indicates that intact rats recognize these animals as abnormal. Also, although detection of abnormalities by intact partners of rats with lesions made around weaning was more evident in the juvenile phase, decreasing by adulthood (Figure 16.4A), detection of abnormalities by partners of the rats with early damage increased with age (Figure 16.4B). These findings suggest that early postnatal damage to the amgydala in rats is more likely to result in persistent changes with a wider effect on social behavior (Diergaarde et al., 2004), and thus is more like the situation in similarly treated monkeys.

As there are overall bigger effects of amygdala damage in primates, it is possible that the amygdala plays a transitory role in rats, where it is crucial, developmentally, as part of the scaffolding that enables social play circuits to be established. After that, the amygdala has either no role or a limited one in enabling play-fighting to occur. Monkeys show a greater reliance on using visual cues from body postures and facial gestures to ascertain the intentions of social partners during play-fighting (Pellis & Iwaniuk, 2000). Because of its important role in assessing such cues for emotional content (Ohman, 2002), the amygdala may continue to play a key part in regulating play-fighting in monkeys even after it fulfils its scaffolding role during development. This expansion of the amygdala's role in regulating play-fighting in primates – and possibly other groups of animals that are similarly reliant on the use of visual signals during play-fighting – likely leads to the evolution of more complex play patterns. Indeed, species that use visual signals during play-fighting to identify past, present, or future behaviors as play have some of the most complex patterns of play-fighting (Bekoff, 1995; Pellis & Pellis, 1996).

In the model we are proposing, the amygdala's initial role is to lay the foundation for the neural capacity to engage in reciprocal exchanges during play-fighting. In some lineages of species, the amygdala's role has become more pronounced as more subtle cues are incorporated into assessing the partner's behavior, enhancing the range and complexity of actions performed during play-fighting. However, to increase the complexity of play further and to enable play to better serve its functions, these subcortical neural circuits need to be modulated by the cortex.

## THE FUNCTIONS OF PLAY-FIGHTING IN RATS

Two functions of play-fighting in rats will be considered. First, it will be shown that adult rats use play-fighting as a means of social assessment and manipulation. Second, it will be shown that play-fighting in the juvenile period leads to enhanced social competence in adulthood. Once the situation with rats is explored more fully, the ongoing debate regarding the functions of play-fighting in humans will be considered.

*Play fighting as social assessment and manipulation:* Within a colony of rats, one adult male is dominant and other males are subordinate, while females are subordinate to all males (Blanchard & Blanchard, 1990; Lore & Flannelly, 1977). When a subordinate male is playfully attacked by another subordinate male or a female, the defender behaves like a typical adult male and most likely uses the partial rotation tactic. However, when a dominant male playfully attacks a subordinate male, the defender reverts to the juvenile pattern and most likely uses the complete rotation tactic. Dominant males are most likely to use the typical partial rotation tactic, regardless of the identity of the attacking rat (Pellis & Pellis, 1990; Pellis, Pellis, & McKenna, 1993). In addition, the subordinate members of the colony direct playful attacks, as well as other amicable social behavior such as grooming, toward the dominant male more than they do toward each other (Adams & Boice, 1989; Pellis et al., 1993). This obsequiousness by subordinates helps maintain friendly relations with the dominant: It reduces the risk of being seriously attacked while also enabling the subordinate to gain benefits of colony living such as food and opportunities for copulation (Pellis et al., 1993).

This strategy is suitable for subordinates that seek to remain subordinates within a colony, but some subordinates seek dominance; for these, play-fighting has another use. Such a subordinate may play more roughly, thus reducing the incidence of juvenile-like defense. By doing so, the subordinate bends the 50:50 rule in its own favor. This incremental bending of the 50:50 rule can continue until the dominant either retaliates aggressively, reaffirming its dominant status, or acquiesces to the changed pattern of play, thus accepting a reversal in its status (Pellis et al., 1993). By altering the 50:50 rule, either in the dominant's favor or in its own, the subordinate can maintain or change its subordinate status (Pellis, 2002a). Similarly, when either dominants or subordinates encounter an unfamiliar adult male rat, they are more likely to use a rougher pattern of play-fighting (i.e., a more frequent use of partial rotation and a less frequent use of complete rotation). In most cases, this behavior can settle their dominance relationship without having to resort to serious aggression (Smith, Fantella, & Pellis, 1999).

Adult male rats thus use play-fighting to assess and manipulate social partners. In rats such assessment and manipulation seems to be limited to sexual encounters and dominance contests, but in other species it can involve a wider range of social contexts (Brueggemen, 1978; Pellis, 2002a; Pellis & Iwaniuk, 1999, 2000). For example, in the period immediately preceding feeding, adult captive chimpanzees (*Pan troglodytes*) were observed to play with unrelated immature partners; this play appears to enhance their tolerance for maintaining proximity with both the immature animals and their mothers during feeding (Palagi, Cordoni, & Tarli, 2004).

As the earlier description suggests, for a subordinate rat to manipulate the behavior of a partner it needs to be able to modify the 50:50 rule. Is the subcortical neural mechanism responsible for reciprocity capable of such modulation? Studies of rats with cortical ablation suggest not. As already noted, rats with such ablations are able to play in a manner that sustains prolonged and repeated encounters – that is, they are able to follow the reciprocation rules necessary for play-fighting to occur. However, adult male decorticate rats interacting with different colony mates do not modify defensive actions, but appear to treat dominants and subordinates in the same way (Pellis et al., 1992). This suggests that the cortex can regulate the subcortical reciprocity circuits and so modulate the pattern of play with different social partners. It is not the entire cortex that is involved, but one specific part, the orbital frontal cortex (OFC) (Pellis et al., 2006), an area known to be involved in social behavior (Kolb, 1984). Although damage to this area allows the rat to engage in play-fighting, it cannot use play-fighting to assess and manipulate its partners.

It seems that a special cortical circuit is crucial for using play-fighting as a tool for social assessment and manipulation, which builds on underlying subcortical neural circuits needed for play-fighting. Indeed, other species with a similar post-juvenile use of play-fighting are also likely to have this cortical mechanism (Pellis & Iwaniuk, 2004). But damage to the OFC also leads to insensitivity toward the social partner in non-playful social contexts (Pellis et al., 2006), suggesting that the OFC is involved in social decision-making in general. That social insensitivity similar to that present in rats with OFC damage is also present in rats that have been deprived of the opportunity to engage in play fighting as juveniles, suggests that one way in which rats and other animals may achieve their social savvy is through the training of the OFC that is provided by playful experience during the juvenile period.

*Play-fighting in the juvenile period as a means of training the social brain:* Direct experimental tests on the role of play in developing adult skills have involved rearing juveniles under conditions of social isolation. When deprived of the opportunity to engage in social play in the juvenile phase, adult rats exhibit a range of social, sexual, and cognitive deficits (Einon, Humphreys, Chivers, Field, & Naylor, 1981; Moore, C., 1985). Although, such isolation deprives young rats of many social experiences in addition to play (Bekoff, 1976); a variety of data consistently point to the absence of play when socially isolated as a critical influence (for a review see Pellis & Pellis, 2006). For example, rats reared as pairs but separated by mesh partitions so they can see and smell each other, as well as lean next to each other, still have cognitive and social deficiencies as adults. Furthermore, rats reared in a cage with an adult so they have direct social contact but little opportunity for play-fighting show similar deficiencies as adults (e.g., Holloway & Suter, 2004). Thus, although the contributions of non-playful social behavior are no doubt important, the experience of play-fighting during the juvenile period appears to be a crucial ingredient for normal development.

The social, sexual, and cognitive deficits in adult rats deprived of play as juveniles seem to be symptomatic of a deeper abnormality. Rats with such deficits are more prone to fight with unfamiliar rats (Byrd & Briner, 1999; van den Berg et al., 1999). They tend to be hyperdefensive in that they respond with inappropriate ferocity to even benign contact (Arakawa, 2002; Einon & Potegal, 1991). These play-deprived rats seem unable to match emotional responses to other rats in an appropriately scaled manner;

instead, they tend to overreact. This inappropriate emotional calibration appears to interfere with the rat's problem-solving ability.

In an experiment in social problem solving, adult rats that had been reared either in isolation or in groups during their juvenile period were placed in an enclosure containing a large, resident male. The group-reared animals decreased their level of activity and moved into a huddle or remained on top of a platform at one end of the cage. In contrast, the isolation-reared rats continued to move around the cage, attracting attacks by the resident male (von Frijtag, Schot, van den Bos & Spruijt, 2002). These isolation-reared rats also had a different endocrinological profile compared with the group-reared rats. In the latter, corticosterone levels spiked quickly, but also dissipated quickly, whereas in the isolation-reared rats, corticosterone persisted at high levels for longer periods (van den Berg et al., 1999). Thus, the isolates' emotional overreaction interfered with their ability to utilize cognitive capacities to solve the social problem effectively.

That such deficits are related to inappropriate emotionality is illustrated further by an experiment involving a non-social task. Isolation-reared and group-reared rats were tested individually for their performance on an elevated plus-maze, a standardized test to measure anxiety. Anxious animals are more likely to remain in the "safer," covered arms of the maze and less likely to explore the open arms. The isolation-reared rats showed more anxiety than the group-reared rats. However, when the experimenters injected the isolation-reared rats with an anxiolytic (a drug that chemically alleviates anxiety), they performed as well as the group-reared rats; and when the group-reared rats were injected with an anxiogenic (a drug that chemically induces anxiety), their performance resembled that of the isolation-reared rats (da Silva, Ferreria, de Padua Gorabrez, & Morato, 1996). Clearly, the difference between the isolation-reared and the group-reared rats was in how anxious they were in the test enclosure.

If play trains animals to calibrate an appropriate emotional response to unexpected problems (Biben, 1998; Pellis & Pellis, 2006; Spinka, Newberry, & Bekoff, 2001), then the movements experienced during play should be highly variable and unpredictable. In juvenile rats, play-fighting seems to provide this varied experience. At this age, by preferentially rotating to a supine position, a defending rat limits its capacity to counterattack (Pellis & Pellis, 1987), and so relinquishes control to its partner. But instead of taking advantage of this situation, the on-top partner does something seemingly peculiar.

Once a rat gains the on-top position over a supine partner, it uses its forepaws to hold, restrain, and position its partner, while keeping its hind

a

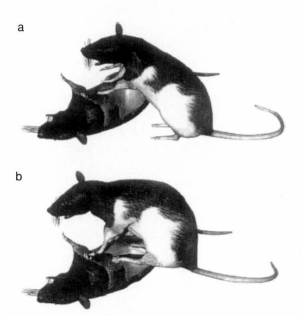

b

**Figure 16.5.** The drawing shows an on-top rat using an anchored posture (a) and an unanchored posture (b). In the unanchored posture, the on-top rat increases its own stability due to the wriggling movements of the supine partner. From Foroud, A., & Pellis, S. M. (2003). The development of 'roughness' in the play fighting of rats: A Laban Movement Analysis perspective. *Developmental Psychobiology, 42,* 35–43. Copyright 2003 by Wiley Periodicals, Inc., A Wiley Company. Reprinted with permission of John Wiley & Sons, Inc.

paws on the ground. From this stable position, the on-top animal can effectively block its partner's movements, allowing the on-top contender to deliver renewed nape attacks (Figure 16.5A). More rarely, the on-top rat stands on its partner with all four paws (Figure 16.5B), a stance that lessens its ability to restrain the supine animal (Foroud & Pellis, 2003). With the on-top rat in this unstable position, the supine rat is better able to launch successful counterattacks, eventually reversing their positions (Pellis, Pellis, & Foroud, 2005). Intriguingly, both as weanlings and following the onset of puberty, rats in the on-top position are more likely to adopt a more stable posture, but during the juvenile period, when play is most frequent and defenders more likely to roll over to supine, the on-top rats are more likely to assume the unstable posture (Foroud & Pellis, 2002).

Thus, during the juvenile period, rats play-fight in a way that reduces control over the movements of their partners, as well as their own movements, which introduces a greater degree of unpredictability into their play.

The age-related modulation of both playful defense and the on-top standing posture is abolished in rats that have had their cortex removed shortly after birth (Foroud, Whishaw & Pellis, 2004; Pellis et al., 1992). Indeed, damage that is limited to the motor cortex is sufficient to abolish the age-related modulation in playful defense (Kamitakahara, Monfils, Forgie, Kolb, & Pellis, 2007). However, removal of either the whole cortex or the motor cortex does not affect how much rats play or their ability to use their full range of defensive tactics or to effectively execute motor actions; rather, it abolishes only the age-related modulation in playful behavior. The existence of such a specific cortical mechanism, ensuring that the organization of juvenile play-fighting produces the experiences that it does, strongly supports the hypothesis that juvenile play in rats fosters development of the ability to take measured responses to unexpected situations – especially social ones.

In rats, then, play-fighting is both an adaptation for assessing and manipulating social partners *and* an adaptation for training juvenile rats to calibrate responses to unexpected and unpredictable situations. The motor cortex ensures that play-fighting is organized to provide the appropriate experiences for juveniles, and the OFC ensures that adults can use play-fighting effectively in varying social contexts. But the OFC does more than modulate play-fighting; it is also involved in a suite of other social behaviors requiring the animal to assess a situation and develop context-specific solutions (Kolb, 1974). The basic behavioral problem of OFC-damaged rats is well illustrated in the food robbing and dodging paradigm.

When a rat is eating a small food item held in its forepaws, it will swerve laterally away from (i.e., dodge) a social partner attempting to steal that item, and the magnitude of the dodge varies with the hardness of the food item (i.e., time to eat it) (Whishaw & Gorny, 1994) and the identity of the robber (rats have idiosyncratic robbing tactics) (Pellis et al., 2006). Following OFC damage, rats are still able to dodge defensively in such situations, but while they can produce dodges of different magnitude for different food items, they can no longer discriminate between robbers (Pellis et al., 2006). In a similar manner, adult rats that were reared in social isolation during the juvenile period are able to dodge a robber to protect a food item, but they show a deficit in their orientation toward the robber. In group-reared males, the dodge ends with the defender orienting its rump to the side of the robber's head, but in isolation-reared rats, the dodger orients on the side of the robber's body (Pellis, Field, & Whishaw, 1999). Thus, both rats with OFC damage and rats with no juvenile play-fighting experience fail to appropriately coordinate their movements with those of the partner.

The similarity of the deficits of OFC-damaged rats and play-deprived rats suggests that a major site of feedback of play experience is in the OFC. Indeed, preliminary data show that the cellular morphology of neurons in the OFC is more complex in rats with more juvenile play-fighting experience (Bell, Kolb, & Pellis, 2007). This conclusion brings us full circle – one cortical area, the motor cortex, ensures that play-fighting provides experiences that enhance the structure and function of another cortical area, the OFC, which, in turn, is able to further use play-fighting to gain immediate benefits from the social environment. So far, so good, for rats, but where does this leave the debate over the functions of play-fighting in the macaques with which we began this chapter?

## JUVENILE VERSUS ADULT PLAY AND THE UNITY OF FUNCTION

A consensus seems to be developing in both the human and the non-human animal literature that play-fighting has different organizational properties in adolescence and adulthood, compared to that in the juvenile period (Biben, 1998; Fry, 2005; Pellegrini, 2003; Pellis, 2002b). Descriptions of play-fighting in older animals indicate that it can vary from rough to gentle; functionally, the former is associated with dominance contests and the latter with maintaining or developing social bonds. As noted for rats, a playful context for establishing and testing social relationships provides a relatively safe setting within which to explore relationships. If one oversteps the boundaries tolerated by one's partner, a message to the effect of "Sorry, I was only playing" provides a graceful exit. Overcoming initial reticence or unfamiliarity is a common problem in the early stages of courtship; in humans, playful flirting, involving wrestling, gentle hitting and tickling, is well documented in both adolescents and young adults (Moore, M., 1985, 1995). Such behavior seems quite prevalent in a wide range of primates and other mammals as well (Pellis & Iwaniuk, 1999). Play-fighting is used by adolescent boys both to assert dominance and to attempt to gain in dominance (Pellegrini, 2003). These motives are also documented for a variety of primates and other mammals (Pellis, 2002a; Pellis & Iwaniuk, 2000). Of course, where boundaries are drawn with regard to what is tolerated as play can vary, depending on the partner and the context. For example, women typically tolerate a narrower range of acceptable playful contact during courtship than do men, even though they allow themselves a broader range of contact (Ryan & Mohr, 2005). Such uses of play-fighting for assessing and manipulating partners can be very taxing both emotionally and cognitively, as actions need to be continually evaluated.

When asked to discriminate between instances of playful and serious fighting, children are more accurate than adults (Smith & Boulton, 1990), while in adults, men are more likely to judge the difference better than women. However, women's accuracy improves if they have had personal experience with play-fighting as children (Conner, 1989). Clearly, experience can make a difference. To our knowledge, no studies are available that have examined whether differential experience with play-fighting leads to more subtle discriminations of playful encounters in adulthood. However, some studies indicate that children who have had more experience with play-fighting are more able to solve social problems (Pellegrini, 1995). The experimental data on rats suggest a direct, causal connection between play-fighting and social competence (Pellis & Pellis, 2007). But some researchers believe that the organization of juvenile play-fighting in humans is best explained as the practice of combat skills (e.g., Fry, 2005).

As we discussed earlier, when comparing degus and rats, play-fighting must contain threshold levels of both competition and cooperation, and irrespective of whether play-fighting is more competitive or more cooperative, every species that engages in it must solve the reciprocity problem. When reciprocation comes late in the play sequence, attack and defense tactics for that species are performed in a manner comparable to such tactics in serious fighting. In such species, play-fighting can serve as practice for adult aggression. But in species that introduce reciprocation early in the play sequence, attack and defense tactics are only superficially similar to tactics in serious fighting. In those cases, play-fighting is a poor means of practicing serious fighting (Pellis & Pellis, 1998b). Whether the play-fighting of human children more resembles that of degus or that of rats awaits empirical determination. Nonetheless, the finding that personal experience with play-fighting can influence one's ability to discriminate between others' playful and aggressive behaviors (Conner, 1989) suggests that even if a child's play-fighting experience enhances later fighting ability, it must also change the ability to differentiate between social actions and weigh them appropriately. Thus, even an extremely competitive form of play-fighting appears to have a built-in mechanism for such social training: Subjects learn that to keep playing means to accept some pain (Biben, 1998; Pellis & Pellis, 1998b). That is, in addition to refining their fighting skills, subjects learn that pleasurable social interactions sometimes involve physical pain as well as psychological pain arising from loss of control. Indeed, for at least one cultural group – the Inuit – the use of playful banter by adults to induce psychological pain in young children has proved a valuable tool for teaching them societal mores (Briggs, 1998). Of course, the flip side is that the ambiguity of play-fighting can be used to punish partners. This appears to be the case when dominant howler monkeys initiate play with subordinates (Jones, 1983).

Regardless of whether the ambiguity of play-fighting is used in positive or negative ways, the juvenile experience of such play would increase the range and subtlety of possible social interactions and thus help resolve the problem of variable boundaries of acceptable contact with a variety of partners. Therefore, whether play-fighting in the juvenile period primarily promotes the development of social skills or combat skills, it would enhance the subject's ability to make more nuanced discriminations about the social actions of others.

REFERENCES

Adams, N., & Boice, R. (1989). Development of dominance in rats in laboratory and seminatural environments. *Behavioral Processes, 19,* 127–142.
Adolphs, R. (1999). The human amygdala and emotion. *Neuroscientist, 5,* 125–137.
Aggleton, J. P. (Ed.). (2000). *The amygdala: A functional analysis.* Oxford, UK: Oxford University Press.
Altmann, S. A. (1962). Social behavior of anthropoid primates: Analysis of recent concepts. In E. L. Bliss (Ed.), *Roots of behavior* (pp. 277–285). New York: Harper.
Arakawa, H. (2002). The effects of age and isolation period on two phases of behavioral response to foot-shock in isolation-reared rats. *Developmental Psychobiology, 41,* 15–24.
Baron-Cohen, S., Ring, H. A., Bullmore, E. T., Wheelwright, S., Ashwin, C., & Williams, S. C. R. (2000). The amygdala theory of autism. *Neuroscience & Biobehavioral Reviews, 24,* 355–364.
Bauer, E. B. & Smuts, B. A. (2007). Cooperation and competition during dyadic play in domestic dogs, *Canis familiaris. Animal Behaviour, 73,* 489–499.
Bell, H., Kolb, B., & Pellis, S. M. (2007). Play: A mind-altering experience? Canadian Spring Conference on Brain and Behaviour, Fernie, BC, Canada.
Bekoff, M. (1976). The social deprivation paradigm: Who's being deprived of what? *Developmental Psychobiology, 9,* 499–500.
Bekoff, M. (1995). Play signals as punctuation: The structure of social play in canids. *Behaviour, 132,* 419–429.
Biben, M. (1998). Squirrel monkey play fighting: Making the case for a cognitive training function for play. In M. Bekoff & J. A. Byers (Eds.), *Animal play: Evolutionary, comparative, and ecological perspectives* (pp. 161–182). Cambridge, UK: Cambridge University Press.
Blanchard, D. C., & Blanchard, R. J. (1990). Behavioral correlates of chronic dominance-subordinance relationships of male rats in a seminatural situation. *Neuroscience & Biobehavioral Reviews, 14,* 455–462.
Breuggeman, J. A. (1978). The function of adult play in free-ranging Macaca mulatta. In E. O. Smith (Ed.), *Social play in primates* (pp. 169–192). London: Routledge.

Briggs, J. L. (1998). *Inuit morality play: The emotional education of a three-year-old.* New Haven, CT: Yale University Press.

Byrd, K. R., & Briner, W. E. (1999). Fighting, nonagonistic social behavior, and exploration in isolation-reared rats. *Aggressive Behavior, 25,* 211–223.

Conner, K. (1989). Aggression: In the eye of the beholder? *Play & Culture, 2,* 213–217.

Daenen, E. W. P. M., Wolterink, G., Gerrits, M. A., & van Ree, J. M. (2002). The effects of neonatal lesions on the amygdala or ventral hippocampus on social behavior latter in life. *Behavioural Brain Research, 136,* 571–582.

da Silva, N. L., Ferreria,V. N. M., de Padua Gorabrez, A., & Morato, G. S. (1996). individual housing from weaning modifies the performance of young rats on elevated plus-maze apparatus. *Physiology & Behavior, 60,* 1391–1396.

Diergaarde, L., Gerrits, M. A. F. M., Stuy, A., Spruijt, B. M., & van Ree, J. M. (2004). Neonatal amygdala lesions and juvenile isolation in the rat: Differential effects on locomotor and social behavior later in life. *Behavioral Neuroscience, 118,* 298–305.

Dugatkin, L. A., & Bekoff, M. (2003). Play and the evolution of fairness: A game theory model. *Behavioural Processes, 60,* 209–214.

Einon, D. F., & Potegal, M. (1991). Enhanced defense in adult rats deprived of playfighting experience as juveniles. *Aggressive Behavior, 17,* 27–40.

Einon, D. F., Humphreys, A. P., Chivers, S. M., Field, S., & Naylor, V. (1981). Isolation has permanent effects upon the behavior of the rat, but not the mouse, gerbil, or guinea pig. *Developmental Psychobiology, 14,* 343–355.

Emery, N., Capitanio, J. P., Mason, W. A., Machado, C. J., Mendoza, S. P., & Amaral, D. G. (2001). The effects of bilateral lesions of the amygdala on dyadic social interactions in rhesus monkeys (*Macaca mulatta*). *Behavioral Neuroscience, 115,* 515–544.

Foroud, A., & Pellis, S. M. (2002). The development of 'anchoring' in the play fighting of rats: Evidence for an adaptive age-reversal in the juvenile phase. *International Journal of Comparative Psychology, 15,* 11–20.

Foroud, A., & Pellis, S. M. (2003). The development of 'roughness' in the play fighting of rats: A Laban Movement Analysis perspective. *Developmental Psychobiology, 42,* 35–43.

Foroud, A., Whishaw, I. Q., & Pellis, S. M. (2004). Experience and cortical control over the pubertal transition to rougher play fighting in rats. *Behavioural Brain Research, 149,* 69–76.

Fry, D. P. (2005). Rough and tumble social play in humans. In A. D. Pellegrini & P. K. Smith (Eds.), *The nature of play* (pp. 54–85). New York: Guilford Press.

Holloway, K. S., & Suter, R. B. (2004). Play deprivation without social isolation: Housing controls. *Developmental Psychobiology, 44,* 58–67.

Jones, C. B. (1983). Social organization of captive black howler monkeys (*Alouatta caraya*): Social competition and the use of non-damaging behavior. *Primates, 24,* 25–39.

Jordan, R. (2003). Social play and autistic spectrum disorders. *Autism, 7,* 347–360.

Kamitakahara, H., Monfils, M.-H., Forgie, M. L., Kolb, B., & Pellis, S. M. (2007). The modulation of play fighting in rats: Role of the motor cortex. *Behavioral Neuroscience, 121,* 164–176.

Kolb, B. (1974). Social behavior of rats with chronic prefrontal lesions. *Journal of Comparative Psychology, 87*, 466–474.

Kolb, B. (1984). Functions of the frontal cortex of the rat: A comparative review. *Brain Research Reviews, 8*, 65–98.

Lewis, K. P., & Barton, R. A. (2006). Amygdala size and hypothalamus size predict social play frequency in nonhuman primates: A comparative analysis using independent contrasts. *Journal of Comparative Psychology, 120*, 31–37.

Levy, J. S. (1979). *Play behavior and its decline during development in rhesus monkeys (Macaca mulatta)*. (Unpublished doctoral dissertation). University of Chicago, Chicago, Illinois.

Lore, R. K., & Flannelly, K. (1977). Rat societies. *Scientific American, 236*, 106–118.

Maaswinkel, H., Baars, A. M., Gispen, W. H., & Spruijt, B. M. (1996). Roles of the basolateral amygdala and hippocampus in social recognition in rats. *Physiology & Behavior, 60*, 55–63.

Meunier, M., Bachevalier, J., Murray, E. A., Malkova, L., & Mishkin, M. (1999). Effects of aspiration versus neurotoxic lesions of the amygdala on emotional responses in monkeys. *European Journal of Neuroscience, 11*, 4403–4418.

Moore, C. L. (1985). Development of mammalian sexual behavior. In E. S. Gollin (Ed.), *The comparative development of adaptive skills* (pp. 19–56). Hillsdale, NJ: Erlbaum.

Moore, M. M. (1985). Non-verbal courtship patterns in women: Contact and consequences. *Ethology & Sociobiology, 6*, 237–247.

Moore, M. M. (1995). Courtship signaling and adolescents: "Girls just want to have fun"? *Journal of Sex Research, 32*, 319–328.

Ohman, A. (2002). Automaticity and the amygdala: Nonconcious responses to emotional faces. *Current Directions in Psychological Science, 11*, 62–66.

Palagi, E., Cordoni, G., & Tarli, B. (2004). Immediate and delayed benefits of play behaviour: New evidence from chimpanzees (*Pan troglodytes*). *Ethology, 110*, 949–962.

Panksepp, J. (1998). *Affective neuroscience*. Oxford, UK: Oxford University Press.

Pellegrini, A. D. (1995). Boys' rough-and-tumble play and social competence: Contemporaneous and longitudinal relations. In A. D. Pellegrini (Ed.), *The future of play theory: A multidisciplinary inquiry into the contribution of Brian Sutton-Smith* (pp. 107–126). Albany, NY: State University of New York Press.

Pellegrini, A. D. (2003). Perceptions and possible functions of play and real fighting in early adolescence. *Child Development, 74*, 1552–1533.

Pellis, S. M. (1988). Agonistic versus amicable targets of attack and defense: Consequences for the origin, function and descriptive classification of play-fighting. *Aggressive Behavior, 14*, 85–104.

Pellis, S. M. (1993). Sex and the evolution of play fighting: A review and a model based on the behavior of muroid rodents. *The Journal of Play Theory & Research, 1*, 56–77.

Pellis, S. M. (1997). Targets and tactics: The analysis of moment-to-moment decision making in animal combat. *Aggressive Behavior, 23*, 107–129.

Pellis, S. M. (2002a). Keeping in touch: Play fighting and social knowledge. In M. Bekoff, C. Allen & G. M. Burghardt (Eds.), *The cognitive animal: Empirical and theoretical perspectives on animal cognition* (pp. 421–427). Cambridge, MA: MIT Press.

Pellis, S. M. (2002b). Sex-differences in play fighting revisited: Traditional and non-traditional mechanisms for sexual differentiation in rats. *Archives of Sexual Behavior, 31,* 11–20.

Pellis, S. M., & Iwaniuk, A. N. (1999). The problem of adult play: A comparative analysis of play and courtship in primates. *Ethology, 105,* 783–806.

Pellis, S. M., & Iwaniuk, A. N. (2000). Adult-adult play in primates: Comparative analyses of its origin, distribution and evolution. *Ethology, 106,* 1083–1104.

Pellis, S. M., & Iwaniuk, A. N. (2002). Brain system size and adult-adult play in primates: A comparative analysis of the roles of the non-visual neocortex and the amygdala. *Behavioural Brain Research, 134,* 31–39.

Pellis, S. M., & Iwaniuk, A. N. (2004). Evolving a playful brain: A levels of control approach. *International Journal of Comparative Psychology, 17,* 90–116.

Pellis, S. M., & Pellis, V. C. (1987). Play-fighting differs from serious fighting in both target of attack and tactics of fighting in the laboratory rat *Rattus norvegicus. Aggressive Behavior, 13,* 227–242.

Pellis, S. M., & Pellis, V. C. (1988). Play-fighting in the Syrian golden hamster *Mesocricetus auratus* Waterhouse, and its relationship to serious fighting during post-weaning development. *Developmental Psychobiology, 21,* 323–337.

Pellis, S. M., & Pellis, V. C. (1990). Differential rates of attack, defense and counter-attack during the developmental decrease in play fighting by male and female rats. *Developmental Psychobiology, 23,* 215–231.

Pellis, S. M., & Pellis, V. C. (1993). Influence of dominance on the development of play fighting in pairs of male Syrian golden hamsters (*Mesocricetus auratus*). *Aggressive Behavior, 19,* 293–302.

Pellis, S. M., & Pellis, V. C. (1996). On knowing it's only play: The role of play signals in play fighting. *Aggression & Violent Behavior, 1,* 249–268.

Pellis, S. M., & Pellis, V. C. (1997a). Targets, tactics and the open mouth face during play fighting in three species of primates. *Aggressive Behavior, 23,* 41–57.

Pellis, S. M., & Pellis, V. C. (1997b). The prejuvenile onset of play fighting in laboratory rats (*Rattus norvegicus*). *Developmental Psychobiology, 31,* 193–205.

Pellis, S. M., & Pellis, V. C. (1998a). The play fighting of rats in comparative perspective: A schema for neurobehavioral analyses. *Neuroscience & Biobehavioral Reviews, 23,* 87–101.

Pellis, S. M., & Pellis, V. C. (1998b). Structure-function interface in the analysis of play. In M. Bekoff & J. A. Byers (Eds.), *Animal play: Evolutionary, comparative, and ecological perspectives* (pp. 115–140). Cambridge, UK: University Press.

Pellis, S. M., & Pellis, V. C. (2006). Play and the development of social engagement: A comparative perspective. In P. J. Marshall & N. A. Fox (Eds.), *The development of social engagement: Neurobiological perspectives* (pp. 247–274). Oxford, UK: University Press.

Pellis, S. M., & Pellis, V. C. (2007). Rough and tumble play and the development of the social brain. *Current Directions in Psychological Science, 16,* 95–98.

Pellis, S. M., Field, E. F., & Whishaw, I. Q. (1999). The development of a sex-differentiated defensive motor-pattern in rats: A possible role for juvenile experience. *Developmental Psychobiology, 35,* 156–164.

Pellis, S. M., Pellis, V. C., & Foroud, A. (2005). Play fighting: Aggression, affiliation and the development of nuanced social skills. In R. Tremblay, W. W. Hartup & J. Archer (Eds.), *Developmental origins of aggression* (pp. 47–62). New York: Guilford Press.

Pellis, S. M., Pellis, V. C., & McKenna, M. M. (1993). Some subordinates are more equal than others: Play fighting amongst adult subordinate male rats. *Aggressive Behavior, 19,* 385–393.

Pellis, S. M., Pellis, V. C., & McKenna, M. M. (1994). A feminine dimension in the play fighting of rats (*Rattus norvegicus*) and its defeminization neonatally by androgens. *Journal of Comparative Psychology, 108,* 68–73.

Pellis, S. M., Pellis, V. C., & Whishaw, I. Q. (1992). The role of the cortex in play fighting by rats: Developmental and evolutionary implications. *Brain, Behavior & Evolution, 39,* 270–284.

Pellis, S. M., Field, E. F., Smith, L. K., & Pellis, V. C. (1997). Multiple differences in the play fighting of male and female rats. Implications for the causes and functions of play. *Neuroscience & Biobehavioral Reviews, 21,* 105–120.

Pellis, S. M., Hastings, E., Shimizu, T., Kamitakahara, H., Komorowska, J., Forgie M. L., et al. B. (2006). The effects of orbital frontal cortex damage on the modulation of defensive responses by rats in playful and non-playful social contexts. *Behavioral Neuroscience, 120,* 72–84.

Power, T. G. (2000). *Play and exploration in animals and children.* Mahwah, NJ: Erlbaum.

Prather, M. D., Lavenex, P., Mauldin-Joundain, M. L., Mason, W. A., Capitanio, J. P., Mendoza, S. P., et al. (2001). Increased social fear and decreased fear of objects in monkeys with neonatal amygdala lesions. *Neuroscience, 106,* 653–658.

Reinhart, C. J., Pellis, S. M., & McIntyre, D. C. (2004). The development of play fighting in kindling-prone (FAST) and kindling–resistant (SLOW) rats: How does the retention of phenotypic juvenility affect the complexity of play? *Developmental Psychobiology, 45,* 83–92.

Reinhart, C. J., McIntyre, D. C., Metz, G. A., & Pellis, S. M. (2006). Play fighting between kindling-prone (FAST) and kindling-resistant (SLOW) rats. *Journal of Comparative Psychology, 120,* 19–30.

Ryan, K. M., & Mohr, S. (2005). Gender differences in playful aggression during courtship in college students. *Sex Roles, 53,* 591–601

Siviy, S. M. (1998). Neurobiological substrates of play behavior: Glimpses into the structure and function of mammalian playfulness. In M. Bekoff & J. A. Byers (Eds.), *Animal play: Evolutionary, comparative, and ecological perspectives* (pp. 221–242). Cambridge, UK: Cambridge University Press.

Smith, L. K., Fantella, S.-L., & Pellis, S. M. (1999). Playful defensive responses in adult male rats depend on the status of the unfamiliar opponent. *Aggressive Behavior, 25,* 141–152.

Smith, P. K. (1997). Play fighting and real fighting: Perspectives on their relationship. In A. Schmitt, K. Atswanger, K. Grammar & K. Schafer (Eds.), *New aspects of human ethology* (pp. 47–64). New York: Plenum Press.

Smith, P. K. (2005). Play: Types and functions in human development. In B. J. Ellis & D. F. Bjorklund (Eds.), *Origins of the social mind* (pp. 271–291). New York: Guilford Press.

Smith, P. K., & Boulton, M. (1990). Rough and tumble play, aggression and dominance: Perception and behaviour in children's encounters. *Human Development*, *33*, 271–282.

Spinka, M., Newberry, R. C., & Bekoff, M. (2001). Mammalian play: Can training for the unexpected be fun? *Quarterly Review of Biology*, *76*, 141–176.

Suomi, S. J. (2005). Genetic and environmental factors influencing the expression of impulsive aggression and serotonergic functioning in rhesus monkeys. In R. E. Tremblay, W. W. Hartup & J. Archer (Eds.), *Developmental origins of aggression* (pp. 63–82). New York: Guilford Press.

Symons, D. (1978). *Play and aggression. A study of Rhesus monkeys*. New York: Columbia University Press.

Thompson, K. V. (1998). Self assessment in juvenile play. In M. Bekoff & J. A. Byers (Eds.), *Animal play: Evolutionary, comparative, and ecological perspectives* (pp.183–204). Cambridge, UK: Cambridge University Press.

van den Berg, C. L., Hol, T., van Ree, J. M., Spruijt, B. M., Everts, H., & Koolhaas, J. M. (1999). Play is indispensable for an adequate development of coping with social challenges in the rat. *Developmental Psychobiology*, *34*, 129–138.

von Frijtag, J. C., Schot, M., van den Bos, R., & Spruijt, B. M. (2002). Individual housing during the play period results in changed responses to and consequences of a psychosocial stress situation in rats. *Developmental Psychobiology*, *41*, 58–69.

Whishaw, I. Q., & Gorny, B. (1994). Food wrenching and dodging: Eating time estimates influence dodge probability and amplitude. *Aggressive Behavior*, *20*, 35–47.

Wilson, S. C. (1981). Contact-promoting behavior, social development, and relationship with parents in sibling juvenile degus (*Octodon degus*). *Developmental Psychobiology*, *15*, 257–268.

Wilson, S. C., & Kleiman, D. G. (1974). Eliciting play: A comparative study. *American Zoologist*, *14*, 341–370.

# SEVENTEEN

# Ethological Vignette

*Social Stress as a Formative Experience: Neurobiology of Conditioned Defeat*

## Kim L. Huhman

## INTRODUCTION

It has been proposed that social conflict, particularly when it results in social defeat or subordination, is a major stressor in humans and that this type of stress contributes to numerous diseases and psychopathologies including a variety of mood and anxiety disorders (Agid, Kohn, & Lerer, 2000; Bjorkqvist, 2001; Gardner, 2001; Nemeroff, 1998). Understanding the dramatic impact that stressful experiences have on social behavior is necessary if we are to develop better ways of treating individuals who develop maladaptive responses to these events. Use of animal models of stress-induced behavioral plasticity are necessary for the exploration of the neural mechanisms and circuitry underlying these changes. This chapter reviews some recent data from experiments aimed at understanding the neural basis of a long lasting, stress-induced change in behavior, "conditioned defeat," which is observed in Syrian hamsters, as well as other species, following exposure to social stress (i.e., social defeat). The purpose of such experiments is to increase our understanding of the basic neural mechanisms that mediate experience-induced changes in social behavior, particularly in response to aversive experience.

An organism's ability to learn about its environment and to alter its behavior in response to external stimuli is critical for survival and reproductive success. In particular, it is vital that organisms have the ability to respond appropriately to, and to remember long-term, potentially threatening events (see Wiedenmayer, this volume). Some of the resulting changes in behavior can be quite striking and long-lasting, having an impact on the organism for extended periods of time or even for its lifetime.

Recently enormous progress has been made to further our understanding of the neural mechanisms underlying aversive learning in animals. Not surprisingly, the neural circuits that have been identified are complex and vary somewhat depending on the nature of the stimulus about which the organism must learn. Many animal models of human stress-related disorders use artificial stressors such as intermittent foot shock or physical restraint to induce stress. These models offer the benefit of being highly controllable, but they may bear little resemblance to stressors normally encountered by animals or humans. Developing animal models that use a social context closer to that which an individual might experience in its natural environment (so-called biological or ethological models) is essential to a better understanding of the neural mechanisms underlying social behavior, in general, and social stress-induced behavioral plasticity, in particular.

The Syrian hamster is one valuable species for use in social stress studies. Although little is known about Syrian hamsters in nature, they are thought to be solitary animals that defend their home territories (Nowack & Paradiso, 1983). In the laboratory, both male and female hamsters readily exhibit agonistic (i.e., conflict) behavior, and their behavioral repertoire has been described in detail (Grant & Mackintosh, 1962; Albers, Huhman, & Meisel, 2002). No complex social housing procedures or co-housing with a female is necessary to induce agonistic behavior in hamsters. Instead, when male or female hamsters are singly housed in the laboratory, resident animals routinely attack and defeat intruders placed in their home cages (resident-intruder model), especially if the resident is larger than its intruding opponent. Thus, agonistic behavior in hamsters is easily produced under laboratory conditions. Another advantage of using hamsters is that their agonistic behavior is highly ritualized and the severity of their agonistic encounters (in terms of bites or tissue damage) is usually quite low in the laboratory, especially when compared with aggressive strains of mice.

The purpose of this chapter is to introduce the reader to a hamster social stress model and to illustrate how this type of model might be used to further our understanding of how social stress can serve as a formative experience. It is also critical to note that the effects of social stress in rodents vary tremendously, depending on when during development the stress exposure occurs, and, further, that very different effects can be observed following repeated versus acute exposure. Additionally, the response to social stress exhibits a striking sex difference and, in females, can vary depending on the stage of the ovarian cycle upon which the exposure

Kim L. Huhman

takes place. Finally, we will demonstrate how such a model can be used to explore the neural underpinnings of stress-induced changes in behavior.

## AGONISTIC BEHAVIOR IN HAMSTERS

### Is Social Conflict Stressful?

Hamsters that are exposed to social defeat, but not those who fight and win, display a "classical" physiological response to stress. That is, following a social encounter, losers, but not winners, display a hormonal stress response that includes elevated plasma adrenocorticotropin, ß-endorphin, ß-lipotrophin, cortisol, and corticosterone (Huhman, Bunnell, Mougey, & Meyerhoff, 1990). The hormonal stress response is not dependent on actual contact between the animals: Exposure of a previously defeated hamster to a dominant opponent stimulates a similar hormonal response in the losing animal, even if the opponents are separated by a barrier (Huhman, Moore, Mougey, & Meyerhoff, 1992), indicating that social defeat in hamsters is a potent psychological stressor. Thus, social conflict in hamsters is stressful if the hamster loses but not if it wins.

### Conditioned Defeat

In addition to the hormonal stress response, defeated hamsters also show a striking behavioral response to social defeat (Potegal, Huhman, Moore, & Meyerhoff, 1993). The initial social defeat occurs when an experimental animal is placed for a brief period of time (either once or repeatedly) in the home cage of a larger, more aggressive opponent (the resident). The experimental animal is thus an intruder in another hamster's home cage. Within seconds, the hamsters "greet" each other in a stereotypical nose-to-nose posture after which the hamsters sniff the body of their opponent. Usually within the first minute of the pairing, the resident will adopt a side attack posture and may or may not attempt to bite the intruder on the flank or rump. A clear dominant-subordinate (winner-loser) relationship generally emerges within a minute or so as evidenced, for example, by the loser adopting either a defensive or a submissive posture (e.g., exhibiting an on-back posture or fleeing from the winner). Dominant-subordinate relationships in hamsters are often established without either opponent being bitten, and tissue damage in these brief encounters is rare. Following a defeat experience, hamsters subsequently fail to defend their own home cage even when paired with a smaller, non-aggressive opponent (a younger, group-housed animal that is non-threatening). Instead of the expected attack and territorial defense of their home cage, previously defeated hamsters subsequently produce high levels of defensive and sub-missive behaviors, such as flee, tail lift, tooth chatter, and side/upright defensive postures, and they exhibit no aggressive behaviors. These ham-sters often attempt to flee from the non-aggressive intruder before the nose-to-nose greeting behavior has occurred, a response we call "antici-patory flight" (Figure 17.1). This striking alteration in agonistic behavior, which can occur in hamsters following a single exposure to social defeat, is what we call "conditioned defeat."

A similar response has been reported in rats and mice following repeated exposure to social defeat. In laboratory rats, however, agonistic behavior is usually quite low unless the animals are housed in complex social con-ditions, while in aggressive strains of mice the level of aggression and wounding is often unacceptably high. Conditioned defeat in hamsters is more easily produced and is robust, reproducible, and easily obtained with-out physical injury to the animals. Conditioned defeat in hamsters can be induced by a single, short exposure to defeat and is long lasting. Following defeat, many male hamsters will continue to exhibit the behavioral profile of conditioned defeat for at least one month despite being repeatedly paired with a non-aggressive intruder (Huhman et al., 2003), a manipulation that one might expect would lead to extinction of the behavioral response and a return of normal territorial aggression. We contend that conditioned defeat is a powerful, ethologically-relevant model that offers a unique opportunity to explore how multiple brain circuits that control fear, social behavior, and motivation interact to modify complex behavior in a social context.

It has been suggested that conditioned defeat might be a laboratory artifact that would not be observed in nature wherein an animal could effectively flee from a threatening opponent. To address this possibility, we allowed hamsters a mechanism whereby they could flee from the cage during an agonistic encounter. In this experiment, we paired opponents three times and the pairings were terminated at 5 min or when one animal escaped the cage. Latencies for the losing animal to flee were 239 ± 58 sec for the first defeat, 64 ± 25 sec for the second defeat, and 113 ± 44 sec for the third defeat. Latency to escape was significantly lower in trials 2 and 3 than in Trial 1, but Trials 2 and 3 were not significantly different from one another. These hamsters exhibited robust conditioned defeat during subsequent testing despite being able to control, to a large extent, the amount of agonistic behavior directed towards them. We believe, therefore, that conditioned defeat is not an artifact but rather that it is ethologically relevant coping strategy in response to social defeat.

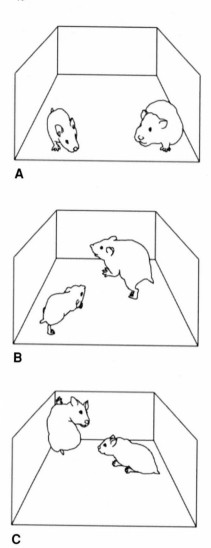

A

B

C

**Figure 17.1.** A previously defeated hamster fails to defend its home cage when paired with a small, non-aggressive opponent. After the smaller hamster is introduced (a), the defeated hamster attempts to flee from the non-aggressive intruder (b) and (c). Drawing by Irene Sukwandi.

## Developmental Effects

It is of critical importance to note that the behavioral response to social defeat in hamsters varies tremendously depending on when the exposure to defeat occurs. Subjects in our experiments are all young adults (i.e., they are post-pubertal). During the pubertal period, the agonistic behavior of hamsters changes qualitatively and quantitatively. Before puberty, attack levels are extremely high and the target of these attacks is largely the face and neck area of the opponent. This behavior is considered "play fighting" in hamsters and other rodents (see Pellis, Pellis, & Reinhart, this volume) and does not result in tissue damage. At puberty, the overall attack frequency declines significantly and the target area of the attacks is redirected towards the rump and belly area (i.e., the adult pattern of aggressive targets). If prepubertal hamsters are exposed to repeated attack, the attack frequency does not decline during puberty as much as it does in undefeated control hamsters. That is, young hamsters that suffer repeated losses are more aggressive as adults. In addition, the shift from "play" targets to adult targets is significantly accelerated by the experience of defeat so that these animals begin to attack the belly and rump of their opponents at an earlier age (Delville, David, Taravosh-Lahn, & Wommack, 2003; Wommack, Taravosh-Lahn, David, & Delville, 2003). These studies clearly illustrate that social defeat can have drastically different – even opposite – effects on subsequent social behavior, depending on when during development the defeat occurs. So-called "formative experiences" clearly vary as a function of the characteristics of the subject at the time the formative experience occurred.

## Gender Differences: Phenomenology by Estrus Cycle

In humans, unlike many other mammalian species, both males and females readily produce spontaneous aggressive behavior. Similarly, both Syrian hamster males and females exhibit high levels of aggressive behavior. Thus, hamsters may serve as a valuable animal model with which to examine sex differences in the response to social stress. When we began to examine whether conditioned defeat occurs in female hamsters following social defeat, we initially found that most females did not exhibit a strong behavioral response to losing even though they do mount a pronounced hormonal stress response to social defeat (Huhman et al., 2003). In addition, even females that did exhibit conditioned defeat when initially tested with a non-aggressive intruder produced normal territorial aggression on subsequent tests. This finding is in contrast to results with males that exhibit conditioned defeat for a prolonged time period following an initial social defeat (Huhman et al., 2003). Because we observed a striking disparity in the behavioral response among females, however, we re-examined the behavioral response to social defeat over the estrous cycle in intact females (Solomon, Karom, & Huhman, 2007). We found an obvious variation in the behavioral response to defeat, apparently dependent on the hormonal status of the female at the time of testing but not at the time of the initial defeat. That is, females in the diestrous 2 and proestrous phases of the four-day ovarian cycle, days in which estrogen levels are rising significantly, exhibit conditioned defeat, whereas females tested on other days of the estrous cycle produce territorial aggression towards an intruder. (Note that female hamsters in behavioral estrus produce only spontaneous lordosis behavior and no aggression or submission, even in the presence of another female.) Thus, it seems that "formative experiences" can have very different effects on female hamsters depending on the stage of the ovarian cycle in which these experiences occur.

## Underlying Neurobiology of Conditioned Defeat

It is challenging to pick a starting point to begin to explore the neurobiological basis for complex social behaviors like conditioned defeat. On one hand there is a relatively well-defined circuit that has been shown to be important for fear learning and responding to stressful stimuli. On the other hand, largely distinct circuits are known to be critical for social behavior. The challenge is to learn how these circuits interact to mediate fear or stress-induced changes in social behavior. As mentioned earlier, the amygdala in the so-called limbic system is a reasonable candidate that is a critical neural component in both the "fear" as well as the "social behavior" circuit. The amygdala, a heterogeneous collection of nuclei, can be divided into four groups based on connectivity, neurochemistry, electrophysiology, and functionality. The groups are (1) the central nucleus (Ce, a major output system of the amygdala); (2) the lateral and basolateral nuclei (referred to herein as the basolateral complex of the amygdala [BLA]), which receives dense sensory afferents and is thought to be critical for the formation of fear memories); (3) the medial nucleus (Me, part of the olfactory system); and (4) the cortical and basomedial nuclei (also part of the main olfactory system; these nuclei may serve to connect the circuitry mediating fear with more medial neurons that relay chemosensory and hormonal information). Based on embryological evidence, reciprocal interconnections, and shared afferents and efferents, the Ce, lateral portions of the bed nucleus of the stria terminalis (BNST), and the nucleus accumbens (NAcc) appear to be part of a functional unit called the "central extended amygdala." The central extended amygdala is thought to be involved in coordinating autonomic function and in producing and integrating behavioral and emotional responses to fearful or stressful stimuli. The Me and more medial portions of the BNST form a parallel circuit, called the medial extended amygdala, believed to be critical for the production of mammalian social behaviors such as aggressive and reproductive behaviors.

The BLA receives highly processed sensory information from a variety of cortical, thalamic, and brainstem sites. Anatomical studies in rats and non-human primates indicate that the BLA then projects directly and indirectly to the Ce as well as to the lateral aspects of the BNST. The Ce and lateral BNST (each of which receive some direct sensory input) in turn project to hypothalamic and brainstem targets to directly activate the behavioral and physiological responses associated with stress or fear. Together, the BLA, Ce and lateral BNST are thought to form a central fear system that is critical for the acquisition and expression of conditioned fear in humans and other mammals.

The Me and the more medial aspects of the BNST form the medial extended amygdala, and these areas have been implicated in the regulation of social behaviors such as reproductive and agonistic behaviors. The medial extended amygdala appears to be an important site for the integration of information from the main and accessory olfactory systems. In addition, many neurons in the medial extended amygdala express substantial numbers of estrogen and androgen receptors, and these areas are sexually dimorphic. Thus, these regions are thought to be responsible for processing chemosensory and hormonal cues that impact social behavior. It has been proposed that the medial extended amygdala is a critical brain "node" within a larger circuit that controls a wide variety of social behaviors. Importantly, the medial extended amygdala and the BLA/central extended amygdala are interconnected, but the functional implication of this link has not been carefully evaluated.

In exploring the role of the amygdala in the acquisition and expression of conditioned defeat, we initially used site-specific microinjections of various pharmacological treatments that temporarily reduce or enhance synaptic transmission in the amygdala to test whether specific nuclei are involved in the learning or production of conditioned defeat. For example, gamma aminobutyric acid (GABA) receptor agonists, such as muscimol, can be used to reversibly inactivate individual nuclei in the amygdala. Muscimol given into the Ce or BLA either before the initial defeat experience (acquisition of conditioned defeat) or before the subsequent testing with the non-aggressive intruder (expression of conditioned defeat) dose-dependently reduces or blocks both the acquisition and the expression of conditioned defeat. That is, when muscimol is present and these nuclei of amygdala is inactivated, the submissive behaviors that characterize conditioned defeat are not produced in response to the non-aggressive intruder

(Jasnow & Huhman, 2001). Glutamate receptors, such as N-methyl-D-aspartate (NMDA) receptors, known to be critical for learning and memory, are also critical for the acquisition and expression of conditioned defeat, as evidenced by the finding that NMDA receptor antagonists such as AP5 are highly effective in dose-dependently blocking the acquisition and expression of conditioned defeat (Jasnow, Cooper, & Huhman, 2004).

One shortcoming of these studies is that it is impossible to determine whether the actual learning underlying conditioned defeat is occurring in the amygdala or whether the amygdala is simply necessary for the production of a behavioral response that is being learned elsewhere in the brain. To address this problem, we used a molecular technique, viral vector-mediated gene transfer, to increase ("overexpress") a gene for an intracellular signal, cyclic AMP response element binding protein (CREB), that is critical for learning and memory. In these studies, experimental animals were exposed to a sub-optimal defeat training procedure (i.e., a single, five minute defeat). This shortened training still results in an absence of aggression in the defeated hamsters but it also stimulates a relatively low level of submissive and defensive behavior when compared to that shown by hamsters that are defeated in our standard protocols (either once for 15 min or four times for 5 min each). Hamsters given a modified herpes simplex virus used to over-express CREB specifically in the BLA during this sub-optimal defeat training exhibit significantly more submissive/defensive behavior (i.e., better conditioned defeat learning) than do hamsters given a control virus (Jasnow, Shi, Israel, Davis, & Huhman, 2005). There is no effect on conditioned defeat if the injection of the virus over-expressing CREB is given after the initial defeat training or into a control brain area just outside the BLA. These data indicate that the learning that occurs in response to social defeat takes place, at least in part, in the BLA.

The Me is critical for a wide variety of social behaviors in rodents and is a site of convergence of chemosensory cues that the animals use to learn about their environment as well as steroid hormone receptors that modify these behaviors. Data exist suggesting that the Me is a site of learning about social status in rodents. We have recently tested whether the Me is part of the neural circuit for conditioned defeat (Markham & Huhman, 2008). Using muscimol to temporarily inactivate the Me either before training or before testing as described above, we have demonstrated that the Me is necessary for both the acquisition and expression of conditioned defeat. We then asked whether actual learning of conditioned defeat occurs in the Me. Because protein synthesis is necessary for the formation of new long-term memories, we can selectively microinject a protein synthesis inhibitor such as anisomycin directly into either the Me or the BLA before the initial defeat training. Anisomycin drastically reduces the submissive behavior associated with conditioned defeat only when given in the BLA, but not when administered in the Me, indicating that while the Me supplies information necessary for conditioned defeat, it is not a site for the actual learning and memory underlying this behavioral change. This study again implicated the BLA as being critical for the learning of conditioned defeat.

Current studies in our laboratory are examining the potential role of brain areas such as the hippocampus and the nucleus accumbens in the neural circuit underlying conditioned defeat. Through these studies, we hope to define a broad circuit that controls conditioned defeat and to begin to understand how a wide variety of brain areas interact to alter complex social behavior in response to past social experience. We maintain that studying ethologically relevant animal models of social stress is critical to promote our understanding of how social stress can serve as an important formative experience. By recognizing the factors that influence responses to social stress and discovering which neural circuits and neurochemical signals regulate behavioral responses to stress, we hope to discern better ways of treating animals and humans that develop maladaptive responses to formative experiences.

REFERENCES

Agid, O., Kohn, Y., & Lerer, B. (2000). Environmental stress and psychiatric illness. *Biomedicine & Pharmacotherapy, 54*, 135–141.

Albers, H. E., Huhman, K. L., & Meisel, R. L. (2002). Hormonal basis of social conflict and communication. In D. W. Pfaff, A. P. Arnold, A. M. Etgen, S. E. Fahrbach, & R. T. Rubin (Eds.), *Hormones, brain and behavior* (pp. 393–433). San Diego: Academic Press.

Bjorkqvist, K. (2001). Social defeat as a stressor in humans. *Physiology and Behavior, 73*, 435–442.

Delville, Y., David, J. T., Taravosh-Lahn, K., & Wommack, J. C. (2003). Stress and the development of agonistic behavior in golden hamsters. *Hormones and Behavior, 44*, 263–270.

Gardner, R. Jr. (2001). Evolutionary perspectives on stress and affective disorder. *Seminars in Clinical Neuropsychiatry, 6*, 32–42.

Grant, E. C. & Mackintosh, J. H. (1962). A comparison of the social postures of some common laboratory rodents. *Behaviour, 21*, 246–251.

Huhman, K. L., Bunnell, B. N., Mougey, E. H., & Meyerhoff, J. L. (1990). Effects of social conflict on POMC-derived peptides and glucocorticoids in male golden hamsters. *Physiology and Behavior, 47*, 949–956.

Huhman, K. L., Moore, T. O., Mougey, E. H., & Meyerhoff, J. L. (1992). Hormonal responses to fighting in hamsters: Separation of physical and psychological causes. *Physiology and Behavior, 51*, 1083–1086.

Huhman, K. L., Solomon, M. B., Janicki, M., Harmon, A. C., Lin, S. M., Israel, J. E. et al. (2003). Conditioned defeat in male and female Syrian hamsters. *Hormones and Behavior*, *44*, 293–299.

Jasnow, A. M., Cooper, M. A., & Huhman, K. L. (2004). N-methyl-D-aspartate receptors in the amygdala are necessary for the acquisition and expression of conditioned defeat. *Neuroscience*, *123*, 625–634.

Jasnow, A. M. & Huhman, K. L. (2001). Activation of GABA(A) receptors in the amygdala blocks the acquisition and expression of conditioned defeat in Syrian hamsters. *Brain Research*, *920*, 142–150.

Jasnow, A. M., Shi, C., Israel, J. E., Davis, M., & Huhman, K. L. (2005). Memory of social defeat is facilitated by cAMP response element-binding protein overexpression in the amygdala. *Behavioral Neuroscience*, *119*, 1125–1130.

Markham, C. M. & Huhman, K. L. (2008). Is the medial amygdala part of the neural circuit modulating conditioned defeat in Syrian hamsters? *Learning & Memory*, *15*(1), 6–12.

Nemeroff, C. B. (1998). The neurobiology of depression. *Scientific American*, *278*, 42–49.

Nowack, R. M. & Paradiso, J. L. (1983). *Walker's mammals of the world*. Baltimore, MD: Johns Hopkins University Press.

Potegal, M., Huhman, K., Moore, T., & Meyerhoff, J. (1993). Conditioned defeat in the Syrian golden hamster (Mesocricetus auratus). *Behavioral and Neural Biology*, *60*, 93–102.

Solomon, M. B., Karom, M. C., & Huhman, K. L. (2007). Sex and estrous cycle differences in the display of conditioned defeat in Syrian hamsters. *Hormones and Behavior*, *52*, 211–219.

Wommack, J. C., Taravosh-Lahn, K., David, J. T., & Delville, Y. (2003). Repeated exposure to social stress alters the development of agonistic behavior in male golden hamsters. *Hormones and Behavior*, *43*, 229–236.

# Commentary on

## "Social Stress as a Formative Experience: Neurobiology of Conditioned Defeat"

Jonathan Hill

Animal models of stress-related mechanisms in psychopathology have enormous potential. Compared to human studies, advantages include that the nature and timing of stressors can be systematically varied; the effects over substantial proportions of the subjects' short lives and over generations can be studied within the duration of a single research grant; and hypothesized neuroanatomical and neurochemical pathways can be examined directly. The research described in Dr. Huhman's chapter realizes this potential in many respects. The challenge is to determine what we can learn from these models. Enumerating the differences between Syrian hamsters and humans might lead to the immediate answer "not much." Equally, the consistency of findings from studies of the key neuronal circuits in fear conditioning – involving not only Syrian hamsters, but many other animal species and humans – would suggest we can learn a great deal. This review considers some of the issues.

### THE INTERPLAY BETWEEN SOCIAL EXPERIENCE AND BIOLOGY

Over a relatively short time, animal studies have informed a transformation from the separate study of the social and the biological to integrated study of the two levels of analysis. It is now well established across several mammalian species that social experiences often have long-term behavioral and biological effects, many mediated by variations in gene expression, and that these occur only over particular, sensitive periods in development (see Wiedenmayer; Szyf et al., this volume). The findings described in Dr. Huhman's chapter concur with this wider body of research and further support these processes as general mechanisms in development.

443

Making more specific links from animal to human research can however be problematic. Studies of human development depend on naturally
occurring variations in social experience that generally correlate with many
other aspects of the social environment and that themselves fluctuate over
their periods of operation. Nevertheless the existence of long-term effects of
early human experience is supported by studies of children adopted after
early institutionalization (Hodges & Tizard, 1989; Colvert et al., 2008); the
importance of timing is supported by studies that find associations between
antenatal stress and development, that are not accounted for by correlated
postnatal stress (O'Connor, Heron, Golding, & Glover, 2003). Some parallels
between mechanisms in antenatal animal and human development exist.
Animal studies find an association between antenatal stressors and alterations in hypothalamus-pituitary-adrenal (HPA) axis regulation, which is
mediated by alterations in gene expression (Meaney, Szyf, & Seckl, 2007).
Consistent with the animal evidence, antenatal stress in humans is associated with an elevation in the stress hormone cortisol, an HPA end product.
Elevated maternal cortisol is reportedly associated with negative temperament in infants (Davis et al., 2007).

Thus far, the principles – while compelling and informative – are quite
general. Once we start to focus on more specific aspects of Dr. Huhman's
findings, generalization becomes more problematic. Numerous species differences have been noted in the nature and long-term effects of the most
salient stressors (Sanchez, Ladd, & Plotsky, 2001). Genetic differences may
be crucial. Rhesus monkeys have provided an excellent model not only
of the consequences of early experiences but also of genotype by environment interactions. In these subjects, peer rearing, in contrast to rearing
by mothers, is associated with poor control of aggression and low serotonin metabolism, but only in the subgroup with a specific polymorphism
("short" allele) in the promoter region of the serotonin transporter (5-HTT)
gene (Suomi, 2006). Studies of humans find similar interactions. Other primates, however, do not appear to possess this allelic variation, so in some
respects they provide less effective models for studying the role of rearing
in development.

Several striking differences exist between the findings on conditioned
defeat that Dr. Huhman reviews and much of the animal literature on stress
and development. For example, in Syrian hamsters, conditioned defeat is
seen only after puberty, and it results from social encounters with other
adult hamsters, whereas this particular species is solitary in its natural
habitat. Contrast this finding with the majority of studies on species that live
in social groups, which have focused on the effects of antenatal and early

postnatal experiences involving variations in mothering or separations from mothers.

When considered in relation to human rearing contexts, the experimental procedures used with Syrian hamsters also look in some ways less convincing than many others used in animal studies. For example a standard paradigm for studying the effects of mothering in bonnet macaques entails imposing unpredictable food provision, resulting in lower maternal sensitivity similar to that seen in humans. Persistent behavioral and neurodevelopmental consequences can result, including increased timidity and social subordinance, as well as alterations in stress-related neuroendocrine profiles (Rosenblum, Forger, Noland, Trost, & Coplan, 2001). By contrast, when compared to contexts of human stress, social defeat among adult Syrian hamsters does not seem so convincing. Furthermore, in humans the case for social defeat as a key stressor leading to psychopathology is not strong. Numerous studies have documented the role of parental neglect, physical and sexual abuse, and interparental discord and violence, but few have addressed the role of social defeat (Nemeroff, 1998; Hill et al., 2001; Kim-Cohen et al., 2006). Three of the four papers referenced by Dr Huhman in support of the relevance of this model do not focus on defeat, but instead consider the roles of parental loss, life events, and maltreatment in childhood. In support of the social defeat hypothesis, a fourth paper cites associations between bullying in school and the workplace and a range of mental health problems (Bjorkqvist, 2001).

Might this line of argument lead to the conclusion that the Syrian hamster social defeat model is too far removed from other animal models and from human functioning to be of value in understanding psychopathology? Certainly it does not look promising as a model of the impact of early experiences with the caregiver or other adult figures.

On the other hand, the model may provide a valuable tool for studying stress-related mechanisms in development. Indeed, it could be argued that the key question is whether the procedure leads to behaviors and neurophysiological changes that would be expected in a stress reactivity paradigm. In this case the answer is clearly "yes." Syrian hamsters show behavioral evidence of fear conditioning and HPA axis dysregulation in response to social defeat. A series of elegant studies reported in the chapter implicates circuits associated with the amygdala, which are consistent with current knowledge of the neurobiology of fear conditioning (Phelps & LeDoux, 2005). Thus, the argument is not that social defeat provides a behavioral model for studying mechanisms in human stress, but that in this species, social defeat may provide a model for studying the biological consequences of social stressors.

## THE CONTRIBUTION TO AN UNDERSTANDING OF SOCIAL DEVELOPMENT AND PSYCHOPATHOLOGY

The author makes the case that organisms must be able to learn about their environments and adapt their behavior to deal with threats. Conditioned defeat may represent an example of an adaptive long-term effect of a social stressor that sensitizes the organism to later threats. Equally, Dr. Huhman claims that processes in conditioned defeat may contribute to our understanding of maladaptive behaviors. The link with psychopathology is made explicit in a previous publication (Huhman, 2006). The possible implication is that conditioned defeat can provide a model both for normal social development and for psychopathology.

Whether this is considered problematic depends in part on the view taken about psychopathology. In most instances there is no clear boundary between normal and psychopathological functioning, so it might be argued, there is no reason to propose distinctive mechanisms. Equally, notwithstanding the unclear boundary, psychopathology is generally assumed to entail maladaptive functioning or impairment, and hence may be expected to entail different mechanisms from adaptive functioning. It is essential therefore, in considering the role of adaptive biological mechanisms in psychopathology, to attempt to specify how they might operate (Bolton & Hill, 2004). I will consider three contrasting proposals and their plausibility in relation to the conditioned defeat model. In the first the mechanisms in normal processes and psychopathology are assumed to be the same, but operating under different conditions in health and disorder. For example, low mood is a universal normal response to threat or loss, and depression occurs when the threat is great or the loss severe. The well-established association between life events and depression is in some respects consistent with this proposal. However their effect is substantially modified by individual vulnerabilities associated with childhood adversities, genetic variations, or previous episodes of depression (Kendler, Thornton, & Gardner, 2001). More generally stress-related disorders do not appear to be simply a function of the severity of the stressor, and therefore it is unlikely that conditioned defeat can in any straightforward way, be a model both for normal functioning and psychopathology.

The second possibility is that, in spite of appearances, the mechanism is in fact maladaptive. This could be argued in relation to conditioned defeat in Syrian hamsters. Far from being sensitized to normal social threats, they react submissively to non-aggressive hamsters that pose no threat. In this case the relevance of the hamster model to human studies will depend on the plausibility of conditioned defeat as a way of understanding psychopathology.

In the case of depression, evolutionary theories have proposed that it arises from a toning down of positive affect following social defeat, which makes it less likely that the defeated individual will further challenge others who are likely to repeat the experience. According to the theory it also increases the likelihood that others will accept the subject's submission and be less likely to initiate further defeat exchanges (Gilbert, 2006). Drawing on this hypothesis, several studies have found that the subjective experience of defeat and of entrapment are associated with depression (Gilbert & Allan, 1998; Gilbert, Gilbert, & Irons, 2004). Most of the relevant research, however, has been cross sectional, focusing on subjective experience rather than on whether depression leads to submissive behaviors in social interactions. Furthermore, it could be argued that conditioned defeat does not look like depression. The animal that is prone to show conditioned defeat appears to behave like other animals except in social interactions. By contrast in depression, low mood and associated symptoms are persistent and present in both social and non-social settings. Thus, social defeat theories of depression have generated productive hypotheses, but current evidence does not strongly support a conditioned defeat model of depression.

A third possibility is that normal functioning and psychopathology share pathways or mechanisms that differ in ways not covered by the animal model under discussion. Studies in Syrian hamsters suggest that conditioned defeat provides an effective way of probing the impacts of social adversity on HPA and amygdala functioning, which are clearly relevant to understanding psychopathology. The technique might be particularly helpful in addressing puzzling and intriguing questions that arise in human studies. Three examples illustrate the point. First, early adverse experiences, particularly child maltreatment, are associated with both internalizing disorders such as depression and externalizing problems, notably aggression (Hill et al., 2001; Jaffee, Caspi, Moffitt, & Taylor, 2004). Second, both hyper-reactivity and hypo-reactivity of the HPA axis are found in association with childhood adversities (Tarullo & Gunnar, 2006). Third, the low expression variant of the MAOA gene is associated with increased amygdala activation (Meyer-Lindenberg et al., 2006) and also with antisocial behaviors related to maltreatment (Kim-Cohen et al., 2006); but psychopathic disorders are associated with reduced amygdala activation (Blair, 2008). These apparent contradictions are probably partly accounted for by sampling and measurement differences. However, developmental explanations involving early adaptations that create vulnerability are also possible. It has been proposed, for example, that early hyper-reactivity of the HPA axis in response to maltreatment or other forms of threat is replaced by hypo-activity as a result of physiological adaptation aimed at reducing stress reactivity. Low HPA activity may then contribute to vulnerability to antisocial behavior problems (Davies, Sturge-Apple, Cicchetti, & Cummings, 2007; van Goozen, Fairchild, Snoek, & Harold, 2007). Similarly, to manage fear, children may develop avoidant social cognitive strategies in the face of threat, leading to down regulation of the HPA axis, and reduced activation of the amygdala (Hill, Murray, Leidecker, & Sharp, 2008). The age-related effects of social defeat in Syrian hamsters, which lead to increased aggression before puberty but to exaggerated defeat after puberty, may thus provide an animal model for further exploring the neuro-physiology of developmentally determined differences in effects of social stressors.

## CONCLUSION

Whether or not studies of social defeat in Syrian hamsters can inform our understanding of mechanisms in humans depends on how we interpret them. It does not appear to be a good model for the long-term effects of social experiences on human biology and behavior; however, in Syrian hamsters social defeat may provide a model for studying the biological consequences of social stressors with application to humans. Similarly, social defeat does not appear to be a promising model for human psychopathology; however, studies of the biology of social defeat in Syrian hamsters may be useful in addressing questions posed by human studies of the neurobiology of psychopathology.

REFERENCES

Bjorkqvist, K. (2001). Social defeat as a stressor in humans. *Physiology & Behavavior*, 73, 435–442.
Blair, R. J. (2008). The amygdala and ventromedial prefrontal cortex: functional contributions and dysfunction in psychopathy. *Philosophical Transactions of the Royal Society of London. Series B, Biological Sciences*, 363, 2557–2565.
Bolton, D. & Hill, J. (2004). *Mind, meaning and mental disorder*. Oxford, UK: Oxford University Press.

Colvert, E., Rutter, M., Beckett, C., Castle, J., Groothues, C., Hawkins, A. et al. (2008). Emotional difficulties in early adolescence following severe early deprivation: findings from the English and Romanian adoptees study. *Developmental Psychopathology, 20,* 547–567.

Davies, P. T., Sturge-Apple, M. L., Cicchetti, D., & Cummings, E. M. (2007). The role of child adrenocortical functioning in pathways between interparental conflict and child maladjustment. *Developmental Psycholology, 43,* 918–930.

Davis, E. P., Glynn, L. M., Schetter, C. D., Hobel, C., Chicz-Demet, A., & Sandman, C. A. (2007). Prenatal exposure to maternal depression and cortisol influences infant temperament. *Journal of the American Academy of Child & Adolescent Psychiatry, 46,* 737–746.

Gilbert, P. (2006). Evolution and depression: issues and implications. *Psychological Medicine, 36,* 287–297.

Gilbert, P. & Allan, S. (1998). The role of defeat and entrapment (arrested flight) in depression: An exploration of an evolutionary view. *Psychological Medicine, 28,* 585–598.

Gilbert, P., Gilbert, J., & Irons, C. (2004). Life events, entrapments and arrested anger in depression. *Journal of Affective Disorders, 79,* 149–160.

Hill, J., Murray, L., Leidecker, V., & Sharp, H. (2008). The dynamics of threat, fear and intentionality in the conduct disorders: Longitudinal findings in the children of women with post-natal depression. *Philosophical Transactions of the Royal Society of London. Series B, Biological Sciences, 363*(1503), 2529–2541.

Hill, J., Pickles, A., Burnside, E., Byatt, M., Rollinson, L., Davis, R. et al. (2001). Child sexual abuse, poor parental care and adult depression: Evidence for different mechanisms. *British Journal of Psychiatry, 179,* 104–109.

Hodges, J. & Tizard, B. (1989). Social and family relationships of ex-institutional adolescents. *Journal of Child Psychology & Psychiatry, 30,* 77–97.

Huhman, K. L. (2006). Social conflict models: Can they inform us about human psychopathology? *Hormones & Behavior, 50,* 640–646.

Jaffee, S. R., Caspi, A., Moffitt, T. E., & Taylor, A. (2004). Physical maltreatment victim to antisocial child: Evidence of an environmentally mediated process. *Journal of Abnormal Psychology, 113,* 44–55.

Kendler, K. S., Thornton, L. M., & Gardner, C. O. (2001). Genetic risk, number of previous depressive episodes, and stressful life events in predicting onset of major depression. *American Journal of Psychiatry, 158,* 582–586.

Kim-Cohen, J., Caspi, A., Taylor, A., Williams, B., Newcombe, R., Craig, I. W. et al. (2006). MAOA, maltreatment, and gene-environment interaction predicting children's mental health: New evidence and a meta-analysis. *Molecular Psychiatry, 11,* 903–913.

Meaney, M. J., Szyf, M., & Seckl, J. R. (2007). Epigenetic mechanisms of perinatal programming of hypothalamic-pituitary-adrenal function and health. *Trends in Molecular Medicine, 13,* 269–277.

Meyer–Lindenberg, A., Buckholtz, J. W., Kolachana, B., Hariri, R., Pezawas, L., Blasi, G. et al. (2006). Neural mechanisms of genetic risk for impulsivity and violence in humans. *Proceedings of the National Academy of Sciences of the U.S.A, 103,* 6269–6274.

Nemeroff, C. B. (1998). The neurobiology of depression. *Scientific American, 278,* 42–49.

O'Connor, T. G., Heron, J., Golding, J., & Glover, V. (2003). Maternal antenatal anxiety and behavioural/emotional problems in children: A test of a programming hypothesis. *Journal of Child Psychology & Psychiatry, 44,* 1025–1036.

Phelps, E. A. & LeDoux, J. E. (2005). Contributions of the amygdala to emotion processing: from animal models to human behavior. *Neuron, 48,* 175–187.

Rosenblum, L. A., Forger, C., Noland, S., Trost, R. C., & Coplan, J. D. (2001). Response of adolescent bonnet macaques to an acute fear stimulus as a function of early rearing conditions. *Developmental Psychobiology, 39,* 40–45.

Sanchez, M. M., Ladd, C. O., & Plotsky, P. M. (2001). Early adverse experience as a developmental risk factor for later psychopathology: Evidence from rodent and primate models. *Developmental Psychopathology, 13,* 419–449.

Suomi, S. J. (2006). Risk, resilience, and gene x environment interactions in rhesus monkeys. *Annuals of the New York Academy of Sciences, 1094,* 52–62.

Tarullo, A. R. & Gunnar, M. R. (2006). Child maltreatment and the developing HPA axis. *Hormones and Behavior, 50,* 632–639.

van Goozen, S. H., Fairchild, G., Snoek, H., & Harold, G. T. (2007). The evidence for a neurobiological model of childhood antisocial behavior. *Psychological Bulletin, 133,* 149–182.

# Commentary

*Interpersonal Violence as a Mediator of Stress-Related Disorders in Humans*

Aaron M. Jasnow and Kerry J. Ressler

The chapter by Kim Huhman, "Social Stress as a Formative Experience: Neurobiology of Conditioned Defeat," is a very interesting description of conditioned defeat in Syrian hamsters as a model of understanding the neurobiology of social stress and its effects on stress-related disorders in humans. This commentary will describe recent data from a large sample of inner-city at-risk subjects who have experienced an enormous amount of inter-personal violence. We find that these traumatic experiences, both in adulthood and childhood, contribute greatly to adult posttraumatic stress disorder (PTSD) and depression. Furthermore, we will describe data suggesting that early unstable family environments in this population are a significant risk factor for these adult stress-related disorders, whereas nurturing caregiving appears to be protective. Finally, we refer to recent data that social support in adulthood appears to be a resiliency factor helping to mediate against the effects of child abuse on adult depression.

## IMPORTANCE OF INTERPERSONAL VIOLENCE AS A CRITICAL MEDIATOR OF STRESS-RELATED DISORDERS

Among civilians, inner-city minority populations appear to be exposed to extreme amounts of trauma (Breslau et al., 1998; Alim, Charney, & Mellman, 2006). For example, economically disadvantaged African Americans living within urban environments experience high levels of inter-personal violence and trauma (Breslau, Davis, Andreski, & Peterson, 1991;

Shakoor & Chalmers, 1991; Fitzpatrick & Boldizar, 1993; Breslau et al., 1998; Selner-O'Hagan, Kindlon, Buka, Raudenbush, & Earls, 1998). Furthermore, a large amount of this exposure occurs during youth (Shakoor et al., 1991; Fitzpatrick et al., 1993; Selner-O'Hagan et al., 1998). The clinical and biological consequences of trauma exposure and neglect during youth and adulthood are well documented and substantially elevate adult risk for mood and anxiety disorders (McCauley et al., 1997; Felitti et al., 1998; Dube et al., 2001; Chapman et al., 2004; Gladstone et al., 2004), as well as for suicide attempts (McCauley et al., 1997; Felitti et al. 1998), substance abuse (McCauley et al., 1997; Felitti et al., 1998), unintended first pregnancy (Dietz et al., 1999), systemic inflammation (Danese, Pariante, Caspi, Taylor, & Poulton, 2007), and a variety of medical illnesses. A graded relationship appears to exist between exposure to trauma and psychiatric/health morbidity in adulthood (McCauley et al., 1997; Felitti et al., 1998). From a sociological perspective, trauma-related psychopathology contributes to intergenerational patterns of violence (Fullilove et al., 1998; Byrne, Resnick, Kilpatrick, Best, & Saunders 1999; Abram et al., 2004; Schwartz, Bradley, Ressler, Sexton, & Sherry 2004; Schwartz, Bradley, Sexton, Sherry, & Ressler 2005), with the potential for psychiatric illness and medical illness in succeeding generations. This psychopathology constitutes a major public health problem.

## INNER CITY TRAUMA, INTERPERSONAL VIOLENCE, PTSD, AND DEPRESSION

In an ongoing study, we are examining the rates of trauma history and stress-related disorders in subjects who are patients in the general medical clinics, OB/Gyn clinics, and pharmacy waiting areas at Grady Memorial Hospital in Atlanta, one of the largest public charity hospitals in the United States. Grady serves a primarily indigent population which is >90% African American, and mostly from the inner-city. We have interviewed >1500 subjects to date, and we find remarkably high rates of trauma history. For example, approximately 50% of our subjects have a friend or family member who has been murdered, almost 2/3 of the men have been attacked with or without a weapon, and approximately 1/3 of the women have been sexually assaulted. Furthermore, rates of PTSD and depression in this population rival the rates of combat veterans, with over 25% of the subjects with lifetime PTSD and a similar high incidence of Major Depression.

**Table 17.1.** *Non–Child Abuse Trauma Exposure and PTSD Symptoms*

| Level of Non-Child Abuse Trauma[#] | N | PTSD Symptom Scale (PSS) Mean ± Sem | 95% Confidence Intervals |
|---|---|---|---|
| None | 159 | $3.58 \pm 0.50^{*,+}$ | 2.60 – 4.56 |
| 1 Type | 183 | $7.30 \pm 0.74^{\$,+}$ | 5.83 – 8.76 |
| 2–3 Types | 265 | $11.57 \pm 0.72^{+}$ | 10.16 – 12.98 |
| ≥ 4 Types | 215 | $16.74 \pm 0.88^{+}$ | 15.00 – 18.47 |

[#] Number of types of non-child abuse (primarily adult) trauma experienced,
[*] indicates $p < .005$ difference in PSS from 1 type of abuse
[\$] indicates $p < .005$ difference in PSS from no abuse
[+] indicates $p < .0001$ difference in PSS from other groups
Table from Binder, E. B., Bradley, R. G., Liu, W., Epstein, M. P., Deveau, T. C., Mercer, K. B., et al. (2008). Association of FKBP5 polymorphisms and childhood abuse with risk of posttraumatic stress disorder symptoms in adults. *Journal of the American Medical Association, 299*(11), 1291–305. Copyright © 2008, American Medical Association. All Rights Reserved.

## INTERACTION OF CHILDHOOD TRAUMA AND ADULT TRAUMA ON PTSD AND DEPRESSION

As shown in Table 17.1 (Binder et al., 2008), we find that a history of increasing adult trauma is associated with adult PTSD symptoms, measured with the PTSD symptom scale (PSS), and depressive symptoms, measured with the Beck Depression Inventory (BDI). Furthermore, as illustrated in Table 17.2, we find a very strong relationship between level of childhood trauma, measured with the Childhood Trauma Questionnaire, and these adult symptoms. Finally, we see a significant interaction between both childhood and adult symptoms. Interestingly, we find that among the strongest single predictors of stress-related disorders in adults is self-report of an "unstable" vs. a "stable" childhood, with unstable predicting significantly higher rates of adult PTSD and depressive symptoms. These data from our group, consistent with some of the data described above, suggests that in humans, early developmental as well as adult interpersonal trauma set the stage for significant stress-related psychopathology in adulthood.

## GENE x ENVIRONMENT INTERACTION TO PREDICT RISK FOR PTSD

In addition to trauma exposure, a number of other factors contribute to the risk for development of posttraumatic stress disorder (PTSD) in adulthood.

**Table 17.2.** *Child Abuse Trauma Exposure and PTSD Symptoms*

| Level of Non-Child Abuse Trauma[#] | N | PTSD Symptom Scale (PSS) Mean ± Sem | 95% Confidence Intervals |
|---|---|---|---|
| No Child Abuse | 566 | $8.03 \pm 0.44$[*] | $7.17 - 8.90$ |
| 1 Type of Child Abuse | 189 | $14.65 \pm 0.87$[$] | $12.94 - 16.36$ |
| 2 Types of Child Abuse | 54 | $20.93 \pm 1.95$[+] | $17.02 - 24.84$ |

[*] indicates $p < .000001$ difference in PSS from other groups
[$] indicates $p < .000001$ and $p < .0005$ difference in PSS from no abuse and 2 types, respectively
[+] indicates $p < .000001$ and $p < .0005$ difference in PSS from no abuse and 1 type, respectively
*Table from Binder et al., JAMA, 2008.*

Both genetic and environmental factors are contributory, with the genetic heritability for PTSD ranging from 30%–40%, and early life stress, such as child abuse, also providing significant risk liability. We predicted that a gene involved in regulating the HPA stress-axis, *FKBP5* (a co-chaperone that regulates the glucocorticoid receptor) would be involved in PTSD. Thus gene x environment interactions of child abuse, level of non-child abuse trauma exposure, and genetic polymorphisms at the stress-related gene, *FKBP5*, were examined to predict the level of adult PTSD symptomatology (Binder et al., 2008).

This cross-sectional study examined genetic and psychological risk factors using a verbally-presented survey, combined with SNP genotyping, in a randomly chosen sample of non-psychiatric clinic patients. Similar to the participants previously described, these participants were primarily low-income, African American (>95%), men and women who were seeking care in the general medical care and obstetrics-gynecology clinics of an urban public hospital. We found that this population had experienced significant levels of childhood abuse as well as non-child abuse trauma. A total of 900 participants were included in the overall analyses, and 762 participants were included for all genotype studies. The primary outcome measure was the severity of adult PTSD symptomatology, as measured with the modified PTSD Symptom Scale (mPSS). Independent factors included in the analyses were non-child abuse (primarily adult) trauma exposure and child abuse measured using the traumatic events inventory (TEI) and eight single nucleotide polymorphisms (SNPs) spanning the *FKBP5* locus.

Although *FKBP5* SNPs did not directly predict PTSD outcome, or interact with level of non-child abuse trauma to predict PTSD, 4 SNPs in the *FKBP5* locus significantly interacted (minimum $p = 0.0004$) with the

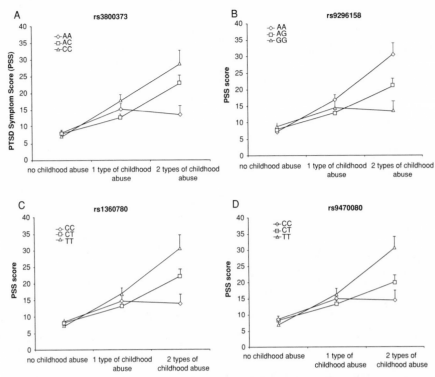

**Figure 17.2.** Polymorphisms within the FKBP5 gene differentially moderate effects of child abuse on adult PTSD. The graphs illustrate the additive effects of child abuse on PTSD symptoms (PSS score), as a function of extent of child abuse and polymorphism at four different FKBP5 single nucleotide polymorphisms (rs3800373, rs9296158, rs1370780, and rs9470080), an additive interaction effect with child abuse on PSS score was observed. Thus the effect of increasing child abuse on level of adult PTSD appears to be carried by a subset of FKBP5 alleles, whereas a group of slightly rarer alleles does not exhibit this additive effect.

severity of child abuse to predict the level of adult PTSD after correcting for multiple testing (Figure 17.2). This gene × environment interaction remained significant when controlling for depression severity scores, age, gender, levels of non-child abuse trauma exposure, and genetic ancestry. This genetic interaction was also paralleled by *FKBP5* genotype- and PTSD-dependent effects on glucocorticoid receptor sensitivity as measured by the dexamethasone suppression test.

These data demonstrate that genes involved in the early development of HPA axis regulation may be critically involved in setting the stage for later psychopathology or resilience, depending on the level of social stress experienced early during development.

## MODERATION OF THESE FACTORS BY SOCIAL SUPPORT

Stice, Ragan, and Randall (2004) explored the relationship between social support and depression in adolescent females, and found a reciprocal relationship between social support and depression. Maher, Mora, and Leventhal (2006) also found a significant bidirectional relationship between perceived social support and depression among an older adult sample. When we examined the effects of perceived social support on adult stress-related symptoms, using the social support behaviors scale (SSBS) within the same population described above, we found a very significant interaction. We found that perceived social support of friendships significantly protected against risk for adult depressive symptoms (p < .01) even after accounting for the variance due to childhood emotional abuse and neglect. These data suggest that supportive friendships can be protective against adult stress-related psychopathology despite significant risks in adulthood from childhood maltreatment and interpersonal violence.

## SOCIAL DEFEAT AS A MODEL OF INTERPERSONAL VIOLENCE

We have presented the above data as part of this commentary to emphasize the importance of interpersonal violence during childhood and adulthood in mediating psychopathology. The model of social defeat described by Kim Huhman appears to be an extremely useful model with tremendous face validity to understanding the development of psychopathology, particularly PTSD in humans. Furthermore, the ability to manipulate the neurobiological underpinnings of social defeat will further allow us to develop potential therapeutic interventions and methods of detection and prevention.

Using a model of social defeat as a basis for understanding the neurobiological underpinnings of stress-related neuropsychiatric disorders involving interpersonal violence has several advantages. First, and most obvious, the nature of the traumatic event precipitating the development of conditioned defeat and PTSD are similar. Both are based on social conflict between individuals, which is one of the most pervasive forms of stress experienced by many animal species, including humans. Second, both result in emotional and behavioral effects that persist over a long period of time and may be resistant to extinction. Third, both can result in generalization of fear responses. Thus, social defeat in rodents may provide appropriate models of interpersonal violence in humans and help us uncover genetic and environmental contributions to the development of stress-related psychopathology.

## RODENT MODELS OF DEVELOPMENTAL CRITICAL PERIODS

As described before and illustrated in Table 17.2, there is a very strong relationship between the level of childhood trauma and symptoms of PTSD and depression as an adult. Specifically, an "unstable" childhood very strongly predicts adult PTSD and depressive symptoms. Thus, early developmental interpersonal trauma has a significant "sensitization" effect on stress-related psychopathology in adulthood. How do models of social defeat in hamsters and other rodents address the issue of childhood trauma influence on adult PTSD and depressive symptoms? As described in the chapter by Kim Huhman, hamsters that are repeatedly defeated as juveniles, at a time when they are acquiring appropriate social interactions, became highly aggressive as adults. Although these data suggest that traumatic experiences during critical developmental periods result in abnormal adult social behavior, little is known about how similar juvenile experience alters emotional behavior in adult rodents and how this might relate to adult risk for PTSD and depression in humans. Some evidence on critical developmental periods comes from the work of Regina Sullivan and colleagues (Moriceau & Sullivan, 2006; Moriceau, Wilson, Levine, & Sullivan, 2006; see also Wiedenmayer, this volume). These data demonstrate that there is a critical period during which a developmental "switch" occurs regulated by the stress hormone, corticosterone, where the response to an aversive stimulus switches from attraction to aversion. Because maternal care modulates corticosterone in the pups, alterations in maternal care may affect the development of fear responses during sensitive critical periods (Moriceau & Sullivan, 2006; Moriceau et al., 2006). This finding may be relevant to the "unstable" versus "stable" childhood as a prediction of adult PTSD, suggesting that an "unstable" childhood may result in a "shift" to a dysregulated neuroendocrine system in adult life.

## BRAIN REGIONS INVOLVED IN CONDITIONED DEFEAT AND PTSD

Several brain regions are thought to be involved in the development of stress-related neuropsychiatric disorders in humans. These include the amygdala, hippocampus, the hypothalamus (HPA-axis), and the medial prefrontal cortex (mPFC). The amygdala is critical for the generation of emotional behavior and the formation of emotional memories. Extensive studies have shown that the lateral and basolateral amygdala in rodents play an important role in the acquisition and expression of conditioned fear. Moreover, recent functional imaging studies in humans suggest that increased activity of the amygdala plays a critical role in the etiology of several psychiatric disorders. As described in the chapter by Kim Huhman, the amygdala plays a critical role in regulating behavioral responses to social defeat, as it does in conditioned fear. Consistent with the data on rodent fear conditioning, studies of PTSD have demonstrated increased activation of the amygdala compared to controls in response to threatening stimuli (Rauch et al., 2000; Protopopescu et al., 2005). The data on amygdala and fear conditioning in rodents and PTSD clearly demonstrates the importance of this region in stress-related neuropsychiatric disorders and provides face validity to social defeat as a model of interpersonal violence. The hippocampus has been a brain region of interest in PTSD because of its involvement in memory and its susceptibility to alteration by the neuroendocrine stress response. Several studies have shown decreased hippocampal volumes in PTSD (Rauch, Shin, & Phelps 2006); however, it has been difficult to determine whether this decrease results from glucocorticoid toxicity, as has been demonstrated in rodent models, or represents a preexisting condition for increased vulnerability to PTSD. Likewise, hippocampal atrophy and/or neuron loss is associated with major depression that may also be a result of neurotoxicity (Sheline, 1996). Stress, which often precipitates the onset of depression in humans, causes cell death, dendritic atrophy, and decreased hippocampal neurogenesis (Gould, Tanapat, McEwen, Flugge, & Fuchs 1998; McEwen, 2008). Moreover, antidepressant treatment increases adult hippocampal neurogenesis, a process that is necessary for the behavioral effects of antidepressants on measures of depression in mice (Malberg, Eisch, Nestler, & Duman, 2000; Santarelli et al., 2003). These data suggest that adult hippocampal neurogenesis may be involved in the etiology and treatment of several neuropsychiatric disorders.

One physiological marker of PTSD that will be particularly difficult to model using rodent social defeat and other stress models is dysregulation of HPA-axis function. Baseline cortisol levels in some studies of PTSD are significantly lower than controls. In addition, PTSD is associated with enhanced cortisol feedback (reviewed in Yehuda & LeDoux, 2007). This finding contrasts starkly with rodent models of chronic stress, social stress, and observations in depressed patients, in which elevated levels of corticosterone/cortisol and a blunted glucocorticoid negative feedback are observed. In this sense, social defeat in rodents seems to be well suited to model depression and several, but not all, symptoms of PTSD.

PTSD and many other fear-related disorders can be thought of as disorders of the process of extinction. Repeated exposure to conditioned stimuli in the absence of the associated unconditioned stimuli results in extinction of the fear response. This active learning process involves the mPFC, which is thought to inhibit the amygdala during the extinction process. Damage to this area in rodents impairs extinction, and evidence in humans suggests that dysfunction of this area is associated with PTSD (Yehuda & LeDoux, 2007). Currently, the role of the mPFC in regulating conditioned defeat in rodents is unknown; however, these data suggest that an overactive amygdala and an underactive mPFC is associated with prolonged responses to traumatic events and PTSD.

## CONCLUSION

In summary, interpersonal violence during development and adulthood is a significant mediating factor in the development of psychopathology in humans. Social defeat in rodents, in particular conditioned defeat, is well suited to model interpersonal violence in humans. Providing an ethologically relevant traumatic event that can be manipulated will undoubtedly lead to a greater understanding of how genetic factors and environmental experience interact to alter basic brain function and ultimately emotional behavior. The convergent data from these different approaches will allow a clearer understanding of how interpersonal violence leads to stress-related psychiatric disorders in humans, and provide insight into the development of novel therapeutic interventions.

## ACKNOWLEDGMENTS

Support was provided by NIH (MH071537 and DA019624), the Center for Behavioral Neuroscience (NSF agreement IBN-9876754), Burroughs Wellcome Fund, and by an NIH/NCRR base grant (P51RR000165) to Yerkes National Primate Research Center.

REFERENCES

Abram, K. M., Teplin, L. A., Charles, D. R., Longworth, S. L., McClelland, G. M., & Dulcan, M. K. (2004). Posttraumatic stress disorder and trauma in youth in juvenile detention. *Archives of General Psychiatry, 61*(4), 403–410.

Alim, T. N., Charney, D. S., & Mellman, T. A. (2006). An overview of posttraumatic stress disorder in African Americans. *Journal of Clinical Psychology, 62*(7), 801–813.

Binder, E. B., Bradley, R. G., Liu, W., Epstein, M. P., Deveau, T. C., Mercer, K. B., et al. (2008). Association of FKBP5 polymorphisms and childhood abuse with risk of posttraumatic stress disorder symptoms in adults. *Journal of the American Medical Association, 299*(11), 1291–305.

Breslau, N., Davis, G. C., Andreski, P., & Peterson, E. (1991). Traumatic events and posttraumatic stress disorder in an urban population of young adults. *Archives of General Psychiatry, 48*(3), 216–222.

Breslau, N., Kessler, R. C., Chilcoat, H. D., Schultz, L. R., Davis, G. C., & Andreski, P. (1998). Trauma and posttraumatic stress disorder in the community: The 1996 Detroit Area Survey of Trauma. *Archives of General Psychiatry, 55*(7), 626–632.

Byrne, C. A., Resnick, H. S., Kilpatrick, D. G., Best, C. L., & Saunders, B. E. (1999). The socioeconomic impact of interpersonal violence on women. *Journal of Consulting and Clinical Psychology, 67*(3), 362–366.

Chapman, D. P., Whitfield, C. L., Felitti, V. J., Dube, S. R., Edwards, J., & Anda, R. F. (2004). Adverse childhood experiences and the risk of depressive disorders in adulthood. *Journal of Affective Disorders, 82*(2), 217–225.

Danese, A., Pariante, C. M., Caspi, A., Taylor, A., & Poulton, R. (2007). Childhood maltreatment predicts adult inflammation in a life-course study. *Proceedings of the National Academy of Sciences of the United States of America, 104*(4), 1319–1324.

Dietz, P. M., Spitz, A. M., Anda, R. F., Williamson, D. F., McMahon, P. M., Santelli, J. S., et al. (1999). Unintended pregnancy among adult women exposed to abuse or household dysfunction during their childhood. *Journal of the American Medical Association, 282*(14), 1359–1364.

Dube, S. R., Anda, R. F., Felitti, V. J., Chapman, D. P., Williamson, D. F., & Giles, W. H. (2001). Childhood abuse, household dysfunction, and the risk of attempted suicide throughout the life span: Findings from the adverse childhood experiences study. *Journal of the American Medical Association, 286*(24), 3089–3096.

Felitti, V. J., R. F. Anda, R. F., Nordenberg, D., Williamson, D. F., Spitz, A. M., Edwards, V., et al. (1998). Relationship of childhood abuse and household dysfunction to many of the leading causes of death in adults. The Adverse Childhood Experiences (ACE) Study. *American Journal of Preventive Medicine, 14*(4), 245–258.

Fitzpatrick, K. M., & Boldizar, J. P. (1993). The prevalence and consequences of exposure to violence among African-American youth. *Journal of the American Academy of Child & Adolescent Psychiatry, 32*(2), 424–430.

Fullilove, M. T., Héon, V., Jimenez, W., Parsons, C., Green, L. L., & Fullilove, R. E. (1998). Injury and anomie: Effects of violence on an inner-city community. *American Journal of Public Health, 88*(6), 924–927.

Gladstone, G. L., Parker, G. B., Mitchell, P. B., Malhi, G. S., Wilhelm, K., & Austin, M. P. (2004). Implications of childhood trauma for depressed women: An analysis of pathways from childhood sexual abuse to deliberate self-harm and revictimization. *American Journal of Psychiatry, 161*(8), 1417–1425.

Gould, E., Tanapat, P., McEwen, B. S., Flugge, G., & Fuchs, E. (1998). Proliferation of granule cell precursors in the dentate gyrus of adult monkeys is diminished by stress. *Proceedings of the National Academy of Sciences of the United States of America, 95*(6), 3168–3171.

Maher, M., Mora, P. A., & Leventhal, H. (2006). Depression as a predictor of perceived social support and demand: A componential approach using a prospective sample of older adults. *Emotion, 6*(3), 450–458.

Malberg, J. E., Eisch, A. J., Nestler, E. J., & Duman, R. S. (2000). Chronic antidepressant treatment increases neurogenesis in adult rat hippocampus. *Journal of Neuroscience, 20*(24), 9104–9110.

McCauley, J., Kern, D. E., Kolodner, K., Dill, L., Schroeder, A. F., DeChant, H. K., Ryden, J., et al. (1997). Clinical characteristics of women with a history of childhood abuse: Unhealed wounds. *Journal of the American Medical Association, 277*(17), 1362–1368.

McEwen, B. S. (2008). Central effects of stress hormones in health and disease: Understanding the protective and damaging effects of stress and stress mediators. *European Journal of Pharmacology, 583*(2–3), 174–185.

Moriceau, S., & Sullivan, R. M. (2006). Maternal presence serves as a switch between learning fear and attraction in infancy. *Nature Neuroscience, 9*(8), 1004–1006.

Moriceau, S., Wilson, D. A., Levine, S., & Sullivan, R. M. (2006). Dual circuitry for odor-shock conditioning during infancy: Corticosterone switches between fear and attraction via amygdala. *Journal of Neuroscience, 26*(25), 6737–6748.

Protopopescu, X., Pan, H., Tuescher, O., Cloitre, M., Goldstein, M., Engelien, W., et al. (2005). Differential time courses and specificity of amygdala activity in posttraumatic stress disorder subjects and normal control subjects. *Biological Psychiatry, 57*(5), 464–473.

Rauch, S. L., Shin, L. M., & Phelps, E. A. (2006). Neurocircuitry models of posttraumatic stress disorder and extinction: Human neuroimaging research – past, present, and future. *Biological Psychiatry, 60*(4), 376–382.

Rauch, S. L., Whalen, P. J., Shin, L. M., McInerney, S. C., Macklin, M. L., Lasko, N. B., et al. (2000). Exaggerated amygdala response to masked facial stimuli in posttraumatic stress disorder: A functional MRI study. *Biological Psychiatry, 47*(9), 769–776.

Santarelli, L., Saxe, M., Gross, C., Surget, A., Battaglia, F., Dulawa, S. (2003). Requirement of hippocampal neurogenesis for the behavioral effects of antidepressants. *Science, 301*(5634), 805–809.

Schwartz, A., Bradley, R., Ressler, K., Sexton, M., & Sherry, A. (2004). Treating posttraumatic stress disorder in urban African American mental health patients. *Journal of the American Psychoanalitic Association, 52*(2), 464–465.

Schwartz, A. C., Bradley, R. L., Sexton, M., Sherry, A., & Ressler, K. J. (2005). Posttraumatic stress disorder among African Americans in an inner city mental health clinic. *Psychiatric Services, 56*(2), 212–215.

Selner-O'Hagan, M. B., Kindlon, D. J., Buka, S. L., Raudenbush, S. W., & Earls, F. J. (1998). Assessing exposure to violence in urban youth. *Journal of Child Psychology and Psychiatry and Allied Disciplines, 39*(2), 215–224.

Shakoor, B. H., & Chalmers, D. (1991). Co-victimization of African-American children who witness violence: Effects on cognitive, emotional, and behavioral development. *Journal of the National Medical Association, 83*(3), 233–238.

Sheline, Y. I. (1996). Hippocampal atrophy in major depression: A result of depression-induced neurotoxicity? *Molecular Psychiatry, 1*(4), 298–299.

Stice, E., Ragan, J., & Randall, P. (2004). Prospective relations between social support and depression: Differential direction of effects for parent and peer support? *Journal of Abnormal Psychology, 113*, 155–159.

Yehuda, R., & LeDoux, J. (2007). Response variation following trauma: A translational neuroscience approach to understanding PTSD. *Neuron, 56*(1), 19–32.

# Commentary on

## "Social Stress as a Formative Experience: Neurobiology of Conditioned Defeat"

## James Wilce

For several years, Huhman has been wrestling with the problems of social stress, and especially social defeat, as a stressor. These studies have all used Syrian hamsters. We can appreciate her motives in using these animals over others, particularly her desire to cause fewer injuries and therefore the methods she uses to induce aggression, particularly the fact that the sort of aggression she induces in them leads to few physical injuries.

Huhman's is one of several chapters in this volume that approaches developmental psychobiology from the perspective of animal behavioral physiology. Huhman uniquely focuses on hormones and brain structure and function, exploring possible homologies between the sort of stress response experimentally induced in hamsters and human stress response. This homology rests, *inter alia*, on the fact that both humans and hamsters "produce spontaneous aggressive behavior," regardless of sex. Both learn. Both are subject to *conditioning*. That is to say that both overreact as it were – developing responses that relate somehow to innate potentials (evolutionary heritage) yet are too intense, last too long, or continue to arise in environments that differ significantly from those in which the response was appropriately learned.

Huhman's work builds on studies like Björkquist's (2001), which have encouraged on the one hand social psychologists (regarding humans) and on the other biologists and physiological psychologists (regarding other animals) to develop shared models of "social defeat." Björkquist proposes that social psychologists, whose convention it is to speak of "bullies" and "victims," should be able to communicate with ethologists, whose convention it is to label animals "dominant" and "subordinate." As a student of semiotics and discourse, I am interested not in what these two sets of terms have in common, but in the separate realities they conjure. To speak of bullies and victims situates action in a *moral* framework, which does not apply to talk of subordination and dominance. This points to problems that arise, as well, when sociocultural or linguistic anthropologists encounter this essay or Huhman's earlier work on social defeat – *among fish*. Claims that anthropologists can learn anything important from the psychobiology of fish, hamsters, or monkeys will provoke laughter in certain circles.

Such laughter, if it implies that studies of social defeat are irrelevant to sociocultural anthropology, would be inappropriate. True, Huhman's model, as presented, is unnecessarily reductionist; the homology between hamsters and humans could have been explored in more detail, rather than being mostly assumed. Yet it turns out that there are rich connections to be made between Huhman's contribution and exciting new work not only in anthropology, but more broadly in the social sciences.

To illustrate, let me start with a recent attempt, certainly not the first, to explain a finding that refuses to go away despite many apparently "promising" critiques – evidence (Hopper, Harrison, Aleksandar, & Sartorius, 2007; Jablensky & Sartorius, 2008) that persons with schizophrenia fare better in "developing" than in "developed" countries. What might be relevant dimensions of the difference between these environments? What might studies of social defeat have to say to this question?

Luhrmann (2007), an anthropologist, invokes the social defeat model to explain why schizophrenia in a developed country such as the United States is particularly likely to be chronic, whereas many individuals diagnosed with schizophrenia in India, for example, have been symptom-free in follow-up contacts, decades after enrollment in the WHO studies that Hopper et al. (2007) review. But the biological model of social defeat needs a bit of translating if it is to be of use to most anthropologists. As Luhrmann puts it, "Sociocultural anthropologists do not typically ground their work in biopsychological models, nor, I suggest, is this model [this grounding] necessary to develop an ethnographic account of social defeat. (The data are at such different levels of analysis.)" (2007, pp. 143–144). What Luhrmann retains as crucial, however, is the focus on individuals experiencing loss in particular (agonistic) encounters with others. Such losses occur not once but repeatedly, even daily, in the lives of one group of persons in the United States in particular – homeless women diagnosed with schizophrenia.

In trying out the social defeat model for schizophrenia, Luhrmann draws inspiration from Selten and Cantor-Graae, who first proposed the link. They hypothesize that "a chronic and long-term experience of social defeat may lead to sensitisation of the mesolimbic dopamine system (and/or to increased baseline activity of this system) and thereby increase the risk for schizophrenia" (2005, p. 101).

To the work on social defeat, Luhrmann adds what sociocultural anthropologists consider fundamental for the understanding of human conduct – an *ethnographic* perspective. Ethnographic fieldwork aims at "an understanding of the ways in which the individual is embedded in social and cultural systems of meaning and practice" (Kirmayer, Lemelson, & Barad, 2007, p. 480). The ethnographer's concern with meaning – situated, sociocultural, richly contextualized meaning – contrasts with the focus of a laboratory scientist like Huhman, who "does everything possible to control the context in order to throw into relief the effect of the experimental manipulation under study. Indeed, for many neuroscientists the concept of 'meaning' is a vague generality that can be replaced by more precise notions of cause and effect in neural systems interacting with an environment" (Kirmayer et al., 2007, p. 480). The question of how to integrate ethnographic and neurobiological data remains.

The amygdala, Huhman demonstrates, can "store" fear-based learning. Anthropologists and sympathizers – including Kirmayer et al. (2007) – recognize the neurological transformations associated with human *trauma*, the subject of their edited collection. But they argue, "*multiple levels of description* [italics added], or disciplinary languages, are needed to encompass the complexity of the phenomena of trauma and healing" (2007, p. 485). Ultimately, meaning – socially distributed, contextually grounded, and symbolically mediated – cannot be ignored in relation to human emotions like fear. Thus no one-to-one mapping of Huhman's results onto a human population will be possible.

Still, rather than despairing over the gap between the laboratory-oriented disciplines of physiological psychology and neuroscience and sociocultural anthropology, let us consider more carefully what "social stress," "social defeat," "fear," and "learning" might mean in a potential collaboration among practitioners of these three disciplines.

The current volume aims at a cross-disciplinary synthesis. It is important, however, to acknowledge the very necessary differences between the objects and methods of study that characterize the collected disciplines. A crucial though seldom recognized distinction is between studies of "behavior" and studies of "action." There are 73 tokens of the word "behavior" and related forms in Huhman's chapter; *interact-* appears thrice (never in relation to two beings interacting), and "act" not at all. As a point of contrast, conversation analyst Charles Goodwin's (2003) article, "Pointing as situated practice," includes 163 tokens of "act" and its derivatives (action, interaction), and not a single token of *behav-* apart from one bibliographic source. What is the difference, how are the two terms used, and why does the choice matter?

Edwin Ardener (1989; compare Farnell, 1994) problematizes the widespread use of "behavior" in social anthropology, tracing the term back to fifteenth-century borrowings from French into English. In its first uses (in elitist discourse about appropriate comportment), the term was marked as "good"; that is, the mere mention of "behavior" already evinced "refinement." By the 1850s, chemists began using the word, but – as Ardener argues – with the awareness that this was a derivative, metaphorical use. It was in that context, however, that "behavior" took on its objectivist sense, so that soon, the extended use became the unmarked use. "Behavior" retains its usefulness in the natural sciences, but the word has never been useful in discussing, for example, how human communities understand their own actions. There is something fundamentally inappropriate about using a single term for chemical processes; animals' activities; and the highly reflected-upon, evaluated, and symbolically classified *actions* of human beings and groups. If animal scientists and sociocultural anthropologists are to have an open and equal exchange, "behavior" cannot define the discourse.

We must also raise a related cross-disciplinary translation issue in relation to "social" and thus to "social stress" and "social defeat." What could enable us to adequately translate, and not simply impose, a notion like "social defeat" vis-à-vis human beings and their social groups and structures (peer groups, families and larger kin groups, communities, institutions, societies, nation-states, and transnational structures)? What is it about the complexities of human sociality, culture, political economies, and various forms of social structure that is most relevant to this translation project? What do anthropologists have to say about emotion and biology in relation to these layers of social complexity?

Let us return to Huhman's work, and specifically to her title. What do we mean by *conditioning*, as in "conditioned defeat," with respect to human social actors? For rats *and* humans, conditioning occurs in *social* environments and hinges on *expectation*, an *emotional* phenomenon. "Conditioning . . . habit . . . mimesis, and emotional contagion" are *embodied socioemotional* phenomena (Lyon, 2003, p. 82). To say that humans are subject to conditioning, or even that large swaths of human social behavior may be conditioned, is to say our learning has dimensions that are just as embodied as is conditioning involving animals. Like them, we are not aware of conditioning or of conditioned responses. Still, human conditioning surely interacts with forms of social learning that are more conscious, mediated by human sign systems including language. Humans may well experience *conditioned defeat*; but in exploring that possibility we must recognize the nontrivial relationship between experience, including unconscious bodily experiences and expectations, and culture as a system of socially produced and circulated *categories* of experience, *inter alia*, that may themselves shape experience itself, as Boas and his students argued (see Parmentier & Sebeok's [1997] insightful discussion).

As Ardener (1989, p. 107) puts it, "Once we enter the human zone, we are dealing with *classes* of action. Unfortunately we [ethnographers] are not the main classifiers. That position is occupied by the human beings who are acting." What is true of "classes of action" applies also to *inter*actions, events, objects, ideas, etc. A "social defeat," for people, cannot be a "natural kind" in the philosophical sense. The fact that we classify – and far more than that, we endlessly talk about, or avoid talking about (in very marked ways), and make up rituals to address – "defeats," "victories," events of "harmonious" or "conflictual" interaction, etc., means that "social defeats" among humans must be what philosopher Ian Hacking (1999) labels *interactive kinds*. Oranges care not what we call them. But labels like "schizophrenia" and "defeat(ed)" matter profoundly to people associated with them, and they act differently in response to what they are called. Thus objectivist approaches to phenomena such as social defeat fail in relation to human beings – not because findings from research with animals are a priori irrelevant, but because people squirm and wriggle and work themselves out from beneath analytic labels, and their meaning-making process relating to even objective (and objectifying) violence is dynamic.

What then of affects like *shame, humiliation, pride, fear,* or *anger,* all of which might accompany human social defeat? Human subjectivity does indeed reflect our biological heritage, as does human sociality. In addition to being related somehow to what is going on when a dog hangs its head, human shame is in a number of different senses a *social* emotion. It is elicited in and focused on social situations; various versions of it are socially constructed, given particular meaning in a particular community; and it contributes to the human social order, especially (but variably) in the many communities where shame is a virtue. Shame, as an affect subject to a high degree of reflexive attention and ideological influence, must be viewed as a co-creation of brain, embodiment in the fullest sense, social structure, and cultural meaning. Thus the stakes for human individuals and groups differ from the stakes for other species. Shame on the scale of peoples, nations, and even larger segments of the total human population has led, and will continue to lead, to spirals of violence.

Many sorts of shame attach themselves to key indexes of the social self – a community's language (Wilce, 2009) or "traditional expressive forms" such as loud wailing with words, i.e., lament (Wilce, 2008). These forms of shame play important roles in the unfolding histories of action and evaluation that define the local-global nexus of cultural production. Thus, scholars have begun to examine the affective correlates of social defeat – shame-humiliation, fear, and anger – on a global scale. Saurrette (2006), writing from the perspective of international relations, argues that only by examining the dynamics of humiliation can we understand "post-9/11 global politics." Scheff (1994), a sociologist, has long warned of the intractability of cycles of humiliation and revenge. Anyone familiar with Al-Qaeda knows the centrality of past defeats and humiliations in its motivations.

We could look at the study of human hormonal responses to defeat as either a very useful beginning, or a dangerous reduction. We could assert the need for careful investigations of the psychoneuroimmunology of human social defeat, or we could warn that reducing what is at stake in defeat and humiliation to individual biology trivializes the human condition and diverts much needed attention from racism, violence, and war.

If psychiatry, currently obsessed with pharmacotherapy, begins to seriously attend to social risk factors for schizophrenia – including the role of social defeat in "sensitisation of the mesolimbic dopamine system" (Selten & Cantor-Graee, 2005, p. 101) – that may signal its nascent "resocialization," the renewal of its dialogue with social sciences (Sapir, 1932/1949). On the other hand, the sorts of macrosocial issues that I have mentioned here, such as cycles of violence driven to some extent by social defeat and accompanying shame (for which there is no pharmacotherapy), demand our attention. They threaten our very existence. Whatever may be the value of fine-grained ethnographic studies (of *personal* shame, for example), or of locating the "seat" of conditioned social defeat in the brains of individuals, we must not lose sight of the larger stakes.

REFERENCES

Ardener, E. (1989). 'Behaviour': A social anthropological criticism. In M. Chapman (Ed.), *Edwin Ardener: The voice of prophecy and other essays* (pp. 105–108). Oxford, UK: Blackwell.
Björkquist, K. (2001). Social defeat as a stressor in humans. *Physiology and Behavior*, 73(3), 435–442.

Farnell, B. M. (1994). Ethno-graphics and the moving body. *Man*, 29(4), 929–974.

Goodwin, C. (2003). Pointing as situated practice. In S. Kita (Ed.), *Pointing: Where language, culture and cognition meet* (pp. 217–241). Mahwah, NJ: Lawrence Erlbaum.

Hacking, I. (1999). *The social construction of what?* Cambridge, MA: Harvard University Press.

Hopper, K., Harrison, G., Aleksandar, J., & Sartorius, A. (2007). *Recovery from schizophrenia: An international perspective: A report from the WHO Collaborative Project, the international study of schizophrenia.* New York: Oxford University Press.

Jablensky, A., & Sartorius, N. (2008). What did the WHO studies really find? *Schizophrenia Bulletin*, 34(2), 253–255.

Kirmayer, L. J., Lemelson, R., & Barad, M. (2007). Epilogue: Trauma and the vicissitudes of interdisciplinary integration. In L. J. Kirmayer, R. Lemelson & M. Barad (Eds.), *Understanding trauma: Integrating biological, clinical, and cultural perspectives* (pp. 475–489). New York: Cambridge University Press.

Luhrmann, T. (2007). Social defeat and the culture of chronicity: or, why schizophrenia does so well over there and so badly here. *Culture, Medicine & Psychiatry*, 31(2), 135–172.

Lyon, M. (2003). "Immune" to emotion: The relative absence of emotion in PNI, and its centrality to everything else. In J. M. Wilce (Ed.), *Social and cultural lives of immune systems* (pp. 81–101). London: Routledge.

Parmentier, R., & Sebeok, T. (1997). The pragmatic semiotics of cultures. *Semiotica*, 116(1 Monograph issue), 1–115.

Sapir, E. (1949). Cultural anthropology and psychiatry. In D. G. Mandelbaum (Ed.), *Selected writings in language, culture, and personality* (pp. 509–521). Berkeley: University of California Press. (Original work published 1932)

Saurette, P. (2006). You dissin me? Humiliation and post 9/11 global politics. *Review of International Studies*, 32(3), 495–522.

Scheff, T. (1994). *Bloody revenge: Emotions, nationalism, and war.* Boulder, CO: Westview.

Selten, J.-P., & Cantor-Graae, E. (2005). Social defeat: Risk factor for schizophrenia. *British Journal of Psychiatry 187*, 101–102.

Wilce, J. M. (2008). *Crying shame: Metaculture, modernity, and the exaggerated death of the lament.* Malden, MA: Wiley-Blackwell.

Wilce, J. M. (2009). *Language and emotion.* Cambridge, UK: Cambridge University Press.

# EIGHTEEN

# The Basic Affective Circuits of Mammalian Brains

*Implications for Healthy Human Development and the Cultural Landscapes of ADHD*

Jaak Panksepp

## INTRODUCTION TO THE SCIENCE OF THE AFFECTIVE MIND

The first half of this essay summarizes the evidence-based affective neu-roscience view of primary-process emotional systems in the mammalian brain, a basic plan of that brain (Panksepp, 1998, 2005a). The second half focuses on the psychological complexities that emerge when this plan, so similar in all animals, interacts with the relatively *blank slate* of the brain-mind's higher regions that need to be epigenetically created through developmental landscapes that vary dramatically among individuals and cultures. I will focus on this complexity through a single topic, gravid with cultural implications: namely, the possibility that our current epidemic of attention deficit hyperactivity disorders (ADHD), perhaps autism too, is being precipitated as much by cultural factors as any intrinsic genetically determined biological flaws. The thesis, already evaluated in animal mod-els, is that our children may no longer get adequate amounts of natural physical-social play – play of their own choosing. Instead, their lives are excessively regimented by adult-guided activities. Such cultural changes, along with diminishing high quality interpersonal interactions with loving adults and peers, often replaced by a deluge of electronic "care-takers" and "companions" (TV, videogames, internet, and cell-phones), are not ideally suited for the epigenetic construction of deeply pro-social brains and minds.

The diminished ability of children to obtain neuro-developmental boosts from abundant self-initiated playful social-interchange with peers – a basic social and cultural meaning-making brain mechanism – may become manifest as impulse control problems. Such problems may emerge in classrooms where children are surrounded by potential playmates but have little opportunity to play – to engage robustly and joyously with each other. Indeed, modern social structures often discourage primal primate engagements – especially rough-and-tumble physical play. In animal models, psychostimulants used to treat our increasingly impulsive children are remarkably effective play-reducing agents (Panksepp, Burgdorf, Gordon, & Turner, 2002), and this may be one reason they are so effective in classroom management. To some extent, medical treatment of childhood impulsivity, much of it within the normal range, is a vast social "experiment." We are medicating increasing numbers of children with powerful psychostimulants before anyone has adequately evaluated the long-term consequences of such practices on brain and psychological development, even in animal models. Some percentage of the problem might result from depriving children of the neural consequences of the natural play that may assist the maturation of higher social-brain structures such as frontal lobes.

Something stable lies at the foundation of the human psyche, an affective substratum, perhaps not that different from the raw mentality of other mammals (Panksepp, 2007b). We inherit emotional systems as part of our core sense of self (Northoff & Panksepp, 2008; Panksepp & Northoff, 2009). As we recognize our deeply affective nature, we must consider the developmental consequences of every emotional system of the brain (Panksepp, 2001). Although abundant neuroscience work remains, we can be confident that the quality of our children's lives depends on early emotional experiences (Kirkpatrick, 1903; Sunderland, 2006; Tronick, 2007).

From an emotional perspective, current "No Child Left Behind" programs, which simply focus on reading, writing, and arithmetic are well suited to leave every child behind in appreciating the arts and the emotional side of life. Early social loss and excessive stress can be disastrous for mental health, with increased likelihood of depression, which is becoming the most common major psychiatric disorder and the second costliest medical problem in our society. Might we reverse such trends by building play sanctuaries for children? Can we diminish the escalating rates of depression by changing child-care policies to maximize playful activities that help construct happy pro-social brains and maximize the likelihood of having healthy societies? Certainly childhood depression disrupts the capacity to play (Mol Lous, de Wit, De Bruyn, & Riksen-Walraven, 2002), and play has abundant potential functions (Power, 2000; Spinka, Newberry, & Bekoff, 2001). Play is nature's way of integrating complex organisms into the social structures in which they find themselves. For instance, animal models indicate that abundant early social play reduces the likelihood of later aggression (Potegal & Einon, 1989). Likewise, biographical analysis of incarcerated young men in Texas has highlighted that most had "playless lives" during childhood (Brown, 1998).

Animal studies also show that abundant tender loving care strengthens the nervous system in many ways, protecting individuals against the "slings and arrows of misfortune" while promoting a robust and confident attitude toward life (Champagne & Meaney, 2001, 2007; Meaney, 2001). This is also true for children (Schore, 2001), and the cross-species database is growing rapidly (Panksepp, 2001).

## Developmental Landscapes

Coherent understanding of emotional development could be further optimized if future work is guided by our emerging understanding of the basic emotional systems all mammals share as affective tools for living (Bekoff, 2007; Grandin & Johnson, 2005; Panksepp, 1998, 2005). Detailed knowledge about emotional systems and their developmental-epigenetic controls may provide solid guidelines to optimize childrearing practices (Sunderland, 2006). Animal models allow us to pursue systematic research on such topics with great rigor. For instance: (1) epigenetic influences and genetic vulnerabilities can be studied in detail (knockout mice, etc.); (2) developmental processes can be isolated and studied; (3) specific environmental toxic factors can be independently manipulated; (4) underlying brain and body systems can be studied in detail, even down to single gene levels within animal brains; (5) new biological therapies for emotional problems (and psychiatric disorders) can be evaluated in model systems; and (6) basic affects – sensory, homeostatic and emotional – can finally be understood (Panksepp, 1998, 2005a, 2005b) even as cognitions remain less neuroscientifically tractable.

Systematic work along these lines provides a coherent strategy to unravel how primary-process affective experiences are constructed within the brain and influence brain development (Panksepp & Moskal, 2008). By triangulating between a neural, behavioral, and mental analysis of the emotional systems of the mammalian brain, we seek a basic science foundation for addressing such issues. Before discussing the implications for child development, I will summarize the affective neuroscience strategy, briefly discuss basic emotional systems that can be supported by solid cross-species neuroscientific evidence, highlight the importance of respecting the emotional lives of other animals, and finally discuss how the PLAY system may be vital to our emotional lives.

Studying animal brains may teach us more about cross-species emotional systems than studying human brains, although many cultural and scientific resistances remain. Perhaps the most long-standing one is the scientific community's general failure to openly recognize that other mammals are feeling creatures and to realize, as did Darwin (1872/1965), that all mammals share the same basic set of emotional proclivities. A neuroscientific understanding of how emotions and affects are organized in the brain requires animal models that can reveal the foundational principles and underlying details (e.g., identification of neuropeptidergic codes) that can guide validation studies in humans. These principles must then be combined with an understanding of how personal experiences and culture program the most abstract, general-purpose reaches of the human brain.

## THE BASIC EMOTIONAL CIRCUITS OF ANIMAL BRAINS

Here, the concept of "emotion" is used to encompass mind-brain entities accompanied by (i) distinct emotional-behavioral displays, (ii) patterns of autonomic and hormonal changes, (iii) characteristic cognitive-thinking-learning effects, and (iv) distinct feeling states. This last attribute, designated by the term "affect," remains the most mysterious aspect of emotion and the most difficult to study. Ever since Wilhelm Wundt's inauguration of experimental psychology, affect has been traditionally envisioned in dimensional terms – psychological states accompanied by different degrees of valence (i.e., positive and negative feelings), marked by different levels of arousal and power (Barrett, 2006). Another view is that varied and distinct feelings (anger, fear, etc.) do exist and each can be discussed in terms of dimensional properties (Panksepp, 1998a).

Clearly, human emotions are constructed from many neural *parts* into complex but psychologically coherent *wholes* that often defy comprehensive neuroscientific analysis. Science is much better at analyzing *parts* than reconstructing *wholes*. Basic emotional systems are envisioned to have specific neuronal network properties, which can serve as a neural definition of an emotional network (see Figure 18.1). Emotional networks function as follows: (1) various sensory stimuli unconditionally access emotional systems; (2) emotional systems generate instinctual motor outputs and (3) modulate sensory inputs, promoting incentive salience; (4) emotional systems have positive feedback components that can sustain arousal following precipitating events, (5) can be modulated by cognitive inputs, and (6) can modify and channel cognitive activities, again modulating incentive salience. The overriding criterion is that such emotional systems create neurodynamics

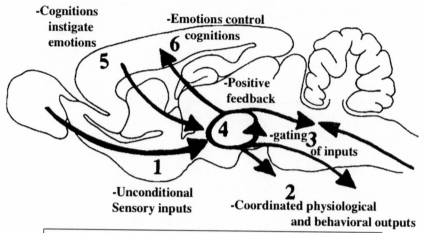

7. Affect arises from activity of the whole system

**Figure 18.1.** Summary of a neural definition of an emotional system. The seven neural interactions schematically highlighted are postulated to characterize all major primary-process emotional systems of the brain. (1) Only a limited number of sensory stimuli can unconditionally access emotional systems; most inputs are gradually developmentally learned; (2) emotional systems promote coherent instinctual action outputs, and they (3) modulate relevant sensory inputs. (4) Emotional systems have internal positive-feedback components that can sustain emotional arousal after precipitating events have passed (for instance, the executive neuropeptides that integrated these responses are not rapidly degraded). Also, (5) these systems can be modulated by cognitive inputs while also being able (6) to modify and channel cognitive activities. The important criterion that emotional systems create affective states is not included, but it is postulated, on the basis of abundant brain stimulation evidence, that arousal of the whole executive circuitry for each emotion is essential for elaborating emotional feelings within the brain, perhaps by interacting with other sub-neocortical brain circuits for organismic-visceral self-representation. From Panksepp, J. (1998a). *Affective neuroscience: The foundations of human and animal emotions.* New York: Oxford University Press. Reprinted with permission of Oxford University Press.

that are isomorphic with primary-process affective states, perhaps by interacting with a widespread neural network for core self-representation in subcortical midline structures that interact with cortical midline structures for self-referential information processing (see Panksepp, 1998b; Northoff & Panksepp, 2008; Panksepp & Northoff, 2009).

It is this last characteristic, the internal feeling state at the heart of emotional experience, that causes much controversy in neuroscience and philosophy. Internal subjective experiences are the hardest aspects of brain function to analyze empirically. Like certain physical properties of the world, such as gravity and the nature of sub-atomic particles, they must be inferred from indirect observation. However, animals clearly tell us in many different ways that they either like or dislike artificial activation of their subcortical emotional networks with localized electrical and chemical stimulation. They do this with traditional behavioral procedures, especially conditioned place preferences (CPPs) and conditioned place aversions (CPAs).

*So what, in a deep neurophenomenological sense, are emotional feelings?* To the best of our knowledge, affects arise from wide-scale neurodynamics that establish mentally experienced "forces" that regulate action readiness within the nervous system. The distinct dynamics are evident in the pounding force of anger, the shivery feelings of fear, the caress of love, the urgent thrusting of sexuality, the painful pangs of grief, the exuberance of joy, and the persistent "nosy" poking about of organisms seeking resources.

*Do other animals have experienced emotional lives?* A credible neuroscientific argument can finally be made for the thesis that animals do have emotional feelings (Beckoff, 2007; Darwin, 1872/1965; Grandin & Johnson, 2006). Although throughout the nineteenth and most of the twentieth century the weight of scientific evidence was insufficient, we can now be confident that various affective feelings exist in all mammals and birds. The most robust evidence comes from the discovery that all vertebrate species studied so far have brain systems for generating various feelings of "goodness" or "badness,'" as shown by their behavioral choices – especially CPP and CPA tasks following direct brain manipulations.

The most compelling evidence comes from the study of emotional responses to specific brain manipulations, such as electrical or chemical stimulation of discrete brain regions. When given control of the stimulation – the power to turn it on or off – animals clearly indicate their likes and dislikes. They also exhibit distinct types of instinctual emotional responses to such stimulation. The emotional vocalizations animals make in various arousing situations often resemble emotional sounds made by humans. For instance, the experience of pain can cause shrieking and crying, and the stronger the pain stimulus, the stronger the vocal response. When we artificially activate the brain circuits that generate spontaneous anger and fear responses, animals rapidly learn to turn off the stimulation. A similar phenomenon has been found in the experience of joy. Humans laugh when they feel joy, and many animals also make laughing-type sounds when they play or when tickled. When allowed to self-stimulate brain systems that generate such happy sounds, rats readily do so (Burgdorf, Wood, Kroes, Moskal, & Panksepp, 2007). The same goes for brain circuits that generate foraging, sexual, and maternal behaviors. Further, all other mammals learn to vigorously self-inject drugs that are addictive in humans, probably because they produce similar desirable feelings. Such findings would be very hard to explain if animals had no emotional experiences. Of course, since nature is adept at building diversities of form and function, types of feelings cannot be identical across species, but this should not be taken as evidence against class similarities. The weight of evidence currently indicates that many other animals possess brain mechanisms that are quite similar to those in humans and mediate a large number of similar emotional states.

Behavioral analysis has long been consistent with this thesis (Darwin, 1872/1965). If animals had no feelings, it would be hard to construct a coherent explanation of the choices they make when confronted by various environmental options. Animals select warm locations when their body temperature is below normal, and colder locations when it is above normal. They exhibit behaviors very similar to those that humans exhibit in response to stimuli easily described as pleasant or unpleasant. If ancient brain mechanisms for affective feelings are evolutionarily related, and hence, similar in humans and other animals, we can finally begin to understand the deep neural nature of human feelings by studying the apparently homologous neuroanatomies and neurochemistries in animal models.

The existence of feelings in other animals is also rich with ethical implications. How we treat animals is partly based on how we perceive their experience of pain, hunger, and thirst. If we respect the existence of anger and fear, desire, and joy in animals, it would be inappropriate to treat them as if they had no such feelings.

At present, the most compelling scientific evidence about animal emotions comes from behavioral brain research, where specific brain systems are manipulated. The most important lines of research have used localized electrical and chemical stimulation of the brain. Walter Hess (1957), who received the Nobel Prize in 1949, initiated his influential work in the 1930s. He found that localized electrical stimulation of cats could transform them from friendly animals into intensely angry creatures. Eventually, distinct forms of attack were identified, the main two being an angry-emotional attack and a methodical stalking-predatory attack. When investigators finally inquired whether animals "cared" about such stimulation, by asking whether they would turn the stimulation on or off, the answers were clear. Animals would turn off the stimulation that provoked angry "affective attack," and activate sites that provoked predatory attack

(Panksepp, 1971). Likewise, animals would terminate stimulation to brain areas that produced fearful behavior and self-stimulate sites that generated exploratory and consummatory (e.g., feeding, drinking, and sexual) behaviors.

Activation of many of these emotion-provoking brain sites also promoted CPPs or CPAs (animals returning to or avoiding places where they had presumably desirable or undesirable experiences). Other studies have evaluated self-administration of various neurochemicals into these brain regions. Taken together, these studies confirm that affective states are organized within primitive regions of the brain that anatomically and neurochemically resemble each other very closely in all mammals.

Various general principles have emerged form this kind of work: (1) A diversity of brain networks for basic emotional instinctual behaviors lie in ancient brain regions that are evolutionarily similar (homologous) in all mammals. (2) Lower regions of the brain are more important than higher regions of the brain for generating raw emotional feelings. (3) Brain systems that generate emotional instinctual behavioral responses tightly correspond with the feelings that accompany those states. (4) The basic chemistries for emotional feelings are similar in all mammals. Through a study of these brain systems in animals, we now have a solid understanding of basic emotional systems of human beings. This work is especially important for the next generation of scientific developments in biological psychiatry (Panksepp, 2004, 2006). Here I will simply provide a general overview of these systems.

### The Basic Affective Circuits of Mammalian Brains

Past work supports the existence of at least seven basic types of highly interactive emotional systems in all mammalian brains (see Panksepp, 1998a, 2005a for fuller descriptions). The names of these systems are capitalized to emphasize that specific neural networks (i.e., functionally dedicated emotional systems) exist in the brain. These systems are all situated subcortically, and consist of large transverse networks that interconnect critical midbrain regions such as the periaqueductal gray and ventral tegmental area, with various basal ganglia nuclei, such as amygdala and nucleus accumbens as well as cingulate, orbitofrontal and medial frontal cortices, via pathways that run through the hypothalamus and thalamus. All emotional systems also share various generalized arousal effects through widespread brain networks that contain norepinepherine and serotonin as transmitters.

Each emotional system has abundant descending and ascending components that work together to generate instinctual emotional responses as well as the raw feelings associated with those behaviors. These systems can be activated and inhibited by higher brain mechanisms, but they can also control how those higher mechanisms process information. There is no longer any doubt that all mammals have a variety of basic emotional systems that coordinate the autonomic, behavioral, and raw feeling aspects of emotions.

In contrast, the functions of the neocortex are not genetically prescribed to the same extent as the brain's subcortical regions. Thus, in the last part of this essay, I will argue that rather than look for biologically deficient evolutionary "modules" in the cortices of young children, we should expend resources on creating social environments that minimize the emergence of childhood problems, such as ADHD and autism, that arise as much from adverse developmental landscapes as from genetic dispositions.

Emotional systems are labeled in capital letters not only to indicate specific neural networks but to highlight that the study of critical neural *parts* does not necessarily constitute an understanding of the *whole*. The seven systems that have the most abundant evidence are the following (Panksepp, 1998a, 2005a). One or two key references are provided that summarize the neural details of these systems:

1) **The SEEKING/Desire System** (Alcaro, Huber, & Panksepp, 2007; Panksepp & Moskal, 2008). This general-purpose appetitive motivational system may be essential for many other emotional systems to operate effectively. It seems to be a major source of the life-energy that has at times been called "libido." It induces animals to be intensely interested in exploring their world and, with learning, excites them when they are about to get what they desire. It eventually allows animals to find and eagerly anticipate all kinds of resources they need for survival, including water, food, warmth, or coolness, depending on the status of thermoregulatory systems, and their ultimate evolutionary survival need, sex. When fully aroused, the SEEKING urge fills the mind with interest and motivates organisms to move their bodies seemingly effortlessly in search of the things they need, crave, and desire. In humans, this system generates and sustains curiosity from the mundane to high intellectual pursuits. When this system becomes under-active for various reasons, such as drug withdrawal, chronic helplessness/stress, or old-age neural deficits, a form of depression results (Watt & Panksepp, 2009). When the system becomes spontaneously overactive, which can happen as a result of various drugs, behavior can

become excessive and stereotyped, guided often by psychotic delusions and manic thoughts.

Neuroanatomically, the SEEKING system corresponds to the major self-stimulation system that runs from midbrain up to the medial frontal cortex. Animals will activate this system readily, whether with drugs such as cocaine or direct electrical or chemical stimulation of the brain (after being surgically prepared with the necessary delivery devices). A critically important chemical in this system is dopamine. Dopamine circuits can energize and coordinate the functions of many higher brain areas that mediate planning and promote normal states of eagerness and apparent purpose in both humans and animals.

2) **The RAGE/Anger System** (Siegel, 2005). Working in opposition to SEEKING, is a system that mediates anger. RAGE is aroused by frustration and attempts to curtail an animal's freedom of action. It has long been known that one can enrage both animals and humans by stimulating specific circuits of the brain that lie rather close to the trajectory of the FEAR system discussed next. The RAGE system invigorates aggressive behaviors when animals are irritated or restrained and also helps animals defend themselves by arousing fear in opponents. Human anger may get much of its psychic energy from arousal of this brain system; a number of well-documented cases record sudden, intense anger attacks with no external provocation in humans stimulated in these brain regions. Key chemistries in this system are substance P, a neuropeptide, and glutamate, both of which activate the system, and endogenous opioids, which inhibit the system; but these chemistries (especially glutamate and opioids) also participate in many other emotional responses. Medicines to control angry behavior in humans and animals could presumably be developed through further understanding of this brain circuitry.

3) **The FEAR/Anxiety System** (Panksepp, 2004). During brain evolution, a coherently operating FEAR circuit evolved to help animals reduce pain and the possibility of destruction. When stimulated intensely, the circuit leads animals to flee as if extremely scared. With much weaker stimulation, animals exhibit a freezing response, which is also common when animals are placed into an environment in which they have been hurt or frightened. Humans stimulated in these same brain regions report an intense free-floating anxiety that appears to have no environmental cause. Key chemistries that regulate this system are neuropeptide Y and corticotropin releasing factor (CRF); specific anti-anxiety agents such as the benzodiazepines inhibit this system.

4) **The LUST/Sexual Systems** (Pfaff, 1999). Sexual urges are mediated by specific brain circuits and distinct chemistries for males and females. They are aroused by male and female sex hormones, which control many brain chemistries including two neuropeptides whose synthesis is strongly controlled by sex hormones: Oxytocin transmission is promoted by estrogen in females and vasopressin transmission by testosterone in males. These brain chemistries help create gender-specific sexual tendencies. Oxytocin promotes sexual readiness and acceptance postures in females, and vasopressin promotes assertiveness, and perhaps jealous behaviors, in males (Panksepp, 2010). Male and female sexual circuits, constructed very early in life, are activated by maturation of gonadal hormones at puberty. Because brain and bodily sex characteristics are independently organized, it is possible for externally male animals to have female-specific sexual urges; likewise, some that are female in external appearance have male sexual urges. Some of the chemistries of sexuality, for instance oxytocin, also mediate maternal care – nurturance and social bonding – suggesting an intimate relationship between female sexual rewards and maternal motivations.

5) **The CARE/Maternal Nurturance system** (Numan & Insel, 2003). Brain evolution has provided safeguards to assure that parents (usually the mother) care for offspring. The massive hormonal changes at the end of pregnancy (declining progesterone and increasing estrogen, prolactin, and oxytocin) set the stage for the activation of maternal urges a few days before the young are born. This symphony of hormonal and neurochemical changes, especially the heightened secretions of oxytocin and prolactin, facilitate maternal moods that assure strong social bonding with offspring. Similar neurochemicals, especially oxytocin and endogenous opioids, promote infant bonding to the mother.

Human infants come into the world as profoundly affective creatures. Their initial cognitive limitations are erased gradually by experiences in loving intersubjective spaces whereby they can become potent actors on the world stage. Their first explorations are not devoted to the inanimate world, but to the eyes, voice, and touch of the caregiver – hopefully, a mother whose brain affective systems have been well prepared not only by culture but also by the loving touch of neurochemical systems that can make engagement with an infant a special delight. It is the rich intersubjective dance of mother and child from which future mental growth possibilities are woven, in both humans and other mammals.

Our society must promote a new and deeper level of emotional education – an affective intelligence that can halt the passing on from parents to children abusive behaviors that are often mental rather than physical. Every emotional system that has been studied exhibits use-dependent plasticity. This means that if one has been exposed to too many horrible experiences, then the brain systems that mediate the resulting feelings will have been strengthened. Infants who have lived at the center of positive emotional engagements with caregivers and have mastered manageable life challenges have received a precious gift of life. Such effects are even evident in laboratory rats (Meaney, 2001). When we begin to understand the nature of separation distress at the neurobiological level, we may learn how to disentangle the damage wrought by emotional misfortunes (Panksepp, 2001).

6) **The PANIC/Separation Distress System** (Freed & Mann, 2007; Panksepp, 1998a, 2003; Swain, Lorberbaum, Kose, & Strathearn, 2007). All young mammals are dependent on parental care, especially maternal care, for survival. Young animals have a powerful emotional system to indicate their need for care, reflected most clearly by intense crying when left in strange places by themselves. These separation calls alert caretakers to seek out and retrieve their offspring, and attend to their needs. The separation distress system has been mapped in several species; it is powerfully inhibited by endogenous opioids, oxytocin, and prolactin – the major social-attachment, social-bonding chemistries of the mammalian brain. These circuits are also aroused during human sadness, which is accompanied by low brain opioid activity. Sudden arousal of this system in humans may contribute to the psychiatric disorder known as "panic attacks."

7) **The PLAY/Rough-and-Rumble, Physical Social-Engagement System** (Burghardt, 2005; Panksepp, 2007a; and also see Pellis, Pellis, & Reinhart, this volume). Young animals have strong urges for physical play in the form of pouncing, chasing, and wrestling. Such actions can seem outwardly aggressive but they are accompanied by positive affect – an intense social joy. During these activities, rats make abundant high-frequency ($\sim$50 kHz) chirping sounds that in many ways resemble human laughter (Panksepp, 2007a). Similarities apparently exist between the subcortical brain circuits that mediate human laughter and play-induced chirping in rats. The most powerful evidence for an evolutionary relationship between positive affect and chirping is seen when humans tickle rats: Tickling often causes vocalizations to increase to maximal levels and the young animals rapidly return to the human hand to solicit more tickling. In contrast, when negative feelings are aroused, animals begin to exhibit 22-kHz "complaint" types of vocalizations and play temporarily ceases. A key function of the social play system is to facilitate the emergence of social dominance. Play helps young animals acquire social interactions that are not genetically coded into the brain but must be learned. Thus, the play urge may be one of the major

emotional forces that promote the epigenetic construction of higher social brains. This emotional system, like all others, is concentrated in specific subcortical brain regions.

To summarize: The primary evidence for the existence of brain systems for basic emotions is our ability to artificially activate various kinds of emotional patterns by applying appropriate chemical or electrical stimulation to specific subcortical regions. Radical decortication (surgical elimination of the dorsal cerebral mantle) generally leaves these emotional-instinctual urges relatively intact, even while impairing the capacity to learn new behavior patterns. Animals are never neutral about such kinds of physical brain stimulation. They are attracted to circumstances that arouse the outwardly positive emotions (SEEKING, LUST, CARE, and PLAY), and they avoid the arousal of negative emotions (RAGE, FEAR, and PANIC). For instance, all brain sites that activate 50 kHz ultrasonic chirps also support self-stimulation behavior. Those that provoke FEAR responses also provoke escape behaviors. Thus, raw affective feeling states that accompany emotional arousal are constituted, in part, from the neurodynamics that generate instinctual emotional responses. Without these systems, and various other affect-generating systems such as hunger, pain, and thirst, animals could not survive for long. Since all mammals share these systems, they are ancestral tools for living.

All affects are intrinsic value systems that inform animals how they are faring in the quest to survive. Feelings are critical for guiding learning. Indeed, the behavioristic concept of "reinforcement" may reflect the manner in which internal affective network processes control learning. (See Panksepp, 2005b for a discussion of the historical biases that led to the elimination of affective terminology during the behavioristic revolution.) The positive affects indicate a return to "comfort zones" that support survival, and the negative affects reflect "discomfort zones" that indicate situations that may impair survival. Indeed, the intrinsic affective states generated by ancient brain regions may be the first kinds of experiences that existed. Without them, consciousness might never have emerged.

Before we return to human developmental concerns, let me close this sub-section by asking a critical question that highlights the issue that we should most worry about in selecting our childrearing practices.

*What difference does it make whether animals have emotional feelings?* The simplest answer to this question is that it surely makes a difference to the animals. Just as we care about how we feel, animals surely care whether they feel good or bad. Since affective feelings are the source of all satisfactions and sufferings, as well as many behavioral choices, scientifically resolving these questions is of momentous importance for our understanding of psychological well-being in animals and humans alike. Feelings inform us about where we stand in terms of health and other survival issues. If we care for our fellow animals, we cannot ignore their feelings. If we care about the future of our children, we must keep their emotional feelings foremost in our minds (Sunderland, 2006).

In sum, the dramatic emotional similarities across mammals, arising from homologous subcortical brain systems, indicate that the basic brain mechanisms are very ancient in mind evolution and ancestrally related in all mammals. These remarkable evolutionary continuities provide a coherent scientific approach for understanding how basic emotional feelings are created in animal as well as human brains. The existence of such systems has profound implications for how we ethically treat other animals, how we treat emotionally disturbed humans, and the main topic of the rest of this essay – how we rear our children.

### Psychiatric Syndromes and the Basic Emotional Systems of the Mammalian Brain

Once we understand the foundational brain systems for affective processes in much greater detail as endophenotypic processes (Panksepp, 2006), we will be in a better position to help humans with emotional problems (Fosha, Siegel, & Solomon, 2009). For instance, we can begin to envision treating the symptomatic manifestations of major emotional syndromes at deep causal levels, as opposed to treating conceptual syndromes generated a century ago to help describe mysteries that could not yet be neurologized. Because emotional symptoms often cut across a variety of psychiatric syndromes, we are now in a better position to treat real human lives. In doing this, we must realize that all classic psychiatric "syndromes" were, and still are, very broad, man-made concepts to categorize poorly understood clusters of psychological problems. ADHD, autism, and the others are not single brain disorders. But first let us consider what evolution did or did not build into the structure of the human brain-mind.

### OF EVOLUTIONARY PSYCHOLOGY AND DEVELOPMENTAL LANDSCAPES

A long-standing battle exists between those who wish to fathom the genetic-evolutionary underpinning of mental processes and others committed to envisioning the fully developmental landscape in which young organisms mature into competent adults (for a recent debate, see Lickliter &

Honeycutt, 2003, and accompanying commentaries). Both viewpoints must be fully integrated, but the historical axes to grind on each side prevent the partisans from seeking middle ground. This is also evident in emotion studies, where those who seek an understanding of basic emotion processes must contend with the fact that emotions in real-life are much more complex than just some basic subcortical circuits that control emotional expressions and raw affective states (for a recent variant of this debate see Barrett [2006] with rebuttals by Izard [2007] and Panksepp [2007b]).

## The Sins of Human Evolutionary Psychology

As far as we know, evolution has provided a set of fundamental tools for living that initially contain no cognitive details. The brain starts with basic neural mechanisms for various sensory and motor processes; sleeping and waking; focused attention; learning and memory; a set of homeostatic interoreceptors to inform an organism that it needs energy, water, warmth and other commodities for survival; and a set of emotional systems that are prepared to respond to the world in certain ways. The least investigative work has been done on the these last brain properties, largely because of disagreement on whether such basic tools for living are built into the brain or constructed by experiences. As already summarized, animal data strongly support that mammals have at least seven built-in emotional systems as ancestral birthrights.

A current difficulty with evolutionary approaches to brain–mind functions is that a vigorous movement in social and personality psychology took up the evolutionary banner and started to suggest that an enormous number of strategic psychobehavioral attitudes, or cognitive modules, are built into the human brain by evolutionary selection processes. This version of evolutionary psychology generated stories about our evolutionary passages toward human complexities, using intuitions, hunches, as well as the most characteristic behavior patterns seen in adults – from "language instincts" to "cheater detection modules" to "courting patterns" and all varieties of "kin selection" dynamics. Much of this sounded eminently reasonable, but our willingness to have strong convictions about such issues could also have been a big mistake. Many of these specializations may not be built into brain. They may emerge ontogenetically, largely through life experiences based upon a limited set of basic emotional systems we share with other animals and a vast neocortical computational space that needs to be "modularized" by experience. Fortunately, there are many approaches to evolutionary psychology, and we should all be committed to a more measured approach to the role of evolution in complex human behaviors (Dunbar & Barrett, 2007).

In any event, to this day, there is no solid neurobiological or genetic evidence for such speculative cognitive adaptive mechanisms in the brain, at least as genetic birthrights, even though there may be a high probability they will be epigenetically engraved there because of our basic emotional attitudes and the regularities in our social environments. Indeed, the regions for abstract cognition in the human brain, the neocortex, has an architectural pattern that resembles random-access memory (RAM) more than any type of specialized modularity. In contrast, the subcortical regions are rich in specialized circuits and networks, and those lower areas of the brain are shared similarly (homologously) with other mammals. The stories about language instincts, etc., have been so compelling that many students have become "true believers" without worrying much about how the brain is really organized. The repetitive columnar structures of the neocortex (metaphorically resembling RAM chips in a desktop computer) were easy to proliferate; one merely needs a developmental genetic message to keep the developmental window for columnar proliferation active for a longer time. In other words, the rule of generating more of a basic brain unit that had already been molded early in brain evolution is not a difficult genetic task. And these RAM fields in the neocortex may functionally specialize largely under the sway of incoming information from more primitive subcortical brain regions and life experiences.

Even primary sensory cortices (e.g., vision) in the mouse are not genetically pre-specified. If one surgically eliminates the occipital cortex *in utero*, mice develop a fully functional cortex in adjacent parietal areas (Sur & Leamey, 2001; Sur & Rubenstein, 2005). It is the "urge" of subcortical thalamic axons to innervate nearby neocortex that allows cortical visual competence to emerge. If one takes this epigenetic rule seriously as a potential general principle for the emergence of neocortical specializations, one should hesitate to ascribe any clear neocortical modularization to adaptations that emerged in the Pleistocene, as is common in non-biological evolutionary psychology (Panksepp & Panksepp, 2000; Panksepp, 2007c). The most robust evolutionary specializations – innate tools for living – are to be found in subcortical brain regions that we share with other mammals. Much of the rest – the higher-order emotions and the accompanying cognitive strategies – are more likely to be gradually built into the brain's higher cognitive regions through life experiences than through the forces of evolutionary selection.

### The Epigenetic Construction of Social Brains

A focus on the social-cultural environments of developing human beings is more important than past evolutionary dynamics for understanding human cognitive tendencies. The growth and maturation of higher aspects of human social brain functions depend more on developmental-epigenetic progressions than on the gene sequences that are critical in construction of our brains and bodies. Family-social-cultural dynamics are more important than Pleistocene evolutionary dynamics for programming higher brain regions that bring forth our uniquely and fully human social qualities. This, as we will see, may have far-reaching consequences for the way we conceptualize childhood disorders such as ADHD and autism.

I will briefly consider the possibility that most of the higher social brain is epigenetically constructed through the use of basic social-emotional tools, especially the CARE, PANIC, and PLAY systems, rather than through genetically prescribed higher brain "adaptations." Epigenetics is our rapidly growing understanding about the semi-permanent non-mutational changes in gene function, which can dramatically modify body and brain functions and be passed down through generations with no modification of the classic nucleotide pairings of DNA sequences (see Szyf, McGowan, Turecki, & Meaney, this volume). These are chemical changes that modify the degree to which specific genes are expressed or not, with profound consequences for bodily cellular specializations and how brain cells develop. The consequences for brain and body functions are as far-reaching as the effects of mutations, but unlike mutations, they remain sensitive to environmental influences. Epigenetic changes can be amplified or diminished, or even undone. The most common epigenetic effect arises from DNA-chromatin methylation and acetylation, which control the extent to which transcription factors can modify the degree to which specific genes are expressed. Indeed, this is the process by which bodily cell differentation occurs during ontogenesis. It is also a major path through which long-term, environmentally induced behavioral changes emerge as a function of the quality of social (Meaney, 2001) as well as physical environments (Dolinoy & Jirtle, 2008).

## ADHD CONCEPTUALIZED AS AN EPIGENETIC SOCIOBIOLOGICAL DISORDER

The epigenetic revolution has profound implications for normal and abnormal child development. Certain variants of autism, especially the female-specific autistic-like genetic disorder, Rett syndrome, partly results from abnormal gene methylation patterns (Shahbazian & Zoghbi, 2002). One can modify schizophrenic-like traits in mice by excessive feeding of methyl-donor amino acids such as methionine, which can be counteracted pharmacologically with widely used anti-epileptic drugs (Tremolizzo, et al., 2005). Although these factors have not yet been identified in environmentally promoted childhood disorders such as ADHD, the general implications for childhood development are vast (Dolinoy, Weidman & Jirtle (2007).

## Potential Environmental Factors in the Genesis of ADHD

At some point in development, every normal child shows characteristics of ADHD. For an official diagnosis, a child of six needs to exhibit 6 of 9 symptoms of inattention or hyperactivity-impulsivity that disrupt functioning at what is deemed an appropriate developmental level (APA, 1994). Although diagnostic practices vary considerably across the United States and other countries, an estimated 5 to 10% of children in different geographical regions are diagnosed with the problem. Children diagnosed with ADHD are now most likely to be placed on psychostimulants (LeFever, Dawson, & Morrow, 1999), which work very effectively to reduce rambunctiousness and increase quiet attentive behavior, especially in classroom settings, where the demand for such behaviors is high. In animal models, all drugs used to reduce ADHD dramatically reduce play (Beatty, Dodge, Dodge, White, & Panksepp, 1982). Might there be a connection between these two observations? May many of the desired (beneficial?) effects of psychostimulants result from their ability to reduce playfulness?

Our recent work on animal PLAY urges may be relevant for understanding ADHD. As we have so little access into the intricacies of children's brains, aside from the correlates provided by modern brain imaging, animal models can help us figure out possible underlying brain substrates of impulsivity such as diminished higher frontal cortical inhibition on primary-process emotionality. From this perspective, it is not surprising that ADHD children are morphologically a bit "short" in the frontal lobes and that these brain regions in ADHD children are a bit sleepy (i.e., have more slow wave activity) than those in typical children. It is noteworthy that frontal lobe damage can markedly increase social play in animal models, leading to the simple idea that much of ADHD is excessive playfulness. Further, it seems reasonable to entertain the possibility that abundant play could reduce ADHD symptoms, perhaps through epigenetic facilitation of frontal lobe maturation. Considering the high probability that children in modern societies are not getting as much physical play as they desire, ADHD children should first be assured abundant physical play. This primary-process emotional need no doubt functions to help program the higher regions of the social brain. Impulse control problems can be difficult in childhood, but our emerging understanding of primary-process PLAY functions encourages us to conceptualize new ways to facilitate pro-social brain-mind maturation, and thereby reduce impulse control problems in children.

Despite years of psychiatric research, *many children* who are diagnosed with ADHD may exhibit no brain abnormality except for being on the lower end of the distribution of age-characteristic brain maturation, a situation that may result partly from genetic factors and partly from social environments. The frontal lobe deficit (~5%) (Castellanos & Tannock, 2002) surely influences the maturation of various executive functions (Figure 18.1). But should this lag be considered a "brain disorder" or simply "maturational slowness"? For most families, this becomes a social problem only when such children enter school. They are simply incapable of being as compliant as typical children with better brain-mind regulatory functions.

Obviously, it would be best for families (and society) to help such children at the earliest and most plastic phases of development, employing interventions that are most likely to facilitate frontal lobe maturation (Barkley, 1997). Clearly, drugs alone could never do that because higher pro-social brain circuits are laid down by the epigenetic effects of lived experiences. Also, one goal would be to decrease the use of psychostimulants because the long-term epigenetic cost-benefit functions of exposing developing brains to such drugs remains inadequately characterized. Wisdom dictates that all natural pro-social interventions be given a chance before resorting to powerful drugs that have been shown to exert long-term effects on brain plasticity in animal models (Robinson & Kolb, 2004). Some effects, such as sustained diminution of dopamine reuptake sites following therapeutic doses of methylphendiate (Moll, Hause, Rüther, Rothenberger, & Huether, 2001), could mean increased incidence of Parkinson's Disease later in life.

Before considering social-therapeutic alternatives to drugs, let's briefly consider several empirically validated problems that might emerge from chronic exposure to psychostimulants.

### ADHD, Psychostimulants, and Drug Abuse

Most psychostimulants used to treat ADHD have neurochemical effects quite similar to cocaine, except they are longer acting, and they enter and exit the brain more slowly, diminishing the addiction-promoting euphoric effects of such drugs. Nevertheless, practically all drugs used to treat ADHD are highly addictive if access is unregulated. Although treatment of children with such drugs may reduce drug use later in life, it is uncertain whether this is due to the drugs' pharmacological and epigenetic effects or simply secondary social benefits.

In fact, looking at all of the data as a whole, we can not yet arrive at any definitive conclusions. Although unmedicated ADHD children develop a subsequent higher-than-normal incidence of drug abuse (Biederman, Wilens, Mick, Faraone, & Spencer, 1998; Wilens, 2004), evidence of a direct relationship between ADHD medications and reduced drug-seeking patterns is inconsistent. Certainly, most adult animal addiction models indicate that prolonged exposure to psychostimulants generally leads to brain "sensitization," a condition that promotes drug abuse tendencies (Robinson & Berridge, 1993; Vanderschuren & Kalivas, 2000). It has been claimed that psychostimulant treatment of ADHD children does not promote drug abuse in adolescents (Mannuzza, Klein, & Moulton, 2003; Willens & Biederman, 2006); however, such studies routinely fail to include amounts of legally prescribed drugs (Biederman, Wilens, Mick, Spenser, & Faraone, 1999). This last study also had a selection bias: children prescribed methylphenidate initially had substantially lower unregulated drug intakes than unmedicated controls (0% and about 38%, respectively, with about 27% and 77% of adolescents consuming drugs after four years). With such baseline differences, and potentially different demand characteristics imposed on the children (e.g., perhaps medicated children receive more supervision), interpretation is difficult.

The central scientific question of such studies is whether there are meaningful psychological changes that are epigenetically promoted by sustained medication with psychostimulants. The scientific question should be: As shown in well-controlled animal studies, do children chronically treated with psychostimulants develop stronger drug cravings when given free access to drugs? Since drug craving has never been measured in psychostimulant-treated ADHD children, the relevant human data stream runs dry.

In animals, long-term psychostimulant exposure "sensitizes" the adult nervous system so that, given access to drugs, addiction occurs more rapidly. In short, the sensitized nervous system desires drugs more intensely (Berridge & Robinson, 1998). And it is not just drugs it desires but, apparently, all varieties of hedonic rewards, from sweets to sex (Nocjar & Panksepp, 2002). This chronic change reflects a broad shift from normal to more intense levels of desire. It seems that psychostimulant sensitization can make organisms more urgently materialistic. To put it simply, the brain has shifted from a normal "I want" state to a "I WANT IT, and I WANT IT NOW" state. If we could choose what to sensitize, surely we would choose empathetic, pro-social brains that are sensitive to the needs and desires of others. Drugs will not achieve that.

Research is needed to determine if human adolescents exhibit changes in their desires after psychostimulant exposure. For this, sensitive depth-psychological studies are needed. Also, various acute physiological and psychological effects of psychostimulants on children about to be medicated (i.e., just getting into the medical pipe-line for pharmacological treatment of ADHD) could be measured and compared with children who have been chronically medicated in the past. At present, the only solace from animal models is that young animals generally fail to sensitize as readily as older ones (Solanto, 2000), although they do sensitize under certain conditions (Laviola, Adriani, Terranova, & Gerra, 1999; Panksepp, et al., 2002). In short, there is an urgent need for better evidence about the nature of brain changes that may arise from chronic exposure to psychostimulants.

Juvenile animals exhibit both stronger and weaker addiction liability after exposure to psychostimulants (Andersen, Arvanitogiannis, Pliakas, LeBlanc, & Carlezon, 2002; Brandon, Marinelli, Baker, White, 2001). Also, pre-clinical evidence is beginning to reveal that such exposure can promote depressive brain changes (Carlezon, Mague, & Andersen, 2003; Mague, Andersen, & Carlezon, 2005). Most importantly for the present analysis, it is clear that psychostimulants are powerful inhibitors of natural social play, using rodent models (Beatty, Dodge, Dodge, White, & Panksepp, 1982). We also know that chronic treatment with methylphenidate reduces social play in juvenile rats, and that the brain substrates for desire-type ultrasonic vocalizations are sensitized by such exposure (Panksepp et al., 2002). Although this issue remains to be evaluated in ADHD children, several clinicians have told me that they have observed diminished playfulness in psychostimulant medicated children.

Many questions remain: What if many children receiving psychostimulants are simply normal, over-rambunctious children with profoundly unsatisfied brain hunger for natural play? What if psychostimulants are partly effective only because they diminish such urges? Might abundant natural play during the pre-school years protect children against ADHD? Might well-regulated natural play promote the epigenetic construction of pro-social brain? Might psychostimulants actually counteract the programming that leads to a well constituted higher social brain? What are the real psychological costs and benefits of anti-ADHD drugs? We have no clear answers to such questions . . . except for some targeted work on animal models.

## ADHD and the Pro-social Effects of PLAY

In our estimation, the play urge is one of nature's foremost tools for the construction of fully social brains (Panksepp, 1998, 2001). It makes little sense for evolution to build cognitive social structures into higher cortical regions of the brain if social environments can vary so greatly. It may be wiser for animals to learn their social place through lived experiences rather than through genetic dictates. The genes merely need to provide organisms with a primal urge to engage with others in positive ways, thus establishing the organism's place in society. Surely such evolutionary dictates guided the evolution of PLAY systems in mammalian brains. We already know that physical-social play can activate growth factors such as BDNF in rodent brains (Gordon, Burke, Akil, Watson, & Panksepp, 2003). We also observed spectacular results in our first micorarray analysis of cortical gene expression changes: Of 1,200 genes analyzed, almost a third were significantly changed one hour after the end of a half-hour play period. The biggest changes occurred in the expression of a brain "fertilizer," Insulin-Like Growth Factor-1 (Kroes, Burgdorf, Schmidt, Panksepp, Beinfeld & Moskal, 2008).

It seems highly unlikely that psychostimulants, in the absence of self-generated social experiences, can simulate such dynamic gene expression patterns. Our working hypothesis is that natural play promotes many brain changes that facilitate cortical maturation, producing deeply pro-social brains that can effectively fit into and compete within existing social structures.

In one experiment, we have formally evaluated the benefits of abundant early social play on later impulsivity, using our well-studied rodent model (Panksepp, Burgdorf, Turner, & Gordon, 2003). Half the animals were subjected to unilateral frontal cortex ablations at 3 days of age to simulate ADHD. These animals were hyperactive, with elevated playfulness, whether right or left frontal poles had been damaged. Then the frontally damaged ADHD-type animals and controls that had undergone surgical procedures without brain tissue aspiration were divided so that half of each group had abundant social play throughout early development; the other half of each category were handled as much but given no opportunities to play with other rats. By early adulthood, the play "therapy" had ameliorated the residual impulsiveness of animals with unilateral frontal damage. The benefits of play were also evident on other measures such as stronger behavioral inhibition in scary environments among the rats given abundant play.

These lines of research need to be extended into situations that evaluate learning (Spinka et al., 2001), assess aggressiveness (Potegal & Einon, 1989), and provide a variety of other social benefits, including learning how to win in social competitions (Panksepp, Jalowiec, DeEskinazi, & Bishop, 1985) and how to lose gracefully (van den Berg et al., 1999). We can conclude that the desire to play is a neurological drive, with many consequences for cerebral maturation. Rather than using psychostimulants, which can abort this drive, it might be wiser to reduce the drive naturally. One solution might be to provide all pre-school children and those in the lower grades with abundant opportunities for joyous physical engagement with others, supervised by intelligent adults who intervene and guide behavioral choices only when bad things happen. Even in animals, at some point, someone will complain when the play becomes too rough. With human children, that is an ideal time for adults to provide guidance on making choices.

This, I believe, is how fully social brains and deeply social minds get organized (Figure 18.2). At a primary-process emotional and epigenetic level, animal work can have profound implications for human clinical practice. Science thrives only through its capacity to generate robust predictions, and the above cross-species predictions may be relevant for human development.

I predict that when properly evaluated, (1) we will find that psychostimulants reduce the urge of human children to play (a prediction perhaps best evaluated by psychoanalytically oriented play therapists); (2) a regular diet of physical play every day during childhood will alleviate ADHD-type symptoms in many children bound for that "clinical" track; (3) play will have long-term pro-social benefits for children's brains and minds that are not obtained with psychostimulants; (4) psychostimulants may sensitize young brains and intensify materialistic and drug desires that may be manifested, *if socio-environmental opportunities are available,* as elevated drug use; and (5) if and when we finally get to relevant genetic studies in children, the profiles of gene activation resulting from lots of play or lots of psychostimulants will be quite different in the brain. In short, we suspect the data will eventually show that different genetic "tunes" are "strummed" in various regions of the brain by the relevant pharmacological and socio-environmental factors.

Systematic work on human physical play remains meager. Indeed, our work with animal models led us to conduct the first formal, well-controlled ethological study of physical play in the young of our species; contrary to what we should have expected from developmental psychology textbooks, there were no major differences in the incidence of play actions between

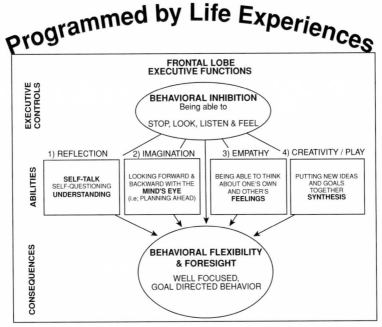

**Figure 18.2.** A synoptic overview of the various major frontal lobe functions that may be slow to mature in children diagnosed with attention deficit hyperactivity disorders. We predict that abundant early social play may facilitate a pro-social organization of these critically important brain systems, especially when children are allowed free play under the supervision of "nurses" or young sports people who only intervene when something negative happens during play (e.g., Figure 18.3), using each of these moments for facilitating social-expectations, social-learning, which may epigenetically facilitate construction of social brains. Summary diagram adapted from Barkley, R. A. (1997). *ADHD and the nature of self-control.* New York: Guilford Press, with permission of Guilford Publications, Inc., permission conveyed through Copyright Clearance Center, Inc.; and Panksepp, J. (2001). The long-term psychobiological consequences of infant emotions: Prescriptions for the twenty-first century. *Infant Mental Health Journal, 22,* 132–173.

pairs of boys and girls (Scott & Panksepp, 2003). We also observed abundant laughter during the play of children, just as the case with rat pups. Tickling is effective in provoking laughter and social joy in both (Panksepp, 2007a; Panksepp & Burgdorf, 2003).

## Play and Early-Learning Social Policies
Important scientific and societal questions remain unanswered about play; for example, what does play do for human brain-mind development?

Without play, can a fully social brain emerge or will it remain socially stunted for life? Have we restricted the playful birthrights of our children? Might abundant early play help reduce the incidence of depression and ADHD? Do animal data already have implications for social policies? I believe the importance of early physical play for brain/mind development has been massively underestimated and needs to be studied and the results applied to early childhood education. Perhaps our modern society has robbed too many of our children of their birthright – "those natural modes of amusement which children find out for themselves when they meet" as Plato said in The Republic [section IV], continuing that "our children from their earliest years must take part in all the more lawful forms of play, for if they are not surrounded with such an atmosphere they can never grow up to be well conducted and virtuous citizens."

In *The Laws* [VII, 794], Plato continued to extol the benefits of free play, suggesting that children from the ages of three to six be gathered at a local sanctuary to engage in games "that nature herself suggests" under the watchful eye of nurses. Although most children can no longer get abundant free play, as they did when the world was a safer place, perhaps it is society's responsibility to make sure that such opportunities are appropriately increased.

In this context, we should remember that Harry Harlow's peer-reared motherless monkeys were not extremely well socialized (Harlow, 1971), which implies that unsupervised peer-play will never provide the degree of socialization that occurs with proper adult/parental supervision. Because physical play takes children to the edges of their emotional knowledge, conflicts will occur that must immediately be resolved with the help of caring adults (the social-educational assistants – Plato's *nurses* – at the periphery of new kinds of play *sanctuaries*). "Bad" things will happen during free play as they do during rat play. As depicted in Figure 18.3, rats during half an hour of play initially exhibit abundant playful 50 kHz chirping ("rat laughter" we have called it: Panksepp & Burgdorf, 2003; Panksepp, 2007a); but as the session proceeds, more and more "complaints" are heard – squeals at 22 kHz – indicating that something bad has happened. It might be a rodent form of excessive roughness, even "bullying," – and it stops play temporarily, but, usually, the animals are so eager to continue the "good stuff" that they begin to emit 50 kHz chirps and resume play. As the session continues, however, complaints often come more frequently, just as with human children. Clearly, complaints are a natural part of play, a time for learning about social processes, and those "bad moments" are ideal times for educating children about social expectations.

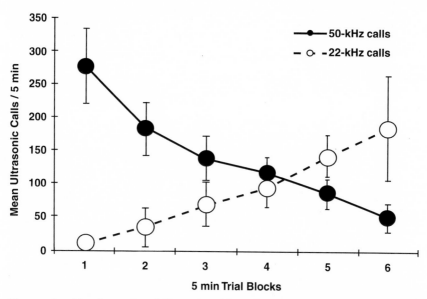

**Figure 18.3.** Numbers of 50 kHz and 22 kHz ultrasonic vocalizations (see representative sonograms in inserts) by pairs of juvenile male rats playing for an half hour period. During this extended play session, the 50 kHz USVs, indicating positive social affect, diminish gradually while 22 kHz USVs, indicating negative affect, increase during the session. This is interpreted to mean that the number of complaints during physical play increase as unsupervised play sessions continue. Unpublished data by Burgdorf and Panksepp (2005).

Without supervision, certain children are bound to bully others and do offensive things, but under watchful eyes of attending "nurses" in "play sanctuaries," those moments could become opportunities for positive social learning. As long as caring people are attending to such critical moments, we are maximizing opportunities to construct fully social brains. To test this theory, we conducted a community-outreach study in a Midwest college town (Scott, 2001), and observed these Platonic ideals in action. During free play sessions, when "bad" things happened and the attending adults gently but firmly conveyed their pro-social expectations – basically "Do unto others . . . !" – children were eager to follow the rules and reap the reward of rapidly returning to the playing field.

In general, it seems that ADHD arises partly from the developmentally slow emergence of frontal-lobe inhibitory-executive functions in certain individuals (Barkley, 1997; Panksepp, 2001). In animal models, such deficits in maturation can be partly corrected by providing abundant social play to frontal-lobe-deficient animals (Panksepp et al., 2003). If a child is heading toward a diagnosis of ADHD, might extra "doses" of physical play be especially "therapeutic"? We don't know, but through our Memorial Foundation for Lost Children in that Midwest college town, we encouraged parents with a child, often an only child on the ADHD track, to energetically play with their children for at least a half hour early in the day and another half hour before bedtime. Many told us how much easier family life had become. Also, we know that physical play in animals has remarkable effects on the gene-expression profiles within the random-access perceptual, cognitive and executive fields of the neocortex (Kroes, et al., 2008).

I look forward to a comprehensive and systematic evaluation of this idea in pre-school children aged 2–6, especially those who might be heading toward a diagnosis of ADHD and a daily diet of psychostimulants. Because it might be difficult for parents with a single child to find consistent play partners, society should consider providing play-sanctuaries for pre-school children. Playful dads and moms can substitute for playmates quite well, perhaps with most of the epigenetic benefits of age-appropriate play companions but the results will not be as beneficial as if children can play with peers. As far as pro-social brain development is concerned, I expect that TVs, video games, using the internet, and the other machine-driven diversions that fill our children's lives will pale by comparison. Also, there is every reason to believe that abundant play may provide prophylaxis against the likelihood of adult depression. Certainly, the antidepressant effects of play have been recognized since Harry Harlow and Steve Suomi's early work with isolate reared monkeys (Harlow & Suomi, 1974; Suomi, Delizio, & Harlow, 1976)

Perhaps abundant early play will tend to protect children against the growing scourge of adult depression, which will soon become the most costly medical problem in America. If animal data is a valid guide, abundant play will facilitate maturation of the frontal cortical inhibitory skills that regulate children's many impulsive primary-process urges. If the epigenetic methylations and other neuronal plasticities happen at just the right places within the maturing pro-social circuits (Szyf, McGowan, & Meaney, 2008), leading to rich expansion of mind-promoting dendritic trees, perhaps the long-term, prosocial benefits of frontal lobe maturation will last a lifetime.

REFERENCES

Alcaro, A., Huber, R. & Panksepp, J. (2007). Behavioral functions of the mesolimbic dopaminergic system: An affective neuroethological perspective. *Brain Research Reviews, 56*, 283–321.

American Psychiatric Association. (1994). *Diagnostic and statistical manual of mental disorders*. 4th ed. Washington, DC: Author.

Andersen, S. L., Arvanitogiannis, A., Pliakas, A. M., LeBlanc, C. & Carlezon, W. A., Jr. (2002). Altered responsiveness to cocaine in rats exposed to methylphenidate during development. *Nature Neuroscience, 5*, 13–14.

Barkley, R. A. (1997). *ADHD and the nature of self-control.* New York: Guilford Press.

Barrett, L. F. (2006). Emotions as natural kinds? *Perspectives on Psychological Science, 1*, 28–58.

Beatty, W. W., Dodge, A. M., Dodge, L. J., White, K., & Panksepp, J. (1982). Psychomotor stimulants, social deprivation and play in juvenile rats. *Pharmacology Biochemistry and Behavior, 16*, 417–422.

Bekoff, M. (2007). *The emotional lives of animals.* Novato, CA: New World Library.

Berridge, K. C., & Robinson, T. E. (1998). What is the role of dopamine in reward: Hedonic impact, reward learning, or incentive salience? *Brain Research Reviews, 28*, 309–369.

Biederman, J., Wilens, T. E., Mick, E., Faraone, S. V., & Spencer, T. (1998). Does attention-deficit hyperactivity disorder impact the developmental course of drug and alcohol abuse and dependence? *Biological Psychiatry, 15*(44), 269–273.

Biederman, J., Wilens, T., Mick, E., Spencer, T., & Faraone, S. V. (1999). Pharmacotherapy of attention-deficit/hyperactivity disorder reduces risk for substance use disorder. *Pediatrics, 104*(e20), 1–5.

Brandon, C. L., Marinelli, M., Baker, L. K., & White, F. J. (2001). Enhanced reactivity and vulnerability to cocaine following methylphenidate treatment in adolescent rats. *Neuropharmacology, 25*, 651–661.

Brown, S. (1998). Play as an organizing principle: Clinical evidence and personal observations. In M. Bekoff & J. A. Beyer (Eds.), *Animal play: Evolutionary, comparative, and ecological perspectives* (pp. 242–251) Cambridge, UK: Cambridge University Press.

Burgdorf, J., Wood, P.L., Kroes, R. A., Moskal, J. R., & Panksepp, J. (2007). Neurobiology of 50-kHz ultrasonic vocalizations in rats: Electrode mapping, lesion, and pharmacology studies. *Behavioral Brain Research, 182*, 274–283.

Burghardt, G. M. (2005). *The genesis of animal play.* Cambridge, MA: MIT Press.

Carlezon, W. A., Jr., Mague, S. D., & Andersen, S. L. (2003). Enduring behavioral effects of early exposure to methylphenidate in rats. *Biological Psychiatry, 54*, 1330–1337.

Castellanos, F. X., & Tannock, R. (2002). Neuroscience of attention-deficit/hyperactivity disorder: The search for endophenotypes. *Nature Reviews Neuroscience, 3*, 617–628.

Champagne, F., & Meaney, M. J. (2001). Like mother, like daughter: Evidence for non-genomic transmission of parental behavior and stress responsivity. *Progress in Brain Research, 133*, 287–302.

Champagne, F., & Meaney, M. J. (2007). Transgenerational effects of social environment on variations in maternal care and behavioral response to novelty. *Behavioral Neuroscience, 121*, 1353–1363.

Darwin, C. (1872/1965). *The expession of the emotions in man and animals.* Chicago: University of Chicago Press.

Dolinoy, D. C., & Jirtle, R. L. (2008). Environmental epigenomics in human health and disease. *Environmental and Molecular Mutagenesis. 49*, 4–8.

Dolinoy, D. C., Weidman, J. R., & Jirtle, R. L. (2007). Epigenetic gene regulation: Linking early developmental environment to adult disease. *Reproductive Toxicology, 23*, 297–307.

Dunbar, R., & Barrett, L. (Eds.) (2007). *Oxford handbook of evolutionary psychology.* Oxford: Oxford University Press.

Fosha, D., Siegel, D. J., & Solomon, M. F. (Eds.). (2009). *The healing power of emotion: Affective neuroscience, development and clinical practice.* New York: Norton.

Freed, P. J., & Mann, J. J. (2007). Sadness and loss: Toward a neurobiopsychosocial model. *American Journal of Psychiatry, 164*, 28–34.

Gordon, N. S., Burke, S., Akil, H., Watson, J., & Panksepp, J. (2003). Socially induced brain fertilization: Play promotes brain derived neurotrophic factor expression. *Neuroscience Letters, 341*, 17–20.

Grandin, T. & Johnson, C. (2005). *Animals in translation.* New York: Scribner.

Harlow, H. F. (1971). *Learning to love.* San Francisco: Albion.

Harlow, H. F., & Suomi, S. J. (1974). Induced depression in monkeys. *Behavioral Biology, 12*, 273–296.

Hess, W. R. (1957). *The functional organization of the diencephalons.* New York: Grune and Statton.

Izard, C. E. (2007). Basic emotions, natural kinds, emotion schemas, and a new paradigm. *Perspectives on Psychological Science, 2*, 260–280.

Kirkpatrick, E. A. (1903). *Fundamental of child study: A discussion of instincts and other factors in human development with practical application.* New York: MacMillan Co.

Kroes, R. A., Burgdorf, J. S., Schmidt, M. E., Panksepp, J., Beinfeld, M. C. & Moskal, J. R (2008). Uncovering the moledualr basis of positive affect using rough-and-tumble play in rats: A role for Insulin-Like Growth Factor 1. *Neuroscience Abstracts, 393.2.*

Laviola, G., Adriani, W., Terranova, M. L., & Gerra, G. (1999). Psychobiological risk factors for vulnerability to psychostimulants in human adolescents and animal models. *Neuroscience and Biobehavioral Reviews, 23*, 993–1010.

Le Fever, G. B., Dawson, K. V., & Morrow, A. L. (1999). The extent of drug therapy for attention deficit-hyperactivity disorder among children in public schools. *American Journal of Public Health, 89*, 1359–1364.

Lickliter, R., & Honeycutt, H. (2003). Developmental dynamics: Toward a biologically plausible evolutionary psychology. *Psychological Bulletin, 129*, 819–835.

Mague, S. D., Andersen, S. L., & Carlezon, W. A., Jr. (2005). Early developmental exposure to methylphenidate reduces cocaine-induced potentiation of brain stimulation reward in rats. *Biological Psychiatry, 57*, 120–125.

Mannuzza, S., Klein, R. G., & Moulton, J. L. (2003). Does stimulant treatment place children at risk for adult substance abuse? A controlled, prospective follow-up study. *Journal of Child and Adolescent Psychopharmacology, 13*(3), 273–282.

Meaney, M. J. (2001). Maternal care, gene expression, and the transmission of individual differences in stress reactivity across generations. *Annual Review of Neuroscience, 24*, 1161–1192.

Mol Lous, A., de Wit, C. A., De Bruyn, E. E., & Riksen-Walraven, J. M. (2002). Depression markers in young children's play: A comparison between depressed and nondepressed 3- to 6-year-olds in various play situations. *Journal of Child Psychology and Psychiatry, 43,* 1029–1038.

Moll, G. H., Hause, S., Rüther, E. Rothenberger, A., & Huether, G. (2001). Early methylphenidate administration to young rats causes a persistent reduction in the density of striatal dopamine transporters. *Journal of Child and Adolescent Psychopharmacology, 11,* 15–24.

Nocjar, C., & Panksepp, J. (2002). Chronic intermittent amphetamine pretreatment enhances future appetitive behavior for drug- and natural-reward: Interaction with environmental variables. *Behavioural Brain Research, 128,* 189–203.

Northoff, G., & Panksepp, J. (2008). The trans-species concept of self and the subcortical-cortical midline system. *Trends in Cognitive Sciences, 12*(7), 259–264.

Numan, M., & Insel, T. R. (2003). *The neurobiology of parental behavior.* New York: Springer.

Panksepp, J. (1971). Aggression elicited by electrical stimulation of the hypothalamus in albino rats. *Physiology & Behavior, 6,* 311–316.

Panksepp, J. (1998). *Affective neuroscience, The foundations of human and animal emotions.* New York: Oxford University Press.

Panksepp, J. (2001). The long-term psychobiological consequences of infant emotions: Prescriptions for the twenty-first century. *Infant Mental Health Journal, 22,* 132–173.

Panksepp, J. (2003). At the interface of affective, behavioral and cognitive neurosciences: Decoding the emotional feelings of the brain. *Brain and Cognition, 52,* 4–14.

Panksepp, J (Ed.) (2004). *Textbook of biological psychiatry.* Hoboken, NJ: Wiley.

Panksepp, J. (2005a). Affective consciousness: Core emotional feelings in animals and humans. *Consciousness & Cognition, 14,* 30–80.

Panksepp, J. (2005b). On the embodied neural nature of core emotional affects. *Journal of Consciousness Studies, 12,* 161–187.

Panksepp, J. (2006). Emotional endophenotypes in evolutionary psychiatry. *Progress in Neuro-Psychopharmacology & Biological Psychiatry, 30,* 774–784.

Panksepp, J. (2007a). Neuroevolutionary sources of laughter and social joy: Modeling primal human laughter in laboratory rats. *Behavioral Brain Research, 182,* 231–244.

Panksepp, J. (2007b). Affective consciousness. In M. Velmans & S. Schneider (Eds.), *The Blackwell companion to consciousness* (pp. 114–129). Malden, MA: Blackwell Publishing.

Panksepp J. (2007c). The neuroevolutionary and neuroaffective psychobiology of the prosocial brain. In R. I. M. Dunbar & L. Barrett (Eds.), *The Oxford handbook of evolutionary psychology* (pp. 145–162). Oxford, UK: Oxford University Press.

Panksepp, J. (2007d). Neurologizing the psychology of affects: How appraisal-based constructivism and basic emotion theory can coexist. *Perspectives on Psychological Science, 2,* 281–296.

Panksepp, J. (2008). The affective brain and core-consciousness: How does neural activity generate emotional feelings. In M. Lewis, J. M. Haviland, & L. F. Barrett (Eds.), *Handbook of emotions* (pp. 47–67). New York: Guilford Press.

Panksepp, J. (2010). The evolutionary sources of jealousy: Cross-species approaches to fundamental issues. In S. L. Hart & M. Legerstee (Eds.), *Handbook of jealousy: Theory, research, and multidisciplinary approaches* (in press). Hoboken, NJ: Wiley-Blackwell.

Panksepp, J., Burgdorf, J., Gordon, N., & Turner, C. (2002). Treatment of ADHD with methylphenidate may sensitize brain substrates for desire. *Consciousness & Emotion, 3*, 7–19.

Panksepp, J., & Burgdorf, J. (2003). "Laughing" rats and the evolutionary antecedents of human joy? *Physiology & Behavior, 79*, 533–547.

Panksepp, J., Burgdorf, J., Turner, C., & Gordon, N. (2003). Modeling ADHD-type arousal with unilateral frontal cortex damage in rats and beneficial effects of play therapy. *Brain and Cognition, 52*, 97–105.

Panksepp, J., Jalowiec, J., DeEskinazi, F.G., Bishop, P. (1985). Opiates and play dominance in juvenile rats. *Behavioral Neuroscience, 99*, 441–453.

Panksepp, J., & Moskal, J. (2008). Dopamine and SEEKING: Subcortical "reward" systems and appetitive urges. In A. Elliot (Ed.), *Handbook of approach and avoidance motivation* (pp. 67–87). Mahwah, NJ: Lawrence Erlbaum Associates.

Panksepp, J., & Northoff, G. (2009). The trans–species core self: The emergence of active cultural and neuro-ecological agents through self related processing within subcortical-cortical midline networks. *Consciousness & Cognition, 18*, 193–215.

Panksepp, J., & Panksepp, J. B. (2000). A continuing critique of evolutionary psychology: Seven sins for seven sinners, plus or minus two. *Evolution & Cognition, 7*, 56–80.

Pfaff, D. W. (1999). *Drive: Neurobiological and molecular mechanisms of sexual behavior*. Cambridge, MA: MIT Press.

Potegal, M., & Einon, D. (1989). Aggressive behaviors in adult rats deprived of playfighting experiences as juveniles. *Developmental Psychobiology, 22*, 159–172.

Power, T. G. (2000). *Play and exploration in children and animals*. Hillsdale, NJ: Lawrence Erlbaum Associates.

Robinson, T. E., & Berridge, K. C. (1993). The neural basis of drug craving: An incentive-sensitization theory of addiction. *Brain Research Reviews, 18*, 247–291.

Robinson, T. E., & Kolb, B. (2004). Structural plasticity associated with exposure to drugs of abuse. *Neuropharmacology, 47*(Suppl. 1), 33–46.

Schore, A. N. (2001). The effects of relational trauma on right brain development, affect regulation, and infant mental health. *Infant Mental Health Journal, 22*, 201–269.

Scott, E. (2001). Toward a play program to benefit children's attention in the classroom. (Unpublished doctoral dissertation). Bowling Green State University, Bowling Green, Ohio.

Scott, E., & Panksepp, J. (2003). Rough-and-tumble play in human children. *Aggressive Behavior, 29*(6), 539–551.

Shahbazian, M. D., & Zoghbi, H. Y. (2002). Rett syndrome and MeCP2: Linking epigenetics and neuronal function. *American Journal of Human Genetics, 71*, 1259–1272.

Siegel, A. (2005). *The neurobiology of aggression and rage*. Boca Raton, FL: CRC Press.

Solanto, M. V. (2000). Clinical psychopharmacology of AD/HD: Implications for animal models. *Neuroscience and Biobehavioral Reviews, 24*, 27–30.

Spinka, M., Newberry, R. C., & Bekoff, M. (2001). Mammalian play: Training for the unexpected. *Quarterly Review of Biology, 76,* 141–68.

Suomi, S. J., Delizio, R., & Harlow, H. F. (1976). Social rehabilitation of separation-induced depressive disorders in monkeys. *American Journal of Psychiatry, 133,* 1279–1285.

Sunderland, M. (2006). *The science of parenting.* London: DK Publishing Inc.

Sur, M., & Leamey, C. A. (2001). Development and plasticity of cortical areas and networks. *Nature Reviews Neuroscience, 2,* 251–262.

Sur, M., & Rubenstein, J. L. (2005). Patterning and plasticity of the cerebral cortex. *Science, 310,* 805–810.

Swain, J. E., Lorberbaum, J. P., Kose, S., & Strathearn, L. (2007). Brain basis of early parent-infant interactions: psychology, physiology, and in vivo functional neuroimaging studies. *Journal of Child Psychology and Psychiatry, 48,* 262–287.

Szyf, M., McGowan, P., & Meaney, M. J. (2008). The social environment and the epigenome. *Environmental and Molecular Mutagenesis, 49,* 46–60.

Tremolizzo, L., Doueiri, M. S., Dong, E., Grayson, D. R., Davis, J., Pinna, G., et al. (2005). Valproate corrects the schizophrenia-like epigenetic behavioral modifications induced by methionine in mice. *Biological Psychiatry, 57,* 500–509.

Tronick, E. (2007). *The neurobehavioral and social emotional development of infants and children.* New York: Norton.

Van Den Berg, C. L., Hol, T., Everts, H., Koolhaas, J. M., Van Ree, J. M., Spruijt, B. M. (1999). Play is indispensable for an adequate development of coping with social challenges in the rat. *Developmental Psychobiology, 34,* 129–138.

Vanderschuren, L. J., & Kalivas, P. W. (2000). Alterations in dopaminergic and glutamatergic transmission in the induction and expression of behavioral sensitization, a critical review of preclinical studies. *Psychopharmacology, 151,* 99–120.

Watt, D. F. & Panksepp, J. (2009). Depression: An evolutionarily conserved mechanism to terminate separation-distress? A review of aminergic, peptidergic, and neural network perspectives. *Neuropsychoanalysis, 11,* in press.

Wilens, T. E. (2004). Impact of ADHD and its treatment on substance abuse in adults. *Journal of Clinical Psychiatry, 65*(Suppl. 3), 38–45.

Wilens, T. E., & Biederman, J. (2006). Alcohol, drugs, and attention-deficit/ hyperactivity disorder: A model for the study of addictions in youth. *Journal of Psychopharmacology, 20*(4), 580–588.

# PUBLIC HEALTH, EDUCATION, AND POLICY IMPLICATIONS

## Carol M. Worthman

### INTRODUCTION

So far, the materials in this book have delineated emerging understandings of development and its relations with experience. These insights lend specificity and weight to the significance of context for development, and provide a basis on which to conceptualize how differences or perturbations in context influence its course. From such a framework, we can then project the consequences for differential function and health. A guiding motive, then, is the support of developmental needs and the realization of human potential. From this orientation, translation from lab to living room, from systematic observation to informed action, and from mutual incomprehension to engaged empathy emerge as important practical goals. Case studies throughout the book have explored lessons learned about decisive developmental contexts, moments, and dynamics from clinical, cross-species, or cross-cultural encounters. The challenge is to scale up from this knowledge for application at the national and international level.

In this section, the challenge is confronted, key issues identified, and solutions suggested for promotion of optimal child development and welfare. The contributions also grapple with an issue long disregarded in developmental research, namely the failure to represent the full range of conditions under which children live and develop. The preponderance of research concerns populations in the affluent countries that conduct it; only a small fraction of our knowledge draws from the widely varied and often impoverished settings where the great majority of humanity lives and develops. What we do know – largely from the databases of WHO and participating countries – documents the significance of three forms of adversity. First is the vast developmental burden of poverty with its attendant material deprivation, frayed social resources, and etiolated infrastructure. Reducing absolute poverty, magnified through its impact on development, exerts enormous leverage for increased human capital and welfare.

Second, social disruption and displacement through human and natural disasters or economic necessity stretches or rends the fabric of early experiences upon which development rests. Rates of family or child displacement and orphanhood continue to escalate while the absolute numbers exponentially increase. Third, inequality – above and beyond poverty – has emerged as a condition with damaging developmental, social, and health effects mediated by pervasive consequences for daily social relations and perceptions, relative conditions of work and living, and self image. Inequality occurs independent of population wealth, and thus may afflict affluent populations such as the United States. Therefore, social transformations and policies to redress inequity have attained importance second only to those against absolute poverty.

Thus, this section's contributions highlight the social restructuring and culture change required to implement what we already know about how to optimize formative experiences and realize developmental potential. Whether it is formation of a coherent child development system (Halfon and colleagues) or income transfers to households (Richter) or emphasis on the primary caregiver and systematic amelioration of inequity (Requejo and Bustreo), such action is a project in culture change. History and culture – established values, assumptions, practices, social arrangements, and power formations – re/produce the status quo and are inscribed on bodies and minds. Even an intervention such as a child vaccination campaign requires culture change in beliefs about what causes and prevents illness, understanding and use of technology, embodied states, and relations among the state, community, parents, and child. Consequently, concerted social action toward the welfare of children in itself must both manifest and drive culture change, and not simply follow from the application of rational evidence-based policy.

# NINETEEN

# Translations from Human Development to Public Policy

Neal Halfon, Emily S. Barrett, and Alice Kuo

Early childhood development (ECD) is receiving increased attention and scrutiny as policy makers attempt to respond to several historical, economic, scientific, and cultural changes that are transforming our understanding of the importance of the early years. This chapter tracks the evolution of our understanding about ECD and discusses the type of policy changes required to ensure that young children have the opportunity for optimal development. We propose a policy transformation framework to help guide the evolution of the current fragmented model of ECD services to a more responsive, comprehensive, integrated, and high performing early childhood system for the twenty-first century.

## OVERVIEW

Our analysis begins with a discussion of the historical, political, and cultural contexts that influence ECD policies, practices, and programs, with a special emphasis on the transactional relationship between cultural norms and policy development, decision-making, and implementation. We then discuss the evolution of early childhood policy in the United States, focusing specifically on outcomes that are reflected in current measures of children's health, development, and well-being and what we know about the performance of services, programs, and policies currently in place to improve child health and developmental outcomes. We introduce the Life Course Health Development framework to link theories of social, cognitive, and emotional development with clinical and policy-oriented approaches toward optimizing health development outcomes. The Life Course Health Development framework also provides the basis for a more integrated approach to ECD, one that is more in tune with the human capital development orientation of a post-industrial society.

The chapter then focuses on the organization and delivery of early childhood services and the gaps that exist in meeting the evolving needs of young children in the twenty-first century. Drawing on one of the dominant metaphors of the post-industrial age, we suggest that the current 1.0 version of the ECD operating system requires not just minor updating, but a comprehensive upgrade to ECD 2.0. We use this computer operating system metaphor to represent the kind of innovative policy change that will be necessary for us to evolve from a fragmented set of unrelated early childhood health, education, and family support services and programs to a universal early childhood system that will assure optimal development of children for a new economy in a new century. Moving from ECD 1.0 to 2.0 and eventually to ECD 3.0 and beyond will require a different way of aligning services, programs, and service delivery sectors, as well as policy, finance, and performance monitoring mechanisms.

Our analysis attempts to provide a new narrative about the nature of the ECD policy problem facing the United States and the solutions that need to be considered. We do not define the problem as a shortage of a particular service or lack of quality, even though there are many services that are in short supply and are of demonstrably poor quality and cry out for performance improvement. Rather, we are addressing a system-level problem with an operating logic that is no longer appropriate and functional to the task at hand. Our analysis implies that creating a high-functioning early childhood system for the twenty-first century will require not only incremental policy changes that update and expand existing services and fill in identifiable gaps, but also major policy jolts that will establish a new national framework for organizing, delivering, financing, and improving the early childhood system.

## CULTURAL BELIEFS SHAPE U.S. POLICY

In the United States, as in all of the Commonwealth countries, the Elizabethan Poor Laws have profoundly shaped our attitudes towards child policy. First established in England in 1601, the Elizabethan Poor Laws outlined how relief was to be distributed to the impoverished. Prior to the passage of these laws, charity to the poor was based on religious principles, with all Christians bound by duty to show mercy to the needy. With the Reformation overturning many of the existing moral codes, and poverty mounting in England, passage of the Elizabethan Poor Laws formalized how the impoverished would be treated. Among the new regulations, each parish was responsible for its own poor, and monies would be collected at the local level to assist them. The "indoor relief" provisos specified that the sick would be admitted to hospitals, the poor to almshouses, and orphans to orphanages. However the laws also specified that poor parents and children were to be responsible for one another, placing some responsibility for care on individual families. In general, parishes were left to administer the laws as they chose, leading to great variation in the stringency with which the laws were implemented.

Disdain for government intrusion into the private world of the family is still evident across Commonwealth countries today. Grounded in the Elizabethan Poor Laws, child and family policy in the United Kingdom, United States, Australia, Canada, and New Zealand is based upon the underlying belief that families should be self-reliant and care for their own needs. By extension, children must also learn the discipline necessary to become self-reliant adults, and they do not need societal investment or government intervention until the family has failed. Thus, rather than investing in child and family welfare in order to prevent problems and optimize development, the values inherent in these policies lead to social service systems that tend to address problems only after they have occurred.

This underlying philosophy, which is a hallmark of the American individualist mentality, contrasts directly with that of more collectivistic societies, in which social solidarity is valued as much as or more than individual autonomy, creativity, and achievement. In the West, Scandinavian countries represent this collectivist mentality; many Asian countries have also been characterized as having a strong collectivist orientation. These countries have developed systems of social services – such as child care, support for single parents, and parental leave – that are heavily financed by the government and available to all families, although there is some cross-national variation on the basis of whether these programs are grounded in social welfare or family policy.

Not surprisingly, differences in policy tend to be accompanied by differences in belief systems: In one study, over half the women in Norway expressed a belief that poverty is a product of social injustice, whereas only a third of American or Canadian women expressed that belief (Phipps, 2001). Reflected in the current policy milieu, this belief represents the prevailing and entrenched attitude in Commonwealth countries that too much charity to the underprivileged will foster laziness. One sign of the difference between Commonwealth and Scandinavian attitudes is that Scandinavian countries show a sense of social responsibility for all children by developing universal programs, as opposed to the targeted programs more common in the Commonwealth.

Along with the historical legacy of the Poor Laws, U.S. child policy has been shaped by the ethos of American independence and individualism. The importance of these twin ideals is obvious in the Declaration of Independence, which outlines protections for the individual against potential tyranny by the state, and in the Puritan/Protestant doctrines, which emphasize individual responsibility (Kamerman & Kahn, 2001). In one survey comparing attitudes about values children should learn in the home, American respondents were more likely than Canadians to report that independence, hard work, imagination, and religious faith are important. Americans were less likely to mention tolerance/respect as a value that should be taught at home (Phipps, 2001). As a result, there has been a historical reluctance to implement policies that interfere with the sovereignty of the family and individual. This has been evident throughout twentieth century American history, as shown by the United State's failure to implement policies to facilitate the entry of mothers into the labor force during World War II, when their contributions were desperately needed (Cooper, 1993). Even during the Progressive Era, when there was great consensus among reformers on the importance of family life and the evils of existing systems of institutionalization, there was still a great deal of discord about the exact role that government should play in reforms (Katz, 1986).

A consequence of our historical context and our long-standing value system, the resulting American reluctance to implement universal child and family-friendly policies means that no explicitly outlined overarching child and family policy exists – not even a suite of policies that together form an integrated American child and family welfare system. Historically, health care was relatively affordable, few mothers worked, and family support networks tended to be strong and local, and an official federal policy on children and family was considered less critical for the successful development of most children (Halfon & McLearn, 2002). But with the transition to a post-industrial economy, the changing face of the American family, growing levels of inequality, and lower levels of educational achievement, it now can be argued that a cohesive national early childhood policy takes on greater import. What exists is a fragmented set of individual problem-specific policies, each of which affects children and families in its own way; not surprisingly, these policies tend to be limited in vision, scope, funding, and coverage (Kamerman & Kahn, 2001).

Characteristic of these programs is a targeted approach that focuses only on sub-populations including the poor, the handicapped, and the severely deprived. Clearly reflecting the Elizabethan Poor Laws, the U.S. government tends to stay out of family life except in situations in which the family proves incapable of providing for itself. In contrast to the Scandinavian model, which emphasizes universal, preventive programs, U.S. child policy has mostly resulted in second-chance types of programs aimed specifically at children or families that have already experienced difficulties or displayed deficits.

For instance, the current program for poor children and mothers, Temporary Assistance to Needy Families (TANF), is limited to mothers who meet a highly restrictive set of criteria. In order to qualify for federal aid, eligible mothers must be "employable" and available to work within three months of giving birth, and they can receive benefits for no more than five years. States administering the block grants must establish teen pregnancy prevention programs, and only teen mothers who participate in educational and training activities can receive aid (Kamerman & Kahn, 2001).

Implementation of TANF policies has been largely left in states' hands, illustrating a second characteristic problem with this piecemeal policy approach: Most programs are state or local-driven, rather than federally regulated. As a result, great variation exists in the extent of and administration of child and family-related social welfare programs. The resulting policy is a disjointed set of partial solutions – disconnected programs and funding streams that have neither clear accountability nor explicit performance goals (Halfon, DuPlessis, & Inkelas, 2007). Integration, organization, and systemization are difficult, if not impossible, because of the patchwork nature of the current system.

This sort of fragmented, second-chance system is at odds with the current movement to optimize health and development in all children by addressing categorical inequalities. Historically unregulated market forces in the United States have generated massive socioeconomic disparities in the post-industrial age. At the same time, there is increasing recognition that optimizing developmental trajectories requires minimizing inequalities early in life and their impact on the developing child. Unless specific attempts are made to redress these inequalities, they tend not only to persist, but to multiply over time. In the post-industrial world, investment in early childhood signifies an attempt to level the playing field and reduce or eliminate the long-term impact of inequalities experienced in early life.

## EARLY CHILDHOOD POLICY AND THE EMERGING EARLY CHILDHOOD DEVELOPMENT SYSTEM

The transactional nature of the policy/culture relationship means that policy can, in essence, frame the cultural scaffolding that supports early childhood development. Policy not only provides legal protections and risk prevention, but it has the potential to promote optimal health development.

Policy effectively shapes the cultural rules, mores, and norms that together determine the relative position, condition, and treatment of children and families in a given society.

In practice, a wide variety of policies with different intents, goals, and scopes influence child development. Most obvious are policies that explicitly address and improve some aspect of early child development. Many of these cater to targeted populations; for instance, Part C (or the early intervention program) of the Individuals with Disabilities ACT (IDEA) provides programs and legal protections for infants and toddlers who have or are at risk for disabilities. In addition to providing early interventions, the program hopes to reduce the costs of and need for special education, reduce institutionalization, promote independent living, and assist families in meeting their children's needs.

Other policies share this focus on early childhood development but have a broader goal of serving all children, rather than targeted populations. For instance, one movement calls for enacting national policies that would provide free, voluntary public preschool to all families nationwide. Having met with a good deal of opposition, the federal movement toward universal preschool has stalled, but several states, including Florida and Illinois, have launched similar efforts to ensure access to high-quality preschool for all 3- and 4-year-olds.

Other policies that do not focus on child development *per se* create conditions that directly or indirectly influence children's welfare. For example, policies on parental leave (both maternal and paternal) are not necessarily designed with early childhood development in mind; however, they clearly affect ECD. Internationally, parental leave rights vary dramatically. Sweden's system guarantees 18 months of parental leave per child and is jointly paid for by state and employers. More typically, nations offer 12–14 weeks of leave for mothers. The United States is a notable exception to this trend; currently there is no federally mandated, guaranteed, paid maternity leave, although the 1993 Family and Medical Leave Act ensured that both male and female employees of middle-sized to large companies are entitled to 12 weeks of unpaid job protection when they engage in birth or adoption. Based on an international comparison of the effects of parental leave policies on child health outcomes, Tanaka (2005) argues that job-protected paid parental leave (but not unpaid leave) has significant effects on reducing post-neonatal infant mortality rates after controlling for social policy and expenditure variables.

Other policies that have little or no intent to influence children's development or families have indirect effects nonetheless. Transportation policy is a good example. In determining the allocation of space, the kinds of public transportation available, and the safety of non-motorized transit, transportation policy affects some behavior patterns of children, such as whether they walk or take bicycles. Policies that promote the extensive use of cars to the detriment of non-motorized transit, for example, can affect not only physical fitness but also mental health and independence.

A logical next step would be to integrate the varied policies that influence early childhood development into a larger human capital investment strategy. While Scandinavian and other European countries have led the way by creating a portfolio of linked policies, programs, and services, recent efforts by the United Kingdom (UK) are perhaps the most illustrative and directly relevant to the United States, given that the countries share many values and have a similar approach to the child welfare state. In 1998 the UK launched a set of policy changes to end child poverty over twenty years; these included a strategy of investing in human capital and upgrading and improving the performance of the children's service systems where that investment would be made. This game-changing strategy launched several major policy initiatives including Sure Start (1998) to build a comprehensive early childhood system; Every Child Matters (2003) to provide a framework and plan for linking services and sectors to achieve uniform outcomes; the Children's Act (2004) to implement changes in local service delivery systems; and the establishment in 2007 of the Department for Children, Schools and Families as a consolidated government department to oversee and administer this major policy transformation. Established originally in some of England's poorest areas, Sure Start delivers integrated family support, health promotion, and early learning and play experiences for children under the age of four. Each Sure Start area is relatively small, targeting about 800 children. Begun with 250 programs, there are now 2500 Sure Start Centers with plans underway for the completion of 3500 by 2010. Encouraged, if not emboldened, by their success, the newly reconstituted Department for Children, Schools and Families recently declared that its intent is "to make this country the best place in the world for children and young people to grow up" (n.d.).

Not surprisingly, differences in policy and in the care and attention paid to formally ensuring children's well-being have dramatic and tangible effects on outcomes. UNICEF Innocenti Research Centre's 2007 report, "An overview of child well-being in rich countries," clearly illustrates how striking and pervasive international differences are. Noting consistent trends across countries, the report compares children of the 21 nations of the industrialized world on six dimensions of well-being (material well-being, health and safety, education, peer and family relationships, behaviors and risks, and subjective sense of well-being), as well as 40 sub-indicators. The Netherlands and the Scandinavian nations ranked at or near the top of every comparison, while the United States and United Kingdom fared poorly on nearly every dimension of child well-being.

In explaining the value of these international comparisons, the report notes that levels of child well-being are not inevitable and do not depend on wealth, but rather result from policy and therefore signify the potential for all countries to actively improve their child development systems. This statement is dramatically underscored by comparing national rates of child poverty before and after the implementation of taxation and income transfer policies. These comparisons demonstrate how child poverty rates, defining poverty as 60% below median national income, are very comparable across advanced nations. But huge differences emerge between the United States and other nations once the levers of government are used to impose greater equality. Even among these wealthy nations, which have agreed upon the *Convention on the Rights of the Child* and which profess to invest in children and their health to the maximum extent possible, the vast variations point to differences in prioritizing children in policy-making and allocating resources.

Building on the results of the UNICEF report, Pickett and Wilkinson (2007) analyzed relationships among child well-being measures and material living standards, income inequality, and poverty across (a) 23 wealthy nations and (b) U.S. states. Whereas material living standards (as assessed by average income) showed little or no relationship to measures of child health and well-being in either analysis, income inequality was associated with worse health and education outcomes. These patterns were present both internationally and across U.S. states, with outcomes significantly worse in nations and states with greater income inequality. These results suggest that at least within economically developed populations, relative income and social position are more important than absolute material standards in determining child health and well-being. It is not clear whether these associations result from a relative scarcity of material resources, effects of relative poverty on family life, heightened awareness of inferior social position and resulting anxiety, or some other factor.

## NEW EPIDEMIOLOGY OF CHILDHOOD

Major social, economic, and health care changes have transformed the risks that children experience, the protective factors available to them, and the

# Children & Youth at Risk

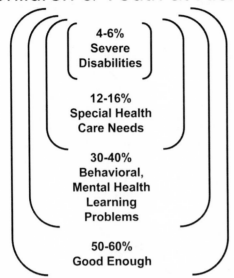

**Figure 19.1.** Distribution of health, developmental, and behavioral problems in children.

kinds of outcomes related to health, development, and education that are observed. While we cannot elucidate all of these changes, we can say that childhood mortality from all causes has been steadily decreasing, with mortality rates for children aged one to fourteen falling by nearly 50% between 1980 and 2003. However, even with this laudable success, more children are being diagnosed with chronic medical problems (affecting 10–14% of all children and youth), mental health problems (affecting 15–20% of children and youth), and developmental problems (such as learning and language delays, affecting 10–17% of all children and youth). While threats of the past, including many deadly and debilitating infectious diseases, have been virtually eliminated as a result of effective vaccines and policies requiring universal immunizations, other threats have emerged, such as the current epidemic of childhood obesity and diabetes. Figure 19.1 attempts to capture the general distribution of health, developmental, and behavioral conditions in children. It suggests a pyramidal distribution: 4–6 % of children and youth with severe disabilities; 12–16% with special medical and mental health needs; 30–40% with developmental, learning, behavioral, or other adaptive disorders, or at risk for developing them; and about 50–60% of the population that is relatively free of any disorder at any one time.

Even while many health problems have improved, disparities in health, developmental, and educational outcomes are increasing. Across a range of outcomes – from infant mortality to childhood obesity – large disparities persist and are increasing in many instances (Wise, 2004; Newacheck & Halfon, 2000). For example, despite the general trend of decreasing child mortality, ratios of excessive mortality in African American children have increased over the past twenty years. Differences in prevalence and impact of disease across family income categories also show large, and in many cases growing, disparities (Wise, 2004).

Child policy can strategically respond to the changing epidemiology of children's health and development in many ways. Policies can be enacted to improve access and availability to services that can screen children, diagnose conditions, and provide appropriate intervention. Policies can also be enacted that attempt to prevent the onset of problems in children by changing their exposure to risk and by increasing protective and promoting factors. The United States has focused much more on screening, diagnosing, and treating individuals than on instituting population-based preventive strategies aimed at shifting risk and optimizing health development trajectories for all children. More comprehensive and integrated policies can utilize individual and population approaches to screen, diagnose, and treat, as well as to prevent, promote, and optimize. By responding to the pyramid of need and understanding the developmental origins and trajectories for many conditions, policy can enable a continuum of appropriate programs and interventions that include:

- Specialized services and programs that target children burdened with the highest levels of need because of chronic and disabling medical or mental health conditions, as well as children with very high risk and stress related to extreme poverty and family dysfunction. Efforts might include school-based treatment services for autistic children, rehabilitation services for children with neurodevelopmental disorders, or a home visitation program by nurses for teen-age mothers living in an impoverished community.
- Broadly targeted services that focus on populations defined by needs (e.g., special health conditions like asthma or ADHD) or by risks, such as extreme poverty. Services might include early enrichment programs similar to Head Start, Reach Out and Read, or other health-care support for children with special health-care needs (CSHCN).
- Universal services that enable all children to achieve optimal health and development and to address routine and predictable problems that

have straightforward solutions. Examples include high quality health care, early care, and education.

Even when powerful treatment results and cost benefit data are available to support the use of a particular program or service, implementing a new service into a fragmented and balkanized early childhood service delivery reality poses a number of challenges. Just as important as the new emerging picture of children's health and development is the realization that reducing risks to children's health and development is quite different from optimizing health and developmental outcomes. In other words, designing public policy with the goal of optimizing health and development outcomes so that all children thrive is quite different from simply trying to minimize insults and treating disease, disability, and dysfunction once they are present.

## EXPOSURE TO POVERTY

In 2004 approximately 12 million U.S. children (17% of total) lived below the federal poverty line, with 5 million (7%) living in extreme poverty, defined as family income less than 50% of the poverty threshold. Compounding the problem, research suggests that our current definition of poverty is insufficient; in reality a family's income must be twice the amount defined as the federal poverty level to meet basic needs. This category, designated as low-income, has 27 million American children (38%) in it. Meanwhile, the number of people living below the official poverty line has increased by 10% in the United States since 2000.

A more in-depth examination of child poverty quickly reveals dramatic variations in risks, exposures, opportunities, and outcomes, however. Well-documented nationwide disparities related to age, race and ethnicity, and region exist, and the children most likely to suffer from poverty are young, African American or Latino, or from the South. Following the Great Society reforms of the mid-1960s, differences in poverty rates among children decreased, but today, 40 years after those measures were passed, racial disparities associated with poverty rates remain particularly persistent.

More generally, economic disparities in the United States decreased from the New Deal (1935) through 1970, but have since increased dramatically. In fact income inequality has grown rapidly since the Great Society. In the United States, the Gini Index (a measure of income inequality) has increased by nearly 25% since 1968 (www.census.gov) and the wealthiest quintile of U.S. households now control 49% of the income and 83% of the wealth (Census Bureau, 2001; Moffitt, Ribar, & Wilhelm, 1998; Wolff, 2001).

The impact of family poverty on the developing child has been extensively studied. Research has demonstrated not only direct impacts of material deprivation on child development, but how family stress and the burdens engendered by a lack of material resources render young children more vulnerable to health, cognitive, behavioral, and social deficits (Evans, 2004). This research has confirmed that poor children are exposed to more turmoil, violence, separation from families, instability, and chaos in their households. They also experience less social support, and their parents tend to adopt a parenting style that is less responsive and more authoritarian. In addition, the air and water they consume is more polluted; their schools and child care are of poorer quality; their neighborhoods are more dangerous and expose them to a host of risks; and their access to health, social, and other services is inferior to that of their more economically advantaged counterparts (Evans, 2004). Research on social deprivation and child development has begun to translate how this legacy of social risk and adverse exposure "gets under the skin" and mediates changes in the programming and response patterns of bio-behavioral systems that influence long-term health and development (Taylor & Reppetti, 2001; others). Recently Gunnar and others have begun to utilize a stress paradigm to explain how exposure to higher levels of what they term "toxic stress" can significantly affect development (Gunnar & Fisher, 2006). Higher levels of toxic stress have been associated with poverty.

## THE LIFE COURSE HEALTH DEVELOPMENT MODEL

The past several decades have witnessed phenomenal advances in our understanding of how health and disease develop (Keating & Hertzman, 2000). We now have the ability to connect the dots between events, experiences, and early-life exposures with educational and health outcomes, including diseases that take decades to become clinically evident. Developmental psychology and neurobiology have transformed our understanding of how biological, chemical, behavioral, and social factors influence developmental trajectories. Some of these studies highlight the role that social adversity (including abuse, neglect, and living in poverty) plays in health trajectories and development of stress-induced mental and physical health problems (Dube, Felitti, Dong, Giles, & Anda, 2003; Felleti et al., 1998; Melchior, Moffitt, Milne, Poulton, & Caspi, 2007). The field of life-course chronic disease epidemiology has yielded hundreds of influential population-based studies demonstrating the link between early life events and many common chronic diseases that usually manifest in adulthood. Meanwhile, research on the developmental origins of adult disease is unraveling how genes and environments interact, pinpointing the mechanisms by which early events are programmed into developing immune, neurological, endocrine, and other physiologic systems. These studies are disentangling, for example, how relative malnutrition of a fetus – because of poor health, smoking, stress, or mechanical problems in pregnancy – can lead to long-lasting physiologic changes in fat and carbohydrate metabolism, thereby increasing the risk of diabetes, heart disease, hypertension, and obesity in adulthood (Kuh & Hardy, 2002; Power et al., 2005; Hertzman, Power, Matthews, & Manor, 2001).

This research has led to a burgeoning interest in Life Course Health Development (LCHD) as a model for better understanding the development of disease and the promotion of health (Halfon & Hochstein, 2002). The LCHD approach builds on the life span (longitudinal connections) and life stage (developmental periods) models by specifying the biological and behavioral mechanisms that determine health trajectories, thus yielding new ways to optimize health outcomes. From a LCHD perspective, health is a developmental process with health status at any given time determined by risk factors, exposures, and events that make us more vulnerable to disease, as well as by protective factors that mitigate risks, enhance resilience, and fortify our health potential.

Figure 19.2 presents a schematic of two different health trajectories. Both show that the earlier years establish different levels of functional health development, followed by stabilization during the middle years, and decline toward the end of life. The different life-long health trajectories are portrayed as the result of competing positive (upward) protective influences, and negative (downward) risk factors. Simply put, optimal health is more likely to occur when risks are minimized and protective and promoting factors are optimized. The implications for our nation's health spending are clear if we can delay disability and compress the period when morbidities are present. This model also provides important insights into the origins of health disparities. Small disadvantages early in life are compounded over time, leading to poorer health at all life stages and persistent gaps between individuals on higher and lower health trajectories.

Building on the strengths and underlying principles of earlier child development models, the LCHD model provides an integrating framework for understanding human development in a more holistic fashion.

# How Risk Reduction and Health Promotion Strategies Influence Health Development

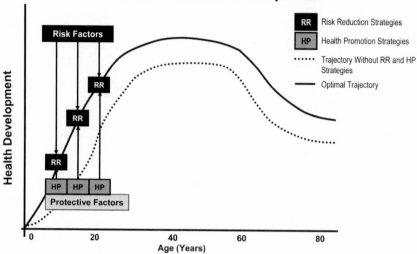

**Figure 19.2.** Model of a health development trajectory. From Halfon, N., & Hochstein, M. (2002). Life course health development: An integrated framework for developing health and financing health intervention. *The Milbank Quarterly, 80*, 433–479. Copyright 2002 by Wiley-Blackwell. Reprinted with permission.

As defined by Halfon and Hochstein (2002), LCHD is "a lifelong adaptive process that builds and maintains optimal functional capacity and disease resistance." The LCHD framework recognizes that multiple determinants of development operate in numerous domains (e.g., physical, cognitive, emotional, social) and at different levels of social organization (e.g., individual, family, community, service delivery system), and that their influences are best understood as dynamic transactions rather than as unidirectional or static relationships. The LCHD model also considers underlying biopsychosocial mechanisms in order to better understand health development and disease outcomes. Not only does this model emphasize a longitudinal perspective that is limited or absent in the previous models, but it is strategically actionable and can be used by public health, social welfare, medicine, education, and other sectors. The utility and generalizability of the LCHD approach enables cross-sector strategies to be created for optimal child health and developmental outcomes.

Therefore the LCHD approach provides:

• a powerful and simplifying theoretical construct to integrate scientific evidence from several fields of study focused on human development;

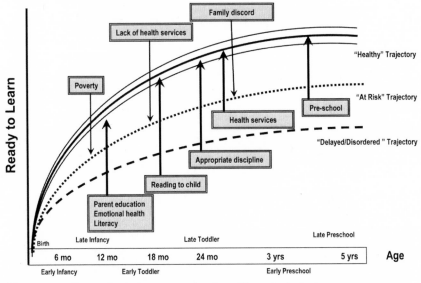

**Figure 19.3.** Strategies to improve school readiness trajectories.

- a conceptual model to connect different types of intervention that have traditionally resided in different agencies, in order to devise new cross sector strategies to optimize health and development;
- a practical approach to link individual and population-focused measurement, assessment, and intervention strategies to address health and developmental risk at a clinical/individual, family, community, service system, or policy level.

Applying the LCHD approach to specific early child development issues helps simplify the abundant empirical evidence about the impacts of various risk and protective factors on health development trajectories, and to begin to formulate policy strategies that focus on optimizing developmental outcomes for all children. Figure 19.3 applies the basic LCHD analytic framework to improving school readiness trajectories. This figure presents three different school readiness trajectories, representing three distinct populations of children. As in the more general model, risk factors impose negative pressures on school readiness trajectories, whereas specific behaviors, programs, and schools can enhance trajectories, often by mitigating risks.

## CURRENT AND FUTURE MODELS OF EARLY CHILDHOOD SERVICES IN THE UNITED STATES

### Current Status of Early Childhood Services in the United States
### ECD 1.0

Our analysis of the current status of the ECD services and the US ECD system is informed by the LCHD approach, and the recognition that an effective ECD system would accomplish the following: Respond to the changing epidemiology of children's health and development; strategically address the pyramid of need for children at different ages and stages of development; and have a clear operating logic, specific outcome goals, appropriate design principles, responsive financing and support, and strategic measures to ensure performance improvement and advancement along the way. We have defined the problem as a systems problem and not just the absence of a particular service (e.g., universal preschool or universal developmental screening). Therefore, it requires a systems-focused solution. Because complex systems evolve in continuous and discontinuous ways, we have utilized the information systems notion of software upgrades (1.0, 2.0, and 3.0) to convey the idea of an ongoing need to significantly upgrade the proposed ECD system, based on the principles outlined above, rather than simply updating our current system or adding some additional services.

Despite the increasing evidence for the need to invest in early childhood development if we are to optimize outcomes for children, our existing service system (version 1.0) poses challenges for families. It focuses on providing *services* to at-risk children and their families through programs that often exist within a specific service sector (Table 19.1). The operating logic of ECD 1.0 is still based on school system needs and the "vantage point of the kindergarten door," that is, the viewpoint of elementary schools toward children who arrive with different kinds of problems, disabilities, and delays. A maturation ECD model depicts a system that continues to focus on whether a child is mature and able to enter school. It eschews the call from the 1992 National Educational Goals Panel for a new approach to defining school readiness, which called on families and communities to work together to create the supports that children need to enhance development from the prenatal period to kindergarten entry. In Table 19.1, we characterize this ECD 1.0 operating logic as focusing on early childhood development, rather than on how to optimize development from birth (as does the LCHD approach).

**Table 19.1.** *ECD System Transformational Framework*

| Components | ECD 1.0 (Current System) | ECD 2.0 (In Progress) | ECD 3.0 (Future Upgrade) |
|---|---|---|---|
| Logic Model | 5 to zero, looking back | Zero to 5, transactional, LCHD | Optimizing Development |
| Organization of ECD Producing Sectors | Isolated sectors | Cross-sector paths to join up services and sectors | Integrated System of functional and geographic based ECD networks |
| Organization & Delivery of Individual Services | Fragmented | One stop FRC/SR Sure Start Centers | Integrated network of Early Learning an Health Centers |
| Education & Workforce Dev't | Ad-hoc | Linking ECE workforce & Economic Develop | New types of providers with new training programs |
| Market Structure | Disorganized, fragmented | Service Sectors embedded in new value production path | New service production networks with more horizontal integration across sectors |
| Funding | Program and service specific, organized in silos, restrictions on combining or pooling | Consolidation of funding streams and filling gaps with new funds focused on enhancing SR | New investment mechanisms, supporting life long development |
| Planning | Very little to none | City, state | National Plan |
| Regulation & Governance | Fragmented across sectors | Joint plan-ning/ECCS | Integrated system |
| Performance Monitoring | Service by service; mostly for financial accountability | New measures like the Early Development Instrument (EDI) | Mapping outcomes and trajectories at neighborhood, community and systems level |

The most obvious challenge for families in navigating the current system of early childhood services is the fragmentation of service delivery and the lack of coordination between programs, organizations, and agencies. Early childhood services are currently situated in multiple sectors, with health, education, and child welfare playing important yet distinct roles in assessing needs, identifying resources and services, and connecting children and families to them. From a family's perspective, discerning which sector is responsible for a certain slate of services can be particularly daunting, especially when the eligibility, application process, and receipt of services from particular programs are not transparent. The location of these programs in specific sectors also reflects problem-based and discipline-defined service-delivery models, as well as the current state of categorical funding, which not only determines financial viability, but also imposes real constraints on how services can be organized and delivered. Attempts to develop cross-sector programs often face financial constraints and challenges related to funding structures. Finally, the currently fragmented service-delivery systems have encouraged significant "cultures" to grow within each service sector; identifying potential collaborations between service sectors often requires in-depth knowledge of the particular processes and criteria of each sector. For example, to improve communication between pediatricians and early care and education (ECE) providers about children with possible developmental issues, it is necessary to understand how both the child health system and the ECE system work; why communication between the two is difficult; and finally, how to improve the referral and response process between the two sectors. To expect families to have the knowledge and expertise to coordinate between such service sectors is unrealistic, given that most families have not only resource challenges but also complex needs that are often beyond the capability of any single service or program.

Families also have difficulty accessing services in the current 1.0 version of the ECD system for a number of reasons. The first is that the demand for services is greater than their availability. Many ECD programs are underfunded because of the categorical nature of funding within service sectors. For example, the amount of funds going toward children with potential or identified developmental problems is miniscule compared with the overall health costs of the entire population, particularly of the growing aging sector. In education, where IDEA has essentially been an unfunded federal mandate since its inception in the 1970s, most funding for special education is aimed at services for children in the K–12 setting, as opposed to 3- and 4-year-olds, an age group targeted by the Part C mandate of IDEA; it specifies support for preschoolers in each school's community catchment area, regardless of enrollment in preschool programs. Lacking a national ECD policy or agenda, sector-specific advocates must compete for a share of funding that is meant to address larger populations, with the result that funding and service availability cannot keep up with demand. With each state designing its eligibility standards, an enormous variation exists in the number of children served. For example, the IDEA screening and referral rates between high- and low-performing states vary as much as fourfold.

In addition to the demand and supply issue, families have difficulty accessing services because of often narrow programmatic criteria for eligibility. In California, for example, developmental disabilities services for children aged 2 to 3 years are organized via a set of 21 Regional Centers established by the Lanterman Act of 1971. These centers provide services to children 0–3 years of age on the basis of the child's at-risk status, regardless of whether the risk comes from health (e.g., having been born prematurely or spent significant time in a neonatal intensive care unit) or from socio-economic status. However, when a child turns 3, the Regional Centers narrow their eligibility criteria by requiring a developmental disability diagnosis in order to continue services. If a diagnosis is not readily available or if a 3- to 4-year-old child would benefit from additional services prior to kindergarten entry, the family faces a challenge. In addition, these Regional Centers consider themselves the "payor of last resort," which means that the education system must provide services for children between the ages of 3 and 21 (or high school graduation, whichever comes first).

In summary, the current 1.0 system of ECD services reflects an outmoded model of care. The focus of the current state is on treatment through services rather than on prevention of problems or early intervention through a more coordinated system of care for children and families. Because the bits and pieces of ECD programs are situated within different and disparate service sectors, contact between programs and families is episodic, and communities are not motivated to improve the situation. Given the separate categorical funding streams, it is virtually impossible to create integrated approaches that would link services and pool funding. Thus, creating more integrated one-stop resource centers on the order of the UK's Sure Start centers becomes all the more difficult.

### Innovative ECD Programs: Going from 1.0 to 2.0

To build ECD systems for the twenty-first century, we must adopt a new operating logic, one that would optimize development of all children and involves moving from a system of fragmented services to a more integrated service delivery model based on multiple sectors. Several U.S. communities are moving toward an ECD 2.0 version by enacting policies and creating new service delivery models and innovative program designed to provide a more comprehensive approach (Table 19.1). These communities have recognized the need to "broadband" services and provide one-stop service delivery platforms that allow families to access a menu of services For example, EDUCARE, with the support of the Buffett Early Childhood Fund, is attempting to place 12–15 Educare Centers in 10 to 12 states as a comprehensive early childhood center-based model. In Los Angeles, the Hope Street Family Center serves 2000 downtown families with a range of early childhood health, development, and support services. If the United States begins to see the value of making community-based early childhood service hubs more available, a policy initiative similar to the United Kingdom's Sure Start might be developed to help establish early enrichment, health development, and family support centers in needy American neighborhoods.

Creating, scaling, and spreading such integrated models will require a transformation in how service sectors are currently organized, a new and differently trained workforce, and an ability to reorganize the currently fragmented and disorganized market into one that can efficiently pool funding streams and fund integrated approaches. Currently, multiple approaches are underway to improve the ECD system, and many innovative approaches are being taken at the program, community, and policy levels. Efforts include implementing evidence-based programs, as well as combining different programs into more integrated service delivery systems.

To promote better health and developmental outcomes, the ECD 2.0 system will need to provide risk-based services that are organized to create the scaffolding that supports an optimal health development trajectory. Figure 19.4 provides a schematic depiction of two developmental trajectories. The more positive trajectory is supported by a scaffolding of evidence-based programs. At each point, children are afforded the benefit of the basic supports they need, including appropriate health care, as represented by the continuous impact of the pediatric medical home (PED); appropriate early learning experiences represented by the early literacy program Reach Out and Read (ROR); Early Head Start, Head Start, early care and education, and school readiness (SR) programs; appropriate family support (as represented by the Nurse Family Partnership home-based visiting program); and access to a neighborhood-based family resource center (FRC). This diagram also shows that these services are both horizontally integrated (across health, education and family support sectors), as well as longitudinally integrated over time. By linking and integrating these evidence-based programs, we can create the scaffolding to support a more optimal

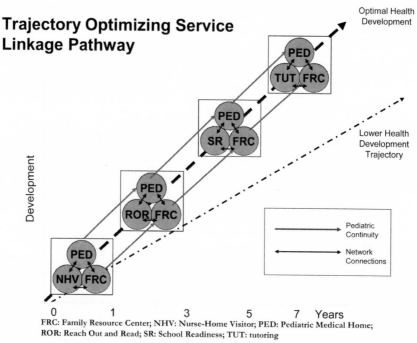

**Trajectory Optimizing Service Linkage Pathway**

Optimal Health Development

Lower Health Development Trajectory

Development

Pediatric Continuity

Network Connections

0   1   3   5   7   Years

FRC: Family Resource Center; NHV: Nurse-Home Visitor; PED: Pediatric Medical Home; ROR: Reach Out and Read; SR: School Readiness; TUT: tutoring

**Figure 19.4.** Trajectory optimizing service linkage pathway. From Halfon, N., DuPlessis, H., & Barrett, E. (2008). Looking back at pediatrics to move forward in obstetrics. *Current Opinion in Obstetrics and Gynecology, 20*(6), 566–573. Copyright 2008, with permission from Wolters Kluwer.

developmental trajectory. In much the same way that building codes provide specifications for scaffolding that protects a building from being damaged by an earthquake, the right kind of service scaffolding is necessary if children and families are to withstand the stressors that inevitably emerge and threaten to knock them off track and into low lifelong health trajectories. ECD 2.0 will need to be built with this level of specification and with new measurement tools and strategies that can demonstrate the desired results.

To facilitate state and local level efforts to develop cross-sector approaches, a number of states have developed new government or quasi-governmental agencies or commissions to oversee efforts to integrate their fragmented services. In addition to California's state and county First 5 Commissions, Michigan in 2005 established the Michigan Early Childhood Investment Corporation (ECIC), which aims to ensure that all children arrive at kindergarten ready for success. To this end, the early care and education, physical health, mental health, family support, and child safety sectors are integrated under a public corporation funded by both public and private sectors. ECIC currently funds 21 Great Start Collaboratives in local communities to train leaders on child health and development and to advocate for policy changes needed to achieve their goals. Ultimately, the ECIC aims to establish such collaboratives throughout the state.

The federal government's Maternal and Child Health Bureau has attempted to help states promote greater service integration through the Early Childhood Comprehensive Systems (ECCS) Initiative. ECCS provides grants to support state and local efforts to develop comprehensive systems of childhood services, including home health care and medical, socio-emotional, and mental health care; early care and education; and family support and parenting education. As with First 5 and ECIC, ECCS attempts to bring together a broad coalition of stakeholders from public and private agencies, parents and community members in order to meet the needs of young children.

These programs are also attempting to institute innovative funding and accountability arrangements that move the involved communities toward a more integrated approach to ECD. In addition, these programs offer improved local coordination, flexibility of services, and increased community and consumer participation. For families, the goal is a one-stop network for the organization and delivery of services, with multiple entry points to the network and cross-sector paths between and among the ECD sectors.

One new aspect of the 2.0 system that was not addressed in the 1.0 system is the focus on outcomes and the measuring of early learning and health development outcomes in the population. Moving toward a systems-improvement approach requires a feedback loop of data and outcomes so that incremental steps can be made to improve the system. Some more advanced 2.0 systems have put into place population-based measures to monitor progress of the system and the cross-sector interventions that have been developed. One such population-based measure is the Early Development Instrument (EDI), developed in Canada, which is being used more widely internationally. It measures school readiness and includes five different scales that account for physical, cognitive, social, emotional, and language development. The EDI is administered to all children entering kindergarten and then is used to develop an aggregate measure of the school readiness of children in a particular neighborhood. EDI results are mapped neighborhood-by-neighborhood and linked to other assets available to children in that locale. Thus, it can be used to monitor progress in improving the ECD system in those communities. Several U.S. communities have also adopted the EDI to monitor progress in changing child development outcomes under their current ECD system.

## Future of Early Childhood Services in the United States 2.0 to 3.0

Just as upgrading from ECD 1.0 to ECD 2.0 requires cross-cutting strategies to accomplish unifying goals such as "school readiness" for all children, upgrading from ECD 2.0 to 3.0 will require ambitious strategies that shift the system toward an integrated and high performing model of service delivery. Clearly focused on the evolving pyramid of needs and risks, the ECD 3.0 system should have well developed approaches for providing specialized, targeted, universal services to the appropriate population of children; it must also demonstrate its impact by measuring shifts in population outcomes, using a common unified measure such as the EDI. Politically, passing legislation to create neighborhood-based, comprehensive ECD centers to house and integrate existing Head Start and Early Head Start and Early Intervention programs could provide the kind of policy jolt and resource base necessary to move the system to the next level.

## Role of Innovation and the Politics of Transformation

In order to transform the ECD system in the United States both collaborative innovation and collective invention are needed. The existing systems will have to be rebalanced, realigned, reengineered, and refinanced as we complete the 1.0 to 2.0 transition and move toward the 3.0 system. Not only will new partnerships be needed, but both problems (and solutions) will have to be redefined as system level problems rather than simply as deficits in particular services.

To shift health development trajectories in a positive direction, an integrated, comprehensive approach will be required. Services need to be more flexible and better aligned, with improved coordination at the community level, as well as increased community and consumer participation. Rather than addressing problems after they occur, efforts (and resources) should be increasingly directed toward prevention, health promotion, early intervention, and developmental optimization, with better data collection and specific targets for outcomes and systems performance. Finally, we will need novel ways to finance these changes through innovative funding and accountability arrangements.

## CONCLUSION

By many measures, U.S. child development policy is not what it could and should be. Many children begin life with far too many risks and experience the kinds of toxic stresses that will impede their development, life-long health, and success. Too many children live in poverty and in low income families that can barely provide the basic resources for their children to survive, let alone thrive. Many children start school with preventable deficits and disabilities, which not only require additional special education resources, but put them at greater risk of dropping out of school and suffering long-term employment, family, and social challenges.

We have argued that child policy reflects its historical era, and that the child-raising expectations of the dominant culture do not necessarily support families by providing the resources they need. With its transition to a post-industrial, globalized economy, the United States is experiencing economic, social and demographic changes that are fundamentally altering the environments in which children live and the context in which they are developing. Like canaries in the coal mine, children often serve to reflect changes in society, especially those that cause alterations in their health and development.

To compete in the current world economy, the United States faces the daunting imperative to re-engineer many of its basic systems, including banking, health care, education, and child development, so that the nation and its citizens can continue to thrive. Moving the nation's ECD system into the twenty-first century requires not just updating old models and ideas, but upgrading the entire system. Our current ECD 1.0 system is a victim of its historical legacy: it is deficit-focused, primarily in the area of detecting disabilities in children and ameliorating their impacts on educational trajectories. The system is fragmented and underfunded, constrained by a piecemeal approach to solving specific problems, and lacking the vision, goals and logic that a well functioning twenty-first century ECD service system should have.

Many policy changes are necessary to move the nation forward, support the emerging ECD 2.0 system, and set in place the operating logic, systems changes, and policies that will usher in a high performing and even more integrated 3.0 system. Much can be learned from the efforts of the many countries that have established ECD systems to meet their specific needs. In particular, the United Kingdom is a good example for the United States to follow because of the shared values and similarities that underlie the organization of our welfare states. Recent policy changes in the United Kingdom have transcended the logic of the Elizabethan Poor Laws and are approaching the developing child in a very different way. Similarly, recent local and state-level innovations in early childhood systems should be studied as models for the national-level reforms that need to occur in order to ensure the healthy development of our nation's children.

REFERENCES

Cooper, S.E. (1993). Discrimination. In K. I. Winston & M. Bane (Eds.), *Gender and public policy: Cases and comments* (pp. 173–175). Boulder, CO: Westview Press.

Department for Children, School and Families. (n.d.). *The children's plan.* Retrieved from http://www.dcsf.gov.uk/childrensplan/

Dube, S. R., Felitti, M. D., Dong, M, Giles, W. H., & Anda, R. F. (2003). The impact of adverse childhood experiences on health problems: Evidence from four birth cohorts dating back to 1900. *Preventive Medicine, 37,* 268–277.

Evans, G. W. (2004). The environment of childhood poverty. *American Psychologist, 59,* 77–92.

Felitti, V. J., Anda, R. F., Nordenberg, D., Williamson, D. F., Spitz, A. M., Edwards, V., et al. (1998). Relationship of childhood abuse and household dysfunction to many of the leading causes of death in adults: The adverse childhood experiences (ACE) study. *American Journal of Preventive Medicine, 14*(4), 245–258.

Gunnar, M. R., Fisher, P. A., & the Early Experience, Stress and Prevention Science Network (2006). Bringing basic research on early experience and stress neurobiology to bear on preventive interventions for neglected and maltreated children. *Development and Psychopathology, 18,* 651–677.

Halfon, N., & Hochstein, M. (2002). Life course health development: An integrated framework for developing health and financing health intervention. *The Milbank Quarterly, 80,* 433–479.

Halfon, N., & McLearn, K. T. (2002). Families with children under 3: What we know and implications for results and policy. In N. Halfon & K. T. McLearn (Eds.), *Child rearing in America: Challenges facing parents with young children* (pp. 367–412). New York: Cambridge University Press.

Halfon, N., DuPlessis, H., & Barrett, E. (2008). Looking back at pediatrics to move forward in obstetrics. *Current Opinion in Obstetrics and Gynecology, 20*(6), 566–573.

Halfon, N., Du Plessis, H., & Inkelas, M. (2007). Transforming the U.S. child health system. *Health Affairs, 26*(2), 315–330.

Hertzman, C., Power, C., Matthews, S., & Manor, O. (2001). Using an interactive framework of society and lifecourse to explain self-rated health in early childhood. *Social Science & Medicine, 53,* 1575–1585.

Kamerman, S. B., & Kahn, A. J. (2001). Child and family policies in the United States at the opening of the twenty-first century. *Social Policy and Administration, 35*(1), 69–84.

Katz, M. (1986). Saving children. In M. B. Katz (Ed.), *In the shadow of the poorhouse: A social history of welfare in America* (pp. 117–151). New York: Basic Books.

Keating, D., & Hertzman, C. (2000). *Developmental health and the wealth of nations: Social, biological, and educational dynamics.* New York: Guilford Press.

Kuh, D., & Hardy, R. (Eds.). (2002). *A life course approach to women's health.* Oxford, UK: Oxford University Press.

Melchior, M., Moffitt, T. E., Milne, B. J., Poulton, R., & Caspi, A. (2007). Why do children from socioeconomically disadvantaged families suffer from poor health when they reach adulthood? A life-course study. *American Journal of Epidemiology, 166*(8), 966–974.

Moffitt, R., Ribar, D. C., & Wilhelm, M. (1998). The decline of welfare benefits in the U.S.: The role of wage inequality. *Journal of Public Economics, 68*(3), 421–452.

Newacheck, P. W., & Halfon, N. (2000). Prevalence and impact of disabling chronic conditions in childhood. *American Journal of Public Health 88*(4), 610–617.

Phipps, S. (2001). Value, policies and the well-being of young children in Canada, Norway and the United States. In K. Vleminckx, & T. M. Smeeding (Eds.), *Child well-being, child poverty and child policy in modern nation: What do we know?* (pp. 79–98). Bristol, UK: The Policy Press.

Pickett, K. E., & Wilkinson, R. G. (2007). Child wellbeing and income inequality in rich societies: Ecological cross sectional study. *British Medical Journal, 335*(7629), 1080–1086.

Power, C., Hypponen, E., & Davey Smith, G. (2005). Socioeconomic position in childhood and early adult life and risk of mortality: A prospective study of mothers of the 1958 British birth cohort. *American Journal of Public Health, 95*(8), 1396–1402.

Tanaka, S. (2005). Parental leave and child health across OED countries. *The Economic Journal, 115* (501), F7–F28.

UNICEF Innocenti Research Centre. (2007). *Child poverty in perspective: An overview of child well-being in rich countries.* Florence: Innocenti Report Card.

Wise, P. H. (2004). The transformation of child health in the United States. *Health Affairs, 23*(5), 9–25.

Wolff, E. N. (2001). The rich get richer: And why the poor don't [Electronic version]. *The American Prospect 12*(3). Retrieved from http://www.prospect. org/cs/articles/article=the_rich_get_richer

# TWENTY

# Global Perspectives on the Well-Being of Children

Linda M. Richter

The conditions under which children grow and develop vary widely according to the combined influences of history, geography, culture, politics, and economics, and also to the unique features of each individual life. The dominant scholarship of the West tends to focus on the childhoods and the circumstances of a minority of children in the world. However, the lot of the greatest number of young children is characterized by tenuous survival, hunger, poor growth, and minimal schooling. Worsening global inequality, disasters, and health threats on the scale of the HIV epidemic add further stress to the formative experiences of young children. Poor children live in what is increasingly a shadow world – a trailing, friable image of the world that children on the better side of the tracks inhabit.

Recent analyses of longitudinal data from developing countries reveal the long-term, intergenerational impact of poverty and under-nutrition on human potential, as expressed in growth, education, and earnings. Yet despite the strong influence of material circumstances in early life, research on resilience across a variety of cultures indicates the presence of three potentially powerful counter forces: warm responsive caregiving in the early years, meaningful family and social relations, and opportunities to learn and succeed. This chapter discusses the well-being of children globally, threats to children's health and development and pathways through which these threats act adversely and, lastly, potential large-scale interventions that protect children and enhance their capabilities.

## DIFFERENCES AND LIKENESSES AMONG CHILDREN GLOBALLY

Every child is different. Genetic predispositions, emerging phenotypical expressions, the worlds into which children are born and raised, and their minute-by-minute experiences – together with their emotions and thoughts – aggregate to render each individual unique. At the same time, all children are alike. Children without serious impairment will learn to communicate with others, have feelings and thoughts that can be shared and understood by others, and strive to be part of one or more social collectives with common purpose.

The most difficult questions for scholars of culture and psychobiology have to do with identifying the similarities and differences that matter, if, in fact, they matter at all, and judging which variation or lack of variation is important and why.

It is abundantly clear that an infant in Oslo, Norway, will come into the world with a different set of potentialities and will experience a widely divergent life from a child in Freetown, the capital of Sierra Leone. On the Human Development Index (HDI), these two cities are poles apart. In 2007, they were number 1, and number 177, the bottom, in terms of standards of living, literacy, education, and life expectancy (United Nations Development Programme, 2007). A baby with a pink and blue elephant pull-toy telephone learns different things about his life and surroundings from a child whose mother ties strips of goat skin on her wrist to recall her family's blessings.

These differences are obvious, as are commonalities among human infants. Apart from having shared anatomy and physiology, infants come into the world prepared to be members of human culture. They are equipped with heightened sensitivities to learn from those around them and from their experiences with the external environment. These are configured in ways that render the human brain, and its associated neurophysiology both experience-dependent and experience-expectant (Thompson & Nelson, 2001). As a result, neurophysiological structure and function mutually influence one another through processes of co-development.

Infants, for example, are primed for communication with other human beings through predisposed *pro forma* sensory and motor capacities. Among other things, newborn babies preferentially focus on the human face, turn to the human voice, and imitate basic mouth movements. Their unfolding development anticipates certain types of experience that creates a curriculum of stimulation and responsiveness to which emotionally involved parents respond (Legerstee, 2005).

Parents and other intimate caregivers also come into relationships with young children with predetermined perceptions and sensitivities. *Motherese* is an example of talk that is unconsciously responsive to the immature baby. The concept *intuitive parenting* refers to parental counterparts to an infant's dependency and expectancy (Papousek & Papousek, 1987). Sensitive caregivers observe infants and young children, respond to their cues, enable their perceived intentions (for example, by pulling a desired object to within the child's reach), imitate infant behavior, and attempt to elicit their baby's communication. These behaviors are not learned and do not proceed from rational analysis and decision. Rather, they are prompted and reinforced by the adult's affection for the child and strong motivation to engage with her. In this sense, motivation to parent a baby primes the adult and opens the way for intuitive responsiveness (Dix, 1991).

Despite variations, the non-verbal emotional and communicative interaction that occurs during caregiving between parents and young children (whether biologically related or not) is universal (Richter, 1995). As language develops, the relationships it makes possible and the material and social world it encounters, transform the mental powers of the young child (Bloom, 2004). The developing child is thus not separated from his environment. There is not a child *and* a culture, but always a child *in* culture. This is what Donald Winnicott, the British psychoanalyst referred to when he asserted that "there is no such thing as a baby.... A baby cannot exist alone, but is essentially part of a relationship" (1970, p. 88).

Human development is a cultural process and young humans are uniquely dependent on particular forms of early experience with other people. Through early interactions and care, babies are inculcated into shared human culture, as well as into their own specific linguistic and ethnic environment. In development they come to be the same as, and different from, other children.

## CHILDREN IN THE WEST – AND THE REST[1]

There is a massive scholarship on young children living in the West. The science of child development has advanced rapidly since the 1970s, particularly with the introduction of new assessment technologies and theoretical cross-fertilization from other disciplines (Rochat, 2001). The most important advances occurred as a result of a number of developments. These include (1) observational technology such as film and videotape, which made it possible to observe infants and young children in real time in everyday situations, especially while interacting with their most

---

[1] The subtitle is taken from the title of William Easterly's book, *The White Man's Burden: Why the West's Efforts to Aid the Rest Have Done So Much Ill and So Little Good* (New York: Penguin Press, 2006).

intimate caregivers (Schaffer, 1977); (2) the influence of psycho-linguistics and Speech-Act Theory, which sensitized researchers to the importance of studying communication and the development of communication and language in context (Bullowa, 1979); and (3) very rapid developments in the neurological sciences, which facilitiated studies using animal and human models of the neurophysiological and behavioral antecedents and the consequences of variations in the care of offspring (Schore, 1994).

Despite these advances, we know comparatively little about the great majority of children born into low-income families and/or non-Western countries (over 90 percent of all children). By and large, these children face the greatest threats to health and development but, as yet, little of our acquired knowledge has been applied to improve their lives (Richter, 2003; Tomlinson & Swartz, 2003). This fact is not unique to the study of children; for example, only 6 percent of studies in leading psychiatric journals come from the so-called "developing" countries (Patel & Sumathipala, 2001).

As previously noted, "The talent and productivity of the West, from which we all enjoy many benefits, does, however, create 'a point of view.'" From this point of view, some things are thrown into relief, noticed, and attended, and other things are not" (Richter, 2003, p. 243). As a result of our bias, we lose the opportunity to use our knowledge to contribute to a fairer and better dispensation for people who have a weak voice, if any, to speak for themselves. We also forgo the prospect of learning more from people whose cultural traditions have helped to buffer them from environmental hardship. *Kangaroo care*, for example, or holding a small or sickly baby against the mother's skin, originates in the child-rearing practices of carrying and co-sleeping of many non-Western groups (Martinez Gomez, Rey Sanabria, & Marquette, 1992). It is now a standard of care for premature neonates and other groups of vulnerable children in high-technology environments in Europe and the United States (Anderson, 1999).

Most importantly, we're unable to see "ourselves" from perspectives that might prompt important questions regarding the interface of culture and psychobiology. For example, if we hold that conscious attributions of mental states and intentionality to infants by caregivers are fundamental to the child's development of a theory of mind (Ruffman, Slade, & Crowe, 2002), how do we account for observations that certain cultures do not engage in this type of talk or interaction with infants? Robert LeVine, for example, argues on the basis of his ethnographic work among the Gusii in Kenya, that mothers avoid eye contact with their infants, rarely behave towards their babies in social and affectionate ways, and regard their young children as incapable of communication other than to signal hunger and distress. Are such observations indicative of reactivity among those observed? Or, as LeVine concludes, do they suggest that "mother-infant conversation is a population-specific pattern and is particularly rare among non-Western agricultural societies" (1990, p. 108).

## THE IMPORTANT EARLY YEARS

We know that the early years are critically important for human development and long-term outcomes. However, our actions to improve life conditions for poor and vulnerable young children lag shamefully behind our information and expertise.

Despite our relative neglect, never before has it been so important to bring the insights of developmental science to bear on understanding and intervening to ameliorate the effects of poverty and underdevelopment on the health and well-being of infants and young children in *the rest* of the world.

Such intervention has become vitally important for three main reasons. First, we are now more aware than ever before of the sentience of young children, and their suffering when they are neglected, abandoned, and abused. From the classic films and work of, among others, Rene Spitz on institutionalization (1946), John Bowlby, James Robertson, and Dina Rosenbluth on separation and hospitalization (1952), and Harry Harlow on maternal deprivation (1959), as well as contemporary research on the impact of orphanage care (Nelson, 2007), we are familiar with both the immediate anguish of young children and its consequences. As a result, social welfare and health care practices in much of the West have changed to improve conditions under which children receive medical assistance and substitute parental care.

Secondly, more than half a century of increasingly sophisticated developmental research attests that early-life conditions and competencies attained in childhood have long-term consequences for individuals and societies alike. For example, differences appear early between children in rich and poor counties with respect to, among others, language abilities and self-confidence. Socioeconomic disparities and persistent lack of opportunity cause these gradients to become entrenched and widen (Keating & Herzman, 1999). Thus, early childhood is now accepted by all major development agencies (including the World Bank) as a critical ingredient of social and economic development in poor countries (Young, 1996), and as an important period for addressing social inequalities.

## POOR CHILDREN – POOR DEVELOPMENT

About 6 million young children in poor countries die each year from preventable causes such as undernutrition, malaria, measles, pneumonia, and diarrhea. These conditions are all associated with poverty and want, poor services, and socioeconomic underdevelopment (Jones, Steketee, Black, Bhutta, Morris, & the Bellagio Child Survival Study Group, 2003). The United Nations Children's Fund estimates that close to 30,000 children die each day because of poverty. "They die quietly in some of the poorest villages on earth, far removed from the scrutiny and the conscience of the world. Being meek and weak in life makes these dying multitudes even more invisible in death" ("The Power of Immunization," 2000).

Premature and needless death is a large part of the picture. But it is not the largest. In 1995, Robert Myers pointed out that 12 of every 13 children born in the world would celebrate their first birthday. He asked what would happen to the survivors, given that they would remain in the same living conditions that put their survival at risk? It was recently estimated that more than 200 million children under 5 years of age in low and middle income countries fail to reach their potential in cognitive development, schooling, and earnings because of poverty, poor health and nutrition, and deficient care (Grantham-McGregor et al., 2007).

Prospective longitudinal studies in developing countries have now made it possible to validate previously established cross-sectional associations between poverty and children's poor linear growth in the early years, with diminished cognitive performance and lags in education. In the first three years of life, both stunting and poverty (assessed through a relative paucity of basic household assets) are associated with declines in measured intelligence quotients in middle childhood and adolescence. The effect sizes are in the region of 1 standard deviation, giving a measure of approximately 10 IQ points (Grantham-McGregor et al., 2007). Similar relationships are found with later educational achievement. Stunting predicts a loss of a grade of schooling. Together, stunting and poverty predict a loss of more than 2 grades. Furthermore, stunted children perform significantly below their classmates in math and reading. In summary, prospective studies corroborate that poor children who are stunted in early childhood experience fewer years of schooling, have lower attained grades, and they learn less per year than their better grown peers from more auspicious socioeconomic circumstances (Grantham-McGregor et al., 2007).

The Consortium of Health Outcome Research in Transitioning Societies (COHORTS) consists of the five largest and longest running birth cohorts in low and middle income countries – Cebu in the Philippines, Guatemala, Pelotas in Brazil, New Delhi, and Birth to Twenty in South Africa. Participants in these studies have been followed for 18 to 40 years. Meta-analyses of human capital data from the five cohorts show that both height- and weight-for-age in infancy predict schooling. In addition, among Brazilian and Guatemalan men, increased height is associated with an 8 percent increase in income, as well as an increase in household assets (Victora et al., 2008). Apart from the direct effects of height on earnings, schooling also affects income; each additional school grade achieved is estimated to correspond with a 12–14 percent increase in lifetime earnings (Psacharopoulos & Patrinos, 2004).

In these studies, follow-up to the next generation indicates that undernutrition in childhood is associated with lower birthweight in the undernourished subjects' children. Given the impacts on schooling and earnings, stunting and poverty are important mechanisms in the intergenerational transfer of poverty. The relationship between poor childhood growth and poverty may also be mediated by later chronic ill-health (Victora et al., 2008).

As important as these long-term findings are, more important is the fact that interventions to affect both stunting and early stimulation have been found to be effective at reducing deficits, especially when they are combined (Pelto, Dickin, Engle, & Obispo, 1999). Program efficacy is enhanced if the interventions start early, target the poorest and most vulnerable children, combine methods such as feeding and enrichment of cognitive development, are of high intensity and long duration, and involve parents and community members. In one of the most comprehensive and longest term follow-ups to date, Guatemalan children who received a protein supplement in early life showed positive effects some 25 years later, compared to those who did not receive the supplement (Hoddintot, Maluccio, Behrman, Flores & Martorell, 2008). The children who received the supplement in their first three years of life later had higher cognitive scores, achieved more years of schooling, and had 45 percent higher earnings than the control group. Importantly, delayed supplementation, that is, receipt between 3 and 6 years of age, had no effect on subsequent schooling or earnings.

The lessons are clear. Poverty and stunting affect growth, cognitive functioning, and future health. They lessen the years of schooling, grades completed, and material learned at school, and they reduce lifetime earnings.

Children of subsequent generations are smaller, entrenching the impacts of poverty and underdevelopment – including stunted growth – and creating a vicious individual and group cycle of deprivation.

## A WORSENING SITUATION

A very large proportion of the world's poor children live in extremely deprived and unsafe conditions. Worsening global inequality, disasters, and health threats on the scale of the HIV epidemic further stress the formative experiences of young children. One in five people (about 1.1 billion) live on less than $1 per day, and half the world's population (about 3 billion) live on less than $2 per day (United Nations Development Programme, 2007). More than 20 million children are displaced either within or outside their country (United Nations High Commission on Refugees, 1994).

Eleven countries (10 in Africa) have under-5 mortality rates above 200 per 1000, and 30 countries (28 in Africa) have under-5 mortality rates ranging between 100 and 200. Close to half of all children (46%) in South Asia are moderately and severely stunted, 38 percent in sub-Saharan Africa. The same number, about half, of all children in developing countries are not taken to an appropriate health care provider when ill, either because of poor access or because the child's sickness is not recognized in the home. An estimated 12 million children in sub-Saharan Africa have lost one or both parents to AIDS, and only three-quarters of primary school entrants in sub-Saharan Africa reach grade 5 (United Nations Children's Fund, 2008). Millions of men and women from poor countries are worldwide labor migrants. While their remittances are often the only income for their family, the long-term separation from their children and the issue of substitute care comprise an emerging global issue (Heymann, 2006). Table 20.1 sets out the proportion of people living on less than $1 together with key child indicators over the last decade and a half in the two poorest regions of the world.

There are few signs that the situation of the worst-off children is improving. The annual Human Development Index (HDI) shows that 18 countries, 12 in sub-Saharan Africa, slipped backwards between 1990 and 1995. These declines are largely associated with the impact of rapid and severe HIV/AIDS epidemics (see Figures 20.1 and 20.2). The other 6 countries with a deteriorated situation belong to the Commonwealth of Independent States (CSI), successors to the Soviet Union. Tajikistan has fallen 21 places in HDI rankings, Ukraine 17, and the Russian Federation 15. The main factors involved are poor health, declining life expectancy, and economic

**Table 20.1.** *Poverty and Child Indicators, 1990–2005, in the Poorest Regions of the World*

| Indicator | 1990 Unless Otherwise Indicated | | 2005 Unless Otherwise Indicated | |
|---|---|---|---|---|
| % of people living on less than 1$ per day[2] | Sub-Saharan Africa 46.8 | Southern Asia 41.1 | Sub-Saharan Africa (2004) 41.1 | Southern Asia (2004) 29.5 |
| Under-5 mortality rate, per 1000 live births[3] | 185 | 126 | 166 | 82 |
| Under-fives suffering from moderate & severe stunting[4,5] | 1990–1997 42 | 1990–1997 52 | 2000–2006 38 | 2000–2006 46 |
| Total net primary school enrolment[6] | 1990/1991 54 | 1990/1991 74 | 2004/2005 70 | 2004/2005 90 |

*Sources:* The Millennium Development Goals Report 2007 (United Nations, New York); UNICEF (1998). The state of the world's children 1998. (Oxford University Press, Oxford and New York); UNICEF (2007). The state of the world's children 2008. (UNICEF, New York).

disruption after the fall of the Soviet Union (United Nations Development Programme, 2005).

## PROMOTING AND PROTECTING CHILDREN'S DEVELOPMENT

Social and material circumstances in early life exert very strong influences on the survival, growth, health and well-being of young children. Evidence discussed both earlier and later suggest the effectiveness of several types of large-scale interventions that protect children and enhance their capabilities. In addition, research on resilience across a variety of cultures

---

[2] The Millenium Development Goals Report 2007, p. 6.
[3] The Millenium Development Goals Report 2007, p. 14.
[4] UNICEF, The state of the world's children 1998, p. 101.
[5] UNICEF, The state of the world's children 2008, p. 121.
[6] The Millenium Development Goals Report 2007, p. 10.

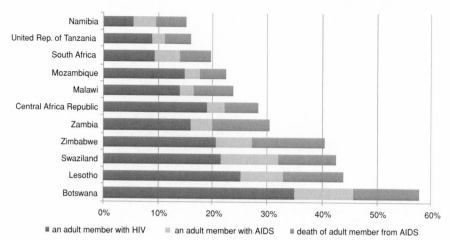

**Figure 20.1.** Percentage of families affected by AIDS illness and death in southern Africa (2005). From Belsey, M. A. (2006). *AIDS and the family: Policy options for a crisis in family capital.* New York: United Nations Department of Economic and Social Affairs. Reproduced by kind permission of the United Nations, Department of Economic and Social Affairs.

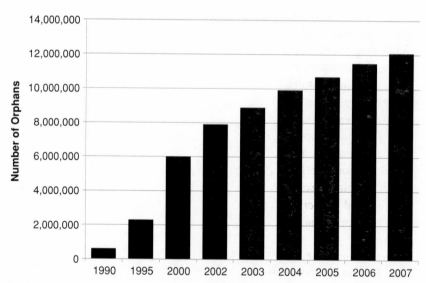

**Figure 20.2.** Estimated number of children who have lost one or both parents to AIDS in sub-Saharan Africa (1990–2007). From Joint United Nations Programme on HIV/AIDS (UNAIDS), 2008. Reproduced by kind permission of UNAIDS. www.unaids.org.

indicates three potentially powerful counter forces – warm responsive caregiving in the early years, meaningful family and social relations, and opportunities to learn and succeed.

Several types of large-scale interventions can protect children in poor countries and enhance their capabilities. Nutritional supplementation and psychosocial stimulation during early child development have already been discussed. Two additional categories of intervention will be outlined: social protection for families in the form of regular income transfers, and the promotion of family care for vulnerable children, as opposed to institutional care. However, efforts to strengthen caregiver-child relationships lie at the heart of all interventions for young children that offer long-term protection of their welfare.

### Social Protection – Income Transfers

As indicated earlier, the majority of young children die because they lack access to the appropriate quantity and quality of food and/or because they live in an environment that directly threatens their health and safety. This lack of basic protection is largely the result of poverty rather than parental neglect (Smith & Haddad, 2000). Directly alleviating poverty through predictable, if relatively small, income transfers to households can address the basis of children's undernutrition and ill health, as well as enable households to cover user costs of accessing clean water, health care, and education (Richter & Desmond, 2008).

An increasing number of developing countries are implementing income transfer programs as part of their social protection agenda. Examples are Brazil (*Bolsa Familia*), Mexico (*Oportunidades*), and South Africa (*Child Support Grant*), and there are non-contributory pension schemes in Namibia, Botswana, Senegal, and Lesotho, among others. Most of these are large-scale – for example *Bolsa Familia* reaches 11 million families (close to 45 million people), *Oportunidades* reaches 5 million households, and South Africa's *Child Support Grant* is approaching 8 million beneficiaries – and some are conditional on recipient service use, such as clinic and school attendance.

Rigorous evaluations of some of these, especially *Oportunidades* (formerly *Progresa*), demonstrate that health service utilization increased in households receiving grants, as did the availability of food (Gertler, 2000). Much of the health benefit was likely due to increased food consumption. Similar positive impacts on health and health-related behavior of income transfers have been observed elsewhere; for example, in Colombia the incidence of acute diarrhea among young children decreased, and in Nicaragua timely immunization rates rose significantly from baseline levels (Rawlings, 2004).

In most developing countries, households with higher incomes provide a healthier diet for their children and have more access to health care and to better quality services (Victora, Vaughan, Barros, Silva, & Tomasi, 2002). Income transfer programs are effective measures to help close that gap. Such programs also are closely associated with improved school enrollment and attendance in a range of countries (Department for International Development, 2005). The emerging evidence is that income transfers, both conditional and unconditional, have positive impacts on children's health, education, and general economic environment.

### Family – Not Institutional – Care for Vulnerable Children

There is no ideal solution to the inadequacy, neglect, abuse by, or loss of a parent, only better or worse alternatives (Williamson, 2004). Institutionalization, or the placement of orphaned and vulnerable children in residential orphanages, is one of the worst alternatives. Nonetheless, historically, institutionalization often has been used to address social and material problems experienced by poor young children and their families.

Increasingly since the Industrial Revolution (Peters, 2000), orphaned and other vulnerable children have been placed in charitable institutions, orphanages, foundling homes, and other forms of group residential care. These placements have frequently been as much to hide or reform *children of poor stock* as to provide for their care; this principle has governed the mass institutionalization of children in the Soviet Union, orphans produced by famine and war in India, and children of mixed Aboriginal heritage in Australia (Sen, 2007). In the western world, such institutions have largely been replaced by community-based social services for families; foster family homes, whether with kin or unrelated families; and small group homes for the most severely troubled children (Tolfree, 1995). Currently, however, in response to the needs of children affected by war, other conflict, and HIV and AIDS (especially in sub-Saharan Africa), orphanages are burgeoning. Human Rights Watch estimates that worldwide, millions of children are in orphanages and forms of non-penal institutions (http://www.hrw .org).

Despite the high cost of orphanages – estimated at about ten times higher than family care (Desmond & Gow, 2001) – very little effort is made in developing countries to undertake family reunification or to support "kith and kin fostering" of separated and orphaned children. When funds for special orphanage projects dry up or are diverted – as occurred, for example, with residential institutions for children established during the Mozambican war of independence – staff pay ceases or becomes inconsistent, infrastructure deteriorates, and the conditions of care decline, often to the point of frank abuse.

Studies of the adverse effects of institutional care on children have been available for nearly a century. Better study design and measurement techniques in recent studies of adoptees from Eastern Europe have confirmed a strong relationship between generally poor health of children and their length of institutionalization or time in group residential care (Judge, 2004). On the basis of a comprehensive review, Frank, Klass, Earls, and Eisenberg (1996) concluded that "infants and young children are uniquely vulnerable to the medical and psychosocial hazards of institutional care, negative effects that cannot be reduced to a tolerable level even with massive expenditure. Scientific experience consistently shows that, in the short term, orphanage placement puts young children at risk of serious infectious illness and delayed language development. In the long term, institutionalization in early childhood increases the likelihood that impoverished children will grow into psychiatrically impaired and economically unproductive adults" (p. 569).

## CONCLUSION – PROTECTING AND STRENGTHENING CAREGIVER–CHILD RELATIONSHIPS

Infants and young children are uniquely prepared by genetic potential, maturing neurophysiology, and growing social capacities to interact with other people emotionally, cognitively, and cooperatively (Cozolino, 2006). Under conditions of physical hardship, hunger, and illness, young children seek human comfort, and they do so more desperately and urgently than they would under comparatively normal circumstances.

We know that close bonds between young children and their caregivers, expressed in mutually satisfying emotional and communicative interaction between infants and more mature individuals, are essential for the unfolding and development of human characteristics such as language, interpersonal and emotional understanding, empathic reasoning and morality, self-regulation, and self-identity (Kaye, 1982; Pinker, 2002; Stern, 1985). The incomplete development of children who are deprived – for a variety of reasons including cruel neglect and isolation – of warm, responsive interpersonal care demonstrates the importance of such care in the phenotypic expression of these human capacities.

Innate and acquired deficits and disabilities in children, including prematurity and other forms of developmental delay, can affect early interactional processes and cause stress in caregiver-child relationships. Separation is particularly difficult for young children. Similarly, material hardship and social dislocation severely challenge the psychological capacities of parents and others to be sensitive and responsive to young children, as do parental depression and demoralization (Richter, 2004).

The fundamental guiding principle for efforts to promote the development of young children, therefore, must be the protection and strengthening of caregiver-child relationships. For this reason, it is essential to avoid separating children from intimate caregivers and, when separation is inevitable, to seek the rapid placement of young children in families, preferably relatives, that have a strong potential for long-term care and commitment. Parents and caregivers must be able to feed and clothe children and meet their fundamental health and education needs, and this goal is best achieved through state provision of basic income security for households. Young children need safe care when parents work, and they require opportunities to socialize with other children as well as to learn under the guidance of responsible adults. Early child developmental programs are important for all these reasons and are especially beneficial to poor children. Parents and other caregivers need social support to mitigate their own mental health problems, especially depression, the gravity of which has been recognized in developing countries only recently (Husain, Creed, & Tomenson, 2000). Follow-up studies suggest that adverse effects of maternal depression on children may persist well into childhood and early adolescence in the form of behavior disorders, anxiety, depression, and attention problems (Galler, Harrison, Ramsey, Forde, & Butler, 2000).

Positive conditions in early childhood build resilience, the *ordinary magic* that prepares children for challenges and stresses, and such conditions also represent experiences of opportunity and hope (Masten, 2001). These conditions include the establishment of strong and secure attachment to parental figures, good nutrition and growth, confident exploration of the world, and rewarding learning encounters facilitated by devoted parents, same-aged peers with whom to play, a community of caring people who support both child and parents, state policies that enable families to bear and rear children, and essential health and education services so that children can reach their potential. At present, for the majority of children in the world, none of these conditions are guaranteed. For many of them, their formative experiences beyond survival are too often hunger, deprivation, and fear. Among children whose early childhood is secure and protected, all credit goes to their parents, family, and immediate community, whose capacity to love and provide endures against the odds.

REFERENCES

Anderson, G. (1999). Kangaroo care of the premature infant. *Acta Paediatrica, 87,* 711–713.

Belsey, M. A. (2006). *AIDS and the family: Policy options for a crisis in family capital.* New York: United Nations Department of Economic and Social Affairs.

Bloom, O. (2004). *Descartes baby: How the science of child development explains what makes us human.* New York: Basic Books.

Bowlby, J., Robertson, J., & Rosenbluth, D. (1952). A two-year-old goes to hospital. *Psychoanalytic Study of the Child, 7,* 82–94.

Bullowa, M. (Ed.). (1979). *Before speech: The beginning of interpersonal communication.* Cambridge, UK: Cambridge University Press.

Cozolino, L. (2006). *The neuroscience of human relationships: Attachments and the developing social brain.* New York: W. W. Norton.

Department for International Development (2005). *Social transfers and chronic poverty: Emerging evidence and the challenge ahead.* London: Department for International Development (DFID).

Desmond, C., & Gow, J. (2001). *The cost-effectiveness of six models of care for orphans and vulnerable children in South Africa.* Pretoria: United Nations Children's Fund.

Dix, T. (1991). The affective organization of parenting: Adaptive and maladaptive processes. *Psychological Bulletin, 110,* 3–25.

Easterly, W. (2006). *The white man's burden: Why the West's efforts to aid the rest have done so much ill and so little good.* New York: Penguin Press.

Frank, D., Klass, P., Earls, F., & Eisenberg, L. (1996). Infants and young children in orphanages: One view from pediatrics and child psychiatry. *Pediatrics, 97,* 569–578.

Galler, J., Harrison, R., Ramsey, F., Forde, V., & Butler, S. (2000). Maternal depressive symptoms affect infant cognitive development in Barbados. *Journal of Child Psychology and Psychiatry, 41,* 747–757.

Gertler, P. (2000). *The impact of progress on health.* Washington: International Food Policy Research Institute.

Grantham-McGregor, S., Cheung, Y., Cueto, S., Glewwe, P., Richter, L., & Strupp. B. (2007). Developmental potential in the first 5 years for children in developing countries. *Lancet, 369,* 60–70.

Harlow, H. (1959). Love in monkeys. *Scientific American, 200,* 68–74.

Heymann, J. (2006). *Forgotten families: Ending the growing crisis confronting children and working parents in the global economy.* New York: Oxford University Press.

Hoddinott, J., Maluccio, J. A., Behrman, J. R., Flores, R., & Martorell, R. (2008). Effect of a nutrition intervention during early childhood on economic productivity in Guatemalan adults. *Lancet, 371*(9610), 411–16.

Husain, N., Creed, F., & Tomenson, B. (2000). Depression and social stress in Pakistan. *Psychological Medicine, 30*, 395–402.

Jones, G., Steeketee, R., Black, R., Bhutta, Z., Morris, S., & the Bellagio Child Survival Study Group (2003). How many deaths can we prevent this year? *Lancet, 362*, 65–71.

Judge, S. (2004). Developmental recovery and deficit in children adopted from Eastern European orphanages. *Child Psychiatry and Human Development, 34,* 49–62.

Kaye, K. (1982). *The mental and social life of babies: How parents create persons.* Chicago: University of Chicago Press.

Keating, D. P, & Herzman, C. (Eds.) (1999). *Developmental health and the wealth of nations: Social, biological, and educational dynamics.* London: Guilford Press.

Legerstee, M. (2005). *Infants' sense of people: Precursors to a theory of mind.* Cambridge, UK: Cambridge University Press.

LeVine, R. (1990). Enculturation: A biosocial perspective on the development of self. In D. Cicchetti & M. Beeghly (Eds.), *The self in transition: Infancy to early childhood* (pp. 99–117). Chicago: University of Chicago Press.

Martinez Gomez, H., Rey Sanabria, E., & Marquette C. M. (1992). The mother kangaroo programme. *International Child Health, 3*, 55–67.

Masten, A. (2001). Ordinary magic: Resilience processes in development. *American Psychologist, 56*, 227–238.

Myers, R. (1995). *The twelve who survive: Strengthening programs of early childhood development in the Third World.* New York: Routledge.

Nelson, C. (2007). A neurobiological perspective on early human deprivation. *Child Development Perspectives, 1*, 13–18.

Papousek, H., & Papousek, M. (1987). Intuitive parenting: A dialectic counterpart to the infant's precocity in integrative capacities. In J. Osofsky (Ed.), *Handbook of infant development* (2nd ed., pp. 669–720). New York: Wiley.

Patel, V., & Sumathipala, A. (2001). International representation in psychistric literature: Survey of six leading journals. *British Journal of Psychiatry, 178*, 406–409.

Pelto, G., Dickin, K., Engle, P., & Obispo, S. (1999). *A critical link: Interventions for physical growth and psychological development. A review.* Geneva: World Health Organization.

Peters, L. (2000). *Orphan texts: Victorian orphans, culture and empire.* Manchester, UK: Manchester University Press.

Pinker, S. (2002). *The blank slate: The modern denial of human nature.* New York: Viking-Penguin.

Psacharopoulos, G. & Patrinos, H. (2004). Returns to investment in education: A further update. *Educational Economics, 12*, 111–134.

Rawlings, L. (2004). *A new approach to social assistance: Latin America's experience with conditional cash transfers programs.* Washington, DC: The World Bank.

Richter, L. (1995). Are early adult-infant interactions universal: A South African view. *South African Journal of Child and Adolescent Psychiatry, 7*, 2–18.

Richter, L. (2003). Poverty, underdevelopment and infant mental health. *Journal of Paediatric and Child Health, 39*, 243–248.

Richter, L. (2004). *The importance of caregiver-child interactions for the survival and healthy development of young children.* Geneva: World Health Organization.

Richter, L., & Desmond, C. (2008). Child health and development. In A. Gatti & A. Boggio (Eds.), *Health and development: Toward a matrix approach* (pp. 168–182). New York: Palgrave Macmillan.

Rochat, P. (2001). *The infant's world.* Cambridge, UK: Cambridge University Press.

Ruffman, T., Slade, L., & Crowe, E. (2002). The relation between children's and mothers' mental state language and theory-of-mind understanding. *Child Development, 73*, 734–751.

Schaffer, H. (1977). *Studies in mother–infant interaction.* London: Academic Press.

Schore, A. (1994). *Affect regulation and the origin of self: The neurobiology of emotional development.* Hillsdale, NJ: Lawrence Erlbaum.

Sen, S. (2007). The orphaned colony: Orphanage, child and authority in British India. *Indian Economic and Social History Review, 44*, 463–488.

Smith, L. & Haddad, L. (2000). *Explaining child malnutrition in developing countries: A cross-country analysis.* Washington: International Food Policy Research Institute.

Spitz, R. (1946). Anaclitic depression: An inquiry into the genesis of psychiatric conditions in early childhood II. *Psychoanalytic Study of the Child, 2*, 313–342.

Stern, D. (1985). *The interpersonal world of the infant: A view from psychoanalysis and developmental psychology.* New York: Basic Books.

Thompson, R. & Nelson, C. (2001). Developmental science and the media: Early brain development. *American Psychologist, 56*, 5–15.

Tolfree, D. (1995). *Roofs and roots: The care of separated children in the developing world.* Aldershot: Arena.

Tomlinson, M. & Swartz, L. (2003). Imbalances in the knowledge about infancy: The divide between rich and poor countries. *Infant Mental Health Journal, 24*, 547–556.

United Nations Children's Fund (1998). *State of the world's children 1998.* New York and London: Oxford University Press.

United Nations Children's Fund (2000). The power of immunization. In *Progress of nations.* Retrieved from http://www.unicef.org/pono0/immu1.htm

United Nations Children's Fund (2007). *State of the world's children 2008: Child survival.* New York: United Nations Children's Fund (UNICEF).

United Nations Development Programme (2005). *Human Development Report: International cooperation at a crossroads: Aid, trade and security in an unequal world.* New York: United Nations Development Programme (UNDP).

United Nations Development Programme (2007). Human Development Report 2007/2008. *Fighting climate change: Human solidarity in a divided world.* New York: United Nations Development Programme (UNDP).

United Nations High Commission on Refugees (1994). *Refugee Children: Guidelines on protection and care.* Geneva: United Nations High Commission on Refugees (UNHCR).

Victora, C., Vaughan, J., Barros, F., Silva, A., & Tomasi, E. (2002). Explaining trends in equalities: Evidence from Brazilian child health studies. *Lancet, 356*, 1093–1098.

Victora, C., Adair, L., Fall, C., Hallal, P., Martorell, R., Richter, L. et al. (2008). Maternal and child undernutrition: Consequences for adult health and human capital. *Lancet, 371,* 340–357.

Williamson, J. (2004). *A family is for a lifetime.* Washington DC: United States Agency for International Development Office of HIV/AIDS.

Winnicott, D. (1970). The mother–infant experience of mutuality. In E. Anthony & T. Benedek (Eds.), *Parenthood: Its psychology and psychopathology* (pp. 245–256). Boston: Little, Brown & Co.

Young, M. (1996). *Investing in the future: Early child development.* Washington, DC: The World Bank.

# TWENTY-ONE

# Response to

## Global Perspectives on the Well-Being of Children

### Jennifer Harris Requejo and Flavia Bustreo

Dr. Linda M. Richter begins her compelling overview of "global perspectives on the wellbeing of children" by discussing in brief the most advanced thinking in the fields of human development and child psychology about what makes each child unique – and yet the same – around the world. She emphasizes in particular that the latest research tells us that all children are born pre-wired for social interaction, and that who they ultimately become is highly dependent upon the types of interactions they experience as they grow. This bio-cultural perspective serves as the basis of her critique of "Western" scholarship's focus on understanding the developmental processes of children living in resource-rich countries while ignoring the increasingly dire circumstances and developmental consequences the majority of children in the world endure.

The remainder of Dr. Richter's text is divided into two parts. She first explains why we must turn our attention towards the lives of the most disadvantaged children, citing a range of contextual factors (e.g., worsening global inequality, the HIV/AIDS epidemic, conflict situations, labor migration patterns, and natural disasters) that negatively impact their formative years. She then reviews the literature on resilience, highlighting the centrality of the child-primary caregiver relationship, as well as other social relationships, to the healthy development of all children. She concludes by describing large-scale interventions targeted at families, reminding us that protecting the welfare of children in poor countries starts with ensuring that those responsible for their care are equipped to meet their material and emotional needs.

We agree with Dr. Richter's view of the primacy of the child-caregiver relationship to the well-being of children around the world, and with her sentiment that "there is not a child *and* a culture, but always a child *in* culture." We have crafted our response as a complement to Dr. Richter's work, building on the conceptualization of the child as "in relation" by more closely examining the life-shaping relationships in which the child is enmeshed, ranging from those with family members, to the local community, the broader society, and the world. With all relationships come responsibilities, and we would stress more forcefully than Dr. Richter does the responsibility shared by the global community, governments, social institutions, local communities, and families in helping children reach their potential. All of these entities must be held accountable for ensuring that children are provided with what they need to thrive. Recognition of this shared responsibility lies at the core of the Countdown to 2015, a collaborative effort aimed at promoting accountability by tracking progress in the coverage and equitable distribution of proven interventions in the 68 countries where 97% of maternal and child deaths occur (Countdown Core Group, 2006; Bryce, Requejo, & the Countdown Core Group, 2008). Results from this effort are presented later.

We also argue that more attention than Dr. Richter allocates be given to the primary caregiver (the other half of the child-caregiver relationship), who is still most often the mother and whose health and well-being is known to be inextricably linked to the health and well-being of her child (World Health Organization [WHO], 2005). In addition, we acknowledge Dr. Richter's point that the situation for children is deteriorating in some parts of the world, and elaborate on this with some recent data from the United Nations Children's Fund (UNICEF) and the Countdown to 2015 analyses. However, we contend that equal attention should be paid to the diverse countries in the world where conditions for children have improved despite the odds and that these successes, if shared, can potentially be repeated elsewhere (e.g., Bangladesh, Cuba, Chile, China, Egypt, Eritrea, Indonesia, Mexico, the Phillipines, Tanzania, Turkmenistan) (Bryce et al., 2008; Masanja et al., 2008; Bahr & Wehrhahn, 1993; Sepúlveda et al., 2006; Casas, Dachs, Bambas, 2001).

Before proceeding, we want to make explicit what is implicit in Dr. Richter's text – that investing in the well-being of children is justified because children are the future of all societies; such investment not only fulfills a basic human right, but also yields significant returns in socioeconomic benefits (Belli & Appaix, 2003; Belli, Bustreo, & Preker, 2005; Brown, Larson, & Saraswati, 2002; Convention on the Rights of the Child, 1989). Nations that neglect to provide for their children will incur the economic and social costs of this neglect as these children reach adulthood, enter the workforce, and assume leadership roles. The Millenium Development Goals (MDGs) ratified by heads of state from 189 nations in 2000 have committed the global community to reducing child mortality (MDG 4 calls for the two-thirds reduction in 1990 child mortality levels by 2015) and to addressing its underlying determinants, both measures being deemed essential to reducing worldwide poverty (http://mdgs.un.org/). In other words, the leaders of most countries in the world have assumed the responsibility of improving child health. This unprecedented step casts an important light on any analysis of progress in child well-being, particularly in the most disadvantaged countries.

The remainder of our response follows the structure of Dr. Richter's chapter, filling in what we perceive as omissions in each chapter section. Specifically, we revisit her discussion of the academic community's complicity in the neglect of the most needy children, contend that more attention to child survival and the international response to meeting MDG4 is warranted, focus on the caregiver side of the child-caregiver relationship – including how persistent gender inequities and lack of access to reproductive health care services contribute to the cycle of poverty and child ill-health – and expand on Dr. Richter's overview of the intergenerational effects of child malnutrition by discussing the long-term benefits of investing in child health and the urgency for increased funding from governments and donors alike.

## THE WEST AND THE "REST": DEVELOPING
## A PRODUCTIVE PARTNERSHIP

Dr. Richter's synopsis of scholarship in human development and psychology is perhaps too negative. We concur that most research in these fields has been conducted in the Western world and is, consequently, rooted in a "point of view [in which] some things are thrown into relief, noticed and attended, and other things are not." We also agree that comparatively little is known about the developmental processes of the majority of children in the world who live in non-Western countries. On the other hand, a significant body of literature does exist on beliefs and practices concerning the care of children living outside the developed world, as indicated in other chapters in this book, as well as in the wealth of social science and pediatric research on childrearing in various cultural contexts. For example, the rich biomedical and anthropological literature generated mostly from the "south" on the benefits of exclusive and long-term breastfeeding has advanced our knowledge about the role of breastfeeding in strengthening the maternal-infant bond, which is so crucial for early child development, and in reducing child mortality from numerous infectious diseases (Victora, Fuchs, Kirkwood, Lombardi, & Barros, 1992; Victora et al., 1999; Stuart-Macadam & Detttwyler, 1995; Cunningham, 1995; DeLoache & Gottlieb, 2000). The "Kangaroo Care" model Dr. Richter describes – derived from non-Western childrearing practices and now considered the standard of care for premature babies and other vulnerable newborns – is another case in point that knowledge from the "rest" is an untapped resource that could lead to important advances in our understanding about what children everywhere need to survive and thrive.

Perhaps the fields of human development and psychology need more theoretical and methodological cross-fertilization with the disciplines of anthropology and sociology. As Dr. Richter notes, this process could facilitate the development of new perspectives and a deeper exploration of unresolved questions concerning the interface of culture and psychobiology, including whether human infants and their caregivers are universally pre-wired to engage with one another in biologically prescribed, mutually beneficial ways. We also assert that Richter's comment about the lack of publications in leading psychiatric journals from low-resource countries is a call-to-action for academic institutions in the north to join forces with institutions in the south. These partnerships could ideally result in capacity building in the southern institutions so that they are able to conduct and disseminate their work through major international journals, enabling the "West" to learn from the "rest."

Dr. Richter's identification of the bias of Western research follows her review of what we now know about the long-term consequences of material and social deprivation during childhood on adult health and life opportunities. We fully agree that our extensive knowledge about the implications of the early years for "individuals and their societies alike" has not been adequately translated into action in resource-poor settings. Going beyond her analysis, we contend that this translation process requires the fostering of productive dialogue between civil society (academics, health care professionals, and others able to advocate for children's well-being), governments, and the international community, including donors. This type of exchange can result in the political prioritization of resources and their harmonized allocation to activities targeted at promoting child well-being at regional, national, and local levels. The success of vaccination programs in Latin America where polio has been eradicated and measles cases are now extremely rare, the African Program for Onchocerciasis Control which has resulted in the removal of this major cause of childhood blindness in seven West African countries, diarrhea-control programs in the Philippines and Egypt resulting in substantial under-five mortality reductions, and smaller scale endeavors like a project implemented in Guatemala aimed at improving the management of common childhood illnesses in local areas are all representative examples (Bryce et al., 2003).

## SURVIVAL IS A PREREQUISITE FOR WELL-BEING AND DEVELOPMENT

We agree with Dr. Richter's poignant observation that child mortality is only a part of the picture, and greater attention must be directed at alleviating the appalling conditions experienced by children living in low-resource countries who do manage to survive. However, we think that the issue of child survival is glossed over too quickly and the mortality situation painted too bleakly in Richter's chapter and deserves greater elaboration. First, UNICEF reports indicate that child deaths recently dropped below 9 million per year for the first time. Other analyses indicate that although child mortality is increasingly concentrated in the most marginalized populations in Sub-Saharan Africa and South Asia, encouraging mortality reductions have occurred in places with historically high child mortality rates such as East Africa (United Nations Children's Fund [UNICEF], 2007a; UNICEF, 2007b; UNICEF 2008; Countdown Coverage Writing Group, 2008). The Countdown 2008 report also indicates that 16 of the 68 countries in the world with the highest burdens of maternal and child mortality are now on track to achieve MDG 4 (Bryce et al., 2008). In sum, there is substantial reason to hope that the lot of the greatest number of young children in many low-resource settings can be improved and is improving.

On the downside, the Countdown to 2015 results reveal sobering trends. Of the 12 countries in the world that have experienced reversals in progress towards MDG 4, almost all have high HIV prevalence rates and/or are affected by conflict (Salama et al., 2008). Coverage levels for key interventions known to reduce child mortality and improve child health are uneven across and within the 68 Countdown countries (Countdown 2008 Equity Analysis Group, 2008). Although these countries are, on average, reaching around 80% of children under five years of age with interventions deliverable through vertical channels such as immunizations and vitamin A supplementation, coverage levels are low and stagnating for interventions that require a functional health care system and 24-hour availability of care, such as the case management of childhood illnesses and postnatal care. For example, the median levels of national coverage for the treatment of child pneumonia, diarrhea, and malaria are 32%, 38%, and 40%, respectively (Bryce et al., 2008). Postnatal care coverage levels in the 5 countries with available data are also low, 4 of the 5 falling below 10%. The lack of available data on postnatal care and the poor coverage levels within those countries with data is an area of major concern because three-quarters of the 4 million annual newborn deaths occur in the first week of life (Lawn, Cousens, & Zupan, 2005). The equity analyses presented in the 2005 and 2008 Countdown reports are equally disturbing. The 2005 equity analysis shows that children from the poorest families are considerably less likely than those from wealthier families to receive at least six essential prevention interventions (Countdown Core Group, 2006). Similarly, the equity analysis in 2008 found substantial disparities in the distribution of services between the poorest and wealthiest population groups in four intervention categories across the continuum of care. These disparities are most pronounced for the maternal and newborn health intervention category and smallest for immunization (Countdown 2008 Equity Analysis Group, 2008).

## THE OTHER HALF OF THE CHILD-CAREGIVER RELATIONSHIP

As child mortality rates have begun to fall in many parts of the world, the overall proportion of under-five deaths occurring during the neonatal period has increased. This epidemiological shift sparked recognition in the international community that the neonatal period has long been a neglected issue (Tinker, ten Hoope-Bender, Azfar, Bustreo, & Bell, 2005). At the same time, growing awareness of linkages between maternal health, care during delivery, and neonatal health resulted in general consensus that maternal and child well-being depends greatly upon every mother and child having the right to access needed health care (WHO, 2005). This awareness also led to the adoption of the Continuum of Care approach and its incorporation into the agenda of the Partnership for Maternal, Newborn and Child Health and the Countdown to 2015. The Continuum of Care, initially described in the 2005 World Health Report Make Every Mother and Child Count, takes a life-cycle approach and views maternal, newborn, and child health as inextricably interconnected; therefore, they cannot be addressed separately through programs focused on single diseases or conditions. It promotes the delivery of care to mothers and children from pre-pregnancy to delivery, the immediate postnatal period, and throughout early childhood. Such a continuum also requires the linkage of service provision across various settings, from households to community-based care to primary health care facilities to hospitals (WHO, 2005; Kerber et al., 2007).

It is noteworthy that countries such as Tanzania, Mexico, and Chile, which have made significant strides in reducing child mortality in recent years, have adopted multi-sectoral and integrated approaches to the delivery of needed health care services (Masanja et al., 2008; Sepulveda et al., 2006; Gonzalez et al., 2009). In Tanzania, for example, important improvements in the health system achieved between 1999 and 2004 have led to rapid gains in child survival; these improvements include doubling public expenditure on health, decentralization and sector-wide basket funding, and increasing coverage of key child-survival interventions (integrated management of childhood illness, insecticide-treated bed nets, vitamin A supplementation, immunization, and exclusive breastfeeding) (Masanja et al., 2008). In Mexico, investments in women's education, social protection, and water and sanitation programs coupled with the introduction of the "diagonal approach," involving the implementation of a selection of highly cost-effective public health interventions bridging clinics and homes, have been identified as factors largely responsible for putting Mexico on track for MDG 4. Strong leadership and continuity of public health policies, along with investments in health care facilities and strengthening human resources, were also key to Mexico's success (Sepulveda et al., 2006).

There is virtually no discussion of the neonatal time period and the importance of maternal health and well-being for neonatal survival and child development in Dr. Richter's chapter. Although she does note in various places that material hardships, social dislocation, and mental health problems challenge the ability of primary caregivers to effectively parent, these issues are not discussed with specific reference to mothers. Indeed, there is no discussion of the issue of gender and its role in the intergenerational transfer of poverty (Merchant, 1993). Demographic factors known to have an impact on child well-being – such as fertility rates, birth spacing intervals, access to family planning services, and maternal age, education and survival – are also given insufficient attention (Black, Morris, & Bryce, 2003; Cleland et al., 2006; Bernstein, Say, & Chowdhury, 2008; Nakiyingi et al., 2003). Dr. Richter merely comments that, "state policy that enables families to enact their motivation to bear and rear children" is one of many positive conditions necessary for enabling children to build "resilience." But this point overlooks findings indicating that the promotion of family planning in countries with high birth rates has the potential to increase school enrollment as well as reduce poverty, hunger, and avert nearly 10% and 32% of all child and maternal deaths, respectively (Cleland et al., 2006).

## INVESTMENTS THAT PAY OFF

Finally, we would like to add to Dr. Richter's convincing discussion of the link between undernutrition during childhood, educational attainment, and later productivity some strong evidence showing a clear connection between childhood infections, ill-health and adult labor market participation (Belli & Appaix, 2003; Belli et al., 2005). These findings, as well as the vast literature on the relationship between child health and the economy, indicate that investing in child health and nutrition can yield long-term benefits for society. These benefits include better educated and more productive adults, favorable demographic changes, and the disruption of the intergenerational transmission of poverty. Safeguarding health during childhood is arguably more important than at any other age because poor health in the early years can permanently impair individuals over the course of their lifetime. Children born into poorer families have also been found to experience poorer health as they age, and lower investment in human capital; both factors are associated with lower earnings in adulthood when they become the next generation of parents (Case, Fertig, & Paxson, 2005).

These significant benefits from investing in child health have not yet been appropriately considered by governments or the international community. The Countdown to 2015 analysis showed that despite increases in aid flowing to maternal, newborn, and child health (donor disbursements increased from US$2119 million in 2003 to $3482 million in 2006), disbursements to the countries with the highest burdens of maternal and child mortality are falling far short of estimated needs. In the 68 Countdown countries, child-related disbursements for the entire year and for all health conditions increased from a mean of only $4 per child in 2003 to $7 per child in 2006 (Greco, Powell-Jackson, Borghi, & Mills, 2008).

The situation is clear: Almost 10 million children die every year from largely preventable and treatable diseases. This loss creates an incredible burden on families and communities, mostly in the developing world. Insufficient investments in maternal, newborn, and child health also mean that children who survive are not receiving the care and nutritional services they need to thrive, reach their potential, and become contributing members of society. We agree with Richter that enabling families to provide loving homes for their children must be prioritized. Delivering the support families and communities need through health and social protection programs, however, depends upon the allocation of additional resources and the creation of greater political commitment to child well-being. This is the ultimate aim of efforts – like the Countdown to 2015 – that hold all partners accountable. In conclusion, the encouraging engagement of parliamentarians with this challenge is a sign that the world is moving in a hopeful direction for the well-being of our children (Bustreo & Johnsson, 2008).

REFERENCES

Bahr, J., & Wehrhahn, R. (1993). Life expectancy and infant mortality in Latin America. *Social Science and Medicine, 36*, 1373–1382.

Belli, P. C., & Appaix, O. (2003). The economic benefits of investing in child health. Health, Nutrition, and Population Discussion Paper. Washington, DC: World Bank.

Belli, P. C., Bustreo, F., & Preker, A. (2005). Investing in children's health: What are the economic benefits? *Bulletin of the World Health Organization, 83*, 777–784.

Bernstein, S., Say, L., & Chowdhury, S. (2008). Sexual and reproductive health: Completing the continuum.Lancet, *371*, 1225–1226.

Black, R. E., Morris, S., & Bryce, J. (2003). Where and why are 10 million children dying every year? *Lancet, 361*(9351), 2226–2234.

Brown, B., Larson, R., & Saraswati, T. S. (2002). *The world's youth: Adolescence in 8 regions of the globe.* Cambridge, UK: Cambridge University Press.

Bustreo, F., & Johnsson, A. B. (2008). Parliamentarians: Leading the change for maternal, newborn, and child survival? *Lancet, 371*, 1221–1222.

Bryce J., el Arifeen S., Parivo F., Lanata C., Gwatkin D., Habicht J. P., & the Multi-Country Evaluation of IMCI Study Group. (2003). Reducing child mortality: Can public health deliver? *Lancet, 362*(9378), 159–164.

Bryce, J., Requejo, J., & the 2008 Countdown working group. (2008). Tracking progress in maternal, newborn, and child survival: The 2008 report. Retrieved from http://www.countdown2015mnch.org

Casas, J. A., Dachs, N. W., & Bambas, A. (2001). Health disparities in Latin America and the Caribbean: The role of social and economic determinants. Retrieved from http://www.paho.org/english/dbi/Op08/Op08_03.pdf

Case, A., Fertig, A., & Paxson, C. H. (2005). The lasting impact of childhood health and circumstance. *Journal of Health Economics, 24*, 365–389.

Cleland, J., Berstein, S., Ezeh, A., Faundes, A., Glasier, A., & Innis, J. (2006). Family planning: The unfinished agenda. *Lancet, 368*, 1810–1827.

Countdown Core Group. (2006). Tracking progress in child survival: The 2005 report. New York: UNICEF. Retrieved from http://www.countdown2015mnch .org/reports

Countdown Coverage Writing Group. (2008). Countdown to 2015 for maternal, newborn, and child survival: The 2008 report on tracking coverage of interventions. *Lancet, 371*(9620), 1247–1258.

Countdown 2008 Equity Analysis Group. (2008). Mind the gap: Equity and trends in coverage of maternal, newborn, and child health services in 54 Countdown countries. *Lancet, 371,* 1259–1267.

Convention on the Rights of the Child. (1989). New York: United Nations Children's Fund.

Cunningham, A. (1995). Breastfeeding: Adaptive behavior for child health and longevity. In P. Stuart-Macadam & K. Dettwyler (Eds.), *Breastfeeding: Biocultural perspectives* (pp. 243–264). New York: Aldine de Gruyter.

DeLoache, J., & Gottlieb, A. (2000). *A world of babies: Imagined childcare guides for seven societies.* Cambridge, UK: Cambridge University Press.

Gonzalez, R., Requejo, J., Nien, J. K., Merialdi, M., Bustreo, F., & Betra, A. P. (2009). Tackling health inequities in Chile: Reduction in maternal, newborn, and child mortality between 1990 and 2004. *American Journal of Public Health, 99*(7), 1220–1226.

Greco, G., Powell-Jackson, T., Borghi, J., & Mills, A. (2008). Countdown to 2015: Assessment of donor assistance to maternal, newborn, and child health between 2003 and 2006. *Lancet, 371,* 1268–1275.

Kerber, K. J., de Graft-Johnson, J. E., Bhutta, Z. A., Okong, P., Starrs, A., & Lawn, J. (2007). Continuum of care for maternal, newborn, and child health: From slogan to service delivery. *Lancet, 370,* 1358–1369.

Lawn, J. E., Cousens, S., & Zupan, J. (2005). Four million neonatal deaths: When? Where? Why? *Lancet, 365,* 891–900.

Masanja, H., de Savigny, D., Smithson, P., Schellenberg, J., Theopista, J., Mbuya, C., et al. (2008). Child survival gains in Tanzania: Analysis of data from demographic and health surveys. *Lancet, 371,* 1276–1283.

Merchant, K. M. (1993). Women's nutrition through the life cycle: Social and biological vulnerabilities. In M. Koblinsky, J. Timyan, & J. Gay (Eds.), *The health of women: A global perspective* (pp. 63–90). Boulder: Westview Press.

Nakiyingi, J. S., Bracher, M., Whitworth, J., Ruberantwari, A., Busingy, J., Mbulaiteye, S.,et al. (2003). Child survival in relation to mother's HIV infection and survival: Evidence from a Ugandan Cohort Study. *AIDS, 17*(12), 1827–1834.

Salama, P., Lawn, J., Bryce, J, Bustreo, F., Fauveau, V., Starrs, A., et al. (2008). Making the Countdown Count. *Lancet, 371,* 1219–1220.

Sepúlveda, J., Bustreo, F., Tapia, R., Rivera, J., Lozano, R., Oláiz, G. et al. (2006). Improvement of child survival in Mexico: The diagonal approach. *Lancet, 368,* 2017–2027.

Tinker, A., ten Hoope-Bender, P., Azfar, S., Bustreo, F., & Bell, R. (2005). A Continnuum of care to save newborn lives. *Lancet, 365*(9462), 822–825.

United Nations Children's Fund. (2007a). *State of the world's children 2008: Child survival.* New York: United Nations Children's Fund (UNICEF).

United Nations Children's Fund. (2007b). *Progress for children: A world fit for children statistical review.* New York: United Nations Children's Fund (UNICEF).

United Nations Children's Fund. (2008). *State of the world's children 2009: Maternal and newborn health.* New York: United Nations Children's Fund (UNICEF).

Victora, C. G., Fuchs, S. C., Kirkwood, B. R., Lombardi, C., & Barros, F. C. (1992). Breastfeeding, nutritional status, and other prognostic factors for dehydration among young children with diarrhea in Brazil. *Bulletin of the World Health Organization, 70*(4), 467–475.

Victora, C. G., Kirkwood, B. R., Ashworth, A., Black, R. E., Rogers, S., Sazawal, S., et al. (1999). Potential interventions for the prevention of childhood pneumonia in developing countries: Improving nutrition. *American Journal of Clinical Nutrition, 70*(3), 309–320.

World Health Organization. (2005). *World Health Report 2005: Make every mother and child count.* Geneva: World Health Organization.

# Index

564

*Index*